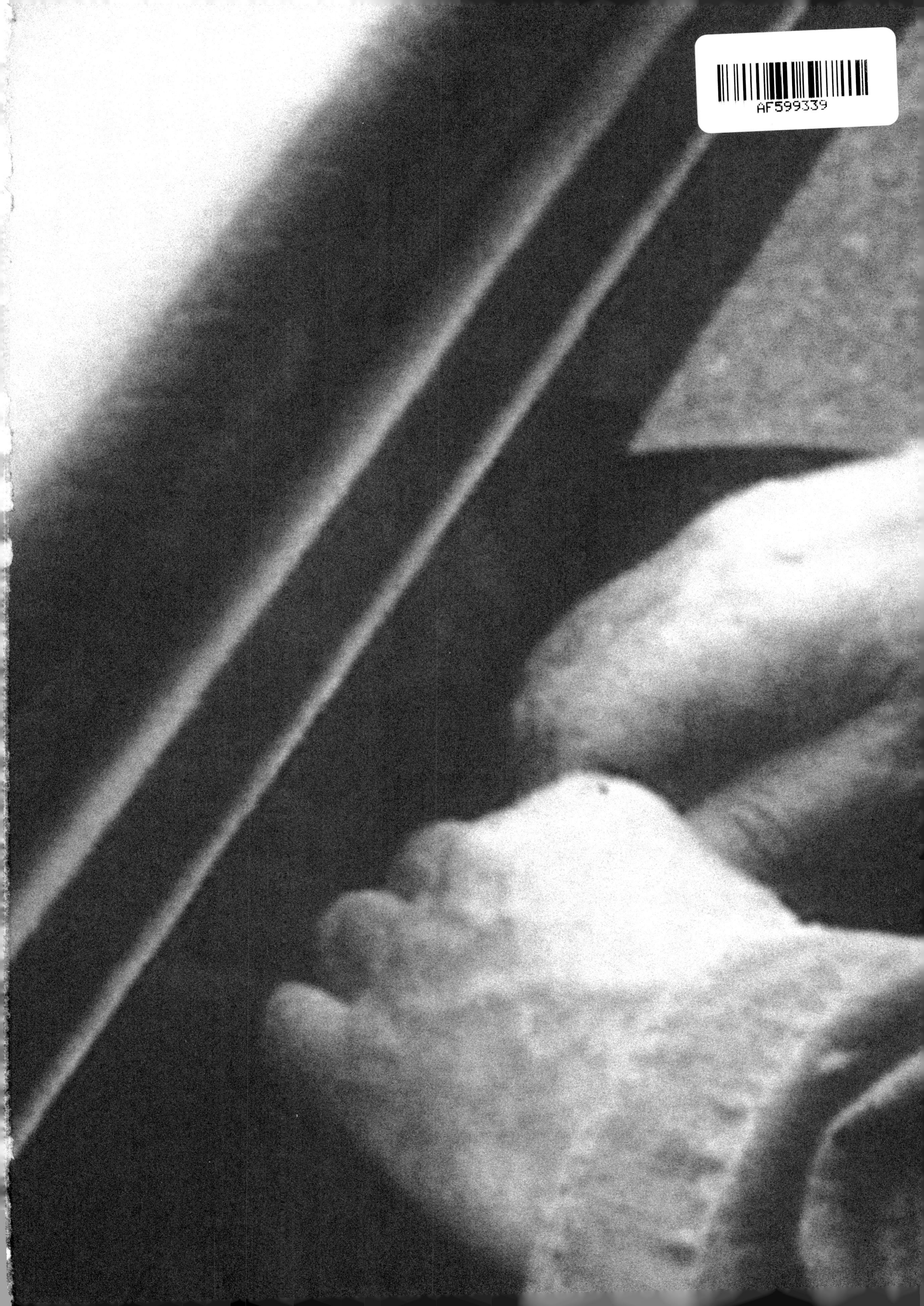

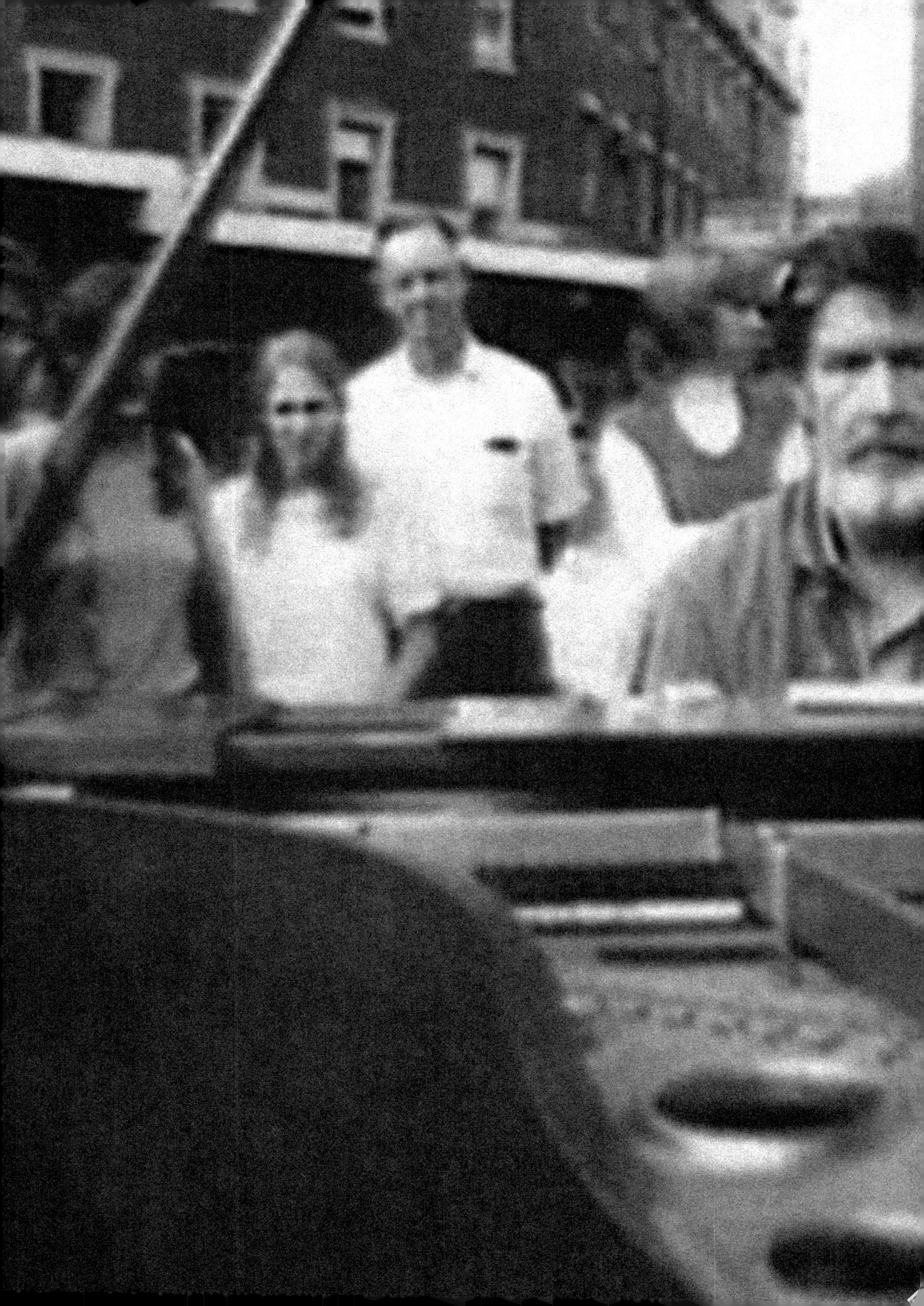

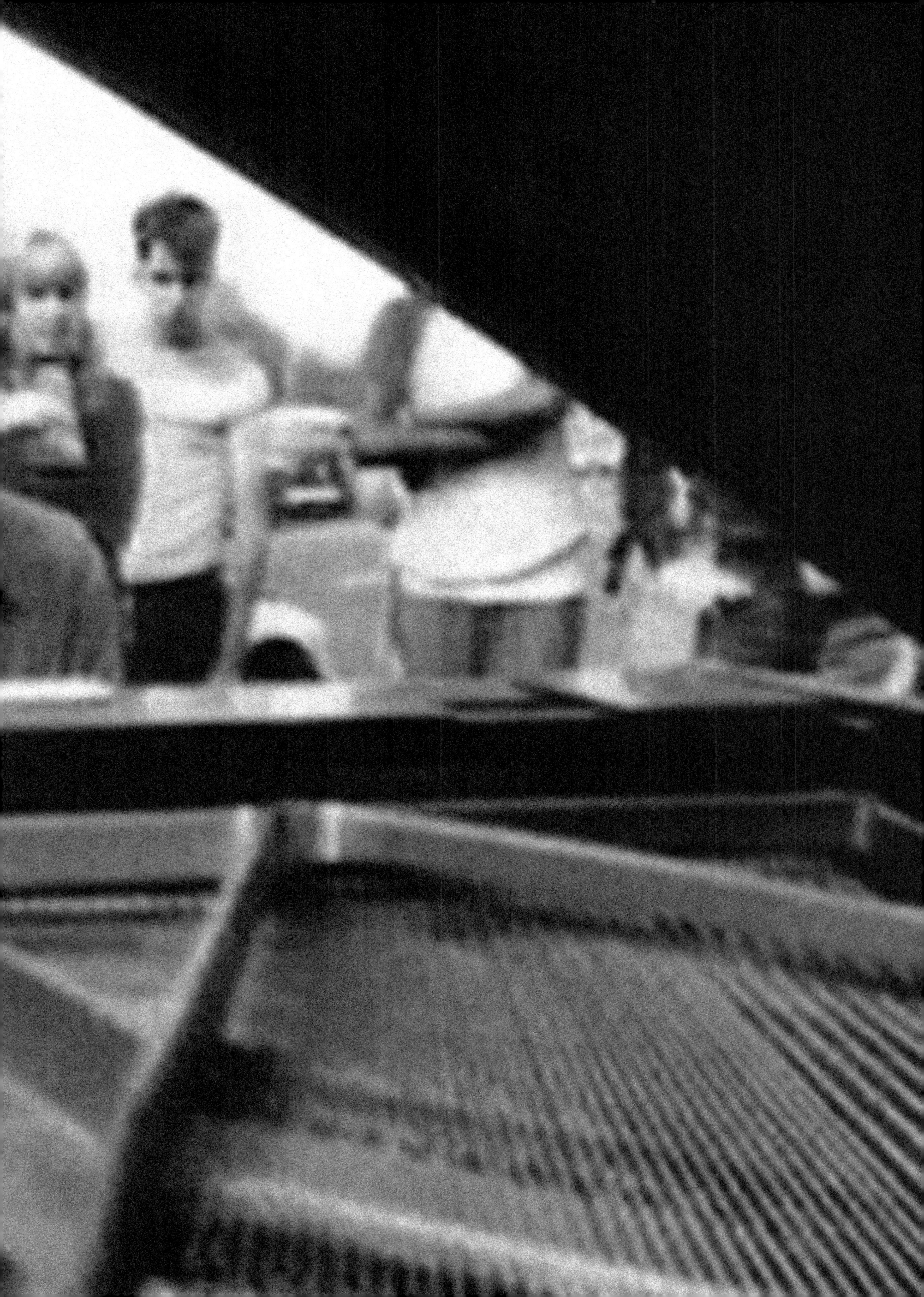

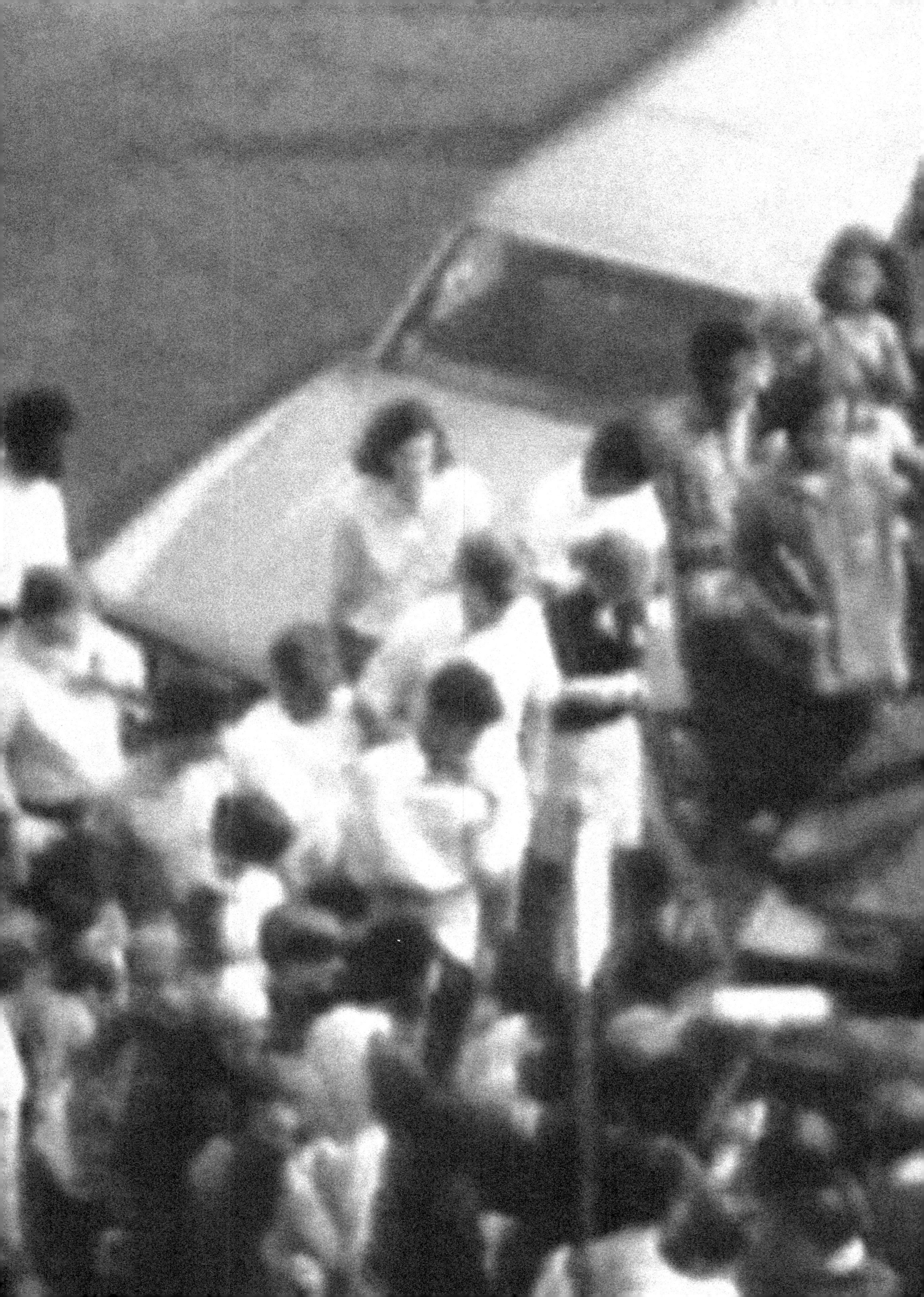

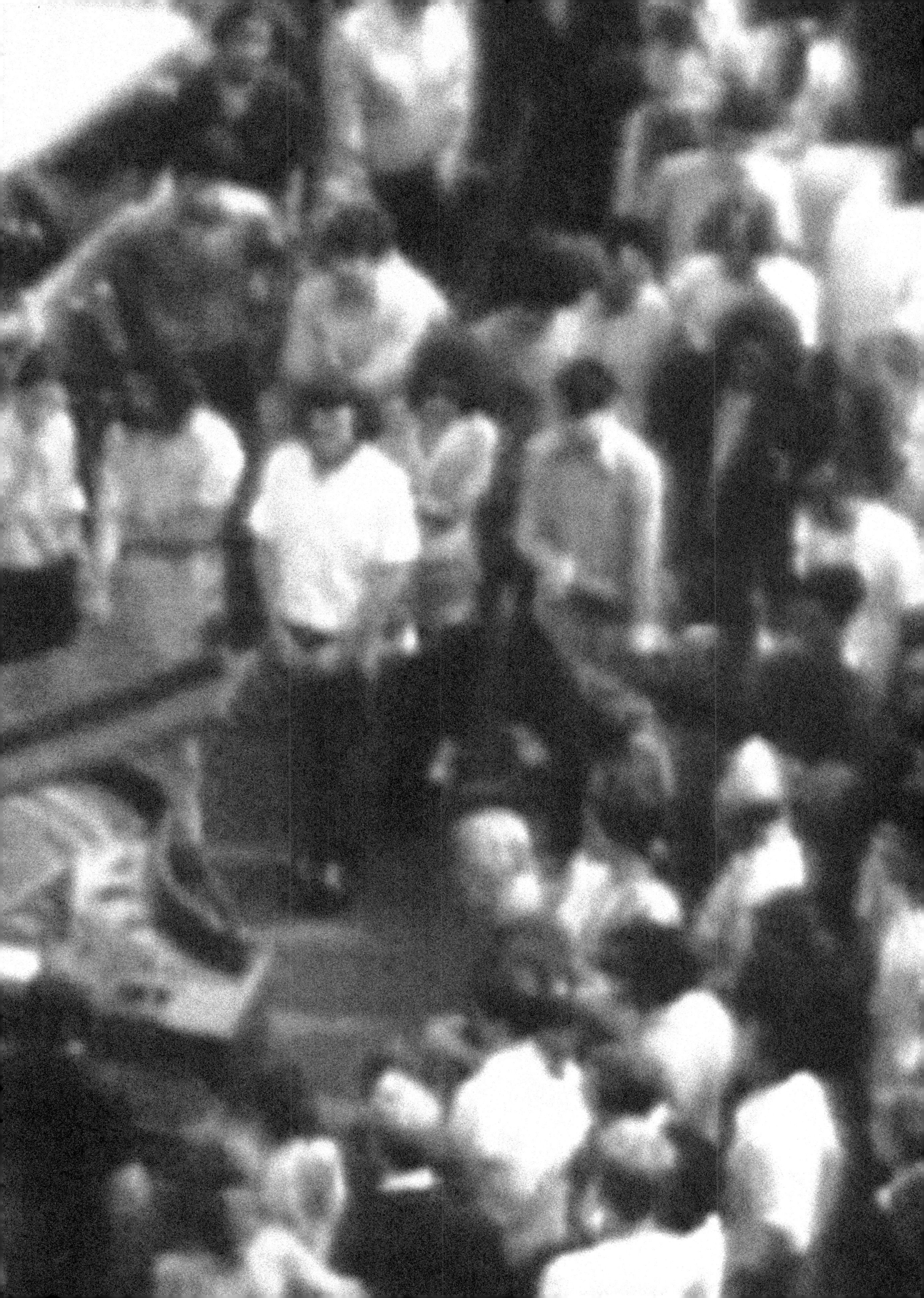

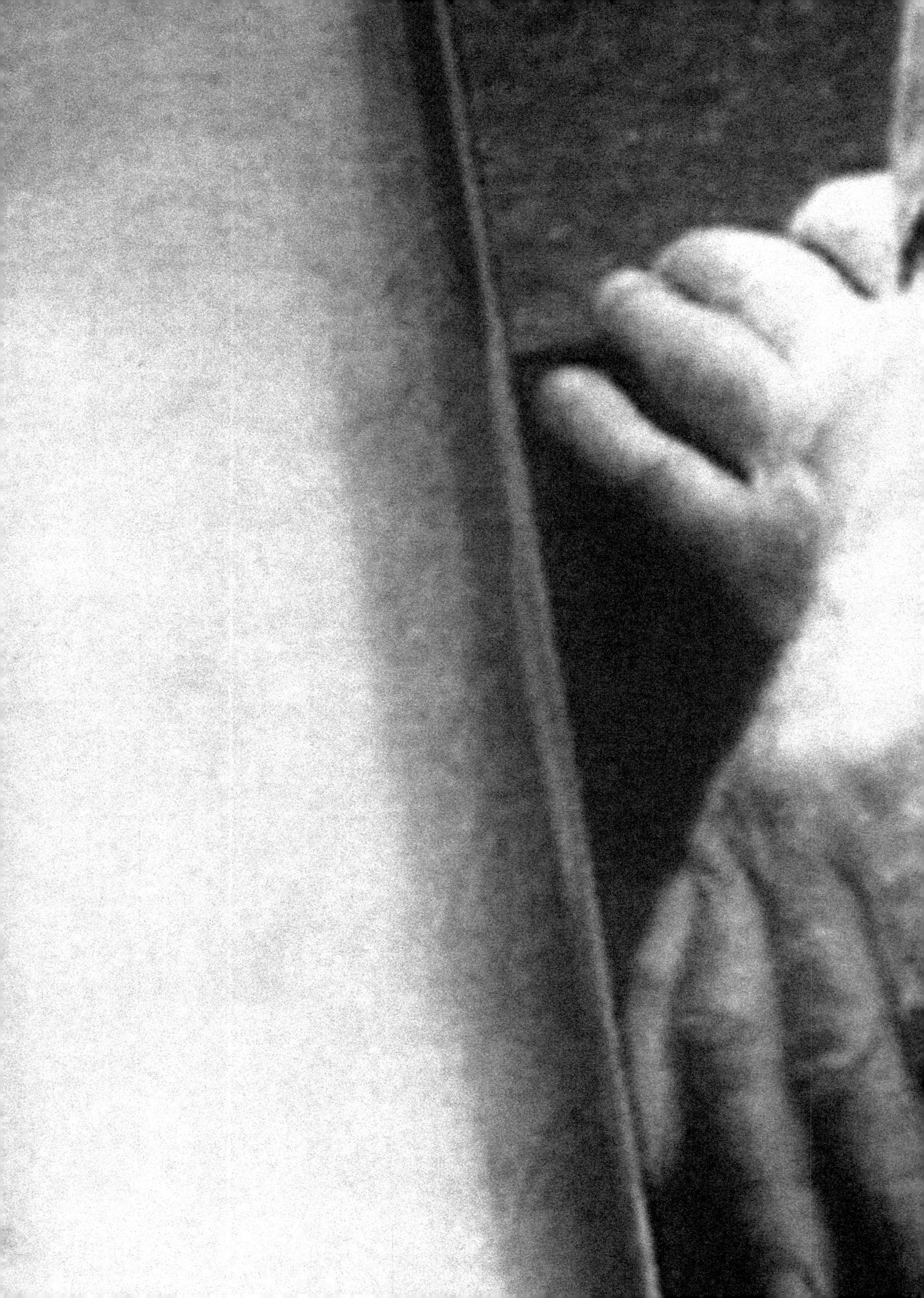

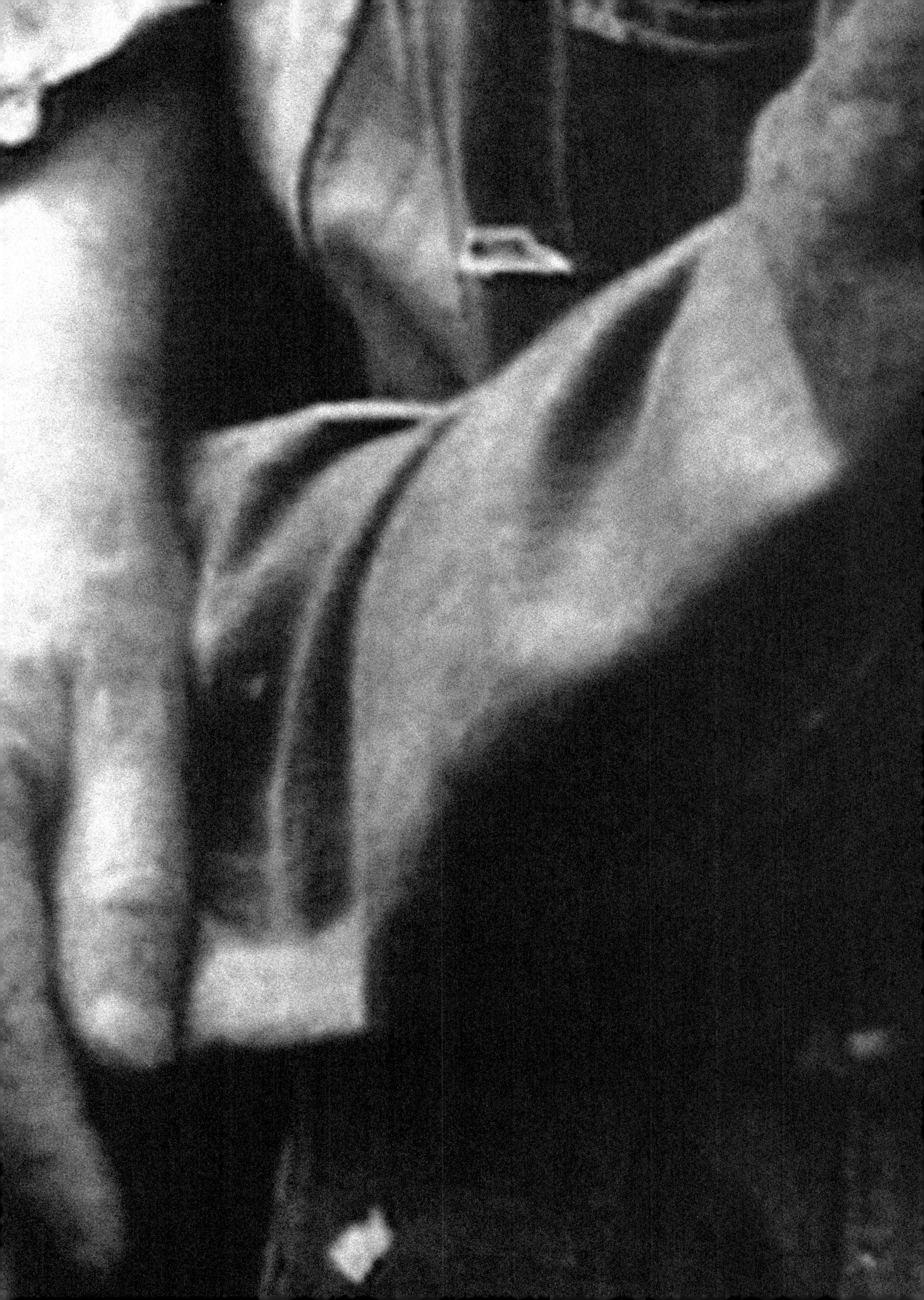

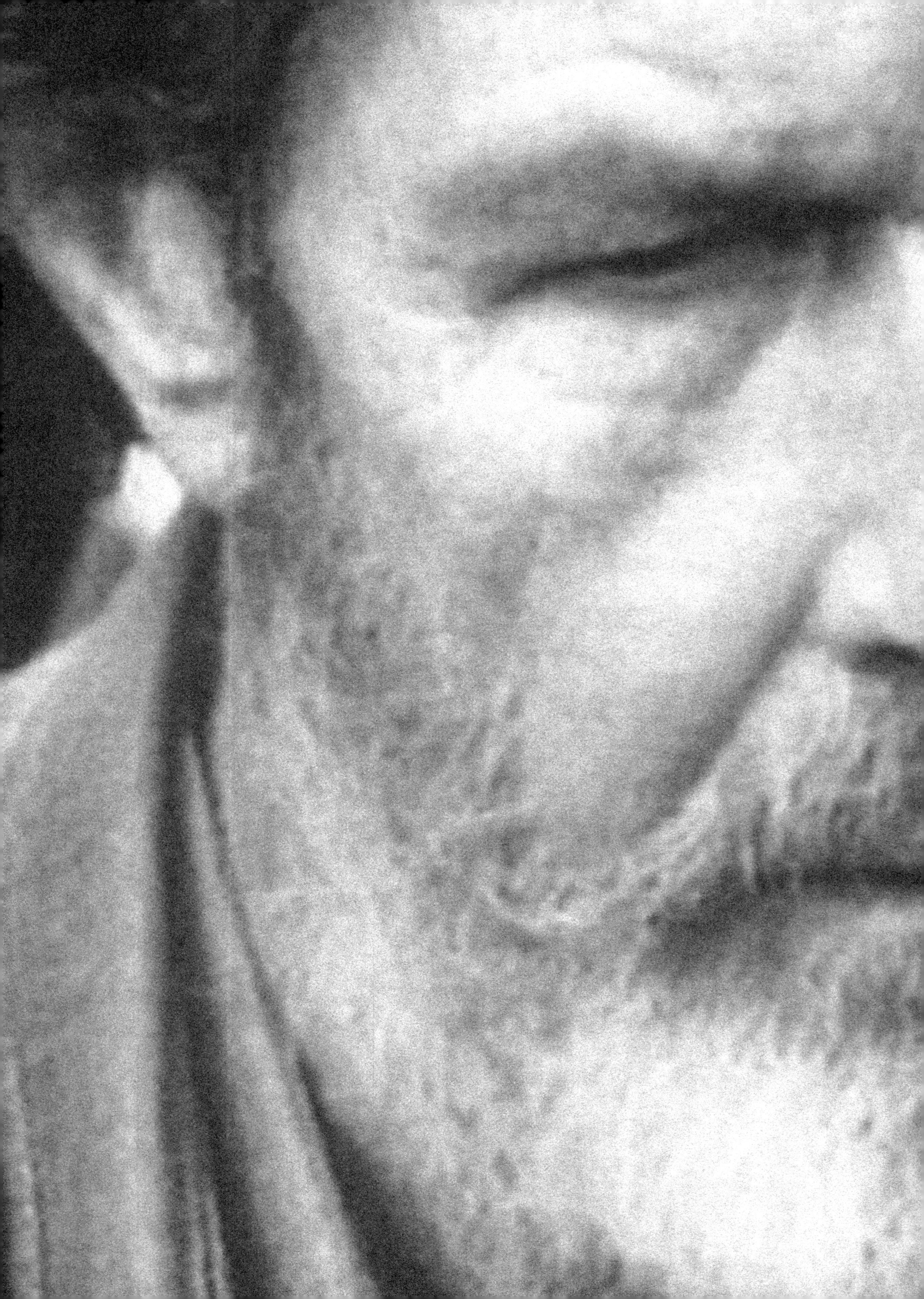

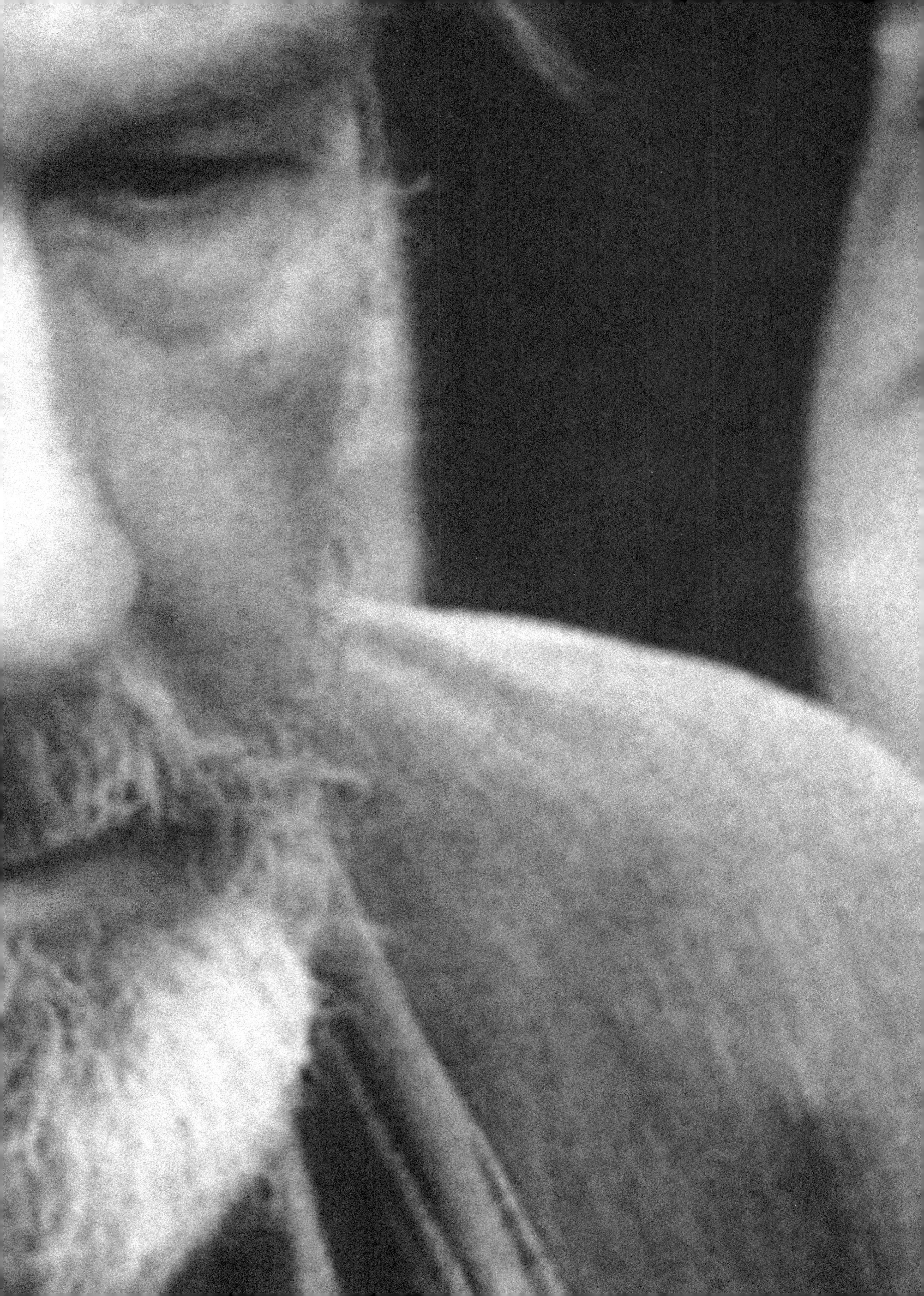

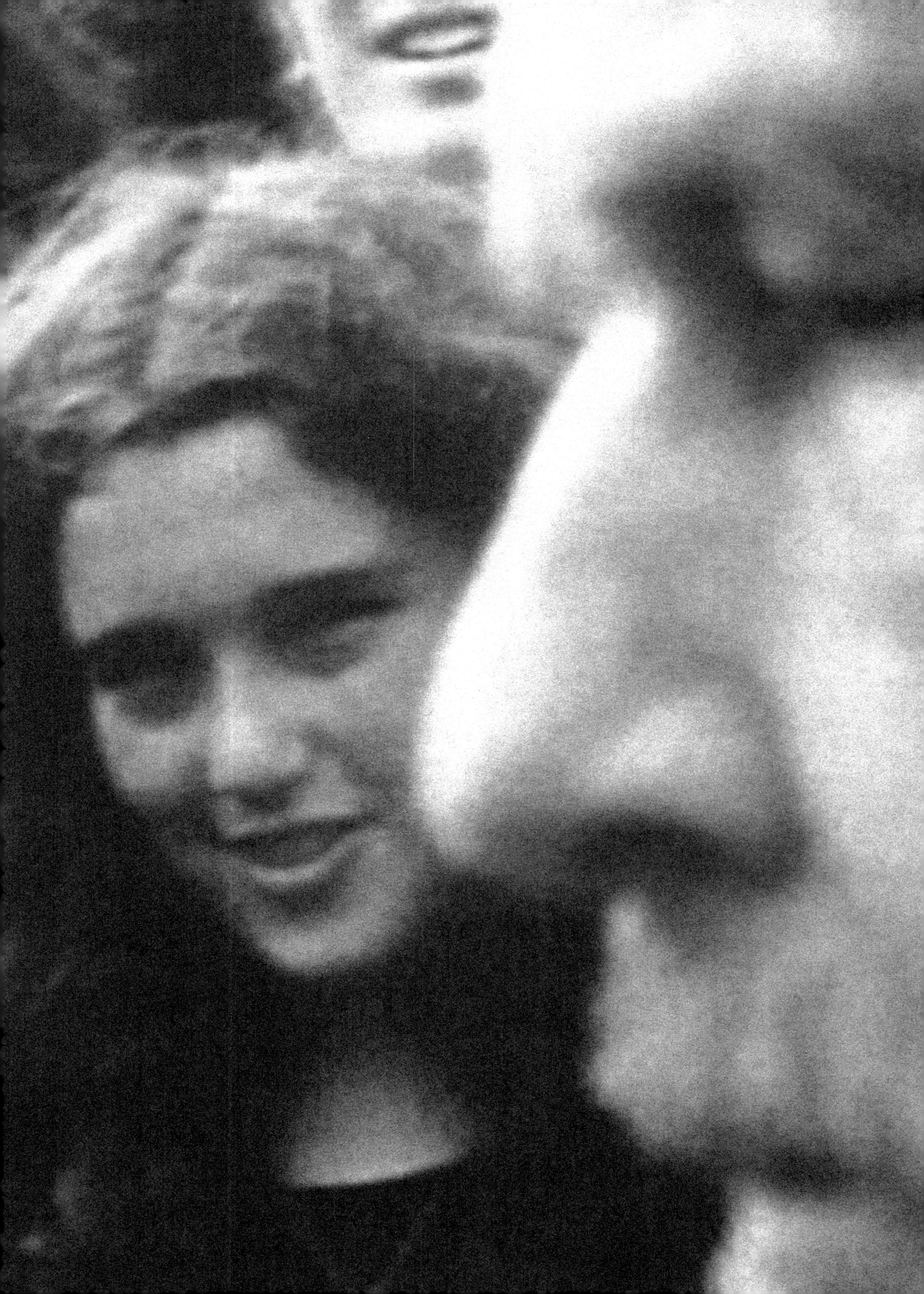

Dieter Daniels / Inke Arns (eds.)

Sounds Like Silence

John Cage
4′33″
Silence Today

1912 1952 2012

Spector Books

Introduction

Essays

A

Scores and Documents

B

Silence: A Reader

C

Exhibition

D

Appendix

Dieter Daniels / Inke Arns

Sounds Like Silence

The title of this exhibition, *Sounds Like Silence,* is ambiguous. On the one hand, silence effectively "sounds"—"There is no such thing as silence," as Cage himself put it. On the other hand, sound needs silence in order to be heard. Even if complete silence does not exist, every sound implicitly conveys the notion of silence: there is no presence without absence. The double meaning of *Sounds Like Silence* therefore touches upon the central issues at stake in this exhibition and the accompanying publication: what do we hear when there is nothing to hear? To what extent do we long for silence? And how much silence can we cope with—provided it even exists?

Points of Departure 1912–1952–2012

In 2012 we celebrate the centenary of John Cage's birth and the sixtieth anniversary of the premiere of the composer's "silent piece" *4'33"* (four minutes, thirty-three seconds) on August 29, 1952. This composition in three movements without intentional sounds is Cage's most prominent work today. As an "art without work" (Cage), it takes up and renews the groundbreaking concepts of the avant-gardes of the early twentieth century, notably Marcel Duchamp's readymades, which the artist himself termed "works without art."

Cage's *4'33"* is often referred to as "four minutes and thirty-three seconds of silence" or the "silent piece." Yet *4'33"* is not so much about silence as about sound, or even noise. It involves the active hearing of ambient sounds—the sounds that are constantly surrounding us, and in this specific case, the non-intentional sounds occurring during the performance of the three movements. In his "silent piece," Cage has listeners experience these sounds as music. In keeping with his personal motto—"Happy New Ears!"—Cage was after a different kind of experience, one which would not be over after four and a half minutes: "Until I die there will be sounds. And they will continue following my death. One need not fear about the future of music."[1]

Publication and Exhibition

Sounds Like Silence combines *research/publication* with *curation/exhibition.* These aspects are structurally related and thematically intertwined; at the same time, each of them opens up a specific perspective on their shared field of research. The publication contains both scientific and essayistic contributions; the exhibition provides information while offering a direct aesthetic experience. Instead of revisiting Cage's œuvre, it aims to analyze and expand on the composer's concepts by concentrating on three main areas.

Firstly, the publication retraces the development of the notion of silence in Cage's work from 1948 (*Silent Prayer*) to 1992. This includes a critical edition of Cage's notations (*Silence Scores*) and an editorial comment by Jan Thoben. Dörte Schmidt also considers the history of *4'33"*'s notation and its changing work concepts. Julia Schröder examines Cage's collaboration with Merce Cunningham to pinpoint the relationships between silence, movement, and sound, and between the presence and absence of the body. In dealing with Cage's work and thought these texts are set in the wider context of an abundant literature

1 John Cage, "Experimental Music" (1958), in *Silence: Lectures and Writings* (Middletown, CT: Wesleyan University Press, 1961), p. 8.

and various scientific methods and theories on Cage's "silent piece." A selection is reprinted in this book in the chapter "Silence: A Reader" [→ pp. 193–238].

Secondly, the exhibition focuses on current artistic and musical references to *4'33"*. We have deliberately omitted a historical account of Cage's work and its impact from the sixties to the eighties, since (parallel to Cage's own developments of the concept of silence) we were mainly interested in taking stock and building bridges: what did silence mean in 1952 and what does it mean today? The essays by Brandon LaBelle and Dieter Daniels retrace how the Cagean notion of silence has branched out in multiple ways and reconsider it in light of topical questions.

The third aspect—the wider questions of how acoustic perception has changed in the course of time and what silence means today—forms the cultural, medial, and social context of our endeavor. This part of the project, which is outlined in the contributions by David Toop and Inke Arns, is likely to appeal to audiences who are unfamiliar either with Cage or with contemporary art, as it can be directly related to aspects of their everyday lives.

Context: Silence Today

The cultural context of this project in turn opens up three perspectives. The first of these is the *need for silence*. This requirement is frequently articulated, but no less frequently avoided, because silence throws us back on ourselves. This is aptly illustrated by Cage's experience in the anechoic chamber at Harvard University, where he was surprised to hear the sounds made by his own body. It taught him that, as long as we are alive, there is no such thing as total silence. Cage's "silent piece" is therefore an invitation to listen, to be attentive to what normally goes unnoticed, and last but not least to become aware of the "liveness" of our acoustic environment and our own physicality. In Cage's thought, silence stands for life rather than death.

The second aspect, which reaches beyond a mere exegesis of Cage's work, addresses the present situation, more precisely the rampant phenomenon of *acoustic pollution*. Besides the noise produced by traffic and industry, this also concerns the unavoidable Muzak in shopping centers, the background noise of electrical home devices (including personal computers), the proliferation of mobile phones in the public realm, and so forth. Initiatives such as the World Forum for Acoustic Ecology and Hörstadt (Acoustic City) Linz are raising public awareness about the impact of noise on the quality of life. It appears that the mentor of this movement, the composer and writer Murray Schafer, was greatly influenced by Cage. In the exhibition visitors are familiarized with this issue by means of a graphic chart by Max Schneider and Frauke Schmidt that retraces the history of Acoustic Ecology. It shows the transformation of the world's soundscape since the beginning of the industrial era, its impact on urbanism, traffic planning, and technological developments in the realms of sound production, acoustic codes, functional sounds, and psychoacoustics.

A third facet of the exhibition is its concern with *silence in the media*, both in terms of content and technology. With the advent of digital technology, the gradual transition from silence to noise has effectively vanished: gone is the traditional white noise, replaced by a signal-less "dead" silence. Similarly, silence has altogether disappeared from mass media programs: in so-called "format radio," for instance, music tracks and announcements follow each other without respite, and today even the news is sometimes presented with background sound. Silence is thus banned in two regards—both in terms of technology and programs. In Germany, for instance, radio broadcasters have fitted an automatic alarm that goes off after more than one minute of silence.

The exhibition addresses this topic through Heinrich Böll's short story *Murke's Collected Silences* (1955) and Guy Debord's film *Howling for Sade* (1952) as well as a series of contemporary works (by Martin Conrads, Matt Rogalsky, Paul Davis, Ultra-red, and others).[2] The confrontation of such varied positions as those of Cage, Böll, and Debord shows that even by the mid-twentieth century, the increasing amount of information and sensory stimuli of modern media society was restricting the available space for self-reflection. Silence thus becomes a metaphor for the need for a non-codified space of reflection. Interestingly, as early as 1948 Cage planned a "silent piece" entitled *Silent Prayer* to be included in a Muzak channel in shopping malls, elevators, and waiting areas: the silence interrupting the "non-listening music" would have sharpened customers' awareness of the presence of Muzak. This idea was revived in 2010 by Cage Against the Machine, an initiative launched via Facebook by a collective of London musicians who succeeded in propelling Cage's *4'33"* to number 21 in the UK Christmas charts. The same year *4'33"* was also performed on German public TV as a piano piece for four hands by the late-night entertainer Harald Schmidt and the musician Helge Schneider.

These three aspects of silence today evidence the timelessness and importance of the subject, which extends far beyond Cage. Simultaneously, they can be linked back to Cage's concepts. *Sounds Like Silence* thus positions itself in the wider context of culture, mass media, media technology, ecology, and perception. By doing so it reaches out to audiences who are not necessarily familiar with Cage and his seminal piece. At the same time the project reflects the multiple aspects that unfold from Cage's silence, focusing not only on the well known work *4'33"* itself, but scrutinizing its philosophical impact and conceptual horizon.

What is *4'33"*?

This question frames the exhibition and the publication. Cage's seemingly straightforward "silent piece" is in fact of dazzling complexity. There are three completely different types of score for *4'33"*, and until his death in 1992 Cage himself created several variations and sequels [→ pp. 485–192]. The contemporary artworks in this exhibition extend Cage's concept of silence into today's media landscape.

In the course of his long creative life Cage repeatedly renewed and re-contextualized the "silent piece," resulting in various performances staged with the composer as a protagonist or collaborator. The premiere of the piece in 1952, with David Tudor in a classic piano situation, has served as a model for performances to this day. But Cage himself also staged performances in the urban space, whether as live renderings or, without any instrument, as an acoustic experience in the urban space designed for TV (as in Nam June Paik's 1973 film *Tribute to John Cage*). Until the end of his life, Cage never ceased to find new forms, as evidenced by his last performance with Henning Lohner in Berlin in 1990.

2 In collaboration with Marcus Gammel, the HMKV has conceived a broadcast around some of these works based on the idea of a "radiophonic exhibition," which reintroduces the artistic reflection on silence into the mass medium of radio. (*Sounds Like Silence*, August 24, 2012, 12.05 am. Curators: Dieter Daniels and Inke Arns. Production: HMKV Dortmund and Deutschlandradio Kultur, 2012. Duration: 54:30 min.) The broadcast is also available on CD, published by Gruenrekorder (Gruen 116, LC 09488).

Besides these various stagings of *4'33"*, Cage also wrote new pieces which directly referred to it, modifying or developing the original idea while embracing different media. In the instructions for *0'00"* (also called *4'33" No. 2*) from 1962, he indicated, "In a situation provided with maximum amplification (no feedback), perform a disciplined action." He thus underlined that electronic amplification could turn even the slightest sound into an intensive listening experience. Based on this idea, he revised his optimistic concept of silence at the end of his life, shifting towards a critical analysis of noise pollution in his piece *One³ = 4'33" (0'00") + 𝄞*, on which he commented in 1990: "... I have another form of it which brings the silence of the room up to the level of feedback but doesn't allow the feedback to be heard, only sensed, so that you realize that you're in an electronic situation that could be painful. But isn't, hmm? But could be ... What I think I'm showing is that we have changed the environment ... it's now a technological silence, hmm? ... that now silence includes technology ... in a way that is not necessarily ... good."[3]

Exhibiting Cage, Curating Silence

The main part of the exhibition consists of works of art and music from the past two decades, some of which explicitly refer to *4'33"*, while others approach the notion of silence from a more general perspective and relate to our acoustic environment. Various positions from the mid-twentieth century (Heinrich Böll, Guy Debord, Robert Rauschenberg, Yves Klein) serve as historical reference. Cage's own developments of the "silent piece" between 1952 and 1992 act as bridge between the historical and contemporary positions.

Sounds Like Silence is therefore not an exhibition about Cage properly speaking; rather, it highlights the timelessness of the questions he raised about the significance of silence. Several exhibitions have addressed his work and influence since the nineties.[4] But how do you actually exhibit the "influence" of an artist or musician—particularly of an artist-musician who was explicitly critical of the concept of "influence" as such? And how do you exhibit a piece of music—particularly a silent one?

Our starting point was a reading of the piece not as a purely musical work, but as a comprehensive conceptual approach to the world. In reference to Duchamp, who spoke of "non-retinal art," we view the "silent piece" as a piece of "non-cochlear sonic art" (Seth Kim-Cohen), namely as something which must not only be perceived with the ears (in the same way that art since Duchamp no longer functions on a mere retinal level).[5] We are not interested in epigonic repetitions of the piece, but in approaches which, in radically different media, reconsider and expand on the reflections that lie at the heart of this piece.[6] The works on display cover a wide range of media—as do all the exhibitions organized by the Hartware MedienKunstVerein (HMKV). More generally, we are looking for works which engage with today's world—a world increasingly relying on media and/or new technologies—without necessarily using these very media to do so.

The centenary of Cage's birth and the sixtieth anniversary of the premiere of *4'33"* are welcome occasions to reconsider the notion of silence and the "experimental" methods introduced by Cage, which have had an impact that exceeds the composer's direct legacy in the realms of art, music, performance, and aesthetic theory. But how could any "succession," in light of Cage's formidable originality, be anything other than epigonic? From the early sixties onwards, the generation after Cage picked up the legacy of *4'33"*: in 1960 LaMonte Young referred directly to it when he wrote his *Piano Piece for David Tudor No. 2*, which asks the pianist to open and close the lid of his piano as softly as possible. Similarly, Paik's *Zen for Film* from 1964/65 explicitly alludes to Cage and Rauschenberg by setting the time-based silence of *4'33"* and the visual emptiness of the *White Paintings* against the space-time dimension of the projection of a blank roll of film. But rather than "perpetuating" the legacy, these works evidence a reciprocal highlighting or obscuring of model and copy, a competition between foresight and retrospection. This also applied to Cage himself, who explicitly referred to his predecessors (among them Erik Satie and James Joyce) and changed his own work in response to the status of model and "myth" he soon enjoyed. Finally, we must also take into account the notion of interdisciplinarity, since the numerous cross-references between art, music, theatre, dance, and literature create a complex network rather than a linear chronology.

Sounds Like Silence seeks to prolong these reflections through variation and renewal. It is not repetition, as Cage remarked in reference to Arnold Schönberg, when someone else appears to be doing the same thing as you. And even when the same artist or musician is repeating something, this something is something else. There was no repetition for Gertrude Stein either, only insistence: "Is there repetition or is there insistence. I am inclined to believe there is no such thing as repetition. And really how can there be."[7] Instead of repeating Cage—an impossible task, as it appears—*Sounds Like Silence* continues the journey on the many paths that he has opened up.

The aim of curating is not to be comprehensive—even (or particularly) in the case of large thematic exhibitions. Instead curating implies making clear choices and balancing out artistic positions so as to sharpen the discursive framework of the exhibition. Independently of this understanding of curating, however, we do regret having been unable to include a number of works that we deemed important—first and foremost Tacita Dean's *Merce Cunningham performs STILLNESS (in three movements)* from 2008—simply because production costs would have exceeded our budget.

The exhibition design holds particular importance if we consider that some of the works, in various ways, resist the very notion of display. This called for an approach that would at once echo the inherent restraint of the subject and help distinguish its various individual aspects, while offering visitors a sensory experience of its conceptual complexity. The exhibition design was conceived and implemented in close collaboration with Ruth M. Lorenz (maaskant, Berlin).

3 Joan Retallack (ed.), *Musicage: Cage Muses on Words, Art, Music* (Middletown, CT: Wesleyan University Press, 1996), p. 77.

4 See for instance Ulrich Bischoff (ed.), *Kunst als Grenzbeschreitung: John Cage und die Moderne*, exh. cat. (Munich: Staatsgalerie moderner Kunst, 1991); Julia Robinson (ed.), *The Anarchy of Silence: John Cage & Experimental Art*, exh. cat. (Barcelona: MACBA, 2009); Wulf Herzogenrath and Barbara Nierhoff-Wielk (eds.), *"John Cage und ..." Bildender Künstler–Einflüsse, Anregungen* (Berlin: Akademie der Künste, 2012).

5 Seth Kim-Cohen, *In the Blink of an Ear: Toward a Non-Cochlear Sonic Art* (London / New York: Continuum, 2009).

6 A related project–although it did not include any historical performance by Cage or works from the fifties–was *4'33"*, held at Magazin4–Bregenzer Kunstverein from 15 to 22 July 2007 (curated by Wolfgang Fetz and Peter Lewis). See *4'33"*, exh. cat. (Bregenz: Magazin4–Bregenzer Kunstverein, 2007).

7 Gertrude Stein, "Portraits and Repetition" (1935), in *Lectures in America* (Boston: Beacon Press, 1985), pp. 166–69.

Essays

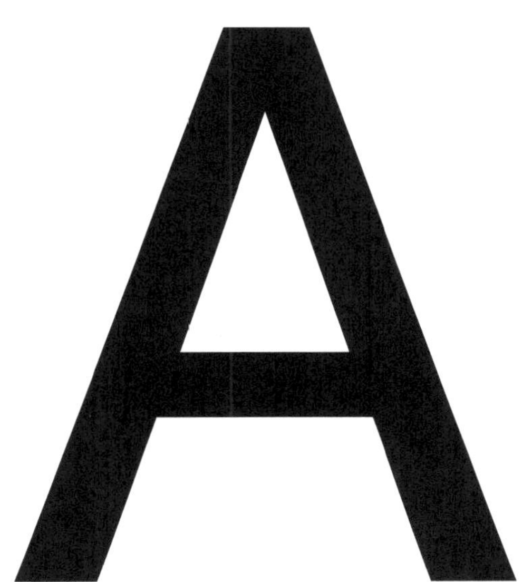

Helen Wolff, photo by Stephanie Wolff, 1994

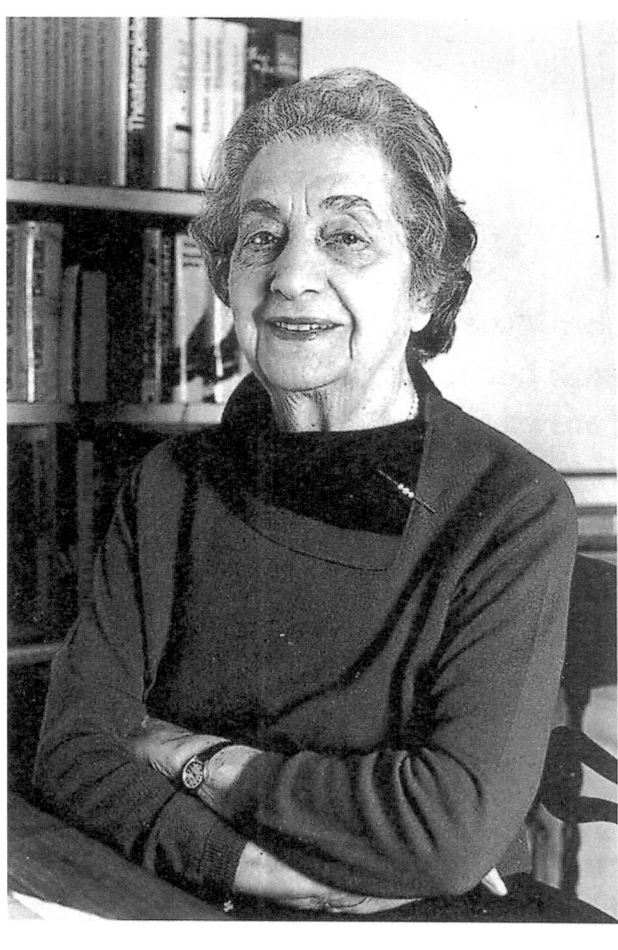

Letter from John Cage to Helen Wolff, facsimile, 1954

This facsimile, along with the complete correspondence in German translation, was first published as "Es wird niemals Stille geben ..." in: *MusikTexte* 106 (August 2005), pp. 47–50.

This letter is John Cage's answer to a letter from Helen Wolff dated April 9, 1954. Her son Christian Wolff had explained the intention of *4'33"* to her, and upon hearing this, she advised Cage with some concern that he wasn't being "sérieux." He would risk putting his serious work in danger and deliberately distressing his critics and audience. Her letter was written in anticipation of the second performance of *4'33"* on April 14, 1954 in New York.

Helen Wolff (who was born as Helen Mosel in 1906 in Macedonia and died in 1994 in New York) was second wife to the publisher Kurt Wolff (1887–1963), who from 1912 on had published the works of Franz Kafka and the German expressionists through his company in Leipzig. After their flight from the National Socialists they founded Pantheon Books in New York in 1942. Following Kurt's death, Helen Wolff continued publishing on her own. As a grande dame of German-American literature, she earned great prestige for the promotion and translation of German authors in the U.S. Uwe Johnson's magnum opus *Jahrestage* [Anniversaries] was dedicated to her.

The composer Christian Wolff (born 1934) was the son of Helen and Kurt Wolff. He belonged to the inner circle of Cage's friends from a young age. Through Christian, Cage discovered, in 1950, the English translation of the I Ching, which Kurt Wolff had published.

1954

12 E. 17

Dear Helen:

(I typewrite because the pen is so bad.)

The piece is not actually silent (there will never be silence until death comes which never comes); it is full of sound, but sounds which I did not think of beforehand, which I hear for the first time the same time others hear. What we hear is determined by our own emptiness, our own receptivity; we receive to the extent we are empty to do so. If one is full or in the course of its performance becomes full of an idea, for example, that this piece is a trick for shock and bewilderment then it is just that. However, nothing is single or unidimensional. This is an action among the ten thousand: it moves in all directions and will be received in unpredictable ways. These will vary from shock and bewilderment to quietness of mind and enlightenment.

If one imagines that I have intended any one of these responses he will have to imagine that I have intended all of them. Something like faith must take over in order that we live affirmatively in the totality we do live in.

With or without my intention, my art is cheapened and made expensive. That is not my concern. A death to myself takes place in composing and in the event of the movement of this composition in the world, a second death to it as mine must take place. Otherwise I shall be in "fear and trembling", in a perilous situation of my own imagination.

You know my constant interest in 'oriental thought' and you may think this has been misused to bring about a musical action which you cannot accept. As I see it useful art has been illustrative or significant of belief, didactic. But what is that art which is not didactic, nor symbolic, but to be experienced following having been taught? Clearly, life itself of which we have only to become aware.

I am therefor not concerned with art as separate from such awareness (nor is the I-Ching (Hex. 22, Grace)).

Another friend of mine was disturbed about 4'33" and said with some heat that I apparently thought him stupid and incapable of hearing the sounds of everyday life which he informed me he could and with pleasure. I asked him why, if in private he could hear, he was disturbed to foresee doing so in public. To this he had to say,"You have a point."

However, I do not wish to win an argument, nor will I. I also consulted the I-Ching after receiving your letter and got Exhaustion (47). 4'33" is also a matter of consultation. Each person present will receive his own hexagram.

I send this not to defend myself but out of love for you and a sense of responsibility to you and to Mr. Wolff (through my relation to Christian) from which I am not free.

It is for that reason, being aware of your concern, that I repeat my practical offer: to warn your friends of the experience in store for them. You have only to give me a list of names and addresses.

Very sincerely,

John

P.S. Incidentally, it was not I but David who decided upon the program. I do not say this to 'shift the responsibility.' But that you may be informed of how things actually take place. I composed the piece nearly two years ago. It was performed by David with mixed reactions at Woodstock, N.Y. The piece exists in the repertoire and he chose to program it at the present time. I myself am detached. I am busy with other things, a new composition, concert details of management, this letter, and this springtime.

I hope your illness disappears quickly.
Reading this letter I find it ministerial. That was my original intention in life: "to become a Methodist minister." I move so easily into a sermon.

Dieter Daniels

Your Silence Is Not My Silence

> Art, if you want a definition of it, is criminal action. It conforms to no rules. Not even its own. Anyone who experiences a work of art is as guilty as the artist. It is not a question of sharing the guilt. Each one of us gets all of it.
> —John Cage, *Diary: Audience*, 1966[1]

Like the exhibition it accompanies, this volume offers multiple perspectives on the very diverse reception/interpretation history that John Cage's "silent piece," *4′33″*, has generated since its premiere in 1952.[2] The overview will focus on three aspects: the various forms that realizations of the piece have taken; the numerous and very diverse theories on *4′33″* that can be found in academic literature, examples of which have been collected in part C of this book: "Silence: A Reader" [→ pp. 193–238]; and works by artists and musicians that are reactions to or re-interpretations of *4′33″* [→ part D of this book "Exhibition," pp. 238–72]. A fourth aspect, which has both accompanied and stimulated the reception/interpretation history, is Cage's own continuous development of his concept of silence and the context it belongs in. This has been documented in his many comments on *4′33″* and in subsequent variants of the "silent piece" from 1952 to 1992 [→ part B of this book "Scores and Documents," pp. 85–192].

Cage's influence is, of course, far wider than that of *4′33″*, and as early as the 1960s it could be seen as so pervasive that some artists of the younger generation felt that his role as a mentor of the scene stifled the development of their own artistic position. La Monte Young remarked on the problem: "It is often necessary that one be able to ask, 'Who is John Cage?'"[3] Walter De Maria's portrait sculpture *Cage* (1962–1965), built in the form of a literal cage after the composer's body measurements, clearly expresses the way in which some contemporaries felt virtually locked up in his body of thought [→ fig. 1]. Cage's own play on his name went in the opposite direction when he gave the title *For the Birds* to a collection of interviews with Daniel Charles, stressing that he was "for the birds, not for the cages in which people sometimes place them."[4] Cage did not like to talk about "influences," least of all about his own influence on others.[5] Still he was aware that his own work and thought had a fruitful effect. When in 1990 I asked him in a letter if George Maciunas wasn't overstating things when he called the detailed Fluxus charts he had made the "travels of Saint John"—because they feature John Cage as their most important protagonist—Cage simply answered: "No."[6] With tender irony, Nam June Paik has retrospectively described meeting John Cage as a turn of eras: "My life began one evening in August 1958 in Darmstadt. 1957 was 1 B.C. (Before Cage). 1947 was the year 10 B.C. Plato lived around 2500 B.C. instead of 500 B.C. [Before Christ]."[7]

1 John Cage, "Diary: Audience" (1966), in Cage, *A Year from Monday: New Lectures and Writings* (London: Calder and Boyars, 1968), p. 51.
2 The two words reception and interpretation belong together in this context, with every performance being a fresh reading of the "silent piece," thus: reception/interpretation.
3 Branden W. Joseph, *Beyond the Dream Syndicate: Tony Conrad and the Arts after Cage* (New York: Zone, 2008), p. 91. Cf. also La Monte Young's *Piano Piece for David Tudor No. 2* from 1960. Here the pianist is instructed to open and close the "keyboard cover without making, from the operation, any sound that is audible ..." Young is thus pushing the implications of *4′33″* to indicate the boundaries of Cage's concept of silence.
4 John Cage, *For the Birds: John Cage in Conversation with Daniel Charles* (New York: Marion Boyars, 1981), p. 11. Presumably Cage used this title, which the original French publisher took for a joke, partly to escape from being "caged" within a particular category.
5 See Christian Wolff, "Under the Influence On John Cage," in Wolff, *Cues: Writings and Conversations/Hinweise: Schriften und Gespräche*, ed. Gisela Gronemeyer and Reinhard Oehlschägel (Cologne: MusikTexte, 1998), p. 148.
6 Dieter Daniels, "Vier Fragen an John Cage," in Daniels (ed.), *Fluxus: Ein Nachruf zu Lebzeiten*, issue of *Kunstforum* 115 (September/October 1991), pp. 214–15.
7 Paik in his obituary for John Cage, published in German: "B.C./A.D.," in *MusikTexte* 46/47 (December 1992), p. 69.

Paradoxically, the very open-endedness of Cage's concepts makes it difficult to escape his long shadow. His influence is felt less in single, easily pinpointed works, but rather through his impact on a complete range of the most diverse artistic areas: music, visual arts, dance, theater, performance, media art, and all the related disciplines of theory. And even this listing of categories cannot do justice to the diversity of his influence, which is first and foremost about an all-embracing attitude, a way of thinking, perfectly embodied in Cage as a person. Maybe Yvonne Rainer found the best way of putting it when, at the start of the 1980s, she spoke of a "Cagean effect."[8] If this effect, which has a bearing on all areas of cultural production, today seems less threatening than it would have done between the 1960s and the 1980s, this is because it has become independent of Cage as a person. Instead the effect impacts recent developments in the arts through filters, refractions, and intermediate agents. Cage's role as a teacher for many of the Fluxus artists, who in turn have become an inspiration for contemporary artistic practices, evidently belongs here.

Fig. 1
Walter de Maria, *Cage*, 1962–65

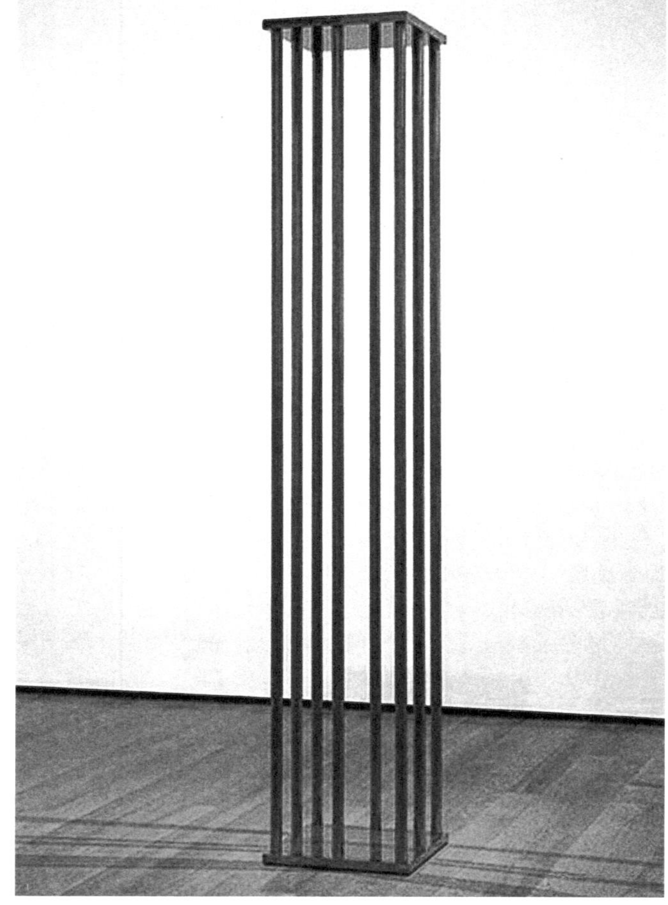

The continued impact of John Cage is best exemplified by his most famous composition, *4'33"*. When in an interview he was asked if, instead of being seen as a joke, it might in fact be taken too seriously today, Cage answered, "I don't think it can be taken too seriously."[9] Taking that as a cue, both the book and the exhibition *Sounds Like Silence* focus on the continued relevance of Cage's concept of silence, without attempting to revisit all the developments of the 1960s, 1970s, and 1980s.

I
Meanings and Readings of *4'33"*

It moves in all directions and will be received in unpredictable ways.
—John Cage on *4'33"* in 1954[10]

The creation of an art without intention or expression was a leading theme of Cage's work. "Yes I do not discriminate between intention and non-intention," he wrote in 1955.[11] The "silent piece" *4'33"* is the cornerstone of this approach to his art. By reducing the composer's work to the creation of a timeframe without intentional sound, he succeeded for the first time in freeing the music from all gestures of expression and transforming it into pure reception and heightened sensibility, an effect he described in a 1958 text, "Composition as Process" [→ excerpt, p. 196].

In 1954 Cage wrote a letter which was only published some fifty years later, in 2005; a facsimile of that letter is at the beginning of this essay. It is addressed to Helen Wolff—mother of the composer Christian Wolff, who was a close friend—and contains one of Cage's earliest comments on his "silent piece."[12] When Cage writes, "it moves in all directions and will be received in unpredictable ways," this may at first come as a surprise. The piece had received decidedly mixed reactions after its premiere two years before.[13] Was there any way of predicting the richness of the reception that *4'33"* would be accorded over the following sixty years? Hardly—and yet the different reactions of his contemporaries seem to have given Cage an inkling of the amazing future reception history of his "silent piece."

This reception history is closely connected to questions of intentionality or non-intentionality as part of the composition. From the creation of the piece through its reception/interpretation one can chart the following steps:

a Cage's motives for his decision to compose the "silent piece"
b the chance operations Cage employed while composing *4'33"*
c the musician/performer's choice of an approach to interpretation
d the sounds which can be heard during the performance
e the audience reactions, both private associations and public comments
f the academic discussion of *4'33"* and its consequences for music history

8 Yvonne Rainer, "Looking Myself in the Mouth" (1981), reprinted in Julia Robinson (ed.), *John Cage: October Files* (Cambridge, MA: MIT Press, 2011), p. 37.
9 William Duckworth, *Talking Music* (New York: Schirmer Books, 1995), pp. 13–15.
10 See note 12.
11 John Cage, "Experimental Music: Doctrine" (1955), in Cage, *Silence* (first edition Middletown, CT: Wesleyan University Press, 1961; in this essay quoted in Cambridge, MA: MIT Press, 1966), p. 15.
12 Helen Wolff chided Cage that he would ruin his reputation with the "silent piece" and that he just wanted to shock people. Her letter is in anticipation of the second performance of *4'33"* in New York 1954. First publication of the correspondence between Helen Wolff and John Cage in *MusikTexte* 106 (August 2005), pp. 47–50. Helen Wolff was wife to the publisher Kurt Wolff, and in 1950 Cage discovered the first English translation of the I Ching, which Kurt Wolff had edited, through their son Christian.
13 *4'33"* remained barely known until the early 1960s. In the complete catalog of scores published by Edition Peters in 1962, the piece is listed on page 25 under the header "Various Solos and Ensembles." During the ten years between the premiere in 1952 and its publication it had received only three documented performances. In an interview with Cage printed in the Edition Peters catalog, the motives of the piece still remain relatively unclear (ibid., p. 61). *Silence*, a 1961 collection of Cage's theoretical writings, has no explicit discussion of *4'33"*, despite the title of the book.

g artistic references to *4'33"* and works by other musicians and artists based on the piece

h variants of and sequels to *4'33"* by Cage himself.

This book and exhibition mostly focus on the last three points. Following the above breakdown, it is clear in retrospect that the diversity and contrariety of the piece's reception history were already inherent in the early steps of conception and realization. But wouldn't such a seemingly linear genealogy of development contradict the non-intentionality that Cage claimed for the creation of *4'33"*? The composer himself touched on this point in his 1954 letter to Helen Wolff: "If one imagines that I have intended any one of these responses he will have to imagine that I have intended all of them," was his comment on the controversial audience reactions.

Following this train of thought, it seems obvious that if we regard *4'33"* itself as free from intentionality, then the many astonishingly diverse versions, variants, and tributes from artists in the sixty years since the premiere in 1952, and the equally multifaceted, often contradictory academic readings of the piece, should definitely not be connected back to Cage's own probable intentions. It would indeed be strange to demand that Cage predict, let alone intend, this rich reception/interpretation history. Could it be that the diversity of reactions, as they are presented in this book, bear out the non-intentionality of the "silent piece?" These thoughts must lead to an aporia, since paradoxically non-intentionality becomes a second-degree intention. The seeming self-contradiction of an intended unintentionality has often been criticized, but it is mostly the result of critics short-circuiting their theoretical analysis of the work with the artistic methods of its production. Verbal comment (either from Cage himself or his critics) and musical composition do not follow the same logic. What sounds contradictory when regarded as an argument can sound completely coherent as music—just as the verb "to sound" will mean something different in each context.[14]

But let us begin with the ending. After studying the works presented in this volume, one question may come up: are in fact all the various readings and meanings of a single composition equally acceptable? Is the "horizon" of possible contexts and multiple layers of meaning contained within *4'33"* so wide that it can allow opposing perspectives on equal footing? Can there even be a false interpretation—in the sense of either an artistic performance or a critical examination—of the "silent piece?" If *4'33"* really expresses neither an aesthetic nor a philosophical intention, would all possible meanings of the piece discussed in print or experienced during a performance be of equal value? At least it can be said that the "quest for truth" approach that still tends to be followed in art history and musicology, the search for the "deeper sense" of *4'33"*, either intended by Cage or legitimized by his testimony, must necessarily fail here. Although Cage's approach often leads to a basic questioning of epistemological or aesthetic principles, it is impossible to resolve these questions from the context of his work or his commentary on it—especially since Cage had always stressed that rational understanding could not offer "final" conclusions with regard to an artwork's ontological mode or interpersonal differences and congruences in its perception. Often, independent of a discussion of Cage's work, factors like "presence," "ephemerality," "immediacy," and "sensibility of the moment," as well as "phenomenological individuality," have been cited as criteria of aesthetic experience.[15] In this sense, *4'33"* offers a *precedent* for aesthetic experience.

It would be too simple to view non-intentionality as indifference. Cage constructed a "purposeful purposelessness," for which he developed a series of complex methodologies that were effective precisely because they were paradoxical.[16] He said: "I believe that by eliminating purpose, what I call awareness increases. Therefore my purpose is to remove purpose."[17] The various chance operations, which Cage employed in his work, served exactly this "purposeful purposelessness"—from the I Ching [→ fig. 2] dating back thousands of years to the computer software custom-designed for Cage by Andrew Culver. Still it is obvious that we cannot ignore the first impulse, the decision, the will, and even the passion to make such a non-intentional work of art. From a philosophical standpoint there is a difference between intention and intentionality. While an artwork can to a large degree be free of any directed intention, the creation of such a work still follows some kind of intentionality, a directedness of actions, feelings, and the human will, which come before any explicit purpose.[18]

Fig. 2
The I Ching, key for identifying the hexagrams from the edition used by John Cage

UPPER TRIGRAM ➤ / LOWER TRIGRAM ▼	Ch'ien	Chên	K'an	Kên	K'un	Sun	Li	Tui
Ch'ien	1	34	5	26	11	9	14	43
Chên	25	51	3	27	24	42	21	17
K'an	6	40	29	4	7	59	64	47
Kên	33	62	39	52	15	53	56	31
K'un	12	16	8	23	2	20	35	45
Sun	44	32	48	18	46	57	50	28
Li	13	55	63	22	36	37	30	49
Tui	10	54	60	41	19	61	38	58

The I Ching or Book of Changes, The Richard Wilhelm Translation rendered into English by Cary F. Baynes, foreword by C.G. Jung, Bollingen Series XIX (New York: Pantheon books, 1950)

14 See Hanns-Werner Heister, "Intentionslosigkeit als Ideologie: Über Cage," in Otto Kolleritsch (ed.), *Über Klischee und Wirklichkeit der musikalischen Moderne, Studien zur Wertungsforschung 28* (Vienna: Universal Edition, 1994), pp. 35–59, and Edward Rothstein, "Cage's Cage" (1990), in *Writings about John Cage*, ed. Richard Kostelanetz (Ann Arbor: University of Michigan Press, 1993), pp. 301–08. For an opposite view cf. Dieter Mersch, *Ereignis und Aura: Untersuchungen zu einer Ästhetik des Performativen* (Frankfurt am Main: Suhrkamp, 2002), p. 288.

15 See Ursula Brandstätter, *Grundfragen der Ästhetik: Bild-Musik-Sprache-Körper* (Cologne: Böhlau, 2008), pp. 100, 116, 117, with reference to, among others, Martin Seel, Gottfried Boehm, Wolfgang Iser, Dieter Mersch, and Hans Ulrich Gubrecht.

16 John Cage, "Experimental Music" (1958), in Cage, *Silence*, p. 12. Compare also: "QUESTION: Then what is the purpose of this 'experimental' music? ANSWER: No purposes. Sounds." John Cage, "Experimental Music: Doctrine" (1955), in *Silence*, p. 17.

17 Cage, quoted in Christopher Shultis, "Silencing the Sounded Self: John Cage and the Intentionality of Nonintention," *The Musical Quarterly* 79, 2 (Summer 1995), p. 344.

18 "Things that are about other things exhibit intentionality. Beliefs and other mental states exhibit intentionality, but so, in a derived way, do sentences and books, maps and pictures, and other representations. The adjective "intentional" in this philosophical sense is a technical term not to be confused with the more familiar sense, characterizing something done on purpose. Hopes and fears, for instance, are not things we do, not intentional acts in the latter, familiar sense, but they are intentional phenomena in the technical sense: hopes and fears are about various things." *The Cambridge Dictionary of Philosophy*, 2nd edition (Cambridge: Cambridge University Press, 1999), p. 441.

To get back to the first stages of the process: does it make sense to question the intentions that led Cage to write such a non-intentional composition? "Numerous reasons have been offered by Cage and others, which should come as no surprise considering how it provides a clean slate, silence, absence, a nothingness rife with potentiality, a blank screen on which so much about so little can be projected."[19] This is what Douglas Kahn, one of Cage's sharpest critics, has to say on the multiple motives that would have led Cage to write this composition. And indeed, the composer has offered autobiographical stories time and again, reaching back even to his own school days.[20] Specifically, his work with children in 1941 has been mentioned by him as a possible source for the "silent piece."[21]

The temptation to read rather too much into Cage's statements is hard to resist. By telling anecdotes from the years before 1952 and relating them to the significance of his concept of silence in retrospect, he himself has only added to the situation. Apart from the biographical framework, though, a study of Cage's musical development makes it clear that silence did not suddenly blast into his work, instead it spread slowly. On the way there were extremely quiet sounds and prolonged rests, before Cage finally arrived at the completely "silent piece."[22] In a lecture four years before he wrote *4'33"*, Cage outlined the idea for a composition without sounds, which was conceived as a media intervention for the Muzak Company. It carried the poetic, spiritually charged title *Silent Prayer*[23] [→ p. 196]. Cage here mentioned four-and-a-half minutes as one of the standard lengths for "canned" music, although the duration of *4'33"* was later supposed to be the result of a series of chance operations. *Silent Prayer* was focused on the context of the mass media and of marketing within an economy of attention, whereas *4'33"* was written for a concert performance, where such matters would not play a role—a fact criticized by Douglas Kahn [→ pp. 201ff]. Obviously, during its lengthy gestation period, possible motives for the creation of *4'33"* became as pluralistic, or even as contradictory, as its future reception history would be.

Approached from yet another angle: can we perhaps redefine our "quest for truth," accept that there are multiple meanings, and see them as the "deeper sense" of *4'33"*? And going one step further: could it be that these multiple meanings are not simply the result of a reception process circling around the "nothingness" of *4'33"*? That it is rather the paradoxical construction of a "purposeful purposelessness" that stimulates the potential for impact? Is not the complexity of the "silent piece" an additional factor in the diversity of its reception?

Here again two different aspects come into play: first the creation of the "silent piece" in 1952, and second its different reworkings into a complete series of compositions up to 1992. The actual process of composing the original version of *4'33"* was more complex than is usually assumed. From his own testimony, Cage worked on the piece note for note over several days.[24] Further arguments for its complexity would be the different versions and methods of notation for *4'33"* as well as the variants and versionings of the piece that Cage wrote and performed until the end of his life.

Each of the three types of scores for *4'33"* underlines a different aspect of the piece:

— The notation on stave paper for the premiere in 1952 (the original has been lost, although two reconstructions by David Tudor from 1982 and 1990 exist) emphasizes the musical character; traditionally notated music can also contain silent moments, which are crucial for the impact of a composition.

— The graphic notation of 1953 (dedicated to Irwin Kremen) depicts the three parts as blank space between lines on six otherwise empty white pages, a time/space notation that offers a visual analogy to Robert Rauschenberg's *White Paintings*.

— The Tacet notation from 1960, first written on a typewriter and ultimately, in the fourth version (1986) in Cage's own handwriting, was the first score to be published, by Henmar Press. This version highlights the textual or conceptual aspect of the piece, which goes beyond the context of musical performance practices [→ Kotz, pp. 212ff/Bormann, p. 222ff].

The three versions, or methods of notation, can also be understood as different modes of the composition: notation as music, as time/space, and as a conceptual text. The three modes have unfolded in academic and artistic references to *4'33"*, where the piece is developed in a variety of ways: as music/performance/setting, as time-space sequence/audiovisual structure, and as concept/instruction/text score.

So if we choose alternative ways to get to the heart of the matter and find the "truth" behind the multiple meanings, which "heart" is it that we are referring to? The premiere on August 29, 1952? The first version of the score (lost but reconstructed by David Tudor)? Cage's original idea, as he had formulated it publicly for the first time in *Silent Prayer* four years earlier? Or the complete long series of variants, the different scores of *4'33"* as well as further compositions up until 1992, which Cage labeled as revised versions of *4'33"*?

The aim of our alternative "quest for truth" appears elusive, and it can lead to the same state of aporia we have experienced before. Indeed the richness of the "silent piece" itself is mirrored by the richness of its reception/interpretation history in music, art, and academic writing. But if, in retrospect, we ascribe the intention of activating all these possible repercussions to the

19 Douglas Kahn, "John Cage: Silence and Silencing," *The Musical Quarterly* 81 (4) (1997), p. 561.

20 Among other things, Cage pointed to a lecture he held at a High School competition when he was fifteen years old, "Other People Think." Here he proceeded from thoughts on the conflict between the U.S. and Latin America to envision a moment of pause, of silence, that would help to come to a pan-American understanding. See a reprint in *John Cage: An Anthology*, ed. Richard Kostelanetz (New York: Praeger, 1970), p. 48.

21 "I was employed by the WPA in San Francisco. I had applied to be in the music section of the WPA, but they refused to admit me because they said that I was not a musician. I said, 'Well, what am I? I work with sounds and percussion instruments, and so forth.' And they said, 'You could be a recreation leader.' So I was employed in the recreation department, and that may have been the birth of the silent piece, because my first assignment in the recreation department was to go to a hospital in San Francisco and entertain the children of the visitors. But I was not allowed to make any sound while I was doing it, for fear that it would disturb the patients. So I thought up games involving movement around the rooms and counting, etc., dealing with some kind of rhythm in space ..." "After Antiquity: John Cage in Conversation with Peter Gena," in *A John Cage Reader*, ed. Peter Gena and Jonathan Brent (New York: C.F. Peters Corp., 1982), p. 170; http://www.petergena.com/aftant.html.

22 See also the detailed musicological analysis of the importance of silence in Cage's music before *4'33"* in Thomas M. Maier, *Ausdruck der Zeit: Ein Weg zu John Cages stillem Stück 4'33"* (Saarbrücken: Pfau, 2001), and Eric De Visscher, "'There's no such thing as silence ...': John Cage's Poetics of Silence," in *Writings about John Cage*, ed. Kostelanetz.

23 The first publication of this lecture from 1948 had to wait until 1991: "John Cage: A Composer's Confession," in *MusikTexte* 40/41 (August 1991), pp. 55–68.

24 Cf. John Cage on the process of composing *4'33"*: "I wrote it note by note. ... It was done just like a piece of music, except there were no sounds – but there were durations." William Fetterman, *John Cage's Theatre Pieces: Notations and Performances* (London: Routledge, 1996), p. 72. Also: "I built up the silence of each movement and the three movements add up to *4'33"*. I built up each movement by means of short silences put together. It seems idiotic, but that's what I did." When asked back by the interviewer if this had been a "very spontaneous creation," Cage said: "No, no it took several days to write it and it took me several years to come to the decision to make it and I lost friends over it." *John Cage I–VI: The Charles Eliot Norton Lectures, 1988–89* (Cambridge, MA: Harvard University Press, 1990), pp. 20–23.

author of a non-intentional work, we return to where we started, since such a proposition is, as we have already seen, manifestly absurd.

If our thoughts move in circles here, they're still not trapped in a vicious cycle that offers no escape. Instead we circle the "silent piece" and get closer to an understanding of it, without having arrived or even wanting to arrive at a conclusion. New facets of the composition open themselves to us and we gain new insights into the influence it exerts. This approach can be described through a term from literary theory: the "hermeneutic spiral."[25] It is a model, though, that is still focused on a fixed core in the center of the spiral. However, *4'33"* is a precedent for the aesthetic experience that Ursula Brandstätter has termed "divergent thinking." In contrast to academic "convergent thinking," characterized by its orientation toward a fixed truth, "divergent thinking" is an aesthetic that allows a variety of interpretations, problem presentations, and solutions, where divergent modes of perception and thinking can coexist without having to lead to a final conclusion.[26]

This opens up another possibility of coping with the fact that there is no ultimate version of *4'33"*. Cage's reformulations, continuations, and new interpretations of the "silent piece" in the years from 1948 to 1992 can be understood as his active participation in the development of multiple meanings for its reception/ interpretation history. Cage, in his 1954 letter to Helen Wolff, stressed the absurdity of any attempt to define his intentions; yet his comments and further compositions helped to multiply and diversify reactions. Why shouldn't the author himself take part in this play of constant transformation? He does so in different ways, mainly by lending a philosophical context to the "silent piece." Cage's comments taken together shape the reception history as much as, if not more than, actual performances of the composition. Christian Wolff has pointed out that Cage's writings and lectures had a vast influence, despite the fact that many ideas he had "characteristically expressed" were explicitly borrowed from others. On the other hand, Cage's music had no real influence; it has stayed sui generis and was not taken up by other composers.[27]

Dörte Schmidt has shown the extent to which Cage's comments on *4'33"* changed over the years [→ p. 67ff]. Nevertheless, these comments are rarely read as single utterances from a specific point in time, but rather as universally valid auctorial statements. Similarly, Cage's own versions and variants of *4'33"* always focus on different aspects of silence. *0'00"* (*4'33" No. 2)* from 1962, for example, stretches the conventions of musical notation even further: there are no prescribed durations and no three movements; instead, a non-musical action is performed in the time that it will take to perform, while all sounds resulting from the action are electronically amplified.[28] On the other hand, *0'00"* (*4'33" No. 2)* stays much closer to the conventions of the musical performance situation than *4'33"*: there are sounds to hear that are produced by a performer in front of an audience. Such compositional reworkings of the "silent piece," as well as the changing commentary from the composer, combine with the reception/interpretation history contributed by scholars and artists to turn the question, "What is *4'33"*?" into an unresolvable, ongoing process. Sixty years after its premiere, the "silent piece" remains a thought-provoking challenge.

Cage has famously said that "there is no such thing as silence," and it would be equally true to extrapolate that "there is no such thing as *4'33"*." Just as silence is, according to Cage, always filled with something other, something unforeseeable, the "silent piece" is filled with multiple meanings that are still never opposed to each other. In contrast to the idea of a musical *presque rien*, which according to Theodor Adorno would be equivalent to a "negative dialectic," which must finally turn against itself, Cage's silence empowers the self-affirmation of the non-intentional by constantly revealing new aspects and augmentations.[29]

II
An Aesthetics of Receptivity

Can one make works which are not works of "art?"
—Marcel Duchamp[30]

Or this form of work: an art without work.
—John Cage on *4'33"*[31]

In his comments and writings, Cage mostly wanted to justify his musical practice.[32] Nevertheless, the comments are often read as if they were a self-contained theory, which can easily lead to misunderstandings.[33] He does not offer an aesthetics of reception with firm theoretical foundations, but rather an artistic aesthetics of receptivity—the creation of artworks, or of aesthetic situations, that are made for active reception.

Cage's practical activity trying to create non-intentional artworks finds a parallel in his theory of a necessarily individual perception of art. In 1965 he said: "The structure we should think about is that of each person in the audience. In other words, his consciousness is structuring the experience differently from anybody else's in the audience. So the less we structure the theatrical occasion and the more it is like unstructured daily life, the greater will be the stimulus to the structuring faculty of each person in the audience. If we have done nothing, he will have everything to do."[34]

25 Jürgen Bolten, "Die Hermeneutische Spirale: Überlegungen zu einer integrativen Literaturtheorie," in *Poetica* 17, H. 3/4 (1985), pp. 362–63.

26 Ursula Brandstätter, *Grundfragen der Ästhetik: Bild-Musik-Sprache-Körper* (Cologne: Böhlau, 2008), p. 104.

27 Christian Wolff, "Under the Influence: On John Cage," in Wolff, *Cues: Writings and Conversations/Hinweise: Schriften und Gespräche*, ed. Gisela Gronemeyer and Reinhard Oehlschägel (Cologne: Musiktexte, 1998), p. 153.

28 In the score *0'00"*, Cage stipulates that the action should fulfill an "obligation to others", making the inherent social factor of *4'33"* explicit. Cage realized this in his own performances of *0'00" (4'33" No. 2)*, when, for example, he chose to write his correspondence on stage, amplifying the sounds of his typewriter through contact microphones.

29 Cf. Lydia Goehr, "For the Birds/Against the Birds: The Modernist Narratives of Danto and Adorno (and Cage)," in Daniel Herwitz and Michael Kelly (eds.), *Action, Art, History: Engagement with Arthur Danto* (New York: Columbia University Press, 2007), p. 43–73.

30 Marcel Duchamp, 1913, from the notes collected in *À l'infinitif*, quoted in *Salt Seller: The Writings of Marcel Duchamp*, ed. Michel Sanouillet and Elmer Peterson (Oxford: Oxford University Press, 1973), p. 74.

31 "I knew that it would be taken as a joke and a renunciation of work, whereas I also knew that if it was done it would be the highest form of work. Or this form of work: an art without work. I doubt whether many people understand it yet." John Cage in William Duckworth, "Anything I Say Will Be Misunderstood: An Interview with John Cage," in *John Cage at Seventy-Five*, ed. Richard Fleming and William Duckworth (Lewisburg, PA: Bucknell University Press, 1989), p. 21.

32 "In his compositions, Cage cannot explain the idea behind his music, he can only demonstrate it. More than anything else, the realization that this problem can't be solved within the music led Cage to develop his ideas in writings and lectures." Sabine Sanio, "Strategien der Unbestimmtheit: Cages Ästhetik und die Zukunft der Musik," in Peter Rautmann and Nicolas Schalz (eds.), *Anarchische Harmonie: John Cage und die Zukunft der Künste* (Bremen: Hochschule der Künste, 2002), p. 116. With this, Sanio also points out the performativity of Cage's "theory."

33 Cf. on the same problem in the fine arts: Ana Dimke, *Duchamps Künstlertheorie: Eine Lektüre zur Vermittlung von Kunst* (Hann. Münden: Scrollheim, 2001), here pp. 13ff. on "artist theory" as a term.

34 Quoted in Fetterman, *John Cage's Theatre Pieces*, p. 92.

While this artistic attitude finds its clearest expression in *4'33"*, it informs Cage's complete musical output from around 1950 on. George Brecht, who, together with other artists who later became part of the Fluxus movement, attended an "experimental composition" course taught by Cage in 1958, took notes of his remarks. The composer characterized his approach in contrast to that of his companions Morton Feldman, Earle Brown, and Christian Wolff: "Cage '4 min 33 sec.' Silence. Tacet. Each observer to have his own experience of the sound in the auditorium."[35] For George Brecht, the consequence lay in developing the concept of a "virtuoso listener:" "The 'virtu' of virtuosity must now mean behavior out of one's life-experience; it cannot be delimited toward physical skill. The listener responding to this sound out of his own experience, adds a new element to the system: composer/notation/performer/sound/listener, and, for himself, defines the sound as music. For the virtuoso listener all sound may be music."[36]

Fig. 3
George Brecht,
event cards from *Water Yam*,
1962

INSTRUCTION

- **Turn on a radio.**

At the first sound, turn it off.

TWO SIGNS

- SILENCE
- NO VACANCY

One can see Cage's theory of an individuality of aesthetic perception as biographically motivated, as a positive outcome of the shocking realization that he could not directly communicate emotions through his music.[37] This shock led him to renunciate intention/emotion/expression in his compositions, and to make the individual reception/interpretation an absolute. This had consequences that went far beyond the biographical motive: for Cage there are no more distinct boundaries between reception and interpretation after *4'33"*. All aesthetic perception at the same time is something actively given shape by the individual—which is also why I have chosen to use the two terms as a single entity, written as reception/interpretation.[38] My thesis is that this individuality of the aesthetic experience can not only be applied to a performance situation of *4'33"*, but also as a guiding theme for the complete spectrum of the piece's reception history. There it applies to the last five stages mentioned above: the perception of the work (by the audience), its performance (e.g. by a musician[39]), but also the reading of the work (through comments or academic analysis), and finally artistic or musical variants or developments (by Cage or others).

"If one imagines that I have intended any one of these responses he will have to imagine that I have intended all of them"—this statement by Cage, already quoted above, was intended to answer the audience reaction to the 1954 performance. While it can be extrapolated to apply to the complete reception history, it cannot be seen as an origination or anticipation of later developments. Otherwise we would have the old circular argument where we are short-circuiting the logic of perception with that of auctorial intent. The above quote follows a model of thought typical for Cage: without transition, he switches from the singular to the universal, and he monopolizes the answer before it has even been given. What started as a logical argument in the end becomes a quasi-theological dictum, like the one Cage immediately follows up with: "Something like faith must take over in order that we live affirmatively in the totality we live in."

Cage's attitude does not lead to indifference, but to an equivalence of all realized receptions/interpretations. They become manifest only in the individual experience during each single performance of the piece. Cage puts the performance over the score, the actual experience is more important than the idea behind it. From the mid-1950s on, he wrote his music without hearing it—he would hear it for the first time at the premiere, most often interpreted by David Tudor.[40] Cage said: "I don't hear music when I write it. I write in order to hear something I haven't heard yet."[41] Thus he himself was in a situation similar to that of his audience: only in the reception of his own work would he hear the sound of his music.[42] This equivalence between listener and

35 George Brecht, *Notebooks I·II·III*, ed. Dieter Daniels in collaboration with Hermann Braun (Cologne: Verlag der Buchhandlung Walther König, 1991): *Vol. I, June–September 1958*, p. 48.

36 George Brecht, *Notebooks I·II·III*, ed. Daniels, Braun: *Vol. III, April–August 1959*, p. 123 (spelling corrected).

37 Cf. Cage on his compositions *Amores and The Perilous Night* and the lack of understanding they met in Calvin Tomkins, *The Bride and the Bachelors* (New York: Viking Press, 1968), p. 97.

38 As early as 1954, John Cage outlined a version of *4'33"* designed purely for reception, without performer or concert context: "I have spent many pleasant hours in the woods conducting performances of my silent piece, transcriptions, that is, for an audience of myself, since they were much longer than the popular length which I have had published. At one performance, I passed the first movement by attempting the identification of a mushroom which remained successfully unidentified. The second movement was extremely dramatic, beginning with the sounds of a buck and a doe leaping up to within ten feet of my rocky podium. The expressivity of this movement was not only dramatic but unusually sad from my point of view, for the animals were frightened simply because I was a human being. However, they left hesitatingly and fittingly within the structure of the work. The third movement was a return to the theme of the first, but with all those profound, so-well-known alterations of world feeling associated by German tradition with the A-B-A." John Cage, "Music Lovers' Field Companion" (1954) in Cage, *Silence*, p. 276.

39 William Fetterman insists that performers of *4'33"* should find their own manner of interpretation instead of simply imitating David Tudor. See Fetterman, *John Cage's Theatre Pieces*, p. 82.

40 "Cage himself could not hear what he had written until Tudor got the score and played it (Cage had given up his own piano when he moved out to the country), and Tudor's solutions to the problems of performance would often open up whole areas of sound that Cage had never foreseen." Tomkins, *The Bride and the Bachelors*, p. 124.

41 Liz Kotz, *Words to be Looked At: Language in 1960s Art* (Cambridge, MA: MIT Press, 2010), p. 50.

42 Cf. also the term "experimental" as used by Cage. While in the natural sciences the repeatability of an experiment serves as proof for the thesis, Cage speaks of an experimental indeterminacy that will lead to an outcome that cannot be foreseen, to a different sound experience. See e.g. John Cage, "Experimental Music" (1958), in Cage, *Silence*, p. 7.

composer, which reached a radical point in *4'33"*, would become an important aspect in the work of other composers too: "For experimental music emphasizes an unprecedented fluidity of composer/performer/listener roles, as it breaks away from the standard sender/carrier/receiver information structure," as Michael Nyman wrote.[43]

In this sense, an aesthetics of receptivity requires that there is no way in which an artwork exists—not, for example, through the intentions or emotions of its creator—independent of its perception: there can be no aesthetics prior to the individual aesthetic experience. Here again we have the same opposition between aesthetic, "divergent" and theoretical, "convergent" thinking: without an artistic intention there can be no "correct" interpretation. But even if criteria like right or wrong no longer apply, an interpretation can still be inadequate or illogical, either in the academic or in the artistic sense. In Cage's collaborations with classical orchestras, for example, it often happened that the professional musicians could not identify with their changed roles and their freedom of interpretation ended up in all manner of antics.[44] Even if there is no absolute final truth, the elemental question as to whether the many, seemingly contradictory interpretations can be of equal value does not lead to a complete free-for-all.

This comes close to Wittgenstein's argument against essentialism in respect to the meaning of language. According to Wittgenstein, there is no hidden essential intention of language beyond the use of words. Instead, "meaning is use"—a dictum that found fertile ground in Cage from 1970 at the latest.[45] Wittgenstein is interested primarily in epistemological questions, not aesthetics. In philosophy, the special importance of aesthetic experience, of its unalienable individuality, can be traced back to Immanuel Kant's *Critique of Judgment*, where matters of taste do have universality, but only as an outcome of generalizing from one's own perceptions and not as a genuinely cognitive achievement. Dieter Mersch, for example, postulates a "reinvention of aesthetics through *aisthesis*," to cut away the many overlayering forms of discourse and get back to the fruitful core of perception. Mersch refers especially to Cage as the protagonist of a "responsive" attitude to an "ethics of performativity."[46] Here Cage's performative "artist theory" itself becomes part of the academic discourse around concepts of performativity.

From this context we understand why Cage had no sympathy for the conceptual art of the 1970s, despite the fact that these artists saw him as their forebear: "Obviously, if under the title 'work of art' I am dealing with nothing but an idea—not an experience at all—then I lose the experience." As an example Cage cites the first New York performance of all 840 repetitions of Erik Satie's *Vexations*, during which he felt something happened which, contrary to expectations, changed everybody's lives: "So if I apply this observation [during the *Vexations* performance] to conceptual art, it seems to me that the difficulty with this type of art, if I understand it correctly, is that it obliges us to imagine that we know something before that something has happened. That is difficult, since the experience itself is always different from what you thought about it."[47]

Cage's understanding of the role of the recipient shows similarities to that of Marcel Duchamp, who thought that the viewer had a constitutive role in every aesthetic experience and thus added "his contribution to the creative act."[48] On another occasion Duchamp radicalized this thought by saying "that a work is made entirely by those who look at it or read it, and ensure its survival through their acclaim or even their condemnation."[49] Duchamp explicitly drew on his experiences in the art world, and especially readings of his work by the *écriture critique*. His statements on creation show clear analogies to his theories of reception. In his lecture on "The Creative Act" from 1957 he said: "The personal 'art coefficient' is like an arithmetical relation between the unexpressed but intended and the unintentionally expressed."[50] One could also put it like this: the production of all art is at least partially non-intentional, and the greater the divergence from an intention, the higher the personal art coefficient.

Much has been written about the common ground in the "art theories" of Duchamp and Cage, which tends to lose sight of the very fundamental differences between them.[51] It is, for example, tempting to compare *4'33"* with the readymades. In both cases artistic self-expression has been replaced by the acceptance of a found object/situation. Duchamp, like Cage, wanted to escape the snares of intentionality. Still there are significant distinctions: the object, once found, remains static for the time being, while the sounds change across the four and a half minutes during every performance. Duchamp's readymades were his answer to the question: "Can one make works which are not works of 'art'?" Cage on the other hand spoke of *4'33"* as "art without work."[52] Both approaches are in a *reciprocal* relationship: Duchamp clung to the idea of the "work," but didn't want to reduce the object to an art context; Cage on the other hand, while he still saw himself in an art or music context, didn't want to create works at all, but preferred to offer a situation for reception. Duchamp started with a solitary experiment in his studio; Cage within a social situation in the concert hall.[53]

One might think that these were genre-specific differences between the visual arts and music, object/work on one side and process/perception on the other. But here one must remember that Duchamp also created "musical" readymades that were based on principles of chance, similar to those used by Cage.[54] Duchamp also saw an element of situative temporality in the readymade, which he characterized as "a kind of rendez-vous."[55]

43 Michael Nyman, *Experimental Music: Cage and Beyond* (New York: Schirmer, 1974), p. 20.

44 Cf. a letter by Cage to the orchestra of the Zürich opera: "My work has been grossly misrepresented, largely, I am sorry to say, by you musicians." Published as "Letter to Zurich" in Richard Kostelanetz (ed.), *John Cage: Writer. Previously Uncollected Pieces* (New York: Limelight Editions, 1993), pp. 255–56. (Thanks to Gisela Gronemeyer for a transcription of the original letter, where Cage had added the word "grossly" by hand.) See also Kotz, *Words to Be Looked At*, p. 55.

45 See Cage, *For the Birds*, p. 154.

46 Dieter Mersch, *Ereignis und Aura: Untersuchungen zu einer Ästhetik des Performativen* (Frankfurt am Main: Suhrkamp, 2002), pp. 9, 289.

47 Cage, *For the Birds*, p. 153.

48 Marcel Duchamp lecture "The Creative Act" (1957), quoted in Robert Lebel, *Marcel Duchamp* (New York: Grove Press, 1959), p. 78.

49 Marcel Duchamp in a letter of 1956 to Jean Mayoux, in Francis M. Naumann and Hector Obalk (eds.), *Affect Marcel: The Selected Correspondence of Marcel Duchamp* (London: Thames & Hudson, 2000), p. 348.

50 Marcel Duchamp lecture "The Creative Act" (1957), quoted in Robert Lebel, *Marcel Duchamp* (New York: Grove Press, 1959), p. 78.

51 Cf. among others Moira Roth and Jonathan D. Katz, *Difference/Indifference: Musings on Postmodernism, Marcel Duchamp and John Cage* (Amsterdam: G+B Arts International, 1998), and Julia Dür, "Glass Wanderers: The Blurring of the Distinction between Art and Life in John Cage and Marcel Duchamp" (M.A. thesis, 2001); excerpts published in: tout-fait 2, 5 (2003), online at http://www.toutfait.com/issues/volume2/issue_5/articles/dur/dur2.html.

52 See footnotes 30 and 31.

53 See Dieter Daniels, "Das Ready-made als privates Objekt," in Daniels, *Duchamp und die anderen: Der Modellfall einer künstlerischen Wirkungsgeschichte in der Moderne* (Cologne: DuMont, 1992), pp. 214–16.

54 See Dieter Daniels, "Zufall und Technik in Kunst und Musik bei Duchamp, Cage und Paik," in Katja Riemer and Andreas Kreul (eds.), *Wunderkammermusik: Die Sammlungen der Kunsthalle Bremen* (Cologne: DuMont, 2011), pp. 246–55.

55 Marcel Duchamp in a note from around 1915 included in the Green Box (1934): "Specifications for 'Readymades'/By planning for a moment to come (on such a day, such a date, such a minute), 'to inscribe a readymade' – The readymade can later be looked for (with all kinds of delays). – The important thing then is just this matter of timing, this snapshot effect, like a speech delivered on no matter what occasion but at such and such an hour. It is a kind of rendez-vous. Naturally inscribe that date, hour, minute on the readymade as information." Quoted in *Salt Seller*, ed. Sanouillet/Peterson, p. 32.

More than anything, the consequences that Cage and Duchamp drew from their discoveries were completely contrary: for Duchamp the readymade was the terminal point of his art, after which the period of his famous retreat from the art world began. He was at first very skeptical when, during the 1960s, the use of found objects became common artistic practice, with the artists concerned invoking him as their forebear. Cage, on the other hand, saw *4'33"* as a starting point for a new working method, allowing him to write more music afterwards than ever before. Duchamp retired from the eyes of the art public, at least for a period of time, and stopped calling himself an artist.[56] Cage always saw himself as a composer and his immense productivity became even greater toward the end of his life.

The substantial significance of quantity in Cage's production has been best recognized by Nam June Paik, whose artistic work was similarly driven by a contrast between reduction and excess. In 1958 Paik asked Cage if he couldn't easily write twenty pieces a day through chance procedures, and then which one he would decide to perform and which reject in the end. "It doesn't matter which," Cage answered, and Paik explained: "This is no lack of responsibility. Instead it is a beautiful submission to nature, leaving behind stubbornness between the intentional and unintentional to reach the center of the sky."[57] Thirty years later, he wrote in his obituary for Cage: "[Buckminster] Fuller said: 'I accept the universe.' I said: 'I accept Cage,' since he was like nature or the universe. His huge quantity disarmed our smaller measure, which we call 'quality' in two different senses: 1. Better ... or worse ... 2. Different ... In Cage's music the huge quantity makes this distinction ineffective."[58] In contrast, Duchamp's influence was based on a small œuvre of few but highly concentrated works.

In 1968 John Cage conceived the piece *Reunion* as a collaboration with Marcel Duchamp, and with it he threw all the commonalities and differences between the two into sharp relief. A chessboard was prepared with electronic light sensors by Lowell Cross, in such a way that movements of the chess pieces would mix the live performance sounds of electronic compositions by David Behrman, Gordon Mumma, David Tudor, and John Cage, fading them in and out, panning them across the room. The collective nature of the composition also inspired its title, *Reunion*. At the chessboard were Cage and guest star Marcel Duchamp, as well as his wife Teeny Duchamp. Cage masterminded the event, which went on for several hours [→ fig. 4].

Reunion is related to *4'33"* through several degrees of variation. The score to Cage's *0'00" No. 2* from 1968 had read: "Two or more performers playing a game on a playing area (table or board) amplified with contact microphones."[59] That piece was in a way subliminally integrated into *Reunion*, where on Cage's express wish Lowell Cross prepared the chessboard with contact microphones.[60] But the sounds the players made moving the pieces around could hardly be heard despite the amplification.[61] The board mainly served as a control matrix for picking out and distributing the sounds of the collaborators' compositions throughout the room.

It was again the social aspect of the piece's title that stood at the core of *Reunion*, something which became increasingly important for Cage in the late 1960s. "Art instead of being an object made by one person is a process set in motion by a group of people. Art's socialized. It isn't someone saying something, but people doing things, giving everyone (included those involved) the opportunity to have experiences they would not otherwise have had," Cage wrote in 1967.[62] There could be no greater contrast to Marcel Duchamp's statement from 1963: "The artist should be alone ... Everyone for himself, as in a shipwreck."[63]

Fig. 4
John Cage, Teeny and Marcel Duchamp in *Reunion* at the Ryerson Theatre in Toronto, 1968

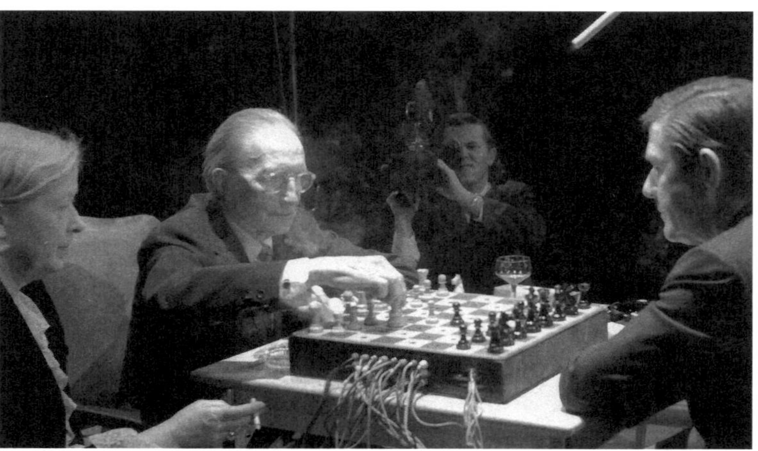

That John Cage started to focus on the social aspect of his art in the 1960s, whereas in the 1950s he had stressed the individuality of the aesthetic experience, is probably also due to the changing spirit of the times. Both views are based on the mutual presence of individuals meeting in a social situation during a musical performance. That is one reason for Cage's lack of interest or even dismissal of conceptual art—the fact that he did not find any shared aesthetic experience in it, but viewed it rather as an intellectual act.[64] For Duchamp, on the other hand, there existed a purely cerebral beauty, for example in the game of chess.[65] Cage insisted that *4'33"* was "a very physical work, not conceptual," which could be grasped only when listening to it and not through reflexive contemplations.[66]

Cage's aesthetics of reception had a bodily and social component, which led him to a very skeptical attitude toward recorded music. It is well known that Cage himself did not own a hi-fi system or record collection, but that he preferred to visit live per-

56 Only after Duchamp's death in 1968 was it revealed that he had worked on his last great work, *Étant donnés*, for twenty years.
57 Translated from the German: Nam June Paik, "Rezension zu den Darmstädter Ferienkursen für Neue Musik" (1958), in: *Nam June Paik: Fluxus/Video*, ed. Wulf Herzogenrath and Sabine M. Schmidt (exh. cat. Kunsthalle Bremen, 1999), p. 22.
58 Paik in his obituary for Cage, published in German: "B.C./A.D.," in *MusikTexte* 46/47 (December 1992), p. 69.
59 John Cage, *0'00" No. 2*, 1968 (C.F. Peters; 6806a 1970, 1987). No score has survived for the *Reunion* performance.
60 For the technical functions of the chessboard and the contact mikes see Lowell Cross, "*Reunion*: John Cage, Marcel Duchamp, Electronic Music and Chess," in *Leonardo Music Journal* 9 (December 1999), pp. 35–42.
61 This was also reflected in the program for the event, which did not list Cage's composition: "The program is full of errors: John's contribution, *0'00" II*, is not announced at all." Letter from Lowell Cross to Pauline Oliveros, March 7, 1969. [→ Schröder, p. 67]
62 John Cage, "Diary: How to Improve the World (You Will Only Make Matters Worse), Continued 1967," in Cage, *A Year from Monday*, p. 151.
63 Duchamp 1963 in a conversation with Jean-Marie Drot, quoted in Calvin Tomkins, *Duchamp: A Biography* (New York: Henry Holt, 1996), p. 93.
64 See Cage, *For the Birds*, pp. 153–54.
65 Seth Kim-Cohen's approach, which takes Duchamp's "non-retinal" art as a model for a conceptual "non-cochlear sonic art," compared to which Cage's *0'00"* would be a "materialist listening activity, still very much about the ear," falls short of the mark here. On the one hand, Duchamp's late work up until *Étant donnés* stressed the corporeality, even the tactility of the gaze. On the other hand, Cage did not insist on corporeality in an empiricist or materialist fashion, but rather focused on a mutual presence in the "there and here," in the act of listening, as has been shown by Brandon LaBelle. Cf. Kim-Cohen, *In the Blink of an Ear*, p. 163; and Brandon LaBelle, "Noise, Over-Hearing, and Cage's *4'33"*" [→ pp. 45ff].
66 Cage in an interview with Alcides Lanza in 1971. Quoted in Richard Kostelanetz, *Conversing with Cage* (2nd edition, New York: Routledge, 2003), p. 218.

formances by his colleagues from the New Music scene.[67] This might seem paradoxical behavior for a composer who utilized records, tapes, and radios in his own music. But Cage used these media like musical instruments in a performance situation, as generators of live sounds, not as reproduction apparatuses. Over the indeterminacy of the score he added a second layer of media-based indeterminacy. Nam June Paik wrote: "The best part of Cage's creation is his LIVE electronic music, which is a whole TIME-SPACE art, which can never be made into either audio or video disc."[68] The fact that Cage did not use any technology in *4'33"* makes this even more obvious.

Within Cage's œuvre, *4'33"* can be set against two of his pioneering efforts for electronic media, which, as it happens, also have a duration of four minutes: the tape montage *Williams Mix* (1952) and *Imaginary Landscape No. 4* (1951) for twelve radios. The latter premiered late at night when most radio stations had already signed off, which led to a silence unexpected by the listeners. This prompted a reaction every bit as controversial as that which greeted the opening performance of *4'33"* a year later.[69] The audience of *Imaginary Landscape No. 4* experienced a similar four minutes of heightened sensibility where the listening act replaced the musical content—although here mediated by the twelve radios used as instruments, whose tuned-in stations would make the ubiquity of the mass media tangible aesthetic source material for a performance. In today's terminology one could even label *4'33"* as an unplugged version of the composition for radios.[70]

A recording of *4'33"* contradicts the mutual presence in the here and now, and the indeterminacy of the unexpected sounds that to Cage were crucial factors of the work. Still there are more than fifty recordings of *4'33"* on LP, cassette, and CD, some of them by popular musicians like Frank Zappa [→ Discography, p. 185–92]. A recording of *4'33"* must necessarily be a paradox—since a live performance is possible at all times anywhere by anyone, and much easier to realize. Storing "silence" on a sound carrier and playing it back at a different time and place leads to the overlayering of minimal noises from the present and recorded situations. A recording of *4'33"* puts the listener into the unaccustomed position of having to permanently switch attention between the "here and now" of the listening space and the "back then" of the recording event. This is very interesting for a theory of reception but has nothing to do with the original composition by Cage. The video installation *Two Times 4'33"* (2007) [→ p. 257] by Manon De Boer plays on exactly this concurrency of playback and live atmosphere, of reproduction and "aura" (if one wants to think in these terms) [→ fig. 5]. First she presents a performance of *4'33"* in a video with location sound, then a second video with the sound completely switched off. That technical reproduction can itself produce an "aura" is proved by Matthieu Saladin in his sound piece *4'33"/0'00"* from 2008 [→ p. 269]. He takes the first LP recording of *4'33"*, interpreted by Gianni-Emilio Simonetti in 1974, and through maximum amplification transforms it into a contemporary digital homage to Cage's *0'00"*. Besides a few obscure background noises the sound is especially dominated by vinyl crackle, which has become amplified to a roaring storm. In a work group without explicit reference to John Cage, Dave Allen recorded the room tone of silence in venues of famous musical performances—for example the Berlin Philharmonie and the Hansa Studios Berlin, where David Bowie had produced his albums *Heroes* and *Low* [→ p. 256]. These *Silent Recordings*, each an acoustic materialization of the respective genius loci, tell us two things: that sounds of the past have in fact not written themselves into the room, and that our knowledge about these places will create a sort of sonic mirage that almost makes us believe we still perceive the reverberations of sounds of long ago—the way J.G. Ballard has suggestively described them in his science fiction story *The Sound-Sweep* from 1960.

Fig. 5
Manon de Boer, *Two Times 4'33"*, 2007

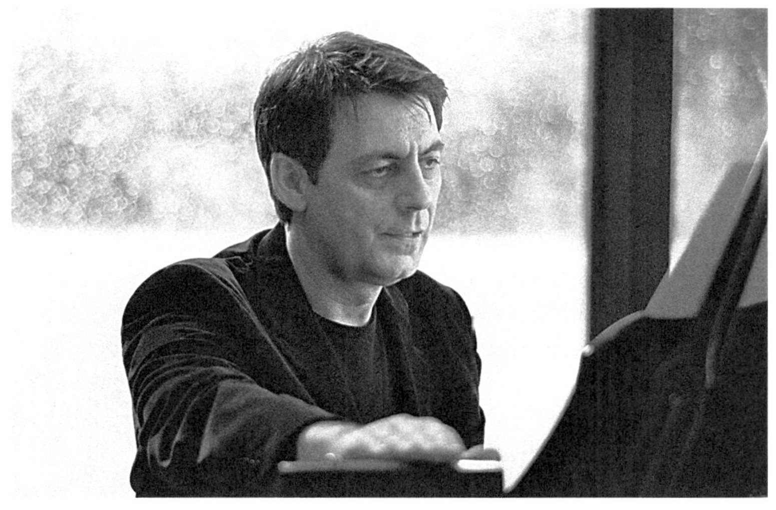

The project "Cage Against the Machine" offers *4'33"* as an intervention into the mass-medial marketing structures of (pop) music [→ p. 258/→ fig. 6]. The artists are, perhaps unconsciously, following Cage's intention here, in that his first idea for a "Silent Prayer" in 1948 was planned as a broadcast on a Muzak channel.

Fig. 6
Cage Against the Machine, recording session for *4'33"*, 2010

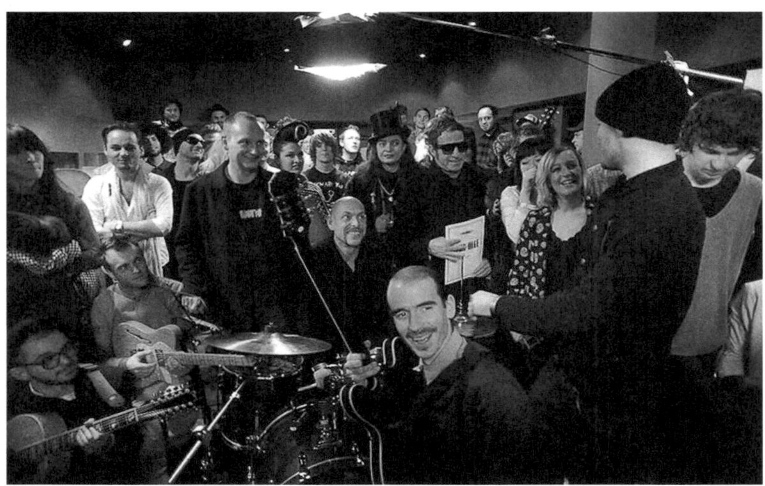

67 See David Revill, *The Roaring Silence: John Cage, A Life* (New York: Arcade, 1992). German edition *Tosende Stille: Eine John Cage Biographie* (Munich: List, 1995), p. 411.
68 Nam June Paik, "Random Access Information," *Artforum* 19, 1 (September 1980), p. 49.
69 Cf. John Hollander, "Silence" (1962), in Richard Kostelanetz (ed.), *Writings about John Cage*, p. 266. Furthermore, *Imaginary Landscape No. 4* was Cage's first piece in proportional notation, though here still combined with conventional notation, a precursor of the proportional score for *4'33"*.
70 For a longer comparison between *4'33"* and both *Williams Mix* and *Imaginary Landscape No. 4* see: Dieter Daniels, "John Cage and Nam June Paik: 'Change your mind or change your receiver (your receiver is your mind)'" in *Nam June Paik*, ed. Sook-Kyung Lee and Susanne Rennert (exh. cat. Tate Liverpool, 2010), especially pp. 110–14.

Petri Söderström-Kelley's online game *4 Minutes and 33 Seconds of Uniqueness* (2009) [→ p. 269], does not attempt to beat the mass media with its own weapons, but instead caters to our desire to be unique: the game can only be played by one player at a time worldwide. It can therefore be understood as a contemporary contribution to the individuality of the aesthetic experience in the Internet age.

III
The Ambivalence of Silence

The thematic spectrum of this book and exhibition reaches beyond John Cage's "silent piece" to include changes in the cultural relevance of silence since the middle of the twentieth century. A multitude of cultural connotations are evident in the different meanings that the term silence may have depending on context.[71] Here one can largely distinguish between the musical and communicative aspects. In classical music, "tacet" signifies that the musician is to remain silent for the complete movement. A musical rest is mainly of aesthetic significance. In verbal communication, on the other hand, silence is a more active proposition. It often equates to a refusal to communicate, for example in Ingmar Bergman's film *The Silence* (1963), which in turn would inspire Joseph Beuys to create an eponymous object in 1973, where galvanized film reels delivered the perfect image for how leaden the silence can become. In contrast to Cage's concept of a receptivity of silence, the term silence in communication refers to a non-compliance: keeping silent, keeping secrets. Heinrich Böll's short story *Murke's Collected Silences* (1955, trans. 1963) addresses this ambivalence: it is about silent moments that have no place in radio as the new mass medium, and also about a silence regarding the national socialist years, during which Murke's chief opponent Bur-Malottke seems to have played an important role.

Besides the musical and communicative aspects, one can also discern a certain corporeality of silence. Cage always insisted that *4'33"* was a physical work.[72] His experience in an anechoic chamber, often quoted by him as an initial moment in the genesis of *4'33"*, illustrates the physiological foundation for his realization that absolute silence cannot exist: the sounds of the involuntary functions of the human organism become perceptible if we are isolated from outside stimulation [→ his account on p. 196]. It is not important here whether the two sounds he heard were really produced by his nervous system and blood circulation —which was his explanation for the experience—or if they were the physiological/physical effect of air molecules in the ears, or even a mild tinnitus, as David Toop [→ p. 53] and Seth Kim-Cohen[73] have suspected. For Cage, the important point was that in "subjective" human perception there is no place for "objective" silence, because the body of the subject will move into the foreground of perception through proprioception. Here Cage's insistence on a corporeality of hearing pertains to theories of "embodiment," from Maurice Merleau-Ponty to recent findings in the cognitive sciences.

One of the most intense connections between corporeality and music is created in dance. It may seem absurd, therefore, to integrate silence and dance. During the long years of their collaboration, John Cage and Merce Cunnigham opened up new areas, where the sounds of dancers' bodies were no longer mere interferences but became part of musical compositions [→ Schröder, p. 59]. Brandon LaBelle took these concepts one step further in his piece *Sonic Body* (2009), where an unheard musical composition becomes perceivable only through the sounds of a dancer's movements [→ LaBelle, p. 45]. The relation between silence and body can also be switched around, so that it isn't about the body used as a sound source, but about silence bodily interpreted as music. As part of his choreography *Enter* (1992), Merce Cunningham held three static poses for the duration of each of the three parts of *4'33"* in a reference both to the death of his partner and to Cage's attitude that death would never come, since "something" would always continue to be—a sentiment, voiced in Cage's 1954 letter to Helen Wolff, that *4'33"* expresses in exemplary fashion. Tacita Dean filmed Merce Cunningham in 2007, a couple of years before his own death, frail now and sitting in an armchair, once more performing this "silent piece" for the camera. Her film installation *Merce Cunningham performs STILLNESS (in three movements) to John Cage's composition 4'33" with Trevor Carlson, New York City, 28 April 2007 (six performances; six films)* from 2008 feels like a memento mori, especially when, in the background, co-performer Trevor Carlson marks the time for Cunningham to change his poses in rhythm with the three parts of *4'33"* [→ fig. 7].

In our Western Christian culture silence is often equated with death. Yet silence for Cage basically means life, both for the individual body and the social organism. Silence is never absolute but only relative to the sounds of the environment and of life itself. The passage referred to from Cage's letter to Helen Wolff—which serves as a kind of leading theme for this text—can be understood in this sense: "The piece is not actually silent (there will never be silence until death comes which never comes)..." And to the music critic of the New York Herald Tribune, Cage in 1956 wrote about his work: "You may call it an affirmation of life. Life goes on very well without me, and that will explain to you my silent piece, *4'33"*, which you may also have found unacceptable."[74]

These words implicitly state Cage's belief that death is not the end of "everything," since there is always "something" that will continue to exist. Cage has said that the "silent piece" was always with him, that to him it wasn't finished after four and a half minutes: "Well, I use it constantly in my life experience. No day goes by without my making use of that piece in my life and in my work. I listen to it every day. Yes I do ... I don't sit down to do it; I turn my attention toward it. I realize that it's going on continuously. So, more and more, my attention, as now, is on it. More than anything else, it's the source of my enjoyment of life."[75] His artistic stance reaches far into the final questions of life and death. The difference in their attitudes toward death tells us about the social vs. solitary understanding of the artist's role in Cage and Duchamp. Where Cage says, "Life goes on very well without me," Duchamp chooses for himself the epitaph: "Besides,

71 For a comparison between the more elegiac negativity of Susan Sontag's notion of silence and Cage's optimistic attitude see Darla M. Crispin, "Some Noisy Ruminations on Susan Sontag's 'Aesthetics of Silence,'" in *Silence, Music, Silent Music*, ed. Nicky Losseff and Jenny Doctor (Aldershot, UK: Ashgate, 2007), pp. 127–40.

72 E.g. in an interview with Alcides Lanza, 1971. See note 66.

73 Kim-Cohen, *In the Blink of an Ear*, p. 161.

74 John Cage, "Letter to Paul Henry Lang, Music Critic of New York Herald Tribune" (1956), in Kostelanetz (ed.), *John Cage: An Anthology*, p. 118. Cf. also: "Until I die there will be sounds. And they will continue following my death. One need not fear about the future of music." John Cage, "Experimental Music" (1958), in Cage, *Silence*, p. 8.

75 John Cage in Duckworth, "Anything I Say Will Be Misunderstood, p. 21. Cf. also: "I think what we need in the field of music is a very long performance of that work." Cage in Kostelanetz (ed.), *Conversing with Cage*, p. 105. And as early as 1954: "I have spent many pleasant hours in the woods conducting performances of my silent piece, transcriptions, that is, for an audience of myself, since they were much longer than the popular length which I have had published." John Cage, "Music Lovers' Field Companion" (1954) in Cage, *Silence*, p. 276.

Fig. 7
Tacita Dean, *Merce Cunningham performs STILLNESS (in three movements) to John Cage's 4′33″, with Trevor Carlson, New York City, 28 April 2007 (six performances; six films)*, 2008

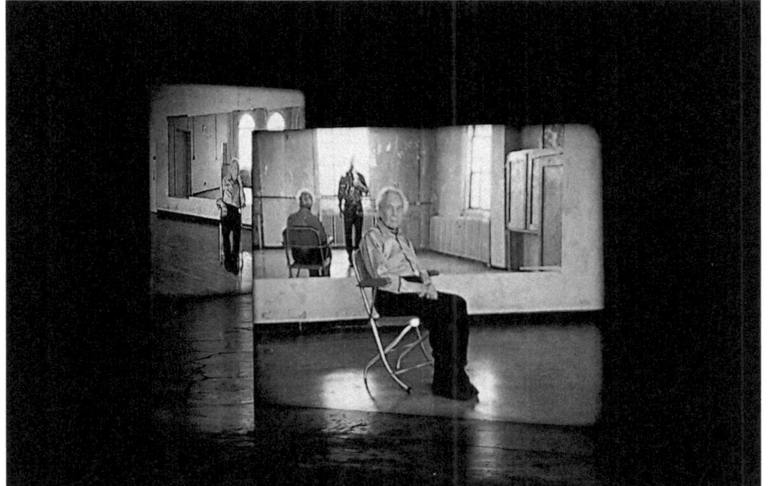

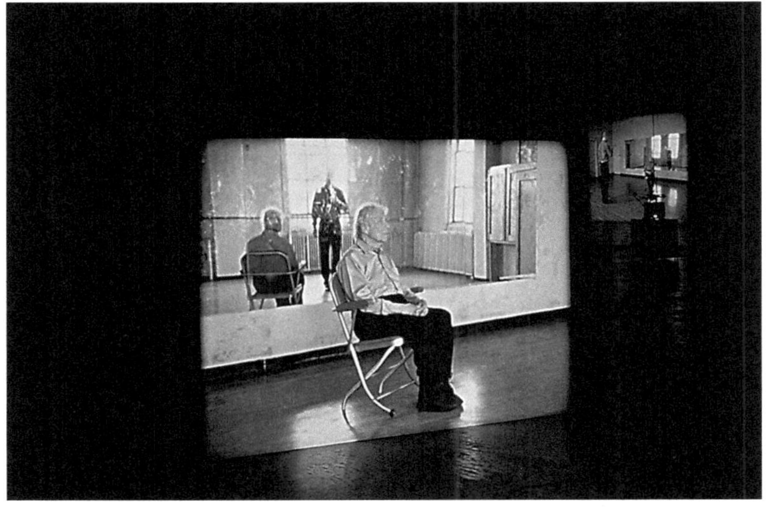

it's always the others that die." Cage doesn't speak of life after death in a religious fashion but in his letter to Helen Wolff he hints at it with mild irony in a handwritten addition below the text: "Reading this letter I find it ministerial. That was my original intention in life: 'to become a Methodist minister.' I move so easily into sermon."

Cage's decade-long, often detailed work on non-intentionality suggests a comparison to religious attitudes, even if the simple thesis of art as a secular religion does not apply. Cage himself made the connection in his letter to Helen Wolff. Directly after his rejection of intentionality in *4′33″* follows the sentence "Something like faith must take over ..." quoted earlier. The same closeness to religion becomes obvious in the title "Silent Prayer" that Cage had planned for his silent piece from 1948. Beyond the musical, communicative, and physiological aspects of silence that we have already mentioned, further connotations of religion, spirituality, and transcendence are always at play. For part of Cage's fanbase, these aspects might be hard to accept, but they belong among the sources of his work. The choice of the Chinese I Ching oracle over neutral, technical charts of random numbers already proves that the spiritual factor was an important part of indeterminacy to Cage. Yvonne Rainer wrote that Cage with his chance operations was "seeming to operate in the space left by the absence of God," but added, "We can't have it both ways: no desire and no God."[76] The debate on these aspects in Cage's work is far from over and its potency can be seen in the two contrary positions of Thomas M. Maier and Douglas Kahn.[77]

If silence is a metaphysically charged term, one must also consider the basic physical criteria. Unlike light, sound is dependent on a material carrier. That is why space outside of the atmosphere is in fact completely silent. To prepare for their spaceflight and the psychological stress of complete silence, Russian cosmonauts during their training would stay in a sound-isolated chamber for days.[78] As Cage's experience in the anechoic chamber proved, the human body will in this situation move its own sounds into the field of consciousness. Physical isolation from the acoustic environment leads to a sensory deprivation that is not tolerable for humans over longer stretches of time. "This space is dead and deadens," reads the report of such an isolation experience in the room installation *Camera Silens* (2002, by Olaf Arndt and Rob Moonen).[79] In all of these examples the "dark side of silence" assumes importance, as Cage, despite his optimistic outlook, was certainly aware.[80]

An additional aspect of silence that leads beyond Cage is noise pollution, a matter of huge relevance for today's living environments. Cage's insight that "silence doesn't exist" is now a threatening everyday experience. Apart from the noise pollution caused by traffic and industry we are also exposed to acoustic irradiation in shopping malls, the background noise of electronic household gadgets, an ever increasing number of mobile phones in public space, etc. Newly founded organizations like the World Forum for Acoustic Ecology or initiatives like Hörstadt (Acoustic City) Linz promote a consciousness of the importance of acoustic environments for our quality of life. A leading mind of this movement is composer and author R. Murray Schafer, who has been greatly influenced by John Cage.

How rare silence has become on Planet Earth: this is the theme of Jens Brand's installation *Stille — Landschaft* (silence / silent — landscape) from 2002 [→ p. 257]. He travelled to the Makgadikgadi Pan, a salt desert in Botswana, to make a recording of one of the last "objectively" silent places on earth. Since today the site has been discovered as a destination for tourists in "Sound of Silence" safaris, soon silence will no longer have a home there.

The evolution of Cage's "silent piece" during the years from 1952 to 1992 can be understood as a reflection of changes in our notions of silence. In 1990 Cage said about *One*³, his last musical variation on *4′33″*, "I thought that silence changed from what it was, and I wanted to indicate that." He continued: "So what I

76 Rainer, "Looking Myself in the Mouth", p. 45.
77 Thomas M. Maier, *Ausdruck der Zeit*, pp. 137–45; Douglas Kahn, "John Cage: Silence and Silencing," *The Musical Quarterly* 81(4), 1997, pp. 556–98.
78 "We humans on earth are not prepared for this kind of silence, since we never meet with it in our lives. Those who can from the very first endure long-lasting complete soundlessness must have a high nervous and mental power of resistance. Man meets with this complete silence in the cosmos, where there is no atmosphere to carry any soundwaves." From the German edition J. Gagarin, M. Melnikov, and N. Kotysch, *Unser Flug in den Kosmos* (Leipzig / Jena / Berlin: Urania-Verlag, 1963), p. 265. (Thanks to Jan Wenzel for this reference.)
79 H. van Boxtel on *Camera Silens* by Olaf Arndt and Rob Moonen. See http://www.robmoonen.nl/2002/2002_camerasilens.htm.
80 A reference to the "dark side of silence" in Cage's hand can be found on one of the proofs to *Sculptures Musicales* (1989) in the New York Public Library: John Cage Music Manuscript Collection. JPB 95–3 Folder 949. Public service copy. *Sculptures Musicales*. Galley proofs, signed. (Thanks to Julia Schröder for the information).

did was to come on stage in front of the audience, and then the feedback level of the auditorium space was brought up to feedback level through the sound-system. There was no actual feedback, but you knew that you were on the edge of feed-back—which is what I think our environmental situation is now.... The thing I was doing ... was showing that the world is in a bad situation, and largely through the way we misuse technology."[81] During his last years Cage revised the earlier optimistic identification of silence with life, which he had made in the 1950s. In a way he returned to his point of departure, to the concept of "Silent Prayer" from 1948 as an intervention against the medial noise carpet of Muzak.

IV
Silence or Emptiness – No Two Nothings Are the Same

Having now delimited the wide horizon of all the ambivalent notions and contexts of silence, the following section will offer a comparative view of artworks with and about either silence or nothingness in different media and genres. The exhibition holds a number of artistic positions that reflect on silence with less than a Cagean optimism and include the ambivalence and the "dark side" of silence. We open with three of Cage's contemporaries, who also took silence, or the void, as their topic, independent of Cage's "silent piece."

The first example is Robert Rauschenberg's *White Paintings* (1951), which form a visual analogy to Cage's silence, and in fact were an inspiration for *4'33"* [→ fig. 8]. Rauschenberg did not see the empty canvas as passive but as a "hypersensitive" picture plane, which made visible the light conditions of the room and the shadow cast by the viewer.[82] The second example is Guy Debord's film *Howling for Sade* (1952), which is based on a text collage, spoken to an empty white screen by four voice-overs, alternating with phases of complete darkness and silence. Debord's film demolished the spectacle, withheld narration, and forced the viewer to remain in the dark of the cinema for twenty-four minutes at the end. The third example is Heinrich Böll's previously mentioned story *Murke's Collected Silences* (1955), which follows radio programmer Dr. Murke as he collects the moments of silence he had to edit from his broadcasts and listens to them on tape at home.

These three almost contemporaneous positions from painting, cinema, and literature show how in the 1950s it was felt that the growing amount of information and the sensory overload of media society allowed the recipient hardly any maneuvering space for autonomous perception. This made silence, or emptiness, into a metaphor for an uncoded space for reflection, withdrawn from the attentions of the media economy.

A study of Cage's *4'33"*, Rauschenberg's *White Paintings*, and Nam June Paik's *Zen for Film* (1964) can offer an ontological differentiation of their respective media and art genres [→ fig. 9]. In 1968 Cage wrote: "Now offhand, you might say that all three actions are the same. But they're quite different."[83] He argued this by pointing to the diverse materialities of the works and the correspondingly different reception situations. Cage's "silent piece" melts into the acoustic surroundings for the duration of the performance. At the same time, sound sources and listeners stay where they are. There is no material transfer, only attention that has been focused or relocated. Against that, Cage called Rauschenberg's paintings "airports for particles of dust and shadows that are in the environment."[84] The textures of the surroundings imprint themselves on the surface of the picture; they touch down like an aircraft on the tarmac, sometimes only to leave it again. Paik's film without images, on the other hand, presents us only with the dust and the scratches on its surface—according to Cage it is more focused than Rauschenberg's work, and "the nature of the environment is more on the film ... and thus less free."[85] Years before Paik's *Zen for Film*, Cage had this to say about the medium in general, "The most important thing to do in film now is to find a way for it to include invisibility, just as music already enjoys inaudibility (silence)."[86] This proposition acts as a kind of contradiction to Paik's work, since Paik made the medium itself visible in its pure material form, while in narrative cinema film as a carrier becomes "transparent" for the course of the action, an invisible medium. Film is technically a storage medium: even if its material stock has not been exposed but is used mechanically, *Zen for Film* stores the traces of dust and scratches and lets them accumulate with every new showing. In contrast to that, the shadows and dust particles on the *White Paintings*, and even more the sounds made during *4'33"*, are in a manner of speaking created "live."

Fig. 8
Robert Rauschenberg,
White Paintings,
1951

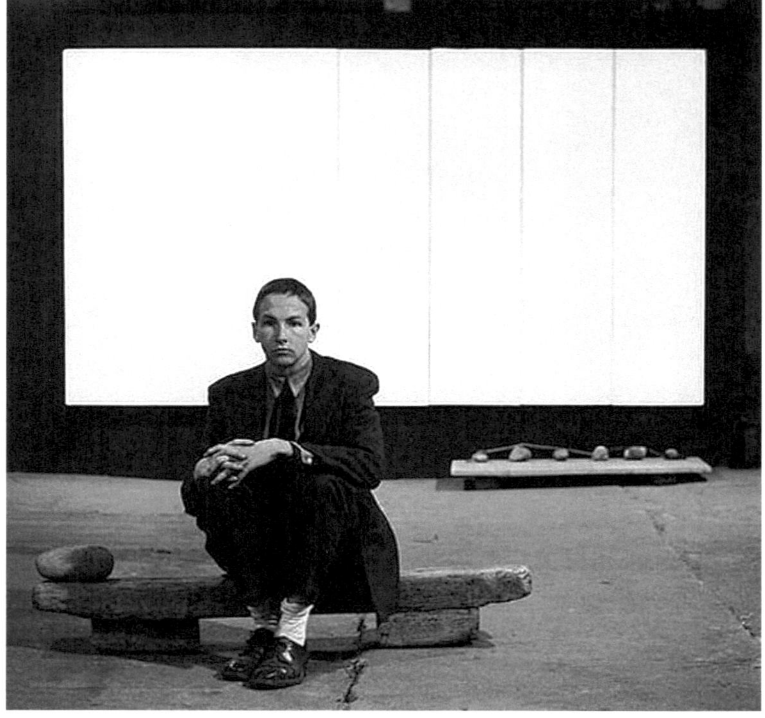

Paik wrote a reply to Cage's 1968 statement concerning *Zen for Film*: "N.B. Dear John: The nature of the environment is much more on TV than on film or painting. In fact, TV (its random movement of electrons) IS the environment of today."[87]

81 Quoted in Fetterman, *John Cage's Theatre Pieces*, pp. 94–95.
82 Tomkins, *The Bride and the Bachelors*, p. 203.
83 John Cage, "On Nam June Paik's *Zen for Film*, 1962–64," in *Nam June Paik: Fluxus/Video*, ed. Wulf Herzogenrath and Sabine M. Schmidt (exh. cat. Kunsthalle Bremen, 1999), p. 150 [→ p. 198].
84 Ibid.
85 Ibid.
86 John Cage, "On Film" (1956), in Kostelanetz (ed.), *John Cage: An Anthology*, p. 116.
87 See note 82.

Fig. 9
Nam June Paik, *Zen for Film*, 1964

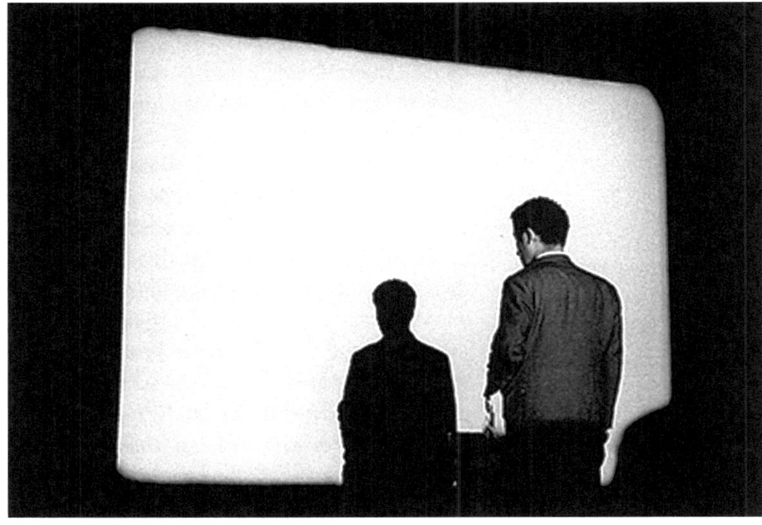

An interesting dialogue on the differences between silence and emptiness began here: Paik's *Zen for Film* drew upon Cage's silence directly. The artist invited Cage and Cunningham to watch the blank film; according to Cage the showing lasted an hour.[88] In his own statement, Paik critized Cage's somwhat old-fashioned notions of the "environment," which was still about Nature in the way the Romantics understood it and not about our "second Nature," technology. Paik also maintained that electronic technology would in and of itself work in random and indeterminate manners. This would make Cage's method of using the Chinese I Ching unnecessary—chance factors were already ingrained in the medium and did not have to be determined from the outside.[89] These views explain why Paik was so enthusiastic about Cage's use of radios as musical instruments: they replaced the roll-of-the-dice randomness of the I Ching oracle with a media technology that was free of cultural baggage.

In contrast to *Zen for Film*, Guy Debord's *Howling for Sade* does not refer to Cage or Rauschenberg, but was planned as a provocative blow against the media of the spectacle. Debord staged a forcible "nothing," which did not aim at developing viewers' sensibilities but at shock and ultimately boredom. The premiere quickly ended in uproar. At the second screening, a "Lettrist commando team" forced the audience to remain seated especially during the last twenty-four minutes of silence and darkness.[90] Similar to Paik's strategies, Debord's film was a reflection on the media, but it was not aimed at the structural and material "apparatus" of film technology. Instead it attacked the institutional role of cinema as an entertainment spectacle. In Debord's words, "The specific conditions of the cinema permit the interruption of the anecdote by masses of empty silence."[91] Several of these lines of argument would later be combined in Ryoji Ikeda's piece *4'33"* from his *time and space series* (2010) into a single, techno-poetical tableau of framed blank 16mm film with AATON timecode [→ fig. 10].

Up to now we have attempted to distinguish between the diverse forms and materialities of "nothing" and have analyzed the concepts and artistic intentions behind realizations of the pieces. In a final analysis, let us now compare the work of John Cage and Yves Klein to explore if it is possible, beyond formal and material criteria, to discriminate their achievements from their respective conceptual or artistic contexts. This leads us back to the question of the "silent piece's" multiple meanings posed in the first section of this text. Beyond Cage's interpretation/reception history, and in the expanded context of an ambivalency of silence, there is an ongoing dialectical play: between the artistic control of reception in framing the musical silence, or staging the emptiness of the exhibition space, and the self-reflection of the listener's or viewer's individuality during the sensory experience.

Fig. 10
Ryoji Ikeda, *4'33"* from his *time and space series*, 2010

Silence has played a significant role in the work of both Cage and Klein, and yet this parallel between them has hardly been examined in academic literature.[92] One reason for that might lie in the fact that Cage and Klein stand for very different artist types: Cage used complex chance operations to erase all traces of subjectivity from the music, while Klein, constantly at odds with his dominant artist's ego, in the end filled the classic European model of artistic genius to perfection. These differences apply similarly to comparisons between Cage and Karlheinz Stockhausen or Pierre Boulez. But between Cage and Klein there are also marked similarities: aside from the silence and the void

88 Cf. John Cage, "Zum Werk von Nam June Paik" (contribution to a panel at the Whitney Museum, New York, May 21, 1982, on occasion of a Paik retrospective), in *Nam June Paik: Video Time – Video Space*, ed. Toni Stooss and Thomas Kellein (Ostfildern: Hatje Cantz, 1991), p. 21. (English edition, New York: Harry N. Abrams, 1993.)

89 Paik sees quantum physics and especially the Heisenberg uncertainty principle, according to which the state of an electron cannot be determined, as a parallel to the random access and participatory liveness of his own artistic work with electronic media. For a more extended account see Dieter Daniels, "John Cage and Nam June Paik: 'Change your mind or change your receiver (your receiver is your mind),'" in *Nam June Paik*, ed. Sook-Kyung Lee and Susanne Rennert (exh. cat. Tate Liverpool, 2010), pp. 107–25.

90 Cf. Roberto Ohrt, *Phantom Avantgarde: Eine Geschichte der Situationistischen Internationale und der modernen Kunst* (Hamburg: Edition Nautilus, 1990), pp. 41–42. Also relevant here is the "force de silence" of Lettrism, according to Isidore Isou, ibid., p. 34. (English translation: *Phantom Avant-Garde: A History of the Situationist International and Modern Art* (Berlin: Lukas & Sternberg, 2006.)

91 Guy-Ernest Debord, "Instructions for the French Federation of Film Clubs. Clarifications on the film *Hurlements en faveur de Sade*," *Internationale Lettriste* 2 (February 1953). Translated from the French by NOT BORED!, http://www.ubu.com/film/debord_hurlements.html.

92 There is no known biographical connection between Cage and Klein. But Klein was present at the scandalous premiere of Debord's *Howling for Sade* in 1952. See for that: Roberto Ohrt, *Phantom Avantgarde: Eine Geschichte der Situationstischen Internationale und der modernen Kunst* (Hamburg: Edition Nautilus, 1990), p. 42.

as a shared theme both had an affinity toward Asian culture and an interest in natural phenomena like fire, rain, or wind. And both artists disassociated themselves from the then reigning aesthetic of abstract Expressionism or Informel.

Before we explore the concept of silence in the œuvre of both artists, let us take a quick look at Klein's most famous work, his exhibition of *The Void*, which in 1958 bore the full title *The Specialization of Sensibility in the Raw Material State into Stablized Pictorial Sensibility, The Void* [→ fig. 11].[93] Just as the silence of Cage's *4'33"* opened up a new chapter in music, Klein emblematically introduced emptiness into the visual arts. With these two works, silence and emptiness have become topoi of momentous consequence for the arts since the mid-twentieth century. The contemporary reception of both pieces differed greatly, though, mostly due to their respective staging. Klein had started a veritable marketing campaign to make *The Void* a great public spectacle with more than two thousand visitors, who had to be led through the hopelessly crowded rooms of the small Galerie Iris Clert at minute intervals. The campaign included trademark blue stamps on the invitation cards, blue cocktails at the opening, and republican guards beside the entrance. Compared to that, the premiere of *4'33"* took place below the threshold of perception. At the first performance in 1952 most of the audience did not understand what was going on: "They missed the point ... because they didn't know how to listen," Cage commented.[94] An ambiguous entry in the program notes, which indicated "4 pieces" to be performed, might have contributed to the situation[95] [→ p. 87]. The concepts of staging are characteristic of their artistic positions: Klein claimed he was charging the void with his sensibility as a painter through his presence in the room and proposed a transfer of that spirit to the audience. Cage's project was to let sounds "be themselves" and provide each and every listener with their own, very individual experience of music or silence.[96]

Fig. 11
Yves Klein, *The Void*, 1958

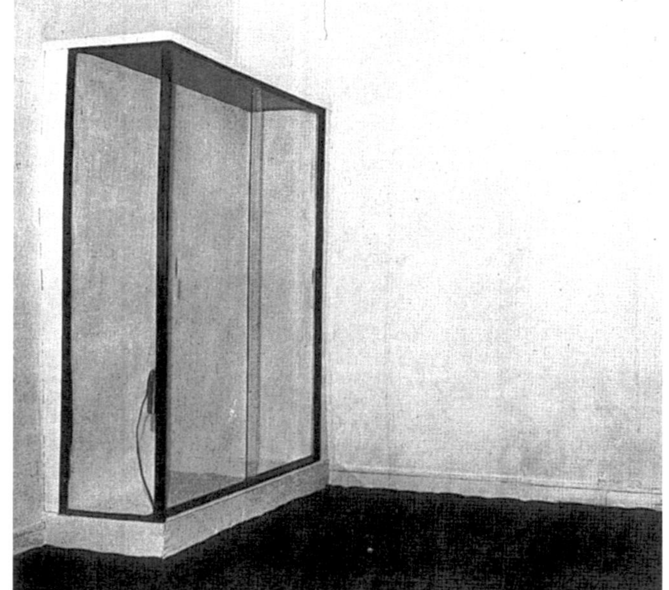

Both Cage and Klein used similar spiritual, religious, and metaphysical elements from a mixture of Eastern and Western traditions. For Cage it was Zen, for Klein judo as a technique for concentration. Just as Cage followed the I Ching as an oracle and discovered the mysticism of Meister Eckhart, Klein explored the mysteries of the Rosicrucians. And while Cage confessed to an early affinity with the Methodists during his youth, Klein became a Knight of the Order of St. Sebastian. The search for something transcending modern rationalism and positivism led both to a certain eclecticism.[97] Their shared dilemma was that their desire for a pre-modern universalism could only be satisfied through a patched-together worldview from the postmodern toolbox.[98]

The many commonalities and the profound differences become especially clear in the way Cage and Klein treated silence in their work.[99] Historically, Yves Klein's interest in silence preceded his interest in the void and the monochrome, which would become his artistic trademarks. According to Klein, he first had the idea for his *Monotone Symphony* around 1949 [→ p. 254].[100] It is not clear to what extent it was then worked out as a composition; probably at that stage it could be compared to Cage's idea for *Silent Prayer* in 1948. In 1957, an electronic version of Klein's symphony was realized by Pierre Henry for an exhibition of Klein's monochrome paintings.[101] In 1960 there followed a live performance, accompanying the execution of *Anthropometries* at the Galerie Clert. The final concept from 1961 was titled *Symphonie monoton – Silence* and comprised two parts, one "symphony" that was simply a D-major chord, and following that a silence of the same length, during which the musicians remained motionless in their seats. Klein wrote: "My old *Monotone Symphony* of 1949 ... was destined to create an 'after-silence' after all sounds had ended in each of us who were present at that manifestation. Silence ... This is really my symphony and not the sounds during its performance. This silence is so marvelous because it grants 'happenstance' and even sometimes the possibility of true happiness, if only for a moment, for a moment whose duration is immeasurable. To conquer silence, to skin it and cover oneself with its hide to never be chilled again spiritually."[102] And elsewhere: "This symphony of forty minutes duration (although that is of no importance, as one will see) consisted of one unique continuous 'sound,' drawn out and deprived of its beginning and of its end, creating a feeling of vertigo and of aspiration outside of time. Thus, even in its presence, this symphony does not exist. It exists outside of the phenomenology of time because it is neither born nor will it die. However, in the world of our possibilities of conscious perception, it is silence—audible presence."[103]

This "after-silence" of Klein's *Monotone Symphony*, which in principle could last forever, recalls how, according to Cage, his "silent piece" would also never end but change into a new, lasting mode of perception. This again touches on the theme of death, or rather of eternal life. While Cage in mysterious words pondered "death which never comes," Klein shortly before his

93 French original: *La Spécialisation de la sensibilité à l'état de matière première en sensibilité picturale stabilisée, Le Vide.*

94 John Cage in conversation with John Kobler (1968), in Richard Kostelanetz, *Conversing with Cage* (2nd edition, New York: Routledge, 2003), p. 70.

95 That the misunderstanding cannot have been due only to the program is shown by an anecdote about the first New York performance two years later, which is related by Calvin Tomkins. Cage's mother, who was aware of what was to follow, "whispered to her neighbor in the audience that *4'33"* could be thought of as being 'like a prayer.' As it happened, *4'33"* was followed on the program by Cage's *Music of Changes*, which took forty-three minutes, and when that was over Mrs. Cage's neighbor leaned across and said, 'Good heavens, what a long and intense prayer!'" Tomkins, *The Bride and the Bachelors*, p. 119.

96 The individuality of experience only moved into Klein's focus with *Theatre du Vide* in 1960.

97 Martin Erdmann in his comprehensive study about Cage and Asia comes to the following conclusion: "Cage's specific appropriation of Asian thought can be labeled selective and eclectic; not at all like an in-depth exploration of a foreign culture, either on the intellectual plane or in terms of lived experience." Martin Erdmann, "Untersuchungen zum Gesamtwerk von John Cage" (unpublished dissertation, Bonn 1993), p. 36.

Fig. 12
Yves Klein, staged photo of Yves Klein as conductor in empty concert hall, n.d.

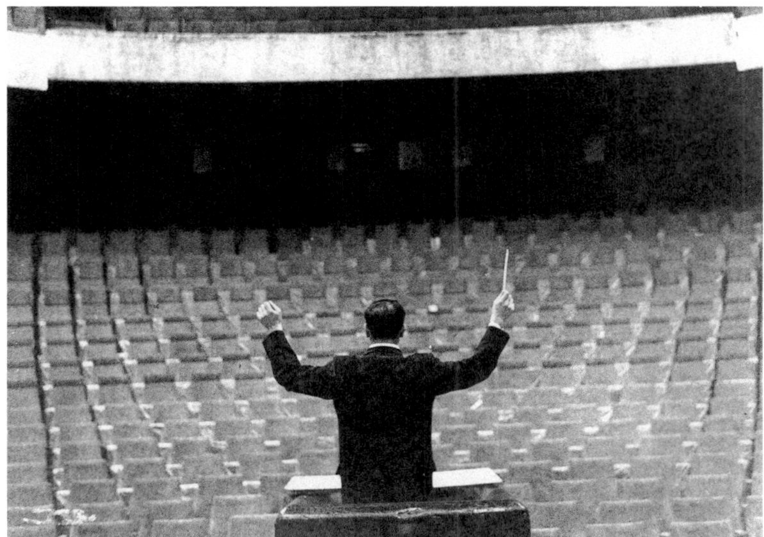

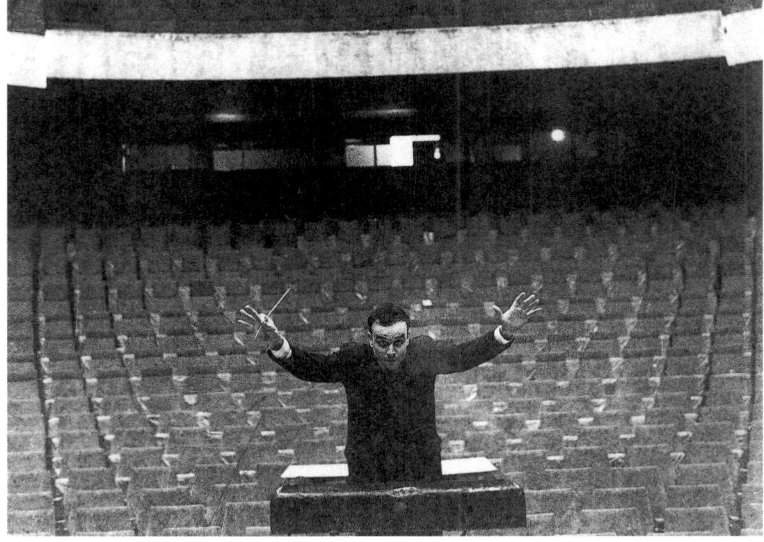

death converted to Catholicism. To him, the body prints of the *Anthropometries* created to the sound of the *Monotone Symphony* did not stand for the physiological side of life, whose importance Cage had repeatedly stressed. For Klein each print was a "mark of the immediate" and the presence of the bodies in his studio "made me understand that I was clearly a product of Western civilization, a true Christian who rightly believes in the 'resurrection of bodies, in the resurrection of the flesh.'"[104] Klein's silence led to a promise of real transcendence. When Klein stylized himself as a kind of messiah of the immaterial sensibility of the universe, he offered a metaphysical-metaphorical bridge to the afterlife, which was both a Christian and a blasphemous concept.[105] Cage's notion of silence likewise connected the corporeal and the transcendent, but for him the outcome was the exact reverse: faith not in the service of a hope of eternal salvation but of life in the present. "Something like faith must take over in order that we live affirmatively in the totality we live in," was how he phrased it in his letter to Helen Wolff. *4'33"* is happening in the here and now in the mutual presence of sounds and listeners.

After Cage and Klein, silence and emptiness have become central topoi for the art and music of the twentieth and twenty-first centuries. But what awaits the viewer or the listener in the silence, the void? At the beginning of this text we explored the multiple meanings of *4'33"*, and the further we went into the diverse contexts and concepts of an auditive or visual "nothing," the clearer it became that "nothing" could be based on the most heterogeneous of ideas and intentions. "Nothing," like silence, has become rather fashionable today: there have been several exhibitions under titles such as *Several Silences* or simply *Silence* as well as *Nothing* and *Nichts* or *Fast nichts*.[106] The project "Voids/Vides/Leeren," which is a kindred undertaking to this book and the *Sounds Like Silence* exhibition, was dedicated to empty spaces in twentieth and twenty-first century art, from 1958 (Klein) to 2006 (Roman Ondak), in a sort of paradoxical retrospective: "Whether as search for novel sensibilities or perceptions, as self-reflexive foregrounding of the exhibition process, as political or ideological position, or even as a springboard for semantic experimentation, these apparently similar exhibitions actually piece together a radical constellation of criticality and refusal."[107]

According to co-curator Mathieu Copeland it finally became obvious that these interventions were not comparable: "The empty space exhibited as such thus became, in a way, a classic of radicalism, and would be repeated and remade in other contexts, other places and other times by other artists whose intentions might be similar, different or even opposed to Klein's ... the affirmation that there is no such thing as nothing."[108] Likewise the different motives for a musical composition without sounds are not really comparable.[109] One can only offer a "media critical" analysis—in the manner we have tried above using Rauschenberg, Cage, Debord, and Paik as instances—or a sort of study

98 From the end of the 1950s, Cage reinterpreted his own intellectual biography. For example, he stressed the importance of Zen in his life and eliminated C.G. Jung's concept of synchronicity. Cage had come across this last term, which would prove very instructive for him, in Jung's foreword to the American edition of the I Ching. See *The I Ching or Book of Changes*, the Richard Wilhelm translation rendered into English by Cary F. Baynes, foreword by C.G. Jung, Bollingen Series XIX (New York: Pantheon Books, 1950), p. IV. Cf. in more detail: Dörte Schmidt, "Die Geburt des Flugzeugs: Cage, I Ching und C.G. Jung," in *Das Andere: Eine Spurensuche in der Musikgeschichte des 19. und 20. Jahrhunderts*, ed. Annette Kreutziger-Herr (Frankfurt am Main: Peter Lang, 1998), p. 353–66.

99 Klein's symphony is still largely ignored by musicologists. See Valerian Maly, "Symphonie monoton-Silence von Yves Klein," in *MusikTexte* 59 (June 1995), pp. 15–17.

100 Klein sometimes also gave a date of 1947–1948 for its creation. See Edward Strickland, *Minimalism: Origins* (Bloomington: Indiana University Press, 1993), pp. 35–36, where the author gives an overview of the diverse versions and suspects Klein backdated the original creation.

101 Sidra Stich, *Yves Klein* (Stuttgart: Cantz, 1994), p. 271, note 23.

102 Yves Klein, "Le vrai devient réalité," *Zero 3*, Düsseldorf 1960; English translation online at http://www.yveskleinarchives.org/documents/vrairealite_us.html.

103 Yves Klein, *Le Dépassement de la problématique de l'art* (La Louvière: Editions de Montbéliard, 1959). English translation of this passage from "Overcoming the problematics of art" online at http://www.yveskleinarchives.org/works/works14_us.html. Klein gave different durations for the length of the symphony on different occasions, sometimes five to seven, sometimes forty minutes.

104 Yves Klein, "Le vrai devient réalité."

105 See Stich, *Yves Klein*, pp. 180–81.

106 For example: *Silence*, The Menil Collection Houston, 2012; *Several Silences*, The Renaissance Society at the University of Chicago, 2009; *[silence]*, curated by Galen Joseph-Hunter and Dylan Gauthier, Gigantic ArtSpace [GAS], New York 2007; *Nothing*, curated by Ele Carpenter and Graham Gussin, August media, London 2001; NICHTS, curated by Martina Weinhart and Max Hollein, Schirn Kunsthalle, Frankfurt am Main 2006; *Fast nichts: Minimalistische Werke aus der Friedrich Christian Flick Collection*, Hamburger Bahnhof, Berlin 2005.

107 *Voids: A Retrospective*, ed. John Armleder, Mathieu Copeland, Gustav Metzger, Mai-Thu Perret, and Clive Phillpot (exh. cat. Centre Pompidou, Paris, and Kunsthalle Bern; Zürich: JRP Ringier, 2009), p. 30 (curators' preface).

108 Mathieu Copeland, http://www.mathieucopeland.net/VOIDS.html.

109 See the comprehensive compilations in *Silence, Music, Silent Music*, ed. Losseff, Doctor, and in Marianne Betz, *Stille: Hörbares und sichtbares Moment in der Musik* (Leipzig: Institut für Buchkunst, HGB Leipzig, 2000), as well as Betz, "'In futurum': von Schulhoff zu Cage," *Archiv für Musikwissenschaft*, 56, 4 (1999), pp. 331–46; and also Craig Douglas Dworkin, "Unheard Music," 2006, online at http://www.ubu.com/papers/dworkin_unheard.pdf.

that offers a critique of "ideology," as in our comparison of John Cage and Yves Klein.

The individuality of experience during a performance of John Cage's *4'33"*, which was addressed at the beginning of this text, corresponds to this incompatibility of ideas behind the concept of "nothing." Every visitor to the Camera Silens, for example, should find "their personal nothing" within "sensory deprivation," according to the artist Olaf Arndt.[110] In the work of Samuel Beckett, one of the great champions of "nothing," the protagonist of ... *but the clouds* ... (1977) must occupy himself on his eternal wait with "nothing—that treasure trove."[111] John Cage's "silent piece" proves to be a derivate of all kinds of absences, which have permeated the art forms of the second half of the twentieth century.

The title of this text, "Your Silence Is Not My Silence," is a reference to this interminable process of an individual "conquest of nothing." That is why no two nothings, and no two silences, are ever the same. Or as Beckett put it: "It is all very well to keep silence, but one has also to consider the kind of silence one keeps."[112] Which is also what we learn from a song by the group Einstürzende Neubauten:[113]

Silence is sexy
So sexy
As sexy as death
Silence is sexy
Silence is sexy
So sexy
So sexy
Just your silence is not sexy at all
Just your silence is not sexy at all
Your silence is not sexy at all!

110 Medien Kunst Geschichte: Medienmuseum, ed. Hans-Peter Schwarz (Karlsruhe: ZKM, 1997), p. 90.
111 Samuel Beckett, ... *but the clouds* ..., television play, 1977, see http://www.medienkunstnetz.de/works/nur-noch-gewolk.
112 Samuel Beckett quoted in *Voids*, ed. Armleder, Copeland, Metzger, Perret, Phillpot, p. 350.
113 For a comment by the lead singer Blixa Bargeld on "My Cage" and a piece of silence in the song *Headcleaner* see: Wulf Herzogenrath, Barbara Nierhoff-Wielk, (ed.) *"John Cage und ..." Bildender Künstler–Einflüsse, Anregungen* (Cologne: DuMont, 2012) p. 102–03.

Inke Arns

On the Dark Side of Silence[1]

> Wherever we are, what we hear is mostly noise. When we ignore it, it disturbs us. When we listen to it, we find it fascinating.
> —John Cage[2]

In his unfinished, posthumously published short story *The Burrow* (1923/24), Franz Kafka describes an animal-like creature's vain attempts to improve the subterranean den he has constructed. His burrow is perfectly quiet ("But the most beautiful thing about my burrow is the stillness."[3])—until one day, waking up after a long sleep, he notices a noise. He begins to listen attentively: "And it is not even constant, as such noises usually are; there are long pauses, obviously caused by stoppages of the current of air." Despite his attempts, he cannot locate the barely audible, "comparatively innocent" whistling, as it is resounding with the same intensity throughout the underground construction: "I don't seem to be getting any nearer to the place where the noise is, it goes on always on the same thin note, with regular pauses, now a sort of whistling, but again like a kind of piping."

Even near the entrance to the burrow, which is camouflaged by moss, the noise is soon heard: "... right enough, the same whistling meets me here too. It is really nothing to worry about; sometimes I think that nobody but myself would hear it; it is true, I hear it now more and more distinctly, for my ear has grown keener through practice; though in reality it is exactly the same noise wherever I may hear it ..." He fails to find a reason for it: "Had I rightly divined the cause of the noise, then it must have issued with greatest force from some given place, which it would be my task to discover, and after that have grown fainter and fainter. But if my hypothesis does not meet the case, what can the explanation be?"

Unable to establish the nature of the noise, he becomes obsessed with it. He loses his sleep and all but stops eating. He manically tries to find out more about the noise, but it stubbornly eludes him: "Sometimes I fancy that the noise has stopped, for it makes long pauses; sometimes such a faint whistling escapes one, one's own blood is pounding all too loudly in one's ears; then two pauses come one after another, and for a while one thinks that the whistling has stopped forever." Yet his hope is short-lived: "But what avail all exhortations to be calm; my imagination will not rest, and I have actually come to believe—it is useless to deny it to myself—that the whistling is made by some beast, and moreover not by a great many small ones, but by a single big one. Many signs contradict this. The noise can be heard everywhere and always at the same strength, and moreover uniformly, both by day and night." Finally, paranoia seems to get the better of him: "The noise seems to have become louder, not much louder, of course—here it is always a matter of the subtlest shades—but all the same sufficiently louder for the ear to recognize it clearly. And this growing-louder is like a coming-nearer; still more distinctly than you hear the increasing loudness of the noise, you can literally see the step that brings it closer to you." The last sentence, however, reads: "But all remained unchanged."

While the animal is unsure whether the noise originates from one or more animals and whether he should be transforming his

1 The title quotes a handwritten note by John Cage on the sketches for the verbal score of his composition *Sculptures Musicales* (1989). In this piece, loud blocks of sounds are framed by "silence." *Sculptures Musicales* (today in the John Cage Music Manuscript Collection at the New York Public Library) was conceived for a choreography by Merce Cunningham and a performance by the musicians of the Merce Cunningham Dance Company, among them David Tudor and Takehisa Kosugi [→ Schröder, p. 71].

2 John Cage, "The Future of Music: Credo" [1937], in *Silence: Lectures and Writings* (Middletown: Wesleyan University Press, 1961), p. 3.

3 This and subsequent quotes from Franz Kafka's "The Burrow," in *Selected Short Stories of Franz Kafka*, trans. Willa and Edwin Muir (New York: Modern Library, 1952), pp. 256–304.

burrow (and whether it was even conceived properly in the first place), readers increasingly ask themselves what it is that he actually hears, as David Toop explains: "Is it [the whistling] produced by air holes created by small tunnelling creatures or by the digging of a great beast, as the narrator believes, *or does it emanate from the narrator himself?*"[4] Indeed, Kafka's narrative offers a myriad of possibilities, which the present essay will aim to retrace. Does his protagonist hear something that is really there? If so, what is it? Or does he rather hear his own physiological sounds ("one's own blood is pounding all too loudly in one's ears")? Is the whistling the sound of his nervous system or a stubborn tinnitus? Or—yet another possibility—does he merely imagine the noise because his burrow is otherwise so perfectly still? Is his mind going mad because it does not have to process any external stimuli, and therefore produces its own? Does his perception tend to recognize patterns where there are no sensory stimuli? This is the structure underlying the present essay, which intends to go beyond what can be seen and heard in the exhibition *Sounds Like Silence*.

Hearing Things (one) (Hearing Things That Are There)

> Focused listening is radical as it makes us "see" a different world.
> —Salomé Voegelin[5]

In summer 1951 the American painter Robert Rauschenberg created his first monochrome paintings—the *Black Paintings* and the *White Paintings*—at Black Mountain College in North Carolina [→ fig. 1]. His works caused a scandal in the New York art scene, which was then wholly preoccupied with Abstract Expressionism. Rauschenberg's *White Paintings*, which Cage described as "landing strips for dust motes, light and shadow" (or, alternatively, as "airports for light and shadow"), encouraged the composer to write his "silent piece" *4′33″* the following year.[6] Like Rauschenberg's paintings, *4′33″* is less concerned with nothingness or emptiness than with the inevitable presence of something. There is always *something*, even when we think that there is nothing to be seen or heard.

The first performance of Cage's *4′33″* also caused a scandal. At the premiere some members of the audience did not even realize that they had heard anything at all. They had, as Cage later said, "missed the point."[7] The work premiered in Woodstock, New York, on August 29, 1952 in a performance by the young pianist David Tudor. The audience were supporters of the Benefit Artists Welfare Fund—people who had embraced the cause of contemporary art. But as Cage recalled: "There's no such thing as silence. What they thought was silence, because they didn't know how to listen, was full of accidental sounds."[8] David Tudor put the manuscript score on the piano, and sat through the performance of the piece in three movements, which he timed with a stopwatch, without striking a single key. He closed the lid of the piano to mark the beginning of the first movement, during which one could hear the wind howling in the trees in front of the Maverick Concert Hall. After thirty seconds he opened the lid to indicate the end of the first movement. For the second movement it was closed again. Now raindrops could be heard falling on the roof of the concert hall. During the second, longer, movement, Tudor turned the pages of the score and stepped on the pedal, but without playing a key. For the last movement the lid was also first opened (pause) and then closed. Now one could hear members of the audience whispering: "... the people themselves made all kinds of interesting sounds as they talked or walked out."[9]

Fig. 1
Robert Rauschenberg, *White Paintings*, 1951

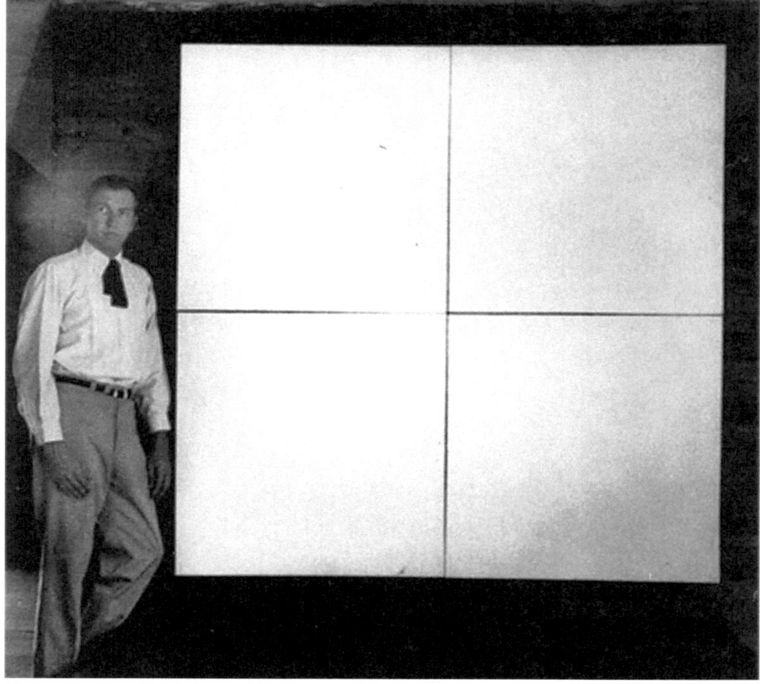

Thirty years later Cage still vividly remembered the premiere: "People began whispering to one another, and some people began to walk out. They didn't laugh—they were just irritated when they realized nothing was going to happen, and they haven't forgotten it thirty years later: they're still angry."[10] When Tudor reached the end of *4′33″*, lifting the lid and rising from his chair, there was a general uproar, as many people were "infuriated and dismayed."[11] *4′33″* was considered "going too far"[12]—even for an avant-garde concert.

Cage continued to develop his "silent piece," which can be performed with as many instruments as wished,[13] until his death in 1992. But Salomé Voegelin has rightly pointed out that the composer's interest in ambient sounds, unlike that of today's sound artists, always remained a musical one. Cage, along with Marcel Duchamp, aimed to expand the realm of art and music alike. Both their "readymades"—Duchamp's *Fountain* (1913) and Cage's *4′33″*—"were primarily concerned with expanding the possibilities of music and visual arts, respectively. Their

4 David Toop, *Sinister Resonance: The Mediumship of the Listener* (London/New York: Continuum, 2010), p. 207 [the author's italics].
5 Salomé Voegelin, *Listening to Noise and Silence* (London/New York: Continuum, 2011), p. 36.
6 Cage personally owned the *Black Painting No. 1*. See Wulf Herzogenrath and Barbara Nierhoff-Wielk (eds.), *"John Cage und…" Bildender Künstler–Einflüsse, Anregungen* (Cologne: DuMont, 2012), p. 35.
7 John Cage, quoted in Richard Kostelanetz, *Conversing With John Cage* (New York: Routledge, 2003), p. 70.
8 Ibid.
9 Ibid.
10 Ibid.
11 David Revill, *The Roaring Silence* (New York: Arcade, 1992), p. 166.
12 See Calvin Tomkins, *The Bride and the Bachelors: Five Masters of the Avant-Garde. Duchamp, Tinguely, Cage, Rauschenberg, Cunningham* (New York: Penguin/Viking, 1965), p. 119.
13 A note by Cage in the Tacet version mentions that "the work may be performed by any instrumentalist or combination of instrumentalists and last any length of time." (EP 6777) [→ p. 138].

proposition works within each one's aesthetic framework, contesting and criticizing its conventions but remaining within and even confirming its domain. The silence of *4'33"* is a musical silence, not a sonic silence. Cage's interest lies in establishing every sound within the musical register. It does not invite a listening to sound as sound but to all sound as music."[14]

In the early fifties[15] Cage not only discovered Rauschenberg's *White Paintings*, but also descended into the vaults of Harvard University to test the faculty's anechoic chamber. Rather than complete silence—which was what he had expected—he experienced the high-pitched buzz of his own nervous system and the low hum of the blood pumping through his veins: "I heard two sounds, one high and one low. Afterwards I asked the engineer in charge why, if the room was so silent, I had heard two sounds. He said 'Describe them.' I did. He said 'The high one was your nervous system in operation. The low one was your blood in circulation.'"[16] Cage had an "epiphany," as Seth Kim-Cohen termed it.[17] The anechoic chamber, the seeming isolation from anything happening in the outside world, effectively sharpens one's sense for one's own bodily sounds. It is quite irrelevant whether the two sounds that Cage describes were actually those of his blood circulation and nervous system or, variously, spontaneous otoacoustic emissions generated inside the ear, the sound of his own brain or even a slight tinnitus, as Toop [→ p. 55] and Kim-Cohen have speculated.[18] What really mattered to Cage was the idea that, as Dieter Daniels [→ p. 32] has suggested, there is no "objective" silence for man's "subjective" perception, because the phenomenon of acoustic proprioception causes the subject to become the focus of perception as exterior stimuli are decreasing. Toop expands on this point when he describes—in lavish detail—the sounds produced by our bodies, which we do not hear unless we pay attention to them: "All hearing animals can audit the body's sonic expulsions of vocalizations, vomiting, sneezes, snores, wheezes, belches and farts, but close listening also reveals a close and interior sound world of corporeal functioning: the beating heart; breath entering and exiting the nostrils; clicking eyelids and jaw; the chewing of food (now recognized as being an important component of taste); contractions of the throat; saliva in the mouth; the gnathosonics of teeth clashing or grinding during sleep (the latter know as noctural bruxism); otoacustic emissions from the ears; bones, joints and ligaments clicking and creaking; the crunching, bubbling sounds of crepitation or rales, heard from diseased lungs; the wonderfully named borborygmi, which are the sounds given off by food and digestive juices passing through the intestines; and the continuous hum and intermittent crackle given off by muscles."[19] In an anechoic chamber the individual therefore turns into a "gigantic ear," as Sabu Kosho writes in an article about Seiko Mikami's installation *World, Membrane and the Dismembered Body* (which uses an anechoic chamber).[20]

Hearing Things (two) (Sensory Deprivation)

In spring 1979 the slogan "In Space No One Can Hear You Scream" announced the science-fiction horror movie *Alien*, which invaded cinemas in autumn that year [→ fig. 2]. Almost two decades earlier, in 1961, Yuri Gagarin had become the first man to fly into outer space. In the early sixties, as part of the efforts to develop manned space travel, scientists on both sides of the Iron Curtain conducted tests on cosmonauts and astronauts trying to establish how they would cope with weightlessness and

Fig. 2
Alien, directed by Ridley Scott, poster, 1979

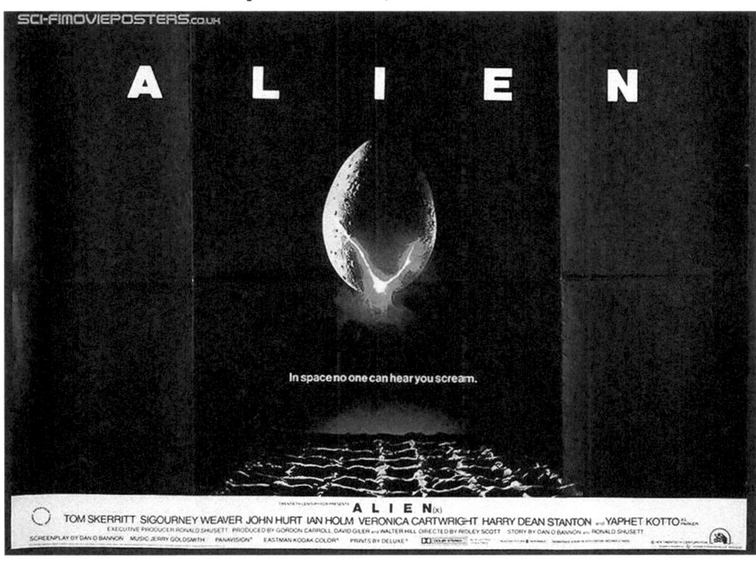

the lack of acoustic stimulation. How would the human mind react when deprived of events? In his autobiography, Gagarin described the training routine that was to prepare cosmonauts for space travel: "After the fast spinning on the centrifuges, we stayed in a specially equipped soundproof chamber over a longer period of time. This 'loneliness' helped determine the cosmonaut's physical and nervous endurance. Sometimes we spent several days in this small isolated room. It was cut off from the rest of the world. No sound or noise filtered through. There was not the slightest movement in the air—nothing. No one talked to you. From time to time we had to operate a radio device according to a given schedule. But it was a one-way connection. We sent the radio message, but we didn't know whether it arrived or not. No one answered, not even a single word [→ fig. 3]."[21]

A few years later, in 1968/69, the artists James Turrell and Robert Irwin started collaborating with Edward C. Wortz within the framework of the Los Angeles County Museum of Art's "Art and Technology" [→ fig. 4] program, initiated by Maurice Tuchman.[22] Wortz, an experimental psychologist and head of the Life Science Department at Garrett Aerospace, was conducting

14 Voegelin, *Listening*, p. 80.
15 Hans-Friedrich Bormann dates Cage's visit between 1948 and 1952, in *Verschwiegene Stille. John Cages performative Ästhetik* (Munich: Fink, 2005), p. 178.
16 John Cage, *A Year from Monday: New Lectures and Writings* (London: Calder & Boyars, 1968), p. 134.
17 Seth Kim-Cohen, *In the Blink of an Ear: Toward a Non-Cochlear Sonic Art* (London/New York: Continuum, 2009), p. xvi.
18 Ibid., p. 161.
19 Toop, *Sinister Resonance*, p. 187.
20 Sabu Kosho, "On Seiko Mikami's World, Membrane and the Dismembered Body," Dutch Electronic Arts Festival, V2_ Rotterdam, 1998, http://www.v2.nl/archive/articles/on-seiko-mikamis-world-membrane-and-the-dismembered-body.
21 Quoted in the German translation: Juri Gagarin, *Mein Flug ins All* (Berlin: Kongress Verlag, 1961), p. 127. The book was published in English under the title *Road to the Stars* (Moscow: Foreign Languages Publishing House, 1962).
22 See Maurice Tuchman, *A Report on the Art and Technology Program of the Los Angeles County Museum of Art, 1967–1971* (New York: Viking, 1971). A full version of the report can be downloaded from http://www.lacma.org/sites/all/themes/custom/lacma/reading_room/A_Report_on_the_Art_and_Technology_Program_of_the_Los_Angeles_County_Museum_of_Art_1967_8211_1971.html. Turrell's and Irwin's project was interrupted in its development stage in 1969. For a survey of the reasons, see Craig Adcock, *James Turrell: The Art of Light and Space* (Berkeley: University of California Press, 1990), pp. 74–75.

Fig. 3
German Titow, the second human to journey into outer space, during training in the anechoic chamber, 1961

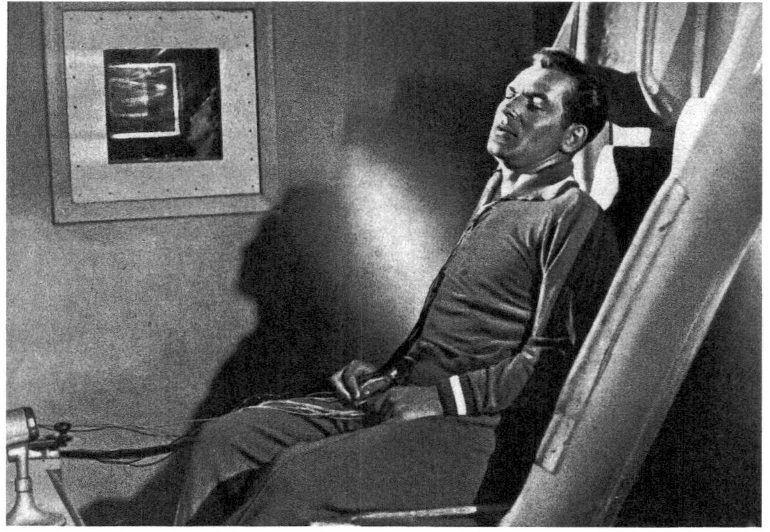

research on human perception in space on behalf of NASA. Turrell, Irwin, and Wortz were particularly interested in questions like up-and-down orientation in zero gravity, the role of (lacking) acoustic stimulation, and how visual perception changes in the emptiness of space. They worked with methods of sensory deprivation (Ganzfeld spheres, which create homogeneous visual fields, anechoic rooms, etc.) and thus started "experimenting with the phenomenon of objectlessness as such."[23] It soon appeared that the exterior world, once it had been deprived of all sensory stimuli, soon gave way to the interior world: "We three," said Turrell in 1969, "are becoming intranauts exploring inner space instead of outer space."[24]

Fig. 4
Maurice Tuchman: *A Report on the Art and Technology Program of the Los Angeles County Museum of Art, 1967–1971*, book cover, 1971

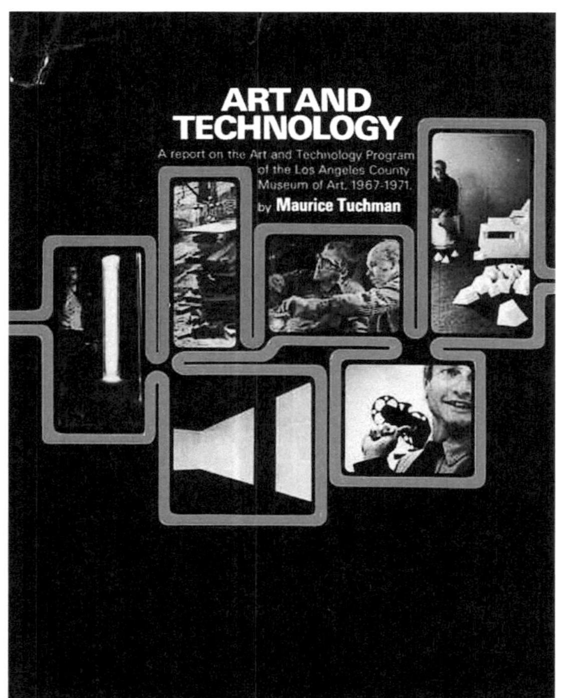

Dead Tract, White Torture

Kosho points to the dark side of these experiments: "It is said that dogs and other animals can live only for a short while in anechoic rooms because of the disorientation, and there are records of anechoic rooms being used for torture."[25] In 1994 the artists Rob Moonen and Olaf Arndt constructed *Camera Silens* [→ fig. 5], an anechoic chamber of which Henk van Boxtel gave the following account: "This space is dead and deadens ... The individual loses himself completely in the *Camera Silens*. The subject becomes an object, becomes a thing. It is the most radical form of isolation. Starving the senses, the space achieves absolute domination of its inhabitant. Reprisal, the potential to take arms against another person or the environment, vanishes. Complete control. Everything remains the same forever, and duration is the assassin. The mind is isolated from the body, is killed in its own way."[26]

Brigitte Kölle describes this bloodless method of torture in more detail: "The *Camera Silens* (Latin for 'silent room') is a completely dark and soundproof room that experimental-psychological research has proven to be able to undermine the human senses within a very short space of time, indeed to provoke the physical and psychological breakdown of the individual. The *Camera Silens* has been used as an instrument of torture, and still is. It is part of the methods termed 'white torture,' or 'clean torture,' as it leaves no visible and verifiable traces ... Belonging to the realm of 'white torture' are methods of social and sensory deprivation such as solitary confinement, confinement in darkness, sleep deprivation, hunger and thirst, but also methods of controlled sensory stimulus (cold or heat, continuous artificial lighting, loud music etc.) ... In Germany the term was first introduced into the public debate at the beginning of the seventies in the context of solitary confinement [the conditions under which the RAF members Ulrike Meinhof and Astrid Proll were detained in a part of the Cologne-Ossendorf prison commonly referred to as the 'dead' or 'silent' tract] and the development of a new type of cell, the so-called F-type cell (which, incidentally, was eagerly adopted in Turkey)."[27]

23 Christoph Asendorf, *Super Constellation. Flugzeug und Raumrevolution. Die Wirkung der Luftfahrt auf Kunst und Kultur der Moderne* (Vienna: Springer, 1997), p. 326. See also Chris Salter, who writes: "Turrell and Irwin's proposed combination of an anechoic chamber, a room that absorbs all reflection such that no sound ever bounces away from its point of origin, with the powerful effect of a visual *ganzfeld*, a horizon without depth or size, only constructs the material conditions for experience. It is, however, the *performance*, the *act* of perception grappling with the process of seeing and hearing in a space on the verge of slipping away that constitutes the work." Salter, "The Question of Thresholds: Immersion, Absorption, and Dissolution in the Environments of Audio-Vision," in Dieter Daniels and Sandra Naumann with Jan Thoben (eds.), *Audiovisuology 2: Essays. Histories and Theories of Audiovisual Media and Art* (Cologne: Verlag der Buchhandlung Walther König, 2011), pp. 201–20, see here pp. 203–04.

24 Adcock, *James Turrell*, p. 76, quoted in Asendorf, *Super Constellation*, p. 328.

25 Kosho, "On Seiko Mikami's World."

26 Henk van Boxtel, "with the face in the mud," http://www.robmoonen.nl/2002/2002_camerasilens.htm.

27 Brigitte Kölle, "Die Zumutung," in Julian Heynen and Brigitte Kölle (eds.), *Weiße Folter. Gregor Schneider* (Cologne: Verlag der Buchhandlung Walther König, 2007), pp. 23–38, see here pp. 27–28.

Fig. 5
Rob Moonen, Olaf Arndt, *Camera Silens*, 1994

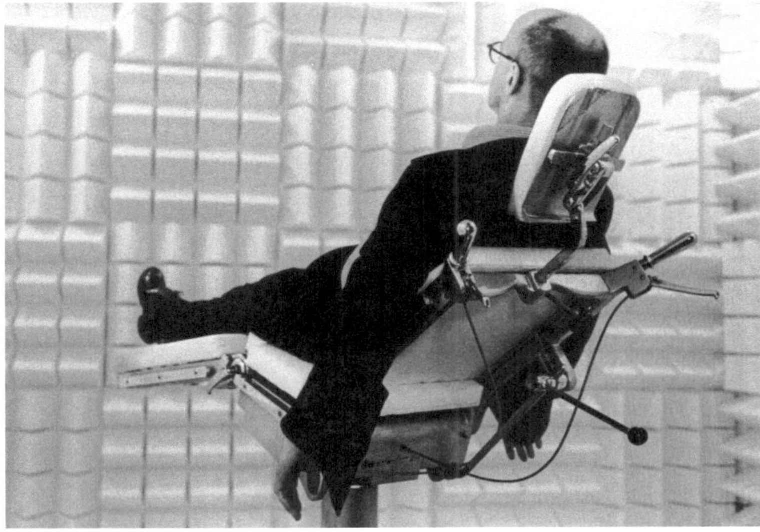

Hearing Things (three) (Hearing Things which Are Not There)

> Daddy, I hear the voices again, waaagh, s-s-s-s-sss, I even hear the foot-tracks.
> —Screamin' Jay Hawkins, *I Hear Voices*, 1962[28]

When the light is turned off, everything turns dark—and quiet. You close your eyes, but your ears remain open, scanning the darkness. As a child, I often heard steps on the carpet at night. If I listened to them carefully, I could hear them slowly approaching my bed, where I was hiding under the blanket, trying to be as quiet as possible, barely able to breathe. "When there is nothing to hear, so much starts to sound. Silence is not the absence of sound but the beginning of listening."[29] "When there is nothing to hear, you start hearing things."[30] The ear wants to recognize patterns—it probes into the darkness, into the silence, or even into monotonous soundscapes, believing it can detect slight differences. In *A Book of Silence*, Sara Maitland identifies the conscious decision in favor of sensory deprivation as the difference between the beneficial effect of floatation tanks and the mechanisms of solitary confinement.[31] Whether silence is deliberately chosen or forcefully imposed has a substantial impact on its regenerative or destructive potential. Numerous descriptions of experiences with silence and loneliness, especially those made in a context of coercion, border on madness. Hearing voices or chanting in silence can be the result of ambient noise that is interpreted as language. This is a common phenomenon at sea, where the combination of silence, loneliness, and the creaking and moaning of men and vessels produces a choir of mythical sounds: this is when sailors start telling stories of sirens luring them to their deaths. How, then, to distinguish between voices that are but a "figment of the imagination" and those that are effectively calling out?

Deserts are monotonous and silent places, too. For *Stille Landschaft* [silence/silent landscape] Jens Brand visited the Makgadikgadi Pans, a salt desert in the North of Botswana and one of the quietest places on this planet, to record the silence there [→ fig. 6].[32] In 1972 the US band America released *A Horse With No Name*, a song dealing with the hallucinations that can occur in the desert: "On the first part of the journey / I was looking at all the life / There were plants and birds and rocks and things / There was sand and hills and rings / The first thing I met was a fly with a buzz / And the sky with no clouds / The heat was hot and the ground was dry / But the air was full of sound." The song describes what could be termed an "acoustic Fata Morgana" produced by the absence of acoustic stimuli in the desert. The chorus refers to the fact of being unable to cope with this silence and losing oneself: "I've been through the desert on a horse with no name / it felt good to be out of the rain / in the desert you can't remember your name / 'Cause there ain't no one for to give you no pain."

Fig. 6
Desert with microphone; graphic design for the exhibition *Sounds Like Silence* (a re-enactment of Jens Brand's *Stille Landschaft*, 2002) 2012

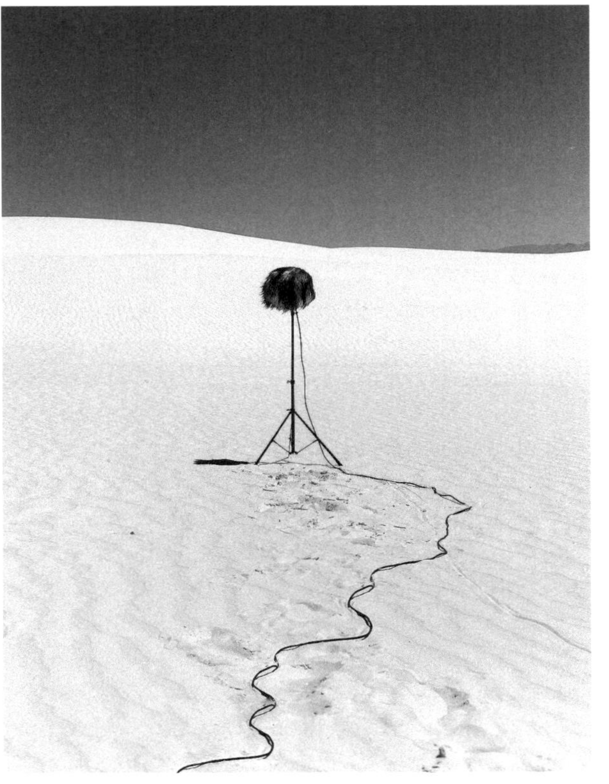

"All silences are uncanny, because we have become estranged from absences of sound."[33] In *The Shining* (1980) [→ fig. 7], Jack Torrance falls victim to the silence reigning at the Overlook Hotel. The writer and former teacher is hired as a caretaker by the remote mountain hotel, where he spends the winter with his family. In the course of the film their deliberate decision to retreat to the isolated hotel progressively turns into a desperate

28 Toop, *Sinister Resonance*, p. 183.
29 Voegelin, *Listening*, p. 83.
30 Voegelin, *Listening*, p. 82.
31 Sarah Maitland, *A Book of Silence* (London: Granta Books, 2008).
32 The graphic design for the exhibition invitation for *Sounds Like Silence* took inspiration from Brand's video recordings and uses a photograph by Andrea Eichardt of the artist's microphone standing in the White Sands Desert in Texas in May 2012.
33 Toop, *Sinister Resonance*, p. 182.

situation as the hotel is snowed in and cut off from the outside world. In Stanley Kubrick's horror film, the ubiquitous snow echoes the silence in which the inner ghosts appear, compelling Jack to commit his horrible deeds.

Fig. 7
The Shining,
directed by Stanley Kubrick,
film still, 1980

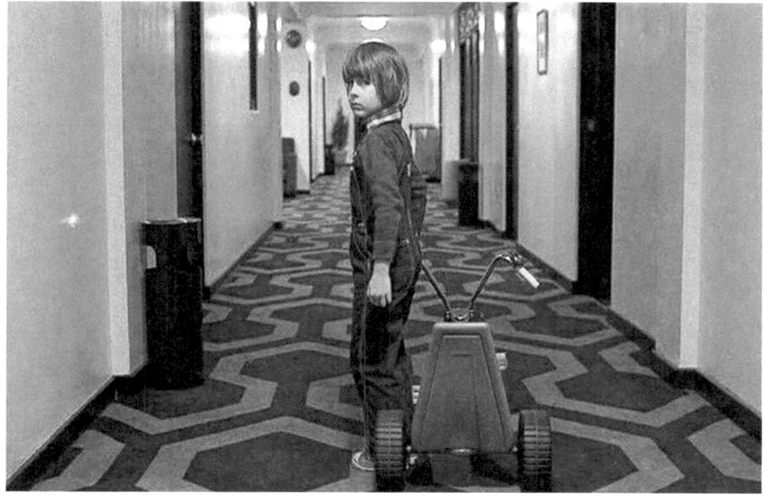

Silent Outlook

The view from the Overlook Hotel opens onto a panorama of white snow-covered woods and mountains. We have heard things that *are there* (we have merely heard them more attentively than usual; we have, so to speak, really heard them for the first time) and we have started hearing things that *are not there at all.* These are the effects of different forms of silence—of rhetoric, anechoic and total silence: "By definition, anechoic (echoless) is different from soundless (which occurs in a vacuum, for example) and, of course, silence, that is a rhetorical rather than physical situation."[34] Whether we are finding respite in silence or whether the silence becomes torture and leads us to the brink of insanity is also dependent on whether we are deliberately exposing ourselves to silence or whether we are being involuntarily exposed to it. In the latter case, the beauty of non-intentional sounds (as in Cage's *4'33"*) will soon fail to impress us. Similarly, the noise heard by Kafka's protagonist in his elaborate, silent burrow is synonymous with uncertainty, unrest, and even paranoia. Kafka died before he could write down what happened to the mole-like being and what was the cause of the noise he heard: the story remains unfinished. Silence, however, in all the cases described in this essay, becomes an at times dangerous test of one's own limits.

34 Kosho, "On Seiko Mikami's World."

Brandon LaBelle

Noise, Over-Hearing, and Cage's *4′33″*

> And with these [memories], the sense of the world's concreteness, irreducible, immediate, tangible, of something clear and closer to us: of the world, no longer as a journey having constantly to be remade, not as a race without end, a challenge having constantly to be met, not as the one pretext for a despairing acquisitiveness, not as the illusion of a conquest, but as the rediscovery of a meaning, the perceiving that the earth is a form of writing, a *geography* of which we had forgotten that we ourselves are the authors.
> —Georges Perec, *Species of Spaces*[1]

The writing of the world that Perec embraces appears through accidental contact, the random passing by of bodies on the move, that is, script shaped by juxtapositions of abrasions and scuffs left on the world by you and me. His reading is attentive to that "geo-graphy" in motion and overlaid onto our surroundings, as diverse writing that only the ebb and flow of so many forces can generate.

Perec's geo-*graphy* is precisely that: a graphing of worldly *intensities*, which draw our attention to the immediate, and to each other. I take from Perec, then, a lesson in attention—not one of fixed reference, or clear focus, but a restlessness that attempts, in its sensual breadth, to *attend* to all that is there. An appreciation for what others are doing as the making of the here and now.

I want to underscore and carry forward such attention also into the realm of listening, and to those spaces marked by sounds, silences, and particularly by what we call *noise*. My interest is to focus on noise as the production of the social, of a geo-graphy through which we may relate. Noise in this sense need not be thought of in terms of volume, nor as having any particular sonic quality. Rather, I emphasize noise as the beginning of confrontation, of negotiation; noise, as Michel Serres suggests, as the "rending" of any system or order.[2] A rending from which new confugrations may arise. I want to locate noise as the initiation of a new sociality: two bodies meeting, and on the threshold of possible community. A mark of audibility that can be heard, as Perec reads, as the making of a collective authorship. *Noise as a special scrawl that demarcates, that territorializes by over-writing, over-stepping, and through acts of over-hearing.*

Noise in this respect is understood as a fundamental aspect of our everyday experiences, as well as a fundamental element within the sound arts. In this regard, noise may be heard or defined as a sound which *over-steps* particular limits; an extreme sound that, as I hope to show, locates us in relation to the other. I'm interested in thinking of noise outside the negative connotations of "nuisance" and "annoyance"—and in contrast, or due to this, to hear it as forming the *basis* for an art of listening. Such a perspective finds resonance with Luigi Russolo's original "art of noises" in which he calls for a broader appreciation for those surges of urban sound abounding throughout modern life. That is, an ear for the "continuous, very strange and marvelous hubbub of the crowd."[3]

To explore this further I want to bring into consideration a particular memory, of attending a concert in Los Angeles in 1998—an event that, while arising out of a personal situation, has come to suggest a larger horizon of ideas. In considering this recollection I am further reminded of another concert, one which I did not attend but which hovers in and around the sound arts, and which I'd like to also address—that is, John Cage's

1 Georges Perec, *Species of Spaces and Other Pieces* (London: Penguin, 1997), p. 79.
2 See Michel Serres, *Genesis* (Ann Arbor: University of Michigan Press, 1995).
3 Luigi Russolo, *The Art of Noises* (New York: Pendragon Press, 1986), p. 45.

concert at the Maverick Concert Hall in 1952 where his *4′33″* was first performed. As an originating work of sound art—as an expanded notion of musicality and listening—*4′33″* historically extends and complicates the project of avant-garde music through its conceptual use of silence and the particularities of context, as well as, and importantly, by explicitly underscoring the differentiating breadth of sound (what I understand as "noise") as a social experience. I take Cage's silence not so much as a deep commitment to quiet, but as a critical move that allows sounds to occur, as well as a device for collapsing distinctions between music and sound, art and life.[4]

I'd like to draw out these two concerts so as to situate noise as an *open horizon* of listening intimately linked to place as well as collective experience, to those always already beside me, whose presence naturally conditions, interferes with, and contours my own.

In recalling this personal memory, and looping it together with the concert of *4′33″*, my aim is to elaborate what I perceive as a vibrant intersection produced by a musical performance, the related sociality of a concert space, and the disrupting verve of noise all coming into dialogue. Such an intersection provides the basis for thinking of noise as geo-graphy, as geo-*phony*, instantiated by audible marks and markings, the abrasions and scuffs of related confrontation and what small worlds might exist therein.

To examine this further, I will point to three coordinates within this mapping, three coordinates within *listening to noise*. These I will call:

I. Acoustics Multiplied
II. The Supplement
III. Difference-Making

I underscore these as coordinates within the field of sonority with which to open a view onto noise: to explore the particular forms and the particular spatial vocabularies noise may be heard to produce. If noise can be thought of as the production of the social, what forms of inhabitation does it make possible? How do we find each other within this open horizon toward which sound tends?

Los Angeles, 1998. I'm at a rock club with a group of friends. We've gone out to see a band and the place is packed. I'm standing a bit to the back, pressed between friends and strangers, drink in hand and the band in front, not too far, but not exactly close: it's a small club, and everyone is listening, focused, interested. All except a few—to my right, roughly six or seven meters away, a group of guys, maybe three or four, are standing, drinking beers and talking, laughing, having a good time and rather oblivious to the situation—that is, that they are breaking the mood, disrupting the scene, causing a ruckus. Suddenly I am caught between two perspectives, two performances, two forms of listening: in front of me, the band, the object of attention, the thing I am here to witness, and to the right, a group of talkers, conversing somewhere between quiet and loud, but still loud enough to unsettle my main focus, my main perspective. The individuality of these strangers blurs into the darkness of the club, into the movements of the general crowd, and still they appear precisely as individuals *out of place*—their laughter, their joking suddenly contrasts with the general situation.

The situation continues for some time: other people start to yell at the group who are talking, the group even starts to yell back, and maybe, I'm not sure, even the band starts to get annoyed. In this moment though, something changes, for myself: I begin to realize that what is happening is extremely provocative, and extremely suggestive—in this moment, I begin to realize what it means to listen. That sound, of course, is never an isolated event, that there are always sounds to the side of another sound, which we constantly over-hear. Listening, in other words, is a process of confronting the expressive movements occurring around us, which act to broaden our attention, even by force.

While this experience of disruption was not necessarily new to me, nor does it necessarily stand out within the normative patterns of rock club behavior—still, at this instant, for some reason, it brought forward a sudden recognition: I became aware that my own annoyance was precisely an opportunity. That if listening is to deepen one's experience of the world, to bring one into contact with the making of those worldly intensities Perec speaks of, then noise provides a dynamic instantiation of such depth, an active education of sound's particular *knowledge structure*. That is, a geo-*phony*, which is precisely the way in which sound inculcates a particular paradigmatic order—*an acoustical spatiality* around which bodies come into contact, and exchange is produced.

I could say more about the specificity of the situation: the fact that these guys were in their twenties, and appeared to be dressed in black, settling into the general fashion of the crowd; I could also say how the club was located on Silver Lake Blvd., and that it acted as an important site for local music culture. These things I could dwell on, in order to examine the particular details of the rock club, as a social structure, and how listening performed at this specific moment: between and within the crowd, and in relation to this band. This would be an interesting analysis, leading to a deeper contextual understanding of the Los Angeles scene of the 90s, and of the normative patterns of attending a rock gig. And further, a means to consider this small group's behavior as a form of "disobedience" precisely as it did not subscribe to the intrinsic social contract underlying the scene. Yet, all of this I plan not to do. Rather, my interest is to extract from this specific situation, this memory, a set of more generalized viewpoints: a theoretical frame from which to enliven a more macroscopic consideration of noise within the social, and how it comes to further participate within the sound arts.

In recalling this concert experience, I am curious to hear a primary lesson or register of an art of listening—a platform for a new ear also active within *4′33″*. We may recall that Cage's own concert begins with a pianist (in this case, David Tudor) entering the stage to sit at the piano. As the score states, there are to be no notes played, instead, an elongated silence that stretches for *4′33″*, along with three small movements of opening and closing the piano lid.[5]

As an audience we are then also caught between two perspectives, two performances, two forms of listening: in front, the piano, the object of attention, the event the audience is here to witness, and to the side, other sounds—someone whispering to their friend, another shuffling their feet, and maybe someone else coughing, even the wind in the trees and birds outside—all these extra-sounds come to unsettle the audience's main focus, the

4 Cage's continual re-investigation and re-writing of *4′33″* reveals his own sense of the work's transversing proposition. From the 1962 version, *0′00″ (4′33″ No. 2)*, whose instructions state simply, "Solo to be performed in any way by anyone," to his own personal performance of the work while identifying mushrooms in the woods (see John Cage, "Music Lovers' Field Companion" (1954) in *Silence* (Cambridge, MA: MIT Press: 1966), p. 276), it becomes clear that the work's operative function is found in its continual restaging, relocation, and rearticulation.

5 These movements were specified at certain times within the work; notably at the Maverick, these were listed on the program as: 30″, 2′23″, and 1′40″. For a consideration of the score of *4′33″* see Julia Robinson, "John Cage and Investiture: Unmanning the System," in *The Anarchy of Silence* (Barcelona: MACBA, 2009).

main perspective. The situation continues for some time: other people start talking louder, someone walks out of the theatre, and yet, the silence continues to be punctuated by the summer evening.[6]

In this moment though, something changes: I want to suggest that a view onto listening is set forward that explicitly places the terms of sound, music, silence, and noise into conversation.[7] The silence of Cage's work declares that music is never an isolated auditory event, and that there are always sounds to the side of another sound, and which we constantly over-hear. Music, following Cage, appears precisely as a space for multiplying perspectives (to which I will return). *4′33″* in this regard instigates two proposals: it problematizes existing conceptions of musical composition, and it lays the ground for sound in its rawest sense, in its *worldliness*, to emerge as the basis for a work.

Such a work, along with my own memory, opens up the possibility of mapping out an "ontology of noise," of ultimately suggesting that what we understand as noise forms the basis, a possible beginning for an art of listening. I would venture to say that the experience of interference, of disruption, of *over-hearing*, rather than being the opposition to a dedicated listening is, instead, the potential of every sound. It's the promise that every sound makes: to say, "Here, I am over here." Cage's continual project to dismantle particular (musical, sensorial, epistemological) heirarchies, what Heinz-Klaus Metzger refers to as "Cage's disorganization of musical coherence,"[8] sets the scene for such pronouncements.

I want to use this notion of "over-hearing," of sounds that appear *over-there*, that moment of interruption, as a fundamental theory of the sound arts, as well as to suggest an appreciation for noise as a productive and generative (social) event. Over-hearing, rather than being a process of "ignoring" (as in the German *überhören*), should be understood here as an expanded listening, where what is in front is complemented by what is beyond—over-hearing, as I will suggest, as a listening to *more than*.

To do so, I'll begin by drawing out my three coordinates of listening, which are equally three forms of spatial thinking, of *over-stepping*. These coordinates aim to give detail to the particular interrupting vitality I'm suggesting hovers at the center of sound. In this way, my intention is not to suggest there is any sharp line dividing the terms "sound," "silence," and "noise." Rather, I understand their relation (as I think Cage also suggests) as interwoven, whereby sound as a flow of audible phenomena necessarily shifts in register, ceaselessly and continually passing through a greater field of sensory experience, which includes silence and noise as edges. I'm interested precisely in these edges, where sound's propagating verve forces negotiation—precisely that point where the audible surprises us. In this sense, "sound" can be understood as always already containing "silence" and "noise," as mobilizing their presence within each oscillation of air pressure. Yet it is my view that "noise" in particular brings forward an opportunity exactly at the point where sound problematizes a relation to others: it is clear that noise behaves to introduce the *unwanted*, and it's here that I want to dwell.

I
Acoustics Multiplied

The first coordinate of listening I'd like to map out, within this *geo-phony*, is that noise *multiplies perspectives*. In other words, there is always a sound outside the frame of a particular listening, which often interferes or occurs to the side, to become immediately part of the experience. Noise in this regard is pluralistic: it registers and highlights our spatial surroundings by explicitly connecting, in many cases, beyond what we can see. It also does so according to a temporality, an explicit time-based flux, toward which our attention is dramatically drawn, fixed, and then unfixed. As Barry Truax proposes, "The sound wave arriving at the ear is the analogue of the current state of the physical environment, because as the wave travels, it is changed by each interaction with the environment."[9]

Sound, in general, turns space into a temporal, fluctuating condition, where each interaction with the environment must be heard to bring into relief, at each moment, the material conditions that surround us. As *4′33″* suggests, sound performs a fundamental multiplication to our experiences of physical space, reminding us that each single room we inhabit contains more than one acoustical perspective.[10] Such multiplication, I'd propose, sets in motion a dynamic transversal across and into architecture, linking and connecting into a simultaneity of events toward an edge of listening. This intrusiveness of sound, as a fundamental instant of noise, can be glimpsed from two sides—while invading one's personal space, or unsettling any particular quietude, it also grants potential to each instant of rupture. That is, to hear *what is out of reach*.

This operation can also be found at work in numerous sound art projects, where sound is used not only as material, but as an extension of a given architectural space, to turn up the volume on our locational perspective. For example, Joel Sanders' *Mix House* project from 2006 [→ fig. 1] aims to fill a domestic architecture with audio-visual extensions. Fitting multiple cameras and microphones to the exterior of a house, the work functions to bring the outside *into* the home. These exterior views and perspectives are amplified through windows that act as screens, as well as a speaker system wired throughout the house, which can be controlled in the kitchen area from a sort of DJ platform integrated into the kitchen counter. Various controls are added, so as to allow active surveying of the exterior, where cameras can

6 The Maverick Concert Hall was opened in 1916 and remains an active venue for chamber music. Built by Hervey White, the wooden hall consists of a large gambrel roof and wall panels which can be opened, allowing audiences to sit outside. In this way, the Hall is an extremely open auditorium, which freely allows the sounds of the surrounding woods to trickle in. See [→ p. 77, fig. 1]

7 While it's hard to fully gauge in what way Cage's original performance was received, I perceive its transformative power solely by the degree to which this work continues to be referred to, discussed, and referenced. The exhibition to which this catalogue relates attests to this.

8 Heinz-Klaus Metzger, "John Cage, or Liberated Music", in *October* 82, Fall 1997, p. 55. (Originally 1959.)

9 Barry Truax, *Acoustic Communication* (Norwood, NJ: Ablex Publishing, 1994), p. 15.

10 It's interesting to note to what degree Cage himself was interested in forms of "multiplicity." The development of his compositional work throughout the 1950s and 60s can be appreciated on this level. Works such as *Williams Mix* (1951–53), a four-minute electronic work for eight simultaneous tapes, or HPSCHD (1969), which incorporated a full range of media, such as sixty-four slide projections, fifty-two tapes of computer-generated sounds, along with seven harpsichords from which works not only by Cage but also Hiller, as well as other classical works, were to be performed (according to chance operations)–these excessive productions, to name but a few, suggest Cage's dedication to "decentering" musical conventions in line with a listener's perspective.

scan the landscape outside, or microphones can zoom in on particular events. The *Mix House* in this way literally extends the single home, creating links to a broader environment.

Fig. 1
Architect: Joel Sanders, Associate Architect: Karen Van Lengen, Media Artist: EAR Studio (Ben Rubin), *Mix House*, 2006

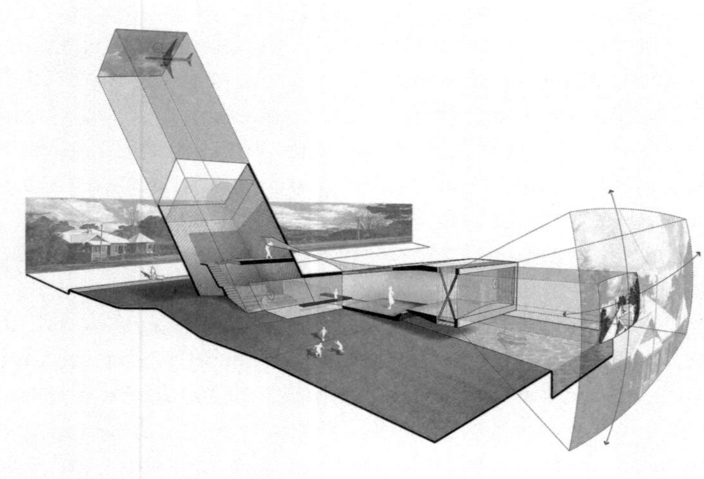

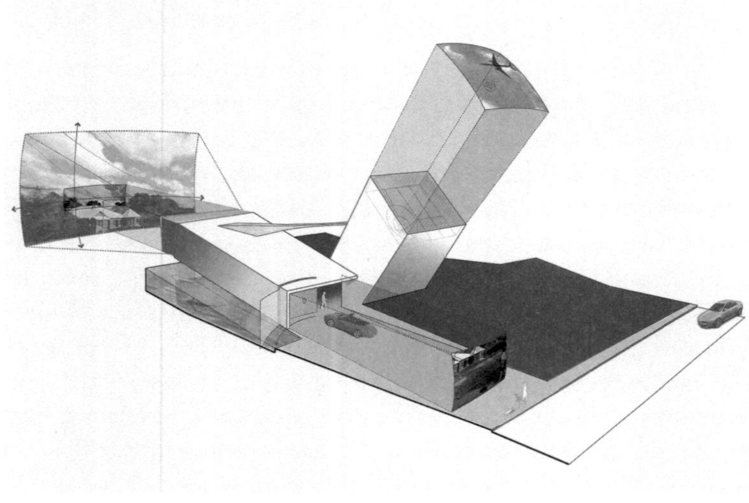

These acts of spatial multiplication, of extension, as well as environmental survey, also feature in the work of artist Carrie Bodle. Her work *Sonification/Listening Up* work (2005) [→ fig. 2] appears as a large-scale sound installation mounted onto the facade of Building 54 on the MIT campus. A series of thirty-five loudspeakers amplify sounds based on data gathered from the MIT Haystack Observatory. In particular, data gathered from the earth's ionosphere functions as the basis for the work's sonification: data is translated into a sonic vocabulary—*ion-acoustic*—and amplified to the exterior of the building. Through such a strategy, the work can be heard to extend this particular architecture, by explicitly linking it to the ionosphere lurking overhead. It starts to demand more from us by dramatically overlaying an excess of sound onto the environment.

I take these projects then as an echo of Truax's environmental listening, whereby a sound wave not only brings forward but multiplies our understanding of the current state of a place. The acoustics of an environment is precisely a territorial layer that often brings into contact things and bodies, events and voices, and from which alliances and resonances as well as ruptures and agitations are experienced and produced. Such productions also radically shift attention from sightlines to a deeper vital materiality: an "energetic" architecture whereby sonic pressures pass through bodies, walls, and objects to generate points of thermodynamic energy.

Fig. 2
Carrie Bodle, *Sonification / Listening Up*, 2005

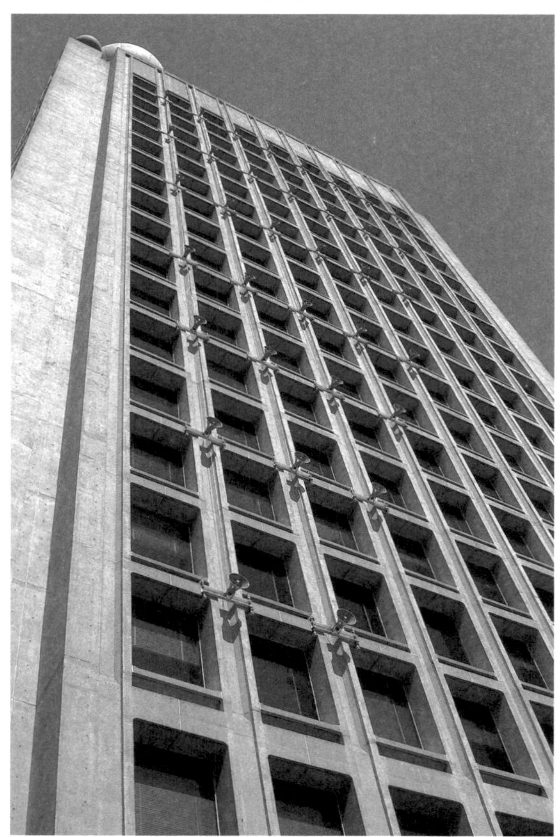

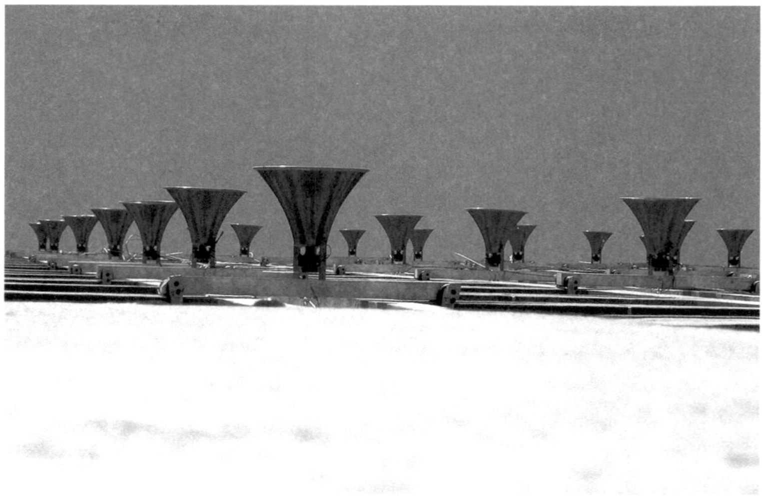

Bodle's project expresses this idea by networking the built environment with sound waves, technologies, dataspheres, and buildings: to hear such sound waves is to also feel oneself located within a greater spatial and acoustical perspective, one deeply connected to the movements of weather. Such a project, along with the extremely dynamic history of sound installation practices in general, should be understood as forming a radical catalogue of spatial experimentation, an *archive of interruption*. The interplay between sound and architecture at work in the legacy of the sound arts materializes a multiplicity of spatial perspectives, and readily suggests acoustics as an "expanded project," a *noise* well beyond conventional understandings of fidelity or unwanted interference.[11] In fact, the multiplying of (architectural) perspectives materialized in the sound arts places noise at the center of spatial experience, where superimpositions and transpositions intentionally dislocate and disorient our perceptual frame. The multiplying of perspectives captures sound's fundamental oscillation to provide a greater spatial experience.

II
The Supplement

The second point or coordinate I'd like to map is that noise *challenges my sense of what I am listening for*. In other words, what I am expecting, what I am waiting for, is constantly supplemented by something else—by that sound there, and then another there.

To return to the Maverick Concert Hall, the sounds happening around the piano interfered with what the audience were expecting, that is, the music; but in doing so, they also started to supplement the musical moment, to add an appendix to their listening, and in that moment, the full presence of the piano, as the point of attention, was undone. Returning also to the club in Los Angeles, my own expectations, that is, what I was waiting for, were supplemented by the laughter and the chattering occuring to the side: what I over-heard did not necessarily block out the presence of the band, the experience of the music, rather, it appeared *alongside*, as a contributing element. Such an instant, of expanded listening, of multiplied perspectives, highlights sound's ability to always demand more, that is, to support the production of an *encounter*. To supplement; *to noise*.

We can understand the supplement as something that adds onto something else; it is not a substitute for something but an addition. Yet in adding on to an original object or phenomenon or music, the supplement also empties out the original, as a full stable presence. The supplement in other words brings into question the wholeness of the original by introducing a *more than*; in doing so, it opens up the original to undo the idea of a stable meaningful reference—the supplement, in other words, makes the original open for sampling, for appropriation, for comment.

It's like being in a cinema during an intensely serious moment in a film, and someone in the audience starts laughing—this laughter, this noise, completely disrupts the scene, but it also begins something else: it says, every expectation, every anticipation is also prone to surprise. This I find to be an extremely vital element to sound and listening: that the process of hearing always already includes the possibility for another narrative to take shape.

This is precisely what Paul Carter suggests when he talks through what he calls "the erotic ambiguity of sound." For Carter, this ambiguity to sound is specifically the "exceeding of representation"—a positive, dramatic ambuigity found within sound that generates what we might think of as "extra-meanings," as part of the condition of listening: something that slips through, or that overflows from any signifying instant.[12]

To explore the idea of the supplement further, I'd like to refer to two works I produced recently, which can be appreciated as acts of supplementing. Working with John Cage's original "Lecture on Nothing" (a lecture originally presented in 1950 and later published in his book *Silence*) I recorded a deaf man reading the text. Through this work I was curious to complicate the ways in which silence is approached or defined, as forming the basis for a dedicated listening. For Cage, silence operates as a frame (as can be seen in *4'33"*) within which non-intentional sounds appear, with a subsequent opening up of our auditory sense, our auditory behavior, to a greater social situation. Following Cage's example, silence continues to inform the sound arts in various ways, often functioning as a positive, nurturing platform for our listening. In recording a deaf individual reading the original text, from my perspective silence may appear also in another way: rather than understand silence as the pre-condition for sound, as an optimistic, democratic frame for *all sounds*, the work poses silence as a particular force, one that carries its own ideological contour, and which ultimately acts to exclude, to territorialize.[13] *Supplementing* the Cage lecture, the voice of the deaf man gives us a silence to listen to, that is, a deafness found in the voice, but one that may reposition Cage's silence to make audible an additional referent: I take this work then, like acts of supplementing, as a possible footnote to Cage's lecture, a footnote that, as Derrida suggests, pulls against the original.[14]

A second work in line with this supplementing feature is *The Sonic Body* [→ fig. 3]. The work is based on making audio recordings of different individuals, as well as selected groups, dancing to music heard through headphones. I was interested to capture the movements of people dancing, and to hear these movements as a detailed translation of the music heard. The subsequent recordings start to give another version of the particular song—the sounds of a body moving to Joy Division's "Transmission" I would propose is the song. It is the song, and it is something *more*. It is the song ingested by a body and forced back out in various pivots and breaks, gyrations and hops. It is a song *and* a body, together, as an assembly: a sonic body. In paying attention to this sonic body, the work gives us a supplementing elaboration of music, to suggest, or to possibly lay bare, the ways in which listening moves us. These supplementing additions and stagings initiate a form of over-hearing, that is, a listening that hears *past* or *through* the original referent, whether Cage's lecture or a musical track, to arrive somewhere *alongside*. It is my view that noise explicitly introduces this potential, this operation, into the sonic imagination, as a method for narrative and criticality, or for countering the encounter.

11 For a thoroughly engaging and informative account of acoustics, see Barry Blesser and Linda-Ruth Salter, *Spaces Speak, are you listening? Experiencing Aural Architecture* (Cambridge, MA: MIT Press, 2007).

12 See Paul Carter, "Ambiguous Traces, Mishearing, and Auditory Space," in *Hearing Cultures: Essays on Sound, Listening and Modernity* (Oxford: Berg, 2004).

13 Questions on the ideological tensions of silence were first developed in my work, *Acoustic Territories: Sound Culture and Everyday Life* (London/New York: Continuum, 2010). It has been my aim to query in what way silence performs to reduce and limit forms of social participation, and how it appears within disciplinary practices (for example, within prisons). Silence and silencing are examined to ultimately challenge some of the overarching assumptions pervasive within the sound arts and related sound culture discussions that cast silence as a positive, "pure" horizon for deep listening and social improvement (e.g. the quiet home initiative in the UK). For more, see *Acoustic Territories*, particularly chapter 2.

14 For more on Derrida's theoretical outline of supplementarity, see Jacques Derrida, *Of Grammatology* (Baltimore: The John Hopkins University Press, 1998).

Fig. 3
Brandon LaBelle,
The Sonic Body,
2009

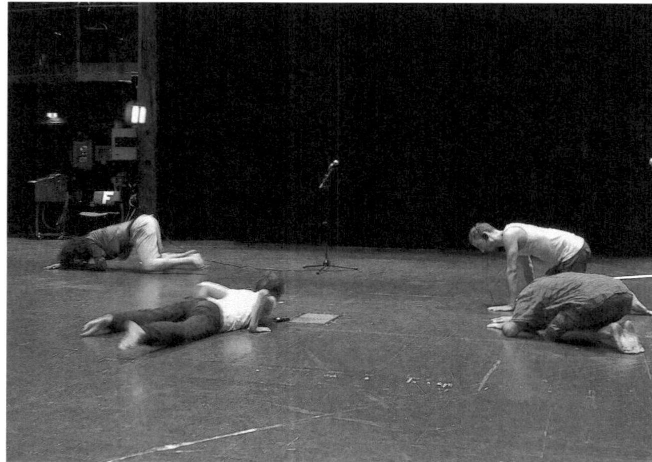

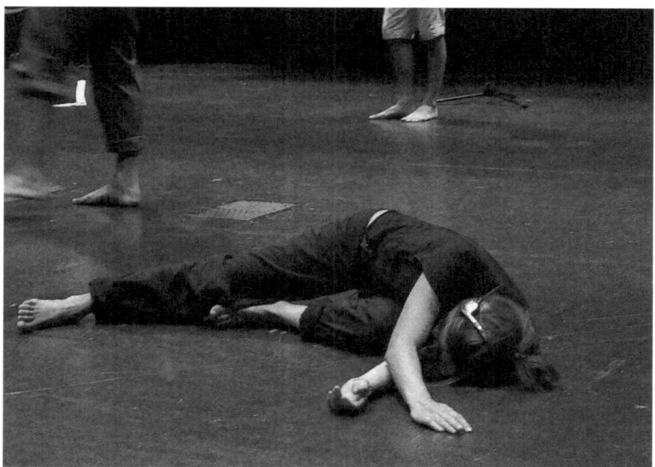

III
Difference-Making

Finally, my last point is that noise *introduces the other onto the scene*. In other words, noise brings the one that is over there to here, in front of me. This elaborates the idea of the supplement, the multiplying of perspective, to suggest that noise delivers a confrontation with the unexpected. This confrontation locates us further in the social, extending the multiplying of perspectives of physical, acoustical space, as well as the supplementing addition initiated by sound's noisy side.

This we find in the work of *4'33"*: by resituating the focus of attention from the piano back onto the audience, the space, and the outside environment, the work explicitly introduces the social onto the scene: that is, sounds that often come from others and that interfere with oneself, that brush up against the skin and unsettle one's attention.

I would propose that if noise has the potential to multiply perspectives, as a spatial acoustic, to supplement what I am expecting, forcing other narratives, it does so by explicitly introducing something, or someone, I do not yet know. It is to bring to my attention something I was not waiting for—in other words, it is to introduce a *difference*. As Aden Evens proposes, "Sound is fundamentally a difference of difference"—that is, a continual introduction of something which was not there before.[15]

I take this difference then as something which broadens my horizon. The multiplying of perspectives, the supplementing of representation, forces me to meet the one that is separate from me, and it does so by immediately collapsing distance: this difference that is over-there forces its way inside, that is, into my ear and into myself. As Steven Connor reminds us: "The self defined in terms of hearing rather than sight is a self imaged not as a point, but as a membrane; not as a picture, but as a channel through which voices, noises, and musics travel."[16] In this regard, the worldly intensities of sound *other* my horizon, as a differentiating production: *as the noise found in relating to the stranger.*

The operations of this *difference-making* can also be found at play in various artistic works. For instance, Richard Serra's video work *Boomerang* from 1974 can be appreciated as a work of difference-making instigated by a voice and its echo. The artist places a microphone in front of a woman. The woman wears headphones and can hear her voice speaking, but delayed—her voice comes back to her slightly after she has spoken. The woman speaks, talks about this experience: she refers to the situation, tries to describe what she is hearing, and how this echoing, this medial device disrupts her speech, her conscious thought. Something is always coming back to infiltrate her speech—she cannot escape herself:

> Yes, I can hear my echo and the words are coming back on top of me
> Uh, the words are spilling out of my head
> and then returning into my ear
> It puts a distance between the words and their apprehension, or their comprehension
> The words coming back seem slow, they don't seem to have the same forcefulness as when I speak them
> I think it's also slowing me down
> I think that it makes my thinking slower
> I have a double-take on myself
> I am once removed from myself
> I am thinking and hearing and filling up a vocal void
> I find that I have trouble making connections between thoughts
> I think that the words forming in my mind are somewhat detached from my normal thinking process
> I have a feeling that I am not where I am
> I feel that this place is removed from reality ...

Serra's *Boomerang* stages the mysterious dynamics of echoing sound. As the woman states, it's as if she leaves her own body, is a stranger to herself, with her voice coming back to her, as though from another reality. Everything staggers within the multiplying movements of the echo.

Such ruptures instantiate the sonorous dynamics I'm aiming for here—over-hearing herself, the participant perfectly describes a condition of *listening subjectivity* that I'd propose is intrinsic to noise.

Over-Hearing / Over-Stepping

Sound can be appreciated as an event that *animates*, and in doing so announces the introduction of *another*, another person,

15 See Aden Evens, *Sound Ideas: Music, Machines, and Experience* (Minneapolis: University of Minnesota Press, 2005).
16 Steven Connor, "Sound and Self," in *Hearing History: A Reader* (Athens: University of Georgia Press, 2004), p. 57.

another event, another animal—whether in the passing of a car, the wind in the trees, the ticking of a clock, a scratching behind the wall, or the voice from across the room, sound gives a body, however shadowy, however immaterial or non-human, to that which surrounds me, that which is other to me. As Mladen Dolar reminds us, even my own sounding presence appears as something separate from me, as another body of myself.[17] Sound as an animating event imparts "voice" to its sources, shifting the distances between bodies and things, spaces and energies.

The introduction of something or someone draws my attention, and yet mostly it is not specifically *for me*. If we appreciate sound as the very phenomenon that animates, that imparts capabilities of introduction and announcement, of *presencing*, even as recorded and synthesized matter, we can also hear it as incidental, as by-product, as something that spills over from haphazard occurrences and that continually brings forward, that instantiates a world where I am always a part of others—and mostly subsumed by surrounding intensities. Sound gives agency, while always already relocating it, in a network of distribution, moving it forward and beyond, away from me: sound thus animates but only moment to moment, and by disregarding separations of body and object, animate and inanimate, human and non-human.

As Cage himself proposed, listening performs as dynamic *inclusiveness* leading to a practice that never stops unsettling expectation, multiplying inputs, and integrating all kinds of materials and gestures. *A restless ear.* It is my view that Cage's *4′33″* establishes noise as the basis for the sound arts by not only opening our ears to a wider horizon, but also by staging sound as an experimental material aimed at the social dynamics of environments—*at multiplying, supplementing, and differencing.* That is, a situational encounter where we are asked to hear not the piano but each other, *along with* everything else. Following Cage's example, noise may be defined in contrast to sound precisely at the point where disorganization is mobilized and located within a particular context, in this case, a musical one. I take Cage's silence then, as his own legendary observations in the anechoic chamber attest, as the antithesis to any notion of "reduced" listening or as an arrest onto musical (and social) expression. In contrast, such silence is precisely the appreciation of noise, of hearing *more*, as the production of the social, the encounter: a sociality that brings you and I into contact, and that places us on a sonic horizon in tune with what is outside of music.

4′33″ is thus a silence that brings forward an environmental perspective and draws out an environmental sociality. I use "environmental" here in its broadest sense: as an expanded perspective or a distribution of agency that draws connections, from human to non-human, that networks existing conditions and, in doing so, demarcates a multitude that integrates the possibility of something entering and something leaving: a growth, a flow, a flux.[18] Such an environmental view is both indistinct and yet absolutely specific; it contains both the individuality of particular bodies as well as their collective identity. Might such work promulgate this movement, of an individuality blurring into the crowd, while the crowd takes on identity?

To refer back to my coordinates of listening, the multiplying and supplementing input of a sound from over-there breaks the separation of particular bodies to redefine the form of collective identity. Cage's silence in this regard might actually be a *withdrawal* of silence, as the condition of loneliness, in favor of a new crowd. Precisely *community in the making.* A becoming, a restlessness. Noise precisely as a coming together.

In returning, however briefly, to *4′33″* I'm interested to further amplify these lessons and this environmental breadth inculcated by the restlessness of Cage—as well as by those strangers found in Los Angeles, who performed to disrupt the settled attention of my own focus. Subsequently, I want to propose noise as an event that *elaborates* the experience of listening: into forms of over-hearing that resituate the lines of here and there, us and them. Whether as vibrations underfoot, a shattering voice coming out of nowhere, or the nebulous cosmic background Serres depicts, noise can be heard to set the foundation for the sound arts by inviting us to hear differently—even our own voice, as if it were not our own. As Jacques Attali claims, noise announces the coming of the new, and it does so by giving us the opportunity to encounter what is outside our usual field of experience or knowledge.[19] Sound in this way appears on a horizon where noise defines its extreme edge, as an *over-hearing* and an *over-stepping*, where each animating, announcing event of sound locates us against the deep rending and intrusiveness noise delivers.

It has been my aim to sketch this horizon: to hear the marks and scuffs of this geo-*phony* as indications of worldly collectivity, as sonic intensities, an authorship always already beyond myself, of which I am nonetheless absolutely a part. Multiplying perspectives, supplementing, and making differences, I suggest, give a deeper view onto this horizon of noise, allowing us to hear it as generative and productive events by which, following Perec's further topographical sensitivity, we might start thinking about place and people.

"Now and again, however, we ought to ask ourselves where exactly we are, to take our bearings, not only concerning our state of mind, our everyday health, our ambitions, our beliefs and our *raisons d'être*, but simply concerning our topographical ... relation to a place or a person we are thinking about, or that we shall thus start thinking about."[20]

17 See Mladen Dolar, "The Phonetic Burrow," in *Parole #2: The Phonetic Skin* (Cologne: Salon Verlag, 2012).

18 I take inspiration from Jane Bennett's work on material vitality and her attempts at exposing a more integrated and dynamic relation between self and surrounding. See Jane Bennett, *Vibrant Matter: a political ecology of things* (Durham, NC: Duke University Press, 2010).

19 Jacques Attali, *Noise: The Political Economy of Music* (Minneapolis: University of Minnesota Press, 1992).

20 Perec, *Species of Space*, p. 83.

“Reading Thoreau’s Journals,
I discover all the ideas
I’ve ever had
that are worth their salt.”

John Cage, *For the Birds: John Cage in Conversation with Daniel Charles*, (New York: Marion Boyars, 1981), p. 23

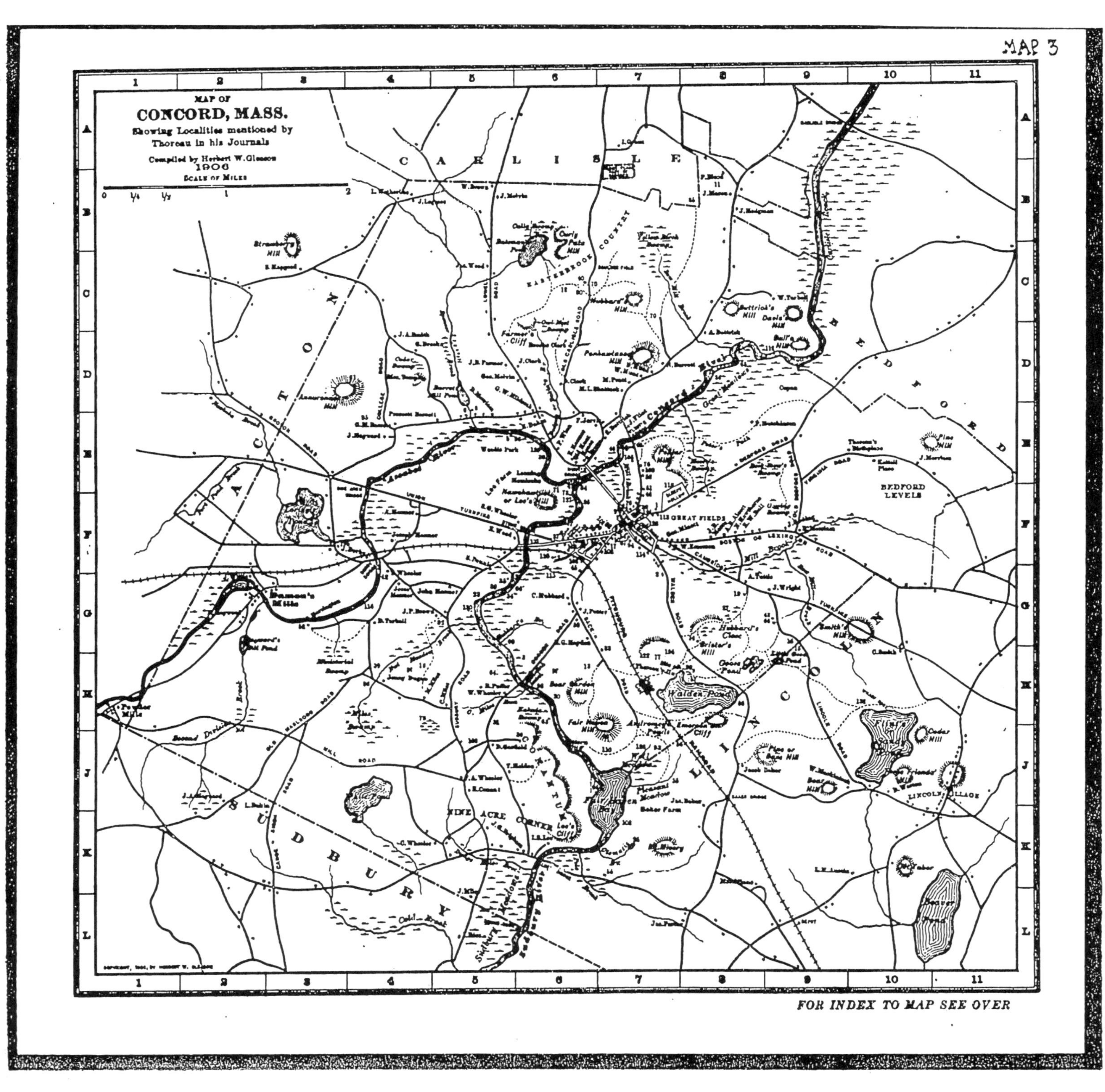

Map of Concord, Massachusetts,
from John Cage *Song Books*,
Vol. III, Instructions,
1970, Edition Peters (EP 6806)

David Toop

Nothing Hear

A recent discovery in the archive of artist John Latham[1] caught my attention in January 2012 for two reasons: first of all because of the ongoing significance of Latham's work within my own research and music practice; also because I had recently developed a music theatre project based on the notebooks of Leonardo da Vinci and had been struck by Leonardo's refrain on the unfinished: tell me if ever anything was finished? "Nothingness has no center," he wrote, "and its boundaries are nothingness."[2]

Latham's text was prepared for the catalogue of a London exhibition by Graham Stevens entitled *Nothing*, held at the Seven Dials Gallery, London, in 1984 (though there seems some doubt as to whether it was published). It begins with a quote from Leonardo:

> Among the great things which are found among us the existence of Nothing is the greatest. This dwells in time, and stretches its limbs into the past and future, and with these takes to itself all works that are past and those that are to come, both of nature and of the animals, and possesses nothing of the indivisible present. It does not, however, extend to the essence of anything.[3]

In less than two pages, Latham expounded a theory of least-event as the converging position of both art and science from the beginning of the twentieth century—the discovery of sub-atomic particles, quantum theory and the monochrome paintings (black or white) of Aleksandr Rodchenko and Kazimir Malevich made in Russia between 1915 and 1918.

"On the basis of actual twentieth century trajectories," he wrote, "both science and art each arrived at the conclusion '*everything = nothing*.' Lacking a reasoning as to how to interpret this finding the next orthodox step has been backwards in both science and art, a retreat. But on line and forwards if unofficially, it has led to a defining of 'event' structure. The dimensional framework of 'event' embodies this equation."

Latham went on to discuss his idea of event-structure as a paradigm distinct from material/mental dualism, an escape route from the 'common sense' reality through which it becomes so difficult (and so undesirable within bureaucracies) to reconcile measurable quantities and observable phenomena with intangibilities, immeasurabilities and qualities (the purpose of art, for example) that resist definitive explanation or quantifiable usefulness. He also proposed the point of *nothingness as a starting point* for this rethink: "'Nothing' is referring in [Leonardo da Vinci's] mind's eye to a nonextended state of everything, a dynamic component in the cosmic *EVENT*."[4]

Nothing to Say

In 1974, artist Marie Yates and I added our names to a letter sent to *The Guardian* newspaper. Printed under the heading "But

1 John Latham (1921–2006) was a British artist who worked in many different media—painting and sculpture, assemblage, performance, text, film, and installation—but whose convictions about the belief systems of the Western world and the role of art led him towards philosophy, science, and art as social action. His use of the spray gun from 1954, in particular the so-called "One Second Drawings" that documented a single burst of spray paint, opened up a way of making statements of non-extendedness, least-events within the frameworks of art at that time that embody a kind of "flat time." As John Walker wrote: "A key characteristic of spray-gun painting was the fact that it was a direct result of the process of production employed. An event—the act of painting—became a two-dimensional configuration: *time was thus translated into a geometry of space*." John Latham/John A. Walker, *The Incidental Person–His Art and Ideas* (London: Middlesex University Press, 1995), p. 24.
2 Leonardo da Vinci, *Notebooks* (Oxford: Oxford University Press, 2008), p. 260.
3 Leonardo da Vinci, Codex Atlanticus 398v, c. 1500.
4 John Latham, unpublished text, 1984, source: John Latham archive.

who deserves patronage?" the letter addressed a contemporary debate on the efficacy and relevance of the Arts Council of Great Britain and its recently published report "Patronage of the Creative Artist." "Sir," the letter began, "A short glance at some journal of current art would show immediately how unrealistic it is to think 'artist' means simply 'poet', 'painter' or 'composer'. However much it might suit administrators to restore those neat distinctions, it is decades since John Cage and Ad Reinhardt (among many) began to reorientate and rephrase the serious capital A activity as quite a different kind of consideration."[5]

Latham had very little time for Cage. They met at one of Cage's events in London (date unknown) and what seems to have occurred is either a monumental misunderstanding or one of those titanic clashes between strong artists in which a kind of negative energy is generated. Latham was impressed by the elaborate setting up of a performance, which led to what he described to me as "just a one-note song." Latham went up to speak to Cage afterwards and was apparently rebuffed: "I told him it was obvious that there was an ordering, that he understood an ordering principle and didn't it have an event kind of structure to it, and he just stared blankly at me and said, 'I don't know what you're talking about.' He could have said, 'No, I don't, I don't think about it', but if he didn't think about it, he couldn't have been that precise about what he did."[6]

This unpropitious encounter did little to enhance Latham's view of Cage's ideas. "Yes, well, I've got a book of his," he told me during the same conversation, "but it's nonsense. It's worse than nonsense. It's not good nonsense, it's just plain boring nonsense. I don't know what it's called because I don't read it but I was very disappointed to try to find ... well where's Cage in all this? And he just didn't show up at all."

Very few people have read all of James Joyce's *Finnegans Wake*, appear to have understood it, and have not only incorporated its implications into their own work but actively promoted it as a key work of twentieth-century literature and art. Cage and Latham are two of the most prominent (and two of the only) exceptions, so their mutual incomprehension is tinged with a degree of pathos.

Despite the famous cross-talk between Rauschenberg's *White Paintings* and Cage's *4'33"*, perhaps artists who stood on the brink of this mid-century void could only properly exist in exclusionary spheres. *Finnegans Wake* is one of the works described by Latham as a "non-spatial continuum." There is narrative but it appears to tunnel down into deep time or mythical time in which all events can happen simultaneously at the beginning of time, in all possibilities and means of communication, and at the most present, microscopic fleeting instant of the now. After this momentous step other writers could only ask themselves, "What now?" The monochrome paintings of Malevich, Rodchenko, Reinhardt, Rothko, and Rauschenberg, Latham's *One Second Drawing*, Nam June Paik's *Zen For Film* (a loop of blank leader film, first projected by Paik in 1964), and John Cage's *4'33"* stand alongside Joyce's final work as finalities in themselves, an end point in the eschatology of art, into great silence.

From the point of view of the composer, what could possibly be committed to manuscript paper once nothingness—no action, no sound—had become a spectacle? This was, of course, an illusion based on a number of myths, exaggerations, and misunderstandings, plus a fatal flaw in Cage's own work, though these are not the reasons why composers decided to forge ahead with their work despite its apparent futility and irrelevance (the pursuit of career offers a more plausible explanation for that). The exaggerations and misunderstandings are too well rehearsed to need reiteration here. As for Cage and his flaws, he was no different to other revolutionaries, one foot stuck in the past. The whole business of *4'33"*, its rituals and formality, its hierarchy, its irritatingly fussy, timings which mean nothing whatever to the audience, its nostalgic deference to the conventions of the concert hall, ensure that Cage kept a tight control on sounds.

Look again at his *Lecture On Nothing*, from 1949,[7] in which he begins, notoriously, by saying, "I am here and there is nothing to say," and then continues, "What we require is silence but what silence requires is that I go on talking." Did silence demand any such thing or did Cage just love to talk? Later in the same lecture Cage expresses allegiance to music structured through the twelve tone row (though not because it is twelve tone), repudiates the phonograph as a musical instrument, and advocates the destruction of gramophone records (my archaic terminology is deliberate here). He imagines listening to Japanese shakuhachi music or the Navajo *Yeibitchai* (or *Yeibichai*—songs performed during the ninth night of the Nightways ceremony) for any length of time, or sitting near Chinese bronzes (perhaps as a way of listening to a form of silence), but then admits that such proximity inculcates the desire to possess. There is much here with which to sympathize and much here to dislike, particularly a kind of folksy nostalgia disguised as revolutionary rigor. Is breaking gramophone records any more acceptable, for example, than burning books? John Latham burned books because he believed that books have dominated and warped our way of thinking about the world; Cage felt that a record was an abomination when you could have a person singing in real time and a particular place. He has a point, though it is deeply conservative. I am reminded of a passage from Norman Lewis's *A Dragon Apparent*, his account of travel through Laos and other South-East Asian countries in 1950 (a coincidence, but striking for being contemporaneous with Cage's *Lecture On Nothing*, and no doubt indicative of a certain remorse among men of a certain age, that those same devices that allowed them to ply their trade—magnetic tape, microphones, passenger aircraft, and motor cars—were destroying a world that they idealized):

> As I arrived the organizers were having trouble with the microphone—an indispensable adjunct to any social occasion in the new Far East. A young man chanted a soft, nasal melody which could only be heard in the *boun* enclosure itself [a *boun* is a Laotian festival]. But suddenly the electricians were successful with their tinkerings and all Vientiane was flooded with a great, ogrish baying. The electricians hugged each other, and, enchanted by the din, the audience began to drift away from the theatre and make for the dancing floor ... By the time the museums turn to the art of the people ... it will be too late. The microphone is an infallible sign of what is to come. Nothing of this kind will survive the era of materialism, under whatever form it arrives.[8]

5 Letters to the editor, *The Guardian*, Thursday July 18 (London, 1974).
6 John Latham interviewed by David Toop, Flat Time House, London, Friday October 8, 2004, published in the catalogue to *The Body Event*, David Toop, Flat Time House, September 2009.
7 *Lecture On Nothing*, printed in John Cage, *Silence: 50th Anniversary Edition* (1961; Middletown, CT: Wesleyan University Press, 2011), pp. 109, 125–26.
8 Norman Lewis, *A Dragon Apparent* (1951; London: Elan Press, 1987), pp. 251–52, 254.

Indifference and Estrangement

My own trajectory with Cage since I first read *Silence* in 1968 has become a slow downward spiral—the writings that I so admired as a young musician now seem riddled with difficulties and contradictions, whereas those few pieces of his music I still enjoy, *Prelude For Meditation*, for example, do the work of the theory far more succinctly and completely without the notoriety of *4'33"*. This is not entirely Cage's fault. Posthumously he is undergoing transformation into a saintly culture hero (even though the status of hero seems no more agreeable than coveting ancient Chinese bronzes—at the present moment auction rooms are growing very rich on that particular trade) and is gradually sinking into a state of orthodoxy, partly because he represents a golden age of the avant-garde which has now passed, and partly because conservative institutions are now beginning to recognize him as part of the canon.

In his introduction to the overly luxurious fiftieth anniversary edition of *Silence,* Kyle Gann tackles some of these difficulties. "Personally, I have tried, at Cage's urging," he writes, "to enjoy a baby crying at a concert, not letting it ruin a piece of modern music; so far I've failed. But that's why I keep coming back to Cage, because I keep thinking that if I could evolve or relax a little more, I *could* enjoy babies crying and fire alarms ringing, and feel as comfortable with the universe as he always seemed to be. He thought his way out of the twentieth century's artistic neuroses and discovered a more vibrant, less uptight world that we didn't realize was there."[9]

Was it really true that Cage was less "uptight?" His persistent critiques of improvisation (hence the entire history of African-American music) suggest not. Of course it may also be true that Cage was indifferent. That would lead us to the arguments presented in Garret Keizer's book—*The Unwanted Sound of Everything We Want: A Book About Noise*—in which he explores the intractable ethical problems of noise in a world increasingly filled with noisy devices and increasingly characterized by claims to personal freedom that are sublimely indifferent to the discomfort and sufferings of others. Keizer's book was published at the same time as other manifestos of silence, all of them arguing for a quieter world and, in the case of Sara Maitland's *A Book of Silence*, documenting a retreat from human habitation and company.

But as Keizer pointed out, personal silence can be illusory, a kind of luxury sustained within a bubble of detachment. "Silence, even the innocent silence of an hour's silent reading, can lie," he wrote. "It can tell us that we're quieter than we really are. It can tell us that our seemingly 'quiet lifestyle' disturbs nobody. Noise, on the other hand, has an uncanny way of telling the truth. Much of the truth it tells is political."[10]

This could also be addressed to Cage's *4'33"*. A contemporary audience arrives en masse to hear a mixed program of Cage's works, including the infamous "silence." The piece is performed with a knowing self-congratulatory irony in which token, painless participation in the crawling historicity of avant-gardism deflates its original claims to be an end point of art. The listeners may also congratulate themselves on their silence, during which they heard their own ardent listening within the arid context of the concert hall. Then they return to their noisy cars to drive home; the many lights, the heating system, air conditioning and all the other utilities that allow the concert hall to function are switched off—the wasteful nature of the exercise is forgotten.

Perhaps this is too cynical? Yet as an affable pioneer of the forbidding, Cage is well suited to our contemporary taste for heroes and celebrities and so we can afford to be critical of the way his ideas enable a form of high-minded hypocrisy, both his and our own. Could it be that one of the difficulties of thinking about Cage in the adulatory atmosphere of an anniversary year is that he is now the man who "invented silence," or, better still, the man who "invented listening?"

Again, this is not entirely his responsibility. Certain stories which even Cage admitted to telling many times over have passed from anecdote into myth. They have come to form an unshakeable, largely unquestioned foundation for so-called audio culture. A perfect example is the famous story of Cage's visit inside one of the anechoic chambers in use at Harvard in 1951, in which he heard two sounds, despite the total absence of reverberation in the room. One was a low pulse, the other a high-pitched singing tone. Being disturbed by these, he was told by the engineer that they were the sounds of his circulation and nervous system respectively. This is so close to the experience of the mole creature in Franz Kafka's short story, *The Burrow* (in which the creature builds a secure burrow underground only to become disturbed by sounds indicating an unseen intruder), as to be uncanny, as if Kafka had struggled with the perpetual disturbance of these same externalizations of interior body processes.

One of the key texts of twentieth-century music, sound art, and American minimalism, the anechoic chamber story may also be incorrect in its details. Cage may have been hearing symptoms of tinnitus, or spontaneous otoacoustic emissions from his own ears, rather than the sound of his brain at work (or as Susan Sontag put it, confusing the issue still further, the blood in his head). These faint sounds of otoacoustics, produced by the expansion and contractions of hair cells within the outer cochlea, could not be measured until the development of sufficiently sensitive low noise microphones in the late 1970s, so the Harvard engineer (and Cage) would have been unaware of their existence.

The origins of the sounds heard by Cage do not affect the sense or impact of the story, but these uncertainties emphasize an estrangement from the emissions of the body. We are left with the conclusion that Cage was a less diligent listener to his own body than Kafka, or indeed those writers whose explorations of listening preceded or were contemporary with his own: Joseph Conrad, Edgar Allan Poe, Virginia Woolf, James Joyce, Samuel Beckett, Herman Melville, William Faulkner, William Wordsworth, and others. The conception of silence as an external phenomenon that can be heard (as opposed to metaphorical, mystical, philosophical, or political silences) presupposes an absence of the body, a neutralization of space as an active presence. My own experiences of anechoic chambers have emphasized the artificiality of this manifestation of silence, a theoretical construct that can only be achieved through extreme measures. In all other environments in which sound waves can meet resistance and be reflected, silence is only a potentiality, aerial yet substantial: the sound of the listener; the sound of space and the air with which it is filled.

9 Kyle Gann, Introduction to John Cage, *Silence*, pp. xxv–xxvi.
10 Garret Keizer, *The Unwanted Sound of Everything We Want: A Book About Noise* (New York: Perseus Running Press, 2010), p. 46.

The Deep Time of Listening

With his references to figures such as Erik Satie, James Joyce, Gertrude Stein, and Henry David Thoreau, Cage began to sketch in a continuum of listening practice of which he was just one part. He was a composer of ideas, not a scholar, not obliged to be in any way comprehensive, and so the compatibility of certain Cagean ideas to the conditions of contemporary life—his arguments against government (borrowed from Thoreau), which might now find followers on both left and right extremes of the political spectrum, his formalizing of the principle of silence, his desire for simplicity—has ensured his centrality within a music scene which might be more true to itself with no heroes at all.

The other factor that consolidates this position is the dearth of composers who continue the work of Cage and his generation with the same impact, or even a similar sense of purpose. As John Latham suggested, after an end point "the next orthodox step is backwards." These sentiments are echoed in Gabriel Josipovici's *What Ever Happened To Modernism?* Josipovi interrogates the conservative literary culture of the present day (particularly that of Britain) and wonders why the innovations of Modernism—its fragmentation, its assault on the subject and its bold experiments with language and time—have been displaced by unchallenging literary fiction.[11]

He argues that Modernism is not an unprecedented phenomenon of the twentieth century, discussing William Wordsworth, of all writers, as one antecedent of the moment when self was swallowed by an abyss. Intriguingly, many examples given from the poems arise out of listening.

In *The Prelude* Wordsworth compared the human mind to music, in both a "dark invisible workmanship that reconciles discordant elements, and makes them move in one society."[12] Cheek pressed to a mossy stone, he listened to subterranean waters as if their murmuring echoed the resonation of his own unconscious. "He used rock to orchestrate the sounds of water," say the authors of *Wordsworth's Gardens*. "He was accustomed to using the flow of water, among other sources of natural music, to balance with the ear what he referred to in the *Prelude* as the domination of the eye."[13] An example of this urge to orchestrate can be seen in a photograph of Wordsworth's garden, taken by Herbert Bell in 1958, *The Well–Dove Cottage garden*, which could be mistaken for a pond in a Kyoto garden. The water continues to pour and we might imagine its sound as a murmur unchanged from the early nineteenth century, but as Heraclitus of Ephesus famously wrote: "We both step and do not step in the same rivers. We are and are not."

In the archaeological discovery of an ancient musical instrument—the vulture wing bone flute dug out of the Hohle Fels cave near Ulm, which is at least 35,000 years old, or 9,000-year-old red-crowned crane wingbone flutes excavated at Jiahu in China—fragile artifacts of auditory technology may be reclaimed from deep time by blowing across an air hole. In itself this is something of a miracle but the original sound, like any sound existing before the age of audio recording, is lost as an actual (though not imaginative) experience. This is true of all sounds, despite the inescapable persistence of certain noise events in contemporary life. Sound is gone before we know it. In Virginia Woolf's *To The Lighthouse*, a novel first published in 1927, the suggestion arises that listening can be an act of composition which grasps at coherence in an attempt to steady, capture, and order all the sounds that are fugitive within a radius of attention. Through its focus on the flow of thought and sensation, Modernist literature opened up new ways of thinking about the intensities of perception. Woolf proposes this mode of creative listening as an extension of such intensities, yet at the same time admits to its futility: a composition made from such transient phenomena decomposes even as it comes together, moving deeper into a level of sounding beyond human perceiving, into that state of apparent absence we call silence.

> And now as if the cleaning and the scrubbing and the scything and the mowing had drowned it there rose that half-heard melody, that intermittent music which the ear half catches but lets fall; a bark, a bleat; irregular, intermittent, yet somehow related; the hum of an insect, the tremor of cut grass, dissevered yet somehow belonging; the jar of a dor beetle, the squeak of a wheel, loud, low, and mysteriously related; which the ear strains to bring together and is always on the verge of harmonizing but they are never quite heard, never fully harmonized, and at last, in the evening, one after another the sounds die out, and the harmony falters, and silence falls.[14]

Think of all the words invented by James Joyce in *Finnegans Wake* to describe intensities of listening: quiet darkenings, flitmansfluh, hushkah, soft belling, amossive silence, lispn. Or think of Bloom's meditations on sound in the Sirens section of Joyce's *Ulysses*. Sounds arc through the complex shift and flow of feelings, sensations, conversations, movements, sighs, and songs of the setting: the bar of the Ormond Hotel in Dublin. The section has been described as musical, which it is, and yet Joyce has passed through this narrow cultural frame already, now placing music within its wider context of sound. "There's music everywhere," he wrote, as if anticipating John Cage, but despite himself, Joyce was a musical conservative. Sea, wind, thunder, water, the sound of cows, hens and snakes, the racket of the cattle market are all music, though not "Ruttledge's door: ee creaking," which Joyce decides is noise.

Joyce gathers up theories of acoustics, Liszt's rhapsodies and the babytalk wordsounds of piss rain within the bowl of the lavatory: the piddling of pearls. Base and elevated, a movement flows between sounds of the spirit, of fire, of creaking shoes, the blind tap-tap of a cane, in finality expelled from Bloom's ciderous arse: "Pprrpffrrppffff" ... end of an end.

For the architecture of the body vessel is mapped also, its sonorous dark innards and their treacherously revealing outer membrane, Joyce dwelling on the organs that emit and receive, the physicality of sound, and its movement through space, syrupy liquor for the lips dealt by the siren who syrups with her voice. Barmaid Miss Douce, that same siren, produces a shell, a seahorn, so that George Lidwell might listen. "Her ear too is a shell," wrote Joyce, "the peeping lobe there ... The sea they think they hear. Singing. A roar. The blood it is. Souse in the ear sometimes. Well it's a sea. Corpuscle islands." Here, the eroticism of Joyce's imagination draws listening more comprehensively into the realm of the senses: Lidwell may as well be lying between her open legs, ear pressed to what Courbet named as *L'Origine du Monde*.

Bodies are shells that hear themselves, instruments to resonate space. Instruments are rooms also: a blade of grass cupped in the shell of the hands, then blown through pursed lips. Sounds

11 Gabriel Josipovici, *What Ever Happened To Modernism?* (New Haven/London: Yale University Press, 2010).
12 William Wordsworth, *The Major Works* (Oxford: Oxford University Press, 1984).
13 Carol Buchanan/Richard Buchanan, *Wordsworth's Gardens* (Lubbock: Texas Tech University Press, 2001).
14 Virginia Woolf, *To The Lighthouse* (1927; London, 1970), p. 161.

to wake the dead. Music of tiny chambers built from the body. The fractured inner thoughts of Bloom chatter and flit like birds, alighting on a female body who is herself a resonating vessel, an instrument: "Play on her lip and blow, body of white woman, a flute alive. Blow gentle. Loud. Three holes all women." Bodies are instruments and instruments are bodies: the double basses with gashes in their sides; the semigrand open piano whose music hath crocodile jaws, the deep, soft, open darkness of the self.[15] But like Cage, capable of great noise, all falls away to forms of fertile silence, as in the monologue of Anna Livia Plurabelle in *Finnegans Wake:* "Soft morning, city! Lsp! I am leafy speafing. Lpf! Folty and folty all the nights have falled on to long my hair. Not a sound, falling. Lispn! No wind no word. Only a leaf, just a leaf and then leaves."[16]

Dying Away Upon the Ear

Nothingness, to return to Leonardo da Vinci, is not empty as an ending, rather, a potentiality through which other beginnings can become born. No wonder music seems to have gone backwards. "Nothingness, one might say, has no properties" wrote Vladimir Jankélévitch, in *Music and the Ineffable.* "One nothing cannot be distinguished from another nothing. How could they be distinguished without having qualities or a manner of being; that is, without, at least, being something? Two nothings are only a single, same nothing, a single, same zero. But silence has differential properties: and as a result, this particular nothingness is not nothing at all—in other words, it is not (like Parmenides' nothingness) the negation of all beings: it is not a nonbeing that totally annihilates or contradicts total being."[17]

Silence is not a "thing," a fixity or common state to be defined by timings or setting but a condition of constant flux subject to the subjectivity of the listener. "The air smells like sulphur," William Faulkner wrote in *As I Lay Dying.* "Upon the impalpable plane of it their shadows form upon a wall, as though like sound they had not gone very far away in falling but had merely congealed for a moment, immediate and musing."[18]

This was an intensity experienced by Wordsworth—*On the Power of Sound*, composed as a poetic essay between 1828 and late 1829, begins with the ineffability of sound passing into the body to register as emotions, sensations, signals of great import that vanish into air at the moment of their becoming:

THY functions are ethereal,
As if within thee dwelt a glancing mind,
Organ of vision! And a Spirit aërial
Informs the cell of Hearing, dark and blind.[19]

Through listening and its decomposition, sound's presence oscillates alongside absence with the potential of a return (through reflection and echo), Gabriel Josipovici reiterates a question raised by Wordsworth—"Is there a way of interacting with nature which is not destructive?" (as Josipovici frames it)—supplying the answer with that section from *The Prelude* in which Wordsworth describes a boy mimicking the hooting of owls through cupped hands. He calls out to the silence of the owls and they respond to his call, the exchange falling away into a deep silence into which rushes another form of echoing, "to a complete incorporation of the landscape into the boy and the boy into the landscape."[20]

Such explorations of echoes (seemingly so modern, despite Monteverdi and the sounding of great trumpets in mountainous countries such as Tibet and Switzerland) were already a listening exercise devised for the pleasure of eighteenth-century explorers of Wordsworth country, the Lake District of northwest England, who fired cannon across the waters in order to enjoy the echoes from surrounding mountains.

W. Hutchinson, a Barnard Castle solicitor, published a detailed account of this practice in *An Excursion to the Lakes in 1773 and 1774.* A barge, fitted with six brass cannon mounted on swivels, sailed to the optimum spot on Ullswater where it discharged one round. "The report was echoed from the opposite rocks," he wrote, "where the reverberation seemed to roll from cliff to cliff, and return through every cave and valley; till the decreasing tumult gradually died away upon the ear."[21]

Anticipating the functionalism of Erik Satie's *Furniture Music* and many subsequent examples of what we now call ambient music or even New Age, two French horns then serenaded Richardson's party with a more ethereal concert of echoes: "All this vast theatre was possessed by innumerable aerial beings, who breathed celestial harmonies." Then, as they finished their lunch, multiple guns were discharged, tipping his perception of the landscape from sublimity into a typically Romantic excess of terror: "For on every hand, the sounds were reverberated and returned from side to side, so as to give the semblance of that confusion and horrid uproar, which the falling of these stupendous rocks would occasion, if by some internal combustion they were rent to pieces, and hurled into the lake."[22]

In the previous year William Gilpin, prebedary of Salisbury, had been entertained with French horns at Ullswater and also heard Windemere's echo and the cannon of Ullswater. Like Hutchinson, he felt overwhelmed by apocalypse when all the cannon were fired in succession. "Such a variety of awful sounds," he wrote, "mixing, and commixing, and at the same moment heard from all sides, have a wonderful effect on the mind; as if the very foundations of every rock on the lake were giving way; and the whole scene from some strange convulsion, were falling into general ruin."[23]

According to Norman Nicholson in *The Lakers*, The King's Arms at Patterdale provided the boat and a small cannon, discharged for what Nicholson describes as trifling expense, though two cannon for four shillings and one for half a crown seems quite pricey for the eighteenth century. He gives short shrift to these dabblers in shock and awe: "Moreover, his echoes give us an analogy for the Picturesque at this stage," Nicholson writes. "To him, to his contemporaries, the landscape was chiefly a sounding board. They sailed into the middle of the lake, fired off the guns of their own ego, and waited, patiently yet excitedly, to hear the echoes return to them. The world itself did not matter—what concerned them was the sound of their own voices."[24]

Improbable as it may seem given this intent to shock nature into life with noise, there is a link between John Cage and these eighteenth century explorers of Romantic nature. Gilpin,

15 James Joyce, *Ulysses* (1922; London: The Folio Society, 1998), p. 258.
16 James Joyce, *Finnegans Wake* (1939; London: Faber & Faber, 1975), p. 619.
17 Vladimir Jankélévitch, *Music and the Ineffable* (1961; Princeton: Princeton University Press, 2003), p. 137.
18 William Faulkner, *As I Lay Dying* (1935; London: Vintage, 2004), pp. 68–69.
19 Wordsworth, *The Major Works*, p. 358.
20 Josipovici, *What Ever Happened*, p. 55.
21 W. Hutchinson, *An Excursion to the Lakes in Westmoreland and Cumberland with a Tour through part of the Northern Counties, In the years 1773 and 1774* (London: Wilkie, 1776), p. 65.
22 Ibid., p. 67.
23 William Gilpin, *Observations on Several Parts of England, particularly the Mountains and Lakes of Cumberland and Westmoreland relative chiefly to Picturesque Beauty made in the year 1772* (London: T. Cadell and W. Davies, 1808), p. 61.
24 Norman Nicholson, *The Lakers. The Adventures of the First Tourists* (London: Robert Hale, 1955), p. 63.

a pioneer of the picturesque, appears in the pages of Henry David Thoreau's *Walden*. Thoreau takes issue with Gilpin's extravagant horror at the drama of landscape by applying a steadier eye and a calmer heart.[25] This quality of engaged detachment may be what attracted Cage to Thoreau and, like Wordsworth, Thoreau was another significant contributor to our fragile history of listening. Sound was simply part of the sensation of living as he did, yet his account of the events that gave auditory texture to his life can seem startlingly modern. He wrote of a winter calling contest between a goose and a cat-owl as follows: "Boo-hoo, boo-hoo. Boo-hoo! It was one of the most thrilling discords I ever heard. And yet, if you had a discriminating ear, there were in it the elements of a concord such as these plains never saw nor heard."[26] In other words, a discord could give pleasure in the nineteenth century and yet there was another music out there, beyond what is known, a music that turned discordance inside out to make concordance. Strongly influenced by these thoughts, Cage was as romantic as Wordsworth; his desire to draw music from unpredictable nature and at the same time eliminate human agency, or at the very most, reduce it to the action of placing a rock here and there to divert the course of a stream, dreams of a human world in which humans have negligible influence. Where John Latham wanted to change the world, Cage only felt he would make matters worse.

Music No Music

In Cage there was always tension between sound and writing (a tension I recognize myself, as writer and musician). Writing is a species of noisy silence. The urge to create a listening music—music that is not played rather than silent (if we can begin to abandon the idea of silence once and for all) is not so contradictory for the writer who instructs in what is not, or draws in nothingness, and is not unprecedented in human history. In the Physics volume of *Science and Civilisation in China,* Joseph Needham quoted from an eighth century commentary on the *Chuang Tzu* book in which the question of where music exists in the playing of the Chinese *ch'in* (described by Robert Hans van Gulik in *The Lore of the Chinese Lute* as "... the lute of antiquity ... chiefly used as a solo instrument, producing a subdued and highly refined music")[27] is answered by the proposition of nothingness:

> Even the most skillful zither player, if he strikes the *shang* (note) he destroys the *chio* (note), if he vibrates the *kung* (note) he neglects the *chih* (note). It is better not to strike them at all; then the five notes are complete in themselves.[28]

As Needham comments, "This extremely Taoist thought might be interpreted in our own idiom as a preference for 'piping to the spirit ditties of no tone', or for a totality in music which cannot be achieved when it is merely played."

But this drive toward nothingness, to silent music, is perhaps more "natural" than we think, or natural in a world divided according to the mental/material dualism that John Latham hoped to resolve with event-structure. Humans are adapted to sight, to looking, to touching and holding, so the listening world is disconcertingly abstract, ambiguous, always to a greater or lesser degree disconnected from objects and sources. These same attributes can become qualities associated with freedom—like a dream of flying—particularly when experienced through music and even more particularly when connecting that which seems natural with that which seems musical, as in birdsong. This is what Cage sought, perhaps, in his desire to listen just to the Japanese shakuhachi. As a man of his time he interpreted such music as an experience of being not being, an art closer to nature than culture.

Easy to see why it should be so—my own response to this particular instrument and its repertoire is similar—yet the Japanese shakuhachi is embedded in theory, history, craftsmanship, a hierarchical lineage of performance and schools. In that sense it is little different to any other music: sanctioning free movement in a sightless, weightless domain, at the same time offering compensatory structures as a form of invisible making. Music is apparently object and order, yet always intangible event, and so, through that tension, pleasure is always underscored with fear in that music reminds us that order may be illusory and that solidity is undone by loss and decay. To privilege a form of listening not wedded to music is to enter a perpetually dynamic space both immeasurable and precise. Listening represents instability, a blurring of boundaries, the feeling of moving out through multiple spaces into sounding events and at the same time drawing sound inward to the place in the self that has no place except as the listening place, the act of listening.

Very few writers have considered the possibility of perceiving the world only through sound. In 1907, Victor Segalen, author, traveller, naval doctor, exoticist, and friend of Debussy, published *Dans un Monde Sonore*, a science fiction story about a man living entirely in the world of sound. To describe an invisible man, a man without mass or image, is easier, perhaps. Is it so unimaginable when writing itself has some intimate relationship to a life lived almost exclusively in sound? Writing listens to the self in silent discourse with the self, detached from performative sounding. Speech is stilled in writing, even though the formation of writing is a form of speech or song; even though writing emerges from a confusion and flow of inner speech. I would say that the ears turn inward, being disengaged from the act of monitoring speech and its effects in outer air, but I'm suspicious of all this ear-talk in the discourse of listening. Maybe R. Murray Schafer started it in 1967 with a book called *Ear Cleaning*, which as a metaphor entraps us within the wrong part of the body. Better to draw upon Joyce and his shell, in which the imaginary and external is joined with the pulsating vessel of the whole body.

Gestures of the hand and other soundings enact this inner listening to the unknown formations of a stranger-self which emerge into resonant space and light to become listening in waiting, a silent text calling for reply, a music without music. Nothing hear: a nothingness falling, to which there is nothing other than to listen.

25 Henry David Thoreau, *Walden* (1854; Oxford: Oxford University Press, 1999), p. 257.
26 Ibid., p. 243.
27 Robert Hans van Gulik, *The Lore of the Chinese Lute* (Vermont: Sophia University; Tokyo: Charles E. Tuttle Company, 1968), p. vii.
28 Joseph Needham, *Science and Civilisation in China, Vol. IV: 1* (Cambridge: Cambridge University Press, 1962), p. 160, footnote d.

Julia H. Schröder

"So that one becomes aware of the presence of a sound – or its absence."[1]

Circling Cage's Concept of "Silence"

John Cage's concept of silence as an absence of intentionally produced sounds or noises did not just pertain to the act of listening but also set the stage for movements that would produce sounds, or held a potential for sound production.

Framing "Silence"

In 1989 John Cage wrote a composition in which he framed noisy blocks of sound with "silences." The piece, titled *Sculptures Musicales*, was performed by musicians of the Merce Cunningham Dance Company, among them David Tudor and Takehisa Kosugi, to accompany a choreography by Cunningham.[2] In the text score, Cage put the word silence in quotation marks: "An exhibition of several [musical sculptures] ... beginning and ending 'hard-edge' with respect to the surrounding 'silence'." In this way he made reference to his concept of silence as non-intentional sounds, i.e. the absence of auditory events that had been produced with a musical purpose in mind.

In *Sculptures Musicales*, Cage focused on blocks of loud, unvarying noise, which he saw as having sculptural qualities: "It's the fact that the sounds start and last without changing, so that they have a kind of fixity that characterizes sculpture."[3] These blocks were flanked by "silences."—"Then there is silence except for the sounds made by the dancers themselves."[4]

During the musical silences, the breathing of the dancers and the shuffling of their feet could be heard with unusual clarity, since before and afterward they were masked by the "sound sculptures." These noises must, however, be differentiated from the everyday noises which can be heard during a performance of *4'33"*. Sounds from the dancers are usually unwanted and, except in tap dancing, they are a mere byproduct of movements to be visually perceived, not created for a musical purpose. Against that, in Cunningham's choreographies the dancers' noises almost become traces of a rhythmically and metrically intricate sequence of movements. Audience noises, on the other hand, cannot be predicted by the artists and are therefore not preconceived. They just happen—like all everyday noises. There is room for those sounds in the "silent" sections of *Sculptures Musicales*. Contrasting with the loud "sound sculptures" that provided the framing, the quiet noises that could occur during the silence would become even more pronounced so that the rustle of cloth when somebody crossed their legs would stand out loud and clear.

1 John Cage in John Cage and Merce Cunningham, "Rehearsing the Human Situation," moderated by David Vaughan, video, 76 min., videotaped at the University of California, Berkeley, on September 29, 1989. New York Public Library, Performing Arts Collection, Merce Cunningham Dance Foundation Collection, *MGZIDVD 5-1422 (at ca. 36 min.). Transcription JHS.

2 Merce Cunningham's choreography was titled *Inventions* (1989). On the creation of Cage's composition see Julia H. Schröder, *Cage & Cunningham Collaboration: In- und Interdependenz von Musik und Tanz* (Hofheim: Wolke, 2011), ch. 8.

3 Cage in Cage and Cunningham, "Rehearsing the Human Situation" (see note 1).

4 Cage in David Vaughan, *Merce Cunningham: Fifty Years*, edited by Melissa Harris (New York: Aperture, 1997), p. 149.

Excursus Duchamp

Infra-mince means super thin, or sub-thin, thinner than thin. ... One way of doing that, [Duchamp] said, to produce an *infra-mince* sound, would be dancers with corduroy trousers. Without any music other than leg against leg.
—John Cage[5]

The title of Cage's composition *Sculptures Musicales* contains a reference to the almost identical "Sculpture musicale" by Marcel Duchamp.[6] Cage also quoted from an explanation of the *infra-mince* concept that Duchamp had offered during an interview.[7] The exact meaning of this concept was purposefully left hanging in the balance. The "infrathin" contains multiple layers of meaning and lends itself to the most varied interpretations.[8] Some of those were launched by Duchamp himself: "Inframince" is the title of a whole chapter in his writings.[9]

Cage struck on the similar idea of "small sounds" at the end of the 1930s, during his first experiments at the radio studio of the Cornish School. In *Williams Mix*, his 1952 composition for magnetic tape, Cage specified "small sounds requiring amplification to be heard with the others." The term gained special importance from *Cartridge Music* (1960) onwards in live electronic compositions for which sounds were produced, amplified, and modulated in real time. It became possible to pay a new kind of attention to very quiet noises, because in live electronic music the amplification transformed the formerly non-audible into an event that could be listened to as music.

Cage knew Duchamp personally and was close friends with the artist and his wife during the 1960s. They played chess together, a shared activity that Cage brought on stage in 1968 with *Reunion*.[10] Two decades later, in 1988, the composer conceived the idea of realizing the musical concepts of the artist, the "complete works of Marcel Duchamp," under the title *Noh-Opera*.[11] It is probable that the *Sculptures Musicales* (1989) grew out of this unrealized music theatre project.

Musical Sculpture

In my case it's a continuation of my work with an idea that begins with Marcel Duchamp, called "musical sculpture." I've simply changed it by pluralizing the word sculpture. So that it consists of undefined combinations of—well, I should say first what Duchamp said of it: It's sounds coming from different points;—and lasting, and thereby producing a sculpture which is resonant and which lasts. And by pluralizing it, it becomes a time in which at least three or more sounds, coming from different points start hard-edge, together, continue and then without going to another sound, stop again hard-edge. So that one becomes aware of the presence of the sound or of its absence. And the kind of sound that it introduces us to, is, of course, the burglar alarm. And the introduction is meant to give us the sense of the pleasure of hearing sounds, that last without changing.
—John Cage on *Sculptures Musicales*, 1989[12]

For a realization of *Sculptures Musicales* [→ fig. 1] the performers themselves first have to compose the diverse, recorded static sounds that together form the "sculptures"[13] of the title and draw up a time plan to decide how long the rests and the sound segments are to last. The text score has to be realized, meaning that each part has to be prepared anew for every performance of the piece, which will each time take on a different musical form. The overall duration originally depended on Merce Cunningham's choreography, for which the piece had been composed.

Fig. 1
John Cage, *Sculptures Musicales*, Edition C.F. Peters (EP 67348), New York: Henmar Press, 1989

Sculptures Musicales "Sounds lasting and leaving from different points and forming a sounding sculpture which lasts" (Marcel Duchamp) An exhibition of several, one at a time, beginning and ending "hard-edge" with respect to the surrounding "silence", each sculpture within the same space the audience is. From one sculpture to the next, no repetition, no variation. For each a minimum of three constant sounds each in a single envelope. No limit to their number. Any lengths of lasting. Any lengths of non-formation. Acoustic and/or electronic.

John Cage 1989

5 Cage in Joan Retallack (ed.), *Musicage: John Cage Muses on Words, Art, Music. John Cage in Conversation with Joan Retallack* (Middletown, CT: Wesleyan University Press, 1996), p. 232.

6 Marcel Duchamp, "Sculpture musicale: Sons durant et partant de différents points et formant une sculpture sonore qui dure." Published 1934 in the *Green Box*, probably conceived between 1912 and 1920, in Duchamp, *Duchamp du signe: Écrits*, ed. Michel Sanouillet (1975; Paris: Flammarion, 1994), p. 47.

7 Duchamp in an interview with Denis de Rougemont (1945) in *Journal de deux mondes* (Paris 1947); quoted in the reprint in *Journal d'une époque* (Paris 1968), pp. 567–68.

8 A fascinating reading of the concept is delivered by Jean-Michel Rabaté, who brings together Walter Benjamin and Duchamp within the notion of *infra-mince*: Jean-Michel Rabaté, "Hauchdünnes Belastungsmaterial oder die Spur einer Spur: Über Duchamps *faits divers*," in Ilja Becker, Michael Cuntz, and Michael Wetzel (eds.), *Just Not in Time: Inframedialität und nonlineare Zeitlichkeit in Kunst, Film, Literatur und Philosophie* (Munich: Wilhelm Fink, 2011), pp. 99–119.

9 Marcel Duchamp, *Notes*, edited by Paul Matisse and Pontus Hulten (Paris: Flammarion, 1999), pp. 19–36, esp. p. 22.

10 For a discussion of *Reunion* see below.

11 Cage in: Retallack (ed.), *Musicage*, p. 230, note 51. Appendix J on p. 341 of the same book is a letter by Cage from April 25, 1988, where he describes the concept of the *Noh-opera*.

12 Cage (1989) in Cage and Cunningham, "Rehearsing the human situation". Emphasis added.

13 On the appropriation of the term sculpture from the visual arts in Cage's composition see also: Peter Becker and Peter Rautmann, "Kann man eine Skulptur hören? Synästhetische Konzepte in der Musik der Gegenwart am Beispiel John Cage," in Frank Schneider (ed.) *Im Spiel der Wellen: Musik nach Bildern* (Munich: Prestel, 2000), pp. 105–27, esp. pp. 122.

Several musicians play synchronously noisy, static sounds, which they have worked out independently of each other. These at the same time are played back through loudspeakers distributed across the space. The innovation of Cage's *Sculptures Musicales* lay in the very immobility of the sounds making up the musical sculptures. In several interviews, Cage told how for a long time he had been interested only in background noises with a fluctuating frequency of acoustic events; one could even call them soundscapes, where the single elements take on the character of events. By contrast, in *Sculptures Musicales* Cage engaged with static sounds of the sort that dominate the electrified everyday of our culture: the buzz of a refrigerator, the humming of the power lines, the continuing wail of a car alarm. These sounds are so uniform that they become sculptural in character:

> I spent so much time loving noises that changed like the noises of traffic and paying no attention to noises that didn't change like hums and burglar alarms and such things. I paid no attention to them and then within recent years [I remembered] Marcel Duchamp's statement about musical sculpture, sounds coming from different places and lasting, forming a musical sculpture. And now, as a result of taking that seriously, I hear all such sounds and immediately listen for another in the neighborhood in order to know what sculpture I'm dealing with. And all the irritation from those constant sounds has gone away, you see? I don't think that that thought has to do with Mozart, nor does it deny Mozart. It's a different pleasure.[14]

Static noises or repetitive sounds can successfully be blocked out from conscious perception. They can in fact be perceived as silence. Only when the sound stops abruptly—"hard edge" is the term Cage used in his score—does a new, much quieter sound situation suddenly become apparent, now no longer masked by the continuous sound. In these quieter sections, the "silences," non-intentional ambience and audience noises, as well as sounds made by the dancers, become clearly audible.

The sounds in *Sculptures Musicales* are framed by silence, which is a completely "normal" situation in a musical context. Expectant silences will mostly occur before and after a musical performance, and within a composition there can be many rests. John Cage's *4′33″* (1952) offers another kind of situation: the composition is set apart from the moments right before and after a performance only through the gestures of the performer—and the noises in the audience. There will be no clearly audible separation between the pregnant silence before and the proper beginning of the piece's four minutes and thirty-three seconds.

Silence before 1952

> A cut in the sound [of a film] would make a hole that is not a silence. What you *heard* was real silence, and I insist on the word "heard" because an attentive ear can detect the thousand and one imperceptible sounds of which silence is composed. There is deliberate silence, yes. But that silence is composed from the locality itself.
> —Jean Cocteau, 1951[15]

In Jean Cocteau's film *Orphée* (1950) [→ fig. 2], there is a book of poetry, titled "Nudisme," which contains only blank pages, offering an analogy to silence.[16]

> *Orphée l'ouvre [la revue].*
> Orphée: Je ne vois que des pages blanches.
> Le Monsieur: Cela s'appelle: "Nudisme."
> Orphée: Mais c'est ridicule …
> Le Monsieur: Moins ridicule que si ces pages étaient couvertes de textes ridicules. Aucun excès n'est ridicule.[17]
> —Jean Cocteau, 1950

But whereas in Cocteau's film the blank pages of the book leave space for imagination, Cage aims to focus perception on that which is already present. If a page has nothing on it to read, then to him the texture of the paper will become interesting:

> And you can say in particular that if you look at a blank sheet of paper—Mallarmé's white page—you can compare it to silence. From the slightest spot or mark, from the slightest hole, from the smallest defect, or from the smallest smudge, you know there is no silence. "Mallarmé's vertigo" is useless![18]

It is probable that Cage saw *Orphée* when it reached U.S. cinemas on November 29, 1950. In the previous year, he and Merce Cunningham had been in Paris, where they enjoyed good contacts with the French artists, and in 1939, Cage and Cunningham's dance teacher Bonnie Bird had written new music and a choreography, re-titled *Marriage at the Eiffel Tower*, to a libretto by Cocteau for a performance at the Cornish School in Seattle.[19]

As Cocteau stated in the above quote from an interview on his film, "real silence" is composed of a "thousand and one imperceptible sounds." Two years before Cage's "silent piece," Cocteau had agreed that there was no noiseless silence. It is interesting to interpret the empty book and the (car) radio in the film in light of Cage's ideas. The film shows the poet listening to numbers and poetical sentences devoid of meaning, which can be received only over the car radio. In Cage's compositions for radio receivers, on the other hand, broadcasts were indeterminate material. To Cocteau's protagonist, the poetical chance element within the sentences coming from the radio opens up layers of meaning. This is why, despite the silent theme, Cocteau's film with its surrealist elements and strong mythical undercurrents still stands for a completely different artistic concept.

14 John Cage, *I–VI* [the Charles Eliot Norton Lectures 1988–89] (Cambridge MA: Harvard University Press, 1990), pp. 131–34, see footer, punctuation added.

15 Jean Cocteau in conversation with André Fraigneau (1951), in: Jean Cocteau, *On the Film*, trans. Vera Traill (London: Dennis Dobson, n.d. [1954]), p. 108.

16 Another French film that comes to mind in the context of silence, non-colors, and emptiness is Guy Debord's *Hurlements en faveur de Sade* [Howling for Sade] (1952), which consisted of a white screen accompanied by sound, in alternation with a silent black screen. Within the film is a quote by Isidore Isou, "Cinema is dead," which has led to a mostly symbolic reading of its final twenty-four dark and silent minutes. See Roberto Ohrt, *Phantom Avantgarde: Eine Geschichte der Situationistischen Internationale und der modernen Kunst* (Hamburg: Edition Nautilus, 1990), pp. 26–49, esp. p. 41; English translation: Phantom Avant-Garde: A History of the Situationist International and Modern Art (Berlin: Lukas & Sternberg, 2006). Cf. Dieter Daniels (2004): "Medien→Kunst/Kunst→Medien," http://www.medienkunstnetz.de/themen/medienkunst_im_ueberblick/vorlaeufer/10/ (retrieved December 29, 2011), and Vincent Kaufmann, *Guy Debord: Revolution in the Service of Poetry*, trans. Roberto Bonono (Minneapolis: University of Minnesota Press, 2006), pp. 21–26.

17 Jean Cocteau, *Orphée: The Play and the Film*, edited by E. Freeman (Oxford: Basil Blackwell, 1976), p. 71. "Orphée opens [the review]. Orphée: I see nothing but blank pages. The Man: It is called 'Nudism.' Orphée: But that's ridiculous … The Man: Not as ridiculous as pages covered with ridiculous text. Excess is never ridiculous."

18 John Cage (1968) in *For the Birds: John Cage in Conversation with Daniel Charles* (New York: Marion Boyars, 1981), pp. 44–45. Cage probably refers to Stephane Mallarmé's typographical poem "Un coup de dés jamais n'abolira le hasard" (1897).

19 Composed in collaboration with Henry Cowell, George Frederick McKay, Silvestre Revueltas, and Amadeo Roldán. Libretto by Jean Cocteau, *Les mariés de la Tour Eiffel*, 1921. See http://www.xs4all.nl/~cagecomp/ (Paul van Emmerik, Herbert Henck, and András Wilheim, *A John Cage Compendium*, an online catalogue of works, chronology, and bibliography).

Fig. 2 Jean Marais as the title figure in Jean Cocteau's film *Orphée* from 1950

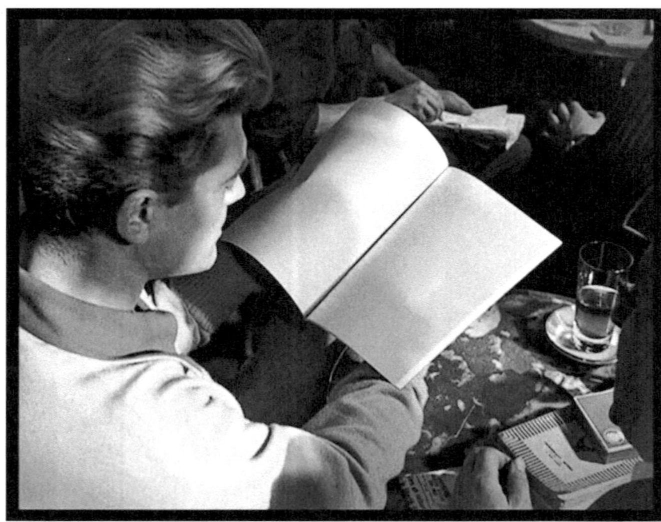

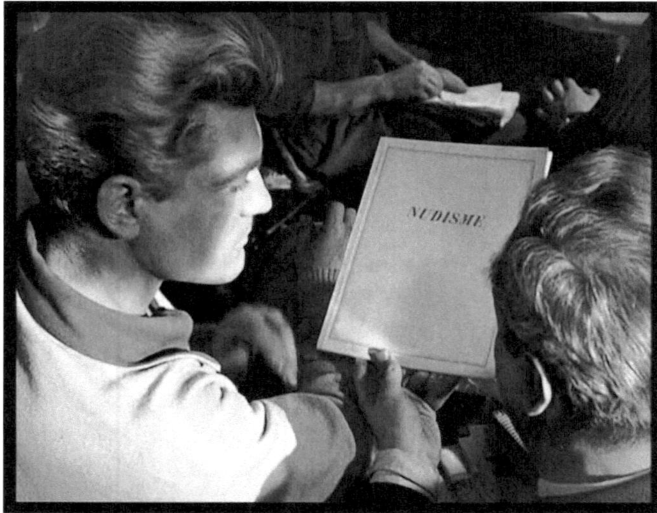

Silence as Metaphor

In many cultural contexts, a measured interval of silence will function as a metaphor for sorrow or even a mourning ritual, for example when a minute of silence is held. I do not think that Cage's composition *4′33″* contains this symbolic reference. The only possible indication to the contrary is the fact that Cage had conceived a silent prayer in 1948, although that was intended as cultural criticism.[20] Cage had planned to interrupt the background Muzak broadcast with a break of silence as a "musical" number in its own right.[21] In this situation, the silence would have been framed by a constant stream of Muzak.

The pre-Dadaist *Funeral March for the Obsequies of a Deaf Man* from 1897 [→ fig. 3], which consisted of twenty-four empty measures, could be seen as an antecedent to Cage's ideas. Its composer, Alphonse Allais, also created monochrome pictures, but in contrast to Rauschenberg's paintings they carried programmatic titles: *Negroes Fighting in a Cave at Night* was a completely black painting, *Anemic Young Nuns Going to Their First Communion in a Blizzard* completely white.[22]

In contrast, Wassily Kandinsky's categorization of black and white carried a symbolic meaning and was meant completely in earnest:

	White	*Black*
1.	wall of infinite strength	infinite, bottomless hole
2.	all possibilities	no way out
3.	maximum light: the sum of all rays	absolute darkness: no rays
4.	highest sound, inaudible	deepest sound, inaudible
5.	birth	death
6.	silence	silence

—Wassily Kandinsky[23]

Black is a non-color here and, together with white, stands for silence, but black also signifies death, motionlessness, and the stillness of the body after death. Interestingly, Kandinsky also sees both the non-colors black and white in relation to inaudible sound waves: ultrasound, the highest sound above, and infrasound, the deepest sound below the threshold of hearing.[24] Cage himself pointed out similar analogies between his concept of musical silence and works from the other arts, such as the *White Paintings* of Robert Rauschenberg[25] or Nam June Paik's film without images.[26] Cage never drew an analogy between his porous silence and Rauschenberg's monochrome *Black Paintings*, and his references never leaned toward the metaphorical. Maybe Cage saw black as an absorption of light, whereas white made the shadows of the surroundings visible, just like the musician's silence enabled noises of the everyday to come through.

20 John Cage, "A Composer's Confession" (1948), in *MusikTexte* 40/41 (August 1991); see also Cage, *John Cage: Writer*, ed. Richard Kostelanetz (New York: Limelight Editions, 1993), p. 43. Douglas Kahn points out a connection to an Aldous Huxley book which Cage had read, *The Perennial Philosophy* from 1946, where successive chapters carry the titles "Silence" and "Prayer:" Douglas Kahn, "John Cage: Silence and Silencing," in *The Musical Quarterly* 81, 4 (Winter 1997), pp. 556–98. See also Douglas Kahn, *Noise, Water, Meat: A History of Sound in the Arts* (1999; Cambridge, MA: MIT Press, 2001), chapter 6.

21 "[A new desire is] to compose a piece of uninterrupted silence and sell it to Muzak Co. It will be 3 or 4 ½ minutes long—those being the standard lengths of 'canned' music—and its title will be 'Silent Prayer.'" John Cage, "A Composer's Confession" (1948), in Cage, *John Cage: Writer*, edited by Richard Kostelanetz (New York: Limelight Editions, 1993), pp. 27–44, esp. p. 43.

22 Alphonse Allais, *Album Primo-Avrilesque* (Paris, 1897; repr. Heidelberg: Das Wunderhorn, 1993). See Michael Glasmeier, "Marcel Duchamp, John Cage und eine Kunstgeschichte des Geräuschs," in Bernd Schulz (ed.), *Resonanzen: Aspekte der Klangkunst* (Heidelberg: Kehrer, 2002), pp. 49–50., engl. pp. 51–52. See also Eric de Visscher, "Die Künstlergruppe 'Les Incohérents' und die Vorgeschichte zu 4′33″," in Stefan Schädler and Walter Zimmermann, John Cage: *Anarchic Harmony* (Mainz: Schott, 1992), pp. 71–76. Peter Dickinson refers to a letter Cage wrote to him from July 22, 1989, where the composer confirmed that when he wrote the "silent piece" he knew neither Alphons Allais's black, white, and colored monochrome paintings nor his "Funeral March." He did know an empty book published in the U.S. during the nineteenth century. Peter Dickinson (ed.), *Cage Talk: Dialogues with and about John Cage* (Rochester, NY: University of Rochester Press, 2006), p. 12, note 39. See also Peter Dickinson, "Book Review," *Musical Quarterly* 75, 3 (1991), pp. 404–09, note 13. Compare the "empty book" mentioned by Cage with the empty book of poems entitled "Nudisme" in Jean Cocteau's *Orphée* (1950). The empty books of the nineteenth century were designed as diaries or notebooks.

23 Wassily Kandinsky, *Cours du Bauhaus: Introduction à l'art moderne*, trans. Suzanne and Jean Leppien (Paris: Denoël Gonthier, 1978), pp. 58–59. Quoted in Rainer K. Wick, *Teaching at the Bauhaus* (Ostfildern: Hatje Cantz, 2000), p. 203.

24 Like Cage, Morton Feldman was interested in the use of "inaudible frequencies" as demonstrated in his composition *Marginal Intersection* (1951) for orchestra, where "2 (high+low) inaudible frequencies" are on the list of instruments (in the final published score, two "high/low oscillators"). Autograph at the Paul Sacher Foundation, Morton Feldman Collection, MF 458-0816.

25 "It was this experience and the white paintings of Rauschenberg that led me to compose *4′33″*." John Cage, "An Autobiographical Statement" (1989), in *Southwest Review* 76 (1991). See also John Cage, "On Robert Rauschenberg" in Cage, *Silence* (1961; Middletown, CT: Wesleyan University Press, 1973), p. 98.

26 "In the case of the Nam June Paik film, which has no images on it, the room is darkened, the film is projected, and what you see is the dust that has collected on the film." John Cage, "On Nam June Paik's Zen for Film (1962–1964)" (1968), in Cage, *John Cage: Writer*, ed. Richard Kostelanetz (New York: Limelight Editions, 1993), p. 109.

Fig. 3 Alphonse Allais, *Marche Funèbre. Composée pour les funérailles d'un grand homme sourd,* 1897

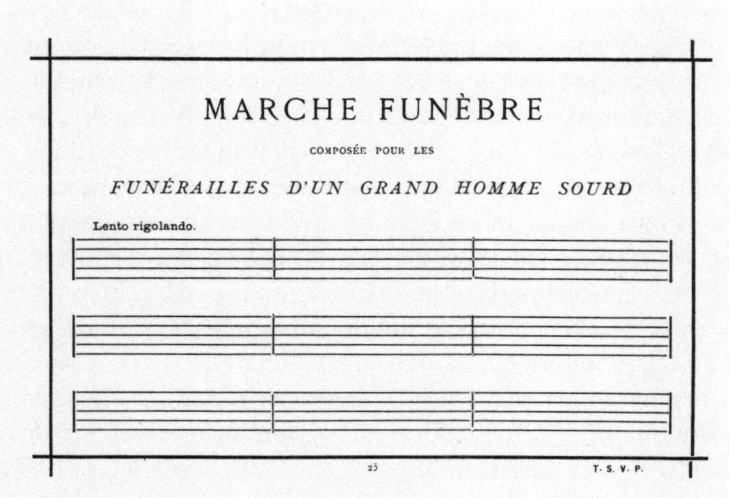

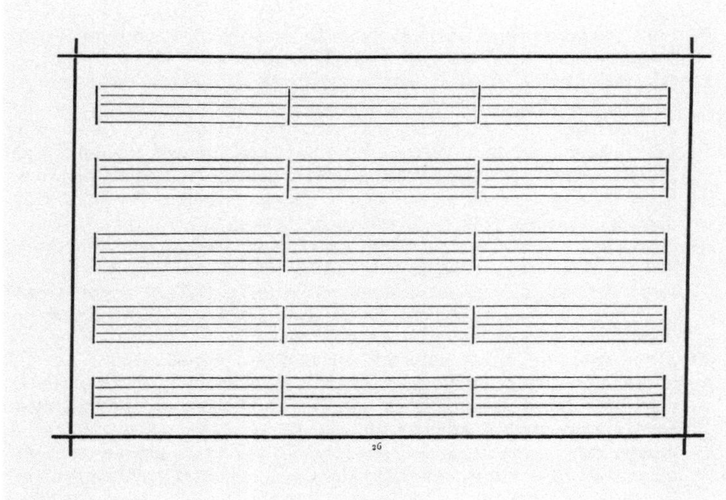

On one of the many computer-printed drafts of the text score for the *Sculptures Musicales*, Cage added by hand: "The dark side of silence."[27] Despite the fact that this note did not make it into the published score, he clearly seems to have been aware of the color metaphors.

Silence and Movement

> Silence consists in the suspension of every movement and is not, as it is generally thought to be in schools, a suspension of the din added to the ordinary noises tolerated in an environment.
> —Maria Montessori, 1926[28]

From 1937 to 1938 Cage worked with children,[29] an occupation he tried to continue as a bread-and-butter job over the following years. During this time, he might have worked with the writings of Maria Montessori,[30] although Cage himself only mentioned exercises by Émile Jaques-Dalcroze, the creator of Eurhythmics, whose method he verifiably knew from the modern dancers and accompanists who played in his percussion ensemble.

> I was employed by the WPA in San Francisco [1940–41] ... and that may have been the birth of my silent piece, because my first assignment in the recreation department was to go to a hospital in San Francisco and entertain the children of the visitors. But I was not allowed to make any sound while doing it, for fear that it would disturb the patients. So I thought up games involving movement around the rooms and counting, etc., dealing with some kind of rhythm in space.[31]

Rhythm in space: Cage explained this concept to the dancers of Bonnie Bird's modern dance class at the Cornish School in Seattle by marking a distance on the floor between lines that they would cross at different speeds, which meant they needed different amounts of time for the same distance in space.[32] He had transferred the discoveries made in media specific compositions using record players or magnetic tape recorders, media that could play back recordings at different speeds. The same notion also led Cage to a so-called "space notation," where a certain duration would be specified through a certain distance, for example, a half inch—of either tape or music paper—equals a second.

Thus, the duration of *4'33"* can be represented by a line in a score, i.e. a distance, or be manifested on a tape or a filmstrip of a certain length, which—if you play it at the determined speed—will run for exactly four minutes and thirty-three seconds.[33]

0'00"—To Play a Game in an Amplified Context

> You see, if music is conceived as an object, then it has a beginning, middle, and end, and one can feel rather confident when he makes measurements of the time. But when it is process, those measurements become less meaningful, and the process itself, involving if it happened to be, the idea of Zero Time (that is to say no time at all), becomes mysterious and therefore eminently useful.
> —John Cage, 1961[34]

The title of Cage's composition *0'00"* negated both temporal duration and spatial distance. This may have been in reference to an idea of his friend and former student Christian Wolff. "Certain time brackets are in zero time," Cage wrote in his 1958 text "Indeterminacy about Wolff's Duo II for Pianists."[35] Wolff's score read: "Zero on the left side of the colon (0:) = tempo 0, or

27 New York Public Library. John Cage Music Manuscript Collection. JPB 95–3 Folder 949. Public service copy. *Sculptures Musicales*. Galley proofs, signed.

28 Maria Montessori "Silence" (1926) in Montessori, *The Discovery of the Child*, trans. Joseph Costelloe (New York: Ballantine, 1967), p. 138.

29 Cage taught "Musical Accompaniment for Rhythmic Expression" at the Experimental Elementary School of UCLA as an assistant of his aunt Phoebe James. See Thomas S. Hines, "Then Not Yet 'Cage'": The Los Angeles Years, 1912–1938," in Marjorie Perloff and Charles Junkerman (eds.), *John Cage: Composed in America* (Chicago: The University of Chicago Press, 1994), pp. 65–99, esp. p. 90.

30 Dickinson points out that the educator Maria Montessori developed a "silent game" in which children learned to keep motionless in order to hear very quiet noises. Peter Dickinson (ed.), *Cage Talk: Dialogues with and about John Cage* (Rochester, NY: University of Rochester Press, 2006), p. 15.

31 Cage in Jonathan Brent, Peter Gena, and Don Gillespie (eds.), *A John Cage Reader: In Celebration of his 70th Birthday* (New York: C.F. Peters, 1982), pp. 169–70. Emphasis added.

32 Bonnie Bird in: David Vaughan, *Fifty Years* (see note 4), p. 17.

33 In fact there is a score of *4'33"* which uses space notation [→ p. 116ff].

34 Cage in an interview with Roger Reynolds 1961, in Robert Dunn, *Werkverzeichnis John Cage* (Frankfurt am Main: C.F. Peters, Henmar Press, 1962), pp. 47–48.

35 John Cage "Indeterminacy" (1958), in Cage, *Silence*, pp. 35–40, esp. p. 38.

any time at all. Zero on the right side (:0) = silence, for the indicated duration (3:0 = three seconds of silence)."[36] These notations specified duration and the number of sound events. "Zero time" meant a temporal freedom for the performer, who acted within a kind of time bubble which delivered him from time regulations in order to realize the action at any desired speed.[37] "(0:0)" in Wolff's composition signified a segment of optional duration during which silence would be held, simply meaning the performers wouldn't play.

> The first one, *4'33"*, involved one or several musicians who made no sound. The second one, *0'00"*, indicates that an obligation towards others must be fulfilled, in a partial or complete manner, by a single person. The third one involves gathering together two or more people who are playing a game in an amplified context. A bridge or chess match, or any game at all can become a distinct—another essentially silent—musical work ... "Distinct" means that there is amplification. It's a work on a work—like all my indeterminate works! I say that it's essentially silent because I believe that it allows the silence of a game of chess to appear for what it really is: a silence full of noises.[38]

With *4'33"* Cage had reduced a composition to its duration. He followed up with further pieces, also titled for their running times, which were meant to dissolve even that temporal element. The score to *0'00"* reads: "In a situation provided with maximum amplification (no feedback), perform a disciplined action."[39] Here sound production in itself is not the aim, but the performance of a gesture, which then would be amplified—so, while the gesture was performed intentionally, it was not intentionally musical. The composition *0'00" No. 2* (1968), identical with "Solo 23" from Cage's *Song Books* (1970), followed a similar strategy. It was written for "two or more performers playing a game on a playing area (table or board) amplified with contact microphones."[40] The score instructs: "On a playing surface (e.g. table, chessboard) equipped with contact microphones (four channels preferably, speakers around the audience, highest volume without feedback) play a game with another person (e.g. chess, dominoes) or others (e.g. scrabble, bridge)."[41] Therefore, the score to *0'00", No. 2*[42] could function as a set of instructions for *Reunion*, also from 1968.[43] This latter performance saw Cage play a game of chess against Marcel and Alexina (Teeny) Duchamp on a chessboard equipped with contact microphones and with light sensors. That way the movements of the chess pieces were not only amplified, but they also controlled which of the live electronic compositions played simultaneously could be heard over the loudspeakers at which moment in time—and which would be muted. David Behrman, Gordon Mumma, David Tudor, and Lowell Cross simultaneously played their separate live electronic compositions and could or could not be heard, depending on the chess game position. The visible course of the game regulated how the music audibly manifested itself. The functional gestures of the chess players became translated into gestures triggering sound—but still one cannot define them as intentionally musical gestures.

Stillness

On October 20, 1957, Paul Taylor[44] performed a choreographic equivalent to the "silent piece" with the "Duet" section of his choreography Seven New Dances. A female and a male dancer remained motionless, standing or sitting in the same pose for several minutes. These immobile poses on stage earned a tribute by critic Louis Horst, whose review in the *Dance Observer* was composed entirely of empty columns. The event was not silent, though—David Tudor performed music by Cage at the piano and using other sound sources. Cage's commissioned three-minute composition was titled *For Paul Taylor and Anita Dencks*, after the dancers whose motionless postures characterized the piece.[45] The other six of Taylor's dances for the event were accompanied by noises: telephone time signals, wind sounds, heartbeat sounds, rain sounds, and something simply labeled as "noise."[46]

Similarly, Merce Cunningham[47] integrated three "static poses" into his choreography *Enter* (1992) [→ p. 251], which he was working on when Cage died. He held these poses for the duration of the three parts of Cage's *4'33"*.[48] Two years later, Cunningham choreographed an event based on *4'33"* for his complete company. Dancers all took poses which they held for the duration of the three parts of the score. The change of positions was introduced by a change in the lighting at the end of each part.[49] At the same time, David Tudor performed Cage's composition, not playing for the duration of four minutes and thirty-three seconds.[50] Strangely, in Cunningham's choreography the silence of *4'33"* metaphorically came to signify commemoration, or even mourning, a reference which I think is not present in Cage's composition itself. *4'33"* is different from holding a minute's silence because it is not about memory but about attention. It is not what is absent that should be perceived, but rather what is present.

36 From the performance instructions in Christian Wolff's score for *Duo for Pianists II* from 1958 (New York: Edition Peters [P6493], 1962).

37 See, for example: "Once, a resulting composed complexity seemed to me so impossible that I declared the tempo at that point to be 'zero'; that is, one constraining factor, the necessary cause of the impossibility, namely time, was removed, or made indeterminate; by 'zero' I meant any time at all." Christian Wolff (1995) in Wolff, *Cues: Writings & Conversations / Hinweise: Schriften und Gespräche*, ed. Gisela Gronemeyer and Reinhard Oehlschlägel (Cologne: Edition MusikTexte 5, 1998), p. 332.

38 John Cage (1968) in *For the Birds: John Cage in Conversation with Daniel Charles* (New York: Marion Boyars, 1981), p. 210. Emphasis added.

39 As per John Cage, *Song Books* (August/September 1970), "Solo for Voice 8," p. 31. The subsequent "Solo 9," by the way, includes an instruction to not perform the text score for longer than 4'32".

40 John Cage, *0'00" No. 2* (1968; C.F. Peters 1970, 1987; 6806a).

41 Score: John Cage, *Song Books* (August/September 1970). Cf. William Fetterman, *John Cage's Theatre Pieces: Notations and Performances* (Amsterdam: Harwood Academic Publishers, 1996), p. 91.

42 A letter from Lowell Cross, who not only took part in the premiere but also designed and built the chess board for Cage, suggests that the composer in fact saw the piece as part of *Reunion* and that it was only by accident that it did not turn up in the program notes: "The program is full of errors: John's contribution, *0'00" II*, is not announced at all." Lowell Cross to Pauline Oliveros (March 7, 1969, two days after the *Reunion* premiere): New York Public Library, JPB 94-5, Pauline Oliveros papers, Box 5, Folder 18.

43 See, for example, Lowell Cross, "*Reunion*: John Cage, Marcel Duchamp, Electronic Music, and Chess," in *Leonardo Music Journal* 9 (1999), pp. 35-42.

44 Paul Taylor (*1930), US-American dancer and choreographer. He danced in the Merce Cunningham Company from 1953 to 1954, and for *Seven New Dances* he collaborated with set designer Robert Rauschenberg, who was the resident designer of the Merce Cunningham Dance Company from 1954 to 1964.

45 Robert Dunn (ed.), *John Cage [Catalogue of Works Published by C.F. Peters]* (Frankfurt am Main: C.F. Peters, Henmar Press, 1962), p. 7.

46 See the internet *catalogue raisonnée* by Paul Taylor: "Paul Taylor Dance Company, Taylor Repertoire," http://www.ptdc.org/repertoire (retrieved December 19, 2011). See also Angela Kane, "Paul Taylor: A Catalogue of Works," in *Dance Research: The Journal of the Society for Dance Research* 14, 2 (Winter 1996), pp. 7-75, esp. p. 14. Kane notes that Anita Dencks had to be replaced by dancer Toby Glanternik for the premiere (while Doris Hering spells the name Glanternick). See also Mark Franko, "Epic Immobility," in Franko, *Excursion for Miracles: Paul Sanasardo, Donya Feuer, and Studio for Dance (1955-1964)* (Middletown, CT: Wesleyan University Press, 2005), pp. 94-95.

47 Merce Cunningham (1919-2009), dancer and choreographer. Cunningham and John Cage collaborated for about fifty years, during which time Cage was musical director of the Merce Cunningham Dance Company.

48 David Vaughan, *Merce Cunningham: Fifty Years*, ed. Melissa Harris (New York: Aperture, 1997), p. 265.

49 Ibid., p. 273. The performance was part of an event called "*4'33"* and Other Sounds Not Intended: A Tribute to John Cage," which was presented at the open-air stage in New York's Central Park.

50 William Fetterman, *John Cage's Theatre Pieces: Notations and Performances* (Amsterdam: Harwood Academic Publishers, 1996), p. 76.

To what extent can stillness and silence be equated? The terms often seem vague. In his notes, Merce Cunningham used the word silence when he wanted dancers to remain immobile.[51] In *Rune* (1959), Cunningham contrasted movement and silence in the dancers.[52] He described the amplitude of possible movements on a scale between the extremes of stillness and maximum physical activity:

> In my choreographic work, the basis for the dances is movement, that is the human body moving in time-space. The scale for this movement ranges from being quiescent to the maximum amount of movement (physical activity) a person can produce at any given moment.[53]

Of course, Cunningham knew the difference between "silences" in music and dance, and in some of his remarks he observed a distinction between the contrasting pairs "movement—stillness" in dance and "sound—silence" in music.[54] Cunningham's solo piece "Stillness" in his choreography *Suite for Five* (1956) was described in these terms for the program notes: "The events and sounds of this dance revolve around a quiet center, which, though silent and unmoving, is their source."[55]

Inventions (1989), the choreography accompanied by Cage's *Sculptures Musicales*, starts with a juxtaposition of the principles of movement and "silence." Half of the dancers remain motionless on stage while the other half begin to dance. One could compare the staggered entrances of the groups of dancers to a musical canon or round. The scene proved that optical "silence" can exist simultaneously with optical movement and not become covered up, whereas in Cage's music for the dance, the musical sound masks the tiny noises which are part of a Cagean "silence." In *Sculptures Musicales*, these are the noises made by the dancers. They become an expected part of the composition, which means they are intended and maybe even composed. When standing still, dancers will not produce these noises, but possibly listen inside themselves and hear the body's internal movement, the way John Cage experienced it himself in the anechoic chamber.

There was a growing tendency to amplify these body sounds from the 1960s on. They demonstrate that the body cannot be absolutely silent, just as it cannot be absolutely still—the living body will always produce some kind of sound. So it is not really a paradox when Alvin Lucier in his *Music for Solo Performer* (1965) uses the brain waves of a performer sitting perfectly still to vibrate percussion instruments. These alpha waves only occur when the body is extremely quiet and relaxed, so in order to produce a sound the performer must avoid making gestures.

Decoding Silence into Sound

> Music, [Thoreau] said, is continuous; only listening is intermittent.
> —John Cage, 1975[56]

Besides amplified body sounds and amplified "small sounds," Cage also made sounds audible which first had to be decoded. He was fascinated by the idea that a room was full of inaudible sounds. In his live electronic compositions he would repeatedly use radios or other kinds of electronic receivers to render the imperceptible, inaudible, but potential sounds into something one could listen to over a predetermined stretch of time.

The concept of a song hidden within all things was a romantic idea which can be traced through New England transcendentalists Ralph Waldo Emerson and Henry David Thoreau and their influence on North American culture to Charles Ives and finally Cage.[57] It was the ideal of something left unfinished, of the fragment central to the Romantic aesthetic which allowed Cage to present the random excerpts of latent sounds—which he made audible at a certain point in time and place through a receiver—as music. These excerpts were part of a "whole beyond comprehension." To Cage, the whole was not nature itself, but comprised of all the sounds and noises of the everyday, something one can already find in Thoreau who listened to the sounds made by a telegraph wire. Cage wanted to give a new and positive meaning to the street noises of a metropolis like New York. This reevaluation required a certain attitude from the listener, who needed to pay the same kind of attention to everyday noises that formerly had been reserved for the perception of artworks.

In *Variations VII* (1966), Cage used only sounds that were already in the room but had to be made audible by amplification (body sounds), by transmission (telephones), or by broadcasting (radio receivers).[58] In his notes on the work he compared his method to catching sound like fish in a net: "Inside composers picking up outside sounds (Fishermen). | (Telephones.) ... | Photocells (V): making audible whatever is already vibrating."[59] From the silence of inaudible noises the composer, with the help of electronic apparatuses, formed a sound one could listen to for a limited duration. Silence became potential sound. But one listened only within that determined duration, which was the timeframe that allowed one to perceive what was present anyway as music.

Christina Kubisch's[60] invention of a set of headphones that renders electromagnetic waves audible is a logical development of these thoughts by Cage. The headphones allow you to listen to the electrical currents in bank terminals or alarm devices on the front of shops or in trams, currents which can neither be heard nor seen without these technical means. Wearing the headphones, the recipient can walk along the streets and string together her or his own composition. All sounds are localized, so the listener, by coming closer or backing away, will perform an interpretation of Kubisch's piece, following the itinerary drawn onto a street map

51 In this context it is interesting to note with Austin Clarkson that *4′33″* is made up of 273 seconds and that -273.2 degrees Celsius is equivalent to absolute zero, the freezing point at which molecular movement stops. Austin Clarkson, "The Intent of the Musical Moment," in David B. Bernstein and Christopher Hatch (eds.), *Writing through John Cage's Music, Poetry, and Art* (Chicago: The University of Chicago Press, 2001), p. 72.

52 David Vaughan, *Merce Cunningham: Fifty Years*, ed. Melissa Harris (New York: Aperture, 1997), p. 118. See also Merce Cunningham, *Changes: Notes on Choreography* (New York: Something Else Press, 1969), no pagination [pp. 167–68]. Cunningham's contrasts also make sense from a neurophysiological point of view: in the brain there are regions and feedback loops that favor movements, while others suppress them, and these can trigger or block each other. They enable both intentional and non-intentional body movements.

53 Merce Cunningham, "Choreography and the Dance" (1970), in Germano Celant (ed.), *Merce Cunningham* (Milan: Charta, 1999), p. 42. Emphasis added.

54 Merce Cunningham, *Changes*, no pagination [p. 161].

55 Ibid., p. 96.

56 John Cage, "Preface to 'Lecture on Weather'," in: Cage, *Empty Words: Writings '73–'78* (Middletown, CT: Wesleyan University Press, 1979), p. 3.

57 See Wolfgang Rathert, "Der amerikanische Transzendentalismus," in Helga de la Motte-Haber (ed.) *Musik und Religion* (Laaber: Laaber, 1995), pp. 189–214.

58 "[In *Variations VII* (1966)] Cage's inspiration was electronic technology's ability to make the inaudible audible ... *Variations VII* is thus similar to *0′00″*, in that it uses electronics to demonstrate that there is a great deal of activity going on even in apparently inactive situations." James Pritchett, *The Music of John Cage* (Cambridge: Cambridge University Press, 1993), p. 153.

59 John Cage, "Variations VII: 7 statements re a performance six years before" (1972). New York Public Library. John Cage Music Manuscript Collection. JPB 95–3 Folder 340, Public service copy, p. 2.

60 Christina Kubisch (*1948), sound artist. On Kubisch's artistic exploration of silence and the work of John Cage see *Über die Stille: Audiovisuelle Installationen von Christina Kubisch* (exh. cat. Fruchthalle Kaiserslautern, 2008).

by the artist. Alternatively, the listener can become composer of her or his own *Electrical Walk*.[61] The distance travelled will be equivalent to the duration of the "composition" and the sounds —always present but usually inaudible noises made perceivable for a short timeframe—will, in their temporal occurrence, structure the "composition."

Absence as Presence

Keeping the silence was for Cage not an act of negation, of oblivion, or mourning.[62] Instead he wanted to turn focus on the present, toward a new listener attitude. If the pianist—or other performer of *4'33"*—abstains from making intentional sounds, this should lead to a perception of the non-intentional sounds in the performance venue. One should expand one's listening from music to the ubiquitous noises of the everyday.

One cannot hear silence, one cannot see absence. Still one can see the shadows of viewers on the white canvases of Robert Rauschenberg, and one can hear the sounds made by the audience and the surroundings during *4'33"*.

> [I]n the anechoic chamber at Harvard University [I] heard that silence was not the absence of sound but was the unintended operation of my nervous system and the circulation of my blood. It was this experience and the white paintings of Rauschenberg that led me to compose *4'33"*.
> —John Cage, 1989[63]

In my reading of *4'33"*, the composition is a study in perception for the listener. In Cage's first concept for a silent composition, "Silent Prayer" from 1948, the composer aimed to realize a silent episode within the interminable tinkling of commercial background music. The listener would have experienced the unexpected silence as a sudden contrast to waken the attention. In *4'33"* (1952), this attention would be directed toward environmental sounds, including those produced by the audience itself. This heightened experience of sounds produced by movements and the body itself was something Cage had become aware of at latest in the anechoic chamber, where he would have expected complete silence and instead heard the sounds of his own body, as the anecdote goes. In the next step, non-musical actions produced sounds which could gain musical interest through being structured by means of a disciplined action. Cage realized this concept on stage through the amplified noises of a game (of chess) in *0'00" No. 2* (1968). From there it was only a small step to the noises of the dancers that filled the "silent" passages of *Sculptures Musicales* (1989), noises that were not made for a musical purpose but produced by a disciplined action (dance) —still in accordance with the instructions to the earlier *0'00"* (1962). The static sound sculptures framing the "silent" passages were taken once more from the everyday and the attention directed toward them could be taken out of the concert hall after the performance by each listener. Every movement, intended or unintended, has the potential to produce sound.

61 See, for example, Christina Kubisch, "Electrical Walks," in Petra M. Meyer, *Acoustic Turn* (Munich: Fink, 2008), pp. 683–88. Kubisch created works from this series for the Museum Ostwall in Dortmund in 2012.

62 Silence in communication is usually read as negation or absence in linguistics or the cultural sciences. See, for example, Efrat Ben-Ze'ev, Ruth Ginio, and Jay Winter (eds.), *Shadows of War: A Social History of Silence in the Twentieth Century* (Cambridge: Cambridge University Press, 2010). In my opinion, such an interpretation is precluded by Cage's work.

63 John Cage, "An Autobiographical Statement" (1989), in *Southwest Review* 76 (1991). Emphasis added.

Dörte Schmidt

"It's important that you read the score as you're performing it." A Philological Perspective on the Various Versions of *4′33″*

It might seem slightly paradoxical to discuss what it means to edit the music of the classic avant-garde of the 1950s and 60s based on an example for which there are no notes. Although *4′33″* is presumably John Cage's most famous piece and has been discussed far beyond the realm of music science, its minutiae remain largely unknown outside specialist circles—first and foremost the fact that, as strange as this may seem, there are different versions of it.[1] These versions reveal the particularities of the written recording of a kind of music that sits at the boundaries of the traditional notion of composition. Here, the notions of composition, text and work are so intricately intertwined that editorial and composition-historical interests conflate. "What happens is a change in function, on which the scores instruct us," augured Heinz-Klaus Metzger as early as 1958[2]—it should therefore be possible to approach the issue from a philological perspective.

Surveying the various versions, developments, and spin-offs of *4′33″* that will be discussed in the following paragraphs, one notices that:

1. there are not only scores to be taken into account but also auctorial performance versions, which are documented in films or written accounts,[3]
2. there are not only versions with the same title but also different forms of spin-offs with modified titles,
3. the versions have been incorporated into cyclical work contexts, and
4. there is a film with published directing instructions, whose title does not refer to the context of the work complex discussed here and whose connection to it will be considered separately.

If the connections are to be ordered, two chronologies must first be distinguished: the compositional genesis on the one hand and the history of its publication on the other, which, although clearly different, has defined public perceptions of it: "The piece began ... a life with unforeseen twists."[4] At the same time one needs to take into account Cage's own statements about his "silent piece," through which he appears to have played an active role in constructing the myth by discussing the piece (essentially in parallel with the changes in the various versions) in light of his philosophical musings of the day. Referring all these statements—as is regularly the case—to *4′33″'s* presumed "work identity" therefore implies that the discussion always revolves around one and the same piece, that one sometimes anticipates or, more often, retrospectively applies philosophical viewpoints which had no bearing whatsoever on the composition at the time the first ver-

1 This text is an unaltered but shortened version of an essay published under the same title in Gabriele Buschmeier, Ulrich Konrad, and Albrecht Riethmüller (eds.), *Transkription und Fassung in der Musik des 20. Jahrhunderts: Beiträge des Kolloquiums in der Akademie der Wissenschaften und Literatur, Mainz, vom 5. bis 6. März 2004* (Mainz: Franz Steiner Verlag, 2008), pp. 11–43. It is noteworthy that it forms part of a long list of nearly simultaneous attempts to approach the phenomenon *4′33″* from a new angle. After William Fetterman [*John Cage's Theatre Pieces: Notations and Performances* (Amsterdam: Harwood, 1996)], Gary J. Salomon [*The Sounds of Silence: John Cage and 4′33″* (1998), http://www.azstarnet.com/~solo/4min33sec.htm], and Thomas M. Maier [*Ausdruck der Zeit: Ein Weg zu John Cages stillem Stück 4′33″* (Saarbrücken: Pfau, 2001)], Hans-Friedrich Bormann in 2005 and Liz Kotz in 2007 (at approximately the same time as this author) focused on this particular work [→ Kotz, p. 212ff/Bormann, p. 222ff].

2 Heinz-Klaus Metzger, "John Cage oder Die freigelassene Musik," in Heinz-Klaus Metzger and Rainer Riehn (eds.), *Musik-Konzepte Sonderband: John Cage* (Munich: Edition Text + Kritik, 1978), pp. 5–17, esp. p. 16.

3 Besides Cage's own performances, Fetterman also discusses other "interpretations." See Fetterman, *Cage's Theatre Pieces*, pp. 79–83.

4 "Über John Cage. David Tudor im Gespräch mit Reinhard Oehlschlägel," in *MusikTexte* 69/70 (April 1997), pp. 69–72, esp. p. 70.

5 Martin Erdmann was the first to show how Cage reinterpreted his own development in hindsight, in *Untersuchungen zum Gesamtwerk von John Cage*, PhD diss., Universität Bonn, 1992.

sion was created (1952), and that by doing so one fails to see the development of Cage's compositional thinking.[5] I therefore want to focus instead on the documented scores and ask if, and to what extent, they reflect Carl Dahlhaus's statement that "a musical writing that fixes texts is not a neutral means of representation but the expression of a system of relationships."[6]

The earliest score recording the initial compositional concept was lost and is only known through two reconstructions created by David Tudor [→ pp. 88 ff]. Cage notated a piano score with clefs. The bar lines, together with the metronome marking, uphold the common relational system of rhythm notation.[7] Instead of a time signature—as in *Music of Changes*—a correlation of tempo, time, and length is established on the stave. On the traditional system of notation, which serves as a guidance to the reader of the score, Cage thus superimposes a "generalized" representation of time, in which minutes and seconds are symbolized as centimeters, or inches as it were. The system comprises no notes—but no pauses either, for that matter—yet it remains readable thanks to the representation of duration by lengths.[8] The premiere performance consisted of three sets lasting 30″, 2′23″, and 1′40″ respectively. The question of the role played by the metronome marking, considering that the time was measured exactly (with the help of a stopwatch), was answered by David Tudor:

> I understood the piece as a composition, and I also understood how it was composed: it was composed with exactly the same method as Music of Changes. I therefore took care to insist, when people asked me about it, that the piece was scored with a metronome marking of quarter = 60. The performance process consisted of reading a score which did not contain any notes, but where all durations were precisely notated.[9]

This can be understood against the backdrop of Cage's compositional process of the time, which was based on ordering the various dimensions of sound in individual charts and determining them by means of chance procedures.[10] In *4′33″* Cage adapted the procedure used for *Music of Changes*: the first compositional question he asked concerned sound or silence. The toss of a coin yielded the answer that only even numbers should appear, which, using the charts developed for *Music of Changes*, produced the result: no sounds.[11] He then determined the tempo, before the time structure of the "silent events" was derived from the charts for duration using chance procedures.[12] The relics of traditional notation refer to the compositional context on the one hand, while, on the other, determining the specific performance situation that characterizes the traditional performance of a piece of music from a score.[13] "It's important that you read the score as you're performing it, so there are these pages you use. So you wait, and then turn the page. I know it sounds very straight, but in the end it makes a difference,"[14] affirms Tudor, not without reason, since the performer thus not only marks the beginning and end of the movements, but also represents their progress in time. The turning of pages that a score written in this way requires appears as a residue of a performance situation based on reading a score rather than as a theatrical action per se.

For his twenty-eighth birthday on June 5, 1953[15] Irwin Kremen received as a gift a specially made "copy" (as Cage himself later called it)[16] of the first notation, which had been "generalized"[17] in many ways: firstly as concerns the orchestration, which was no longer confined to the piano or a solo piece, but was destined explicitly "for any instrument or combination of instruments," and secondly (as a consequence thereof) with regard to the form of notation as such [→ p. 116]. In a "proportional notation" (according to Cage) a space limited by vertical lines at the beginning and at the end of movements and defined in two dimensions replaces the systems of notation: the two times five lines of the traditional pitch system, which also defined the number of voices, have disappeared, as have the breakdown of measures and the metronomization relating to the traditional notation of duration. What remains is the indication of the scale as "1 page = 7 inches = 56″." The horizontal line represents the timeline defined by this scale, whereas the indeterminate vertical line of the page represents the pitches. The reading conventions of traditional notation still apply. However, the notation no longer just concerns distinct parameters (measures, tone locations specified by way of note lines), but a geometrically defined continuum.[18] Again, no sound incidents have been registered, and the surface within the coordinate system remains blank.

Cage—as his use of the term "copy" suggests—understands this "generalization" of notation as a special form of "transferability" of writing, a principle which, according to Dahlhaus, stipulates that "the notation in which a work of music is edited need not coincide with the writing in which it has been conceived."[19] This transferability—for Dahlhaus one of the fundamental premises of "writing" in the actual sense—is an abiding principle. When this version was first published in *Source*

6 Carl Dahlhaus, "Notenschrift heute," in Ernst Thomas (ed.), *Notation Neuer Musik* (Mainz: Schott, 1965) [= *Darmstädter Beiträge zur Neuen Musik* IX], pp. 9–34, esp. p. 10.

7 Dahlhaus actually cites the system of duration notation in traditional notation, as kept up by Cage, as an example of the "system of relations" characteristic of a notation that "fixes texts." See Dahlhaus, "Notenschrift heute", pp. 10–11.

8 This is what principally differentiates it from Alphonse Allais's *Marche funèbre*, which various authors have related to *4′33″*. See Andreas Bee (ed.), *Alphonse Allais: Album Primo-Avrilesque* [1837] (Heidelberg: Wunderhorn, 1993) and Eric de Visscher, "Die Künstlergruppe 'Les Incohérents' und die Vorgeschichte zu *4′33″*," in Stefan Schädler and Walter Zimmermann (eds.), *John Cage: Anarchic Harmony* (Mainz: Schott, 1992), pp. 71–76.

9 "Über John Cage," p. 70. It is not surprising that Tudor reconstructed the lost score of the initial version several times for his performances: firstly for a concert on March 13, 1982 (fourteen pages in total, first movement on pages 1 and 2, second movement on pages 3 to 9, page 10 empty, and third movement on pages 11 to 14; the score is part of the estate; see Fetterman, *Cage's Theatre Pieces*, p. 75) and secondly for a video production in 1990 (*I Have Nothing to Say and I Am Saying It*, video documentation on John Cage, dir. Allan Miller and Vivian Perlis, 55 min., PBS, New York, 1990).

10 See John Cage, "To Describe the Process of Composition Used in 'Music of Changes' and 'Imaginary Landscape No. 4'," first published in *trans/formation* I/3 (1952), pp. 57–59, and republished in *Silence: Lectures and Writings* (Middletown, CT: Wesleyan University Press, 1961), pp. 57–59.

11 "Über John Cage," p. 70.

12 See John Cage, *I–VI (The Charles Eliot Norton Lectures 1988–89)* (Cambridge, MA: Harvard University Press, 1990), pp. 20ff. On the use of tarot cards, see Cage's interview with Fetterman in 1990, in Fetterman, *Cage's Theatre Pieces*, p. 72, as well as Maier, *Ausdruck der Zeit*, pp. 146 ff.

13 The score is thus distinguished by the very duplicity that Dahlhaus demands of musical writings: to be simultaneously representatives of a musical context and an encouragement to performance. See Dahlhaus, "Notenschrift heute", pp. 24–25.

14 From an interview with Fetterman on June 21, 1989, quoted in Fetterman, *Cage's Theatre Pieces*, p. 75.

15 See Kremen's preface to the facsimile edition of this version (EP6777a), published in 1993 [→ p. 173].

16 In a note to the Tacet version published in 1986.

17 The term "generalization" was introduced to describe these processes by Earle Brown, whose Folio cycle unfolds a similar movement. See Earle Brown, "Notation und Ausführung Neuer Musik," in Ernst Thomas (ed.), *Notation*, pp. 64–86, esp. p. 84. On Folio, see Dörte Schmidt, "Schrift-Graphik-Bild: Zur Notation in Earle Browns *December 1952* und dem Zyklus Folio," in Wolfgang Budday (ed.), *Musiktheorie: Festschrift für Heinrich Deppert zum 65. Geburtstag* (Tutzing: Hans Schneider Verlag, 2000), pp. 183–207.

18 In Cage's work this notion goes hand in hand with a critique of the Serialists' parametrical thinking, which is dependent on distinct tone locations. See for instance the notes taken by George Brecht during Cage's composition course at the New School of Social Research, in Dieter Daniels (ed.) in collaboration with Hermann Braun, *George Brecht: Notebooks I·II·III* (Cologne: Verlag der Buchhandlung Walther König, 1991), particularly those relating to the session of July 17, 1958, in *Notebook I*, p. 41.

19 Dahlhaus, "Notenschrift heute", p. 12.

magazine in 1967, the issue had clearly not been identified, since it appeared as a scaled-down facsimile of the handwriting without any adjustment of the indicated scale; in other words the individuality of the autograph was deemed more important than the "writtenness" of the recording.[20] This inevitably led to the situation where the structure of the work was no longer comprehensible and therefore seemed necessarily random.

A consequence of the "generalized" time grid was that it allowed for any kind of activity to be structured as a musical one. Cage experimented with this in his famous "happening" in Black Mountain in the summer of 1952 by setting the task of completing an activity within timeframes defined with the help of random operations, the type of activity being left to the choice of the participants.[21] It is mainly based on accounts that this "happening," which became famous as a kind of founding act of the Fluxus movement, is today associated with "the 'discovery' of the performative."[22] The notations and their specific consequence for a generalized organization of time hardly play any role in this and are rarely ever seen as relevant for Fluxus, where such actions executed in "measured time" played an important role. In actual fact, however, this is precisely one of the central conditions of numerous Fluxus actions, as epitomized by George Maciunas's scores [→ fig. 1]. It is no coincidence that, in the early sixties, Maciunas saw Cage as a central figure of New Music.[23] Obviously at the time there had been no deeper analysis of the function of notations in this context—this was also true for *4'33"*, the next version of which was published in 1960 and coincided with the foundation of Fluxus.

Fig. 1
George Maciunas, "Solo for Violin (for Sylvano Busotti)," 1962

seconds
play any sentimental tune
scrape strings with nail
loosen strings and pluck
break string by overtentioning peg
insert bow between strings & sound board & oscillate bow
hold bow to shoulders & bow with violin
strike with bow over sound board
scrape inside of sound box with bow
blow through sound holes
put pebbles inside sound box & shake violin
scrape floor with violin
push-pull violin over table or floor
scratch violin with sharp tool
saw violin or part of it
drill violin
drive a nail into violin
hammer violin with hammer
bite violin
step over violin and crush it
rip violin appart
drop violin over floor
throw violin or parts of it to the audience

In the two versions of *4'33"* that we have discussed so far, Cage wrote scores, which are determined in all the dimensions of sound: for the durations, he used the random procedures developed for *Music of Changes* to establish exact values, and for all the other dimensions of sound, the—equally unambiguous—value zero (which implies that the durations are without pitch, volume, etc.). In the best-known version, which was also first published in 1960 by Henmar Press in New York, Cage's compositional interest shifts from structured silence to what can still be heard besides this "silence." Fundamentally, it is no longer a determinately notated "silent piece," but an indeterminately notated piece consisting of random sounds. Consequently, Cage no longer actually notates a score recording everything that makes a sound, but only a voice, which, in the concert of everything that sounds, has its own task, namely to suspend play [→ p. 131].[24] This is precisely what the term "tacet" refers to.[25] Looking up the word in a relevant dictionary, we find yet another example for its use: "tacet: a direction indicating that a particular instrument or singer does not take part *in a movement or part of a movement*."[26]

For the convention to be effective, Cage has to keep the division into movements. To a certain degree, this version conflates the conception of *4'33"* with what he achieved in the *Concert for Piano and Orchestra* (1957/58): even the non-performance of all voices is a conceivable performance here.[27] The Tacet version of *4'33"* reads almost like an implementation of this particular case.[28] As in his *Concert*, Cage here leaves any decision regarding time to the performer, since it effectively depends on the sound which he does not determine and which the musician with the "tacet" voice awaits. In the preliminary remark he does not specify how the alternative timeframes should be determined, but he does make it clear in the first sentence that there must be a determination which structures the performance—and gives it its title, hence conferring it the status of a work: "The title of the work is the total length in minutes and seconds of its performance."[29] The fact that it is important to mark the beginning and end of the timeframes of the three movements is corroborated by Cage's remarks on the premiere in the foreword: he is obviously not concerned about the documentation of the performance history, since he merely describes how David Tudor visualized the limits of the movement by closing (at the beginning) and opening (at the end) the piano lid, not the turning of the

20 See *Source. Music of the Avant-Garde* 1/2 (1967), pp. 46–55. The same error had previously been committed by Henmar Press when they published *Music of Changes*. Here, too, the composer's handwriting, noted to scale, was scaled down in the reproduction. For more details, see Rosângela Pereira de Tugny, *Le Piano et les dés: Étude sur 'Music of Changes', 'Constellation-Mirroir' et 'Klavierstück XI'*, (Thèse de doctorat, groupe de formation doctorale, Université de Tours, École normale supérieure et Conservatoire national supérieur de Paris, 1996), pp. 13–14. The author would like to thank Robert Piencikowski (Basel) for drawing her attention to this parallel.

21 There are several, partly contradictory, accounts of this happening. See Mary Emma Harris, The Arts at Black Mountain College (Cambridge, MA: MIT Press, 1988), pp. 226–27, and, for more detail, Fetterman, *Cage's Theatre Pieces*, pp. 97–104.

22 See, for instance, Erika Fischer-Lichte, "Grenzgänge und Tauschhandel. Auf dem Wege zu einer performativen Kultur," in Uwe Wirth (ed.), *Performanz: Zwischen Sprachphilosophie und Kulturwissenschaften* (Frankfurt: Suhrkamp, 2002), pp. 277–300.

23 He interprets Cage's step, in musical terms, as a movement towards concretion, which must be systematically pursued. See Dörte Schmidt, "Flugversuche. Serialismus und Experimentelle Musik in den 50er und frühen 60er Jahren," in Hannes Grossek and Thomas Reischl (eds.), *Zeit-Wart/Gegen-Geist: Beiträge über Phänomene der Kultur unserer Zeit; Festschrift für Sigrid Wiesmann* (Vienna/Sydney: Reischl & Grossek, 2001), pp. 219–61, 253–54.

24 Edition Peters schematically list all versions of the piece as a "score" according to the rule (which here no longer applies) that when something is a piece, its notation is a score.

25 Reinhard Kapp, "Cage," in Horst Weber (ed.), *Metzler Komponisten Lexikon* (Stuttgart: 2003), pp. 95–103, esp. p. 100. Interestingly, both Fetterman and Petra Maria Meyer provide a definition of "tacet" that points in this direction, yet omit to draw the obvious conclusion. See Fetterman, *Cage's Theatre Pieces*, p. 78, and Meyer, "Als das Theater aus dem Rahmen fiel," in Erika Fischer-Lichte, Friedemann Keuder and Isabel Pflug (eds.), *Theater seit den 60er Jahren: Grenzgänge der Neo-Avantgarde* (Tübingen/Basel: UTB, 1998), pp. 135–95, esp. p. 139.

26 http://woerterbuch.reverso.net/englisch-definitionen/tacet [May 20, 2012].

27 In the foreword to the piano voice, he writes: "The whole is to be taken as a body of material presentable at any point between minimum (nothing played) and maximum (everything played), both horizontally and vertically: a program made within determined length of time (to be altered by a conductor, when there is one) may involve any reading, i.e. any sequence of part or parts thereof." (EP 6705)

28 Ulrich Mosch had already pointed out the link between *Concert* and *4'33"*, although he did not emphasize that the version of *4'33"* to which this parallel really applies was created later. See Mosch, "Boulez und Cage: Musik in der Sackgasse?," in Sabine Ehrmann-Herfort, Ludwig Finscher and Giselher Schubert (eds.), *Europäische Musikgeschichte* (Stuttgart/Kassel: Bärenreiter/Metzler, 2002), vol. 2, pp. 1253–316, esp. p. 1299.

29 John Cage, note, in *4'33"*, EP 6777 (1969 and 1986).

pages during the performance, which visualizes the reading of the score and must have been equally noticeable to the audience.

The notation published by Henmar Press in 1960 is a typescript, most probably from Cage's typewriter [→ p. 131].[30] Remarkably, in 1986[31] the publisher exchanged this version, using the same catalogue number, for a facsimile of an autograph version that was notated later, as several differences suggest. While the typescript version consists of a single sheet of paper, Cage here notated the "voice" on a separate page, preceded by a cover sheet and a slightly expanded note [→ pp. 136 ff].

When comparing the two versions, one notices two additions. Firstly, Cage deems it necessary to specify that the durations of the individual movements can be freely altered and that the title of the piece derives from the sum of these durations. By doing so, he possibly reacts to misunderstandings that have occurred in the execution of the first Tacet version and wants to prevent performers from dismissing the division into movements. Secondly, by adding information about the Kremen version he clearly intends to show two things: the durations of the movements indicated here differ from the premiere, thus providing an auctorial example of the changeability of the durations of the movements,[32] and the situating of the autograph notation of the Tacet version in a line of "copies"—from the original to a "proportional" version, and from there to the one at hand, which (as we must remember) exists as a typescript and an autograph version. Cage thus underlines the transferability of the piece into various writings, especially in the context of the version that represents the fundamental change of the concept from silence determined by random procedures to indetermination.

But what happens to this transferability if we look at the substitution of the reproduction of a typescript with that of an autograph at the end of this line? Are we again dealing with a transfer based on a structural analogy of writings—which would thus have come to an end and could merely be copied by facsimile? From the perspective of the performer, the question of the *type* of writing is certainly irrelevant in this case, as the text could also be copied in other writings without influencing the result of the performance. From the viewpoint of the composer, however, an element comes into play which could eventually also convince the editor to opt for a facsimile or at least comment on the issue: to the extent that composers relinquish the determination of sound events, the question is where they inscribe their "handwriting" (this has been an issue for many composers since the end of the fifties). Artists react to this situation with the personalization of the "gesture of writing," in which the performative aspect of the act of writing also remains enshrined in the handwriting, and a shift from writing towards drawing (which extends one aspect of this movement). Notations which were initially created as an abstraction of writing are not infrequently reinterpreted into an image by the authors themselves, the most famous example being Earle Brown's *December 1952*.[33] The autograph Tacet version of *4′33″* stands on the brink between being a text and "something written," as the document of auctorial and intentional artistic action. This clearly demonstrates that the reason for the acute problem facing editors of the "non-transferability" of texts is not the indetermination of musical structures as such, but its consequence: the ensuing question of where the artistic action of the author inscribes itself.

The step after the Tacet version seemed so important to Cage himself that he changed the title and identified the subsequent pieces as variations or developments. In 1962 Henmar Press published the first in this series, *4′33″ (No. 2) (0′00″)* [→ pp. 142 ff]. As soon as this step—from the "silent piece" to the indetermination of the noises produced involuntarily during the performance—was taken, it opened up a new kind of compositional conception: Cage could now dictate "actions" that produce noises without necessarily aiming to do so in various determinations, and thus make these noises or sounds the focus of attention.[34] *4′33″ (No. 2) (0′00″)* is explicitly a "solo," which is why no further "voices" have been allowed for.

The notation of *0′00″* consists of an instruction which is no longer connected to traditional forms of notation and dispenses with instruments. The performer is asked to perform a "disciplined," i.e. intentional, action which, firstly, refers at least partly to others (and should therefore have some sort of communicative nature); and, secondly, may not be repeated as a performance of the piece nor consist of the performance of a musical composition; and during which, thirdly, no attention should be paid to the performance situation. The resulting noises, towards which the intention of the executed action must explicitly not be directed, are to be amplified as much as possible without causing feedback.

As soon as this step from the performance of a work-text into action was taken, Cage replaced the predefined time structure—which was determined by the composer in the two earlier versions, and by the performer prior to the performance in the Tacet version, and had to be checked with a stopwatch—with the inherent time of the action (which in the final instance cannot be predicted exactly). This, indeed, was what led to the need for a change in title.[35] Cage here completes the "shift of the compositional effort as such from the results to actions, the results of which cannot be predicted," as Heinz-Klaus Metzger had underlined as early as 1958.[36] The concept and the performance of *One³* in Leningrad in 1989 demonstrate how Cage, as a final consequence of *0′00″*, deleted the action itself without resorting to the predetermined times of the Tacet version: he transferred the amplification on the edge of feedback to the public sound system, thus making the space itself audible, and now used his "inner clock" as a "metronome," since neither a predetermined structure nor an action could possibly assume this function.[37]

In *4′33″ (No. 2) (0′00″)* writing is of striking importance: the score, not without ambiguity, indicates that the writing of this manuscript was the first performance. The publication of the autograph version of the Tacet variation might have been a reaction to this. Obviously, the question shifts from the transferability of writing and its consequences for the performance to

30 The author would like to thank Laura Kuhn from the John Cage Trust, New York, for sharing this information (in a letter to the author dated August 15, 2008). According to Kuhn, Don Gillespie, who supervised the publications of Edition Peters, New York, recalls that the first typescript was replaced by yet another one, which had been created at the publisher's by Hank Haffner. However, the exact genealogy could not be reconstructed.

31 Dated as per Fetterman, *Cage's Theatre Pieces*, p. 259, and Maier, *Ausdruck der Zeit*, p. 154. Don Gillespie recalls that the publisher asked Cage for an autograph version. (Kuhn in a letter to the author dated August 15, 2008.)

32 The durations of the Kremen version do not match those of the published score. Whether Cage failed to recollect correctly or changed them deliberately to document the changeability, or whether a version with these times actually existed, cannot be established retrospectively. For a discussion of this topic, see Fetterman, *Cage's Theatre Pieces*, p. 79, Solomon, *The Sounds of Silence* , pp. 8ff, and Maier, *Ausdruck der Zeit*, pp. 148–49.

33 See Schmidt, "Musik-Graphik-Bild," pp. 183 ff.

34 The impact on *4′33″ (No. 2)* only becomes fully visible when taking into account the intermediate step of the Tacet version; even James Pritchett still related this directly to the "silent piece." See Pritchett, *The Music of John Cage* (Cambridge: Cambridge University Press, 1993), p. 147.

35 Cage's estate holds a manuscript version of this piece, which explicitly states that no stopwatch should be used. See the transcription in Fetterman, *Cage's Theatre Pieces*, p. 87.

36 Metzger, "John Cage," p. 16.

37 Cage's description in the interview with Fetterman in 1990, in Fetterman, *Cage's Theatre Pieces*, p. 94.

the relationships between writing and text. The fact that Cage, in subsequent performances of *4'33" (No. 2)*, pursued the topic of writing in numerous variations (with a pencil, typewriter, or fountain pen) is certainly no coincidence.

Among the accounts of Cage's own public performances, we find only one instance in which Cage did not choose an act of writing as the action.[38] He also perpetuated this subject explicitly when incorporating *4'33" (No. 2)* into his *Song Books* (as *Solo for Voice 8, 24, 28, 62* and *63*), published in 1970, and in his further developments of them. Other variations (such as *0'00" No. 2 = Solo for Voice 23* and *0'00" No. 2B = Solo for Voice 26*), in which Cage presents versions for two performers playing a board game, are less interesting for our enquiry than the developments of *(0'00")* in which he determines the action: in both cases "writing" is required. In *Solo for Voice 15* the instruction reads: "Using a typewriter equipped with contact microphones (four channels preferably, speakers around the audience, highest volume without feedback), typewrite the following statement by Erik Satie thirty-eight times: *L'artiste n'a pas le droit de disposer inutilement du temps de son auditeur.*"[39] And *Solo for Voice 71* demands: "Write a card or note with sketch in ink."[40]

One is tempted to see this move towards "writing" as an artistic pendant to Roland Barthes's reflections on the "death of the author," superseded by the writer—or scriptor as it were—whose relation to the text has considerably changed:

> In complete contrast, the modern scriptor is born simultaneously with the text ... there is no other time than that of the enunciation and every text is eternally written here and now. The fact is (or, it follows) that writing can no longer designate an operation of recording, notation, representation, "depiction" (as the Classics would say); rather, it designates exactly what linguists, referring to Oxford philosophy,[41] call a performative, a rare verbal form (exclusively given in the first person and in the present tense) in which the enunciation has no other content (contains no other proposition) than the act by which it is uttered ...[42]

As long as we presume the unity of composer and performer, the parallel might work. But this perspective leads us to question the possible text status of a note that Cage formulated in order to produce such a performative, detached from the writer of the instruction, and which he published under his name as an author. This potentially leaves us with two text levels. Provided we do not throw overboard the notion of work in such cases, music —and maybe paradigmatically Cage's music—manifestly provides a field where we can observe crossovers that make it possible to hold on to the work-text, while simultaneously moving towards performativity.

The fact that this lay at the heart of Cage's interests is corroborated by yet another approach of *4'33"* and *0'00"*. If we systematically address the "shifting" text status, on which, as Metzger promised, "the scores instruct us," the versions and variations we have considered so far are first of all divided into three groups: scores, voices, and performance instructions. All subsequent developments play with the reciprocal relation of these systematic possibilities, showing that Cage did not by any means see the step into action as severing the ties with previous standpoints. A particularly eloquent case in point is *WGBH-TV for a Composer and Technicians* (1971) [→ fig. 2].[43] This piece exists in two different formats, which in point of fact represent the two text levels we distinguished earlier, namely a directing sketch for a TV film and its filmic implementation. It is noteworthy that, in contrast to Cage's other films, this "work" is available in both formats from the publisher, who lists the directing sketch as a "score" in his catalogue. The publication of the directing instructions initially followed a very pragmatic impetus related to the traditional appreciation of composers' autographs, as it was Cage's reply to a request by the Caledonia Women's Club for a contribution to a charity auction: "For your auction I am enclosing your envelope on which I made a composition for TV. This envelope together with your letter+ this one of mine will constitute a m[anu]s[cript] to be published by Henmar Press of C.F. Peters, NYC. Cordially + Best wishes, John Cage."[44]

Fig. 2
John Cage, *WGBH-TV*, 1971

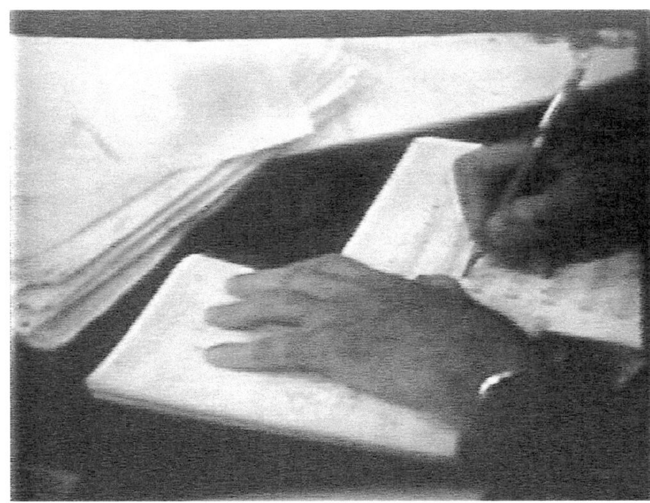

This letter and the sketch on the back of the envelope have been published in facsimile and with a cover page bearing a dedication to Nam June Paik under the catalogue number EP 6808. But there is more to this than just a joke for a good cause: with *WGBH-TV*, which, not coincidentally, explicitly requires a "composer" to be the perfomer, Cage almost programmatically reformulated the question of the writing and the work-text by exaggerating two aspects of the notes to *0'00"*: these excluded the possibility of the action consisting of the performance of a "musical composition," but, on the other hand, stipulated that the writing of the manuscript had been the first performance; "composing" as an "act of writing" is therefore not excluded, and "that which has been written" can obviously live on as a text, which in turn can trigger performances.

The film [→ fig. 2], which follows the directing instructions, shows only Cage's hand (filmed from the left with a static camera so that neither the body nor the head are in the frame) writing a

38 In 1965, at the University of Illinois, the action consisted in producing and drinking vegetable juice. To be compared with the accounts (all quoted in Fetterman, *Cage's Theatre Pieces*, p. 88) of performances at Brandeis University, Waltham, on May 5, 1965, which saw him writing letters with an amplified typewriter (Alvin Lucier); in Berlin in the mid-sixties, which involved writing his correspondence with an amplified typewriter and a pencil fitted with a contact microphone (David Tudor); and at the Lincoln Center, New York, in July 1988, where he used a black fountain pen (Neely Bruce).

39 "The artist has no right to waste the audience's time." John Cage, *Song Books* (New York: Henmar Press, 1970), vol. 1, 56. This action was in turn developed in *Solo for Voice 69* and *80*.

40 Ibid., vol. 2, p. 256.

41 Ibid.

42 Roland Barthes, *Death of the Author* [1967], quoted in Stephen Heath (ed.), *Image, Music, Text* (New York: Hill and Wang, 1977), pp. 142–48.

43 Fetterman was the first to point out the relation between this film and the body of work around *4'33"*. Fetterman, *Cage's Theatre Pieces*, pp. 93ff.

44 Quoted in Gabriele Leupold and Katharina Raabe (eds.), *In Ketten tanzen: Übersetzen als interpretierende Kunst* (Göttingen: Wallstein Verlag, 2008), p. 60.

piece in traditional notation. The "act of writing" plainly leads to a musical work-text in the old sense, but the writer is both bodiless and headless—he is not shown as an "author." The writing noises are heard as a heavily amplified spatial sound recording. The recording is overlaid five times with Cage's voice uttering the statement: "Music is being written but isn't finished yet. That's why there isn't any sound."[45] The published sketch shows that the film is based on a painstaking management of time (even the length of the statement is precisely structured). Here, Cage directly stages the transition between "work" and "*écriture*" by bringing together the requirements of the first scores of *4'33"*, whose performance supposes a predefined temporal structure, and *0'00"*. The writing creates a piece that cannot sound because the proper time of the writing exceeds the predetermined temporal structure. This writing can nevertheless become an aesthetic object if it finds a "means of storage" that suits its specificity (and is entirely predefined): sound film.

Fig. 3
John Cage, two versions of *4'33"*, in: Nam June Paik, *A Tribute to John Cage*, video, 1973

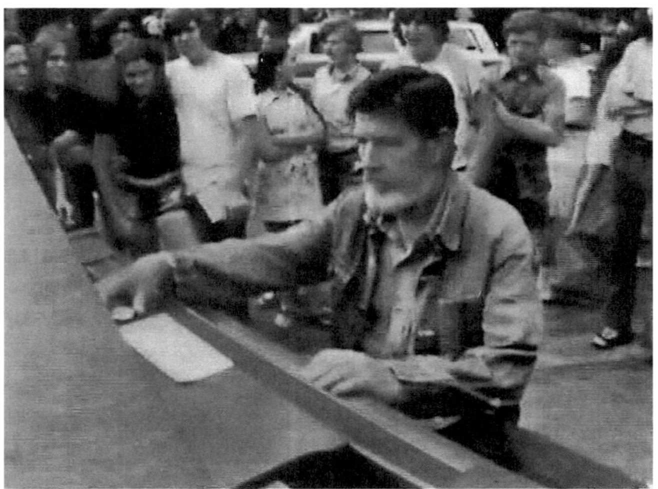

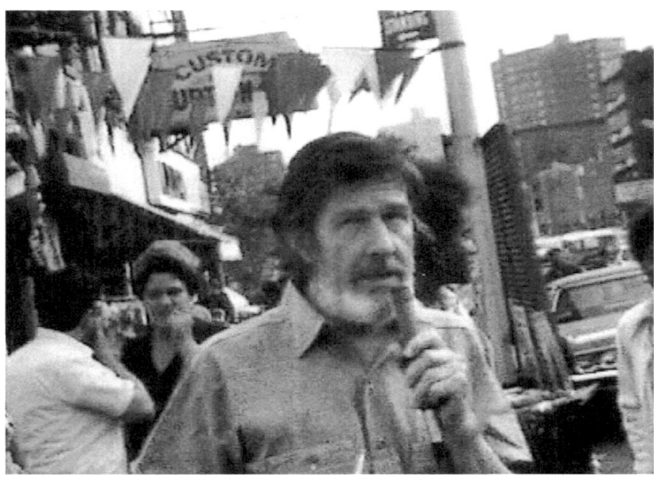

Two years later, film allowed Cage to implement a further consequence from the Tacet version, which profits from the possibility, introduced in *0'00"*, of working without instruments but with a sound amplifier. For Nam June Paik's film *A Tribute to John Cage* (1973/76) [→ fig. 3] he performed two versions of *4'33"* in which he demonstratively left the concert hall and relocated the performance to an outdoor venue. First of all, he asked for a grand piano to be installed on Harvard Square in Cambridge, where he filmed a concert performance of the Tacet version with an audience, applause, and so forth.[46] He then accepted the consequences of the filmic situation and left the concert situation itself: Cage dispensed with both an instrument and an actual performance situation, instead of which, in spots determined by random operations and at previously determined times, he held a microphone in the air to record ambient sounds, which were then added as a soundtrack to the film recordings of the action (this is clearly sensed by spectators, because the short off-mike conversations that Cage has with passers-by during the recording can be seen but not heard): the idea was obviously to visualize the split between the action and the sound object it produces.

The purposeful confrontation of the filmic recording of an "instrumental" performance of *4'33"* with a veritable film version evidences the shifting meaning of outside noises: Cage uses the possibilities of film to dismiss the unity of place for the performance, while retaining it for spectators/listeners. Whereas, initially, they identify with the spectators/listeners in the filmed performance and so in turn adopt their listening attitude (thus also including their respective ambient sounds at the time of hearing/seeing), Cage's second version confronts them with the recorded ambient sounds as a sound structure, which they now hear as a fully determined performance.[47]

A second film version of *4'33"* involving Cage and created in 1990 can be found in John Cage & Hennig Lohner, *4'33"* at the former checkpoint Invalidenstraße, Berlin [→ fig. 4].[48] Here, Cage and Lohner tellingly modify several aspects of the piece. Firstly, the place and time of the performance become an integral part of this version, giving the "random" sound events a meaning, and are therefore also mentioned in the final credits: "8 January 1990, during the dismantling of the checkpoint Berlin Invalidenstrasse." Secondly, the unity of place and time of the "action" is consequently reintroduced, and the events are interpreted as a continuum. Thirdly, for the first time in *4'33"*, there are two performers whose sole task is to be present at the chosen time and place. There are no instruments, the performers do not perform any action and do not—as in Paik's film—hold a microphone, nor do they visibly monitor the passage of time, but they essentially function as figures of identification—protagonists, rather than performers, in a self-contained filmic action framed by a director and confronting the spectator/listener as an aesthetic object. The step into action thus ultimately leads again to a result that can be re-performed.[49]

4'33" epitomizes the qualitative move away from the traditional aesthetic principles of the musical work of art, which are so closely linked to the instance of the notated text. Heinz-Klaus Metzger saw in Cage the embodiment of the move towards the performative described by Barthes. This is precisely why he

45 Directions for the realization of a TV film, EP 6808, sheet 4.
46 In the film Cage explicitly refers to his decision to relocate the concert hall.
47 A similar attitude also underpins the CD recording of the Amadinda Percussion Group, which consists of recordings of natural sounds, while the movements correspond to the different recording locations (Hungaroton HCD 12991, 1989).
48 Broadcast as part of Henning and Peter Lohner's film essay *John Cage: 22708 Types – Utopie im Niemandsland*, 3Sat, 1992, 44:59 min. The author would like to thank Albrecht Riethmüller (Berlin) for directing her to this film.
49 A concert recording by the public broadcaster WDR, which was later turned into a feature film, documents an auctorial development of the Tacet version, also without music instruments (i.e. a kind of intermediate step on the way to the version performed at the Berlin Wall), which was staged in 1986 as part of the opening of the exhibition *Die 60er Jahre* at the Kölner Kunsthalle in Cologne. Here, however, Cage still indicated the beginning and end of the movements by turning around a glass standing on its head. See video by Klaus vom Bruch. [→ pp. 180f.]

introduced the distinction between a "result writing" aimed at the representation of aesthetic objects and an "action writing" that ignores such objects and highlights the process.[50] Dahlhaus saw this as aesthetic propaganda and replied sharply:

> "Action writing" is a slogan. The meaning is vague, the tendency unmistakable. It is aimed against the "work" as an aesthetic object ... The claim that result writing should be replaced by action writing betrays the notion that it is appropriate for the state of composing not to denote tonal characteristics as part-moments of a musical system of reference, but types of the production of sounds and noises.

Fig. 4
John Cage & Henning Lohner, *4'33"* at the former checkpoint Invalidenstraße, Berlin, video, August 1, 1990

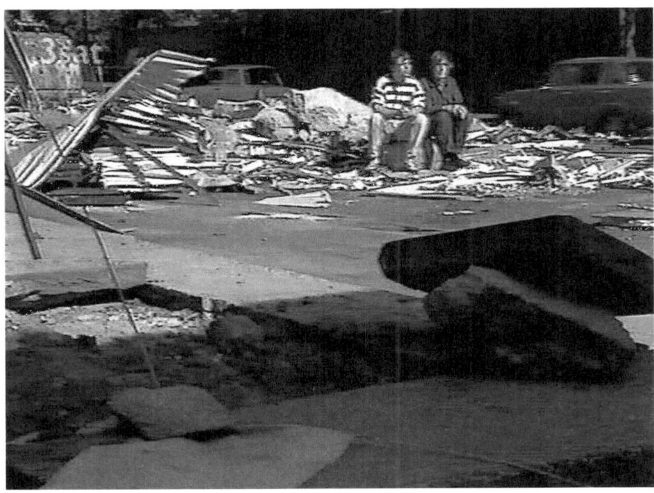

This, he contended, was a regression into the primitive stages of conceptualization.[51] He considered the abandonment of the notion of work also as a near-malicious abandonment of the edifying function of music, to which he repeatedly objected, emphasizing the importance of writing as "a medium of musical reflection."[52]

The debate was a highly emotional one: at stake was the status of the "work of art," and hence the fundamental categories of composing. Notation itself, however, which Metzger so heatedly invoked as a defining category, clearly shifted out of focus: hardly anyone really read it. Yet it is precisely Cage's transition between "text" and "*écriture*" which indicates that he obviously cultivated an interest in the agency of writing as a "medium of aesthetic reflection" and that, in principle, he never departed from the idea that the purpose of composing is the marking of "aesthetic objects" through writing (which is corroborated by his further development as a composer). Rather, he aimed to investigate the possibilities and limits of musical notation and gather them under "work titles." The versions of *4'33"*, and all the off-shoots that we have surveyed here, form such a complex, which is available to us in various types of sources: work-texts, films, which can be regarded as aesthetic objects invested with the status of works, and variously recorded documents of auctorial performance versions. And while there is a hierarchy of sources, they do not lead towards a *single* valid text (to which all the discussions around *4'33"* seem to refer), but to a constellation of equal versions. The editor here inevitably becomes a commentator.[53] He or she must clarify the text status of the various sources and will soon realize that the crucial philological question regarding the music of the experimental avant-garde does not so much concern the parts of indetermination as such, but how they are notated how long is the claim of the "transferability" of writing valid, and when does the text tip over into "something written" or even into drawing, such that it can only be reproduced as a facsimile?

The fact that these transitions are so deliberately and systematically marked out in Cage's work suggests that he never dissolved the relation between the author and the work (which would ultimately mean that signing his pieces with his name must be disqualified as a convention or a mere safeguarding of financial rights). Rather, he was looking for alternatives to occupy the place traditionally held by intentionality—in some eras also by genius (which did not always have to be primarily intentional, as is evidenced by numerous composer myths): the concept of synchronicity actively propagated by Carl Gustav Jung, which established the link between author and action via coincidence rather than intention and so forth, provided Cage with a point of departure that bears clear parallels to the idea of performance postulated by Barthes, with its absolute focus on the first-person present tense; here lies one of the roots of Cage's interest in Far Eastern practices.[54] This does not, however, preclude the function of the work-texts. If music theory and theatre theory want to do justice to these pieces, they must start to look at the changes in the notion of text and its functions. In the same way that music science will have to abandon the idea that the "work-text" is the last absolute piece in the historic process and that "autonomous" art ends where its traditional function is challenged, theatre science should probably give up on the idea that the "discovery" of the performative dispenses with the necessity of philological readings of the "work-texts" and warrants an exclusive focus on the event of the performance. In any case, this cannot be justified with Cage, as, in my opinion, the example of *4'33"* shows.

However, taking this step presupposes a better knowledge of these texts. A scientific and critical edition of a piece such as *4'33"*, or of any of Cage's pieces for that matter, is therefore not as devious an idea as it might seem. From the perspective adopted here, it would by no means aim to elevate yet another composer to god-like status and preserve his works in the Museum of Editions, but it would, on the contrary, contribute to demystifying a much-loved myth, one that substantially skews our vision of the history of composition in the second half of the twentieth century and has developed a momentum of its own through a history of performances marked, on the one hand, by randomness (and hence meaninglessness) and, on the other, by the influence of an almost orthodox, oral tradition of performances from the composer's environment. Both ultimately ignore the significance

50 Metzger, "John Cage," p. 16.
51 Dahlhaus, "Notenschrift heute," p. 25.
52 Dahlhaus, "Über den Zerfall des musikalischen Werkbegriffs," in *Beiträge 1970/71 der Österreichischen Gesellschaft für Musik* (Kassel: Bärenreiter, 1971), here quoted in *Schönberg und andere: Gesammelte Aufsätze zur Neuen Musik* (Mainz: Schott, 1978), p. 285. See also Dahlhaus, "Plädoyer für eine romantische Kategorie: Der Begriff des Kunstwerks in der neuesten Musik," in *Neue Zeitschrift für Musik* 130/1 (1969), pp. 18–22.
53 The debate around Cage invokes traditional notions in an attempt to defuse this situation, which from a philological standpoint is not new. This is also evidenced by the fact that Peters, on the sleeve of the 1993 Kremen version, terms it the "original" version. Thanks to Fetterman, we could now recreate an "*ur*-version."
54 On the significance of Jung and his concept of synchronicity for Cage's reading of the I Ching, see Dörte Schmidt, "Die Geburt des Flugzeugs: Cage, I Ching und C.G. Jung," in Annette Kreutziger-Herr (ed.), *Das Andere: Spurensuche in der Musikgeschichte des 19. und 20. Jahrhunderts* (Frankfurt: Peter Lang, 1998) [= *Hamburger Jahrbuch für Musikwissenschaft*, 15], pp. 353–66, esp. pp. 358ff.

and changing function of the work-texts.[55] This explains why the points, which Cage, in his course at the New School in the summer of 1959, dictated to his student George Brecht, are still valid: what New Music lacks most are reliable editions of works, which are accessible, and performances based on the reading of these texts [→ fig. 5].[56]

Fig. 5
George Brecht, *Notebooks*, entry for July 22, 1959

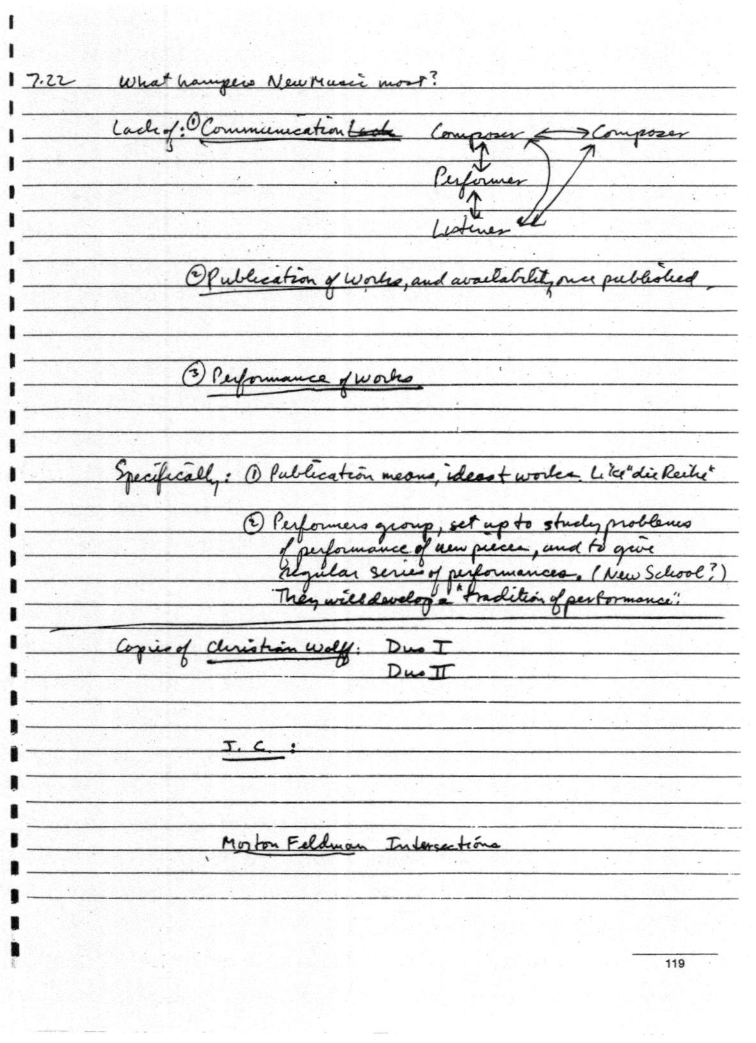

7.22 What hampers New Music most?

Lack of: ① Communication

Composer ⟷ Composer
Performer
Listener

② Publication of Works, and availability once published.

③ Performance of works

Specifically: ① Publication means ideas + works. Like "die Reihe"

② Performers group, set up to study problems of performance of new pieces, and to give regular series of performances. (New School?) They will develop a "tradition of performance".

Copies of Christian Wolff: Duo I
Duo II

J. C.:

Morton Feldman Intersections

119

55 A perfect example of this is the debate around the authority of the work-texts on the one hand, and the oral tradition of Cage's performance principles on the other, which emerged during the 1995 John Cage Symposium at the Hochschule der Künste in Berlin, where Eberhard Blum, for instance, voiced the opinion that it was impossible to interpret the meaning of the scores without additional information.

56 George Brecht, *Notebooks I·II·III (June 1958–August 1959)*, ed. Dieter Daniels with Hermann Braun (Cologne: Verlag der Buchhandlung Walther König, 1991), entry for July 22, 1959, in *Notebook III*, p. 119.

Jan Thoben

John Cage's Silent Scores

The relationship between author, score, performer, and audience has always been an issue in John Cage's compositions and the same is true for his silent pieces. In fact, Cage's silent scores should be considered part of his aesthetic reflection on silence as much as his or David Tudor's performances of them and their numerous contemporary enactments and documentations. A philological perspective on Cage's notations—their textuality, visuality, and conceptual implications—enriches the notorious ear-focused understanding of his silent pieces by pointing toward a broader frame of reference. The scores are part of a "non-cochlear" sonic discourse beyond the confines of what we call the phenomenology of sound and the apparent act of pure listening.[1] Throughout his career Cage consistently addressed issues of silence in his compositions. Probably his best-known composition *4'33"* is anything but a silent solitaire. It was premiered on August 1952 in the Maverick Concert Hall in Woodstock. Being his first composition entirely lacking intentional sounds, *4'33"* was followed by numerous derivative works forming a significant body of silent pieces within Cage's complete œuvre. The scores reproduced or transcribed in this catalogue are the notations of the following silent compositions:

4'33"	[1952]
0'00" (4'33" No.2)	[1962]
0'00" No.2	[1968]
Solos for Voice 8, 23, 24, 26, 28, 62 and *63* from *Song Books*	[1970]
WGBH-TV	[1971]
One³ = 4'33" (0'00") + 𝄞	[1989]
One¹¹	[1992][2]

The scores of *4'33"* encompass numerous versions and also reconstructions of Cage's now lost first notational version by David Tudor. They are displayed in this book [→ pp. 85–192] in typological rather than chronological order so that the complex interplay between composition, edition, and reconstruction history can be understood.

1948–1952 The Generative Years of *4'33"*

The four years between 1948 and 1952 can be regarded as the time period during which John Cage put his concept of a silent composition into concrete terms. Cage prominently mentioned his ideas on silence as musical parameter in his lecture *Defense of Satie* during the Black Mountain College Satie Festival in 1948. Here, silence is characterized as the necessary partner of sound, and duration is considered the most fundamental characteristic of musical material: "If you consider that sound is characterized by its pitch, its loudness, its timbre, and its duration, and that silence, which is the opposite and, therefore the necessary partner, is characterized only by its duration, you will be drawn to

1 For the concept of a "non-cochlear sonic art" see: Seth Kim-Cohen, *In the Blink of an Ear. Toward a Non-Cochlear Sonic Art* (London/New York: Continuum, 2009). Not unlike Douglas Kahn, Kim-Cohen takes a critical view: "By insisting on *4'33"* as an engagement with materiality; with sound-in-itself ... Cage and his adherents fail to realize the fundamental thought of a non-cochlear sonic practice: sound is bigger than hearing." Ibid, p. 167. Consequently, Kim-Cohen suggests a re-reading of the piece, showing in fact that *4'33"* does not address the ear alone.

2 *One¹¹* is Cage's first and only film. It is included in this text because it visually addresses the issue of nothingness or emptiness in a similar way to the silent compositions.

the conclusion that, of the four characteristics of the material of music, duration, that is, time length, is the most fundamental."[3] The wording is reminiscent of Feruccio Busoni's remarks on silence in his *Sketch Of A New Esthetic Of Music* (first version published in 1907). He addressed the rest and the pause (fermata) as features, which come closest to the essential nature of the art of music.[4]

However, the step from fermata to tacet is an important one. Cage's first idea for an actual silent musical piece has more direct conceptual relationships with Eric Satie's and Darius Milhaud's *musique d'ameublement*. Satie urged the listeners "to take no notice of it and to behave during the intervals as if it did not exist. This music ... claims to make a contribution to life in the same way as a private conversation, a painting in a gallery, or the chair on which you may or may not be seated." And Milhaud clearly defined it as proto-Muzak: "It is *musique d'ameublement*, heard, but not listened to."[5] Cage also explicitly refered to Muzak in his lecture *A Composer's Confessions*, delivered on February 28, 1948 at the *National Inter-Collegiate Arts Conference* held at Vassar College. In his attempts at exploring new musical materials, Cage announced his intention "to compose a piece of uninterrupted silence and sell it to Muzak Co. It will be 3 or 4 ½ minutes long—those being the standard lengths of 'canned' music—and its title will be *Silent Prayer*."[6]

But Cage's and Satie's strategies are crossed. Whereas Satie and Milhaud were proposing a shift from the everyday audiosphere into the artworld in order to create an absence of attention, Cage suggested distributing a musical artifact—namely a silent composition—through an established everyday media network, and thus creating aesthetic presence through absence. The subtle interventionist potential of silence becomes apparent, when we realize that a previously unnoticed auditive phenomenon enters our consciousness. Cage declares *Silent Prayer* to be a piece of functional music and therefore paradoxically suspends its apparent function as Muzak. This implicit paradox creates a sense of irony without losing its serious impetus. It reveals a conceptual idea of what silence can reveal if only we listen to it.

"It [*Silent Prayer*] will open with a single idea which I will attempt to make as seductive as the color and shape of a flower." The flower alludes to the icon of Zen tradition and—together with the title of the composition—makes reference to Cage's engagement with oriental philosophy, which he admitted was "full of" when giving his talk at Vassar College.[7] According to the founding legend, known as the Flower Sermon, Buddha silently passed on his entire teaching (dharma) in an instant to one of his disciples simply by smiling and holding up an *udumbara* flower.[8] This process of transmission can be regarded as the metaphysical background of Cage's concept of distributing a godless *Silent Prayer* through the Muzak network, even though at the time Muzak was not yet wireless and *Silent Prayer* remained a conceptual sketch.[9] The collective aesthetic reception of mediated silence turns into a techno-spiritual experience.[10]

Cage has never been a practicing Buddhist, but believed in the potential of sense perception. Hence, his often-quoted statement about his experience in the anechoic chamber at Harvard University doesn't necessarily provide any physiological, but rather phenomenological insights. Cage reported, he "heard two sounds, one high and one low. When I described them to the engineer in charge, he informed me that the high one was my nervous system in operation, the low one my blood in circulation."[11] The engineer's claim that the ear can detect nervous impulses lacks scientific proof entirely. But whether these high sounds were caused by tinnitus or some kind of otoacoustic emission isn't the prime issue. More important is the fact that John Cage wasn't able to experience silence in a technically silent environment: "I found out by experiment (I went into the anechoic chamber at Harvard University) that silence is not acoustic. It is a change of mind, a turning around. I devoted my music to it. My work became an exploration of non-intention. To carry it out faithfully I have developed a complicated composing means using I Ching chance operations, making my responsibility that of asking questions instead of making choices."[12] The conclusion that there is no such thing as silence is not an insight provided by the ear only, but by a change of mind, which is something superior to the auditive domain.

In fact, composing *4'33"* finally became necessary because of developments in the visual arts: "The thing that gave me the courage to do it ... was seeing the white empty paintings of Bob Rauschenberg to which I responded immediately not as objects but as ways."[13] Cage later added, "When I saw those, I said, 'Oh yes, I must; otherwise I'm lagging, otherwise music is lagging',"[14] and thus positioned *4'33"* within the discourse of Paragone, which has been a crucial art-historical topos since the Italian Renaissance. Cage credited Rauschenberg's influence for the genesis of *4'33"* in his article *On Robert Rauschenberg, Artist, and His Work* from 1961: "To whom it may concern: The *White Paintings* came first; my silent piece came later."[15] Rauschenberg had approached Betty Parsons in 1951 in order to exhibit his white paintings, but she had declined.[16] Although the paintings were part of the *Theater Piece No. 1 (Black Mountain Piece)* at Black Mountain College in North Carolina in 1952, which was initiated

3 John Cage, "Defense of Satie," *John Cage, An Anthology*, ed. Richard Kostelanetz (New York: Da Capo Press, 1991), p. 81
4 See Ferruccio Busoni, "Entwurf eine neuen Ästhetik der Tonkunst," *Von der Macht der Töne: Ausgewählte Schriften* (Leipzig: Reclam, 1983), p. 72; also see Douglas Kahn, *Noise Water Meat: A History of Sound in the Arts* (1999; Cambridge, MA: MIT Press, 2001) p. 179. Parallels can also be drawn between Busoni and Henry David Thoreau's conception of silence as being in partnership with all possible sound, recounted in his journals [Bradford Torrey (ed.), *The Writings of Henry David Thoreau: Journal I: 1837–1846* (Boston/New York: Houghton Mifflin, 1906), p. 66.], a book which became highly relevant for Cage decades after his "Defense of Satie."
5 Darius Milhaud as quoted in Matthew Shlomowitz, "Cage's Place In the Reception of Satie," (PhD diss., University of California at San Diego, 1999). Accessed June 11, 2012. http://www.satie-archives.com/web/article8.html #note.
6 John Cage, "A Composer's Confessions," in *Musicworks* No. 52 (Spring 1992), p. 15. In 1949, Cage again commented on this idea in an interview in *Time*: "The first step in describing silence ... is to use silence itself. Matter of fact, I thought of composing a piece like that. It would be very beautiful, and I would like to offer it to Muzak." Quoted in William Fetterman, *John Cage's Theatre Pieces: Notations and Performances* (Amsterdam: Harwood Academic Publishers, 1996), p. 70.
7 John Cage, *I–VI (The Charles Eliot Norton Lectures, 1988–89)* (Cambridge, MA: Harvard University Press, 1990), p. 23.
8 See William Harmless, S.J., *Mystics* (New York: Oxford University Press, 2008), p. 192.
9 In the 1940s Muzak was still wired radio distributed via telephone landlines. By the end of the 1950s, Muzak had begun switching from telephone lines to FM subcarriers.
10 See also Thomas M. Maier, *Ausdruck der Zeit: Ein Weg zu John Cages stillem Stück 4'33"* (Saarbrücken: Pfau, 2001), p. 138.
11 John Cage "Experimental Music," in *Silence: Lectures and Writings* (1961; Middletown, CT: Wesleyan University Press, 1973), p. 8.
12 John Cage, "An Autobiographical Statement," in *Southwest Review* (1991), p. 4. According to Kyle Gann, determining the exact date of Cage visiting the anechoic chamber seems almost impossible. See Kyle Gann, *No Such Thing As Silence: John Cage's 4'33"* (New Haven, CT: Yale University Press, 2010), pp. 163–64. The "late forties," to which Cage attributes his experience in his "Autobiographical Statement," is unlikely; in other texts he mentions 1951, and there are also some indications that Cage went to the anechoic chamber in 1952. Ibid, p. 165.
13 Cage, *I–VI*, p. 25.
14 John Cage in a conversation with Alan Gillmor & Roger Shattuck (1973), in Richard Kostelanetz, *Conversing with Cage* (New York: Limelight Editions, 1988), p. 67.
15 John Cage, "On Robert Rauschenberg, Artist, and His Work," in *Silence*, p. 8.
16 See letter from Rauschenberg to Parsons from *October* 18, 1951 quoted in Gann, *No Such Thing As Silence*, p. 157.

by Cage and is now known as the first "happening," they would not be on public display in a gallery space until the 1953 exhibition at Stable Gallery in New York.

The *White Paintings* incorporated the surrounding environment by changing according to what was happening outside of them and thus created a framework for non-intentional processes, in the same way as *4′33″*. Cage characterized them as "airports for the lights, shadows, and particles," a metaphor that puts them in context with Man Ray's *L'élevage de poussière (Dust Breeding)* from 1920. Man Ray photographed the surface of Duchamp's *Large Glass*, as it had collected a considerable amount of dust and appeared like a landscape (possibly an airport) as seen from above.[17] Indexicality in this case equals the movement of the non-art realm into an aesthetic setting, or, as Rauschenberg puts it with regard to the *White Paintings*, "They take you to a place art has not been (therefore it is)."[18] Seen with light, shadows and particles in mind "a canvas is never empty," as Cage commented.[19] Neither is silence. It provides a frame, within which the unnoticed gets noticed.

Finally, Rauschenberg's *White Paintings* establish the link to Cage's most radical notational version of *4′33″*, the "Original Version in Proportional Notation"—which is not, in fact, the original version. Moreover, it is questionable whether there is such a thing as an original version at all. This question directly points to the complex composition and edition history surrounding *4′33″*. It is important to realize that Cage continuously rethought *4′33″* in the course of his career and influenced the reception of this composition by altering the identity of the work.[20] Thus, reconstructing the composition history of *4′33″* and the following silent pieces can help to understand not only the historical but also the conceptual development of Cage's engagement with silence.

Composing *4′33″*

4′33″ was first performed by pianist David Tudor at the Maverick Concert Hall, Woodstock, New York, on August 29, 1952 [→ fig. 1]. It is very likely that Cage finished the composition in New York City shortly before the premiere. John Holzaepfel reports that "[i]n the latter part of August, Cage returned to New York from Black Mountain College, where he had viewed Robert Rauschenberg's series of all-white paintings." He refers to a letter in which Tudor writes "he hoped Cage would complete the composition in time for a recital he was planning to give in Woodstock, NY, at the end of the month." Holzaepfel emphasizes that "if it was the implications of Rauschenberg's radical art ... that emboldened Cage to begin composing the piece, it was Tudor's interest in performing it that persuaded him to finish it."[21] Cage had the idea that for the premiere Tudor should close the keyboard lid of the open grand piano at the beginning of each movement and open it again at the end.[22] This gesture emblematically symbolizes the silencing of traditional musical practice and at the same time shows how profoundly Cage's concept of silence is tied to the notion of performativity. Tudor's appearance on stage and his gestures were the only indication that there was anything to listen to at all. There's a certain irony in the anecdote that Cage apparently staged his own performance of *4′33″* at the piano in the house of Du Mont publisher Ernst Brücher in Cologne on November 26, 1956 in a way that almost nobody recognized. Only later in the evening when asked if he would still perform *4′33″*, he replied—it is said—that it had been performed hours ago.[23]

4′33″ consists of three movements of silence, which add up to the length of its title. Cage himself recalls the compositional process as follows:

> When I wrote *4′33″* I was in the process of writing the *Music of Changes*. That was done in an elaborate way. All the work was done with chance operations. In the case of *4′33″*, I actually used the same method of working and I built up the silence of each movement, and the three movements add up to *4′33″*. It seems idiotic but that's what I did. It took several days to write it and it took me several years to come to the decision to make it.[24]

Remembering Cage's 1948 statement about the length of his silent composition being derived from the length of canned music, it is hard to imagine that the result of his chance operation in 1952 just came out to be *4′33″* coincidentally.

Fig. 1
Maverick Concert Hall
in Woodstock

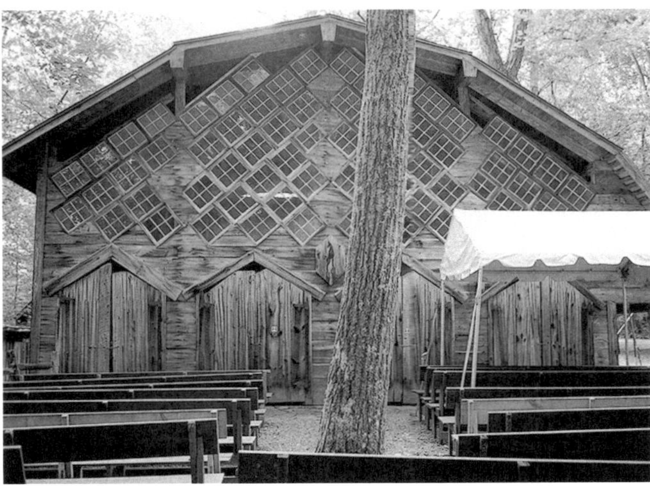

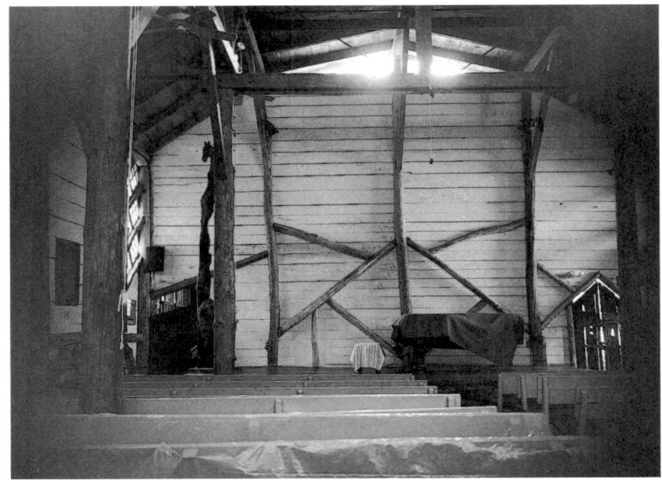

17 See also Branden W. Joseph, "White on White," in *Critical Inquiry*, Vol. 27, No. 1 (Autumn, 2000), p. 97.
18 The collaborative work *Automobile Tire Print* (1953) for which Cage printed a black line on a glued paper roll by driving across it with his Model A Ford can also be seen in this conceptual frame.
19 Cage, "On Robert Rauschenberg," p. 103.
20 See also Dörte Schmidt's text in this catalogue [→ pp. 67 f].
21 John Holzaepfel, "Cage and Tudor," in *The Cambridge Companion to John Cage*, ed. David Nicholls (Cambridge: Cambridge University Press, 2002), p. 174.
22 David Tudor in an interview with William Fetterman, June 21, 1989. Tudor also recalls using a different pedal in each movement. Fetterman, *John Cage's Theatre Pieces*, p. 74.
23 See Karin Thomas, "Ernst Brücher und die Neue Musikszene–Erinnerungssplitter," in *Ernst Brücher: Ein Erinnerungsbuch* (Cologne: Dumont, 2008), pp. 120–25.
24 Cage, *I–VI*, pp. 20–22.

There is also some confusion about how exactly Cage composed *4'33"*, as there are no records or sketches of the composition process.[25] Cage and Tudor both described the working process as an accumulation of chance-determined lengths of silence comparable to the process of composing *Music of Changes*. The latter composition is notorious for having been composed using complex chance operations based on the I Ching, whereas for *4'33"* Cage recalled using a home-made deck of cards with durations written on them and determining the durations using the Tarot:

> "I wrote it note by note, just like the *Music of Changes*. That's how I knew how long it was, when I added all the notes up. It was dealing these cards—shuffling them, on which there were durations, and then dealing them—and using the Tarot to know how to use them. The card-spread was a complicated one, something big.
> [Question: Why did you use the Tarot rather than the I Ching?]
> Probably to balance the East with the West. I didn't use the [actual] Tarot cards, I was just using those ideas; and I was using the Tarot because it was Western, it was the most well-known chance thing known in the West of that oracular nature."[26]

Cage went even further and characterized the compositional process as remote: "I didn't even know I was writing *4'33"*. I built it up very gradually and it came out to be *4'33"*."[27] The piece evolved as much as the composer's notion of it, and as a matter of fact, the altering of *4'33"* can be depicted in the numerous versions and variations of its scores as well. There are four different types of notations of *4'33"*, henceforth referred to as versions with different variants:

1 The lost original diastematic version of stave paper dedicated to David Tudor (reconstructed by David Tudor in two different variants, 1982 and 1989).[28]

2 The graphic version (dedicated and given to Irwin Kremen in 1953; first published in *Source* 1967; republished posthumously by C.F. Peters in 1993 as EP 6777a with an annotation by Irwin Kremen; again republished by C.F. Peters in 2012 as *4'33": John Cage Centennial Edition*, EP 6777c).

3 The typewritten linguistic version (the original typescript, composed probably in the late 1950s, is lost; facsimile variant from original backdated to 1953 probably by David Tudor; variant published in 1960 as EP 6777 by C.F. Peters; variant copied on a different typewriter by Hank Haffner from C.F. Peters; variant with handwritten additions by John Cage prior to the publication of the calligraphic linguistic version), now out of print.

4 The calligraphic linguistic version (handwritten facsimile version of the typewritten linguistic notation with significant changes made by Cage; published as EP 6777 by C.F. Peters in 1986).

Another score from 1986 has appeared recently. Cage composed this version on the occasion of the exhibition *Die 60er Jahre – Kölns Weg zur Kunstmetropole: Vom Happening zum Kunstmarkt*. This score can be regarded as an auctorial performance score of the linguistic version.

The Lost Original Score and David Tudor's Reconstructions

The original score is considered lost. According to David Tudor the first notation was dedicated to him. In an interview with Reinhard Oehlschlägel from October 1992 Tudor explains that, in order to compose a piece for Irwin Kremen—which was to be the second graphical version of *4'33"*—Cage borrowed the original score from Tudor, because it was (besides the concert program of the premiere) the only document in which the durations of the single movements were notated.[29] Cage lost the original before he gave Kremen the graphical version as a gift for his birthday on June 5, 1953.[30]

Tudor made two reconstructions of the original score from memory, the first one on the occasion of his performance at the Symphony Space *Wall to Wall John Cage* concert in New York on March 13, 1982. Like the original, the reconstructed score is chronometrically notated in time-space proportion, meaning that unlike traditional musical scores, the horizontal axis equals the linear passage of time: 1 sec. = ½ in. The chronometrical proportionality visually emphasizes the nature of *4'33"* as a time-grid framing non-intentional sounds. The tempo is sixty. This reconstruction encompasses fourteen pages with just two single hand-drawn staves per page and no clefs. Bars mark every fifteen seconds. The durations in this score are: 0'33", 2'40", 1'20".[31]

In contrast to the 1989 reconstruction—and presumably also the original notation for Woodstock—this score doesn't call for the use of a keyboard instrument. There are no clefs and it also does not contain any time signature. Bearing in mind that this score was made in 1982, and hence after Cage's graphical and linguistic notations had been published, it is very likely that the process of reconstruction was an explorative one, comparable to reverse engineering. When asked to re-enact the version of *4'33"* that was performed in the piece's premiere, Tudor tried to figure out the durations and contacted Irwin Kremen, who described Cage's graphic score in a written reply and included a Xerox copy of the graphic manuscript.[32] This is why Tudor's first reconstruction bears as many similarities with the graphic version as with the supposed original. There are timing notes in the Tudor papers illustrating the reconstruction process [reproduced on p. 105]. Tudor derived the proportions from the ratio of the graphic score 56 sec. = 7 in. (1 sec. = ⅛ in.). By multiplying this ratio: 1 sec. = ⅛ in. × 4 = ½ in., he arrived at the time-space proportion for his 1982 reconstruction.

25 David Tudor, "Über John Cage. David Tudor im Gespräch mit Reinhard Oehlschlägel," in *Musik Texte*, Vol. 69/70 (April, 1997), p. 70.
26 John Cage in an interview with William Fetterman, New York, 10 August 1990, in Fetterman, *John Cage's Theatre Pieces*, p. 72.
27 Cage, *I–VI*, p. 21.
28 For William Fetterman's publication Tudor made an illustration of the first page of the original manuscript in 1989. Again, this notation example differs from the two complete reconstructions with regard to certain details. See Fetterman, *John Cage's Theatre Pieces*, p. 74.
29 Tudor, "Über John Cage," p. 70. The fact that Tudor didn't mention the Maverick program in the interview is remarkable and further discussed on page 81 in of this text. Tudor also dated the composition of the graphic score incorrectly in the interview.
30 Kremen recalls that Cage mentioned the lost original score when he visited him on his birthday in June 1953. Irwin Kremen in an email to the author, May 30, 2012 [full quote → p. 79].
31 These durations are very likely not identical with the time lengths in the original score [detailed discussion of the durations → pp. 80f].
32 Irwin Kremen, letter to David Tudor, February 5, 1982, Getty Research Institute, Los Angeles, Special Collections ID 980039, Box 55, Folder 7.

The second reconstruction was made in 1989 for a performance for the video documentation about John Cage *I Have Nothing to Say, And I Am Saying It* by Allan Miller and Vivian Perlis for PBS, New York.[33] As John Holzaepfel noted, this 1989 reconstruction resembled that of *Music of Changes* and is more likely to accurately reflect the original score of *4′33″* than Tudor's first reconstruction.[34] Tudor must also have recalled that Cage's *Music of Changes* was scaled in centimeters instead of inches and that the bars were spaced in intervals of 10 cm. He described the original in an interview with William Fetterman from 1989:

> The original was on music paper, with staffs, and it was laid out in measures like the *Music of Changes*, only there were no notes. But the time was there, notated exactly like the *Music of Changes* except that the tempo never changed, and there were no occurrences—just blank measures, no rests—and the time was easy to compute. The tempo was 60.[35]

Corresponding to Tudor's description, the 1989 reconstruction is written on music paper with staves. He indicated the three movements of the composition using red Roman numerals and added page numbers for the eight pages. G and F clefs indicate the instrumentation. Although this score contains the same durations as in 1982, Tudor used a different scaling factor. One second equals 2.5 cm (approximately one inch). In 4/4 time signature (four seconds) one bar equals 10 cm. Tudor added time values every sixteen seconds (with exceptions) creating a time-space grid so that each page ended with a value that was a multiple of sixteen. Interestingly Tudor left out every other stave between the systems on pages 1, 5, 6, 7, and 8. Consequently those pages contain thirty-two seconds of silence, whereas pages 2, 3, and 4—which make up most of the second movement—are condensed using every available stave. These pages contain forty-eight seconds of silence. Tudor has not commented on this spatial compression procedure, but it logically results in fewer pages having to be turned during the performance of the second (the longest) movement of *4′33″*. It is also important to note that this method of notation caused the end of the first movement at 33″ to be written on the second page of the score. This would have required that the page had to be turned one second before the ending of the first movement. Obviously, for practical but also aesthetical reasons, when performing the score for the video production, Tudor did not turn the page.

As indicated on the first page in the lower right corner, this small but nonetheless relevant detail was already part of the score. The arrow pointing to 33″ instructs the performer to have already turned the page before the beginning of the performance. At first sight, this seems surprising, since Tudor explicitly pointed out the importance of actually reading the score and turning the pages to convey the idea of time passing.[36] But here the difference between actually reading and performing a reading of the score becomes apparent. In order to perform the reading of the score at an accurate pace, the first page cannot be read—a paradox similar to the many others surrounding *4′33″*.

Whether Cage himself had notated the second movement in spatial compression cannot be verified, but it is rather unlikely. The page turning instruction and the spatial compression were likely added from the perspective of a performer rather than from a composer's point of view. There is no indication that Cage had included these practical aspects of performing a reading of the score in his original version the way Tudor did. Moreover, since David Tudor was known for solving notational problems of indeterminate scores, it should come as no surprise that he may also have modified the original. The modification or renotation of an indeterminate score is a preparatory procedure resulting in a functional rewriting of the score. Therefore, the status of this score as a reconstruction of the original document may be put into question without undermining its relevance as an important document in itself.[37]

The Graphic Version Dedicated to Irwin Kremen

The second version of *4′33″* is dedicated to visual artist and psychologist Irwin Kremen. Cage gave it to him as a gift for his twenty-eighth birthday on June 5, 1953. It is the oldest notational document of *4′33″* and the only original handwritten manuscript by the composer, since the original diastematic version and the original typescript are both considered lost. According to Holzaepfel, John Cage wrote the original manuscript "in the latter part of August" (1952), after he had returned to New York City from Black Mountain College.[38] Thanks to Irwin Kremen, who assembled the following evidence regarding the dating, we now know that this graphic score was written in May 1953 and Cage wanted it dated as the original manuscript:

> John gave me the score on June 5, 1953. In handing it to me as he entered my wife's apartment—if I recall correctly, he came with Merce [Cunningham], M.C. [Richards], and David [Tudor]—he mentioned that he had made it recently, had borrowed the Woodstock score from David and that that subsequently had gotten lost. I have a Xerox of a letter from Cage to David that John Holzaepfel sent me in 2000. In that letter Cage writes that he "... had copied *4′33″* in another way," and on the Xerox Holzaepfel noted that what John was referring to was the score he made for me. In an accompanying letter to me, Holzaepfel further said that "it does seem pretty clear that he [John Cage] wrote the letter [to David Tudor] in 1953." Certain other events Cage writes of in his letter to David suggest that the copy of *4′33″* was made in May. Yes, "8.52; N.Y.C." appears at the end of the final movement of the score in proportional notation. That's the way John wanted it to be. And from what I write above he probably produced that score well after August 1952, quite likely in May 1953.[39]

33 It is important to note that in 1989 Tudor made an illustration for inclusion in William Fetterman's book *John Cage's Theatre Pieces*, p. 74. This illustration may be regarded as a third variation of Tudor's. From a genealogical perspective, this illustration represents an intermediate state between the reconstructions of 1982 and 1989. As it is a notation example and not the actual score, this single page is supposed to give an impression of the original notational principle; it is an exemplification given by Tudor, who also signed it "dt." In this 1989 illustration Tudor notated the tempo 60 M.M. just as in his 1982 reconstruction, and wrote in grand stave just as in the later 1989 variation, not yet including the time signature of 4/4. According to Fetterman a quarter note still equals half an inch as in the 1982 reconstruction. Moreover, and in contrast to the 1982 reconstruction, the illustration already shows the division of sixteen seconds into four measures each of four seconds. Finally, in the 1989 reconstruction Tudor chose a metric notation system closely resembling that of *Music Of Changes*.

34 See Holzaepfel, "Cage and Tudor," p. 175.

35 David Tudor in an interview with William Fetterman, June 21, 1989. As quoted in Fetterman, *John Cage's Theatre Pieces*, p. 72.

36 David Tudor, "Über John Cage," p. 70.

37 For a detailed discussion and reconstruction of Tudor's performance scores see John Holzaepfel, *David Tudor and the performance of American experimental music, 1950–1959*, (Ann Arbor, MI: University Microfilms International, 1997).

38 Holzaepfel, "Cage and Tudor," p. 174.

39 Irwin Kremen in an email to the author, May 30, 2012. Kremen adds, "at least three other reasons come to mind why not in August 1952. For one, he would not have left the manuscript lying around for nine months before giving it to me. Secondly, he would not so early have 'copied *4′33″* in another way' and, then, suddenly the next May inscribed my name on it as the dedicatee. Finally, the manuscript Score including its dedication is—empirically and critically—all of a piece as written, calligraphically without hesitation or abruptness and with the inking consistent throughout. Descriptively 'backdated' may apply. That doesn't tell one much, and John could have had his good reasons for what he did."

According to Kremen's description, the manuscript of the graphic score "is made up of three sheets of paper, approximately 11 × 17 [inches], which were folded in half to give a page approximately 11 × 8 ½. The three sheets give altogether 12 such pages, the last two being blank and not part of the score. The 2nd page is also blank, as is the 7th but the latter is part of the actual score!"[40] The first page displays title, instructions, and signature, the second page is empty, the third page contains the dedication, and the fourth page indicates the proportionality, "1 PAGE = 7 INCHES = 56." Hence, six of the twelve pages make up the actual score. Kremen described the page progression again in detail in a letter to Larry Austin, publisher of *Source* magazine, when it was about to be published in 1967 [→ pp. 168 f]. It must be emphasized that the structure of the components of the unbound manuscript differs from the published versions. The first folded manuscript sheet serves as the wrapper of the score with two folded sheets inserted one after another.[41]

The graphic score contains neither staves nor clefs, just vertical lines on blank pages indicating the beginnings and endings of the three movements. The pages are not numbered. The tempo 60 indicates the beginning of each movement on top of each line, the length in minutes and seconds is added on the bottom of each line at the ending of each movement. Just like the original diastematic version, this score was written in proportional notation. But when compared with the original, it becomes apparent that Cage had erased almost all the traditional features of a musical composition.[42] All that remains is the title, the signature, and the temporal grid, which constitute *4'33"*. This version doesn't even contain instrumentation. Accordingly, it is subtitled "for any instrument or combinations of instruments." No longer a composition for a keyboard instrument, *4'33"* stipulates indeterminate instrumentation. At this point we can only speculate as to whether Cage regarded his original score as a piano version for David Tudor, or if *4'33"* had been a piano piece in the first place and became a composition for indeterminate instrumentation afterwards.

Another aspect, which has often been ignored, is the fact that each page of the graphic score measures eight and a half inches in width, but Cage's benchmark for the time-space relation designates only seven inches. It is important to understand that—as indicated by the lines at the beginning of each movement—there is an invisible margin on the left and right side of each page. This space doesn't contain any time and the score cannot be easily read during a performance. Imagining the resulting difficulties for a performer reading the score probably explains why most interpreters make use of the linguistic version when performing 4'33". More than any other version, the graphic score closely resembles the *White Paintings* with its black lines being reminiscent of the gaps between the canvases. It was first published in *Source: Music of the Avant Garde* in reduced size in July 1967, and in 1993 and 2012 by C.F. Peters in true size.[43]

The Linguistic Versions and the Riddle of the Durations

Just as with the original diastematic version of *4'33"*, the location of the original typescript of the linguistic version is unknown.[44] Furthermore, there is no reliable data on when exactly Cage produced the typewritten version of the linguistic *Tacet* score. Unlike in the graphic version and probably deliberately, Cage did not add a date. William Fetterman dated it 1960 according to the copyright annotation, but a letter that Cage wrote to Tudor on July 7, 1960 informs us that he had signed a contract with C.F. Peters/Henmar Press and was recording this copyright on all compositions: "Together with the words 'Copyright c. 1960 by etc,' I have been writing that on everything: title pages and first music pages (scores and parts) for a week now."[45] It was the third version composed, but got published first. Liz Kotz, who did detailed research on the linguistic versions of the *4'33"* scores, pointed out that, on July 17, 1958 in his notes for Cage's class in experimental composition at the New School, George Brecht referred to Cage's "4 min. 33 sec." as "Silence. Tacet."[46] James Pritchett also stated that the linguistic version must be dated to 1957 or later, since it reflected Cage's abandonment of structure in the late fifties.[47] However, all commentators agree that this version was written after the graphic score and thus represents the third notational version of *4'33"*. The original linguistic score was probably typewritten on Cage's own typewriter and published by C.F. Peters in 1960. It has been replaced by a second typescript written by Hank Haffner of Peters.[48]

The first typewritten variant has been copied several times. In the Tudor papers, a copy can be found which had obviously been made before Cage added the Henmar Press copyright annotation. Like several copies of other scores in Tudor's collection that date prior to Cage's signing with Peters, it is stamped: "COMPOSER'S FACSIMILE EDITION copyright 195_." Judging from the handwriting it may have been Tudor who added "1953" and "John Cage."

However, the compositional changes also indicate a reworking of the piece: Cage had further erased the determining constituents of *4'33"*. The most important change with regard to the

40 Letter from Irwin Kremen to David Tudor, February 5, 1982. Getty Research Institute, Los Angeles, Special Collections ID 980039, Box 55, Folder 7.

41 In an email to the author dated June 16, 2012 Irwin Kremen precisely described the manuscript components: "The separate components of the manuscript are not bound together. Consisting of three separate sheets of thin, onion-skin paper 11 inches by 17 inches, these sheets of the score are folded in two, thus making 12 pages altogether. One folded sheet serves as the wrapper of the score and the two other bifolia are inserted within it, Folio 1 followed by Folio 2. On the wrapper is the title, instructions, and Cage's signature with its three remaining pages being blank. Folio 1 contains the dedication 'For Irwin Kremen' on its first page, the time instruction on its second, the first movement on its third, and the beginning of the second movement on its fourth. Folio 2 begins where Folio 1 leaves off, with a blank page that is the continuation of the second movement, which ends on Folio 2's second page; the final movement of *4'33"* occupies the third and fourth pages of Folio 2.

42 For parallels between Cage's act of erasing and Rauschenberg's *Erased de Kooning Painting*, see Kim-Cohen, *In The Blink of An Ear*, pp. 163–67.

43 In a note written for the 1993 and 2012 editions of the graphic notation, Irwin Kremen describes the misprinting in detail. Quite peculiarly, while Peters New York published a correct version of the graphic score EP 6777a, the copy from Peters Frankfurt still contains errata to this day. Former mistakes in reproduction size and page order have been corrected, but in the copy ordered by the author in March 2012, the tempo-indication for the third movement is cut off.

44 Jonathan Hiam, head of the American Music Collection of The New York Public Library for the Performing Arts in an email to Inke Arns dated June 11, 2012.

45 Letter from John Cage to David Tudor, July 7, 1960, as cited in Liz Kotz, *Words to Be Looked At: Language in 1960s Art* (Cambridge, MA: MIT Press, 2007), p. 270.

46 George Brecht, *Notebooks I·II·III (June 1958–August 1959)*, ed. Dieter Daniels with Hermann Braun (Cologne: Verlag der Buchhandlung Walther König, 1991).

47 James Pritchett in an email to Liz Kotz, August 25, 2005, as cited in Kotz, *Words to Be Looked At*, p. 270.

48 According to Laura Kuhn of the John Cage Trust, New York, Don Gillespie remembered that Cage's first typescript had been replaced by Hank Haffner–letter from Kuhn to Dörte Schmidt [→ p. 70]. This typescript is reprinted in Kotz, *Words to Be Looked At*, p. 21, and Fetterman, *John Cage's Theatre Pieces*, p. 79. Interestingly, Fetterman describes this second variant as "[t]he first published version of *4'33"*, now out of print," and does not mention the two typewritten variants.

preceding version is the relaxing of a rigid time-grid. As a result, the typewritten version does not come with a title but with a note. The note informs the reader that "[t]he title of this work is the total length in minutes and seconds of its performance" and it may "last any length of time."[49] The indeterminacy of the temporal grid also emphasizes the fact that Cage's chance operations simply could have led to another result. *4'33"* "could have been some other length so that we can listen at any time to what there is to hear ... in ordinary circumstances or in extraordinary circumstances."[50] Moreover, as Reinhard Kapp and Dörte Schmidt have emphasized, "tacet" by definition refers to only one voice of an ensemble.[51] A performance of *4'33"* is always embedded in its social context: remaining silent while other things are happening. Cage also replaced "any inst[r]ument" from the graphic version with the more personal "any instrumentalist," a tiny but nonetheless revealing detail with regard to this shift of perspective towards human agency.[52]

Fig. 2 Woodstock Artists Association, invitation card for August 29, 1952

WOODSTOCK ARTISTS ASSOCIATION

invites you to attend a concert and lecture-demonstration by

JOHN CAGE and DAVID TUDOR

Maverick Concert Hall Friday August 29 8:15 P. M.

The program will include works by John Cage, Pierre Boulez, Morton Feldman and Christian Wolff

Admission $1.00 plus tax Benefit - Artists Welfare Fund

The note also gives an account of the durations that Tudor supposedly used in the premiere. While these durations (0'33", 2'40", 1'20") must have been the source for Tudor's reconstructed scores, they neither correspond to the graphic version nor to the program for the premiere in Woodstock (30", 2'23", 1'40"). As if this wasn't discrepancy enough, the program announces 4'33" as: "4 pieces ... john cage. 4'33", 30", 2'23", 1'40"." The fact that three movements were announced as "pieces" and that *4'33"* appears to be the first of four pieces could be a printing error of comparatively little relevance. On the other hand, Tudor himself selected the program and arranged the order carefully.[53] Furthermore, as indicated by the invitation card for the Woodstock concert, it was announced as "concert and lecture-demonstration" [→ fig. 2]. Whether the lecture was part of the performance cannot be determined conclusively.

It is also possible that there was some confusion about the fourth Cage piece in the concert, because, besides *4'33"* with its three movements, Tudor also performed Cage's *Water Music*. The title of this work is supposed to be changed to the name of the city where one performs the composition, followed by the date of performance. That Friday evening it was called "aug. 29, 1952." However, in a 1972 video performance of the silent piece, which took place in four different locations in Manhattan, Cage himself announced *4'33"* as a composition with four movements.[54]

Still, all this doesn't explain the confusion about the durations of the movements as such in the different documents. One hypothesis might be that the durations in the original score did not differ from either the Woodstock program or the graphic version at all. Larry Solomon's discussion of the durations also points in this direction.[55] In the end, this would mean that Tudor, while reverse-engineering the original score in 1982, was not sure about the original durations. The timing notes indicate that he speculated about the two different sets of durations and took both possibilities into account. He decided on 33", 2'40", and 1'20", presumably because Cage had said so in the typewritten score: "At Woodstock, N.Y., August 29, 1952, the title was 4'33" and the three parts were 33", 2'40", and 1'20"." It is very likely that these durations in the typewritten linguistic version emerged from Cage's error of recall. Later he acknowledged that he "might have made a mistake in addition."[56] Kyle Gann made the interesting observation that the digits of the contradictory durations are identical, which would further indicate a slip of the memory.[57] All in all, it must be emphasized that the different sets of durations became an issue only after Cage had written the linguistic notation.

In 1982 Tudor included the durations in his reconstructions of the original score based on a questionable comparison he mentioned in an interview with Peter Dickinson in 1987 and later with Reinhard Oehlschlägel in 1992. Tudor reports that he had discovered that the times of his Xerox copy of the Kremen score were different from those in his programs and that he concluded that Cage "instead of trying to reproduce the original score for Irwin Kremen ... must have tossed the coins and come out with three different lengths in the movements."[58] Irwin Kremen comments: "Both the Xerox copy and the *Source* reproduction clearly indicate the time lengths of the movements, again 30", 2'23", and 1'40", precisely those of the Woodstock performance and presumably of the lost score. David could not have made his claimed comparison! He imported it into his account." Furthermore, according to Kremen, "what David says he figured out —that John instead of trying to reproduce the original score tossed the coins and came up with different time lengths for the Kremen score—goes entirely counter to what John wrote in the Tacet publication."[59] Here Kremen refers to the fourth version of *4'33"*, the calligraphic linguistic version. Most importantly, Cage changed the note when approached by Peters in 1986 to provide an autograph of this score. He added the remark that "a copy in proportional notation was made for Irwin Kremen." The fact that Cage calls it a copy clearly rules out Tudor's assumption. Cage also added the time lengths of the movements from the graphic score to the note of the calligraphic version. This results in two contradictory sets of durations, which obviously did not

49 As with *Water Music*, the identity of the piece is subject to the actual circumstances of its performance.
50 Cage, *I–VI*, p. 26–27.
51 See Dörte Schmidt's text in this book [→ p. 69].
52 This issue will also occur in the instructions for *0'00"* described in detail in Hans-Friedrich Bormann's text in this book [→ pp. 222ff].
53 See Holzaepfel, "Cage and Tudor," p. 174. The program is reproduced in this book [→ p. 87].
54 This performance is part of the experimental video documentation *A Tribute to John Cage* by Nam June Paik, 1973 [→ pp. 178f].
55 Larry Solomon, *The Sounds of Silence: John Cage and 4'33"* (2002), accessed June 11, 2012. http://solomonsmusic.net/4min33se.htm.
56 Cage, *I–VI*, p. 21.
57 Gann, *No Such Thing As Silence*, p. 177.
58 David Tudor in an interview with Peter Dickinson, 1987, Dickinson (ed.) *CageTalk: Dialogues With and About John Cage*, (Rochester, NY: University of Rochester Press, 2006), p. 87.
59 Irwin Kremen in an email to the author, May 30, 2012.

cause any artistic problems for the composer. Accordingly, they should not be interpreted as mistakes, but rather as a result of Cage welcoming the effects of indeterminacy:

> Error is drawing a straight line between
> anticipation of what should happen and
> what actually happens. What actually
> happens is however in a total not
> linear situation and is responsible
> generally. Therefore error is a fiction, has
> no
> reality
> in fact.
> Errorless music is written by not giving
> a thought to cause and effect.
> Any other
> kind of music always has mistakes in it.[60]

John Cage made another notational version of *4′33″* on August 31, 1986. It was written on the occasion of his performance of the piece in the exhibition *Die 60er Jahre – Kölns Weg zur Kunstmetropole: Vom Happening zum Kunstmarkt*. It can be regarded as an autographic performance score of the linguistic version. Cage glued it into the artists guestbook of Wulf Herzogenrath, the curator of this exhibition, who kindly provided the score for publication in this book [→ p. 141]. As an instrument Cage chose an empty glass, which he put upside down on a table. When the performance began, Cage pressed the stopwatch and turned the glass around. After the first and second movement, Cage turned the glass upside down again for ten seconds each time to indicate the "pauses" between the movements. The empty glass is a metaphor for silence and emptiness used in Cage's *Lecture on Nothing*, first printed in August 1959:

> I have nothing to say and I am saying it and that is poetry as I need it. This space of time is organized. We need not fear these silences,—we may love them. This is a composed talk for I am making it just as I compose a piece of music. It is like a glass of milk. We need the glass and we need the milk. Or again it is like an empty glass into which at any moment anything may be poured.[61]

Herzogenrath recalls Cage sitting in his office throwing dice to determine the durations for the performance, so obviously Cage was able to re-compose *4′33″* using more time-efficient chance operations than those which took four days to perform in 1952. Again, Cage came up with a new set of durations:
I. 54″ (10″ pause)
II. 2′09″ (10″ pause)
III. 1′30″.[62]

These durations used in the performance are notated in seconds in the left column of the score. Additionally, in the right column, which probably represents a conversion from seconds to minutes and seconds, the score shows yet another set: 54″, 2′49″, 1′, adding up to 4′43″. While this right column might be the result of an incorrect conversion and was clearly not followed during the performance, the actual performance durations are only specified in seconds. If Cage used a regular stopwatch counting in minutes and seconds, he must have either worked out the conversion in his head while performing or used another sheet with the correct conversion. However, what Cage decided to include in the artists guestbook was the preparatory document—his own interpretation of the linguistic version—showing that it simply "could have been some other length."[63]

In Zero Time: *0′00″ (4′33″ No. 2)* and Its Derivatives

The first performance of *0′00″* was the writing of the score by the composer during a concert in Tokyo on October 24, 1962 (first margination only).[64] This causality dilemma of a performance constituting its own notation is reminiscent of the changing title of *4′33″*. Cage's precise and yet highly indeterminate use of language characterizes all silent pieces based on linguistic notation. The score consists of a single US-Letter page in Cage's calligraphic handwriting. *4′33″ No. 2* lacks any temporal frame and its title, *0′00″*, rather than indicating the duration of its performance, refers to the fact that it is a composition "in zero time." "Zero time" is a term coined by Christian Wolff, which Cage refers to at the beginning of the ninth interview in *For the Birds*. He explains: "'Zero time' exists when we don't notice the passage of time, when we don't measure it."[65] Wolff himself had expounded: "[T]he zero I take to mean no time at all, that is, no measurable time, that is any time at all."[66] Thus, *0′00″* addresses the very aporia of experiencing time which is highly subjective. The composition is consequently subtitled as a "solo to be performed in any way by anyone." And as a solo it is subject to the performer's individual concept of time. Avoiding the self-organization of materials—no feedback—Cage endeavors a "silence full of noises"[67] by allowing things to appear with the aid of technology: "In a situation with maximum amplification (no feedback), perform a disciplined action." For a detailed discussion of this work, its score and its composition sketches see Hans-Friedrich Bormann's text [→ pp. 222 ff].[68]

0′00″ reappears as *Solo for Voice 8 (0′0″)* [sic] in John Cage's *Song Books*, which were published in 1970 by C.F. Peters. In this version, not only has the title been modified but Cage has also left out the subtitle, dedication, dating, and parts of the directions. *Solos for Voice 24, 28, 62,* and *63* are variants of *Solo for Voice 8 (0′0″)* denoting with algorithmic precision that the performer should "engage in some other activity" than before. Also, *0′00″* was the origin for two new compositions, both included in *Song Books* as *Solo for Voice 23. 0′00″ No. 2* and *Solo for Voice 26. 0′00″ No. 2B*. William Fetterman interpreted *0′00″ No. 2* as the written score, made after the fact of *Reunion*, performed by John Cage, Marcel Duchamp, Teeny Duchamp, Gordon Mumma, David Tudor, David Behrman, and Lowell Cross at the Ryerson Theatre in Toronto on March 5, 1968.[69] For this performance, Lowell Cross had constructed a chessboard with a photo-electric

60 Cage, "45′ for a Speaker," in *Silence*, pp. 167–68.
61 Cage, "Lecture on Nothing," in *Silence*, pp. 109–10. (The position of the words in the original text has not been reproduced). The first line of this quote was recorded for the 1990 video production introducing Tudor's re-enactment of the premiere of *4′33″*.
62 Remembering the peculiar listing of *4′33″* in the Woodstock program as four pieces, it is remarkable that in this performance score [→ p. 87] Cage also refers to the movements as pieces.
63 Cage, *I–VI*, p. 26.
64 See Fetterman, *John Cage's Theatre Pieces*, p. 84, and the score *4′33″ (No. 2) (0′00″)* published by C.F. Peters (EP6796) [→ p. 143].
65 John Cage, *For the Birds. John Cage in Conversation with Daniel Charles* (London / New York: Marion Boyars, 2009), p. 209. Cage added a footnote: "This expression 'zero time' comes from Christian Wolff. He was the first to use zero time in his compositions, concurrently with clock time."
66 Christian Wolff, 1965, as quoted in Daniel Charles, "Music as Antimetaphor," in Eero Tarasti (ed.), *Musical Signification: Essays in the Semitic Theory and Analysis of Music* (Berlin/New York: Gryter, 1955) p. 32.
67 Cage, *For the Birds*, p. 210.
68 See also Fetterman, *John Cage's Theatre Pieces*, pp. 86 ff.
69 Ibid., p. 91.

switching mechanism, through which the whole audio system was routed.[70] When Cage and the Duchamps played a game of chess, the audio of all the musicians involved was controlled by the position of the chess figures on the board.

As Cross reports, Cage insisted that the chessboard be equipped with contact microphones even if the amplified sounds were hardly noticeable during the performance.[71] This anecdote illustrates Cage's conceptual concerns, because according to the score of *0'00"*, which *Reunion* was supposed to be a realization of, a disciplined action had to be performed with maximum amplification. Thus, *0'00" No. 2* was implemented in the *Reunion* performance, even if this performance encompassed several other aspects. *0'00" No. 2B* is very much akin to *0'00" No. 2*; the type of game and number of players is changed.

Correspondence as Score: *WGBH-TV*

The score of *WGBH-TV for a Composer and Technicians*—a "composition for TV," as Cage calls it—consists of three items: A handwritten letter from Eva Smerchek from the Caledonia Woman's Club asking for an artistic donation for an auction for the benefit of retarded children, a reply message from John Cage and a sheet with notes for a 30 min. telecast written on the back of the original envelope from Smerchek. "This envelope together with your letter and this one of mine will constitute the m[anu]s[cript], to be published by the Henmar Press of C.F. Peters," wrote Cage in his reply. This score was dedicated to Nam June Paik and published by C.F. Peters in 1971. The notes indicate how the TV composition is to be recorded: "Camera to focus without movement on work table [–] no face (just ms; hands, etc.) [–], microphones [–] high amplification [–] (not contact) to pick up sound of work." Cage's instruction not to use contact microphones is interesting with regard to the fact that he himself had performed *0'00"* with a pencil picked up by a contact microphone while doing his correspondence.[72] The relationship between *0'00"* and *WGBH-TV* can be seen as derivative. Writing the correspondence is seen as a disciplined action. In this case, the result constitutes a new notation. For a more detailed analysis of the work please see Dörte Schmidt's text [→ pp. 71f].

Cage's Final Reworking of the Silent Piece: *One³ = 4'33" (0'00") + 𝄞*

One³ has only been performed by John Cage himself, first on November 14, 1989 in Kyoto, Japan, and again at Symphony Space in New York, on December 4, 1990. A manuscript draft exists which must have been made in Acrosanti, where John Cage had participated at the second "Minds for History" conference, October 15–19, 1989. Arcosanti is an experimental town in the high desert of Arizona, seventy miles north of metropolitan Phoenix. It was designed by Paolo Soleri showing his concept of *arcology* (architecture + ecology). David Mayne, whose name, address, and phone number appear on this draft manuscript, was involved in filming the conference and also shot an interview with Cage at the conference. Later, in 1993, he produced a documentary film on Soleri.

Furthermore, a faxleaf including the score is addressed to Yutaka Fujishima from Mimi Johnson of Artservices, and is dated October 19, 1989. Mimi Johnson's nonprofit organization Performing Artservices, Inc., founded in 1972, promoted and presented Cage's work and concert activities at this time. Cage had been asked to perform *4'33"*, but as he explains in an interview from 1990, he didn't want to do the silent piece, because he thought that "silence had changed from what it was and I wanted to indicate that." Further pushing the instruction from *0'00"* "in a situation with maximum amplification (no feedback)," Cage asks for an arrangement of the sound system so that "the whole hall is just at the edge of feedback ... not actually feeding back, but feeling like it might." Probably still in the frame of mind of the "Minds for History" conference and the ideas of *arcology*, Cage added that being on the edge of feedback "is what I think our environmental situation is now.... The world is in a bad situation, and largely through the way we misuse technology." Furthermore in *One³* the act of listening, and thus sharing the perspective with the audience, becomes the actual performance. Cage described the performance as follows:

> I went into the auditorium and sat with the audience and listened to this situation, to the silence which was on the edge of feedback, and without a watch measuring the time as I had in *4'33"*—so that was my inner-clock. In Leningrad [now, again St. Petersburg], Sofia Gubaidulina had said that she liked my music but she didn't like the watches, and I should remember that there was an "inner-clock." So I was doing the inner-clock (laughs), and it turned out that I sat there for twelve minutes and a half, more or less (laughs); and then I went back on the stage in front the audience and the feedback level was reduced, and that was the end of it. [73]

One³ represents the last re-working of *4'33"*, but in 1989 Cage started to transfer his concept of nothingness to the visual domain and composed his first and only film *One¹¹*.

The Computer-Generated Score of *One¹¹*

The 93:00 min long 35 mm film *One¹¹* was produced in collaboration with filmmaker and film score composer Henning Lohner from 1989 to 1992. *One¹¹* is synchronized with a soundtrack containing Cage's *composition 103* (for 103 musicians). Both compositions—visual and auditive—contain seventeen scenes, equaling the number of chapters in James Joyce's *Finnegans Wake*. In a conversation with Henning Lohner in New York on December 23, 1989 Cage mentioned, that "the film will be about the effect of light on an empty room. But no room is actually empty."[74]—a comment clearly reminiscent of his article on Rauschenberg from 1961.[75]

Just like *One³*, *One¹¹* is a part of Cage's series of number pieces for solo performer, in this case Van Carlson, the cameraman. The movements of the lights, the movements, lens-angles

70 See Michael Nyman, *Experimental Music: Cage and Beyond* (Cambridge: Cambridge University Press, 2002), p. 98.

71 See Dieter Daniels's text in this book [→ pp. 23ff]; see also Lowell Cross, "*Reunion:* John Cage, Marcel Duchamp, Electronic Music and Chess," *Leonardo Music Journal*, Vol. 9 (December, 1999), pp. 35–42.

72 David Tudor recalled this performance version of *0'00"* from the 1960s in an interview with William Fetterman from March 8, 1989, in Fetterman, *John Cage's Theatre Pieces*, p. 88.

73 John Cage in an interview with William Fetterman, August 10, 1990, in ibid., p. 95.

74 John Cage in an interview with Henning Lohner from the film essay *Making of "One¹¹"* by Henning Lohner, Accessed June 11, 2012. http://vimeo.com/14869738.

75 John Cage, "On Robert Rauschenberg," p. 103.

and fades of the camera, and the editing of the film were directed by means of chance operations using the I Ching. These three categories also constitute the three different parts of the score: the light movements, the camera operations, and the editing process. The score for *One[11]* was first generated in New York using custom computer software and then realized in the Munich TV Studios, Germany. Each of the seventeen scenes consists of various takes with chance-determined instructions. Thanks to Henning Lohner's support we can reproduce six exemplary sheets of the score within this book [→ pp. 161 ff].

On June 12, 1992 *One[11]* was completed. The editing also followed a composed score, which required fades, superimpositions of the film material, and film scenes played in reverse motion.

Discarding the socio-political metaphors of feedback in *One[3]* and once more referring to the Kantian concept of the disinterested pleasure in the observation of the aesthetically beautiful, Cage commented on *One[11]* in 1992:

> Both music and laughter—and I think we can say now: light, too—give pleasure without having any meaning whatsoever. And it's through their changes; the changes that take place with sounds, and the changes that take place in the sound of laughter, and the changes that take place in intensity, and differences between light and dark. Noticing such things, one is free of the problems of politics and economics, I think. Even perhaps free of oneself.[76]

Having nothing to say and saying it represents Cage's notion of a poetics of art that is in accord with the reception aesthetics of disinterested pleasure. After all, his continuous reworking and the many versions of his silent piece show the paradoxical diversity of nothingness within this poetical framework. In his *Lecture On Nothing* he put it as follows: "What silence requires is that I go on talking ... Slowly, we have the feeling we are getting nowhere. That is a pleasure, which will continue."[77]

76 John Cage in an interview with Henning Lohner from the film essay *Making of "One[11]"* by Henning Lohner.
77 John Cage "Lecture on Nothing," p. 109 and 119.

Scores and Documents

Versions, Derivatives, Sequels,
Reconstructions, and Recordings of *4′33″*

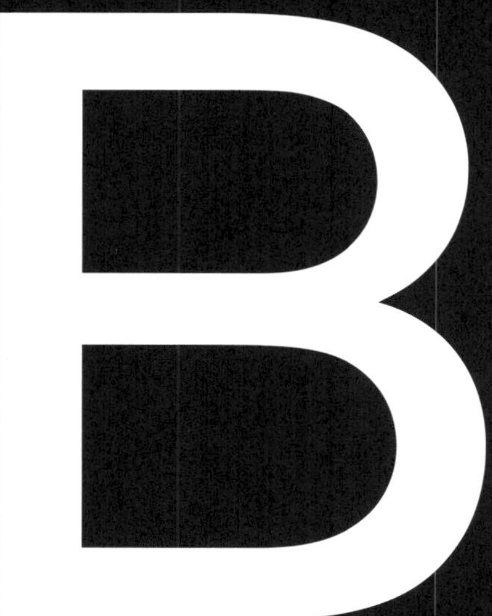

Compiled by
Jan Thoben, Dieter Daniels,
and Inke Arns

The reproduced materials include editions of scores by C.F. Peters
as well as manuscripts and composition sketches.
Unless otherwise indicated, all the documents are reproduced in true size.

Woodstock Artists Association

Program for August 29, 1952
Maverick Concert Hall

6½ × 8½ in.
Woodstock Artists Association
and Museum Archives and Library

Program from a concert with piano music played by David Tudor including the premiere of John Cage's *4′33″*. It is listed as "4 pieces."

Woodstock Artists Association

presents

john cage, composer

david tudor, pianist

PROGRAM

aug. 29, 1952 .... john cage
for piano .... christian wolff
extensions #3 .... morton feldman
3 pieces for piano .... earle brown
premier sonata .... pierre boulez
2 parts
5 intermissions ..... morton feldman
for prepared piano ... christian wolff
4 pieces .... john cage
4' 33"
30"
2' 23"
1' 40"
the banshee .... henry cowell

PATRONS: Mrs. Emmet Edwards, chairman; Mr. and Mrs. Sidney Berkowitz, Dr. and Mrs. Hans Cohn, Mr. and Mrs. Henry Cowell, Mr. and Mrs. Rollin Crampton, Mr. and Mrs. Roland d'Albis, Mr. and Mrs. Pierre Henrotte, Dr. and Mrs. William M. Hitzig, Mrs. Charles Rosen, Dr. and Mrs. Harold Rugg, Mr. and Mrs. Alexander Semmler, Mr. and Mrs. John Striebel, Mr. and Mrs. Richard Thibaut, Jr., Capt. C. H. D. van der Loo, Miss Alice Wardwell.

MAVERICK CONCERT HALL

Friday, August 29 8:15 P. M.

BENEFIT ARTISTS WELFARE FUND

David Tudor

First reconstruction of John Cage's now lost original score of *4′33″* used at its premiere 1982

Pencil on paper
15 pages, 8½ × 11 in. (US Letter)
Getty Research Institute, Los Angeles, Special Collections ID 980039
Box 7, Folder 11

David Tudor, the pianist for the premiere of *4′33″* in the Maverick Concert Hall in Woodstock, NY on August 29, 1952, wrote this score on the occasion of a reenactment of the original performance. This reenactment took place as part of the Symphony Space *Wall to Wall John Cage* concert in New York on March 13, 1982. This score is dated as of Aug. 1952, the date when *4′33″* was composed.

4' 33"

JOHN CAGE

1/2" = 1 SEC.

1

2

3

60

15

4

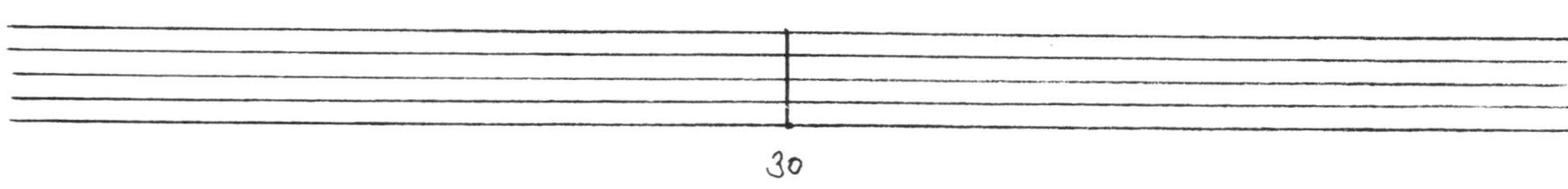

45

5

1.

6

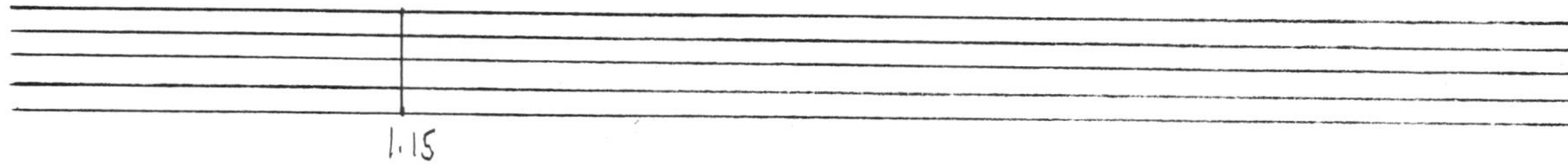

1.30

7

2.

8

2.15

Courtesy of the Getty Research Institute, Los Angeles

9

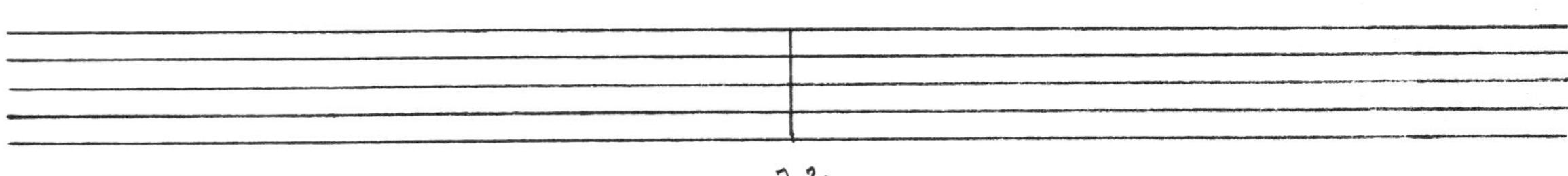

Courtesy of the Getty Research Institute, Los Angeles

10

11

60

.15

12

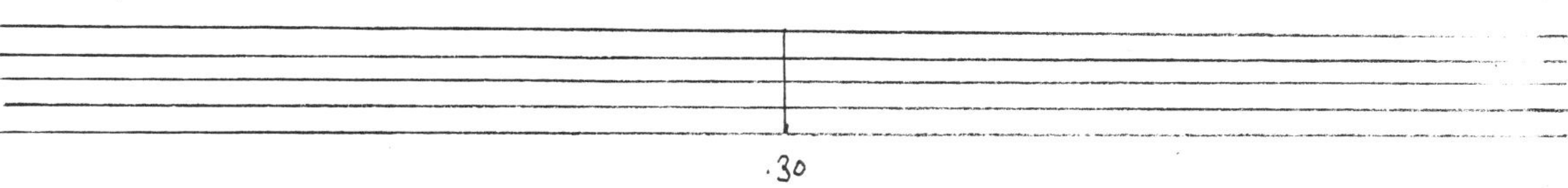

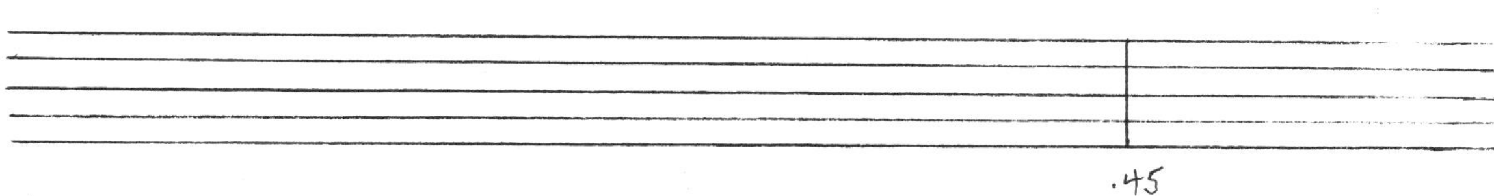

13

1.

Courtesy of the Getty Research Institute, Los Angeles

14

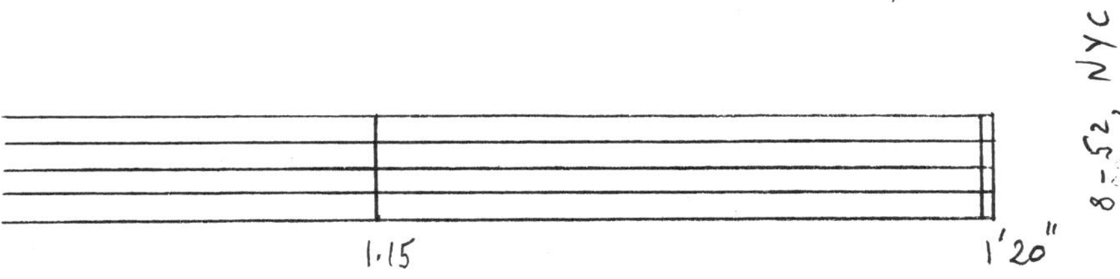

David Tudor

Timing notes
for the first reconstructed score of *4′33″*
1982

Pencil on paper
1 page, 8 1/2 × 11 in. (US Letter)
Getty Research Institute, Los Angeles, Special Collections ID 980039
Box 7, Folder 11

David Tudor noted the durations to establish the measurements for his first reconstruction of the original score of *4′33″* [for a discussion of the durations → pp. 78, 80 ff].

16 1/2
80
40

[1 = 6 + 6 = 12
[2 = 4 1/2

[3 = 6 + 6
[4 = 6 + 6

[5 = 6 + 6
[6 = 6 + 6

[7 = 6 + 6
[8 = 6 + 6

[9 = 6
[10 = 2

[11 = 6 + 6
[12 = 6 + 6

[13 = 6 + 6
[14 = 4

15 = 7 1/2
30 = 15
45 = 22 1/2
60 = 30

33″ 4 1/8 8 1/4
2′ 40″ 20 40
1′ 20″ 10 20

30″
2′ 23″
1′ 40″

7″ = 56″
1″ = 1/8″

30/8 = 3 3/4
143/8 ~~18 5/8~~ 17 7/8
100/8 12 1/2
273/8 = 34 1/8

[1 = 6″
[2 = 2 1/4″

[3 = 6″
[4 = 6″

[5 = 6″
[6 = 6″

[7 = 6″
[8 = 6″

[9 = 4″
[10 = 0

[11 = 6″
[12 = 6″

[13 = 6″
[14 = 2″

15/4 = 3 3/4
30/4 = 7 1/2
45/4 = 11 1/4
60/4 = 15

David Tudor

Second reconstruction of John Cage's now lost original score of *4′33″* used at its premiere 1989

Pencil and ink on commercial stave paper
8 pages, 9½ × 12½ in.
[Reproduction in 92% of original size.
The editiors and the publisher have decided to include the score in reduced size to fit our format.
This reduction renders Tudor's durational marking "60 ♩ = 2½ cm." moot.]
Original manuscript written on 2 folded sheets, 12½ × 19 in.
Getty Research Institute, Los Angeles, Special Collections ID 980039, Box 7, Folder 11
Also published in reduced format by C.F. Peters in 2012 as part of the
4′33″: John Cage centennial edition (EP 6777c).

David Tudor's second reconstruction was written for a performance on the occasion of the video production *I Have Nothing to Say, And I Am Saying It* by Allan Miller and Vivian Perlis for PBS (video documentation about John Cage), New York, 1990.

I

60 ♩ = 2½ cm.

4/4

.16

.32

→ .33

1

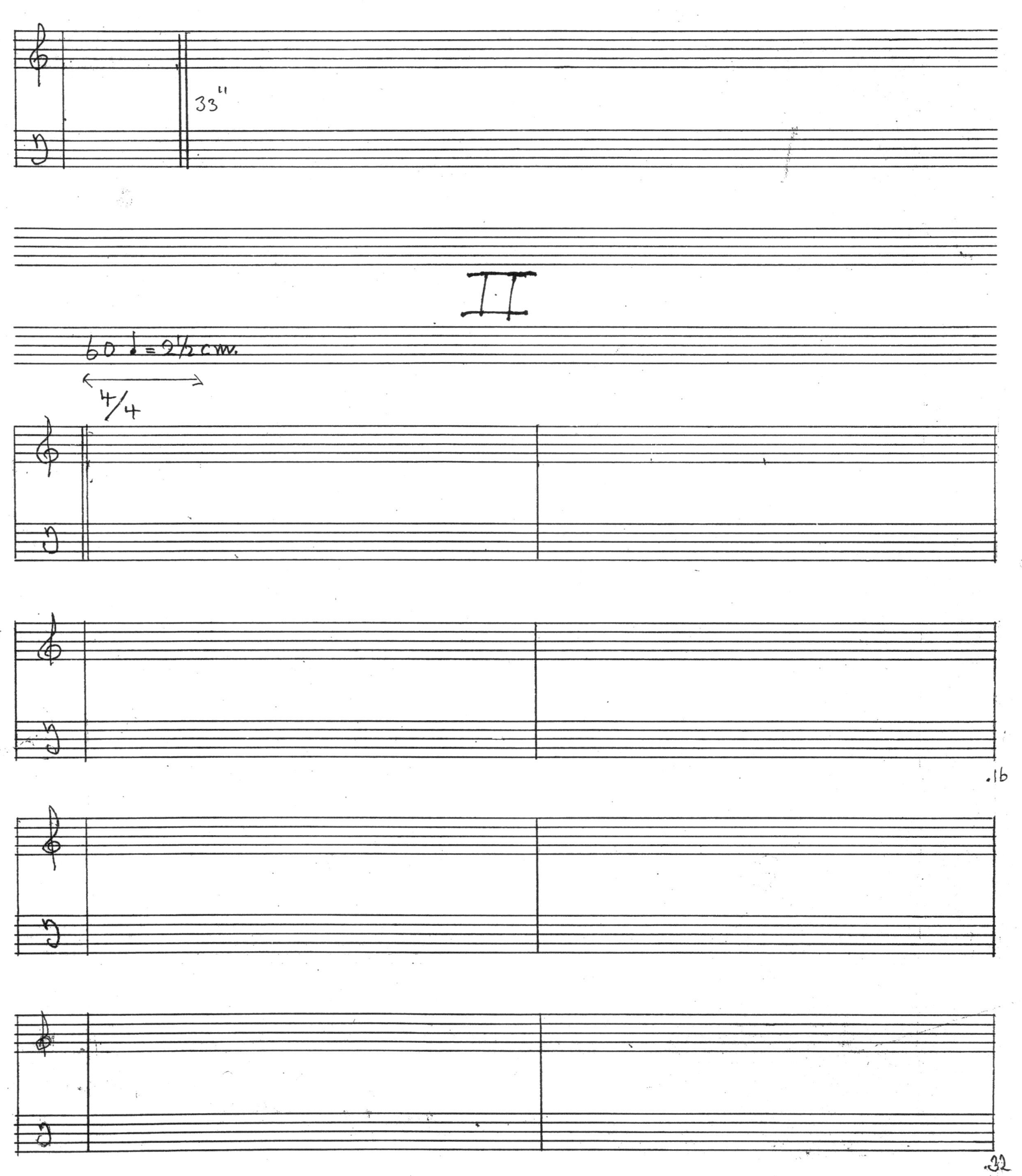
33"
II
60 ♩ = 2½ cm.
4/4
.16
.32
2
ROBBINS MUSIC CORPORATION
NEW YORK

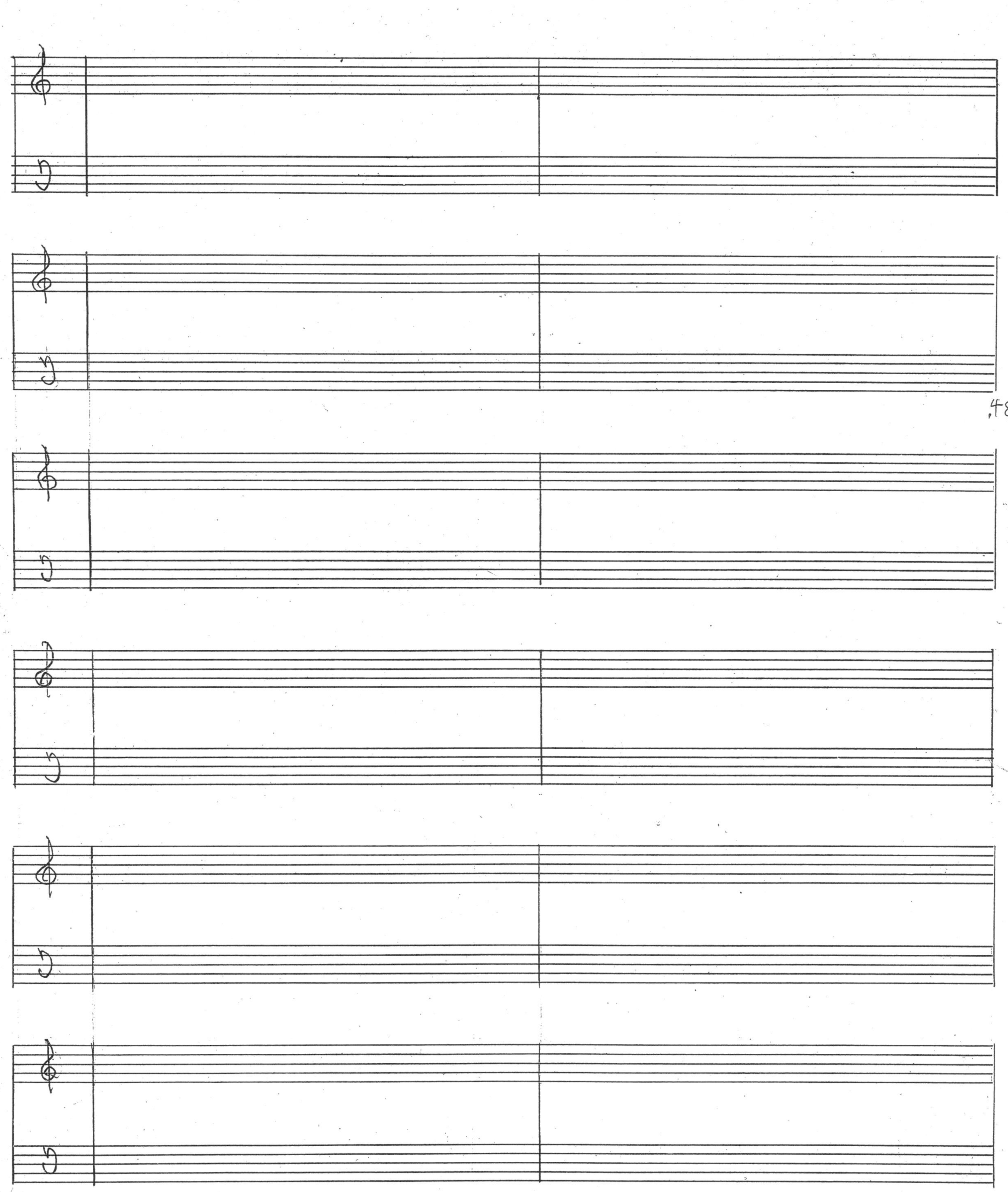
.48
1.20
3

1.36

2.

2.08

4

ROBBINS MUSIC CORPORATION
NEW YORK

2.24

2.40″

5

ROBBINS MUSIC CORPORATION
NEW YORK

III

60 ♩= 2½ cw.

4/4

.16

.32

6

.48

ROBBINS MUSIC CORPORATION
NEW YORK

1.12

1'20''

8

John Cage

4′33″: For Any Inst[r]ument or Combination of Instruments
Graphic score in proportional notation
1953

Printed version of ink on paper manuscript
10 pages, 8½ × 11 in. (US Letter)
As published by C.F. Peters in 1993 (EP 6777a);
first published in 1967 in *Source: Music of the Avant-Garde* #2, July 1967,
also published by C.F. Peters in 2012 as part of the *4′33″: John Cage centennial edition* (EP 6777c).
The original manuscript consists of 3 folded sheets, 11 × 17 in. (US Tabloid),
Museum of Modern Arts, New York, Object Number: 1636.2012

This score represents John Cage's second version of the *4′33″* notation. It is dated as of Aug. 1952, the date when *4′33″* was composed. Cage dedicated this score to Irwin Kremen and gave it to him as a gift for his 28th birthday on June 5, 1953. It is the oldest existing notational document of *4′33″* handwritten by Cage.

4′ 33″

FOR ANY INSTUMENT OR COMBINATION OF INSTRUMENTS

John Cage

FOR IRWIN KREMEN

1/8 PAGE = 7 INCHES = 56"

60

2'23"

60

8-52; N.Y.C.

1'40"

John Cage

Typewritten linguistic version of *4′33″* (Tacet) Probably late 1950s

Facsimile version of the original typescript
1 page, 8½ × 11 in. (US Letter)
Getty Research Institute, Los Angeles, Special Collections ID 980039
Box 7, Folder 11

This facsimile of the now lost original typescript can be found in the David Tudor papers at the Getty Research Institute, Los Angeles. It was made before John Cage signed a contract with C.F. Peters/Henmar Press. The composer's earlier facsimile copyright annotation is stamped on the paper. Judging from the handwriting it may have been David Tudor who added "John Cage" and backdated it to 1953. The typewritten linguistic score is dedicated to Irwin Kremen.

I

TACET

II

TACET

III

TACET

NOTE: The title of this work is the total length in minutes and seconds of its performance. At Woodstock, N.Y., August 29, 1952, the title was 4' 33" and the three parts were 33", 2' 40", and 1' 20". It was performed by David Tudor, pianist, who indicated the beginnings of parts by closing, the endings by opening, the keyboard lid. However, the work may be performed by any instrumentalist or combination of instrumentalists and last any length of time.

FOR IRWIN KREMEN JOHN CAGE

John Cage

Typewritten linguistic version of *4′33″* (Tacet) ca. 1960

As published by C.F. Peters in 1960 (EP 6777), out of print
1 page, 8½ × 11 in. (US Letter)
Also published in reduced format by C.F. Peters in 2012 as part of the *4′33″: John Cage centennial edition* (EP 6777c)

As the third version composed, the typewritten linguistic score was first published in 1960 by C.F. Peters. The original typescript was probably written on Cage's own typewriter.

I

TACET

II

TACET

III

TACET

NOTE: The title of this work is the total length in minutes and seconds of its performance. At Woodstock, N.Y., August 29, 1952, the title was 4' 33" and the three parts were 33", 2' 40", and 1' 20". It was performed by David Tudor, pianist, who indicated the beginnings of parts by closing, the endings by opening, the keyboard lid. However, the work may be performed by any instrumentalist or combination of instrumentalists and last any length of time.

FOR IRWIN KREMEN JOHN CAGE

John Cage

Typewritten linguistic version of *4′33″* (Tacet) n. d.

Typewritten copy
1 page, 8½ × 11 in. (US Letter)
As published by C.F. Peters (EP 6777)
Out of print

Copy of the typewritten original made with another typewriter by Hank Haffner of C.F. Peters.

I

TACET

II

TACET

III

TACET

NOTE: The title of this work is the total length in minutes and seconds of its performance. At Woodstock, N.Y., August 29, 1952, the title was 4' 33" and the three parts were 33", 2' 40", and 1' 20". It was performed by David Tudor, pianist, who indicated the beginnings of parts by closing, the endings by opening, the keyboard lid. However, the work may be performed by an instrumentalist or combination of instrumentalists and last any length of time.

FOR IRWIN KREMEN JOHN CAGE

John Cage

Modified typewritten linguistic version of *4′33″* (Tacet) ca. 1986

Copy of published typographic score from ca. 1960
additional remarks by hand ca. 1986
1 page, 8 1/2 × 11 in. (US Letter)
NYPL Music Division, John Cage Music Manuscript Collection
JPB 94-24, Folder 171

In 1986 C.F. Peters published a calligraphic linguistic version of *4′33″* for which Cage revised the note of the typewritten version and made additional remarks added by hand.

I

TACET

II

TACET

III

TACET

NOTE: The title of this work is the total length in minutes and seconds of its performance. At Woodstock, N.Y., August 29, 1952, the title was 4' 33" and the three parts were 33", 2' 40", and 1' 20". It was performed by David Tudor, pianist, who indicated the beginnings of parts by closing, the endings by opening, the keyboard lid. However, the work may be performed by any instrumentalist or combination of instrumentalists and THE MOVEMENTS MAY last any lengths of time.

AFTER THE WOODSTOCK PERFORMANCE A COPY IN PROPORTIONAL NOTATION WAS MADE FOR IRWIN KREMEN. IN IT THE TIMELENGTHS OF THE MOVEMENTS WERE 30" 2'23" and 1'40". It

FOR IRWIN KREMEN JOHN CAGE

30"
223
140

112
1/2
2/24

6777

John Cage

4′33″: For Any Instrument or Combination of Instruments
Linguistic score in calligraphic handwriting (Tacet)
1986

Printed version of ink on paper manuscript
3 pages, 9 × 12 in.
[Reproduction in 97% of original size.
The editiors and the publisher have decided to include the score in reduced size to fit our format.]
As published by C.F. Peters
in 1986 (EP 6777)

The calligraphic linguistic notation of *4′33″* is a reworking of the earlier typewritten score. It is dedicated to Irwin Kremen.

4′ 33″

FOR ANY INSTRUMENT OR COMBINATION OF INSTRUMENTS

John Cage

NOTE: THE TITLE OF THIS WORK IS THE TOTAL LENGTH IN MINUTES AND SECONDS OF ITS PERFORMANCE. AT WOODSTOCK, N.Y., AUGUST 29, 1952, THE TITLE WAS 4'33" AND THE THREE PARTS WERE 33", 2'40", AND 1'20". IT WAS PERFORMED BY DAVID TUDOR, PIANIST, WHO INDICATED THE BEGINNINGS OF PARTS BY CLOSING, THE ENDINGS BY OPENING, THE KEYBOARD LID. AFTER THE WOODSTOCK PERFORMANCE, A COPY IN PROPORTIONAL NOTATION WAS MADE FOR IRWIN KREMEN. IN IT THE TIMELENGTHS OF THE MOVEMENTS WERE 30", 2'23", AND 1'40". HOWEVER, THE WORK MAY BE PERFORMED BY ANY INSTRUMENTALIST(S) AND THE MOVEMENTS MAY LAST ANY LENGTHS OF TIME.

FOR IRWIN KREMEN

I

TACET

II

TACET

III

TACET

John Cage

For Wulf Herzogenrath with friendship silently
Performance score of *4′33″*
1986

Red ink on paper
1 page, 8¼ × 9¾ in.
Handwritten performance score of *4′33″*

This score was used by John Cage for his performance at the opening of the exhibition *Die 60er Jahre – Kölns Weg zur Kunstmetropole*: *Vom Happening zum Kunstmarkt* in Cologne on Aug 31, 1986. When asked for an entry, John Cage glued this score into Wulf Herzogenrath's artists guestbook. The performance was recorded on video by Klaus vom Bruch [→ pp. 180 f].

for Wulf Herzogenrath with friendship silently

1st piece	0	I	0	
	54		54	
10"	64		(1'04")	
2nd piece	193	II	(3'53")	
10"	203	203	4'03"	
	303	III	5'03"	

John Cage 8/31/86

Courtesy of Wulf Herzogenrath

John Cage

0′00″ (4′33″ No. 2)
1962

Printed version of ink on paper manuscript
1 page, 8½ × 11 in (US Letter)
As published by C.F. Peters in 1962 (EP 6796)

The score consists of a single US Letter page in Cage's calligraphic handwriting. It is dedicated to Yoko Ono and Toshi Ichiyanagi.

0'00"
SOLO TO BE PERFORMED IN ANY WAY BY ANYONE

FOR YOKO ONO AND TOSHI ICHIYANAGI
TOKYO, OCT. 24, 1962
John Cage

IN A SITUATION PROVIDED WITH MAXIMUM AMPLIFICATION (NO FEEDBACK), PERFORM A DISCIPLINED ACTION.

WITH ANY INTERRUPTIONS.
FULFILLING IN WHOLE OR PART AN OBLIGATION TO OTHERS.
NO TWO PERFORMANCES TO BE OF THE SAME ACTION, NOR MAY THAT ACTION BE THE PERFORMANCE OF A "MUSICAL" COMPOSITION.
NO ATTENTION TO BE GIVEN THE SITUATION (ELECTRONIC, MUSICAL, THEATRICAL).

10·25·62

THE FIRST PERFORMANCE WAS THE WRITING OF THIS MANUSCRIPT (FIRST MARGINATION ONLY).

THIS IS <u>4'33" (NO.2)</u> AND ALSO PT. 3 OF A WORK OF WHICH <u>ATLAS ECLIPTICALIS</u> IS PT. 1.

John Cage

Silent pieces from *Song Books* (*Solos for Voice 8, 23, 24, 26, 28, 62* and *63*) 1970

6 pages, 8 1/8 × 11 5/8 in.
As published by C.F. Peters in 1970 in two volumes (EP 6806a, EP 6806b)

The silent pieces from *Song Books* contain linguistic instructions. *0′00″* reappears as *Solo for Voice 8 (0′0″)* [sic]. Not only has the title in this version been modified but Cage has also left out the subtitle, dedication, dating, and parts of the instruction. *Solos for Voice 24, 28, 62,* and *63* are variants of *Solo for Voice 8 (0′0″)*. *0′00″* was the basis for two new compositions, both included in *Song Books* as *Solo for Voice 23. 0′00″ No. 2* and *Solo for Voice 26. 0′00″ No. 2B.*

0′00″ No. 2 can be regarded as a score of *Reunion*—made after the fact—performed by John Cage, Marcel Duchamp, Teeny Duchamp, Gordon Mumma, David Tudor, David Behrman, and Lowell Cross at the Ryerson Theatre in Toronto on February 5, 1968.

31

SOLO FOR VOICE 8 THEATRE USING ELECTRONICS (IRRELEVANT)
(0′0″)

DIRECTIONS

In a situation provided with maximum amplification (no feedback), perform a disciplined action.

With any interruptions.
Fulfilling in whole or part an obligation to others.
No attention to be given the situation (electronic, musical, theatrical).

87

SOLO FOR VOICE 23
0'00" No. 2

THEATRE WITH ELECTRONICS (IRRELEVANT)

DIRECTIONS

On a playing area (e.g. table, chessboard) equipped with contact microphones (four channels preferably, speakers around the audience, highest volume without feedback)

Play a game with another person (e.g. chess, dominoes) or others (e.g. scrabble, bridge).

88

SOLO FOR VOICE 24 THEATRE WITH ELECTRONICS (IRRELEVANT)

DIRECTIONS (SEE SOLO 8)

Engage in some other activity than you did in Solo 8 (if it was performed).

91

SOLO FOR VOICE 26 | THEATRE WITH ELECTRONICS | (IRRELEVANT)

0'00" No. 2B

DIRECTIONS (SEE SOLO 23)

Play a game of solitaire (or play both or all sides of a game ordinarily involving two or more players.

94

SOLO FOR VOICE 28 THEATRE WITH ELECTRONICS (IRRELEVANT)

DIRECTIONS (SEE SOLO 8)

Engage in some other activity than you did in Solos 8 and 24 (if either of these was performed).

231

SOLO FOR VOICE 62 THEATRE WITH ELECTRONICS (IRRELEVANT)

DIRECTIONS (SEE SOLO 8)

Engage in some other activity than you did in Solos 8, 24, and 28 (if any one of these was performed).

232

SOLO FOR VOICE 63 THEATRE WITH ELECTRONICS (IRRELEVANT)

DIRECTIONS (SEE SOLO 8)

Engage in some other activity than you did in Solos 8, 24, 28, and 62 (if any one of these was performed).

John Cage

WGBH-TV
1971

3 pages, 8½ × 11 in. (US Letter)
As published by C.F. Peters in 1971

The score of *WGBH-TV* consists of three items: a handwritten letter from Eva Smerchek from the Caledonia Woman's Club asking for an artistic donation for an auction for the benefit of retarded children, a reply message from John Cage, and a sheet with notes for a 30 min. telecast written on the back of the original envelope from Smerchek. This score was dedicated to Nam June Paik. The notes indicate how the TV composition is to be recorded [stills from the video → pp. 174 f].

Caledonia Woman's Club

Member of General Federation of Woman's Clubs

Dear Mr Cage;

The Caledonia Woman's Club is going to present a Celebrity Auction Sale for the benefit of the Racine County Opportunity Center for Retarded Children.

We are asking prominent people in many fields to help us. Would you as a noted composer donate an item for our auction? Should you decide to help please enclose a card with your name and address.

Please accept our thanks now for your cooperation with our efforts on behalf of Retarded Children.

Sincerely,
Mrs. Eva Smerchek
7634 Hwy G
Franksville, Wisc 53126

JOHN CAGE

[illegible] BANK STREET • NEW YORK, NEW YORK [illegible]

MESSAGE	REPLY
TO Mrs. Eva Smerchek 7634 Hy 6 Franksville, Wisc. 53126	DATE
DATE Sept. 15, 1971	
For your auction sale I am enclosing your envelope on which I made a composition for TV. This envelope together with your letter & this one of mine will constitute a ms. to be published by The Henmar Press of C.F. Peters, NYC. Cordially & Best wishes, John Cage	
BY	SIGNED

DETACH AND FILE FOR FOLLOW-UP

Mrs. Eva Smerchek
7634 Hy 4
Franksville, Wisc 53126

WGBH TV
for composer & technicians
John Cage NYC 9/11/71

Recording 30"+ ~~announcement~~ statement for WGBH 30' Telecast 9/11/71:

0" "Music is being written, 15" but is not ~~not~~ finished yet. ~~finished.~~ 30" That's why there isn't any sound."

every 45
15
225
45
60 | 675 seconds
11 + 15
2 | 5 min 37 1/2 sec.

(Camera to focus without movement on work table; microphones (not contact) to pick up sound of work. high amplification. no face (just arms, hands, pen etc.))

John Cage

One^3 = *4′33″ (0′00″)* + 𝄞
1989

Manuscript and faxleaf containing the score
8½ × 11 in. (US Letter)
NYPL Music Division, John Cage Music Manuscript Collection
JPB 94-24, Folder 782

The manuscript of *One*^{3} was written on a sheet of paper probably also used during the second "Minds for History" conference in Arcosanti, October 15–19, 1989, in which John Cage participated. In addition, a faxleaf including the score is addressed to Yutaka Fujishima from Mimi Johnson of Artservices, and is dated October 19, 1989.

One 3

is David Mayne

602 468 1459

hall should be on edge of feedback

4′33″ (0′00″) + = 1 3

=

4130 E Glenrosa Ph. Ariz 85018

Mimi's office (102) 1-212-941-8911 – 33

Arcosanti 602-632-7135

10/19/89 17:27 212 334 5149 ARTSERVICES INC.

Artservices

FACSIMILE MESSAGE

FROM: Mimi Johnson
ARTSERVICES
105 Hudson Street, Room 200
New York, NY 10013

Telephone: 212/941-8911
Fax: 212/334-5149

SAMPLE

TO: Yutaka Fujishima
Fax: 011/81/75/882-4358

Number of Pages: 1 Date: October 19th, 1989

Dear Mr. Fujishima,

Mr. Cage would like to perform a new work, rather than 4'33". Here is the title....written exactly as it should be.

One[3] = 4'33" (0'00") + [treble clef on staff]

Note: [treble clef on staff] = Sofia Gubaibulina (There Is An Inner Clock)
III International Music Festival in the USSR

You should arrange the sound system so that the whole hall is just on the edge of feedback...not actually feeding back, but feeling like it might.

No piano is necessary.

use treble clef sign
on not the five staff lines

PERFORMING ARTSERVICES, INC. | 105 HUDSON STREET, NEW YORK, NY 10013 | 212-941-8911 FAX: 212-334-5149 TELEX: 66842

John Cage

One[11]
1992

Digital printouts
Pages of the score for the 35 mm film, 93:00 min

The score for Cage's first and only film *One*[11] was computer generated and contains about 250 pages (of which only six exemplary pages are reproduced here).

The movements of the lights, the camera movements, the angle of view of the lenses, the fades, and the editing of the film were directed based on the I Ching. They are represented in the score as numeric listings and also as computer generated drawings in a grid mapped to the space of the TV studio.

The producer and director of the film was Henning Lohner. The executive producer was Peter Lohner. The light environment was designed and programmed by John Cage and Andrew Culver, who also wrote the software which carried out the I Ching operations for the score. The film *One*[11] is synchronized with a soundtrack containing Cage's *Composition 103* (for 103 musicians).

Cage's introductions for the cameraman and the crane operations.

One[11] Takes

Instructions for each take are given in drawing and table form.

The table shows the time bracket for each take - a time within which a take must begin together with a time bracket in which the take must end. In most cases, successive takes overlap (by 10, 15 or 20 seconds). Some takes, however, have fixed beginnings and endings (these are very short), and the different scenes abut at fixed times.

The lens for each take is also given in the table.

Finally, the table gives the use of crane or not (on "foot"), and the "from" and "to" grid positions. If no "to" position is given the take is without movement. Crane "from" positions are that of the base of the machine. The crane "to" position may be used to indicate the direction that the crane arm takes. Further details of crane direction, rotation, movement etc. will be determined on the spot by chance operations with respect to practicality.

On the drawing, "foot" "from" positions are circles, those for the crane are squares. The dotted line shows the trajectory to the "to" position.

Courtesy of Henning Lohner

Page 2 of the score for the cameraman

One^{11}

2

Take	Begin time bracket	End time bracket	Lens	Foot/Crane	From	To
SCENE 1						
1	0:00:00<->0:00:45	0:00:30<->0:01:15	32mm	Foot	H 1	I 1
2	0:01:00<->0:01:45	0:01:30<->0:02:15	24mm	Crane	I10	F 7
3	0:02:05<->0:02:35	0:02:25<->0:02:55	40mm	Foot	E 5	I10
4	0:02:35<->0:03:35	0:03:15<->0:04:15	100mm	Foot	B 8	M 9
5	0:03:55<->0:04:55	0:04:35<->0:05:35	20mm	Crane	J10	D 4
6	0:05:15<->0:06:15	0:05:55<->0:06:55	40mm	Crane	L 3	J 7
7	0:06:40<->0:07:25	0:07:10<->0:07:55	100mm	Crane	H 3	B 7
8	0:07:55	0:08:35	85mm	Foot	K 4	
9	0:08:35<->0:09:05	0:08:55<->0:09:25	50mm	Foot	H 6	L 5
10	0:09:10<->0:09:55	0:09:40<->0:10:25	85mm	Crane	O 3	N 9
11	0:10:05<->0:11:05	0:10:45<->0:11:45	100mm	Crane	H 5	J 9
12	0:11:25<->0:12:25	0:12:05<->0:13:05	85mm	Foot	B 9	M 9
SCENE 2						
1	0:13:05<->0:13:35	0:13:25<->0:13:55	20mm	Crane	G 1	G 7
2	0:13:40<->0:14:25	0:14:10<->0:14:55	24mm	Crane	H 2	D 1
3	0:14:45<->0:15:30	0:15:15<->0:16:00	32mm	Crane	L 7	N 3
SCENE 3						
1	0:16:00<->0:16:30	0:16:20<->0:16:50	100mm	Crane	J 1	A 6
2	0:16:50	0:17:00	20mm	Crane	N10	D 8
SCENE 4						
1	0:17:00<->0:17:30	0:17:20<->0:17:50	50mm	Foot	G 2	E 8

Courtesy of Henning Lohner

The positioning of the different types of light sources in a grid mapped to the space of the TV studio for Scene 2

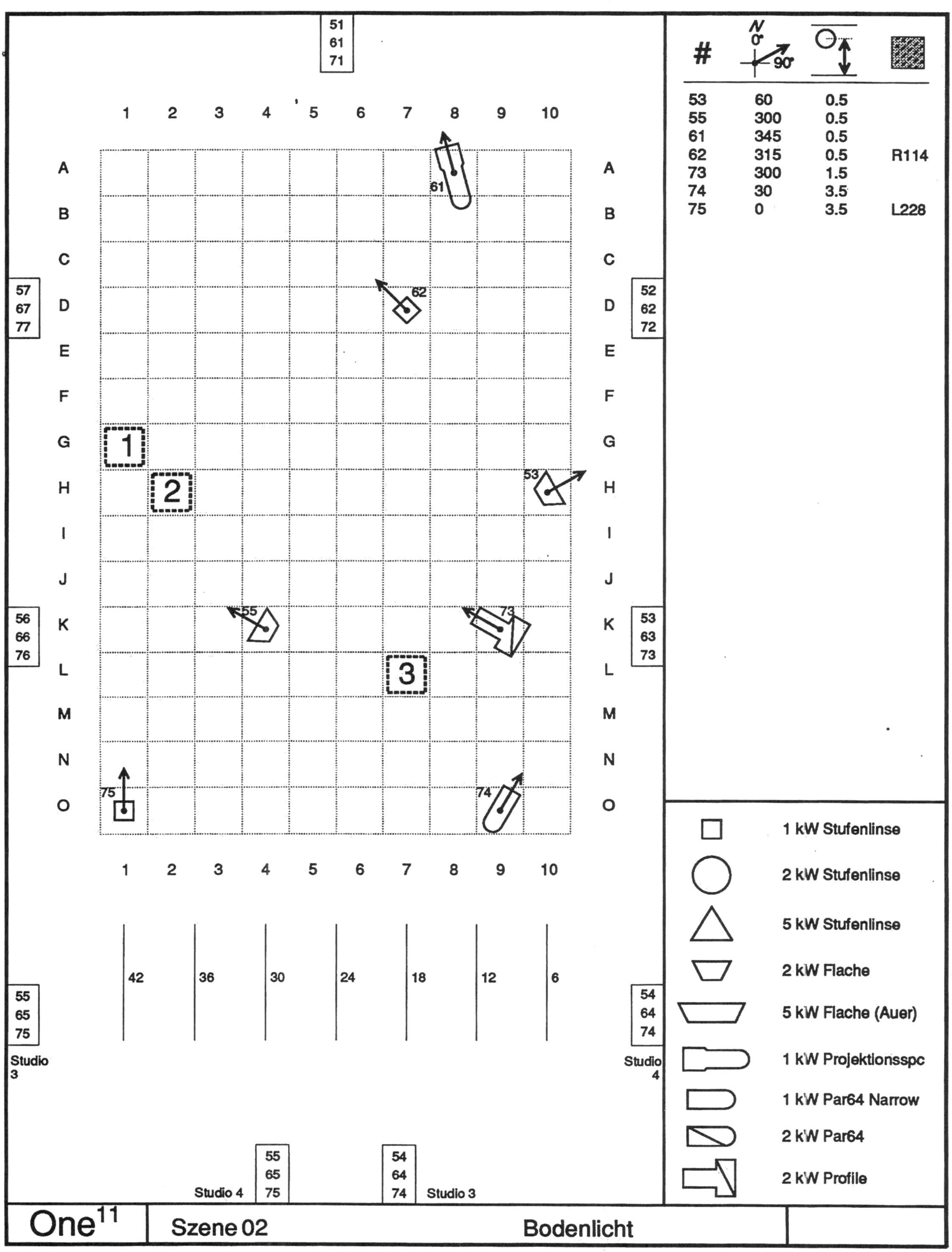

Courtesy of Henning Lohner

The above positions for Scene 4

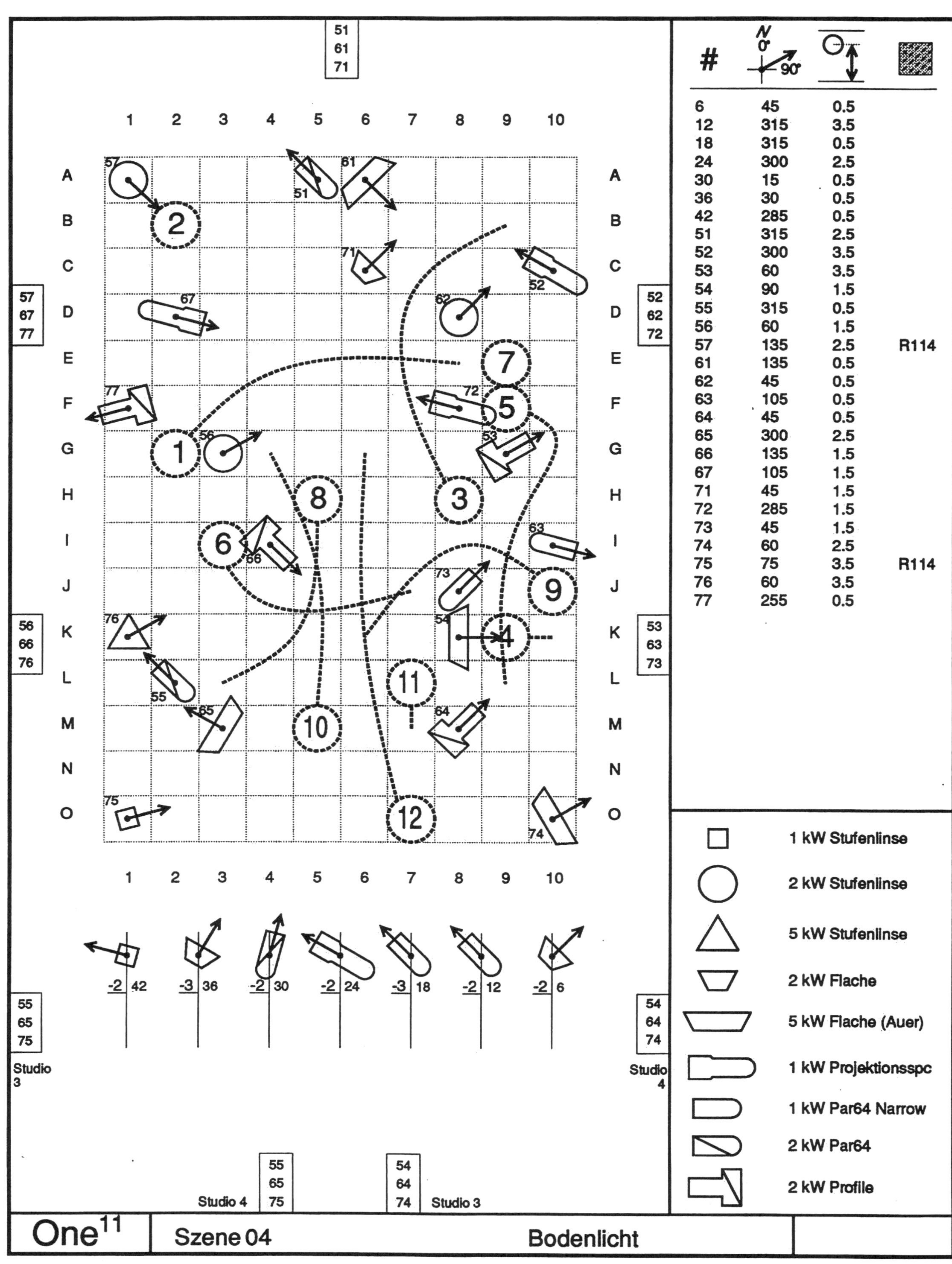

#	N 0° / 90°		
6	45	0.5	
12	315	3.5	
18	315	0.5	
24	300	2.5	
30	15	0.5	
36	30	0.5	
42	285	0.5	
51	315	2.5	
52	300	3.5	
53	60	3.5	
54	90	1.5	
55	315	0.5	
56	60	1.5	
57	135	2.5	R114
61	135	0.5	
62	45	0.5	
63	105	0.5	
64	45	0.5	
65	300	2.5	
66	135	1.5	
67	105	1.5	
71	45	1.5	
72	285	1.5	
73	45	1.5	
74	60	2.5	
75	75	3.5	R114
76	60	3.5	
77	255	0.5	

Courtesy of Henning Lohner

Page 11 of the light score indicating the cues for the programmable light control engine in the TV studio

One11 Scene 02 11

CUE: 0 PERFTIME: 00:13:05 DURATION: 00:00:00

5<035 10<035 17<093 18<078 19<088 21<035 24<035 26<077
29<035 32<035 34<072 53<035 55<035 61<035 62<035 73<035
74<035 75<035

CUE: 1 PERFTIME: 00:13:05 DURATION: 00:00:08

10<042 17>058 18>070 19>074 24<042 26>059 29<062 34>053
53<052 74<090 75<053

CUE: 2 PERFTIME: 00:13:13 DURATION: 00:00:05

10<046 17>035 18>065 19>065 24<046 26>047 29<079 34>041
53<062 74>063 75<064

CUE: 3 PERFTIME: 00:13:18 DURATION: 00:00:01

10:046 17<036 18>064 19>064 24:046 26>045 29<083 34>038
53<064 74>058 75<066

CUE: 4 PERFTIME: 00:13:19 DURATION: 00:00:01

10:046 17<037 18>063 19>063 24:046 26>043 29>082 34>035
53<066 74>053 75<068

CUE: 5 PERFTIME: 00:13:20 DURATION: 00:00:03

10<049 17<042 18>060 19>057 24<048 26>035 29>077 53<073
74>035 75<075

CUE: 6 PERFTIME: 00:13:23 DURATION: 00:00:03

10<052 17<047 18>057 19>051 24<051 29>072 53<080 74<074
75<082

CUE: 7 PERFTIME: 00:13:26 DURATION: 00:00:03

10<055 17<052 18>054 19>045 24<054 29>067 53<087 74>069
75<089

CUE: 8 PERFTIME: 00:13:29 DURATION: 00:00:03

10<058 17<057 18>051 19>039 24<057 29>062 53>079 74>063
75<097

Courtesy of Henning Lohner

Sheet of chance operations by John Cage, with Cage's hand-written executions during the shooting of *One*[11]

33 numbers non-repeating, sorted, between 1 and 34

1 2 3 4 5 6 7 8 9 1Ø 11 12 13 14 15 16
17 18 19 2Ø 21 22 23 24 25 26 27 28 29 3Ø 31 32
33

1Ø numbers non-repeating, sorted, between 1 and 31

3 8 11 15 16 17 18 21 27 28

11 numbers non-repeating, sorted, between 1 and 3Ø

5 6 9 1Ø 2Ø 21 22 24 28 29 3Ø

31 numbers non-repeating, sorted, between 1 and 33

1 2 3 4 5 6 7 8 9 1Ø 11 12 14 15 16 17
18 19 2Ø 21 22 23 25 26 27 28 29 3Ø 31 32 33

15 numbers non-repeating, sorted, between 1 and 32

1 2 3 4 6 7 1Ø 11 13 15 19 22 25 29 3Ø

2Ø numbers non-repeating, sorted, between 1 and 29

1 2 3 4 5 6 7 9 11 12 15 16 17 18 19 2Ø
21 24 25 29

7 numbers non-repeating, sorted, between 1 and 3Ø

2 11 17 21 22 24 3Ø

26 numbers non-repeating, sorted, between 1 and 31

1 2 3 4 5 6 7 8 9 1Ø 11 12 13 14 15 17
18 19 21 23 24 26 27 28 29 3Ø

13 numbers non-repeating, sorted, between 1 and 37

Courtesy of Henning Lohner

B

Related Material

Texts by Irwin Kremen
on the proportional notation
of *4′33″*

Auctorial performances
of *4′33″* on video

Irwin Kremen

Carbon copy of a letter to Larry Austin regarding the publishing of John Cage's graphic score of *4′33″* 1967

3 typewritten pages, 8 ½ × 11 in. (US Letter)
Getty Research Institute, Los Angeles, Special Collections ID 980039
Box 55, Folder 7

This letter written by Irwin Kremen shows the order of the single pages of the graphic score of *4′33″*.

June 1, 1967

Mr. Larry Austin
Source: Music of the Avant Garde
330 University Avenue
Davis, California
95616

Dear Mr. Austin:

Here are 8 "lith" negatives of the written (inked) portions only of the title page, the dedication page, the scale page (where time is given as a function of spatial extensity), and the score pages, of 4' 33". The printer here insists that negatives only of the written (inked) portions of the various pages are needed to reproduce those pages, providing you have an adequate dummy or mock-up, for which the actual-size Xerox copy that you already have, will do. This means that there is no "lith" negative for the 3rd score page, the one that is entirely blank. Though without anything written on it, still it is spatially extended (the horizontal) and so contributes to the time count; without it you could not get 4' and 33". I am concerned that this page, even though blank, be included. It is an integral part of the score and must be reproduced unlike the back of the title page or the two blank pages at the very end, which can be omitted. Perhaps this model will help you:

Title page

Blank (back of title page) | Dedication Page

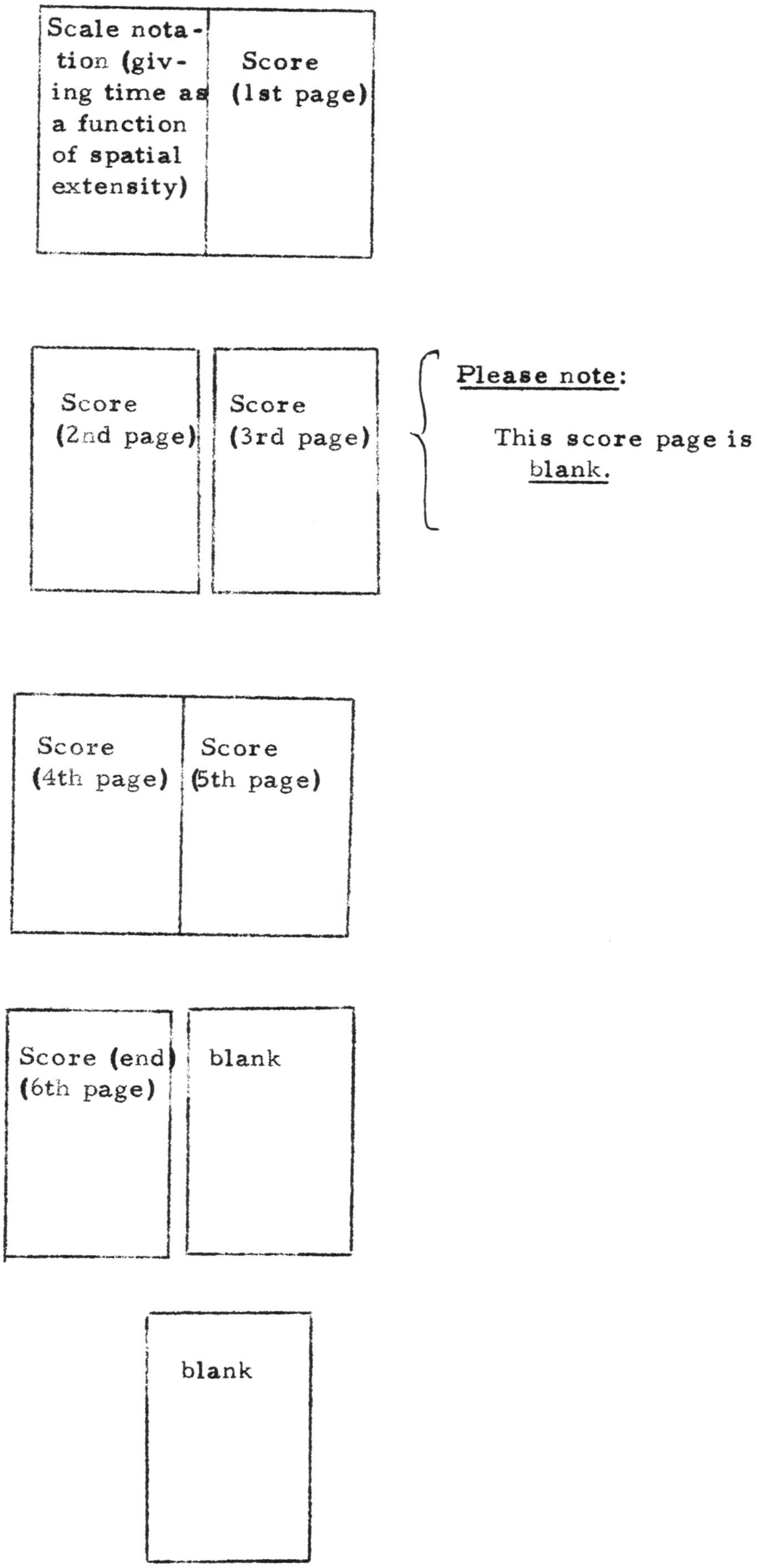

Scale notation (giving time as a function of spatial extensity)
Score (1st page)
Score (2nd page)
Score (3rd page)
Please note:
This score page is blank.
Score (4th page)
Score (5th page)
Score (end) (6th page)
blank
blank

-3-

You may reprint portions of my earlier letter. But, to my dismay, I find that in it I described the manuscript incorrectly. I was doing so from memory and found my error as I was checking the arrangement of the pages for the model above. In that letter, I say:

> Also, the manuscript actually consists of three large sheets folded together. Thus, if you were to connect the first with the last, there being a fold between them, and similarly the second and the fifth, and finally the third and the fourth-- you'd have it as it is.

I was instructing you on how to connect the Xerox sheets that you have, the numbers referring to them in the order I sent them to you. While the first connection is correct, the last two are not. Below I give you the way I suggest connecting the pages in the quote above and <u>how they should correctly be connected:</u>

<u>Above</u>	<u>Correct Connection</u>
1 and 6	1 and 6
2 and 5	2 and 3
3 and 4	4 and 5

I also enclose a model, 3 folded sheets, of the manuscript which you can match with the correct version of connection given in the second column above, and match further with your Xerox copies. (Please do not quote my incorrect description but change it to the correct order.)

John gave me this as a birthday gift long ago. We ate black-cherry ice cream at Barbara Herman's (she is now my wife,) ~~We ate black-cherry ice cream~~ in New York, on the roof outside her window. M. C. Richards was there, and Merce Cunningham, and David, and John.

I enclose a paid receipt from the printers here, according to your instructions.

Thank you for offering to send me a copy of <u>Source</u>. May I have two? And would you please send one to John and one to David. Thank you ever so much. I hope I am not asking too much. If I can be of further help, please feel free to call upon me.

Very sincerely yours,

Irwin Kremen

IK/mw
Enc.

Irwin Kremen

Note for the 1993 edition of the graphic score of *4′33″*
1993

Included in the C.F. Peters edition of the graphic score from 1993

Irwin Kremen's comments on the erroneous facsimile reproduction of the graphic score in *Source: Music of the Avant-Garde* #2, July 1967, and the new corrected C.F. Peters edition from 1993.

The published score of ***4'33"*** (Edition Peters No. 6777) is a later version of it. As John Cage writes in his note to the published version, after David Tudor gave the first performance of ***4'33"*** at Woodstock in 1952, John made a copy "in proportional notation" which he gave to me as a gift for my twenty-eighth birthday (June 5, 1953). A noteworthy feature of this score is its manner of indicating time, here made a function of continuous space with the direction "1 PAGE = 7 INCHES = 56"."

In 1967, John and David, on a trip to North Carolina, asked me, because of this version's significance, to arrange for its facsimile reproduction in ***SOURCE, Music of the Avant Garde***. Accordingly, I contacted that journal and then sent it lifesize photostats of the entire manuscript, this so it could *exactly* reproduce the score of ***4' 33"*** "in proportional notation." But ***SOURCE*** printed its reproduction (July 1967, Vol. 1, No. 2) *reduced* in size, 7¼ x 10 11/16 inches rather than the 8½x 11 inches of the manuscript itself, and without anywhere specifying the actual dimensions. However inadvertently it happened, this unacknowledged reduction changed, hence falsified, the space x time relationship of the original, a fact I grasped at the time but did nothing further about. Then, this past year, I was scheduled by the Tampa Museum of Art to give a short talk about Black Mountain College for the opening of its exhibition ***The Black Mountain College Connection: John Cage, Merce Cunningham, Irwin Kremen, M. C. Richards*** - - by happenstance a month after John's death. I decided to forgo Black Mountain as a topic and, instead, give a talk in honor of John, focusing on ***4'33"***. In preparing this talk, I realized how necessary it was to correct the distortion introduced by the reduced reproduction in ***SOURCE*** and I, therefore, approached Don Gillespie and Stephen Fisher of C. F. Peters Corporation in the hope of rectifying it. They saw immediately the need to publish a correct version.

-Irwin Kremen
Durham, North Carolina

John Cage

Video of *WGBH-TV*
1971

28:00 min., color
Digital copy from PAL VHS tape
by C.F. Peters, New York

TV composition recorded as indicated in the score with the same title [→ pp. 152 f].

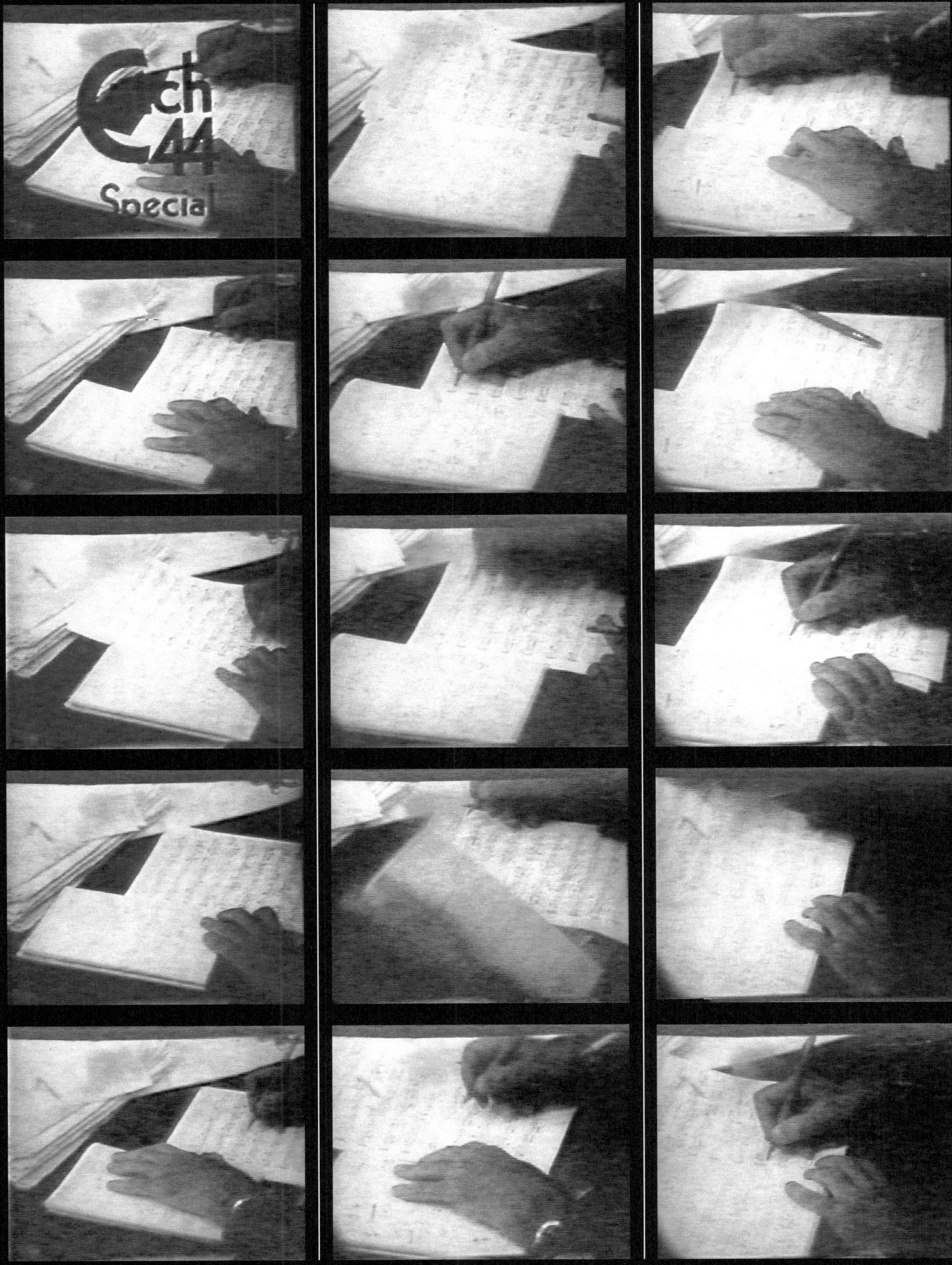
Cch
44
Special

First version: Harvard Square, Cambridge, Massachusetts

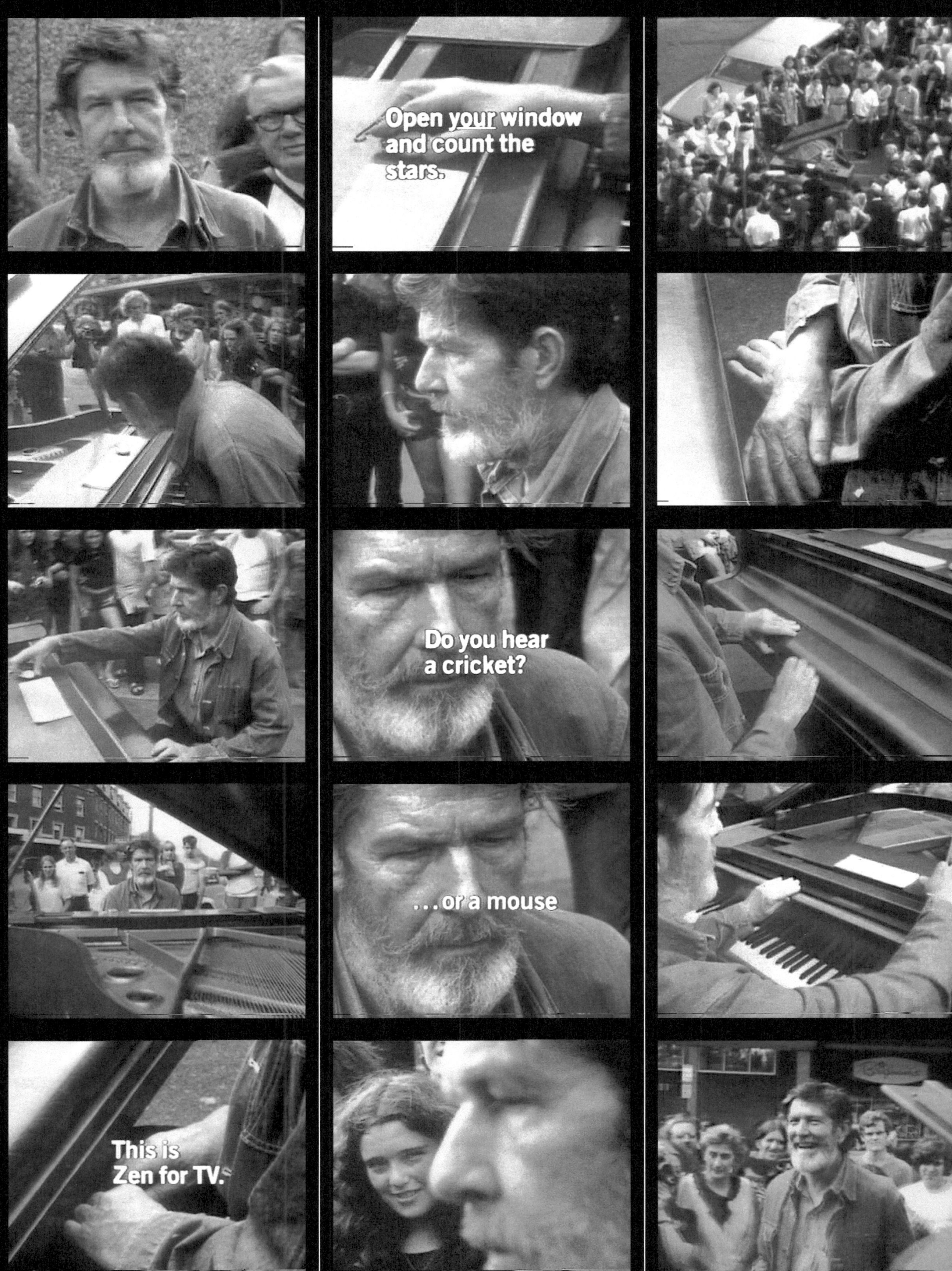

Courtesy of Electronic Arts Intermix, NYC

Comments by John Cage on the second version of *4′33″* in Paik's video

What we are going to do is perform my Silent Piece. Somewhere in Manhattan. We are assuming that the entire island is, so to speak, a concert hall. And what we're trying to do is find out where we should go to hear the concert.

For that purpose I have counted the number of streets and avenues given on this map. Including the piers and coming to the number 981. On this chart I have related the number 981 to the I Ching number of 64. I have this computer printout of the I Ching so that it is possible for me to locate first a group of 15 or 16 locations and then one in that group of 15 or 16. The first number I have is the number 50. That gives me locations 746 to 760. The next number is two and that gives me the first of that group of 15, namely location number 746.

Counting backwards from 750 I get 49, 48, 47, 46 [counts off on the city map] *and that gives me as our first location – we're going to have four of them – somewhere between 1700 and 2100 on 3rd Avenue. The next is the first group 50 and 32, in that group of 15, which is the 8th. That's 46, 47, 48, 49, 50, 51, 52, 53* [counts off on the city map]. *753, which is Times Square.*

First movement

Here we are between 104th and 105th Street on 3rd Avenue. This is the location given to us by the I Ching for the first movement of this four movement performance in Manhattan of the Silent Piece. The time length given is one minute and 49 seconds. I will be silent during that period so that we can listen to the sounds of this environment.

[Paik takes the microphone out of Cage's hand and begins interviewing people on the street.]

Paik: *Do you like this street sound?*
Woman: *Yes.*
Paik: *Do you love this street sound?*
Man: *Yes.*
Paik: *What do you like – this music more or this street sound more?*
Man: *The music. You know, I think the music more, because, you understand, the music is what's happening and all this here, all this here, all the buses and airplanes and stuff, you know, and fire engines – they don't have to make all that noise – at night you're trying to sleep, they don't have to make all that noise.*
Paik: *Okay, thank you.*

[Paik hands the microphone back to Cage.]

That's the end of the first movement. Now we'll go to the second movement, which is between 203rd and 204th Street, probably overlooking the river.

Second movement

We're now at a dead end of 203rd Street and Harlem River. This is the location for the second movement, which will only be 14 seconds long.

That's the end of it.

Third movement

[The third movement begins without introduction. The stop watch can be briefly seen at the start and end of the movement.]

Fourth movement

Mitchell Place is at the foot of Beekman Place and this is the position the I Ching gave us for the last movement.

This is the kind of music that anyone can make. All you have to do is open your ears and listen.

Second version: Manhattan, New York

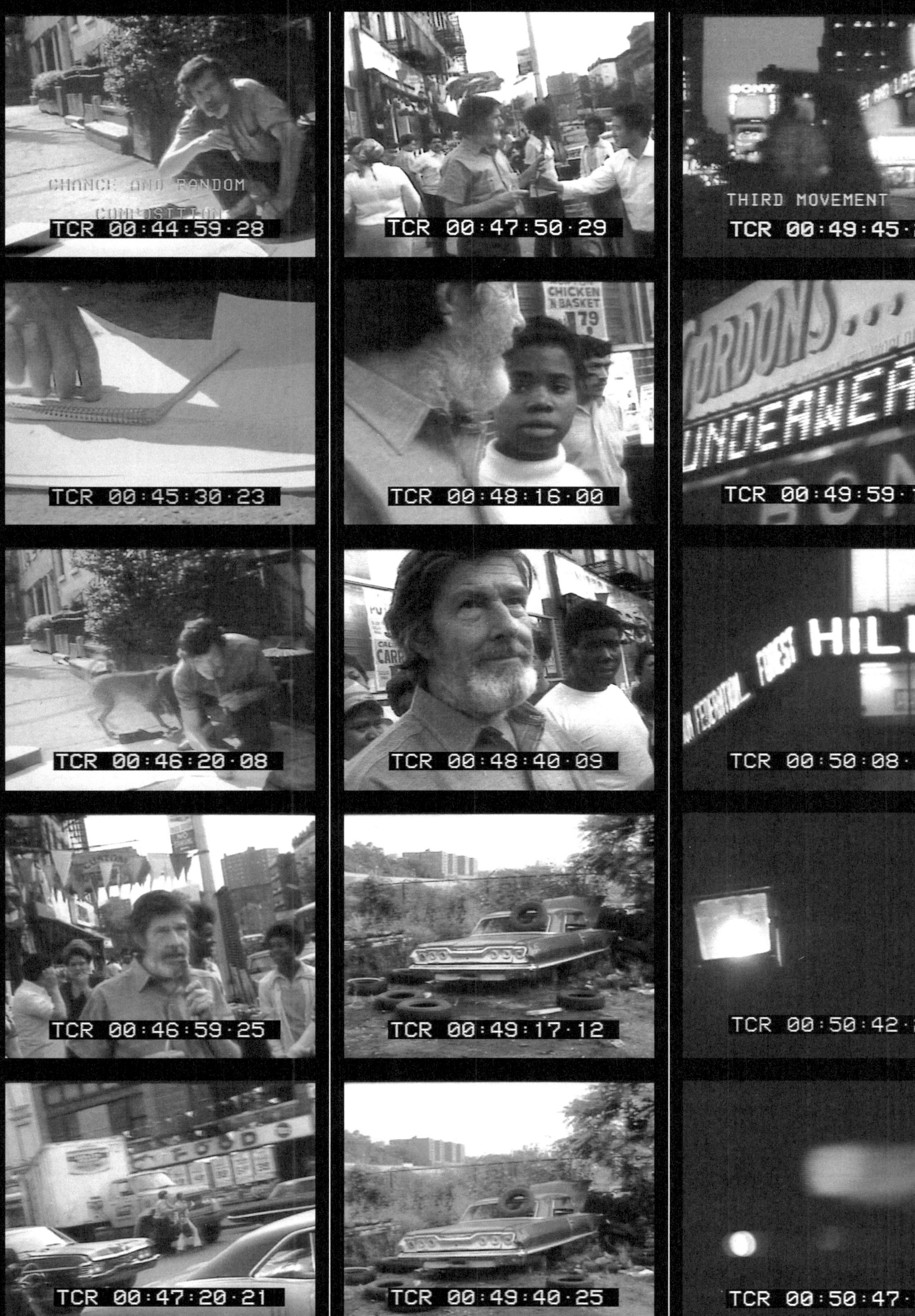

Courtesy of Nam June Paik Art Center, Korea

John Cage

4′33″
1986

Video recording by Klaus vom Bruch of the *4′33″* performance by John Cage at Kölnischer Kunstverein in front of Sigmar Polke's painting *Schimpftuch*, Cologne, 6:12 min.
Courtesy of Klaus vom Bruch

Performance of *4′33″* by John Cage at the opening of the exhibition *Die 60er Jahre – Kölns Weg zur Kunstmetropole: Vom Happening zum Kunstmarkt* in Cologne on Aug 31, 1986 [for the notation of the performance → pp. 140 f].

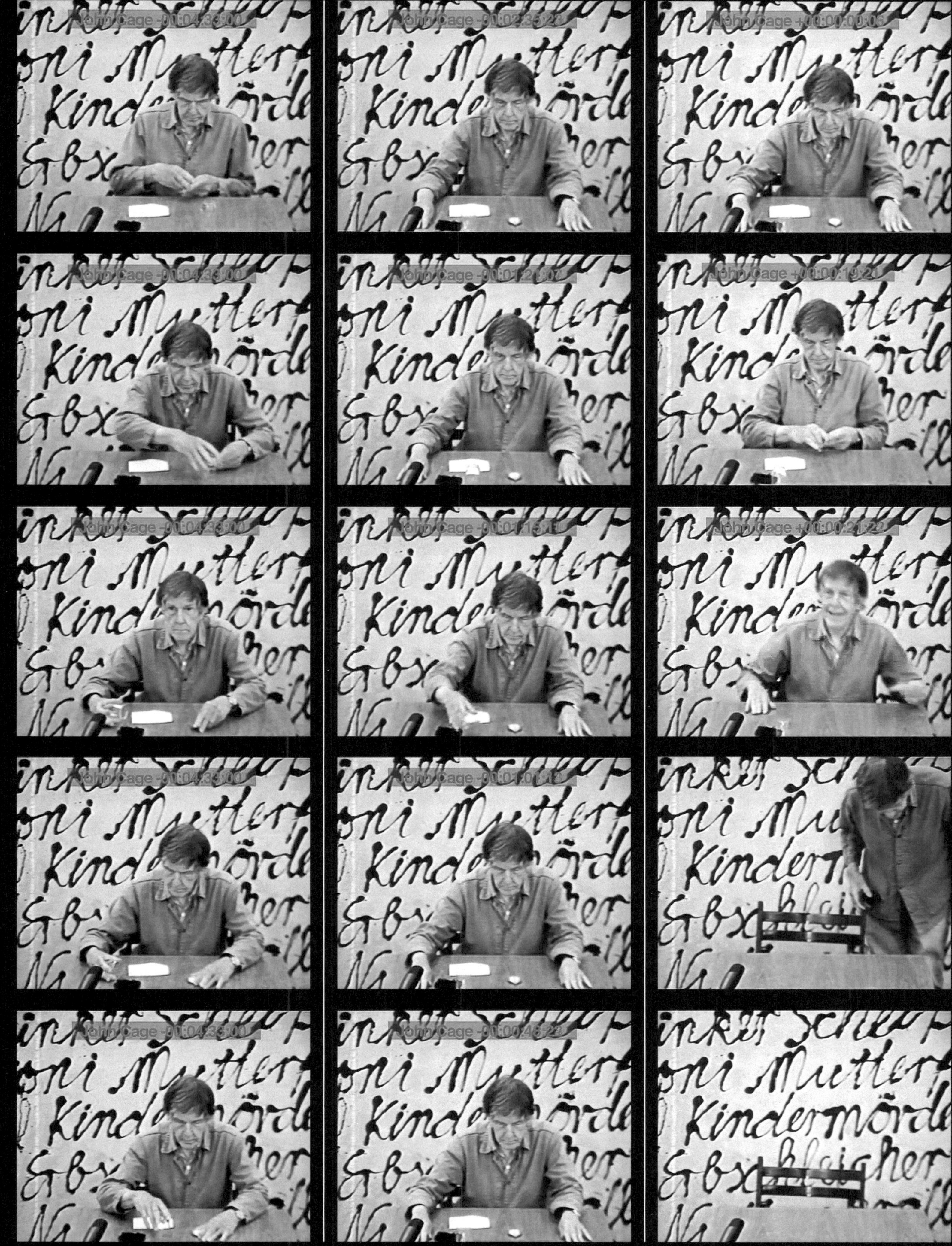

Courtesy of Klaus vom Bruch

John Cage & Henning Lohner

4′33″
1990

Video documentation
of the performance of *4′33″* at the former German-German border checkpoint Invalidenstraße, Berlin, August 1, 1990
4:33 min., no sound
Courtesy of private collection Berlin and Los Angeles

This performance of *4′33″* from 1990 represents an interesting filmic adaptation of the composer's famous piece. Recorded shortly after the fall of the Wall near a former checkpoint on Invalidenstrasse, the film consists of a still sequence shot. In the lower third of the image one recognizes the rubble of the checkpoint, which has been torn down. In the middle of the frame one sees Cage and Lohner sitting silently in front of a crane, which was evidently used to take down the checkpoint. The demolition site is framed by a busy road branching out to the left behind the crane, with a slow but steady and seemingly endless succession of cars winding past. Occasionally the shadow of a passer-by falls on the rubble waiting to be cleared. Instead of staging a classic concert situation and sharpening the audience's senses for ambient sounds, Lohner's filmic adaptation focuses on the two men's silence, whose lack of pathos underlines the historic eventfulness and turns it into a lasting, quiet moment of introspection. All the while the hustle and bustle of everyday life goes on in the background, creating a dynamic momentum that unfurls around a gravitational point in the center of the frame. The video thus becomes a silent, unclichéd, and uncommented metaphor for a historic moment of bliss. [FSL]

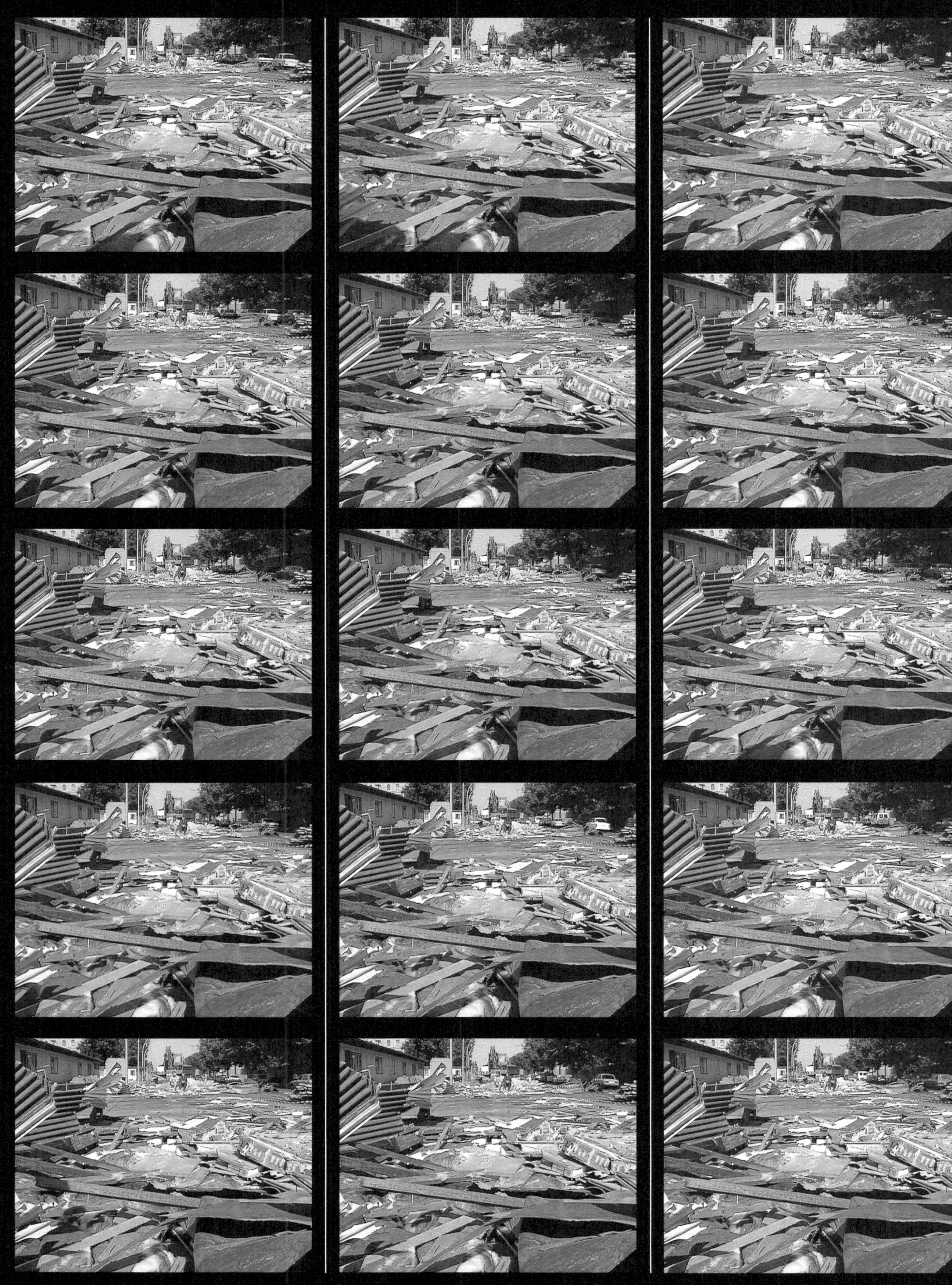

Courtesy of Henning Lohner

Various
Nova Musicha Nr 1: John Cage

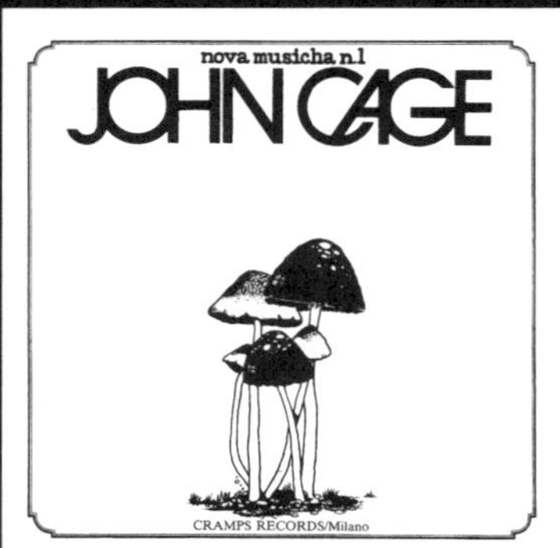

1974, Cramps Records (CRSLP 6101 N.1), Italy, LP.

Gianni-Emilio Simonetti interpreted *4′33″ (In Three Parts: 0′30″ / 2′23″ / 1′40″)*. This LP was rereleased on CD in 1989 on the same label, Cramps CRSCD 101. Currently available on LP on Get Back Records GET 5201 (1999) and on CD Edel 0136582CRA (2002).

Amadinda Percussion Group
4′33″

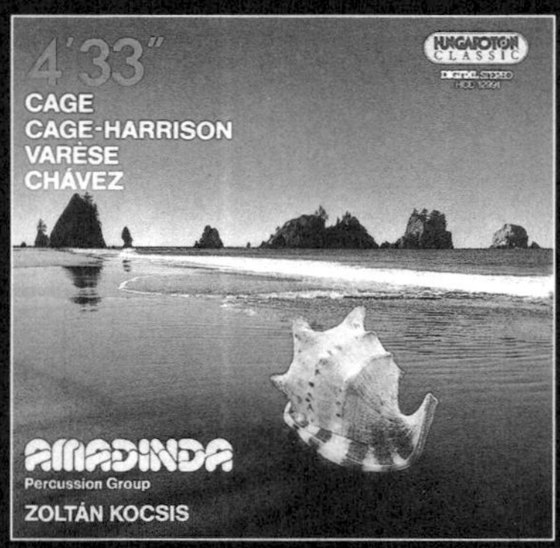

1989, Hungaroton (SLPD 12991), Hungary, LP.

Digital recording: Hungaroton Studio, Budapest, Bartók Concert Hall, Szombathely, Börzsöny Hills, 1988. Also released on Cassette (MK 12991). Currently available on CD: HCD 12991, released in 1994.

Ex Novo Ensemble di Venezia
Da Capo

1989, IB Office (IB Office 3), Cassette tape.

John Cage
Music For Five

1991, hat ART (hat ART CD 2-6070), Switzerland, CD.
4′33″ (No. 2) (0′00″).

Wayne Marshall
Cage

1991, Floating Earth (FCD 004), UK, CD.

Yann Tomita
Music For Astro Age

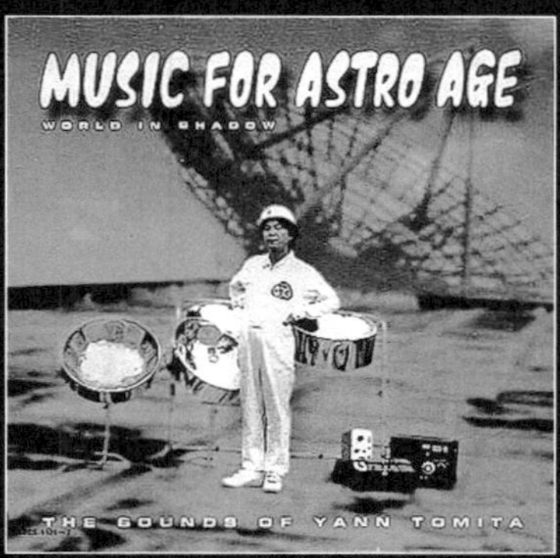

November 1, 1992,
Sony Music Entertainment (Japan) (SRCS 6526~7), Japan, CD.
The album contains two *4′33″* tracks.

The Cassandra Complex
Sex & Death

1993, Play It Again Sam (PIAS) (BIAS 255 CD), Belgium, CD.
Track no. 12: *4′33″*.

Various
A Chance Operation: The John Cage Tribute

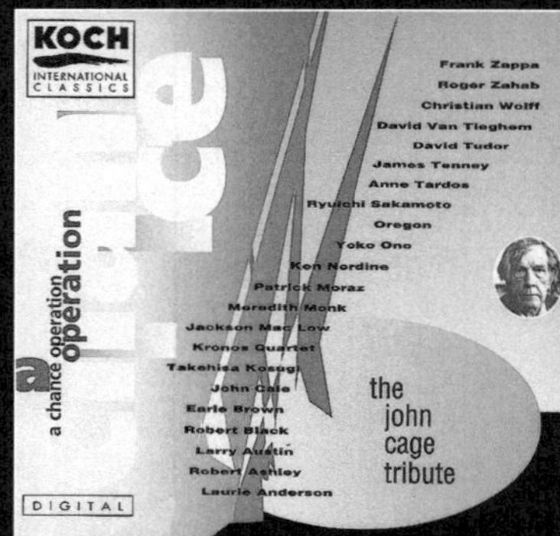

1993, Koch International Classics (3-7238-2), US, CD.

Kronos Quartet combined with words spoken by John Cage, Patrick Moraz, and Charles "Vision" Turner; Earle Brown, trumpets; David van Tieghem, percussion and voice; Frank Zappa (*4′33″* split into five pieces), Meredith Monk, and others. Each piece is divided into short tracks. There are 98 tracks on disc one and 85 tracks on disc two. This allows the disc to be played in random/shuffle mode to further enhance the Cage experience.

Kazue Sawai Koto Ensemble
live at Dacapo in Bremen ’93

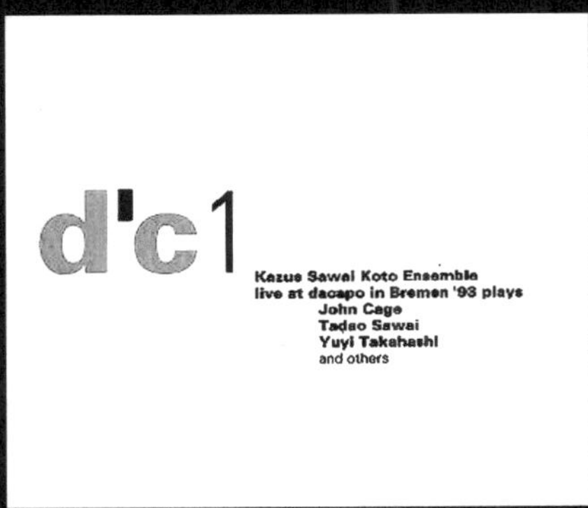

1993, d'c records gmbh / Dacapo e.V. (d'c 1), Germany, CD.
Track no. 6: John Cage – *4′33″*, 5:04 min., recorded in June 1993 live at 274. Dacapo concert at Galerie Katrin Rabus.

Various performers
Music of the 20th Century

1994, United (88088), CD.
4′33″ performed by Colin Stone.

Carl Michael von Hausswolff
CM von Hausswolff Plays John Cage

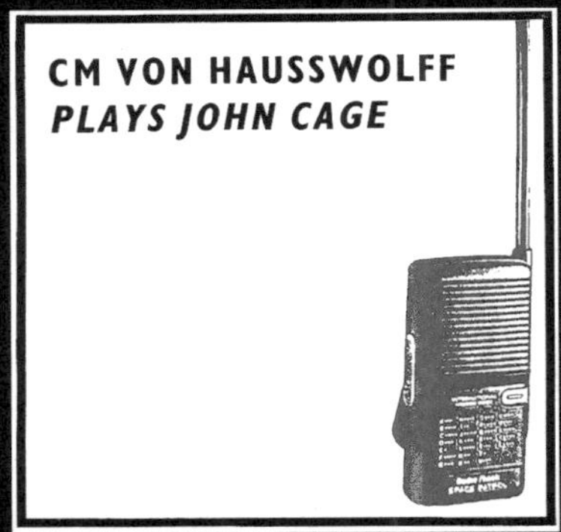

1996, Povertech Industries (PAT 38), US, LP.

Band Of Pain
You’re Miss Fortune

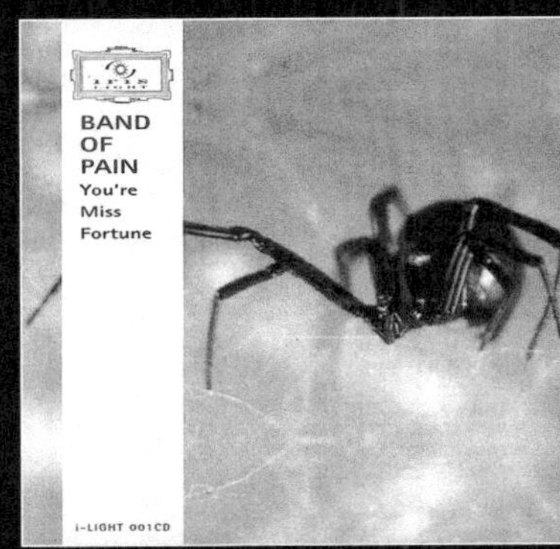

1996, Iris Light Records (i-light 001CD), UK, CD.
Track no. 5: *4′33″*.

Various
Revista De Arte Sonoro 2

May 1997, Centro De Creación Experimental (2), Spain, CD, Album, Compilation.
Track no. 7: José Iges, *Homenajes En 4′33″*.

George Wolfe & The New Millenium Ensemble
Lifting the Veil

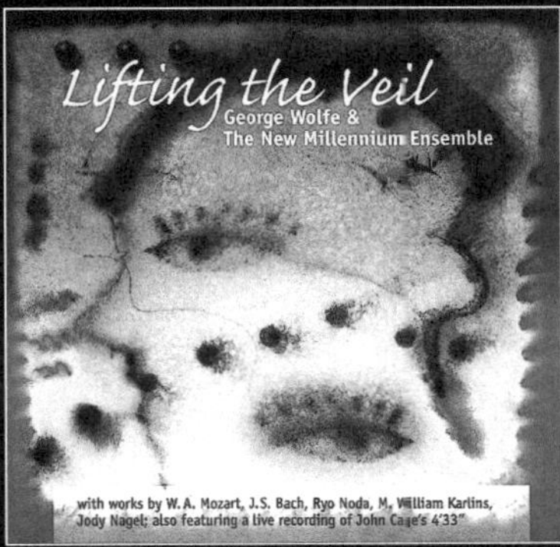

1997, Soundwind (SW 1133), US, CD, also published in 1998 by Arizona University Recordings (3066), US, CD.
Track no. 5 is an interpretation of John Cage’s *4′33″*.

Deep Listening Band
Non-Stop Flight

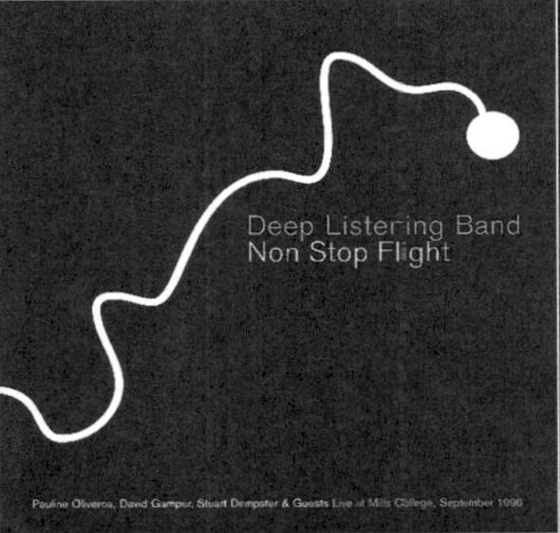

1998, Music And Arts Programs Of America, Inc. (CD-1030), US, CD.

Various performers
Wagner’s Rinse Cycle

1999, ABC Classics (465 260-2), Australia, CD.

Performers include Victoria de los Angeles, Elisabeth Schwarzkopf, The Cambridge Buskers, P.D.Q. Bach, and others. Various recording dates and locations.

Mimetic Mute
Negative

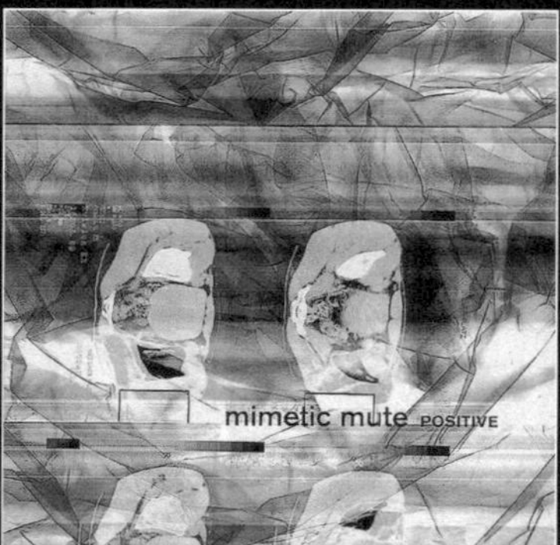

2000, Prikosnovénie (PRIK036), France, CD.

Boole
Boole

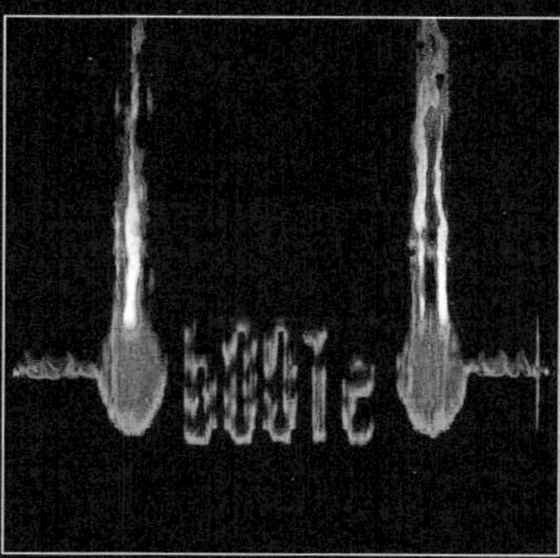

2000, Dancing Bull Productions (DBP05), US, CD.
Track no. 12: *4′33″*.

Yann Tomita
An Adventure of Inevitable Chance

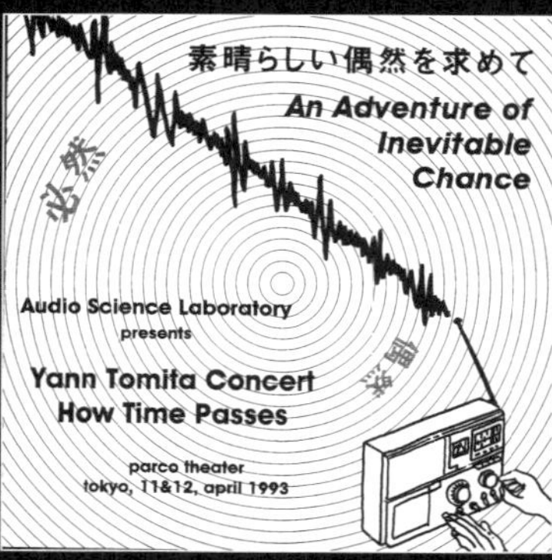

June 25, 2000, P-Vine Records (ASL-5809), Japan, CD, Album.
Recorded live at the Parco Theater, Tokyo,
on April 11/12, 1993.

Covenant
United States Of Mind

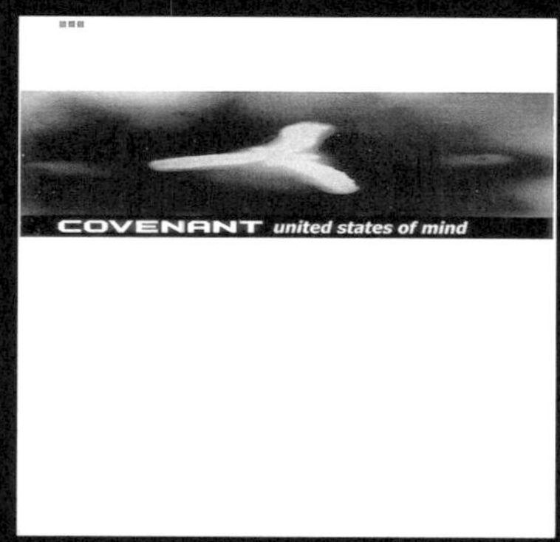

February 2000, Dependent Records (mind 010), Germany, CD.
Track no. 11: *You Can Make Your Own Music* (4′33″)
consists entirely of silence.
It is a tribute to John Cage's famed *4′33″*.

DJ Quietstorm
Damare

2001, Nakameguro Yakkyoku Recordings (NMYKCD03), Japan, CD.
Track no. 15: *4′33″*.

Steve Roden
Schindler House

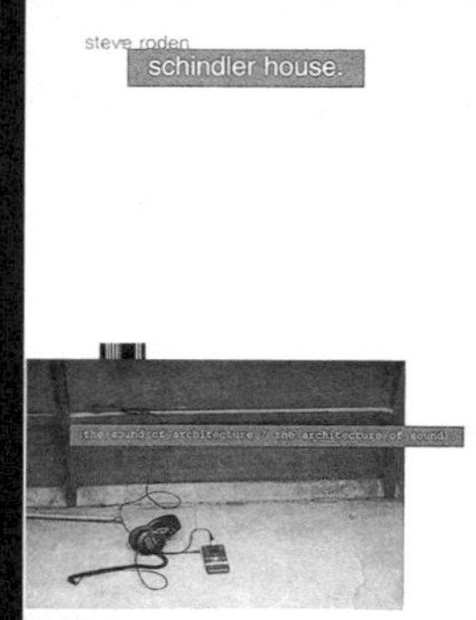

2001, Mak Center (npibmak-001), US, CD.

Alexandre St-Onge
Kasi Naigo

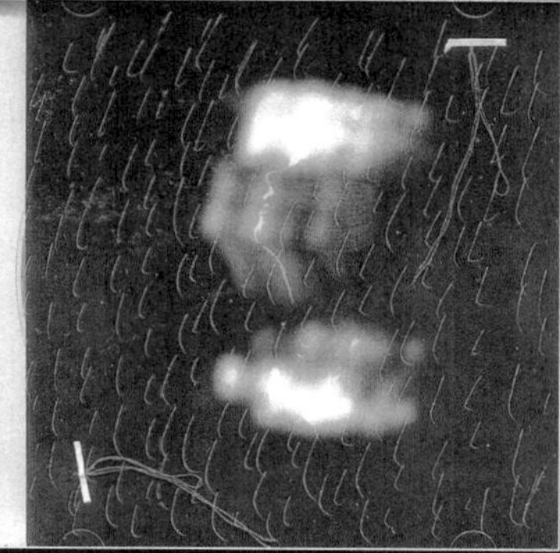

2001, Squint Fucker Press (squint 00C), Canada, CD.
Track no. 3: *4′33″*.

Various
45'18"

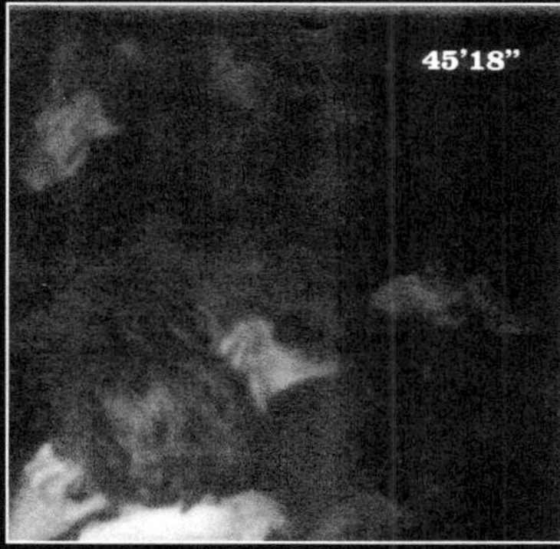

2002, Korm Plastics / Staalplaat (KP 3005), The Netherlands, CD.

Nine variations of *4'33"* by Keith Rowe, Artificial Memory Trace, Thurston Moore, Pauline Oliveros, Deep Listening Band And Guests, Jio Shimizu, Voice Crack, Clive Graham, Toshiya Tsunoda, Alignment. The booklet also contains a text by Frans de Waard on not recording Cage's *4'33"*.

Various
John Cage – Into Silence

2002, OBST (P 330.14), Germany, CD.
Track no. 11: *4'33"*, performed by Dietmar Bonnen.

Alexei Borisov + K.K. Null
Xenoglossia

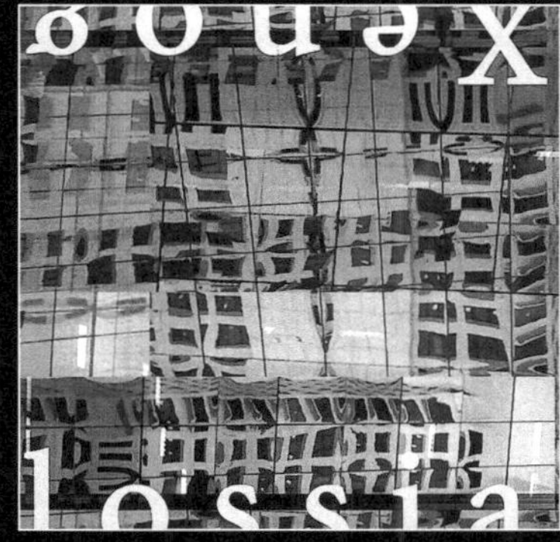

2003, Insofar Vapor Bulk (IVBCD11), Russia.
Track no. 4: *4'33"*.

Margaret Leng Tan
Art of the Toy Piano: The World of Margaret Leng Tan

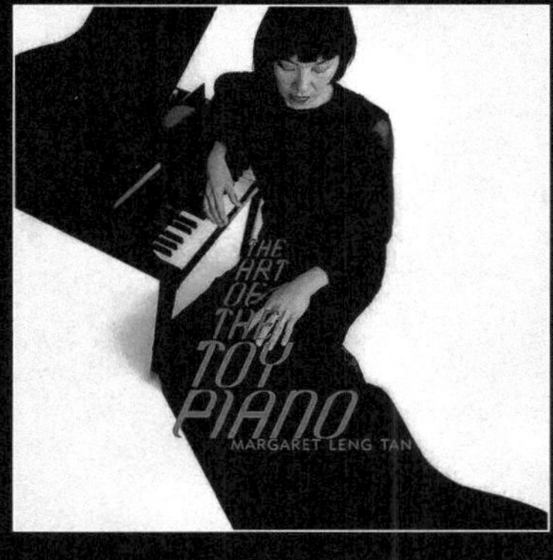

2004, Philips, DVD.

Stephanie McCallum
The Classic 100 Piano

2005, ABC Classics (476 720-2), Australia, CD.
4'33": first movement only.

Ensemble o (Sylvain Chauveau, Stéphane Garin, Joël Merah, Maitane Sebastian)
John Cage / 0

June 2006, Onement #0 (limited edition CD-R).

Ultra-red
An Archive Of Silence

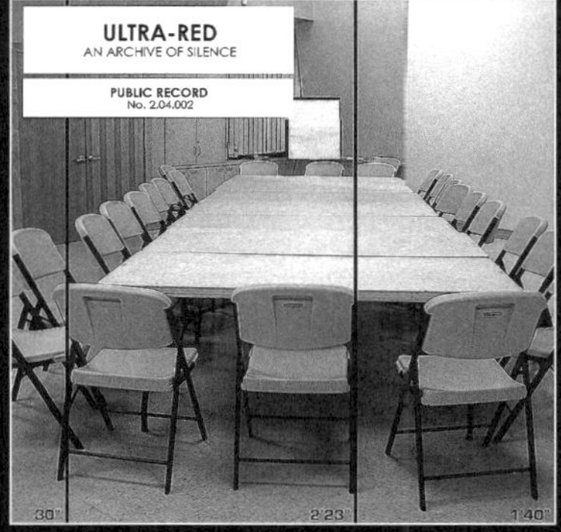

September 1, 2006, Public Record (2.04.002), US, File, MP3.

Susanne Kessel
... es wehet ein Schatten darin ...

2006, OBST (CD P 330.23), Germany, CD.

The recording of *4'33"* was made at the Schumann house, Bonn-Endenich, in the room where Robert Schumann died.

Susanne Kessel
Californian Concert Music of European Immigrants and their American Contemporaries

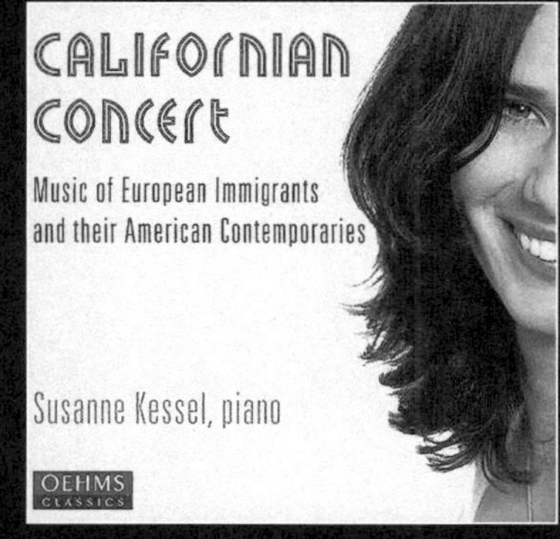

2006, Oehms Classics (OC 534), Germany, CD.

4'33" recorded on May 30, 2004 at Villa Aurora in Los Angeles, California, USA.

Cilia Erens
Uit 'T Zicht

March 2007, Not On Label (De Kunst Van Het Wandelen Series), The Netherlands, CD, Limited Edition

The two tracks are entitled Zonder Uitzicht (Without a View) and Met Uitzicht (With a View). The duration of each track is 5:33 min. which is written as *"4'33"* + 1'" on the label. The "+ 1'" notation refers to the final minute of silence meant for the listener to experience the difference of silence before and after hearing the compositions.

Various
The Sonics Of Art Spaces

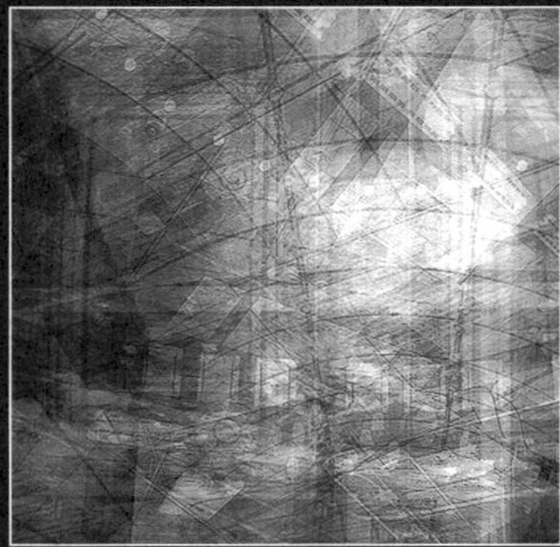

December 17, 2007, Stasisfield (SF-6001), US, 15 × File, MP3, Compilation
Track no. 15: Steve Roden, *4'33"* (Schindler House).

Oh Yes, By All Means
Greatest Hits, Vol. 1

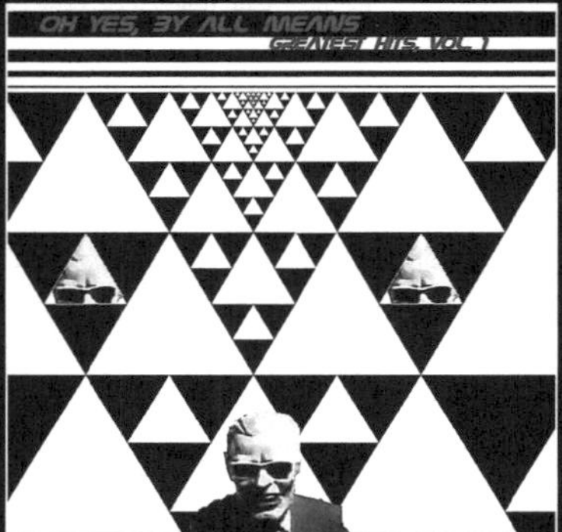

December 27, 2007, Glitch City (GC022), The Netherlands, 10 × File, MP3.
Track no. 10: *4'33"*.

Tickets Go Past
Twelve Songs About Numbers

2008, Cryptic Recording (TGOP 001), The Netherlands, CD.
Track no. 3: *Waiting For Zero* (4:33 min.).

Margaret Leng Tan
Sorceress of the New Piano

2008, Mode (194 [DVD]), Country, CD.

Matthieu Saladin
4'33"/0'00"

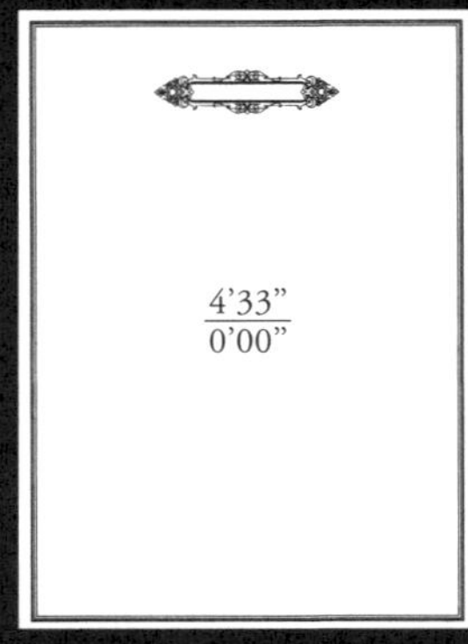

2008, Editions Provisoires (none), France, CD-R, Mini.

Maximum amplification of the first release (Cramps, 1974) of *4'33"* (1952) by John Cage, performed by Gianni-Emilio Simonetti. Play at high volume. Price: □ 4.33.

Nigel Tomm
John Cage's 4'33"

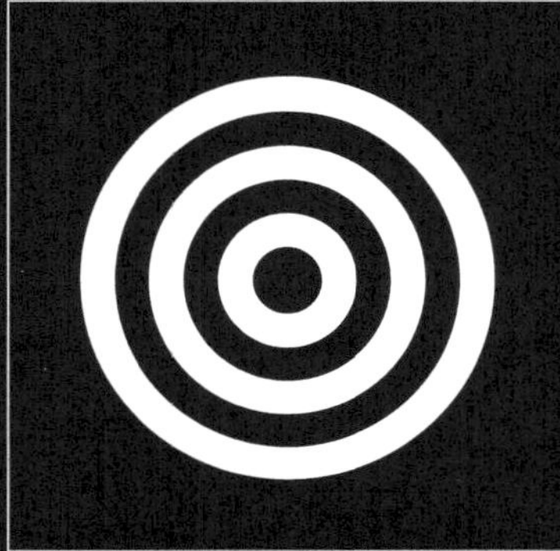

December 8, 2008, Remix Culture (ASIN: B001N0LDY8), CD, MP3.

魔ゼルな規犬
090-9170-6987

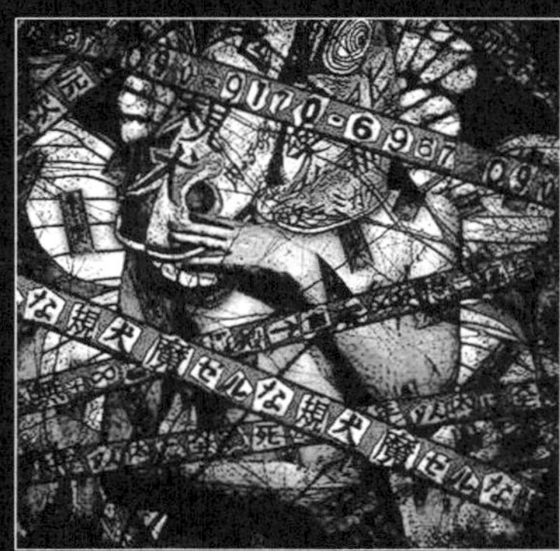

2008, 人間大學レコード (none), Japan, CD.
Track no. 12: *4'33"*.

Stjerneheimen
Star Mountains

2009, Velvet Blue Records (VB-02), Brazil, CD-R, Album.
Track no. 10: *4'33" (John Cage Cover)*, 4:33 min.

John Cage (Ulrich Krieger)
The Complete John Cage Edition

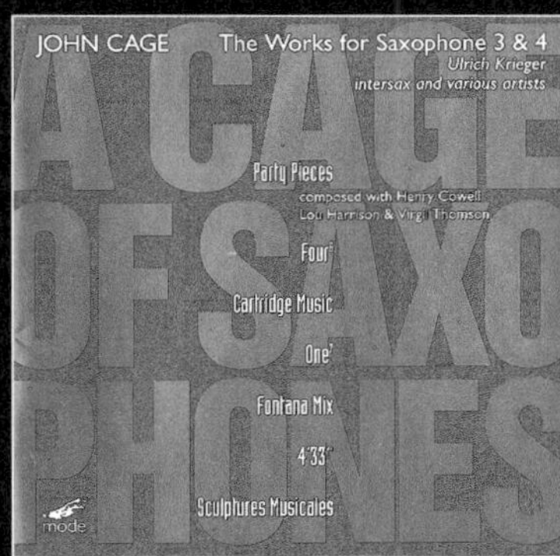

Volume 42: A Cage of Saxophones, Vol. 3 and Vol. 4 (Indeterminacy 1 & 2), 2010, Mode Records (MODE 222, 223), US, CD.

Essenz
KVIITIIVZ – Beschwörung Des Unaussprechlichen

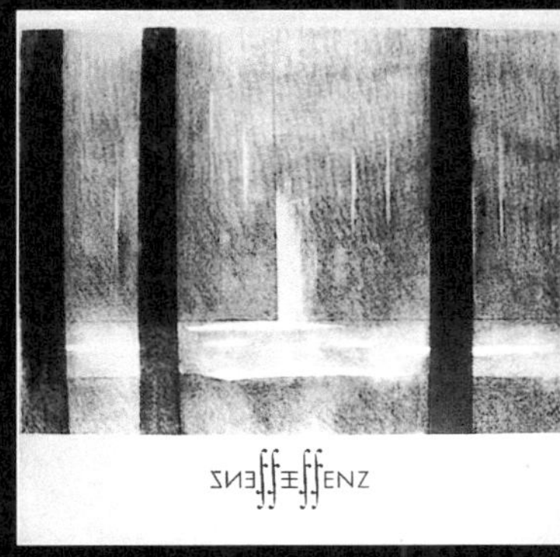

July 28, 2010, Amor Fati (AFP 005), Germany, 2 × Vinyl, LP, Album. Track D1: *Silenzium 4'33" (Tribute to John Cage)*.

John Kannenberg
Audio Tour: The 4'33" Museum

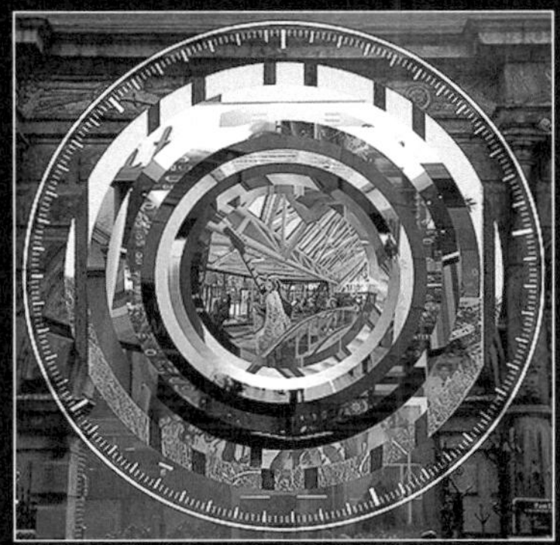

July 26, 2010, Stasisfield (SF-8003), US, 11 × File, MP3, 320 kbps, Album.

Stasisfield founder John Kannenberg presents an initial sampling of an ongoing practice that began in 2005: "performing" John Cage's *4'33"* in various museums around the world. Instead of not playing an instrument, however, these tracks of unmanipulated phonography are the product of actively recording a space, perhaps more fully realizing one of Cage's motivations behind composing *4'33"*: the encouragement of active listening. By placing this practice within the context of museums, it both translates a primarily visual experience into a purely sonic one, and reaffirms the long-standing relationship that museums have with the experimental music world, serving as venues for avant-garde performances. *4'33"* recordings were made in the Rijksmuseum, Amsterdam, NL; Motown Museum, Detroit, US; SFMOMA, San Francisco, US; Internet Archive Backup Server, Bibliotheca Alexandrina, Alexandria, Egypt; Art Institute Of Chicago Modern Wing, Chicago, US; Tate Modern, London, UK; Milwaukee Art Museum, US; Van Gogh Museum, Amsterdam, NL; Open Air Museum, Memphis, Egypt; Art Gallery Of

Cage Against the Machine
4'33"

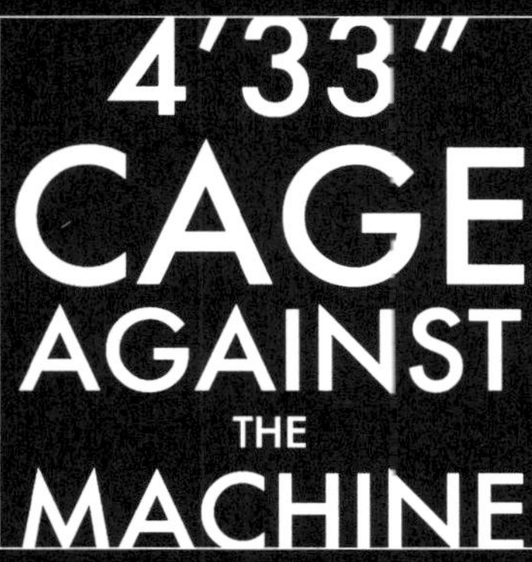

December 12, 2010, Wall of Sound (WOS099D), UK, 8 × File, MP3, Single

09CORDES1106
4'33"

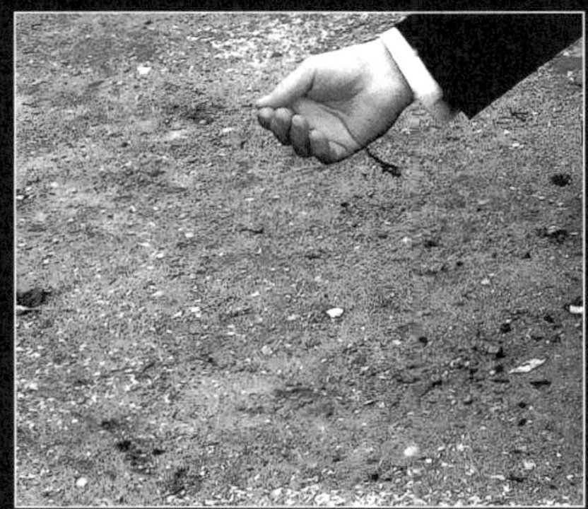

December 14, 2010, Not On Label (09CORDES1106 Self-released – 213.251.145.96), Germany, CD-R, EP, Limited Edition.

Various
Con-vpilation [Lithuania]

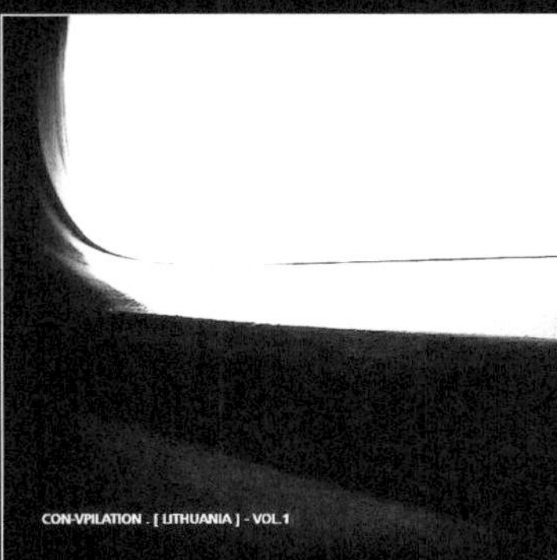

December 30, 2010, CONV (CNV66), Spain, 13 × File, MP3, Compilation, 320 kbps. Track no. 2: Diissc Orchestra. *4'33"*.

Mystified
4:33

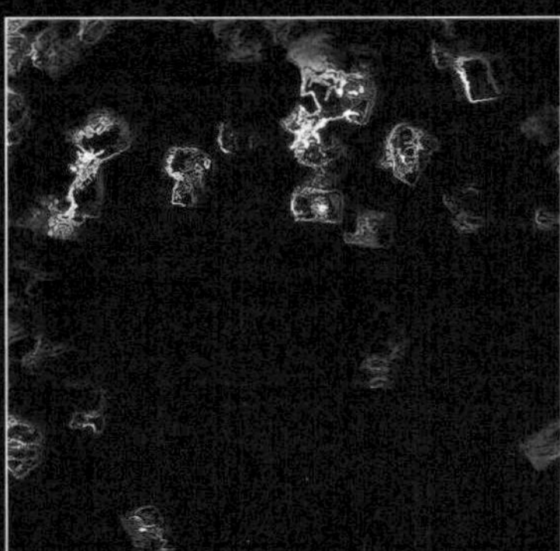

March 19, 2011, *4'33"* music (433/002), The Netherlands, File, WAV.

The Musk-rat Cult
The . . . Of

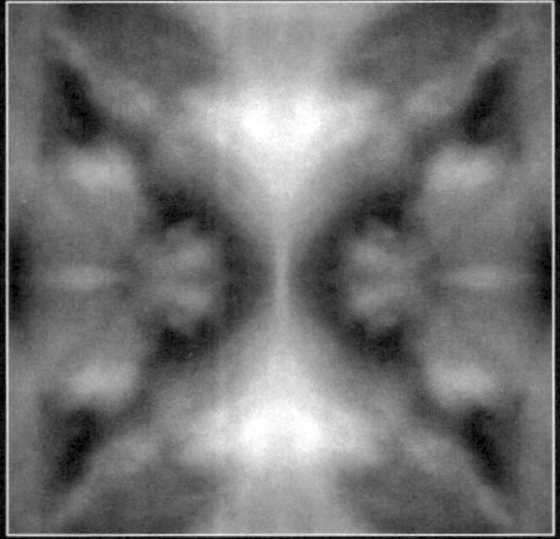

April 22, 2011, Sirona-Records (Siro034), France, 8 × File, MP3, 320 kbps Track no. 8: *Interpretation Of John Cage's 4'33"* (4:33 min.).

Various
IFAR
Musique Concrète 4'33"

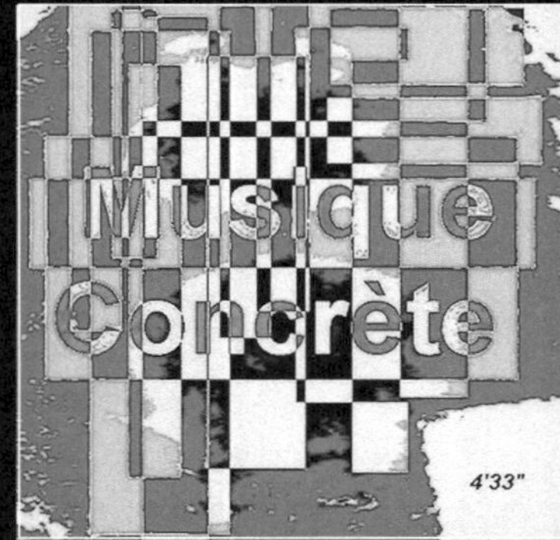

December 10, 2011, Institute For Alien Research (none), UK, CD-R, Compilation, 15 × File, MP3. All tracks are of the same length of 4:33 min.

Various
Sounds Like Silence

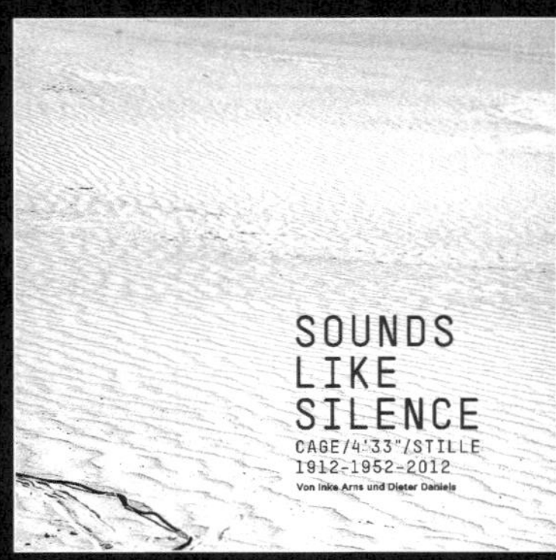

Ed. Inke Arns, Dieter Daniels, August 24, 2012, DeutschlandRadio Kultur (radio broadcast), Grünrekorder, Germany, CD (Gruen 116/LC 09488).

Reader

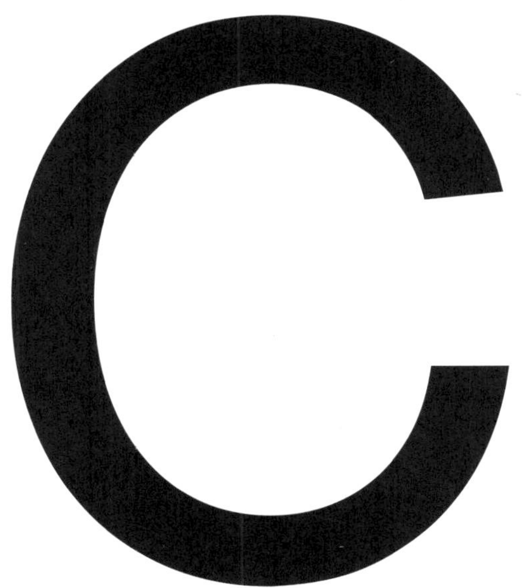

Dieter Daniels / Eva Wilson
Silence: A Reader

Cage's seemingly simple "silent piece" is in fact a highly complex work. The composer has written several different scores as well as a series of variations and sequels. In the course of his long creative career, he repeatedly updated and recontextualized the piece. The scholarship on *4'33"* is similarly variegated, approaching the piece and its sequels from the angles of musicology, art history, media theory, philosophy, perception theory, theater studies, and gender studies. Simultaneously, scholars have pointed out numerous links to other fields and issues, including Zen Buddhism, conceptual art, performance art, the debate regarding the liveness of music, the development of pop music, and even Cage's homosexuality.

The anthology compiled for this publication provides an overview of these different approaches and, in addition to the various methodologies presented in the excerpts from the selected authors' essays, the texts offer a wide range of background information to the work. The excerpts are arranged following the chronology of Cage's own development of his "silent piece" from 1948 (*Silent Prayer*) to 1962 (*0'00"*). As most of the authors mention similar basic facts about the piece, strict editing was necessary to avoid repetitions. The texts are chosen to represent the author's main focus of interest and the core thesis of his/her approach, but they do not always give complete coverage to the author's argument. Similarly, some relevant studies could not be included because the areas of redundancy relative to other texts proved too great.[1]

Some recent texts were published around the same time (notably those by Hans-Friedrich Bormann, Branden W. Joseph, Liz Kotz, and Dörte Schmidt). The authors thus could not cross-reference each other and their theses are juxtaposed here for the first time. They vary in focus and have their background in such diverse discourses as performance theory, art history, textuality, and musical philology. However, they are not contradictory but rather combine to produce complementary perspectives.

The anthology as a whole is not meant to offer a clash of interpretations. It aims to unfold a spectrum of approaches, of convergences and differences, which enhance our ability to come to grips with the ongoing multiplicity of meanings and readings of the "silent piece." In this sense, the theoretical "interpretations" are perhaps not so distinct from the musical "interpretations," each one different, but most of them equivalent with regard to the wide range of individual ways to fill the silence. Like the literature on Duchamp's ready-mades, writing on *4'33"* seems to be a never-ending story — one, however, that becomes more and more interesting and complex over time. The essays and thoughts compiled here present us ultimately with a polyphonic discourse, without ever coming to any final or finite conclusions. [DD]

1 E.g.: Thomas M. Maier, *Ausdruck der Zeit. Ein Weg zu John Cages stillem Stück 4'33"* (Saarbrücken: Pfau, 2001) and Eric de Visscher, "'There's no such thing as silence…': John Cage's Poetics of Silence" in: *Writings About John Cage*, ed. Richard Kostelanetz (Ann Arbor, MI: University of Michigan Press, 1993).

Texts by John Cage

John Cage, “A Composer’s Confessions. Adress given before the National Inter-Collegiate Arts Conference, Vassar College, February 28, 1948,” in *MusikTexte. Zeitschrift für neue Musik,* 40/41 (August 1991), p. 67.

A Composer’s Confessions

However, as long as this desire exists in us, for new materials, new forms, new this and new that, we must search to satisfy it. I have, for instance, several new desires (two may seem absurd but I am serious about them): first, to compose a piece of uninterrupted silence and sell it to the Muzak Co. It will be 3 or 4½ minutes long—these being the standard lenghts of “canned” music, and its title will be *Silent Prayer*. It will open with a single idea which I will attempt to make as seductive as the color and shape or fragrance of a flower. The ending will approach imperceptibility. And, second, to compose and have performed a composition using as instruments nothing but twelve radios. It will be my *Imaginary Landscape No. 4*.

John Cage, “Composition as Process” (1958), in John Cage, *Silence. Lectures and writings by John Cage* (Middletown, CT: Wesleyan University Press, 1961), pp. 22–23.

Composition as Process

[...]
And what happens
to a piece of
music when it
is purposeless-
ly made? ¶ What hap-
pens, for instance,
to silence? That
is, how does the
mind’s perception
of it change? For-
merly, silence
was the time lapse
between sounds, use-
ful towards a va-
riety of
ends, among them
that of tasteful
arrangement, where
by separat-
ing two sounds or
two groups of sounds
their differen-
ces or rela-
tionships might re-
ceive emphasis;
or that of ex-
pressivity,
where silences
in musi-
cal discourse might
provide pause or
punctuation;
or again, that
of architec-
ture, where the in-
troduction or
interruption
of silence might
give defini-
tion either to
a predeter-
mined structure or
to an organ-
ically de-
veloping one.
Where none of these
or other goals
is present, si-
lence becomes some-
thing else—not si-
lence at all, but
sounds, the ambi-
ent sounds. The na-
ture of these is
unpredicta-
ble and changing.
These sounds (which are

called silence on-
ly because they
do not form part
of a musi-
cal intention)
may be depen-
ded upon to
exist. The world
teems with them, and
is, in fact, at
no point free of
them. He who has
entered an an-
echoic cham-
ber, a room made
as silent as
technologi-
cally possible,
has heard there two
sounds, one high, one
low—the high the
listener’s ner-
vous system in
operation,
the low his blood
in circu-
lation. There are, dem-
onstrably, sounds
to be heard and
forever, giv-
en ears to hear.
Where these ears are
in connection
with a mind that
has nothing to
do, that mind is
free to enter
into the act
of listening,
hearing each sound
just as it is,
not as a phe-
nomenon more
or less approx-
imating a
preconception.
[...]

[...] (each line of the text whether speech or silence requiring one second for its performance)—J.C.

Richard Kostelanetz, *Conversing with Cage*, 2nd Edition (New York and London: Routledge, 2003), pp. 70–71, pp. 196–98, p. 217.

Conversing with Cage

I think perhaps my own best piece, at least the one I like the most, is the silent piece [*4′33″* (pronounced four minutes, thirty-three seconds ❧ or four feet, thirty-three inches ❧), 1952]. It has three movements and in all of the movements there are no sounds. I wanted my work to be free of my own likes and dislikes, because I think music should be free of the feelings and

ideas of the composer. I have felt and hoped to have led other people to feel that the sounds of their environment constitute a music which is more interesting than the music which they would hear if they went into a concert hall.
—Jeff Goldberg (1974)

They missed the point. There's no such thing as silence. What they thought was silence [in *4'33"*], because they didn't know how to listen, was full of accidental sounds. You could hear the wind stirring outside during the first movement [in the premiere]. During the second, raindrops began pattering the roof, and during the third, the people themselves made all kinds of interesting sounds as they talked or walked out.
—John Kobler (1968)

People began whispering to one another, and some people began to walk out. They didn't laugh—they were irritated when they realized nothing was going to happen, and they haven't forgotten it 30 years later: they're still angry.
—Michael John White (1982)

I had friends whose friendship I valued and whose friendship I lost because of that. They thought that calling something you hadn't done, so to speak, music was a form of pulling the wool over their eyes, I guess.
—Ellsworth Snyder (1985)

Most composers like some of their own pieces better than others, or feel some are more important than others. Which piece or pieces of yours would you consider the most important?
Well, the most important piece is my silent piece.
That's very interesting. A lot of people would agree with that.
Uh-huh.
But you feel that way as well.
Oh yes. I always think of it before I write the next piece.
Really? Tell me how you came to do that piece?
I had thought of it already in 1948 and gave a lecture called *A Composer's Confessions*. It was given at Vassar College in the course of a festival involving artists and thinkers in all fields. Among those was Paul Weiss who taught philosophy at Yale University. I was just then in the flush of my early contact with Oriental philosophy. It was out of that that my interest in silence naturally developed: I mean it's almost transparent. If you have, as you do in India, nine permanent emotions and the center one is the one without colour—the others are white or black—and tranquillity is in the center and freedom from likes and dislikes. It stands to reason, the absence of activity which is also characteristically Buddhist … well, if you want the wheel to stop, and the wheel is the Four Noble Truths. The first is Life is Activity, sometimes translated as Life is Pain. If the wheel is to be brought to a stop, the activity must stop.

The marvellous thing about it is when activity comes to a stop, what is immediately seen is that the rest of the world has not stopped. There is no place without activity. Oh, there are so many ways to say it. Say I die as a person. I continue to live as a landscape for smaller animals. I just never stop. Just put me in the ground and I become part and parcel of another life, another activity. So the only difference between activity and inactivity is the mind. And the mind that becomes free of desire. Joyce would agree here, free of desire and loathing—that's why he said he was so involved with comedy, because tragedy is not so free from these two. So when the mind has become in that way free, even though there continues to be some kind of activity, it can be said to be inactivity. And that's what I have been doing, and that's why critics are so annoyed with my work. Because they see that I am denying the things to which they are devoted.
—Stephen Montague (1982)

You see I was afraid that making a piece that had no sounds in it would appear as if I were making a joke. In fact, I probably worked longer on my "silent" piece than I worked on any other. I worked four years—
Just to get up the guts.
Actually what pushed me into it was not guts but the example of Robert Rauschenberg. His white paintings that I referred to earlier: When I saw those, I said, "Oh yes, I must; otherwise I'm lagging, otherwise music is lagging."
—Alan Gillmor and Roger Shattuck (1973)

What other works of yours do you feel have also been very important?
All the others.
But the silent piece stands above all the rest.
It's more radical. I think the pieces since the silent piece in a sense are more radical than the ones that precede it, though I had an inclination toward silence that you can discern in very early pieces written in the 1930s. One of my early teachers always complained that I had no sooner started than I stopped. You can see that in the *Duet for Two Flutes*, or those early piano pieces that were written in the thirties. Then I'm always introducing silence right near the beginning. When any composer in his right mind would be making things thicker and thicker, I was getting thinner and thinner.
—Stephen Montague (1982)

[…] *Could you explain the function of silence in your music compared to the "white page" of Mallarmé?*
I've always felt very close to Mallarmé; and the book that was published posthumously, *Le Livre*, also is very involved with chance operations, is it not? I often think of him, though I haven't studied Mallarmé closely. But one has the feeling of space in which a variety of things can be present.
But didn't you say, on the other side, at least concerning your music, that there is no such thing like silence?
Right. There always are sounds.
Well, just in comparison to Mallarmé's fear of the "white page"?
He had a fear of it?
In some ways, yes, he had to write something on it at least—the fear of every author of having a white page in front of him.
Well, clearly, my silent piece doesn't express that fear but expresses the acceptance of whatever happens in that emptiness. And the same thing was expressed by that empty painting, that white painting of Bob Rauschenberg, which I mention in the note which precedes [the article on him in] *Silence*. It saw that the white paintings came first and my silent piece came afterwards. And Mallarmé preceded both.
—Birger Ollrogge (1985)

[…] *Is it possible to say that the "Cagean" influence is also present in conceptual art?*

I don't agree with that notion. I think that we are all together and that ideas are also equally available to us. For instance, two inventors invent the same thing at the same time. This must be that they didn't influence each other, but that they were influenced by the possibility of having that idea. So I think that what appears to be my influence is merely that I fell into a situation that other people are also falling into. And what is so nice about the situation is that it admits a great deal of variety. I would say that it admits more variety than if you fell into the twelve-tone system.

I have thought, for instance, that *4'33"*, which could be thought to be the source of my influence on conceptual art, was a very physical work, not conceptual. I thought of it as a quick way of hearing what there was to hear.

—Alcides Lanza (1971).

John Cage on Robert Rauschenberg's *White Paintings*

John Cage, *Silence, Lectures and Writings by John Cage* (Middletown, CT: Wesleyan University Press), 1961, p. 98.

"To Whom It May Concern:
The white paintings came
first; my silent piece
came later."
—J. C.

John Cage, *An Anthology,* ed. Richard Kostelanetz (New York: Praeger, 1970), p. 111–12.

To Whom
No subject
No image
No taste
No object
No beauty
No message
No talent
No technique (no why)
No idea
No intention
No art
No feeling
No black
No white (no and)

From Emily Genauer's column. Reprinted with her permission.

After careful consideration I have come to the conclusion that there is nothing in these paintings that could not be changed, that they can be seen in any light and are not destroyed by the action of shadows.

John Cage
Hallelujah! the blind can see again; the water's fine.

John Cage, "On Nam June Paik's Zen for Film", with a remark by Nam June Paik, in *Nam June Paik* (New York: Galeria Bonino, 1971).

On Nam June Paik's *Zen for Film*

On the nature of silence: Well now, you know that I've written a piece called *4'33"*, which has no sounds of my own making in it, and that Robert Rauschenberg has made paintings which have no images on them—they're simply canvases, white canvases, with no images on them—and Nam June Paik, the Korean composer, has made an hour-long film which has no images on it. Now, offhand, you might say that all three actions are the same. But they're quite different.

The Rauschenberg paintings, in my opinion, as I've expressed it, become airports for particles of dust and shadows that are in the environment.

My piece, *4'33"*, becomes in performance the sounds of the environment.

Now, in the music, the sounds of the environment remain, so to speak, where they are, whereas in the case of the Rauschenberg painting the dust and the shadows, the changes in light and so forth, don't remain where they are but come to the painting. In the case of the Nam June Paik film which has no images on it, the room is darkened, the film is projected, and what you see is the dust that has collected on the film. I think that's somewhat similar to the case of the Rauschenberg painting, though the focus is more intense. The nature of the environment is more on the film, different from the dust and shadows that are the environment falling on the painting, and thus less free.

University of Cincinnati. 1968
"Cinema Now"
(edited by H. Currie & M. Porte)

N.B. Dear John:
The nature of environment is much more on TV than on film or painting. In fact, TV (its random movement of tiny electrons) IS the environment of today.

N.J.P. (1971)

Preconditions / Prehistory

Branden W. Joseph, selection of "White on White," chapter 1 from *Random Order: Robert Rauschenberg and the Neo-Avant-Garde* (Cambridge, Mass.: MIT Press, 2003), pp. 42–49.

White on White / *Silent Prayer*

Cage has always been clear that his infamous *4'33"* of silence was composed after seeing Rauschenberg's *White Paintings*.[1] In this, the most controversial of Cage's works, a performer sits at his or her instrument for the requisite amount of time without sounding a single note, while the audience members are given to hear the sounds that occur in their surroundings. Cage would explain that not only did Rauschenberg's *White Paintings* give him the "courage" to compose a piece of such radicality,[2] they made him fear that the development of music had fallen behind that of art. "Oh, yes, I must," Cage recalls thinking, "otherwise I'm lagging, otherwise music is lagging."[3]

Despite Cage's insistence that the *White Paintings* preceded the composition of *4'33"*, historians have been tempted to backdate Cage's silent piece from the summer of 1952 to early 1948.[4] The reason derives from a comment Cage made in the lecture "A Composer's Confessions", delivered at Vassar College in February of that year. Cage explained to his audience that he had "several new desires," the first of which was:

> to compose a piece of uninterrupted silence and sell it to Muzak Co. It will be 3 or 4½ minutes long—those being the standard lengths of "canned" music—and its title will be *Silent Prayer*. It will open with a single idea which I will attempt to make as seductive as the color and shape and fragrance of a flower. The ending will approach imperceptibility.[5]

Although *Silent Prayer* undeniably represents an early stage in the development of *4'33"*, the two works ... rightfully belong within two separate aesthetic paradigms.

As noted by Eric de Visscher, who has most carefully charted the rapid evolution of Cage's concept of silence during these years, an important component of *Silent Prayer* is its antagonistic relationship to Muzak.[6] Indeed, on one level, *Silent Prayer* appears as nothing more than the abstract negation of the unceasing stream of piped-in, commercial background music. In 1948 Cage had not yet formulated his mature concept of silence, and the "uninterrupted silence" of *Silent Prayer* was still understood in terms of the complete absence of sound. Nevertheless, even at this early stage, Cage's piece was not conceived simply in negative terms and was not intended primarily to shock its audience through musical withdrawal. Instead, with *Silent Prayer* Cage sought to revalue silence as a distinct essence, presenting it with a positivity of its own.[7]

More than simply the negation of Muzak, Cage's *Silent Prayer* was to serve as an acoustical manifestation of a metaphysical concept derived in part from Cage's study of the medieval European mystic, Meister Eckhart.[8] His metaphorical description of the piece in terms of "the color and shape and fragrance of a flower" distinctly echoes the line found in Eckhart: "I am come like the fragrance of a flower."[9] In Eckhart, this phrase occurs as one of a series of analogies provided by St. Augustine to describe the manner in which the "eternal Word" can be "uttered in the Person of the Son while remaining God by nature in his nature."[10] Thus, Cage's initial view of his silent piece closely resembled Rauschenberg's earliest understanding of his *White Paintings* in relation to incarnation. Like them, *Silent Prayer* seems to have been conceived as an earthly manifestation of a divine essence, the embodiment of "an organic silence." Indeed, in the immediate context of this quotation, Eckhart describes the indivisible and all-encompassing nature of the divine essence precisely in terms of "absolute stillness" and "silence."[11]

Between 1948 and 1951, however, Cage's idea of silence began to change rapidly and significantly. Instead of seeing sound and silence as opposites, Cage came to understand them as inextricably interrelated. In part, this transformation in Cage's thinking parallels a deeper understanding of Eckhart's theology.[12] For Eckhart, God's divine essence was presented in the form of an all-encompassing and all-supporting "Ground"—"from which," Cage summarized, "all impermanencies flow and to which they return."[13] By 1951, Cage's ideas of sound and silence were further coupled with an emerging interest in Zen Buddhism which conceived of being and nothingness not as opposed to one another but as necessarily intertwined.[14] But though this understanding of the relationship of sound and silence more completely integrated the existence of one within the other, Cage had not yet overcome the duality between them.[15] While he saw them as more closely interrelated, sound and silence still remained distinct and different—resembling, as he stated in the "Lecture on Something," the positive and negative of "an alternating current."[16]

It was Cage's oft-recounted experience within an anechoic chamber at Harvard in 1951 that enabled him to overcome the remaining distinction between silence and sound. Once inside the room, specially dampened so that no sound could either penetrate the walls or reverberate on the inside, Cage heard not the absolute silence he had been expecting but rather two distinct sounds emanating from his own body: one was the low tone of his blood circulating, the other the high tone of his nervous system.[17] As a result, Cage came to understand the strict impossibility of silence, famously redefining it as the presence of unintentional noises. "The situation one is clearly in," Cage concluded, "is not objective (sound-silence), but rather subjective (sounds only), those intended and those others (so-called silence) not intended."[18]

This event is among the most significant and most frequently recounted in Cage literature. Nevertheless, it seems so far to have gone unobserved that whatever his actual experience in the anechoic chamber, both Cage's story and the insight derived from it were, in essence, a recasting of Henri Bergson's "The Idea of 'Nothing'" from *Creative Evolution*. In that discussion, with which Cage was familiar, Bergson imagines a scene directly analogous to Cage's within the anechoic chamber in order to demonstrate the futility of attempting to imagine nothing.[19]

"I am going to close my eyes, stop my ears, extinguish one by one the sensations that come to me from the outer world," declares Bergson:

> Now it is done; all my perceptions vanish, the material universe sinks into silence and the night.—I subsist, however, and cannot help myself subsisting. I am still there, with the organic sensations which come to me from the surface and from the interior of my body, with the recollections which my past perceptions have left behind them—nay, with the impression, most positive and full, of the void I have just made about me.[20]

Significantly, this section of *Creative Evolution* was devoted to a critique of the reification of the idea of nothing—precisely the same type of reification Cage had been attempting in *Silent Prayer's* elevation of the concept of silence to a substantive essence.[21] Through his demonstration, Bergson sought to prove that such nothingness was in fact devoid of ontological status: that it was merely a "pseudo-idea" resulting from confusion within the subject.[22] What was perceived as the absence of an object or the negation of an idea actually corresponded only to the finding of one thing while searching for, or expecting, another. It was—to use one of Bergson's examples—like declaring "this is not verse" when, while searching through a bookshelf in order to find verse, one happens upon a book filled with prose.[23]

In the story of the anechoic chamber, Cage imported Bergson's critique of negation from philosophy into music, applying it to sound in specific rather than to being in general; but the conclusion was the same. Indeed, a substitution of the term "sound" for "reality" in Bergson's writing provides Cage's mature understanding of silence exactly. This is Bergson:

> Now the unreality which is here in question is purely relative to the direction in which our attention is engaged, for we are immersed in realities and cannot pass out of them; only, if the present reality is not the one we are seeking, we speak of the absence of this sought-for reality wherever we find the presence of another. We thus express what we have as a function of what we want.[24]

It is Bergson's critique of negation, expressed in his contention that "there is no absolute void in nature,"[25] that ultimately underlies Cage's statement that "There is no such thing as silence," as well as Rauschenberg's later pronouncement that "A canvas is never empty."[26]

Yet, although inextricably related to his understanding of Bergson's critique of negation, Cage's experience in the anechoic chamber was still not, as existing literature would have it, sufficient to produce the understanding of silence showcased in *4'33"*.[27] In the chamber, environmental noises were completely shut out, and what Cage heard was entirely predicated on their exclusion. In *4'33"*, by contrast, the sounds of the environment are allowed to resonate freely within the composition. What connects these two is the idea of transparency developed by Moholy-Nagy in *The New Vision*—hence the profound effect that Rauschenberg's *White Paintings* had on Cage at Black Mountain College. Understood in terms of Moholy-Nagy's incorporation of external events, they indicated to Cage a means of escaping the solipsism of his Harvard experience and revealed to him that music was, as he put it, "behind."[28] With *4'33"*, then, Cage succeeded in moving music into the same "modern" (we would now say "postmodern") paradigm occupied by Rauschenberg. Following on his understanding of the *White Paintings*, Cage's criterion of musical modernity became an acoustical "transparency" to sounds outside the work. As he later noted, "A cough or baby crying will not ruin a good piece of modern music."[29]

In the following year, Cage further clarified the connection between Rauschenberg's *White Paintings* and his *4'33"* in a version of the score dedicated to Irwin Kremen. The original score for *4'33"* was measured out on conventional music paper, with staffs and bar lines but without notes or rests. A second version notated the piece linguistically as "I. Tacet / II. Tacet / III. Tacet." The Kremen version, however, consists of six sheets of entirely blank paper onto which Cage drew six long, vertical lines.[30] Each line represents the beginning or the end of one of the work's three separate movements, which last, respectively, thirty seconds; two minutes, twenty-three seconds; and one minute, forty seconds. Clearly recalling the edges of Rauschenberg's abutted canvasses, these lines form the empty structure of *4'33"*. A key provided at the bottom of the page reads "1 page = 7 inches = 56" [seconds]" and provides the means by which the score can be read horizontally across the page to give the timing of the movements. Visually, the score acts just as does one of Rauschenberg's *White Paintings*; the lights, shadows, and particles falling onto it become analogues of the environmental sounds occurring within the piece when "performed."

1 As Cage wrote in the preface to his article on Rauschenberg in *Silence:* "To Whom It May Concern: The white paintings came first; my silent piece came later" (Cage, "On Robert Rauschenberg," in *Silence*, p. 98). Rauschenberg has recently stated that, "[Cage] wrote the silent piece because of my paintings. And there were lots more".

2 Richard Dyer, "A Refreshing, Surprising Exchange with John Cage," *Boston Globe*, 20 October 1988, p. B8; and Deborah Ann Campana, "Form and Structure in the Music of John Cage" (Ph.D., Northwestern University, 1985), p. 103.

3 Kostelanetz, *Conversing with Cage*, p. 67.

4 See, for example, James Pritchett, *The Music of John Cage* (Cambridge: Cambridge University Press, 1993), pp. 59–60.

5 John Cage, "A Composer's Confessions," (1948) in *John Cage: Writer*, ed. Richard Kostelanetz (New York: Limelight Editions, 1993), p. 43.

6 Eric de Visscher, "'There's no such thing as silence...': John Cage's Poetics of Silence," in *Writings About John Cage*, ed. Richard Kostelanetz (Ann Arbor: University of Michigan Press, 1993), p. 118. See also the discussion of the relations and differences of *Silent Prayer* and *4'33"* in Kahn, *Noise Water Meat*, pp. 161–99.

7 See de Visscher, p. 120.

8 Eckhart's aesthetic philosophy was discussed in the writings of Indian art historian Ananda Coomaraswamy, also read by Cage. Beginning in the mid-1940s–most likely upon the suggestion of the mythologist Joseph Campbell, a close friend at the time–Cage became interested in South Asian and medieval European philosophy and religion. For a discussion of Cage's Eastern influences, see David W. Patterson, "The Picture That Is Not in the Colors: Cage, Coomaraswamy, and the Impact of India," in Patterson, ed., *John Cage: Music, Philosophy, and Intention, 1933–1950*, pp. 177–215. Patterson dates Cage's initial interest in Asian philosophy and aesthetics to the years of World War II (p. 179). James Pritchett has related *Silent Prayer* and *4'33"* (between which he makes little distinction) to Cage's adoption of Eckhart's ideas of "ignorance" or self-negation which was a means of being able to perceive the divine (Pritchett, pp. 46, 60, and 206 n. 11).

9 Eckhardt, in Franz Pfeiffer, *Meister Eckhart*, trans. C. de B. Evans (London: John M. Watkins, 1924), p. 284; this collection of Eckhardt's writings is cited in Ananda K. Coomaraswamy, "Meister Eckhart's View of Art," in *The Transformation of Nature on Art* (Cambridge: Harvard University Press, 1934), p. 83.

10 Eckhart, in Pfeiffer, *Meister Eckhart*, p. 284.

11 Eckhart, in Pfeiffer, *Meister Eckhart*, pp. 284, 283.

12 This pattern–that a reference, after entering his thinking, becomes progressively more complexly understood as he engages with it over a period that may last several years–recurs often in Cage's work.

13 John Cage, "Composition as Process II: Indeterminacy," (1958) in *Silence*, p. 39. See, for example, Eckhart: "Three things are to be noted about the divine essence. First and foremost, it is the principle preserving all things; in his divine essence God is in all things upholding them" (in Pfeiffer, *Meister Eckhardt*, p. 284). Pritchett, as noted above, discusses *Silent Prayer/4'33"* in terms of an idea, found in Eckhart, of opening oneself up to the universal. However, as de Visscher has indicated, in 1948–1949 Cage still held, "a relatively classical position about silence: silence is considered as absolutely necessary to the existence of sound, but still as the absence of sound" (de Visscher, p. 120). Thus, it would seem that an understanding of *Silent Prayer* as a representation of a stillness rather than as an opening onto the totality of the universe lies closer to Cage's interpretation of *Silent Prayer* as expressed in "A Composer's Confessions." Clearly, this notion of silence has Heideggerian implications as well. For an investigation of Cage's work from this perspective, see Marc Froment Meurice, *Les Intermittences de la raison: penser Cage, entendre Heidegger* (Paris: Klincksieck, 1982).

14 See, de Visscher, p. 121, who also notes that, in that their sounds, soft and somewhat isolated, never seem fully to emerge from their silent surroundings, Cage's compositions of the time served to illustrate this mutual interdependence.

15 de Visscher, p. 123.
16 Cage, "Lecture on Something," (1951) in *Silence*, p. 135.
17 This story is recounted many times in Cage's writings. See, for example, "Experimental Music," in *Silence*, p. 8: "For certain engineering purposes, it is desirable to have as silent a situation as possible. Such a room is called an anechoic chamber, its six walls made of special material, a room without echoes. I entered one at Harvard University several years ago and heard two sounds, one high and one low. When I described them to the engineer in charge, he informed me that the high one was my nervous system in operation, the low one my blood in circulation." See also *Silence*, pp. 13–14, 23, 168, and *A Year from Monday*, p. 134.
18 Cage, "Experimental Music: Doctrine," (1955) in *Silence*, p. 14.
19 Henri Bergson, *Creative Evolution*, trans. Arthur Mitchell (New York: Henry Holt & Co., 1911), pp. 272–298. To my knowledge, the impact of Bergson's thinking upon Cage has not previously been noted. Cage explicit refers to Bergson at the end of the article "Experimental Music," where he writes: "Here we are concerned with the coexistence of dissimilars, and the central points where fusion occurs are many: the ears of the listeners wherever they are. This disharmony, to paraphrase Bergson's statement about disorder, is simply a harmony to which many are unaccustomed," in *Silence*, p. 12. This idea forms part of Bergson's larger critique of negation (*Creative Evolution*, pp. 241 ff.).
20 Bergson, *Creative Evolution*, p. 278.
21 Bergson, *Creative Evolution*, pp. 295–96.
22 Bergson, *Creative Evolution*, p. 277.
23 Bergson, *Creative Evolution*, pp. 221, 232.
24 Bergson, *Creative Evolution*, pp. 273 (emphasis in original).
25 Bergson, *Creative Evolution*, p. 281.
26 Cage, "45′ for a Speaker," in *Silence*, p. 191; Rauschenberg, quoted in Dorothy C. Miller, ed., *Sixteen Americans* (New York: Museum of Modern Art, 1959), p. 58.
27 In his discussion of Cagean silence, de Visscher remarks upon an apparent one-year delay in Cage's drawing upon the consequences of his experience at Harvard (de Visscher, p. 125).
28 Despite the decisive impact that Rauschenberg's *White Paintings* had on Cage's thinking, the concept of transparency began to enter Cage's mind. The earliest quotation in which he relates transparency and music occurs in a lecture delivered on 27 March 1952: "It acts in such a way that one can 'hear through' a piece of music just as one can see through some modern buildings or see through a wire sculpture by Richard Lippold or the glass of Marcel Duchamp" (Cage, "Juilliard Lecture," in *A Year from Monday*, p. 102). The date of this lecture is given in David Wayne Patterson, "Appraising the Catchwords, c. 1942–1959: John Cage's Asian-Derived Rhetoric and the Historical Reference of Black Mountain College" (Ph.D., Columbia University, 1996), p. 336; and in John Holzaepfel, "David Tudor and the Performance of American Experimental Music, 1950–1959" (Ph.D., City University of New York, 1994), p. 223, note 32.
29 Cage, "45′ for a Speaker," in *Silence*, p. 161.
30 The version of the score for *4′33″* dedicated to Irwin Kremen initially appeared in *Source* 1, no. 2 (July 1967), and has been published, in a corrected version, by C.F. Peters as Edition 6777a. For a discussion of the important implications of the second version of the score for postwar art, see Liz Kotz, "Post-Cagean Aesthetics and the 'Event' Score," *October* 95 (Winter 2001), pp. 55–89. For a documentation of the different versions of the score of 4′33″, see William Fetterman, *John Cage's Theatre Pieces: Notations and Performances* (Amsterdam: Harwood Academic Publishers, 1996), pp. 69–84.

Douglas Kahn, "John Cage: Silence and Silencing," in *The Musical Quarterly,* 1997, 81(4), p. 556–598. www.douglaskahn.com/writings/douglas_kahn-cage_silence_and_silencing.pdf

John Cage: Silence and Silencing

In this article, I will examine Cagean sounds at the amplified threshold of their disappearance—silence, small and barely audible sounds—and how the social, political, poetic, and ecological aspects correspondingly disappear. I will not venture into what Yvonne Rainer has called Cage's "goofy naiveté" when it comes to politics, nor explore how Cage dealt with the theatrical, organizational, or institutional practices of Western art music, nor discuss Cage's compositional prowess. I will concentrate primarily on how his concept of sound failed to admit a requisite sociality by which a politics and poetics of sound could be elaborated within artistic practice or daily life.

[...] [W]hen questioned from the vantage point of sound instead of music, Cage's ideas become less an occasion for uncritical celebration (as is too often the case among commentators on Cage) and his work as a whole becomes open to an entirely different set of representations. What becomes apparent in general is that while venturing to the sounds outside music, his ideas did not adequately make the trip; the world he wanted for music was a select one, where most of the social and ecological noise was muted and where other more proximal noises were suppressed.

[...] These considerations made their first coordinated impact on his thinking during the critical years 1948–52, from the proposal for his first silent composition, *Silent Prayer* (1948), to his most notorious composition, *4′33″* (1952).[8] The link between these two silences, moreover, demonstrated how he developed techniques and rationale, while engaging the sounds and silences of the world, to musically silence the social.

8 The year 1952 was a good one for nothing to happen. Following Rauschenberg's white and black paintings of the year before, there was Beckett's *Waiting for Godot* (1952), with its not-so-pregnant pauses scattered throughout a larger non-event. If Godot was a play "where nothing happens twice," then *4′33″*, with its three movements, was a composition where nothing happens thrice. In 1952 also appeared the final version of Guy Debord's film *Hurlements en faveur de Sade,* which consisted of black and white *imageless* screens with a pared-down sound track of people speaking. Debord used another form of withholding in his 1961 address to the Group for Research on Everyday Life by not participating in the everyday life of the conference and, instead, delivering his speech using a tape recorder. "These words are being communicated by way of a tape recorder, not, of course, in order to illustrate the integration of technology into this everyday life on the margin of the technological world, but in order to seize the simplest opportunity to break with the appearance of pseudo collaboration, of artificial dialogue, established between the lecturer 'in person' and his spectators." Guy Debord, "Perspective for Conscious Alternations in Everyday Life," *Situationist International Anthology,* ed. and trans. Ken Knabb (Berkeley: Bureau of Public Secrets, 1981), 68–75. For an account of reductionism within the arts of this period, see Edward Strickland, *Minimalism: Origins* (Bloomington: Indiana University Press, 1993).

Douglas Kahn, *Noise Water Meat: A History of Sound in the Arts* (Cambridge, Massachusetts: The MIT Press, 1999), p. 159, pp. 165–183, Part III: The Impossible Inaudible.

Much to Confess about Nothing

Some may take this as a critique of Cage, whereas I would argue that he merely begins to look like someone of his time. [...]

In *4′33″*, commonly known as the *silent piece*, the performer sits at the piano and marks off the time in three movements, all the while making no sound.[9] An unsuspecting audience (if one still exists) might attempt to reconcile the silence with its expectations before discovering, perhaps, what the piece might be. The initial absence of music might be taken as an expressive or theatrical device preceding a sound. When that sound is not forthcoming, it might become evident that listening can still go on if one's attention (and this is Cage's desire) is shifted to the surrounding sounds, including the sound of the growing agitation of certain audience members. Ostensibly, even an audience comprised entirely of reverential listeners would have plenty to hear, but in every performance I've attended the silence has been broken by the audience and become ironically noisy.

It should be noted that each performance was held in a concert setting where any muttering or clearing one's throat, let alone heckling, was a breach of decorum. Thus, there was already in place in these settings, as in other settings for Western art music, a culturally specific mandate to be silent, a mandate regulating the behavior that precedes, accompanies, and exceeds musical performance. As with prayer, which has not always been silent, concert-goers were at one time more boisterous; this association was not lost on Luigi Russolo, who remarked on "the cretinous religious emotion of the Buddha-like listeners, drunk with repeating for the thousandth time their more or less acquired and snobbish ecstasy."[10] *4'33"*, by tacitly instructing the performer to remain quiet in all respects, muted the site of centralized and privileged utterance, disrupted the unspoken audience code to remain unspoken, transposed the performance onto the audience members both in their utterances and in the acts of shifting perception toward other sounds, and legitimated bad behavior that in any number of other settings (including many musical ones) would have been perfectly acceptable. *4'33"* achieved this involution through the act of silencing the performer. That is, Cagean silence followed and was dependent on a silencing. Indeed, it can also be understood that he extended the decorum of silencing by extending the silence imposed on the audience to the performer, asking the audience to continue to be obedient listeners and not to engage in the utterances that would distract them from shifting their perception toward other sounds. Extending the musical silencing, then, set into motion the process by which the realm of musical sounds would itself be extended.

Silence can be derived from the idleness of an instrument or from the object status of the accouterments of music; thus, any sheet music or instrument becomes music in potentia, or the corpse of a music that has lived its life. In her 10 May 1951 diary entry Judith Malina wrote about a concert in which there was a performance of "*Imaginary Landscape No. 4* ... scored for 12 radios and 24 players. Silence is an important component." After the concert the instruments are moved out to the sidewalk, and a friend drives up in a hearse to take them away: "John and Remy [Charlip] pile the silent music into the vehicle, which drives off trailing a funereal gloom."[11] A similar objecthood overtakes certain performers in an orchestra when they are instructed by the score to remain silent; they join a tableaux as still and mute as their instruments and sheet music. The only difference between them and the performer of *4'33"* is that the latter is performing solo.

4'33" was not a gesture for Cage but something he sincerely took to heart and one of the key moments within the development of his mature philosophy and practice. From this point on he would typically make comments such as, "If you want to know the truth of the matter, the music I prefer, even to my own or anybody else's, is what we are hearing if we are just quiet. And now we come back to my silent piece. I really prefer that to anything else, but I don't think of it as 'my piece.'"[12] What could have moved him to legitimize and compose (or vice versa) such a radical piece? Numerous reasons have been offered by Cage and others, which should come as no surprise considering how it provides a clean slate, silence, absence, a nothingness rife with potentiality, a blank screen on which so much about so little can be projected. The earliest precedent occurred, as Cage recollected (we shall propose an earlier, deeper constituent), in 1940 while Cage was living in San Francisco:

> I had applied to be in the music section of the WPA, but they refused to admit me because they said that I was not a musician. I said, "Well, what am I? I work with sounds and percussion instruments and so forth." And they said, "You could be a recreation leader." So I was employed in the recreation department, and that may have been the birth of the silent piece, because my first assignment in the recreation department was to go to a hospital in San Francisco and entertain the children of the visitors. But I was not allowed to make any sound while I was doing it, for fear that it would disturb the patients. So I thought up games involving movement around the rooms and counting, etc., dealing with some kind of rhythm in space.[13]

With its rules regarding silence, the hospital resembles the setting for a music concert. Recreation introduces performance into this space because recreation, unlike a concert, turns everyone into performers. Thus, in keeping kids quiet Cage is keeping both the audience and performers quiet, ostensibly while a grander therapy ensues all around, and by doing so thus extends the hospital's requisite silence.

Cage's recollection, which came during a conversation with Peter Gena, is interesting because it was raised so rarely (perhaps once?) in reference to the genesis of *4'33"*. Instead, for Cage the most obvious motivation for the piece arose from his interest in Eastern thought. When he first thought of the idea in 1948, he was "just then in the flush of my early contact with oriental philosophy. It was out of that that my interest in silence naturally developed: I mean it's almost transparent."[14] By *oriental* Cage mainly meant South Asian and East Asian, although early Christian mystical texts and practices were often included and inferred. By 1952 Cage was familiar with several individuals and many texts that could have served as sources bridging orientalism and silence. Since the number of possible sources increased in retrospect over the years as Cage commented on *4'33"*, commentators have had difficulty in convincingly pointing out what may have played a key role and how. Thus, more precise determinations of what Cage called *oriental philosophy* are hard to come by, and, as will be argued, the restriction to "oriental" itself is not very accurate. The more accurate term at the philosophical locus of his generation of silence would be, if anything, *perennial*.

Cage also said that *4'33"* was provoked by his encounter with the white paintings of Robert Rauschenberg. Cage had probably seen them in New York at the Betty Parsons Gallery. Irwin Kremen, to whom Cage dedicated a version of *4'33"*, remembers seeing the white and black paintings of Rauschenberg (December 1951) in Cage's New York apartment—in other words, prior to Cage's incorporating of the white paintings, along with Rauschenberg himself, into his 1952 Black Mountain event:[15] "Actually what pushed me into it was not guts but the example of Robert Rauschenberg. His white paintings.... When I saw those, I said, 'Oh yes, I must; otherwise I'm lagging, otherwise music is lagging.'[16] He noticed how, on a canvas of nearly nothing, notably absent of the expressive outpourings characteristic of the time, another plenitude replaced the effusiveness in the complex and changing play of light and shadow and the presence of dust. Correspondingly, environmental sounds rushed in to fill the absence of musical sound in *4'33"*. Rauschenberg's paintings may have provoked Cage's *silent piece* or given him the courage to go ahead with it, but in this case their influence cannot be confused with an earlier development of the piece, since Cage had already had the idea in mind since at least 1948.

If we look back to 1948, to the first glint of the whiteness of what was to become *4'33"*, we find a number of factors that, in their totality, require a general reappraisal of Cage. The key factor is a document entitled "A Composer's Confessions," the text of a lecture delivered at the National Inter-Collegiate Arts Conference held at Vassar College (28 February 1948). When asked in a 1982 interview about the type of silence involved in *4'33"*, Cage replied, "I'd thought of it already in 1948 and gave a lecture which is not published, and which won't be, called A Composer's Confessions.'"[17] The curious thing about this statement is not that he had already been thinking about doing a silent piece four years prior to the 1952 date of composition of *4'33"*, but why in

1982—nearly thirty-five years later in die context of a discussion about the thirty-year-old piece *4'33"*—would Cage assert that the lecture *won't be published*? This interjection may have been just an offhand comment underscored by largely inconsequential considerations about the administration of his writings. On the other hand, the text of the lecture is very long and informative and, in retrospect, indispensable for understanding Cage's career and the genesis of his notion of silence. In it he proposed a new composition called *Silent Prayer* that would consist of three to four and a half minutes of sustained silence (the maximum time being just three seconds short of *4'33"*) to be played over the Muzak network. Most texts from the period were published in *Silence* and *A Year from Monday*, several of them much less important and none that would duplicate the material covered in "A Composer's Confessions." Was this a departure from his usual openness? Was he concerned about this text being touched by the light of day? Why would Cage wait to have it published until around his eightieth birthday?[18] One could speculate that Cage chose not to publish the text because it would have unnecessarily complicated the specter of silence as it had developed over the course of the 1950s—that is, the folkloric Cage first presented in *Silence* (1961) would have run counter to the Cage involved in the silencings at the birth of silence.

What are these complications? To begin with, in the supposed *transparency* of Cage's oriental thought there are several relevant texts, individuals, and activities leading up to 1948, many of which will never be known.[19] David Patterson has summarized many of these and observed Cage's overall predilection for South Asian references, a shift to East Asian ones, with a "rhetorical lurch" occurring between "Forerunners of Modern Music" (1949) and "Lecture on Nothing" (1950).[20] In this respect, the South Asian sources would be of greatest relevance for Cage's Vassar lecture, and, thus, the original genesis of Cage's silence would be Indian and not related to East Asian, or more specifically Zen, sources as has often been noted in discussions about *4'33"*. Among the most notable South Asian sources were his friendship with Gita Sarabhai, who assisted Cage in learning about Indian music and aesthetics; Joseph Campbell; texts by Ananda K. Coomaraswamy, including *The Transformation of Nature in Art* (1934) and, to a lesser extent, *The Dance of Shiva* (1948); and *The Gospel of Sri Ramakrishna*.[21] Yet as we shall see, there are at least two more texts that play an important role within "A Composer's Confessions": Carl Jung's *The Integration of the Personality* (1940) and Aldous Huxley's *The Perennial Philosophy* (1946).[22]

What becomes apparent when these texts are examined is that all, with the exception of *The Gospel of Sri Ramakrishna*, are transparently concerned with cross-cultural perspectives.[23] Coomaraswamy and Huxley both subscribe to Leibniz's *philosophia perennis*, evidencing the same global reach as Jung's *collective unconscious*. Therefore, although Cage's texts through 1949 cite South Asian and Christian mystics, his operant sources were much broader.[24] For instance, Cage's motto—"Art is the Imitation of Nature in her manner of Operation"—was not from Coomaraswamy, as Cage repeatedly states, but from St. Thomas Aquinas, from whom Coomaraswamy had borrowed the idea: *Ars imitatur naturam in sua operationen*.[25] In all of these perennially philosophical sources—tranquillity, quiescence, austerity, blankness, nothingness, emptiness, and any number of other ideas related to silence, including silence itself—were quite common. Jung summed it up when he wrote, "We are always surprised by the fact that something comes out of what we call 'nothing.'"[26] It should come as no surprise, then, that there are so many nothings and that they should be, all of them, so fecund.

The reason for Cage's reading in spirituality has been attributed to changes in his personal life during the 1940s, yet it was also significant that he, as an American, was attracted to timeless, global ideas during and after the World War II.[27] The war and its aftermath presented the United States with a cultural problem: how to estrange the character of its enemies while securing sympathies from certain domestic populations? For instance, one of Cage's compositions, *A Book of Music* (1944), was used by the Office of War Information, renamed *Indonesian Supplement No. 1*, and broadcast to the South Pacific "with the hope of convincing the natives that America loves the Orient."[28] This schism became intensified immediately following the war, since the domestic American populace was required to reconcile the decimation of the civilian populations of Hiroshima and Nagasaki with appeals to global commonality. The universalism and world betterment fervor that swept the United States after the war—after the world had become its oyster, especially as it served as the ideological frontline in the cold war—provided the cultural environment for popular projects of self-improvement; that most were detached, touristic, imperialistic, and appropriative did not rule out the possibility for more plausible engagements with cultures outside the Eurocentric sphere.

In this respect, the war repeated a problem posed by Jung in *The Integration of the Personality*. The "white man," as the translation went, was unable to contemplate the metaphysical conundrums by Lao Tze in the *Tao Tê Ching*, let alone answer them, because "he is forced to reject [it] as if it were a foreign body, for his blood refuses to assimilate anything sprung from foreign soil."[29] There are indications that Cage read Jung's text closely, yet he chose to frame the sentiment through reference to Coomaraswamy, who "convinced me of our naiveté with regard to the Orient. At the time—it was at the end of the war, or just afterwards—people still said that the East and the West were absolutely foreign, separate entities. And that a Westerner did not have the right to profess an Eastern philosophy. It was thanks to Coomaraswamy that I began to suspect that this was not true, and that Eastern thought was no less admissible for a Western than is European thought."[30] Jung had suggested, in the tradition of perennial philosophy, that Westerners assume a disposition toward the wisdom of *the East* which, although they could not hope to repeat it, would at least lead them to traditions closer to home:

> One must be able to *let things happen*. I have learned from the East what it means by the phrase "Wu wei": namely, not-doing, letting be, which is quite different from doing nothing. Some Occidentals, also, have known what this not-doing means; for instance, Meister Eckhart, who speaks of "sich lassen," to let oneself be.[31]

For Jung, the *way* of the Tao was to be developed in the West through the development of the personality, and the key to this development was the integration of the different parts of the psyche, primarily conscious mind ("the ego and the various mental contents") and the unconscious.[32] A non-integrated psyche was not merely an obstacle to spiritual development; it impacted on all psychological matters and a range of physiological conditions:

> Medical psychology has been profoundly impressed with the number and importance of the unconscious processes that give rise to functional symptoms and even organic disturbances. These facts have undermined the view that the ego expresses the psychic totality. It has become obvious that the "whole" must include, besides consciousness, the field of

> unconscious events, and must constitute a sum total embracing both. The ego, once the monarch of this totality, is dethroned. It remains merely the center of consciousness.[33]

Many American artists during the 1940s, under the influence of Surrealism, Freud and Jung were interested in dethroning the monarchy of the ego to tap the unconscious. Such a mission provided ample opportunity for individuals to engage in selfexpression while imagining an ineluctable communication at a level above or below society and culture (oneiric, instinctual, archetypal) and for a socialization of figures of the unconscious in ideas of a *primitivism* based in the body. Jung in *The Integration of the Personality* believed in a connection between the Eastern and Western psychic states that subtended the ego: "The psyche called the superior or the universal mind in Hindu philosophy corresponds to what the West calls the unconscious."[34] Yet he was unwilling to subscribe to the body disciplines by which adepts reach the state of contact with universal mind: "This is all very well, but scarcely to be recommended anywhere north of the Tropic of Cancer."[35] Cage was not interested in self-expression, whether it was in music or in painting; he was also becoming less sure about communication, and his appropriation of other cultures for musical purposes was centered more on the operations of the mind than the body. Like Jung, Cage was interested in choosing among the ideas of the adepts without taking up any body practices. Over the course of a thousand pages Sri Ramakrishna was forever slipping off into *samadhi*, but Cage's interest remained solely with his wisdom and not in the practices that lent to its development. Overall, Cage was less interested in getting the ego out of the way to enable the unconscious to come out into the world than in removing the ego so more of the world could get *in* unobstructed. He wanted to be open to "divine influences" but not to the extent of fusing them with a world within.

"A Composer's Confessions" consists primarily of a long autobiographical sketch, the bulk of which pertains to a time before his most recent activities. At the very moment in the text in which Cage moves into the present and recent past he invokes Sarabhai, Coomaraswamy, and Jung: "After eighteen months of studying oriental and medieval Christian philosophy and mysticism I began to read Jung on the integration of the personality."[36] He reiterates Jung's concerns regarding psychological and physiological health and applies them to the topic of people's occupations in contemporary society as a basis from which to focus on the vocation of composition.[37] Composers, like everyone else, are prone to neuroses; however, "If one makes music, as the Orient would say, *disinterestedly*, that is, without concern for money or fame but simply for the love of making it, it is an integrating activity and one will find moments in his life that are complete and fulfilled."[38]

The term *disinterestedness* thereby becomes a tangible link between Cage's orientalism and his initial formulation of silence. I have not been able to locate where Cage might have derived the specific word—although it has cropped up in several texts, it has not occurred with the emphasis that might explain adoption into his vernacular—but there is no shortage of sources when it comes to the concept. Sentiments similar to "letting things happen" and "not-being" can be found in Coomaraswamy's discussions of self-naughting, dementation, anonymity, and impersonality,[39] and more specifically, both Cage and Coomaraswamy mention a similar disposition as it pertains to musicians. Coomaraswamy quotes the great poet Rabindranath Tagore in describing Indian musicians: "Our master singers never take the least trouble to make their voice and manner attractive. [...] Those of the audience whose senses have to be satisfied as well are held to be beneath the notice of any self-respecting artist [while] those of the audience who are appreciative are content to perfect the song in their own mind by the force of their own feeling."[40] Cage emphasizes disinterestedness in performers and does so with a source from the Orient ("if one makes music, as the Orient would say, *disinterestedly*"). Within "A Composer's Confessions" Cage explained that he found a concert of music by Ives and Webern pleasurable because "when the music was composed the composers were at one with themselves. The performers became disinterested to the point that they became unself-conscious, and a few listeners in those brief moments of listening forgot themselves, enraptured, and so gained themselves."[41] Making and listening to music disinterestedly is the means to integrate the personality "and that is why we love the art."[42]

Disinterestedness is also associated with Aldous Huxley's explanation of self-mortification and nonattachment in *The Perennial Philosophy*, including his own observation that "spiritual authority can be exercised only by those who are perfectly disinterested and whose motives are therefore above suspicion."[43] He also cites St. François de Sales's "holy indifference" and Chuang Tzu's story of Confucius lending advice to a disciple regarding "the fasting of the heart," which links indifference with a model for Cagean listening: "Cultivate unity ... You do your hearing, not with your ears, but with your mind; not with your mind, but with your very soul. But let the hearing stop with the ears. Let the working of the mind stop with itself. Then the soul will be a negative existence, passively responsive to externals ... Living in a state of complete indifference—you will be near success."[44] Fortified through its opposition to self-expression, *disinterestedness* remained an operative term through "Lecture on Something" (1951–1952) and was abandoned only as chance and indeterminacy transformed it from an attitude and disposition into a reproducible and consistent technique.[45] Later, disinterestedness took the most familiar form of a supercession of taste, which itself superseded style and genre, extramusicality and silence. Recounting its roots, Cage said in a 1984 interview:

> I wanted to be quiet in a nonquiet situation. So I discovered first through reading the gospel of Sri Ramakrishna, and through the study of the philosophy of Zen Buddhism—and also an important book for me was *The Perennial Philosophy* by Aldous Huxley, which is an anthology of remarks of people in different periods of history and from different cultures—that they are all saying the same thing, namely, a quiet mind is a mind that is free of its likes and dislikes. You can become narrow-minded, literally, by only liking certain things, and disliking others. But you can become open-minded, literally, by giving up your likes and dislikes and becoming interested in things.[46]

Canned Silence

Disinterestedness, despite signaling the presence of a cultural other, when used within the context of "A Composer's Confessions" becomes implicated within an array of not-so-foreign values. It also becomes a means to commend the music of certain composers and celebrate the love of art, against the Western art music repertoire with its inflated importance, its claims to genius, posterity and masterpieces. And it becomes a means to counter academization and commercialization of the arts, self-expression, and art appreciation. In short, *disinterestedness* is the best response to all matters animated by "sheer materialistic nonsense."[47] The first call for silence in Cage's lecture comes when his disinterestedness shifts from the sheer materialistic nonsense of Western art music and the arts in general to commercial music proper and the mass media in general. He invoked silencing through the power of someone who had already in effect silenced music, James Petrillo, president of the American Federation of Musicians (AFM): "Since Petrillo's recent ban on recordings took effect on the New Year, I allowed myself to indulge in the fantasy of how normalizing the effect might have been had he had the power, and exerted it, to ban not only recordings, but radio, television, the newspapers, and Hollywood."[48]

When the vitaphone, the system that synchronized the phonograph with cinema, was introduced by Warner Brothers Studios in the late 1920s, many musicians whose job it was to accompany the silent film were no longer necessary; sound film made them even less necessary. Since in the 1920s such musicians constituted 30 percent of the AFM membership, the union was from that point on acutely conscious of the effects of recording technologies and over the next two decades countered by demanding proper remuneration from those who profited handsomely from the disembodied repetition of their members' performances. Petrillo and the AFM responded in 1942 with a strike to enforce their decree that record companies pay royalties to their musicians on every pressing. The strike lasted for over two years during the middle of the war and cost AFM members millions of dollars in lost wages. Since Petrillo's base of operation was in Chicago, his presence must have been felt by Cage, who was living in Chicago in 1942 and working with professional musicians during the Columbia Workshop (CBS) radio production of *The City Wears a Slouch Hat*, his collaboration with Kenneth Patchen. Indeed, Petrillo's reputation would have been unavoidable, for he was notorious for aggressively pursuing grievance not only through legal union tactics but also through gangsterist means at home in Chicago. In this respect, was Cage being tongue in cheek when he pondered whether Petrillo "had the power, and exerted it?"

In his lecture (28 February 1948) Cage was referring to Petrillo's second assault on record company practices, when a decree was issued (midnight on 31 December 1947) that extended the labor action to dance halls and radio shows dependent on recorded music. In Cage's fantasy, he wanted to extend Petrillo's silencing further still, to all of radio and other forms of mass media, whether they were audible or not. However, with the experience of the first decree in mind, the record companies put contingency plans in place, and, consequently, only working musicians were silenced.[49] Cage did go on to state what he hoped for from his fantasy: "We might then realize that phonographs and radios are not musical instruments, that what the critics write is not a musical matter but rather a literary matter, that it makes little difference if one of us likes one piece and another; it is rather the age-old process of making and using music and our becoming more integrated as personalities through this making and using that is of real value."[50] Of course, for nearly a decade Cage had used phonographs and radios as musical instruments —phonograph records, turntables, a radio station in 1939 in *Imaginary Landscape No. 1*, and a radio again in 1942 in *Credo in Us*—and was liable to use absolutely anything to make music. He was, in this instance, speaking rhetorically from inside Western art music as a practitioner and purveyor of "live" goods and even more immediately as a listener. Seemingly, by arguing for *liveness*, Cage was siding with the AFM against the record companies, but by 1948 the issue was not between live and recorded; it was a labor issue that seemed to Cage to be a distraction from the real social project of music. Phonographs and radios, the targets of the AFM decrees, are not important. In the terms of the text itself he was still attending the performance of Ives and Webern as a listener, where disinterestedness in *making and using music* had already led to "and that is why we love the art," but then he directed his attention to the performances reproduced on phonographs and radios, which followed a very different program.[51] Instead of acknowledging the obvious differences between the two spheres of music or contemplating the political realities of working musicians outside Western art music who act in an *interested* manner regarding their occupations, he returns again to the question of the integration of the personality and attempts to socialize it by implicating all musical activity in self-improvement. From where he sat in the text listening to music, all of music became "music," and the politics of music dissipated among the dispositions of individual personalities.

There is certainly the possibility that Cage's fantasy may have been an offhanded remark, a quick way to snub commercialism in favor of the integrity of the individual. However, there is more than just the kernel of truth in this particular jest, since the fantasy of a grand silencing of society had long been within his personal repertoire:

> One of the greatest blessings that the United States could receive in the near future would be to have her industries halted, her business discontinued, her people speechless, a great pause in her world of affairs created, and finally to have everything stopped that runs, until everyone should hear the last wheel go around and the last echo fade away.... then, in that moment of complete intermission, of undisturbed calm, would be the hour most conducive to the birth of a Pan-American Conscience. Then we should be capable of answering the question, "What ought we to do?" For we should be hushed and silent, and we should have the opportunity to learn that other people think.[52]

This was the text of Cage's speech "Other People Think" for the Southern California Oratorical Contest in 1927, where he represented Los Angeles High School and won first prize. The rhetorical device of imagining a large social silencing was placed in a context very similar to that in "A Composer's Confessions."

Both instances of silencing create conditions for asking questions, which in turn lead to large transformations in consciousness. The social silencing in "Other People Think" provides the opportunity to ask the question "what ought we to do?" and to learn *that*, not *what*, other people think ("It is the produce of the mind of man, and in that it is truly great"),[53] and this in turn promises a Pan-American Conscience. Within "A Composer's Confessions" a smaller quiet provokes the key question about making and using music with which the remaining text is concerned. Cage had moved into a "new apartment on the East River in Lower Manhattan which turns its back to the city and looks to the water and the sky. The quietness of this retreat brought me finally to face the question: to what end does one write music?"[54] And then this question soon leads to a larger social silencing if Petrillo "had the power, and exerted it, to ban not only recordings, but radio, television, the newspapers, and Hollywood,"[55] in recognition of the unimportance of reproduced commercial music, music critics, and musical tastes versus the real value of making and using music, integrating the personality, and cultivating disinterestedness and the wisdom of the Orient.

In "Other People Think" Cage implied only that the social transformation would come about through individual transformation of consciousness, whereas in "A Composer's Confessions" social transformation would come about only through personal acts by legions of solitary individuals: "That island that we have grown to think no longer exists to which we might have retreated to escape from the impact of the world, lies, as it ever did, within each one of our hearts."[56] Both instances share what Yvonne Rainer has called Cage's "goofy naiveté" when it comes to politics,[57] the earlier speech in thinking that United States imperialism within Latin America would be moved by conscience (an opinion that might be expected from a high school student) and the Vassar lecture in conflating an issue of the political economy of music with self-improvement.

The second call for silence in "A Composer's Confessions" narrowed down the scope of the fantasy from silencing all the mass media to silencing just one aspect: Muzak. He planned "to compose a piece of uninterrupted silence and sell it to Muzak Co. It will be 3 or 4½ minutes long—those being the standard lengths of 'canned' music—and its title will be *Silent Prayer.* It will open with a single idea which I will attempt to make as seductive as the color and shape and fragrance of a flower. The ending will approach imperceptibility."[58] In the late 1940s Muzak was piped over telephone lines into restaurants, workplaces, and other institutions and was thus primarily a transmissional service like radio. The company was just beginning to make a transition to recorded systems situated in-house. Although it would be difficult to say whether the Muzak Co. would have been amenable to Cage's idea, failure to realize the project would not have been due to a lack of courage on Cage's part to approach the company. The unbridled confidence for which he was known had been boosted by the nationwide reception, in both senses of the word, of *The City Wears a Slouch Hat*, and his *Book of Music* was broadcast throughout the South Pacific on military radio. He had always been very enterprising, unafraid to approach anyone who might be able to advance his projects, including a number of companies when he sought support for his Center of Experimental Music. There should be no reason to believe that his proposal was a ruse.

There are several possible art connections. It is obvious that *4'33"* is just three seconds over the upper limit for canned music, and, although much happened in the four years between the two pieces, if it was indeed chance that finally arrived at this duration, then it was at least a moment of objective chance, unwittingly, in the Surrealist sense. The fact that it was *canned* recalls the *ready-mades* of Marcel Duchamp, with whose work Cage was quite familiar. Although Duchamp transposed a mass-produced object into an art venue whereas Cage wanted to place an art object of canned silence alongside the other cans on the narrow-casted Muzak shelf, *Silent Prayer* could be thought of as a musical version of *Air de Paris*, Duchamp's bottled air. Then there was Ferruccio Busoni's well-known *Sketch of a New Esthetic of Music* (available in English translation from around 1911), in which he stated that consummate players and improvisers "most nearly approach the essential nature of the art" during their employment of holds and rests. If properly isolated, the product of such playing could very well describe one of the bases for Cagean silence: "The tense silence between two movements—*in itself music*, in this environment—leaves wider scope for divination than the more determinate, but therefore less elastic, sound."[59] I am not saying that Cage was thinking of Duchamp or Busoni at the time, and he certainly was not aware of F. T. Marinetti's radio *sintesi* written in the early 1930s and entitled *I Silenzi Parlano fra di Loro* (Silences speak among themselves), the most notable precedent of an art-work in which silence took on its own presence.[60]

The most plausible connection with the past becomes apparent when we ask what could have attracted Cage to Muzak in particular, among all the other forms of mass media? What more so than Erik Satie's *furniture music*? Cage had a long-standing interest in Satie (he arranged the first movement of the *Socrate* for a Merce Cunningham dance, *Idyllic Song*, in 1945), and by the time of his Vassar lecture he was deeply engaged with Satie's work. He was no doubt preparing for the Satie Festival lectures and concerts to be held at Black Mountain College that summer. At Black Mountain, concerts took place in the dining hall, or pieces would be played by Cage on the piano in his cabin while people roamed about outside, the latter suggesting the ambiance of furniture music.[61] Anyone involved in even modest research would have known about the two primary biographical texts on Satie—if Rollo Myers's *Erik Satie* (1948) was too late, then Pierre-Daniel Templier's *Erik Satie* (1932) was not—as well as the prominence of the "Erik Satie and His *Musique d'Ameublement*" section in Constant Lambert's *Music Ho!* (1934).[62]

Although usually solely attributed to Satie, *musique d'ameublement* (furniture music or furnishing music) was a collaboration with Darius Milhaud. It first took place in 1920 at an art gallery to act as an interlude for a play by Max Jacob. The introduction, read by Pierre Bertin, was included in Myers's book: "We present for the first time, under the supervision of MM. Erik Satie and Darius Milhaud and directed by M. Delgrange, 'furnishing music' to be played during the entr'actes. We beg you to take no notice of it and to behave during the entr'actes as if the music did not exist.

This music … claims to make its contribution to life in the same way as a private conversation, a picture, or the chair on which you may or may not be seated."[63] To put music in the intermission required an unobtrusive music—otherwise it would be another performance and not an intermission at all—and this not-to-be-listened-to music evokes immediate comparison with Muzak. The association with Muzak would have been particularly noticeable in Templier's book where he cites a note from Satie assigning certain of his compositions their respective *musique d'ameublement* settings: "*The Banquet*—'Musique d'ameublement'—For an assembly-hall … *Phèdre*—'Musique d'ameublement'—For a lobby … *Phédon*—'Musique d'ameublement'—For a shop window."[64] This type of shift in settings from art to nonart and vice versa has been a regular feature of art through the twentieth century, having perhaps its most notable demonstration with the institutional tactics of Duchamp's ready-mades, while eliciting a certain circularity in the relationship of Cage's *Silent Prayer* and Satie's *musique d'ameublement*. Satie's performance was a displacement of one of his café haunts (people talking, ignoring the music) into an artistic space, whereas *Silent Prayer* returns to the cafés and other nonart settings to replace Muzak with silence—that is, an unobtrusive music with something even more unobtrusive. Cage was not, like the protagonist in Heinrich Böll's story "Murke's Collected Silences," inside the institution trying to patch together some reprieve but was instead trying to seek a bit of reprieve, an *entr'acte*, from a daily life where Muzak had become obtrusively and insultingly pervasive. And there may have been a special consideration for choosing to silence Muzak among other forms of auditive mass media: if one was to be involved in silencing, there was little danger of being accused of censorship, for in its unobtrusiveness Muzak had already assumed a certain self-censorship, and a hiatus of four and a half minutes would do nothing to disturb the pervasiveness. Silencing would only impose a brief intermission.

In his book Myers also discussed Satie's composition *Cinema* (1924) as another instance of *musique d'ameublement*. Indeed, it was likewise intended to take place within an intermission, yet this time it did not stand alone but accompanied René Clair's film *Entr'acte*, which was to function as the intermission to Francis Picabia's ballet *Relâche* (the name *Relâche*, posted when a performance is canceled, is itself suggestive of the revoked performances of *Silent Prayer* and *4'33"*). *Cinema* was comprised of segments of music, incidental both in itself and to the images in the film, cut in regularly measured lengths with no regard for conventional continuity (the simple structure is perhaps the clearest statement of Satie, the measurer of sounds). Cinema in general affords its own unobtrusiveness and silence with regard to sound in at least two ways. First of all, since film music must as a rule never overwhelm the images, action, or speech, it is relegated to a music heard but not to be listened to. Silence enters the picture with segments of *Hörspielstreifen*, the delicate atmosphere of recorded silence whose purpose is to imperceptibly confirm the presence of a reproduction under way and not frighten the audience into thinking there has been a technical malfunction (which would require a break in the silence of the audience itself). The silence of cinema audiences is—like that of concertgoers, people praying, and kids being entertained in hospitals—culturally specific, and a true silence, without the presence of the *Hörspielstreifen*, would have the same effect as *4'33"*.

Apart from *musique d'ameublement*, another influence on *Silent Prayer* could have been derived from Cage's understanding of how structure in Satie's music worked to equalize the status of silence with that of sound. In his lecture "Defense of Satie" at Black Mountain College, Cage gave a great deal of importance to structure, specifically as practiced by Satie and Webern and heralded by music from, following his *perennial* motif, Asia and the middle ages.[65] Both Satie and Webern worked in a *short form* conducive to canned music, but Cage had more fundamental concerns. He figured that structure was determined by duration, which sound and silence shared, and in turn determined being from nonbeing: "Music is a continuity of sound. In order that it may be distinguishable from nonbeing, it must have structure."[66] Pitch, loudness, and timbre, although they could be heard in musical sound, were not intrinsic to the being or nonbeing of music because they did not require duration, whereas "silence cannot be heard in terms of pitch or harmony: it is heard in terms of time length.[67] This line of reasoning was one of Cage's platforms against harmony (thus Beethoven) and could be found in his earlier arguments for percussion and noise. Indeed, Satie's structure was "extramusical in its implications ... into Satie's continuity come folk tunes, musical cliches, and absurdities of all kinds."[68] Cage now called Satie's structure into service to privilege yet another element historically downplayed within Western art music: silence. Music was composed most fundamentally of sound and silence, and silence became a way of hearing time within the *being* of musical structure. Nevertheless, he was still thinking of sound and silence as being conventionally distinct from one another, a presence and an absence of sound. By the time of *4'33"*, silence became only the absence of an intentional sound, whereas musical sound had become ever-present and omnipresent, filled with intentional or unintentional sound. Thus, *Silent Prayer* was not underscored by the same sense of silence as *4'33"*; it was not a way to begin hearing and musicalizing the surrounding sound. If anything was meant to be heard, it was conventional silence—in this case, the absence of the sound of Muzak, along the measured lengths of canned music.

But why the prayer in *Silent Prayer*? I believe the reason can be found in Aldous Huxley's *The Perennial Philosophy*—specifically, at the juncture of chapters 15 and 16, entitled "Silence" and "Prayer," respectively. Huxley's book consists of his commentary on perennial philosophy, with substantial quotes from mystics, saints, monks, philosophers, and psychologists. Among the people quoted—many passages are nothing but a sequence of quotes—one can find all the individuals and approaches favored by Cage; moreover, one could find them within a relatively secular context. The problem with Coomaraswamy, Eckhart, and others, after all, was the difficulty of appropriating spiritual ideas without committing oneself overtly to deism. Huxley's chapter on silence is one of the shortest in the book, perhaps because three-quarters of the chapter is devoted to appeals to stop talking. The remaining section consists of one paragraph consisting of Huxley's own appeal for silence over the mass media. It is only one paragraph, but it cannot be taken lightly. Throughout the book Huxley maintains an evenhandedness about timeless, global matters. Here he steps out of character and forthrightly condemns the present-day media:

> The twentieth century is, among other things, the Age of Noise. Physical noise, mental noise and noise of desire—we hold history's record for all of them. And no wonder; for all the resources of our almost miraculous technology have been thrown into the current assault against silence. That most popular and influential of all recent inventions, the radio, is nothing but a conduit through which prefabricated din can flow into our homes. And this din goes far deeper, of course, than the ear-drums. It penetrates the mind, filling it with a babel of distractions—news items, mutually irrelevant bits of information, blasts of corybantic or sentimental music, continually repeated doses of drama that bring no catharsis, but merely create a craving for daily or even hourly emotional enemas. And where, as in most countries, the broadcasting stations support themselves by selling time to advertisers, the noise is carried from the ears, through the realms of phantasy, knowledge and feeling to the ego's central core of wish and desire. Spoken or printed, broadcast over the ether or on wood-pulp, all advertising copy has but one purpose—to prevent the will from achieving silence. Desirelessness is the condition of deliverance and illumination. The condition of an expanding and technologically progressive system of mass production is universal craving. Advertising is the organized effort to extend and intensify craving—to extend and intensify, that is to say, the workings of that force, which (as all the saints and teachers of all the higher religions have always taught) is the principal cause of suffering and wrong-doing and the greatest obstacle between the human soul and its divine Ground.[69]

If one needed spiritual impetus or moral justification to silence any aspect of the mass media—to remove the obstacles that would *prevent the will from achieving silence*, no less—here it was in an emphatic end to a chapter entitled Silence. On the facing page began the chapter called Prayer.

9 The piece was initially made up of three fixed lengths of silence (30", 2'23", 1'40") arrived at by using chance operations and then underwent modification when it was published in 1960. It may be played on other instruments besides the piano, and involve more than one performer.

10 For the historical nature of silence among audiences, see James H. Johnson, *Listening in Paris: A Cultural History* (Berkeley: University of California Press, 1995).

11 Remy Charlip was one of Merce Cunningham's dancers and the lover of Lou Harrison, who also had music performed the same evening. See Judith Malina, *The Diaries of Judith Malina, 1947–1957* (New York: Grove Press, 1984), p. 163.

12 *John Cage*, ed. Kostelanetz, p. 12. On the question of whether it was or was not "his piece," he could go either way: "I think perhaps my own best piece, at least the one I like the most, is the silent piece." John Cage, *Conversing with Cage*, ed. Richard Kostelanetz (New York: Limelight Editions, 1988), p. 65.

13 John Cage in conversation with Peter Gena, "After Antiquity," in *A John Cage Reader*, ed. Peter Gena and Jonathan Brent (New York: Peters, 1982), p. 169–70.
14 Stephen Montague, "John Cage at Seventy: An Interview," *American Music* (Summer 1985): p. 213.
15 Michael Kirby and Richard Schechner, "An Interview with John Cage," *Tulane Drama Review* 10, no. 2 (Winter 1965): p. 53, reprinted in *Happenings and Other Acts*, ed. Mariellen R. Sandford (London: Routledge, 1995), p. 53; Irwin Kremen, e-mail message to Larry Solomon (17 June 1997), posted to the *Silence List*. One of the other interesting, if fanciful, reasons that have been entertained is based on the observation that 273, the number of seconds in four minutes and thirty-three seconds, is the positive value of absolute zero (minus 273 degrees Centigrade).
16 John Cage, Roger Shattuck, and Alan Gillmor, "Erik Satie: A Conversation," *Contact*, no. 25 (Autumn 1982): p. 22.
17 Montague, "John Cage at Seventy," p. 213. James Pritchett cites the lecture in connection with *4'33"* but then steers clear of the social implications within the text itself and states instead, "Thus the silent piece's origins lie not in Cage's works of the 1950s and 60s, but rather in the aesthetic milieu we are considering here: the late 1940s, the *String Quartet in Four Parts*, and the 'Lecture on Nothing.'" James Pritchett, *The Music of John Cage* (Cambridge: Cambridge University Press, 1993), p. 59.
18 *MusikTexte*, nos. 40–41 (Cologne, August 1991) and *Musicworks*, no. 52 (Toronto, Spring 1992). Subsequent citations to "A Composer's Confessions" will be to the *Musicworks* publication. Calvin Tomkins apparently had access to this text, perhaps from a publication of which I am unaware, when he wrote his portrait of Cage for The New Yorker, but he did not mention information relevant to the genesis of *4'33"*. See Calvin Tomkins, *The Bride and the Bachelors* (New York: Penguin Books, 1976), pp. 69–144.
19 Cage did not make matters easier by selling off portions of his library, including many of his Asian books, during some financially difficult times.
20 David Wayne Patterson, "Appraising the Catchwords, C. 1942–1959: John Cage's Asian-Derived Rhetoric and the Historical Reference of Black Mountain College" (Ph.D. diss., Columbia University, 1996), 129. The inclusion of Meister Eckhart and other Christian mystics within the period of South Asian influence is explained by the chapter on Eckhart appearing in Coomaraswamy's *The Transformation of Nature in Art*.
21 Coomaraswamy, *The Transformation of Nature in Art* (1934); Ananda K. Coomaraswamy, *The Dance of Shiva* (Bombay: Asia Publishing House, 1948); Mahendranath Gupta, *The Gospel of Sri Ramakrishna* (New York: Ramakrishna-Vivekananda Center, 1942).
22 Carl Jung, *The Integration of the Personality*, trans. Stanley M. Dell (London: Kegan Paul, Trency, Trubner, 1940); Aldous Huxley, *The Perennial Philosophy* (London: Chatto and Windus, 1946).
23 Coomaraswamy's *The Transformation of Nature in Art* contains much Chinese, medieval Christian material, most significantly Meister Eckhart, and some Zen sources. *The Dance of Shiva*, more consistently Indian, contains chapters of "Intellectual Fraternity" and Nietzsche. The Huxley and Jung texts are based entirely on cross-cultural comparisons and contain explicit references to East Asian sources. In 1923 Jung also wrote about Meister Eckhart in *Psychological Types* (Princeton: Princeton University Press, 1971).
24 See Patterson, "Appraising the Catchwords," pp. 72–73. In the same respect, his reliance on Jung should temper his well known rejection of psychoanalysis as well as place him closer to the abstract expressionists, to whom he was supposedly diametrically opposed.
25 Ibid., pp. 95–99.
26 Jung, *The Integration of the Personality*, p. 11.
27 This is the point around which could pivot a fruitful comparison of avant-garde and modernist musics with that other postwar impulse of lounge, easy-listening, novelty, and exotica musics—what Ken Sitz has called Deep 50s music.
28 Cage, "A Composer's Confessions," p. 13. Henry Cowell advised the OWI "on serious works, American pieces, and music especially selected to go out to particular districts.... We used art music, old and new from all countries, and found that pieces by modern Americans whose style is not too complex were well received." Henry Cowell, "Shaping Music for Total War," *Modern Music* 22, no. 4 (May–June, 1945): pp. 223–26.
29 Jung, *The Integration of the Personality*, pp. 30–31.
30 John Cage and Daniel Charles, *For the Birds* (Boston: Marion Boyars, 1981), p. 105.
31 Jung, The Integration of the Personality, pp. 31–32.
32 The last paragraph of his book states it explicitly: "When all is said and done, the hero, the leader, and saviour is also the one who discovers a new way to greater certainty. Everything could be left as it was if this new way did not absolutely demand to be discovered and did not visit humanity with all the plagues of Egypt until it is found. The undiscovered way in us is like something of the psyche that is alive. The classic Chinese philosophy calls it 'Tao,' and compares it to a watercourse that resistlessly moves towards its goal. To be in Tao means fulfillment, wholeness, a vocation performed, beginning and end and complete realization of the meaning of existence innate in things. Personality is Tao." Ibid., pp. 304–05.
33 Ibid., p. 4.
34 Ibid., p. 15.
35 Ibid., p. 26.
36 Cage, "A Composer's Confessions," p. 13.
37 The question of how spiritual matters relate to the workaday world of occupations runs throughout all the readings, which move closer to one another in discussions of "vocations," or callings. Coomaraswamy expands the field of what Westerners might think as artists by listing more than eighteen professional arts, the sixty-four avocational arts in India, embracing "every kind of skilled activity, from music, painting, and weaving to horsemanship, cookery, and the practice of magic, without distinction of rank, all being equally of angelic origin." *The Transformation of Nature in Art*, 9. See also Patterson, "Appraising the Catchwords," pp. 73–75.
38 Cage, "A Composer's Confessions," pp. 13–14. In "Defense of Satie," a lecture given at Black Mountain College the summer after the Vassar lecture, Cage repeated the link between Jung and music: "Music then is a problem parallel to that of the integration of the personality: which in terms of modern psychology is the co-being of the conscious and the unconscious mind, Law and Freedom, in a random world situation. Good music can act as a guide to good living." *John Cage*, ed. Kostelanetz, p. 84.
39 Patterson, "Appraising the Catchwords," pp. 86–92. There is a temptation to identify Cage's disinterestedness with Duchamp's indifference, but his engagement with Duchamp's ideas would come later.
40 *The Transformation of Nature in Art*, p. 28.
41 Cage, "A Composer's Confessions" p. 14.
42 Ibid.
43 Huxley, *The Perennial Philosophy*, p. 143.
44 Ibid., pp. 115, 134.
45 In "Lecture on Nothing" (1950), Cage extended his idea of disinterestedness by associating it with a lack of interest in possessing things ("a piece of string or a sunset," "one's own home") or in possessing moments in time ("We need not destroy the past: it is gone") and specified it by setting it against the conventional forms of continuity within Western art music ("themes and secondary themes; their struggle, their development; the climax; the recapitulation"). *Silence*, pp. 110–11.
46 Cage, *Conversing with Cage*, p. 231.
47 Cage, "A Composer's Confessions," p. 15.
48 Ibid.
49 Among them were the members of Spike Jones's band, who chose to satirize Petrillo openly, following his every command as though given by military top brass. Cage had no apparent interest in Spike Jones, although the band would be celebrated in the post-Cagean ranks of Fluxus. See Jordan R. Young, *Spike Jones and His City Slickers* (Berkeley: Disharmony Books, 1984), pp. 36, 77. See also Russel Sanjek, *American Popular Music and Its Business* (New York: Oxford University Press, 1988), pp. 229–30, p. 286. The big companies also had a new technology on their side: the same month as Cage's talk, ABC Radio Network announced it was going "all-tape" for nighttime programming, using the latest improvements on the German Magnetophone that had been discovered by American troops.
50 Cage, "A Composer's Confessions," p. 15. What critics wrote was also a *literary* matter, in accord with other instances of Cage's use of the term, because they were interested almost entirely in the playing of the literature —the repertoire—and not new music.
51 Two years later in "Lecture on Nothing" (1950) he stated, "Record collections, that is not music. The phonograph is a thing, not a musical instrument. A thing leads to other things, whereas a musical instrument leads to nothing." *Silence*, p. 125. The idea of an instrument literally leading to nothing that is music is, of course, the foundation of *4'33"*.
52 John Cage, "Other People Think" (1927), in *John Cage*, ed. Kostelanetz, p. 48.
53 Ibid.
54 Cage, "A Composer's Confessions," p. 13.
55 Ibid., p. 15.
56 Ibid.
57 Yvonne Rainer, "Looking Myself in the Mouth," *October*, no. 17 (Summer 1981): pp. 65–76.
58 Ibid. The last two sentences are less enigmatic when taken as rhetorical devices. In this capacity, there is no synesthetic shift away from in/audibility. The *idea* is to be made seductive as a means (short of interrupting his lecture with several minutes of standing quietly at the podium) to induce his Vassar audience into imagining what it might be like to actually *listen* to "silence" for such a length of time and not immediately understand it as a withholding of utterance. And in lieu of the type of markers of time or development that might provide an anticipation of an end, the end approaches imperceptibly and, thereby, approaches imperceptibility. He had, after all, associated disinterestedness with his own brand of continuity in music two years later in his "Lecture on Nothing," and it would be understandable that, within the realm of all the ends of disinterestedness, imperceptibility would lie near the end of the trajectory from quietness to silence.
59 Busoni, *Sketch of a New Esthetic of Music*, included in *Three Classics in the Aesthetic of Music* (New York: Dover, 1962), p. 89 (emphasis in the original).
60 Translated by Victoria Kirby in Michael Kirby, *Futurist Performance* (New York: Dutton, 1971), p. 293.
61 See Patterson, "Appraising the Catchwords," pp. 204, 232. Patterson interviewed W. P. Jennerjahn, who places the invention of "happenings" not with Cage's *Black Mountain Piece* (1952) but with these cabin performances in 1948: "The music of Satie, played on two pianos inside the open window of one of the cottages on campus while the audience sat on the ground outside, or strolled about."
62 Rollo H. Myers, *Erik Satie* (1948; New York: Dover, 1968); Pierre-Daniel Templier, *Erik Satie* (Paris: Les Editions Rieder, 1932); and Constant Lambert, *Music Ho! A Study of Music in Decline* (London: Faber and Faber, 1934). Cage was fluent in French by the time of his study of Satie.
63 Myers, *Erik Satie*, p. 60.
64 Templier, *Erik Satie*, p. 46, and cited in Alan M. Gillmor, *Erik Satie* (New York: Norton, 1988), p. 232.
65 "It took a Satie and a Webern to rediscover this musical truth, which, by means of musicology, we learn was evident to some musicians in our Middle Ages, and to all musicians at all times (except those whom we are currently in the process of spoiling) in the Orient." Also: "There can be no right making of music that does not structure itself from the very roots of sound and silence—lengths of time. In India, rhythmic structure is called Tala. With us, unfortunately, it is called a new idea." Cage, "Defense of Satie," in *John Cage*, ed. Koslelanetz, p. 81.
66 Ibid., pp. 78–79.
67 Ibid., p. 81.
68 Ibid., p. 83.

69 Huxley, *The Perennial Philosophy*, pp. 249–50. Jung's *The Integration of the Personality*, 10, contains a similar passage: "The enormous increase of technical facilities only serves to occupy the mind with all sorts of sensations and impressions that lure the attention and interest from the inner world. The relentless flood of newspapers, radio programs, and movies may widen or fill the external mind, while at the same time, and in the same measure, consciousness of the inner world becomes darkened and may eventually disappear altogether. But 'forgetting' is not identical with 'getting rid of.'"

Julia Robinson, "John Cage and Investiture: Unmanning the System", in: *John Cage, October Files 12*, ed. Julia Robinson (Cambridge, Massachusetts: The MIT Press, 2011), pp. 191–96. Substantially revised version of the essay of the same title in *The Anarchy of Silence: John Cage and Experimental Art* (Barcelona: Museu d'Art Contemporani de Barcelona, 2009).

The Anechoic Chamber, Technology, and the Landscape of the Postmodern

The period 1950–1952 was critical in the development of what we might think of as a Cagean System. The "Lecture on Nothing" generated a textual enactment of his new deployment of structure, and positioned Eastern philosophy as the touchstone of his practice; it cleared the way for a new field of experimentation. Soon thereafter, the "Lecture on Something" (1951) *appropriated* Feldman's advance for the new discourse, and the vast and complex *Music of Changes* then definitively staked Cage's claim to the new musical territory being charted. More ephemeral and anecdotal, Cage's visit to the anechoic chamber would turn out to buttress the whole. Taken together, these events become the marks of symbolic investiture.

Cage's visit to the anechoic chamber has developed into a crucial origin story marking a "founding" moment: the founding of his concept of "silence." At this stage of the history it is crucial to separate the anecdotes—whether true or false—from the symbolic value that Cage gave them to articulate his aims. The raw material of the anechoic chamber story is that Cage entered this putatively "silent" environment, and proceeded, in a sense, to defy technology with his listening capacities, managing to hear, after a while, two distinct sounds: his blood in circulation and his nervous system in operation.[80] If the interpretation of these sounds seems far-fetched, Cage anticipated that reaction; in later retellings, he relinquished his own claim to this part of the story, instead attributing the diagnosis to the engineer at Harvard.

Cage made the event critical because of what he said about it. As he told and retold the story, the point became that in a space where all the sound is removed, one still hears something—sounds one does not intentionally make—and therefore that sound is not governed by intentionality. The story is crucial not only for what was being instated but for what was being dismantled. The model of symbolic investiture with which we began, the case of Daniel Paul Schreber, has at its center the concept of "unmanning" (*Entmannung*). For the many readers of this case, notably Jacques Lacan, this will to dismantle a powerful system, from individual subjectivity outward, is what makes it "symbolic." In opposition to his own field of the law, which reflects the social order at large, Schreber develops a new vocabulary of symbols by which he is able to dismantle that System *for himself*. Lacan speaks of a "signifying chain" through which Schreber creates his survival model of unmanning, which, Lacan insists, must be read symbolically rather than literally.[81] The extraordinary relevance of this model for our reading of Cage's developing system of symbolic investiture is in its parallel strategy. Cage's moves are negations—albeit rendered positive philosophically and structurally in his work—modes of unmanning his own discipline, its systems, and even its content. The anechoic chamber event, which Cage converts to a critique of intentionality, is the symbol of this process *par excellence*.

The anechoic chamber provided a concrete form, even an architecture, for all Cage's previous "negations." In his polished account, the chamber accomplished a number of feats: it made the space of *no-sound* physical, it made the nonintentional palpable, and crucially, it ushered in these new theoretical premises under the auspices of "technology." Vital in Cage's retelling is that the protagonist, a composer, had an experience of sound that he could not instantly identify. Strategically, Cage first *unmanned* himself, deskilling the masterful arranger of sound, the composer, in order to *unman* the priority of Western music and its laws. It is not a mere detail in the story that he deferred to the Harvard engineer; this is what accomplishes the symbolic unmanning, both micro and macro. Cage would use this "expert" explanation of sound under "silent" conditions to *authorize* his next moves. This technologically created environment—with its silence punctuated by incidental sound—begins to make the structured spaces that Cage generated, exhaustively, in the *Music of Changes* infinitely more meaningful. The complete story (developed retroactively) created a profound logic for Cage's next two landmark scores: *Imaginary Landscape No. 4* (1951) and *4'33"* (1952).

For Cage, musical expertise had limited what could be composed to a stifling degree. If the anechoic chamber is an environment in which the subject is sound, its palpable (and putatively empty) physical space materialized as a countermodel to the sonic plenum controlled by composers and allowed Cage to redefine sound as part of a spatial field. Pritchett explains that the concurrent chance techniques with which Cage was working freed him from musical form, opening up a new idea of "infinite space." He adds that Cage would spend "the next decade finding compositional methods which ... would make more of that space available to him."[82]

In *Imaginary Landscape No. 4*, a work often considered alongside *Music of Changes* because its composing methods were the same, Cage attempted to render this new, desubjectivized "sound-space" mediated by technology as a score/performance.[83] The "instruments" for the piece are twelve radios, operated by twenty-four performers (two on each: one for tuning, one for volume), perhaps implicitly confronting the formidable "twelve" of Schoenberg.[84] The move made in *Imaginary Landscape No. 4* is as striking as the voiding of composerly intention in the subsequent *4'33"*—though the two scores are rarely examined side by side—and its symbolic move is as great. Given that *Imaginary Landscape No. 4* includes whatever will come up in the radio broadcasts, its sounds cannot be predicted.[85] Since Cage was not a fan of radios, this score reveals all the more clearly his efforts to contend with the inevitable changes that audio technology brought to the field of perception; this is the first such instance, of which many more would follow. By confronting what he found antithetical to the composer, Cage mediated the function of authorship and the effects of technology, qualifying the power of both, to reclaim some agency for the subject. Explaining this score, he wrote:

> It is thus possible to make a musical composition the continuity of which is free of individual taste and memory (psychology) and also of the literature and "traditions" of the

> art. The sounds enter time-space centered within themselves, unimpeded by service to any abstraction, their 360 degrees of circumference free for an infinite play of interpenetration. Value judgments are not in the nature of this work as regards either composition, Performance, or listening.... A "mistake" is beside the point for anything that happens authentically is.[86]

Technological means thus dismantle the traditions of music and restructure attention. Generating the idea of a "landscape" with a cluster of twelve radios as the expanded field of the contemporary "imaginary," Cage used the piece to give a new form to the unpredictability he was introducing into the act of composing. *Imaginary Landscape No. 4* positioned the work as part of a network of communication in which perception is subjected to *reception.*

4′33″

Cage's renowned score, *4′33″*, is at the center of the most comprehensive period of change in his oeuvre. However, its vast notoriety derives in large measure from the fact that it has been simplified, and also that it is usually understood as one definitive thing. *4′33″* is situated between two Cagean landmarks: "Silence" and "Indeterminacy." A more hybrid object than is commonly surmised, Cage completely changed the score at least three times in the course of the 1950s, as he extended the concept of chance operations in composing to indeterminacy in the realm of performance. In a process that included his parallel work on lectures, the changes in the format of the score reflect a period of consolidation and expansion. *4′33″* spearheaded Cage's aims to shift the foundations of the discipline of music, which opened out conceptually to a redefinition of the creative act. As a dismantling of the composer's power of authorship and control—with a new emphasis on "receptiveness," and "nature" (as incidental sound)—it is the very inscription of Cage's unmanning of musical convention.

An "empty" score with only a temporal framework (defined initially and then later removed), *4′33″* gave Cage's stunning assertion of "silence" a notated form. In effect, he realized the contained "silence" of the anechoic chamber as a score, sutured in perpetuity to a changing world of sounds. Rarely discussed is the way in which the format of *4′33″* actually developed with Cage's rhetoric; both were directed toward what he needed that score to accomplish as the decade unfolded. The first version of 1952 was measured out on grand staff pages, albeit emptied of notes, asserting the way in which chance can compose "nothing" as well as "something"—that time is all that need remain to concern the composer. The second, graphic, line-drawing version of 1953 opened Cage's project to an intervention beyond the confines of music since it was linked to the landmark statement of Robert Rauschenberg's *White Paintings* (1951).[87] Making this point allowed him to suggest that the "statement" of *4′33″* brought music into sudden alignment with advanced art. It was an ambitious move, which he evoked as a highly conscious act. With brevity, and artful humility, he managed to position himself as representing the most advanced position in "music." Cage said he *had* to write *4′33″*: "otherwise I'm lagging, otherwise *music* is lagging."[88] The inference being that having written it when he did, the stakes were changed.

The third version of *4′33″* was written in the late 1950s. As Cage had largely dispensed with the score per se, as he established his concept of indeterminacy, this version took the form of pure text. Three words—tacet, tacet, tacet—defined three movements, separated on the page by roman numerals: I, II, III. There was no timing. The score included a note at the bottom of the page describing the specific temporal unfolding of the first performance, since the "reader" had little else to go on. The description of the August 1952 realization implied that those timings were circumstantial. Cage later commented to Richard Kostelanetz that movements were not actually needed anymore, adding that he did not even need *4′33″* anymore.[89] Over the three versions, the score became less obviously musical—first dispensing with staff lines, then time measures—and seemingly more abstract. Another way of thinking of this is that *4′33″* became *symbolic*. The fact that Cage spoke of needing/not needing *4′33″*—an odd observation, made of this piece alone—indicates the value of this unfathomably open composition as more symbol than score. If Cage's "silence" signified a dismantling of musical convention as well as intention, *4′33″* was its first important matrix of articulation. The three versions of *4′33″* developed this theoretical position progressively: (1) by removing musical notation, in the 1952 version; (2) by echoing (if not rivaling) advanced painting using the template of a score in 1953; and (3) by converting the musical notation to a textual proposition.[90]

[...] Cage unmans the composer as well as the performer, and empowers the listener. Schreber's state as an open, hypersensitized, receiver, converts the bounded modern subject into a dispersed, uncentered process. The Cagean score—as a desubjectivized matrix of relations—effectively performs this radical dispersal of subjectivity on the unidirectional control of composing. With *4′33″* the composer gestures toward such receptive conditions, asserting a fragile structure to evacuate old content. What we are left with is a new dynamic between composer-performer-audience, without the power relations, an *unmanned* creative (un)structure, in a word: "indeterminacy."

80 Evidence of Cage's performative repetition of this story to instantiate his model of silence appears in George Brecht's (June–September 1958) notebook from Cage's "Experimental Composition" course at the New School. On the first page, the first day of class, Brecht notes, "At one time Cage conceived of a sound-silence opposition, but after the anechoic chamber experience (hi-note nervous system noise, low note blood circulating) concluded silence was non-existent." George Brecht, *Notebooks*, vol. 1, ed. Dieter Daniels (Cologne: Walther König, 1991), p. 3.

81 Lacan, "On a Question Preliminary to Any Possible Treatment of Psychosis," pp 445–88.

82 Pritchett, *The Music of John Cage*, pp. 78–79.

83 Cage links the concept of "sound-space" to the anechoic chamber experience in the New School class of 1958. After the abovementioned note on the anechoic chamber, George Brecht writes, "Events in sound-space (J.C.)." See Brecht, *Notebooks*, 1: p. 3.

84 Since Cage later defined his "automatic minimum" for a sufficiently diversified sound experience as *two* (radios for example), this twelve stands out all the more. See John Cage, "Experimental Music: Doctrine," in *Silence*, p. 14.

85 The first performance happened late at night, when many of the radio stations had stopped broadcasting for the evening, which produced a more silent piece than expected. Henry Cowell, who was present in the audience, was apparently disappointed that the "instruments" could not capture sound "diversified enough to present a really interesting, specific result." Cowell found it striking that such a negligible effect did not bother the composer: "Cage's own attitude about this was one of comparative indifference, since he believes the *concept* to be more interesting than the result of any single performance" (my emphasis); cited in Michael Nyman, "Towards (a definition of) Experimental Composition," in *Experimental Music: Cage and Beyond* (Cambridge: Cambridge University Press, 2002), p. 24.

86 Cage, „Composition: To Describe the Process of Composition Used in *Music of Changes and Imaginary Landscape No. 4*," in *Silence*, p. 59.

87 Cage would go on record, connecting the two moves, in the form of a statement in *Silence*. In the head note to his text "On Robert Rauschenberg, Artist and His Work," Cage wrote: "To Whom It May Concern: The White Paintings came first; my silent piece came later" (*Silence*, 98). Perhaps the most developed and complex theorization of the relationship of these two works to date is Branden W. Joseph's "White on White," in *Random Order: Robert Rauschenberg and the Neo-Avant-Garde* (Cambridge: MIT Press, 2007).

88 Cage, interview with Alan Gillmor and Roger Shattuck (1973); reprinted in *Conversing with Cage*, ed. Richard Kostelanetz (New York: Limelight, 1994), p. 67.

89 Ibid.

90 In 1962 Cage wrote a score called *0′00″* (also referred to as *4′33″ No. 2*, though as we have discussed, with three preceding versions it would

technically be No. 4), which points to the most radical outcome of *4′33″* and clarifies its applicability beyond music. The instructions read, "In a situation provided with maximum amplification (no feedback), perform a disciplined action." Pritchett, has discussed the mystifying place this piece holds within his oeuvre: "The fact remains that it stands apart from all that Cage had composed before it." "Part of the problem of approaching *0′00″*," he continues, "is that it does not appear to be 'music' in any sense." He offers a possible explanation: "Later in the 1950s, Cage taught classes in composition at the New School for Social Research in New York City, classes that were attended by artists who would go on to develop the performance art genre: George Brecht, Allan Kaprow, Al Hansen, and Dick Higgins, among others. *0′00″*, with its simple prescription of a concrete action, is similar to many of their performance art pieces, especially the 'events' of George Brecht, where the focus is on a single action described in simple prose." Pritchett, *The Music of John Cage*, p. 139.

Work Structure / Score / Composition

Liz Kotz, *Words to Be Looked At: Language in 1960s Art* (Cambridge, Massachusetts: The MIT Press, 2007), pp. 14–28, p. 39, pp. 46–49, pp. 51–54.

Proliferating Scores and the Autonomy of Writing

As language enters 1960s' visual art from all sides, one tendency stands out: the use of words to propose or record a set of procedures for making a work. This notion—of a work as something that can be notated or realized in language—derives from music, specifically from the experimental music of the 1950s.

To understand how the turn to language challenged the very nature and structure of the work of art, we need to address this trajectory from musical composition to the visual arts. In turn, this will necessitate coming to terms with the deep structural transformations occurring in modern music, musical notation, and sound phenomena in the middle of the twentieth century. Central to this story is the work of the American composer John Cage, and in particular, his landmark silent composition *4′33″* (1952). Although composed as a piece of music, *4′33″* could also be described and notated entirely in words and numbers—a quality that helped make it accessible to people without musical training. Indeed, this version of the score, the text score published in 1961, circulated widely in the 1960s.

To grasp the impact of this work, we must consider what it means for words to occupy the space of the musical score, not merely as auxiliary annotation but as a primary material that displaces conventional musical notation. In his compositions of the 1930s and 1940s that led to *4′33″*, Cage gradually eliminated from his work many of the properties conventionally considered musical—melody, harmony, rhythm, and even notes—and instead came to reconceive music as the "organization of sound" and the muscal composition as something like a time structure—a series of time lengths or "time brackets" that could be filled with any material, or none. It is precisely because conventional musical syntax is voided in *4′33″* that verbal language can take the fore.

This crucial relationship between *4′33″* as a durational structure and the fact that it can be notated entirely in language will take some work to tease out. For it is no coincidence that these permutations in modern music happened around midcentury. The composition of *4′33″* is overdetermined by its relation to then-new technologies of sound recording and sound production. First phonography, then radio broadcast, microphony, loudspeaker technologies, and the like had already greatly altered the sensory experience and scientific understanding of sound before magnetic tape, oscillators, sine wave generators, and other electronic means of recording and producing sound became available in the 1940s and 1950s. These technologies radically challenged composers' perceptions of what sound was and what music could be. Many eccentricities of postwar experimental music are incomprehensible without this larger technical and historical context, from the so-called crisis in notation and the strange fetishization of the score as an independent graphic object to Cage's programmatic insistence on dissociating sound from intentionality, a move that mirrors what some have described as audiotape's "acousmatic" property, its tendency to separate sound from its source.[1]

Viewing *4′33″* in this context will require rethinking what has long been a canonical (if highly eccentric) work. For instance, the opposition to hierarchy and the radical openness to "whatever happens" that characterize Cage's work of the 1950s are often understood as the expressions of a philosophy or worldview, and particularly, as results of Cage's sustained encounter with Zen Buddhism. While not discounting the importance of that encounter, I want to propose a different logic, in which the much-celebrated Cagean philosophy is partly the result of changes in material support and medium. Understanding *4′33″* in this way, as part of a perverse turn to language that occurs in reaction to the electronic inscription of sound, will help elucidate why the piece was so productive for 1960s' visual artists, poets, and performers who were also absorbing the perceptual effects of new recording technologies.

Proliferating Scores

As various accounts attest, *4′33″* was first realized in August 1952 by the pianist David Tudor, who sat silently at the piano and carefully raised and lowered the keyboard lid to mark three irregularly timed sections consisting of chance-determined time brackets of 30″, 2′23″, and 1′40″, thereby providing a minimal compositional frame that would open up the performance to unanticipated environmental sounds and transfer responsibility for the experience on to the perceptual capacities of audience members.[2]

For all its simplicity, the piece did not come easily. Cage had apparently struggled with the idea of writing a "silent piece" since at least 1948, when he half jokingly described his plan to compose a piece of uninterrupted silence and sell it to the Muzak Company: "It will be 3 or 4 ⅓ minutes long—those being the standard lengths of canned music—and its title will be *Silent Prayer*."[3]

If, as Cage has insisted, the example of Robert Rauschenberg's 1951—1952 *White Paintings* emboldened him to proceed with the project, according to John Holzaepfel, "It was Tudor's interest in performing it that persuaded him [Cage] to finish it" in time for a concert the pianist had planned for the end of August for the Woodstock Artists Association at the Maverick Concert Hall, where the work "was played alongside compositions by Cage's friends and fellow new music pioneers Earle Brown, Pierre Boulez, Henry Cowell, Morton Feldman, and Christian Wolff.[4] The initial reaction apparently was not positive, as members of the audience began to talk and walk out. Cage later recounted losing valued friendships over the work.[5]

Existing as rumor, scandal, and verbal description far more often than as a performed work, *4′33″* since its debut has had a curious status. Much about its genesis remains unclear, and it may seem as though the piece cannot always bear the weight of its subsequent history and impact. By its nature, the composition's radical abstraction produces radical ambiguity. *4'33"* represents both a crystallization of certain Cagean imperatives into their clearest and most influential "statement," and a work that is in many respects highly atypical of Cage's overall production, a limit point from which one could argue that Cage himself gradually withdrew, leaving its implications for others to take up.[6]

The goal of this chapter is to present an account of *4'33"* and Cage's work more generally that allows us to understand its rich and diverse legacy for subsequent work in the visual arts and poetry. To do this effectively, we need to understand key aspects of Cage's work as a composer. From his early percussion music of the 1930s and 1940s to his turn to chance-based and indeterminate compositions in the early 1950s, Cage pursued a series of unorthodox musical moves that paved the way for *4'33"*: reconceiving the musical composition as a time structure, voiding the work's internal musical syntax by gradually abandoning conventional musical notes in favor of noise sounds and quantitatively defined "sound parameters," and moving toward an indeterminate relationship between score and performance in which the musical notation ceases to be a system of representation and instead becomes a proposal for action. Understanding the conceptual and historical roots of these moves requires looking closely at Cage's own accounts, yet also reading them critically and against the grain, to clarify not only the internal musical logic of Cage's unorthodox choices, but their relation to the larger ruptures introduced by new technologies that altered our relationship to time and seemed poised to displace older systems of writing and inscription.

Critics have argued that *4'33"* was central to the altered function of the score in postwar music. Michael Nyman declares, "As notation, *4'33"* is early evidence of the radical shift in the methods and function of notation that experimental music has brought about."[7] Within this trajectory *4'33"* is the work in which the Cagean score fully breaks from an older representational model to assume a new "operational" function, in which the notation no longer describes what we hear but what we do. As Ian Pepper argues, *4'33"* marks the breakthrough to "'composition' as an autonomous process of writing, as a graphic production that is not secondary to, and has no determined relation to, the sound of the work in performance."[8] This potential autonomy of writing was not authorized by Cage, who always insisted on the sounding of the composition; but it would be taken up by others who saw *4'33"* as a license to sever writing from the production of sound.

Curiously, however, in such discussions it is not clear which score we are dealing with. Complicating any analysis of *4'33"* is the fact that the work has had at least three quite distinct notations: a handwritten score in conventional grand staff notation with blank measures of silence that Tudor used for the initial Performance at Woodstock in August 1952, and that was subsequently lost and later reconstructed; the proportionally notated graphic version of the score that Cage gave to Irwin Kremen (the work's dedicatee) in June 1953, a version of which was published in Source 2 (July 1967) and later issued in a corrected scale by C. F. Peters as Edition 6777a; and the typewritten text-based version published in 1961 by Peters as Edition 6777, which despite its 1960 copyright, has never been clearly dated.[9] In addition, there are certain discrepancies between these scores and the information recorded in the program for the work's August 29, 1952 premier at the Maverick Concert Hall that records the work as "4 pieces": 4'33", 30", 2'23", and 1'40".[10]

Cage himself routinely dated the "work" *4'33"* to 1952, without differentiating between scores, despite their distinct notational modes. In interviews and statements, he repeatedly dodges questions about the differences between them, and his own accounts are patently inconsistent—although the overall length of *4'33"* was supposedly arrived at through random methods, Cage's late 1940s' idea for a composition of uninterrupted silence already entailed a standard pop song length. His plan for a piece of "silent Muzak" not only implies that *4'33"* was designed to have a curious interface with vernacular and commercial music practices but also suggests the repressed aggressivity of the piece, one that performs, in Douglas Kahn's analysis, not only "silence" but also "silencing," carried out on and within forms of industrial standardization.[11]

Since the 1960s, *4'33"* has often been flattened into a conceptual provocation, or an unstructured gesture of rebellion or revolt. Yet as debuted in 1952, the work was a highly structured composition and a publicly performed intervention into both musical and extramusical discourses, a public "speech event" whose social or political valence continues to elude definition. However seductive, efforts to read a specific politics of negation into Cage's project consistently neglect the musical and aesthetic specificity of *4'33"*. Despite the work's fame and the endless discourses around it, detailed accounts of its composition, notation, and initial performance are limited. In his 1988–89 Charles Eliot Norton lectures at Harvard University, Cage described the piece as having been built up gradually, "note by note," with procedures like those used in *Music of Changes*, Cage's legendary 1951 piano work composed by means of chance procedures:

> When I wrote *4'33"* I was in the process of writing the *Music of Changes* that was done in an elaborate way there are many tables for pitches for durations for amplitudes all the work was done with chance operations in the case of *4'33"* I actually used the same method of working and I built up the silence of each movement and the three movements add up to *4'33"* I built each movement up by means of short silences put together it seems idiotic but that's what I did I didn't have to bother with the pitch tables or the amplitude tables all I had to do was work with the durations ... it took several days to write and it took me several years to come to the decision to make it.[12]

In an interview with William Fetterman, Tudor insisted that "the original score was on music paper, with staffs, and it was laid out in measures like the *Music of Changes*, only there were no notes. But the time was there, notated exactly like the *Music of Changes*, except that the tempo never changed, and there were no occurrences—just blank measures, no rests—and the time was easy to compute. The tempo was 60."[13] Tudor scholar John Holzaepfel concurs that *4'33"* was originally written on staff paper, in proportional notation that graphed time according to bars, indicating silences as rests, just as one would conventionally notate a part for an instrument that remains silent for a specified length of time or movement during a larger work. In performance, Tudor read these by a stopwatch. In Tudor's 1989 reconstruction, the piece is notated in grand staff form, with a time signature of 4/4—precisely the system used to notate the *Music of Changes* (which Holzaepfel terms "the parent work" of *4'33"*). Holzaepfel concludes that the 1989 reconstruction "accurately reproduces Cage's lost score," although in other texts he has emphasized Tudor's practice of constructing, for the purposes of performance, conventionally notated scores of works originally written in proportional and graphic notation.[14]

By situating *4'33"* within Cage's musical production, these accounts help us understand the work not merely as a perceptual experience or conceptual "idea" but as a structured composition, and as the product of a radical reconfiguration of the relation between sound and notation. As Tudor recalled in an interview for the German journal *MusikTexte*, Cage insisted that "it was very important to understand that every note of the piece had been composed ... It is, in philosophical hindsight, very important to understand that he had completed a compositional process in order to produce this piece."[15] *4'33"* is a composition whose performance parameters can be indicated in a series of different notations, *and* the richness and material specificity of those notations. My insistence on the specificity of the scores for *4'33"* may be puzzling to those who would see the transposition between metered and graphic notations as a "trivial translation," or who insist, for instance, on the fact that current music notation software often allows one to show a score in either regular or "piano roll" notation that roughly resembles Cage's space = time rendering. While Cage may have seen these notations as equivalent, the process by which he came to do so is of tremendous interest. If in the shift from metered to graphic notation vestiges of Cage's early approach to phrasing drop out, it is also the concision and extreme reduction of the piece that allow it to be so elegantly rendered in language, since the work comprises three silent durations and no notes.

Within this collection of different notations, the typewritten text score has had a particularly strange status. Despite its influence on visual art and conceptual projects, there has been a longstanding tendency to dismiss it as a secondary, later adaptation, and instead view the graphic score as more authentic and "original."[16] This is a curious claim, since the prior existence of a conventionally notated version suggests that neither published version could be held to be original, whatever such a concept might mean in this context.[17]

As various commentators have observed, only the time brackets for the graphic version correspond to the original printed program, while the more frequently used text version records a different set of movements: 33", 2'40", and 1'20". The published version of the text score carries the copyright date of 1960, the year Cage signed with music publisher C.F. Peters, leading many observers to assume that it was written in 1960, even though many of Cage's earlier scores also carry a copyright date of that year.[18] In his book on Cage, James W. Pritchett describes *4'33"* as having been "revised ... sometime around 1960, creating a wholly different work."[19] And the text score's ambivalent note that the work "may last any length of time" indeed seems to open the door to the popular conception of the piece as simply an exercise in activated listening.

While trying to trace out the relation of Cage's text score to subsequent word-based compositions, I have at times considered that the early event scores of George Brecht and La Monte Young, composed in 1959–1960, might have triggered the straightforward typewritten notation. Yet this sequence appears unlikely, given that Brecht, in his July 17, 1958, notes for Cage's class in experimental composition at the New School, refers to Cage's "4 min 33 sec" as "Silence. Tacet"—a jotted record that suggests Cage already referred to or notated the work in linguistic terms.[20] Nonetheless, I was surprised to find in the David Tudor papers a copy of the typewritten score, nearly identical to the one issued by Peters, dated 1953. Of course, this dating may be far from conclusive. Several copies of scores in Tudor's collection that date prior to Cage's signing with Peters are similarly stamped "COMPOSERS FACSIMILE EDITION Copyright 195_" with the exact date handwritten in. The fact that the handwriting on this copy of 4'33" does not appear to be Cage's (it could be Tudor's) makes it possible that it was backdated to 1953, the year of the graphic score.[21]

We will probably never know exactly when Cage produced the typewritten notation for *4'33"*, but the tendency among many musicians and musicologists to discount or denigrate this version strikes me as curious. That it was likely produced after the two earlier versions of the score—the grand staff notation, and the graphic score—is no reason to treat it as secondary or a corruption of the conceptual purity of the initial composition. Instead, the fact that *4'33"* can be inscribed as a time signature on staffpaper, vertical lines on otherwise-blank pages, or a terse set of verbal instructions is integral to the work. That the existence of three distinctly notated scores of *4'33"* is no mere historical accident is confirmed in Young's better-known series *Composition 1960 #7, Composition 1960 #9*, and *Composition 1960 #10,* which explicitly renders the "same" structure as a musical note, a straight line on an index card, and a verbal inscription. While unaware of the three versions of *4'33"*, Young cites Cage's and Sylvano Bussotti's graphic scores as inspirations for his awareness that a line or drawing was "something you could play."[22]

The typewritten text score consists of minimal indications for the performer of an unnamed intrument, presenting simply three sections "I", "II" and "III", each marked "TACET". This term is generally used in orchestral music, and particulary in percussion parts, to indicate a rest performed by one player while others continue to play their instruments. Thus, it indicates a bracketed silence while other things are going on—and not, say, an absolute silence or the absence of a work altogether. Centered on the page and vertically stacked, the three numbered movements are sparsely rendered and suspended in white space. This centrality inverts the norm in which words have remained visually and structurally marginal in the musical score. Besides indicating a title and an author, written language generally serves only as annotation, as a mean of specifying aspects of the realization for orchestral performances like tempo, mood, and instrumentation (aspects Cage leaves unspecified). Hence, displacing the signs of musical notation with words in a sense involves a historical inversion, as almost all codified forms of musical notation are themselves modeled, structurally and materially, on a culture's existing written language.[23]

Perhaps most surprisingly, the score carries no title. Instead, a typed "NOTE" below the main notation declares that "the title of this work is the total length in minutes and seconds of its performance," and records that the debut performance was "*4'33"*", and the three parts were 33", 2'40", and 1'20" (figures that do not accord with the 1952 program)—adding "the work may be performed by any instrumentalist or combination of instrumentalists and last any lenght of time." This practice of retitling the work based on contingent factors of performance resembles the instructions used for *Water Music*, which debuted at the New School in May 1952, and initially carried the title of the date or place or place of its performance—for example, "66 W. 12" or later "Aug. 12, 1952."[24] This constant retitling (later suspended) was presumably designed to name each performance a distinct "work" (hence the work carries the title "Aug. 29, 1952" on the Woodstock program).[25] In addition, it is precisely the text score's apparent evacuation of structure—the idea that the work can last "any length of time" rather than consisting of precise durations—that understandably leads critics like Pritchett to conclude it could not have been written before 1957 or 1958. For as we will see, the principle that organized Cage's compositions from the late 1930s through the mid-1950s was duration.

Durational Structures

By the early 1960s, Cage would promulgate a free-form version of *4'33"* that he could "perform" in the woods while searching for mushrooms; it could last any amount of time and consisted simply of attentively listening to the world around one—as if the score simply read "listen." Given Cage's growing discomfort with any imposed structure, many of his later remarks effectively denied the formal specificity of *4'33"* as a composed work with three movements consisting of externally generated durations. Cage himself even compared *4'33"* less favorably to his 1962 refashioning of it as *0'00"*, judging the earlier piece "a more conventional musical work in the sense that it marks its own temporal limitation, and has a time signature."[26]

Going against Cage's own rewriting of the project to instead situate *4'33"* in his long-term work with durational structures and sustained experimentation with both sound and notation, we can retrieve another, perhaps more useful reading of the piece: one in which performance is by no means a formless "anything that happens," but the activation of a text. And this text, significantly, describes a time structure. Whichever score is employed, a performance of *4'33"* is a structured experience in three movements that occurs in relation to a written inscription. In a 1989 interview, Tudor comments, regarding his performance using one of the conventionally notated versions he prepared, "It's important that you *read* the scores as you're performing it, so there are these pages you use. So you wait, and then turn the page. I know it sounds very straight, but in the end it makes a difference."[27]

In its three chance-composed movements, the compositional structure of *4'33"* presents time as a kind of neutral container, like an empty frame that could contain whatever events or sounds might happen during its course. While it is most evident in an abstract work like *4'33"*, Cage's practice of structuring compositions according to preestablished lengths of time began with his percussion works of the late 1930s. While Cage's organization of compositions by means of lengths of time may initially resemble more traditional uses of musical meter and phrasing, he gradually adopts arbitrary quantification schemata structurally unrelated to his unconventional sound materials.[28] Cage termed this practice "rhythmic structure" or "structural rhythm." Its emergence had far-reaching implications for his work. By breaking the organic relation between the sound material and their overall structure, these "time brackets" gradually evacuate the internal syntax of the work and disrupt the function of notation.

[...] What Cage terms indeterminacy is, first and foremost, a relation between notation and realization. It represents one outcome of this reconfiguring of notation, from an idealized representation to something resembling an operational model, like a list of instructions or a set of procedures. Although subsequent artistic projects of the 1960s, such as the proto-Fluxus event scores, would associate this instructional or procedural function with *language*, it is important to note that this operational mode first arises within conventional-looking musical notation, and is only later transferred to numbers, graphic inscription, and written text. In a 1970 interview with Daniel Charles, Cage states, "Once I developed the prepared piano, notation became a way to produce something."[56] If notation is now a way to do a job, any tools—writing, graphics, diagrams, and even musical bars and notes—can be used.

Cage's use of proportional graphic marks to notate time structures—such as those used in the graphic version of *4'33"*—emerged from working with magnetic tape in the early 1950s. This experience would be decisive for remapping his understanding of sound and transforming his measure of time from conventional metrical counting to one based on spatial extension. In the long run, it would not only completely transform Cage's scores but also move him fully toward indeterminacy, as he took his failure to archieve technical control as an "omen to go to the unfixed". It is in the context of magnetic tape that Cage describes the discrete properties of scale, modes, counterpoint, and harmony as "musical habits" that behave like a "cautious stepping" inconsistent with the continuous nature of sound:

> In mathematical terms these all concerns discrete steps. They resemble walking—in the case of pitches, on steppingstones twelve in number. This cautious stepping is not characteristic of the possibilities of magnetic tape, which is revealing to us that musical action or existence can occur at any point or along any line or curve or what have you in total sound-space; that we are, in fact, technically equipped to transform our contemporary awareness of nature's manner of operation into art.[57]

The Work of Art as Notation and Realization

What is it about Cage's work—and *4'33"* in particular—that would prove such a potent model? The most compelling reception of this work, I believe, occurs in the visual arts, where the concept of the work as a neutral time structure, and an inscription to be activated, could be applied to all manner of material and procedure.

By prying open the regulatory relation between sign and realization, Cagean indeterminacy repositioned writing as a kind of productive mechanism, thereby giving notation a functional and aesthetic autonomy—an autonomy that opened the door for the scores, instructions, or snippets of language to themselves *be* the work, while individual realizations occur as "instances," "samples," or "examples" of it. From the vantage point of Conceptual art, this strategy could appear as the elevation of the concept or idea over the sensuous material or temporal realization, or as an understanding of the produced object, mark, or enactment primarily as the execution or testing out of a conceptual premise or linguistic proposition—as in Sol LeWitt's oft-cited words, "The idea becomes a machine that makes the art." LeWitt adds that "all the intervening steps—scribbles, sketches, drawings, failed works, models, studies, thoughts, conversations—are of interest," acknowleding that "preparatory" materials may be as interesting or even more so than the produced work.[69] Thus, as postwar compositional experiments bring the forms and functions of notation to a kind of crisis within music, the proliferation of forms they generate allowed models from musical practice to disseminate out into other art forms.[70]

As this notational function is adapted to divers media beyond music—to work in language, sculpture, performance, video, photography, and beyond—the crucial model is indeed *4'33"*, in which the most widely circulated notation is comprised mostly of words. While many readings of *4'33"* emphasize its gestural, visual, and theatrical qualitites, or its minimally structured focus on nonart experiences, others target the work's inherently linguistic dimensions, reading it as the activation of a text, mobilizing the capacity of a simple structure to generate multiple realizations, and situating the listener or reader as a kind of performer. Language is central to the expanded concept of notation, in which the simplicity and reduction of the list, for instance, will become a paradigmatic form of the work or score.

If the musical score no longer aspires to "represent" sounding material or tightly control the realization of a work, what does notation do? The generativity of notation comes from its contingency, as a flexible template or schema that can be used to produce more realizations. As Roman Ingarden contended, writing in the late 1920s, the score is a kind of schema that "fixes the musical work only incompletely". It is precisely this "incomplete determination of the work by the score" that is its advantage over recording technologies since it permits "on the one hand, the 'fixed' relatively invariant schema, and on the other hand, the multiplicity of possible profiles through which the work manifests itself."[71] As already evident in Cage's compositions of the late 1950s, language, graphic inscriptions, and diagrams all provide a means of defining parameters or indicting a structure, while retaining sufficient ambiguity to permit distinct performances or instantiations.

[...] Yet the typewritten score for *4'33"* represents an opposing notational strategy: reconstituted in vernacular signs so repeatable and translatable that no original appears to exist, it disseminates into the culture by reproduction, reputation, hearsay, and verbal accounts whose reach far exceeds the circulation of any of the score versions or score copies. However hermetically, it offers a set of *instructions to the performer*, a set of *words to be read*. By its nature, this unregulated circulation permits considerable deviation, degradation, and factual "inaccuracies"—a complex dissemination made possible by the concision and simplicity of the piece. By tapping into the power of the vernacular and the productivity of such proliferation, *4'33"* carries a capacity for rereading and reuse that potentially exceeds the more programmatic indeterminacy of Cage's other works. In its sparse presentation as well as its minimal, elegantly condensed structure, *4'33"* is the most important model and precedent for much subsequent work in other media.

1 The term acousmatic stems from French musique concrète composer Pierre Schaeffer and writer Jérôme Peignot; the concept has disseminated through the work of, among others, François Bayle and R. Murray Schaeffer as well as film theorist Michel Chion. I thank Eric Drott for his insights here.

2 Most accounts of the debut performance of *4'33"* rely on Cage's recollections of the performance (independent audience accounts are quite rare): see Calvin Tomkins, *The Bride and the Bachelors: Five Masters of the Avant-Garde* (New York: Viking Press, 1965), and *Off the Wall: Robert Rauschenberg and the Art World of Our Time* (New York: Doubleday Books, 1980); Cage's various interviews, many of which are collected in Richard Kostelanetz, ed., *Conversing with Cage* (New York: Limelight Editions, 1988); the much later and quite different description Cage gave in his 1988–89 Harvard University lectures, collected in *John Cage I–VI* (Cambridge, MA: Harvard University Press, 1990), pp. 20–25. Certain key discrepancies will be addressed below.

3 John Cage, "A Composer's Confessions" (1948), in *John Cage: Writer*, ed. Richard Kostelanetz (New York: Limelight Editions, 1993), p. 43.

4 John Holzaepfel, "Cage and Tudor," in *The Cambridge Companion to John Cage*, ed. David E. Nicholls (London: Cambridge University Press, 2002), p. 174.

5 Kostelanetz, *Conversing with Cage*, pp. 66–68.

6 Even if we are to accept, for instance, Douglas Kahn's diagnosis that Cage offered a series of "end game" strategies that merely "performed the last possible modernist renovation of Western art music," the use of these strategies in other contexts appears far from exhausted. Douglas Kahn, "Track Organology," *October* 55 (Winter 1990), p. 71.

7 Michael Nyman, *Experimental Music: Cage and Beyond* (New York: Schirmer, 1974), p. 3.

8 Ian Pepper, "From the 'Aesthetics of Indifference' to 'Negative Aesthetics' John Cage in Germany, 1958–1972," *October* 82 (Fall 1997), p. 33.

9 In *John Cage's Theatre Pieces: Notations and Performances* (Amsterdam: Harwood Academic Publishers, 1996), William Fetterman provides the most sustained account of the different scores and dates the "linguistically notated version" to 1960. Yet he subsequently acknowledged that this was an assumption made without any evidence beyond the copyright (Fetterman, letter to the author, March 2001). The single-page manuscript held in the Cage archives at the New York Public Library is considered the original typewritten score, though who produced it—or when—is unclear. And complicating this scenario, the text score was later reissued by Peters in 1986 in a version printed in Cage's distinctive handwriting; the current version, printed as a booklet, has been typeset with each movement on a separate page.

10 For conflicting accounts of these versions, see Fetterman, *John Cage's Theatre Pieces*, pp. 69–84; Larry J. Solomon, "The Sounds of Silence: John Cage and *4'33"* (1998), at http://solomonsmusic.net/4min33se.htm; Irwin Kremen's 1996 account of the graphic score, available in the online archives of "Silence: The John Cage Discussion List" at http://newalbion.com/artists/cagej/silence/; Tudor's recollections in "Interview with Reinhard Oehlschägel," translated by Daniel Wolf, in *MusikTexte* 69/70 (1997): 69–72. While I had tended to read the billing of *4'33"* on the Woodstock program as a misprint, Tudor scholar John Holzaepfel disagrees: "Since Tudor selected the program and arranged the order, and Cage was presumably involved in preparations for the concert, what would have led the printer to think there were four pieces unless someone made it clear that each of the three movements constituted one piece and all of them, together, a fourth?" (email to the author, August 20, 2005).

11 The most insistent critic arguing for such contextualization is Douglas Kahn, who in a series of essays culminating in *Noise, Water, Meat. A History of Sound in the Arts* (Cambridge, MA: MIT Press, 1999), proposes that Cage's reaction to the modern conditions of aurality was a fundamentally conservative or recuperative strategy that sought to musicalize all sound by minimizing or eliminating its associative, social dimensions, thus contributing to a project of what Kahn terms "noise abatement."

12 Cage, *John Cage I–VI*, pp. 20–22; punctuation in the original. In an interview with William Fetterman, Cage reiterated that "I wrote it note by note just like the *Music of Changes* ... That's how I knew how long it was, when I added all the notes up. It was done just like a piece of music, except that there were no sounds—but there were durations" (Fetterman, *John Cage's Theatre Pieces*, p. 72).

13 Fetterman, interview with David Tudor, June 21, 1989 (*John Cage's Theatre Pieces*, p. 72).

14 John Holzaepfel, "David Tudor, John Cage, and Comparative Indeterminacy" (lecture, the Art of David Tudor: Indeterminacy and Performance in Postwar Culture Conference, Getty Research Institute, Los Angeles, May 2001).

15 Tudor, "Interview," p. 70.

16 In his 1998 essay "The Sounds of Silence," Solomon goes so far as to decry the text version as "bogus"—and a notion of the graphic score as the original goes back to the 1960s, since it was often preferred by musicians who embraced the abstraction and indeterminacy of proportional visual notation. In *Music in the United States: A Historical Introduction*, 2nd ed. (Englewood Cliffs, NJ: Prentice-Hall, 1988), H. Wiley Hitchcock writes: "The original version of *4'33"*, which shows its relation to the earlier (non-experimental) music by Cage and is quite different from the published 'score,' is reproduced in *Source* 1/2 (Jury 1967)" (266).

17 Solomon's argument that the graphic score, in which long vertical lines on an otherwise-blank page indicate the three temporal "movements," visually resembles the vertical panels of Rauschenberg's white paintings is valid, and acknowledges the role of the proportionately notated graphic score as an analogue to painting. This similarity is also noted by Branden W. Joseph, who reproduces a portion of the graphic score in "White on White," *Critical Inquiry* 27 (Autumn 2000), 90–121. Complicating this resemblance is the fact that unlike the rigidity and detail of Cage's strict space-time notation, the visual format of the 1953 Kremen manuscript more closely resembles the graphic scores produced as early as 1950–1951 by Morton Feldman.

18 In a July 7, 1960 letter to Tudor, Cage notes that he has just signed a contract with C.F. Peters/Henmar Press and is now recording this copyright on all his compositions: "Together with the words Copyright c. 1960 by etc, I have been writing that on everything: title pages and first music pages (scores and parts) for a week now." Getty Research Library, David Tudor Papers.

19 James W. Pritchett, *The Music of John Cage* (New York: Cambridge University Press, 1993), 208–22.

20 George Brecht, *George Brecht Notebooks* (June 1958–August 1959), ed. Dieter Daniels with Hermann Braun (Cologne: Walther König, 1991), p. 48.

21 This was Holzaepfel's suggestion (email to the author, August 20, 2005). Pritchett (email to the author, August 25, 2005) elaborates that he considers the text score "a rethink of the work": "the 'original' *4'33"* is very much of a piece with the rest of Cage's work in the early 50s," while "the text version reflects his abandonment of structure in the late 50s," and therefore must date to 1957 or later. I take his comments seriously, although I am aware that in the past, everyone assumed that the type-written version dated from 1960 simply because of the copyright.

22 John Holzaepfel, "La Monte Young and Marian Zazeela, New York City, July 25, 1999" (unpublished interview).

23 Musical notation, Ian Bent notes, "rarely fashioned its own signs"; instead it has "generally been content to take over systems in use for other purposes" including signs of language, speech inflection, and arithmetic. These provide not just materials but structural devices: "The ordering of letters in an alphabet offers a ready-made base for notation, as it can be directly related to the intrinsic acoustical order of musical sound," Bent adds. This relation extends to its implicit visual graphing of time: "The act of writing a succession of notational syllables is graphic because it traces a path across the writing surface.That path is the analogue of the passage of music through time.The direction of the path tends to follow the prevailing direction of writing." Ian Bent, David Hiley, Margaret Bent, and Geoffrey Chew, "Notation," in *The New Grove Dictionary of Music and Musicians*, ed. Stanley Sadie (London: Macmillan, 1980), 13, pp. 336, 341.

24 See Robert Dünn, ed., *John Cage* (New York: Henmar Press, 1962), p. 43.

25 This inscription of the contingency of each specific realization into the work in-evitably recalls later works like Dan Grahams 1966 "poem" *Schema*, and

subsequent site-based projects that self-reflexively seek to inscribe their physical and institutional location.

26 John Cage and Daniel Charles, *For the Birds: John Cage in Conversation with Daniel Charles* (London: Marian Boyars, 1981), p. 169.

27 Cited in Fetterman, *John Cage's Theatre Pieces*, p. 75.

28 Cage's terms "rhythmic structure" and "structural rhythm" are confusing, since his practice eliminates the regularized time beats usually connoted by the term "rhythm." In fact, Cage's aversion to regularized time beats was the stated basis for his repeated dismissal of jazz, and his use of externally generated durational structures emerged hand in hand with the complete evacuation or suppression of the pulsational dimension of time—indeed, the most striking quality one encounters in listening to Cage's otherwise-heterogeneous music is a general absence of beat or propulsive energy.

[...]

56 Cage and Charles, *For the Birds*, p. 160.

57 John Cage, "Experimental Music" (1957), in *Silence* (Middletown, CT: Wesleyan University Press, 1961), p. 9.

[...]

69 Sol LeWitt, "Paragraphs on Conceptual Art," *Artforum* 5, no. 10 (Summer 1967), pp. 80. 82.

70 For a concise account of the changing nature and role of musical notation in the United States, see H. Wiley Hitchcock, "Notation," in vol. 3, *The New Grove Dictionary of American Music*, ed. H. Wiley Hitchcock and Stanley Sadie (London: Macmillan, 1986). A more historically extensive and comparative overview can be found in Bent, Hiley, Bent, and Chew, "Notation," pp. 333–420.

71 Roman Ingarden, *The Work of Music and the Problem of Its Identity*, trans. Adam Czerniawski (1928; repr., Berkeley: University of California Press, 1986), pp. 157, 158.

James Pritchett, *The Music of John Cage* (Cambridge: Cambridge University Press, 1993), pp. 138–140, pp. 146–148, pp. 150–152.

Signs of Change: *0′00″*

In May of 1965, concert-goers entering the Rose Art Museum at Brandeis University were treated to an unusual musical experience. They were attending a concert of contemporary music, organized by Alvin Lucier, which featured works by Lucier, John Cage, and Christian Wolff. As the audience entered the museum, they were greeted by loud noises—squeals, gulps, clacks—coming from Speakers located at various locations in space. They soon discovered the source of the strange sounds: John Cage, sitting in a squeaky chair on a staircase landing between the two floors of the museum, was writing letters on a typewriter, and occasionally drinking from a glass of water. He was equipped with microphones connected to the museum sound system, so that every movement he made—every squeak of the chair he sat in, every tap of his typewriter, every gulp of water was greatly amplified so that it filled the space of the museum. When Cage was finished writing letters, the sound equipment was shut off, and the next work on the program was prepared.

What the Brandeis audience witnessed that night was a performance of Cage's composition *0′00″ (4′33″ No. 2)*. Composed in 1962, the score for the work consists of a single sentence: "In a situation provided with maximum amplification (no feedback), perform a disciplined action." The first performance of the piece, given in Tokyo during Cage's first tour of Japan, consisted of Cage writing that very sentence. The day after the Tokyo performance, he added four qualifications to the basic score: the performer should allow any interruptions of the action; the action should fulfill an obligation to others; the same action should not be used in more than one performance, and should not be the performance of a musical composition; and finally, the performer should pay no attention to the situation he finds himself in, whether electronic, musical, or theatrical. These qualifications were perhaps suggested by that first performance, their inclusion in the score thus clarifying Cage's intention for the work.

Given the history of Cage's compositions of the 1950s, *0′00″* is a difficult piece to understand. It is astonishing to realize that this is the work that immediately follows *Variations II* and *Atlas Eclipticalis:* nothing in these earlier works prepares the ground for *0′00″*, which at first glance seems to be completely unlike the chance and indeterminate music Cage composed in the 1950s. Any similarities one might find lie entirely on the surface. The use of amplification suggests a connection with *Cartridge Music*, but in that work the amplified objects are treated as instruments to be played, and the amplification system is used as a source of other musical parameters to manipulate; there is no sense of either "instrument" or "parameter" in *0′00″*. Similarly, while the focus on action and theatre calls to mind the earlier *Theatre Piece*, in fact no comparison is possible. The one work consists of a fragmented series of actions distributed among random time frames, while the other is a single deliberate and directed action that recognizes no measurement of time at all.

Part of the problem of approaching *0′00″* is that it does not appear to be "music" in any sense that we might use the term —even in the somewhat expanded sense of Cage's music of the 1950s. Its character instead would seem to place it under the category of theatre, or more properly what has come to be known as "performance art." Cage, in fact, has a long-standing connection to the performance art movement. Some authors cite the event he organized at Black Mountain College in 1952—a joint performance with Merce Cunningham, Robert Rauschenberg, David Tudor, M.C. Richards, and Charles Olsen —as the first example of a "happening." A simple structure of random time brackets was used to control the performance, which included film, slides, poetry, music, and dance. Later in the 1950s, Cage taught classes in composition at the New School for Social Research in New York City, classes that were attended by artists who would go on to develop the performance art genre: George Brecht, Allan Kaprow, Al Hansen, and Dick Higgins, among others. *0′00″*, with its simple prescription of concrete action, is similar to many of their performance art pieces, especially the "events" of George Brecht, where the focus is on a single action described in simple prose—Brecht's *Piano Piece 1962* consists of the phrase "a vase of flowers on(to) a piano."

But whatever affinities *0′00″* may have with early 1960s performance art, the fact remains that it stands apart from all that Cage composed before it. In it, we find a different relationship between Cage as a composer and the external world of sounds that was his medium. In general, we might say that his earlier chance and indeterminate works were indirect in their approach to music. In all of them—even such open-ended compositions as *Variations II*—a score (or a score-making tool) is used to act as a buffer between mind and sound. Uppermost in Cage's thoughts at that time was the image of a world of interpenetrating sounds, a world in which each sound was unique and centered on itself. The actions of the performer were methodically worked out via the score so that this external sound world could be apprehended unconditionally, without the obstruction of the mind. In *0′00″*, this situation is reversed. There is no score to speak of here at all, and there is no sense of an objective sound world to be apprehended. Instead, there exists a totally subjective situation, in which the performer acts in a deliberate and personal fashion. The actions of a performer in *0′00″* are not arranged according to any elaborate plan or process, but are arrived at simply and directly. In its clear presentation of a musical world quite different from that of the 1950s, *0′00″* represents that rarity in music history—a clear line of stylistic demarcation. [...]

Process and Action

Let me return now to the issue of *0′00″* and how one is to understand such a composition in the context of Cage's prior work. The best course, I believe, in dealing with a difficult piece such as this is to try to see what is *there* in the work—in this case, to ask the question of just what is given in the score to *0′00″*. All that Cage has supplied is a direction to act—to perform some disciplined action that will fulfill an obligation to others. Cage has also indicated some of the circumstances surrounding this action: it should be amplified and performed in an unselfconscious way. This is all that the score contains. What probably accounts for the difficulty in reconciling it to Cage's earlier work is what it does *not* contain: it lacks any reference to sound. The only acoustic information given at all is the instruction that the action be amplified, and this only *implies* that sound will be heard. Because there is no mention of sound, and no means for describing or measuring the sorts of sounds that the piece will entail, *0′00″* does not exist as a compositional object—a series of sounds—but only as a process, an action by the performer.

This distinction between objects and processes is at the heart of the change in Cage's music from the 1950s to the 1960s. *0′00″* is not an isolated case, but is in fact quite typical in its emphasis on action and process. A quick examination of the scores Cage produced during this period shows that few of them mention sounds directly. None at all (with the possible exception of *HPSCHD*, which was, in any event, a collaborative effort) is primarily involved with describing or ordering sounds. This attitude is made explicit in the instructions to *Variations VI*, where Cage indicates that "the notations refer to what is to be done, not to what is heard or to be heard." That statement fairly describes all Cage's music of the 1960s: he had moved from arranging *things* to facilitating *processes*.

[...] A concomitant to this replacement of objects by processes was Cage's avoidance of any sort of measurement in his musical scores. The title of *0′00″* is a reference to this: it refers to the notion of "zero time" as derived from the work of Christian Wolff. In response to Wolff's notations of "zero time" in his *Duo for Pianists II* (an event so notated can have any duration at all), Cage changed his notion of time in music so that it became "less tangible than it was." As he explains:

> You see, if music is conceived as an *object*, then it has a beginning, middle, and end, and one can feel rather confident when he makes measurements of the time. But when it [music] is *process*, those measurements become less meaningful, and the process itself, involving if it happened to, the idea of Zero Time (that is to say no time at all), becomes mysterious and therefore eminently useful.[14]

[...] Cage refers to *0′00″* as *4′33″ No. 2*, thus implying that this is another silent piece. However, it is obvious that the piece is not at all silent, but in fact is quite noisy, given the extreme amplification involved. To understand this subtitle, it is necessary to consider what Cage meant by "silence" in the original *4′33″*. There, he drew upon his experience in the anechoic chamber to point out that what we refer to as silence is in fact just the occurrence of sounds not intended; *4′33″* embraces these unintentional sounds, and thus connects with Cage's chance works. *0′00″* represents a similar realization, but this time in the field of actions, not sounds. In the early 1960s, Cage began to realize that his identification of silence as unintentional sound could be extended to inactivity, which he now saw as unintentional action. Where his music of the 1950s was an attempt to blur the distinctions between intentional and unintentional sounds, so with his music of the 1960s he became concerned with blurring the distinctions between intentional and unintentional actions.

In *0′00″* this emphasis on unintentional action is manifested in various ways. The amplification system, for example, functions as a microscope, magnifying every tiny, uncontrollable detail of the performer's actions. Thus an action (such as writing letters) which is fully intentional on the part of the performer is transformed into a non-stop stream of minute, unintended acts. The encouragement of interruptions given in the score to *0′00″* (and in other works) also represents the unintentional. When dealing with sound and silence, Cage had been fond of testing a musical work's validity by seeing if it could accommodate ambient noises (i.e., unintentional sounds); by 1966, the criterion had changed to whether it "can include action on the part of others."[15] Finally, the instruction that the action of *0′00″* is to be performed in an unselfconscious fashion serves to de-emphasize the intentional side of the action—to make it appear as though the performer is doing what he would do anyway, without thinking of it as music or even as a performance. [...]

Electronic Technology in Cage's Music

I have already noted a difference in the use of electronics in *0′00″* as opposed to works such as the *Imaginary Landscape* series or *Cartridge Music*. Cage's treatment of electronic technology in those earlier works is, in essence, instrumental: the various devices are used as sources of particular sorts of sounds, and the musical scores—whether traditional, chance-composed, or indeterminate—are concerned with describing the ways in which these devices are to be played. In *0′00″*, on the other hand, the technology is that of amplification, which does not suggest the instrumental, but rather acts as a transforming force, elevating the mundane action of the performer to the realm of art. Cage used amplification in performances of all kinds during the 1960s; the gulping of water in his performance of the *Variations III* is one such example among many. Virtually any action he made or any device he used was likely to be amplified: in *Variations VII*, some of the performers' bodies were wired for sound, and in *Musicircus*, the sounds of the light switches were amplified. Cage saw amplification as a means to examine areas of action where nothing is definite, a way of making it clear that what one thought was inactivity is really full of uncontrollable, unintentional actions that produce sounds. In this way, he used technology in a more thorough way in the 1960s than he had in the past; the *spirit* of the music is electronic, not just its material.

Cage's attitude towards technology was shaped in part by his reading of the work of Marshall McLuhan, the prominent critic of media and technology. Cage read McLuhan's two major studies, *The Gutenberg Galaxy* (1962) and *Understanding Media* (1964), but he cites McLuhan's article "The Agenbite of Outwit" (1963) as the work "that I rank above all his [McLuhan's] books."[18] Cage refers to McLuhan repeatedly throughout his diaries and other writings, and McLuhan, in turn, quotes from Cage in his own book *The Medium is the Message* (1967).

McLuhan's work is wide-ranging and hence precludes any quick summation; I will limit myself here to outlining the points that are essential for understanding Cage's attraction to his ideas. First, McLuhan saw all technologies as extensions of the human body: a wheel, for example, is an extension of the feet. Electronic media, he felt, were extensions of our own senses and central nervous system, thus producing a good deal of uneasiness in society. McLuhan felt that such changes in media and technology, no matter what specific uses they are put to, in turn change people—that, regardless of the content communicated, the way one interacts with a medium is built into the technology. This is the meaning of his oft-quoted dictum "the medium is the message"—as he puts it in *Understanding Media*: "any technology gradually creates a totally new human environment. Environments are not passive wrappings but active processes".[19] In McLuhan's view, much of the change in society in the twentieth century resulted from the weakening of the old mechanical environment (created by the technology of printing), and the ascendancy of the new electronic environment (created by the new technologies of telegraph, radio, and television). Print culture emphasized "*lineality*, a one-thing-at-a-time awareness and mode of procedure" that included detached analysis, specialization, and fragmentation. The new electronic media, on the other hand, "deal in *auditory space*," with total involvement, unification, and simultaneity. In "Agenbite of Outwit" McLuhan uses the structure of the newspaper page as an example of this way of thinking: the news items and advertisements on the page "have no interconnection of logic or statement ... It is a kind of orchestral, resonating unity, not the unity of logical discourse."[20]

It was this description of the new electronic environment —the new "global village" created by instantaneous electronic communication—in which Cage found a compelling and informative parallel to his own work. In his essay "McLuhan's Influence" (1967) Cage makes the connection between what he saw as McLuhan's message and his own ideas:

> We are now, McLuhan teils us, no longer separate from this environment. New art and music do not communicate an individual's conceptions in ordered structures, but they implement processes which are, as are our daily lives, opportunities for perception (observation and listening). McLuhan emphasizes this shift from life done for us to life that we do for ourselves.

But McLuhan did more than provide an explanation of the changes in society: he affirmed the primacy of the artist in dealing with those changes. Because the artist deals with the senses, he is best equipped to understand the changes in perception caused by new technology. McLuhan saw experimental artists such as Cage as prophets of the new technology, and offered them a new purpose: the instruction of society on "how to rearrange one's psyche in order to anticipate the next blow from our own extended faculties."[21] This is the point at which Cage and McLuhan converge: Cage had always seen music as a means of "changing one's mind," and McLuhan provided a good reason to change it. After encountenng McLuhan, Cage saw himself as the creator of musical experiences that would allow people to adjust to the new electronic media environment.

14 John Cage "Interview with Roger Reynolds" (1961), in *John Cage* [catalog of works], p. 49. Cage first mentions Wolff's "zero time" notations and their implication of music as process in "Composition as Process: Indeterminacy," in *Silence*, p. 38.
15 Cage, "Diary: How to Improve the World (You Will Only Make Matters Worse) Continued 1966," in *A Year From Monday*, pp. 58–59.
[...]
18 Cage, *For the Birds* (Boston: Marion Boyars, 1981), p. 225.
19 Marshall McLuhan, *Understanding Media: The Extensions of Man*, p. viii.
20 Marshall McLuhan, "The Agenbite of Outwit," p. 43.
21 Marshall McLuhan, *Understanding Media*, p. 71.

Performativity / Theatricality / Visuality

William Fetterman, *John Cage's Theatre Pieces: Notations and Performances* (Amsterdam: Harwood Academic Publishers, 1996), pp. 75–76, pp. 80–82.

John Cage's Theatre Pieces: Notations and Performances

The first performance of *4'33"* by David Tudor is still considered to be the most important realization of this compositum. Calvin Tomkins describes it as follows:

> In the Woodstock hall, which was wide open to the woods at the back, attentive listeners could hear during the first movement the sound of wind in the trees; during the second, there was a patter of raindrops on the roof; during the third, the audience took over and added its own perplexed mutterings to the other "sounds not intended" by the composer. (Tomkins 1968, 119)

Tomkins's documentation is most accurate in describing the ambient sounds that occurred, but does not focus upon the actual performance of the composition, and is misleading if one considers *4'33"* to only be for piano. Tomkins's focus on the incidental sounds, rather than the score and its performance, is the usual interpretation of *4'33"*, and this closely follows Cage's own philosophical reflections. David Tudor, however, also characterizes the piece in more mystical terms:

> It is ... one of the most intense listening experiences one can have. You really listen. You're hearing everything there is. Audience noises play a part in it. It is cathartic—four minutes and thirty-three seconds of meditation, in effect. (Schonberg 1960, 49)

The gestural quality of David Tudor's performance is the most significant aspect of *4'33"* being a theatre piece, something to hear as well as to see. In addition to the previously mentioned gestures of closing the keyboard cover and starting the stop-watch, and depressing one of the three piano pedals, the *New York Times*, in reviewing the New York City premiere at Carl Fisher Concert Hall on April 14, 1954, adds that "At the appropriate time, Mr. Tudor seated himself at the piano, placed a hand on the music rack—and waited" ("Look, No Hands! And It's Music" 1954). The understated quality of gesture has, perhaps, become even more refined in Tudor's recent videotaped performance in 1990. Here, one can see very graceful, rounded gestures in such details such as starting the watch, closing the keyboard cover, as well as Tudor's close attention between reading the score and checking the reading by looking at the stop-watch. Except for turning the pages, Tudor had his hands folded in his lap during the three movements, his back erect, his expression very serious and concentrated (Miller and Perlis 1990). Apart from the ambient sounds that occur while watching this performance on television at home, the non-intentional sounds recorded in the videotape session primarily consist of the ticking of the stop-watch.

Tudor's most recent performance was on a program of various performing artists's responses to Cage's seminal composition, held at the New York Central Park Summer Stage on July 15, 1994. The highlights consisted of a talk by Irwin Kremen on the importance of Cage's score as an open-content notation of space equal to time, Margaret Leng Tan doing the prepared piano version of *Waiting* (1952), with Tudor's performance of *4'33"* as the finale. There was no noticeable deviation from his previous practice. The most extraordinary aspect of this performance was the choreographie accompaniment by Merce Cunningham. Cunningham and his company of dancers each occupied a position on the stage and held a different static gestural/postural attitude for the duration of each movement. The combination of Tudor's presence with Cunningham's choreography made for a moving and concise instance of mysterious calm and reflective stasis. [...]

Most performances of *4'33"* after David Tudor have been in four minutes and thirty-three seconds, but not always in three movements. Most have been imitations of David Tudor, using the piano with the third score timings but without the gestures of page turning or making any alternative chance-determined durations.

Ellsworth Snyder has performed *4'33"* several times since the 1960s. When doing it as a solo, he has always used the piano, as that is his instrument. He recalls first doing it as one extended movement. Later, he divided it into three movements as indicated in the third score, using chance procedures to determine different durations adding up to four minutes and thirty-three seconds. His next performance was using the *Source* score. For still another variation, Snyder recalls a solo performance:

> I think one time I did it with how time was passing. I did it with the watch to show the beginning and ending, but I did the movements by feeling whatever length they should be. (Snyder 1989)

He also recalls a totally impromptu ensemble performance when John Cage came to Milton College around 1970 and met with a large group of students. A student in the assembly asked if they could all perform *4'33"*. Snyder fondly recalls:

> We performed it then. The piece began, and we simply let the time elapse. Then at four minutes and thirty-three seconds it ended, with nobody doing anything intentional. This was in the spring, and it was done with the doors and windows open. (Snyder 1989)

Don Gillespie recalls two very different performance versions, both from the summer of 1970. In August, 1970 at the University of North Carolina at Chapel Hill, there was a chamber ensemble performance by harpsichord, piano, flute, and clarinet. Gillespie was at the piano and led the ensemble. He recalls that the third score timings were used and that all the instrumentalists had their own score copy from which to read. Gillespie used a stop-watch and made the same closing and opening gestures as done by David Tudor. He also recalls that the other performers made gestures to show that they were engaged with their instrument, but that the wind-players did not bring the instrument up to their mouth or do anything to be too obvious or comical. The performance was done in a very serious manner, and at the conclusion the audience shouted "encore!" (Gillespie 1988).

Don Gillespie also recalls witnessing another performance, one which he was not involved in, given by the full student orchestra at the North Carolina School of Arts at Winston-Salem during the summer of 1970. Roger Hannay was the conductor. Gillespie recalls that Hannay apparently did not approve of what happened, for the students performed *4'33"* by throwing paper airplanes and making noise (Gillespie 1988). Although it might be correctly argued that Cage's score/s are indeterminate of actual performance, there is nothing in any of the scores or in his comments about this work to suggest that this interpretation was an accurate performance.

Three performances in Germany present other subtle variations. The first example was performed at Stuttgart in June, 1979, by the The-Ge-Ano Ensemble as a trio for piano, an oboe, and a female vocalist (Urmetzer 1979). The second performance of note was by the RSO Ensemble at Berlin in December, 1982, with oboe, clarinet, and bassoon. The review mentions that the performers had their fingers poised over the instrument keys in mimically playing, and that the performance lasted three minutes and fifty-six seconds (Kneit 1982). The reviewer continues by questioning whether or not the musicians were actually playing *4'33"* since the actual duration was different from the title. This is a moot point, and one which reveals an ignorance of Cage's notes in the third and fourth score versions published by C.F. Peters. Closer to an informed criticism is the fact that the performers were mimically playing their instruments, which is antithetical to both David Tudor's performance as well as John Cage's general aesthetic approach. The final German performance of note was at Stuttgart by the Südfunkchores under the direction of Rupert Huber in November, 1991 (Pschera 1991). It is important to note that the The-Ge-Ano Ensemble included a vocalist, and that the Südfunkchores performance was a completely "vocal" version, as *4'33"* is almost always performed as a purely instrumental work.

The most obviously theatrical version of *4'33"* to date was performed by Jeffrey Kresky at William Paterson College in Wayne, New Jersey, in April, 1985. Kresky used a page-turner, which one review describes as a "red-headed girl in a purple dress" who sat on a "bright orange chair" (Avignone 1985). Another review describes the complete performance in more detail:

> The piano player entered with a flourish, bowed elaborately, and was greeted with loud applause…
>
> Jeffrey Kresky raised the lid of the piano and took his seat at the piano bench. Dissatisfied, he got up and lowered the lid, then raised it again, greeted each time by knowledgeable members of the audience.
>
> Next he put a large blank sheaf of paper on the piano's music rack and propped a stopwatch next to it.
>
> Then he sat. After a while he adjusted the stopwatch…
>
> The page turner rose and turned the page. Kresky made another adjustment to the stopwatch, then wiped his hands on a handkerchief and mopped his brow. He clicked the watch again. She turned more pages.
>
> People coughed…
>
> Someone yawned. Out in the middle of the audience someone else began whistling softly.
>
> Kresky clicked the stopwatch again, stood, and bowed to sustained applause. The piece was over. (Groenfeldt 1985)

Judging from this documentation, Kresky's performance of *4'33"* has been the most overtly theatrical version. While it is a rare later performance to include page turning, it is far different from David Tudor. Kresky's blank pages were not a score to read from, but simply a theatrical prop, a cute distraction from any serious attention to be given to the situation. In his gestures, Kresky was being obvious, humorous, and rather egotistic; while David Tudor has always been subtle, serious, and almost transparent as a physical presence.

The understated gestural quality of David Tudor is reinterpreted in Margaret Leng Tan's performance of *4'33"*, given since November, 1989. Tan asked me to attend a practice session for criticism in October, 1989. She performed *4'33"* using the out-of-print linguistic score issued by Peters, in the manner of David Tudor. I then told her that the problem with *4'33"* is that most performers do a David Tudor imitation rather than finding their own approach. I then suggested to her one way that I would do it, by using a stop-watch and silently depressing individual keys, chords, or clusters to visually show the durations of the three movements. Tan was delighted, and together we then tried out various combinations. Tan has followed my suggestion and has found critical success with this approach, although Cage commented that he was ambivalent about her performance (Tan 1990).

Perhaps the most unique performance of *4'33"*, apart from David Tudor, was a videotaping session at The Kitchen in New York on March 21, 1990, for the PBS "American Masters" documentary on John Cage directed by Allan Miller. The performance consisted of a large blank piece of white posterboard affixed to the music rack of a grand piano. Miller used a stopwatch, and the piece was videotaped as one movement. In this version, the most active performer was the video-camera operator, who photographed the piano and posterboard. This performance was later excised in favor of David Tudor's videotaped performance, which appears in the final documentary (Miller and Perlis 1990).

Simon Shaw Miller, *Visible Deeds of Music: Art and Music from Wagner to Cage* (New Haven, CT: Yale University 2002), p. 212, pp. 213–216, pp. 224–225.

Visible Deeds of Music: The Borderline of Sound

But let us *look* more closely at this work (and I choose my words carefully). Conceived within the conventions of Western art music, Cage's piece seems to deny the very raison d'être of music itself: sound.

[…] Whereas the first two versions of the score will not elicit any sound in the mind of the musical performer (who might otherwise sound the notation internally), in the third version the word "TACET," a signifier of silence, will internally "sound" as it is read.

Paradoxically, this final version implies a sound through its employment of language rather than "silent" graphics. In contrast, the language used in Fluxus textual scores, discussed below, was prosaic and straightforward. A linguistic instruction thus produces not sound but simply a visual transformation, a performance action. But in *4'33"* as Cage conceives it, the textual element is almost always present. There is, of course, no technical reason for it; if a performer can memorize the solo part of a Rachmaninoff concerto, for example, he or she can memorize the timings of *4'33"* with no difficulty. The text is there solely for its visual impact, as a point of focus for the performer and audience, demonstrating the visual as a constituent of all performance ritual.

Given this centralization of the visual elements of the performance of *4'33"*, it is significant that the origins of the work are in part derived from the visual field: the all-white paintings Cage's friend Robert Rauschenberg produced in 1949. As Cage himself noted, these paintings are no more empty or blank than his own piece was silent, for they act as environmental surfaces, on which motes of ambient dust or shadows may settle.[15] They are a *field* of focus for the spaces they occupy. The frame acts for the painting as the "concert occasion" acts for the "music," as a point of elision between art and nonart, text and context. These paintings gave him, he said, "permission" to compose a silent work.[16] The silence is also a critique of modernist terms of aesthetic engagement. The view that art requires a detached aesthetically emotive response, one that for visual art is divorced from any other sense, "purely" visual and self-sufficient, is parodied in Cage's silence, which is anything but pure. If modernist criticism requires silent contemplation in the presence of the art work, suppressing any elements outside the medium, *4'33"* shows that no such pure state is possible, no such absolute silence exists, such suppression ultimately fails.

It is worth highlighting two issues that arise as consequences of the performance of *4'33"*. First, the piece allowed the audience to recognize its role in producing this noise and the potential for hearing such sounds as music: the audience members were the composers as well as the listeners, the literal embodiment of the music. Second, because the piece gave the audience members nothing to listen to from the performer, they were made even more aware of the spectacle, the "theater," the visual nature of musical performance. In short, as the audience shifted to listen to something that was not there (the conventional sound of music), they watched something that was: the ritual of performance. This involved the performer and his limited actions—page-turning, pedaling (in the first version), consulting the stopwatch, sitting still, and so on—the concert hall itself, the object of the piano, each other, and so on, and then (but I do not wish to imply a sequence), the audience members recognized themselves as the producers of the "cultural" sound.[17] Sight (and site), sound, performance, and audience are thus shown as inextricably linked and interdependent. To recall Fried's objections, such a work cannot be seen as modernist, for it makes no attempt to transcend the contingencies of the viewer's or listener's time and place. It is "literalist," encountered as part of, or actually made up of, the everyday context. But, we should add, this "everydayness" is filtered through the conventions of music and art within the frame of the concert hall.

Yet we also need to see Cage's piece as a work that is not just about absence but also about presence. In this way *4'33"* is a Gesamtkunstwerk, but one that is in many ways antithetical to Wagner's. For here there is a concern with silence over amplification, and thus coexistence over synthesis. "Music" does not sublimate the other arts, volume does not drown out the other arts' voices. Rather, through Cage's silence, the other arts can be seen to be a part of the discourse of music. The textual (score), visual, and theatrical elements are already part of the fabric of music, here exposed as parts in the chorus of voices that make up the concept "Music." The difficulty some might have in seeing this work by Cage as music is precisely that the sound acts as a conduit through which we can observe the other elements of musical discourse.

[...] Fluxus "notation" aims at accessibility through simplicity of description; there is no requirement for acquiring technical language or Jargon. However, such a score describes a series of actions; it does not describe or stand for the music in a conventional sense. The "music," or sound, that results from these actions is ancillary to the score. It takes a large number of words to describe even a simple conventional musical perimeter; the scores used by Fluxus artists almost always provide instructions (they are not descriptive) for setting up a situation in which the consequent actions are to be *seen* as music: "The score is the agent that engages the reader-performer in the theater of the act."[38] This they share with Cage, as the examples of *4'33"* and *Variations IV* make clear.

However, many such text-scores (or event-scores, as they are also known)—those that are concerned with simple situations—are performable in the mind, as a thought; they do not a priori require physical Performance or actual sounding. This is also, of course, the case with more conventional scores (at least for the trained musician), and, as Hauer's example attests, it is even something desired by some composers to achieve a pure musical experience. The difference is that in conventional scoring the recreation of sound is the intended outcome. In text-scores the intention is the creation of a Situation (mental or actual) in which music takes place. A large part of the impact of such scores comes from the imaginative work in conceiving the appropriate Situation; they are consulted in advance rather than used as a guide during Performance. The active creation of the event by the performer or reader can, therefore, be private or public, and in their challenge to authorial power the scores meet Marcel Duchamp's claim that the creative act "is not performed by the artist alone; the spectator brings the work in contact with the external world"; or we might add, their own internal world (external to that of the composer).[39] In this sense the scores are also *incidental*. They clearly stand apart from the realization of the sound of the music, and in so doing they draw attention to the conventional structures and syntax of notation, reminding us that notation is a semiotic of sound, part of the field of music, an dement of "music."

15 Cage, *Silence*, p. 103.
16 See R. Kostelanetz, ed., *Conversing with Cage* (London, 1988), p. 188.
17 For a more recent discussion of embodiment in Performance, an essay that provides a useful summary of a small but growing "body" of research on the intitnate links between musical sound and the bodily movement involved in its production, see E. Clarke and J. Davidson, "The Body in Performance," in W. Thomas, ed., *Composition-Performance-Reception: Studies in the Creative Process in Music* (Aldershot, 1998), pp. 74–92.
[...]
38 Stiles, "Between Water and Stone," *in In the Spirit of Fluxus* (Minneapolis: Walker Arts Center, 1993), p. 66.
39 M. Duchamp, "The Creative Act," in G. Battcock, ed., *The New Art* (New York, 1966), p. 25.

Hans-Friedrich Bormann, *Verschwiegene Stille, John Cages performative Ästhetik* (Munich: Wilhelm Fink Verlag, 2005), pp. 229–48 (revised by the author for the English translation).

A Theatre of Writing: *0'00"*[1]

A detailed analysis of the various scores of John Cage's "silent piece" entitled *4'33"* brings to light the composer's manifold, and at times contradictory, strategies of writing and reading: rather than a mere negation of the work of music, *4'33"* supposes its conventionality, which it subjects to a constant process of repetition, dismissal, and re-writing. This viewpoint runs counter to the widely held belief that the "silent piece" is a proclamation of the "pure" event and breaks with the logic of the work, the text, and writing.[2] But any such approach focusing on "presence" will surely fail to understand why, of all pieces, the "silent piece" inspired Cage to create several (literally countless) developments. There are many reasons to assume that the "silent piece" does not open up a field of sensorial experience, but on the contrary allows the audience to experience the precedence of writing in its distortions and disguises: writing and reading, emptiness and fullness, presence and absence are related to each other and mirror each other. The resulting tensions—between reading and understanding, between hearing, remembering, and recounting, between the reassurance of identity and its questioning—prove to be an essential aspect of aesthetic experience.

The fact that this also concerns the performance (or the relationship between the performance and the score) becomes particularly manifest in the 1962 version of the "silent piece" which may be regarded as Cage's first explicit development [*Fort-Schreibung*] of *4'33"*: a composition entitled *0'00"*, which bears the addendum *4'33" (No. 2)*.[3] The score is comprised of a single sheet of US letter-size paper (21.59 × 27.94 cm) with capital letters in Cage's handwriting on one side. It can be roughly divided into four segments:

- a title section with the inscription "*0'00"*", the instrumentation: "solo to be performed in any way by anyone", a dedication: "for yoko ono and toshi ichiyanagi", the date: "tokyo, oct. 24, 1962", and a signature: "[John Cage]",
- a middle section with playing instructions and a commentary,
- the separate addition "this is *4'33"* (no. 2) and also pt. 3 of a work of which atlas eclipticalis is pt. 1.",
- the copyright information.

The title and the instrumentation alone radicalize the issues already raised in *4'33"*. If it is true that in *0'00"* as well, the title stands for the duration and vice-versa, then we must acknowledge that this composition has *no* length of time *whatsoever* and can therefore strictly speaking not have a title either—except, precisely, a non-title that questions the possibility of its identity or at least the possibility of a scenic implementation. This is also true for the indication of instrumentation, which merely determines that it is a "solo" and does not specify which action could be performed in the non-time that lends its non-title to the work.

Even so, the conventionality of these directions is important. As in other compositions, Cage strictly follows the rules of framing the notation of a piece. The title section moreover provides several important clues for the reading of the subsequent text and, consequently, for the understanding of the composition as such—the fact that it is a *musical composition*, that it is a musical composition for a single performer, that it is a musical composition *for a single performer* which *is to be performed*. This composition is furthermore *dedicated*, in this case to two people equally. The date and signature refer to the space-time of its making and to an author. We can therefore say: Cage presents a composition that fulfills all the formal requirements of a work, and it isn't until after this has been done that the indeterminacy, which is simultaneously obscured and revealed by the mask of convention, can unfold.

The "zero time" that lends the work its title takes place, but it cannot be apprehended through a program (not even through Cage's "silent piece" entitled *0'00"*); therefore *nothing is less* sure than that it takes place. Speaking to Daniel Charles, Cage nevertheless claimed: "'Zero time' exists when we don't notice the passage of time, when we don't measure it." In reference to *0'00"*, he added: "I mean when I work on the piece … or, 'in' that piece, I am indeed 'in' zero time." But rather than a privileged moment or the "event" of a performance, this implies a reversal of daily life and work practice: "… that doesn't stop me from working, from doing what my work requires. The difference is that I am no longer working towards an envisaged end, in line with the economy."[4] This means that Cage is precisely in zero time—of which (the title/piece) *0'00"* is an "outstanding" example—when he *does something else*, when he finds himself simultaneously inside and outside an activity. The economy of aims and means should be suspended as much as possible, without implying the need to interrupt the activity as such—but does this not also entail a dismissal of zero time as such (as a notion and premise of artistic activity)? And would not any reading and intentional performance of zero time be synonymous with its eradication?

Against this backdrop Cage's instruction to the interpreter of *0'00"* is of particular interest: "in a situation provided with maximum amplification (no feedback), perform a disciplined action." This may be an insufficiently determined instruction, but by no means senseless or absurd. Clearly, a performance that would fulfill Cage's guidelines is conceivable, the more so as the musical framing restricts the meaning of "amplification" and "feedback." It effectively means *electro-acoustic amplification*, which should be as loud as possible without producing *feedback* between the microphone and the loudspeaker. In this sense the score of *0'00"* does point to its implementability in and as a performance, not to say a concrete scenic implementation. Cage elaborates on this in the score, in the commentary after the instruction, which is set off with a smaller font size and an indentation. The premises and conditions of the performance are defined in greater detail. In reference to the first movement, Cage writes:

> with any interruptions. / fulfilling in whole or part an obligation to others. / no two performances to be of the same action, nor may that action be the performance of a "musical" composition. / no attention to be given the situation (electronic, musical, theatrical).

This is followed by a further date, "10.25.62", which refers to the day after the date indicated in the title section. Under it appears another sentence, which was clearly also added subsequently: "the first performance was the writing of this manuscript (first margination only)." In principle, none of these explanations raises any question in terms of meaning. They let us imagine a potential implementation: on a stage or a podium a single, everyday performance is carried out, which becomes recognizable as *0'00"* merely by way of certain framings. The title could be understood, if not as a precise indication of imparted time, then as a practical advice, for instance if we suppose an extremely short, non-repeatable, and non-repetitive action or, in other words, an "event." However, we must keep in mind that Cage, in the very first sentence of the commentary, identifies the interruption of the action as a possibility, if not a premise. "With any interruptions" means *with all possible interruptions*. This could be construed to mean that the action must not or should not be present (in each and every moment) or be itself (in each and every moment). Rather, it can or must be split and/or split itself up—stopping and resuming, as often as needed or possible. In a conversation with Lars Gunnar Bodin and Bengt Emil Johnson held in 1965, Cage outlined his intention in yet more detail:

> Just briefly, *0'00"*, which is about two years old now, is nothing but the continuation of one's daily work, whatever it is, providing it's not selfish, but is the fulfillment of an obligation to other people; done with contact microphones, without any notion of concert or theater or the public, but simply continuing one's daily work, now coming through loudspeakers. What the piece tries to say is that everything we do is music, or can become music through the use of microphones; so that everything I'm doing, apart from what I'm saying, produces

sound. When the sounds are very quiet, they become loud only through the use of microphones. And I may not do again in performance what I did once before.[5]

Above all, this statement clarifies the framing function of acoustic amplification: even the slightest noise accompanying the disciplined action would now become perceptible (and even if the action did not produce any sound, there would still be the latent white noise of the loudspeakers: a technically produced and insofar audible silence). Contrary to Cage's accounts of the premiere and subsequent performances of *4'33"*, where audiences were unsure *what, if anything at all,* could be heard[6], in *0'00"* the audience's attention is captured with the help of technical, i.e. controlled and regulated, means. Cage himself confirmed this: "That's how I *act*, with the aid of technology."[7] The underlying premise, however, does not merely concern the technical, but also social regulations, which any reading (of a text or a performance) must take into account.[8] This explains why Cage (regardless of the possible or required interruptions) wants the uniqueness of each performance to be guaranteed. Yet the criterion for the success of *0'00"* is not this regulated eventfulness, but the discipline demanded by Cage, which presumably refers to the "discipline of the ego" he invokes in various instances, mostly in connection with reference to Arnold Schönberg and Daisetz T. Suzuki.[9]

The action, according to the commentary of *0'00"*, should fulfill "in whole or part an obligation to others." This highlights an aspect that indicates a prior externalization [*Ent-Äußerung*] of the will, a dedication and a non-identity that cannot be embraced by any understanding of presence. This is consistent with the fact that Cage defines neither the significance nor the content of the obligation. The obvious question—to whom and in which way the performer is (or is supposed to be) obliged—thus remains unanswered. Cage merely demands that this obligation should be linked to discipline; he does not indicate to what extent the latter is implied by one's daily work. In any case we can posit a double exclusion: the obligation should neither concern the person of the performer nor the scenic situation—and therefore not the audience, who are certainly not the "o/Others" mentioned in the commentary.

Here, the aporetic constitution of *0'00"* manifests itself, albeit almost unnoticeably. It affects both the performer and the/their audience: *who* dedicates himself to *whom* and through *which* action? Moreover, who could say that their action (or any action) is sufficiently disciplined, who may judge whether through their own or someone else's action (or any action) an obligation, if any, is being fulfilled? This calls into question the possibility of judgment and, consequently, the possibility of the success of *0'00"*. In other words, even if the use of a program leaflet or electro-acoustic amplification seems to ensure that *0'00"* will be heard, no one (not even Cage himself) can ever be sure to perform *0'00"*, and therefore no one can be sure to hear (or see) it.

But there is even more to it. The last, added sentence of the commentary causes the conventional relation between composition and performance to collapse: "the first performance was the writing of this manuscript (first margination only)." Once again it makes sense to read this indication as a concrete reference to a scenic implementation. Based on his conversations with Cage, William Fetterman states:

> It was composed during a concert tour of Japan with David Tudor. The first performance was the writing of the score by the composer during a concert in Tokyo on October 24, 1962. … For the first performance of *0'00"*, the act of notating the score was done in front of the audience, and was the example of the described action. Cage recalled that the obligation to others, referred to in the score, was a fulfillment to make a new piece.[10]

It is perfectly plausible to see the activity of composing as a fulfillment of some (cultural or social) obligation. Yet *every* composition could potentially achieve this. If we consider *0'00"*, on the other hand, which evokes and works with the very notion of obligation, we are faced with an irreducible temporal-logical conundrum. After all, the composition of *0'00"* can only be seen as a fulfillment of a specific obligation, if it follows the instructions outlined in the score. But since these instructions (at least according to Fetterman) only emerge in the process of or after the action, and become readable at best as an addendum, there cannot be a "first" performance (in the sense of the making of the score).

This also has consequences for the graphic design and the chronology suggested by the commentary. Cage's addition "(first margination only)" indicates that there are at least two *indentations*, which derive from two separate writing actions: the left margin of the page holds the notations which were possibly created during the performance; the greater indentation denotes the commentary declaring them to be the fulfillment, in whole or in part, of an obligation. The key sentence, however, with which the writing of the score and the (first) performance are conflated, was also excluded from the second dating. It is therefore an addendum to the addendum, which Cage would not or could not date. Although its font size and spacing indicate that it belongs to the "second indentation", it is impossible to assign it an unequivocal place in the web of cross-references.[11] This in turn means that the very sentence by which this score is declared to be the score of *0'00"* was not written during the premiere, nor even the next day, but *at some time* (and this also leads us to acknowledge that Cage's writing in the concert of October 24, 1962 cannot have been the writing of *0'00"*).

This, however, also allows us to say that this performance does not merely become the *performance of 0'00"* in the addendum, but that the obligation signified by *0'00"* precedes every performance (including the premiere): *it will already have written itself.*[12] In this context we should consider a remarkable proposition, which is again cited by Fetterman as a thought expressed by Cage: "The disciplined action that someone other than Cage would first do would be reading the score (usually one writes or studies a score in private) previous to doing an action in public."[13] According to this view, the writing scene entitled *0'00"* simultaneously creates and evidences a reading scene. In light of the conundrum outlined earlier, we could also say that the one stands for the other. Before he writes, Cage is already a reader, in this case *his own reader.* The notion of obligation is thus invoked once more: the writing of *0'00"* is dedicated to the reading and the readers, and this also means that it *answers* subsequent readings.[14]

This is also suggested by the remark in the comment according to which the performance of *0'00"* should not be a performance of a "musical composition." Cage presumably wants to make sure that *0'00"* is not substituted with another work. (After all, the possibility exists!) At the same time we have to acknowledge that, as discussed earlier, a consistent ("complete") fulfillment of the self-obligation is even compatible with the forsaking of *0'00"* (insofar as it is a musical composition). Even the non-writing (or a non-performance) would correspond to an obligation which has not yet been formulated, which has not yet been pre-scribed.

The consequence arising from the incessant postscript of the (self-)reference also precludes any (self-)identity of the concrete performance, which *is* already split as soon as it *appears* (as a performance of *0′00″*). This aspect also becomes manifest in an account of another performance offered by the composer Alvin Lucier. He describes a performance by Cage at the Rose Art Museum at Brandeis University on May 5, 1965:

> Cage began performing *0′00″* before the audience came in. He sat in his amplified squeaky chair with a World War II aircraft pilot's microphone strapped around his throat, writing letters on an amplified typewriter, and occasionally taking drinks of water. Part of the intention of this piece is to do work you have to do anyway, and John chose to answer some correspondence. Every move he made, every squeak of his chair, tap of his typewriter and gulp of water was greatly amplified and broadcast through speakers around the museum.[15]

In this case the writing of letters obviously supplants the writing of the score. This observation can be interpreted in two different ways. Firstly, we can say that Cage equates the writing of letters with the writing of a work of music, and secondly, that the writing of the work is equated with the writing of letters.

In relation to the dedication in and of the book Silence—"To whom it may concern"—the question has already been raised as to who the sender and the recipient are and what the message might be, and whether there are in fact a "sender", "recipient", and "message".[16] This movement of undecidability also manifests itself in Lucier's account, according to which Cage was writing his *correspondence* on a stage or a podium. The obligation here appears as a literal and simultaneously non-transparent correspondence, a reciprocal answering, a mutual and always incomplete fulfillment of an essentially invisible and therefore unenforceable obligation. The mechanical noise of the keyboard, Cage's involuntary body noises, the squeaking chair: all this *happens*, not only because of the writing, but also because this writing is preceded by the obligation to answer. If the obligation itself were communicated, if it became the subject, the economy of the everyday could take place, but not *0′00″*. Writing and reading are related to each other—in their discretion. The audience do not know what Cage is writing, whether his letters arrive, whether they will ever reach their addressees, whether they will (or can) ever be read. And even if that were the case—would the (fulfillment of the) obligation be readable?

And yet *there is* the literal marking of the void (namely the title *0′00″*/the time indication *0′00″*) and there is also the *gift of giving*, its relentless motion, which possesses no space-time (and therefore not even the space-time of the score of the performance of the score). The gift arrives by withdrawing itself. The duration enshrined in (the) zero time is deprived of any possibility to be thematized or objectivized. It manifests itself in the permanence of a having-begun, which is radically (dis-)continuously situated outside of any measurability, in the ineluctability of the acceptance of the gift.[17] The writing precedes itself in the act of writing: no matter where and in which form the "silent piece" appears (on a stage, podium, score, book, or sheet of paper), it is neither *its* place nor *its* form. Each representation (necessarily and ineluctably) masks the processuality of writing, even or particularly when it explicitly invokes it, proclaims it as the program, or makes it the work itself.

This also concerns the contextualization that Cage brings about in the score of *0′00″* with the sentence: "this is *4′33″ (no. 2)* and also pt. 3 of a work of which *atlas eclipticalis* is pt. 1." Its positioning in the left margin of the sheet indicates that Cage wanted it to be understood as a notation from the "first" performance. In other words, he considered this indication to be so important that he put it on the same level as the title segment and the playing instructions. Yet what is its significance for this composition, what does it say about the "silent piece?"

Cage writes that *0′00″* is both a number two (namely of *4′33″*) and the third part of a non-identified work, the first part of which is *Atlas Eclipticalis*. By doing so he attributes the composition *0′00″* to two independent registers.

Firstly, he declares it to be a repetition of the non-identity of *4′33″*, which means that the "silent piece" here does not (only) appear for the second time, but as a reiteration of itself. *0′00″* is *4′33″ (No. 2)* as a renewal of the structure of permanent indeterminacy/indeterminability, which can be regarded as the essential characteristic of the Tacet editions of *4′33″*, including the aspect of a general self-substitution.[18] Although the two compositions (from the instrumentation and playing instructions to the commentary) are not identical, they do converge in the notion of this very self-difference: that which, respectively, distinguishes them from themselves is that which links them.

Secondly, he summons up a piece in three parts and without a title of its own, the second part of which is not specified here.[19] Looking at *Atlas Eclipticalis* itself hardly clarifies the issue. It is a composition for 86 musicians that Cage created with the help of celestial maps. Apart from the fact that *Atlas Eclipticalis* and *0′00″* were created at around the same time and share a number of general characteristics (such as the indeterminacy of the instrumentation and the freedom of interpretation, which do however apply to many of Cage's compositions from the fifties onwards), the connection with *0′00″* seems random. If we consider this in relation to the dizzying precision with which Cage implements this attribution, we might conclude that instead of a definition of the music or content, it is the importance of contextuality as such that reveals itself. Cage says—without saying—exactly this: *0′00″* is in context(s), and this means: it is obliged to its exterior.

Talking to Cage, Charles also addressed this contextuality, although with a different reference: "When you composed *Atlas Eclipticalis*, you wrote it as the first line of a haiku." Cage answered:

> The allusion to the haiku comes from one of my Japanese friends, Hidekazu Yoshida, who suggested that I consider the first line of each haiku as referring to nirvana, the second to samsara, the third to a specific individual action—which, however, is completed through non-action. So I planned *Atlas Eclipticalis* as the first line of a haiku that included *Variations IV* as its second line, and *0′00″* as its third line.[20]

This explanation seems to clarify what the three-part work consists of. At the same time it prompts the question of the relation between the haiku as a form and the work mentioned in the score of *0′00″*. In light of the differences between the three compositions, the idea that the macro-structure of the ranking is directly transferable onto the poem structure can be excluded.[21] And, in fact, Cage seems to be less interested in the literary form as such than in its relation to the two essential principles of Buddhism: in Cage's vision "samsara" (the eternal cycle of birth and death), "nirvana" (extinguishment, exit from the cycle) and "a specific individual action" are to relate to each other both in the haiku and in the compositional sequence.[22] However, this relation itself appears rather like an assertion of relatedness, an arbitrary positing, which as such eludes all justification and justifiability.[23] We must also take into account that this positing does not originate from Cage himself, but from one of his Japanese acquaintances. When Cage tells Charles that it was Hidekazu Yoshida "who suggested that I consider the ... haiku as ...", this means that he took up someone's suggestion or, to be precise, a suggestion related to his (Cage's) own considerations. One's own and the other's thinking thus enter into an idiosyncratic, grammatically quite dubious relation. Yet this very dubiousness is the key aspect, since it rather accurately illustrates not only Cage's discursive approach to Buddhism, but also the relationship of the three compositions to each other. It marks a dis-possession of thinking that manifests itself in Cage's oeuvre, in the "silent piece" and particularly in *0'00"*.

This aspect becomes clearer if we include the composition *Variations IV* (EP 6798), which Cage introduced in his conversation with Charles as the second part of a three-part work and whose defining structural characteristic is that it devolves the compositional process to the interpreter. *Variations IV*, as the title suggests, is part of a another series of works initiated in 1958, which can largely be understood as *scores for the writing of scores*. Cage here delegates the choice of musical or scenic material to the interpreter(s). Based on self-chosen parameters and structural premises, the exact processes are determined with the help of random graphic operations. The choice of instrumentation is largely left to the performer(s). *Variations IV* indicates: "for any number of players, any sounds or combinations of sounds produced by any means, with or without other activities" (EP 6798). The score requests [the interpreter(s)] to choose a map of the area where the performance takes place and to randomly distribute on it circles and points on transparent foil according to certain rules. On the backdrop of *Atlas Eclipticalis*, the use of a map seems to establish a correlation, but again this connection is so generic that it may end up being misleading: the maps are not only totally different, but they are also used in totally different ways.

However, if we take a closer look at the score of *Variations IV*, we notice a particularity, which in turn refers to the aspect of contextualization. Cage here evokes the connection with the three-part work from *0'00"*, and this appears to be so important for him that he makes it explicit on the title page, immediately after the title "variations iv" and even before the indication of instrumentation: "second of a group of three works of which *atlas eclipticalis* is the first and *0'00"* is the third." The problem of the order thus seems to have been solved once and for all. The date, however, which is also indicated on the title page—"malibu. july 19, 1963"—shows that *Variations IV* was created after *0'00"*. This means, firstly, that in this case the second part must actually have been created after the third, and secondly, that *Variations IV* as such could not have been a part of the work (or have been named as one) when, on October 24, 1962, Cage declared in *0'00"* that the work was made up of three compositions.[24] The missing title now appears in a different light: Cage here conceives a self-referential circle that ascribes different compositions to a macro-structure, the significance of which is apparently limited to the aspect of reciprocal reference, without yet being linked to the specificity of certain compositions.

But even this does not fully describe the contexts of *0'00"* evoked by Cage himself. In his conversation with Charles, he identified another series—the "silent pieces". In the context of our analysis, the following passage is particularly important:

> D.C.: The Peters catalog entry *0'00"* bears the subtitle, *4'33" no. 2*. This then is your second silent work?
> J.C.: Yes, and I have still another.
> D.C.: That's rather intriguing. How do you manage to differentiate among them?
> J.C.: The first one, *4'33"*, involved one or several musicians who made no sound. The second one, *0'00"*, indicates that an obligation towards others must be fulfilled, in a partial or complete manner, by a single person. The third one involves gathering together two or more people who are playing a game in an amplified context. A bridge or chess match, or any game at all, can become a distinct—another essentially silent—musical work.
> D.C.: You said a "distinct" work? That presupposes that the work already exists ...
> J.C.: Yes, in nature, at every moment. "Distinct" means that there is amplification. It's a work about a work—like all my indeterminate works! I say that it's essentially silent because I believe that it allows the silence of a game of chess to appear for what it really is: a silence full of noises.
> D.C.: It can't appear exactly as it is, since it's amplified.
> J.C.: That's how I act, with the aid of technology.
> D.C.: Then your "action" consists in choosing a particular situation: the game.
> J.C.: But my music isn't a game. I don't like the idea of a game, if by game you mean rules and measurements.[25]

This statement provides several clues for our analysis of the problem of the "silent piece". First among these is Charles's choice of the word "intriguing", which evokes both the idea of raising interest or curiosity and the possibility of fraud. It appears that the order of the "silent pieces" suggested here is by no means unquestionable and that it puts into doubt (both as a whole and as concerns certain details) a series of commonly held views and historical findings (or is put into doubt by them). Let us nevertheless start by following the path outlined by Cage: the first composition in the series of "silent pieces" is *4'33"*, the second *0'00"* (*4'33" No. 2*). The third remains largely undetermined: Cage cites as its essential characteristic the circumstance of "gathering together two or more people who are playing a game in an amplified context." One difference between this composition and *4'33"* is that the interpreters are neither (not) playing an instrument nor (not) reading a score; the difference with *0'00"* is that it is not a solo and that no obligation needs to be fulfilled—except, we might add, that of performing this piece. Another important aspect is the technical dimension, which again takes the shape of electro-acoustic amplification. Yet it does not have a title of its own—or at least its title is not stated here. This becomes apparent in retrospect, because there actually exists a performance of several composers and artists initiated by Cage in 1968 and called *Reunion*, which seems to match the succinct description of the third "silent piece." *Reunion* is in fact mentioned in *For the Birds*, but in a different context and without a reference to the "silent piece", which means that its relation to it remains unclear. Cage describes the performance of *Reunion* as follows:

> The first performance took place in Toronto in 1968. David Behrman, David Tudor, and Lowell Cross were there. Each had his own sound sources and systems, that is, means of modulation and amplification, and loudspeakers. All these systems were active, each one of them connected to the squares of a chess board that Lowell Cross had wired electronically; movements took place on the chess board, then outside the chess board. The chess board acted as a gate, open or closed to these sources, these streams of music. The first time, it was Marcel, Teeny Duchamp, and I who played. Our game affected all the sound sources, but it was not one itself.[26]

At this point it must be pointed out that the series of "silent pieces" that Cage evoked was already incomplete at the time the conversation with Charles took place. In Cage's *Song Books* (EP 6806a/b), dated from August to October 1970, we find two groups of "solos", one of which follows the instructions of *0'00"*, while the other resembles the game project outlined to Charles. There, *0'00"* also appears as *Solo for Voice No. 8, 24, 28, 62, 63*, and the electro-acoustically amplified game as *0'00" No. 2* as *Solo for Voice No. 23* and *26*. Even this quick survey convincingly demonstrates the complex ramifications of the series of "silent pieces"—and how this perpetuates the problem of positive attribution.[27]

What's more, at least two further "silent pieces" can be identified for the period after the conversation published as *For the Birds: WGBH-TV* from 1971 (EP 6808), directions for the realization of a TV film that shows Cage sitting at a table and writing a score, and *One*^{3} from 1989. *One*^{3} had manifestly been planned as a further development of both *4'33"* and *0'00"*; the complete title reads: *One*^{3} *= 4'33" (0'00") + [𝄞]*. Thus, even its genealogical order is potentially suspended—*4'33"* and *0'00"* become one and are in turn supplanted with the violin clef, which (as Cage indicated to Fetterman) denotes a "G", for Sofia Gubaidulina, Gorbachev, or Glasnost. Cage recalls the performance:

> So what I did was to come to the stage in front of the audience, and then the feedback level of the auditorium space was brought up to feedback level through the sound system … So, after that was reached, I went into the auditorium and sat with the audience and listened to the situation, to the silence which was at the edge of feedback, and without a watch, without measuring the time as I had in *4'33"*—so that was my inner-clock … I sat there for twelve minutes and a half, more or less [laughs], and then I went back on the stage in front of the audience and the feedback level was reduced, and that was the end of it.[28]

Here, too, electro-acoustical amplification appears as an essential aspect of the later "silent pieces". In light of this fact, it is worth reconsidering Cage's remark to Charles, according to which "a distinct—another essentially silent—musical work"[29] already exists. If we disconnect this passage from the notion of game, the fundamental ambivalence of any "silent piece" emerges:

> D.C.: You said a "distinct" work? That presupposes that the work already exists …
>
> J.C.: Yes, in nature, at every moment. "Distinct" means that there is amplification. It's a work about a work—like all my indeterminate works![30]

Two interpretations become possible. The first one stipulates that "essential silence" (the non-intended noises) already exists before each "silent piece", but it is *not distinguished*, which means that it is identical unto itself and therefore not perceptible. Hence, the role of amplification would be to interrupt the discretion of the silence as such and bring it to the fore. According to the second reading—which would explain Cage's reticence to name it—the "silent piece" itself also seems to already exist, namely in such a way that it could not have been noticed. The *silence of the work* (the silence that is the work)—says Charles, and Cage agrees—will always already have been there. It precedes itself—*at every moment*. Accordingly, the *work of silence* (the work that is the silence) is an irretrievable delay of itself. That which can be heard or seen is not "nature", but "a work about a work" (about a work etc.). The "silent piece" refers to itself, i.e. that it (also) distinguishes itself from itself. It is not itself, especially since it does not proceed from the (acoustically amplified) perception of sounds, but from the conventionality (of writing and reading, of hearing and seeing).

1 This text is a shortened and amended excerpt from the author's book *Verschwiegene Stille. John Cages performative Ästhetik* (Munich: Fink, 2005), pp. 228–48.

2 A good example of this viewpoint can be found in Dieter Mersch, *Was sich zeigt. Materialität, Präsenz, Ereignis* (Munich: Fink, 2002), p. 197.

3 In the following I am referring to a score published by Edition Peters under the catalogue number EP 6796, which was bought in 2003.

4 Tom Gora and John Cage, *For the Birds: John Cage in Conversation with Daniel Charles* (Boston and London: Marion Boyars, 1981), p. 209. Cage and Charles use the term "zero time" in reference to the composer (and Cage scholar) Christian Wolff. Interestingly, Wolff himself does not expand systematically on this term, but rather seems to view it as an operative characteristic of the musical performance: "The zero I take to mean no time at all, that is, no measurable time, that is, any time at all, which the performer takes as he will at each performance." Gisela Gronemeyer and Reinhard Oehlschlägel (eds.), *Christian Wolff: Cues/Hinweise. Writings & Conversations/Schriften und Gespräche* (Cologne: MusikTexte, 1988), p. 46. Compare this with the theoretical ennobling of "zero time" by Charles in *Musketaquid. John Cage, Charles Ives und der Transzendentalismus* (Berlin: Merve, 1994), pp. 95–118.

5 Quoted in Richard Kostelanetz, *Conversing with Cage*, 2nd ed. (London and New York: Routledge, 2003), p. 74.

6 Cage's criticism of the audience, who are *unable to hear* and therefore miss not only the specific experience of the silence of *4'33"*, but the composition as a whole, is a recurring detail in these accounts. See Bormann, op. cit., pp. 198–206.

7 Gora and Cage, op. cit., p. 210.

8 Douglas Kahn has highlighted this aspect in his critique of Cage, *Noise Water Meat. A History of Sound in the Arts* (Cambridge: MIT Press, 1999), pp. 194–99.

9 Gora and Cage, op. cit., p. 58. See also the corresponding paragraphs in Bormann, op. cit., pp. 78–86 (on Schönberg's theory) and pp. 166–70 (on Cage's attitude to Zen Buddhism).

10 William Fetterman, *John Cage's Theatre Pieces: Notations and Performances* (Amsterdam: Harwood, 1996), p. 84.

11 Fetterman proceeds on the assumption that only the sentence in which the indication is formulated should be seen as a "primary performance notation", which excludes the title area (and the dating therein), the explanatory addition, and the copyright information, although they are also situated in the left margin. See Fetterman, ibid. James Pritchett also writes that "the score of the work consists of a single sentence", in *The Music of John Cage* (Cambridge: Cambridge University Press, 1993), p. 138.

12 This structural precedence also manifests itself if we assume a scenic implementation (of any kind) that supposes a previous conception or, at any rate, last-minute arrangements with the organisers and technicians: for an action to be amplified acoustically (notably, or particularly, during a premiere), adequate equipment needs to have been allowed for; moreover, the microphone and amplifier must be adjusted so as to make the noises audible without producing feedback.

13 Fetterman, ibid.

14 In this context we need to take into account the documents in Cage's estate at the New York Public Library–sketches (for scores) and writing samples that lead us to ask what was written when. For an exemplary analysis of some of these documents, see Bormann, op. cit., pp. 236–39.

15 Alvin Lucier, "Notes in the Margin", unpublished manuscript, 1988, quoted in Fetterman, op. cit., p. 88.

16 See John Cage, *Silence. Lectures and Writings* (Hanover: Wesleyan University Press, 1961), n. p. See also Bormann, op. cit., pp. 106–08.

17 On the significance of the gift in Cage's oeuvre (following his promise to Arnold Schönberg and in light of Jacques Derrida's reading of the speech act theory), see also Bormann, op. cit., pp. 49–94.

18 Bormann, op. cit., pp. 221–28.

19 One is tempted to believe that it is *4'33"*, but there is no further indication to support this–not to mention the fact that this would imply that the first part was created ten years after the second.

20 Gora and Cage, op. cit., p. 211.

21 The traditional form of the haiku consists of seventeen syllables, arranged in three lines according to the following distribution: first line–five syllables; second line–seven syllables; third line–five syllables. Connecting the three compositions by way of the haiku is further confused by the fact that in other instances, Cage has worked with explicit equivalences between the musical and the literary form. See for instance his composition *Seven Haiku* for piano from 1952 (EP 6745): "The composing means are those of the *Music of Changes*. The seventeen-syllable Japanese poem-structure is rendered as a space of time where a quarter-note equals ½ inch, having seventeen units (5, 7, 5), within which chance operations determined the musical events." Quoted in Richard Kostelanetz (ed.), *John Cage: Writer. Selected Texts*, 2nd revised ed. (New York: Cooper Square Press, 2000), p. 53.

22 In conversation with Fetterman, Cage even mentions a certain haiku, but it remains unclear whether this is one example among many or whether it is specific. The poem in its English translation by Suzuki reads: "The old pond, ah! / A frog jumps in: / The water's sound!" Quoted in Fetterman, op. cit., p. 84.

23 Thomas M. Maier has pointed out that "Cage's correlation of the three lines of a haiku to nirvana, samsara and the Zen Buddhist notion of action and non-action … does not correspond to any traditional correlation", in *Ausdruck der Zeit. Ein Weg zu John Cages stillem Stück 4'33"* (Saarbrücken: Pfau, 2001), p. 172.

24 We must remember that Cage explicitly ascribes the sentence by which this connection is effectuated in *0'00"* to the premiere by placing it in the left margin. It is therefore–by definition–not an addition.

25 Gora and Cage, op. cit., p. 210.

26 Gora and Cage, op. cit., p. 168. The game of chess was manifestly not the object of the acoustic amplification itself, but only a way to modulate the

musical processes unfolding outside of it. This could be seen simultaneously as a decisive difference and a precise analogy to the "silent piece".

27 In this context it is also interesting to consider the question of dating: if we consider the conversations in *For the Birds* to be in chronological order, the passage concerning the series of "silent pieces" could most likely be dated to after the premiere of the *Song Books* on October 26, 1970 at the Théâtre de la Ville de Paris, which took place one day before the first "Dialogue with John Cage" and was attended by Charles. See Gora and Cage, op. cit., pp. 33, 54. Charles's disbelief only makes sense if *0′00″/0′00″ (No. 2)*, was not performed or, which is more likely, not (sufficiently) emphasized, so that Charles did not perceive them (as such).

28 Fetterman, op. cit., pp. 94–95. There exists no published score for *One*[3]. Related sketches can be found at the New York Public Library under JPB 94–24, folder 782.

29 Gora and Cage, op. cit., p. 210.

30 Ibid.

Contexts / References / Biography

Jonathan David Katz, "John Cage's Queer Silence or How to Avoid Making Matters Worse", GLQ, Duke University Press, April, 1999. Reprinted in *Here Comes Everybody: The Music Poetry and Art of John Cage*, ed. David Bernstein (Chicago: University of Chicago Press, 1999).
http://www.queerculturalcenter.org/Pages/KatzPages/KatzWorse.html

John Cage's Queer Silence or How to Avoid Making Matters Worse

> To know of some is good; but for the rest, silence is to be praised;
> —Ser Brunetto speaking of his fellow sodomites to Dante in the Inferno[1]

John Cage never did quite come out of the closet.[2] Nonetheless, nearly everybody in the art world who knew him knew of his lifelong relationship with Merce Cunningham, and some even about the other men in his life. His sexuality was a kind of open secret within the avant-garde, and, as his fame spread, so too did knowledge of his personal life. Still, direct public acknowledgement of Cage's sexuality was, until quite recently, hard to find, consigned to the realm of gossip and understood to be tangential to his historical import and achievements. Cage himself, while never denying his sexuality, preferred instead to duck the question: when asked to characterize his relationship with Merce, he would say, "I cook and Merce does the dishes."[3]

Gay Life

John Cage first met Merce Cunningham in 1938 at the Cornish School in Seattle, after having taken a job as piano accompanist to the dance classes. In a rare personal revelation, Cage remarked that he and his wife Xenia had an open marriage and that both were attracted to the teenage Cunningham. Following their menage a trois, "Cage stated that he realized he was more attracted to Cunningham than to Xenia."[4] The two men moved together to New York, without Xenia, in 1942 and there collaborated on their first joint endeavor, entitled *Credo in Us*. Its title is an acknowledgement for the first time of the personal and professional partnership that would animate so much of their subsequent work. Though they had already been involved with one another for nearly four years, *Credo in Us*, a collaboration born of this new independent life together in New York, marks the public emergence of the relationship as muse.

[...] Finding John Cage advocate such a situated, even biographical approach to music criticism is perhaps a surprising, albeit happy, antecedent for my own analysis of the social dynamics of his silences. But it isn't difficult to reconcile Cage's infamous anti-expressionism with his example of a situated, social historical inquiry, for there is a substantial difference between saying that the work is not about the life (anti-expressionism) and saying that the life has nothing to do with the work. There are, after all, modes of revelation of self that have nothing to do with expressionism. And one of the points of silence, Cage was fond of reminding his audiences, was to give life itself a more ample hearing. As Cage once said: "Sometimes we blur the distinction between art and life; sometimes we try to clarify it. We don't stand on one leg. We stand on both."[28]

Indeed, it is only from such a symmetrical, two legged stance that we can see how the development of Cage's anti-expressive aesthetic correlates with these wholesale changes in his personal life. Repeatedly, Cage's referencing of "disturbances" in his life slips so easily between the spheres of his creative work and his daily existence as to "blur the distinction between art and life." And indeed, as we've seen, personal trauma could prove to be artistically fecund. Cage has remarked:

> I saw that all the composers were writing in different ways, that almost no one among them, no one among the listeners could understand what I was doing in the way that I understood it. So that anything like communication was not possible. I determined to find other reasons, and I found those reasons because of my personal problems at the time, which brought about the divorce from Xenia.[29]

In understanding himself as homosexual, Cage came to accept as corollary a new creed as well: an injunction against self-expression in daily life. Cage's newly embraced gay life—in the context of Cold War homophobic culture—made clear in a very personal way that "anything like communication was not possible." This is not to say that the closet alone motivated Cage's deepening involvement with Zen and concomitant turn towards an anti-expressive art, nor is it to confine his powerfully felt theoretical investments to a species of identity politics. Yet it seems clear that through Zen Cage finally found a means to quiet what had once been so disturbing, to transmute trauma into peace. Indeed, in explicitly crediting his embrace of Zen to the "personal problems" that brought about his divorce from Xenia, Cage himself reframed the origins of his Zen sensibility from theoretical to autobiographical grounds.

A developing relationship with Cunningham thus pointed in the direction of a new musical voice not tied to the desire for communication. That voice, he would shortly conclude, was most at home in the definitionally "noble" (which is to say, detached) aleatory mode, which achieved its most crystalline form, for 4 minutes, 33 seconds, in the embrace of silence.

Silent Lives

A new generation of scholars have been trying to break through Cage's silence, ascribing his coy reticence with regard to his sexuality to his membership in the pre-Stonewall, pre-liberationist generation of gay men. As to why a person of Cage's radical, unconventional lifestyle, disdain for public opinion, and anarchistic leanings would nonetheless uphold the highly restrictive social compact of the closet, one long-time acquaintance of Cage's (who wishes to remain anonymous) remarked, "Well, he's a fifties queen, you know." And surely according to our contemporary modeling of gay and lesbian identity, which holds being out of the closet as perhaps the central measure of freedom and psychic health, John Cage was a fifties queen, his conspicuous silence regarding his sexuality an index of a time thankfully receding into the past.[30]

That Cage's increasingly unexpressive mein [*sic*] was at least partly strategic is clear from his friend Morton Feldman's account of the culture in which Cage traveled throughout the 1940's, the macho, often homophobic community of Abstract Expressionism.[31] Feldman underscored the degree to which Cage's unexpressiveness may have done double duty as shield, answering an interviewer's question self-consciously, as if fearful of violating a confidence, "I don't want to exaggerate this point, because John was very sensitive to it. I remember there was a little gathering in a Chinese restaurant, and Jackson Pollock was taunting John."[32] For his part, Cage has remarked of Pollock, "Well, I more tried to avoid him. I did this because he was generally so drunk, and he was actually an unpleasant person for me to encounter. I remember seeing him on the same side of the street I was, and I would always cross over to the other side."[33]

The audience for avant-garde music was notably small, and the Abstract Expressionist painters, as the chief advocates for an experimental and self critical art in the post-war American context, became Cage's friends and allies.[34] But for a closeted gay man, not only was the Abstract Expressionist premium on self-expression anathema, but so too its too-anxious rehearsal of a performative machismo. The Abstract Expressionist agreement with dominant cultural attitudes regarding sexuality and gender—including a general assumption of masculine privilege premised at least in part on the exclusion of women and gay men—made the painters' alliance with Cage somewhat tenuous. Morton Feldman, who was not gay, perceived just such homophobic bias in the Abstract Expressionist painter Robert Motherwell's relationship to Cage, despite the fact that the composer was his former co-editor of *Possibilities*:

> I became quite close to Motherwell. I think that they may have had some kind of intellectual or artistic falling out. John never talked about Motherwell ... Although everybody cared greatly for him (Cage), and they weren't overly critical, I would say there was a homosexual bias ... Well, not only against him, but against the younger people who began to associate with him: Rauschenberg, and Jasper, and Cy Twombly. I would say there was a homosexual bias.[35]

To be homosexual in a homophobic culture was to forcefully realize that conversation was not always about expression; that it could in fact be about the opposite—dissimulation, camouflage, hiding. But is there another frame through which to assess Cage's conspicuous silence? For if Cage's silence was an attempt to escape notice—as the silence of the closet presumably is—it was a manifest failure. Cage became notable precisely for his silences—clear proof of its unsuitability as a strategy of evasion. Closeted people seek to ape dominant discursive forms, to participate as seamlessly as possible in hegemonic constructions. They do not, in my experience, draw attention to themselves with a performative silence, as John Cage did when he stood before the fervent Abstract Expressionist multitude and blasphemed, "I have nothing to say and I'm saying it."[36]

My point is that if silence was, paradoxically, in part an expression of Cage's identity as a closeted homosexual during the Cold War, it was also much more than that. Silence was not only a symptom of oppression, it was also, I want to argue, a chosen mode of resistance. This silence is not the passive stratagem of a closeted homosexual unwilling and unable to declare his identity within a hostile culture. On the contrary, in contrast to the codes of the closet, if the point of Cage's silence was to escape notice, its effect was surely the opposite.

[...] Hence, for Cage, freedom from meaning was also freedom from domination, definition, and control in a very real world sense. After all, to be a subordinated subject is to be defined by power. To articulate the social body, and one's place or investments in it, was thus to divide that body against itself. In silence, there was instead a wholeness, healing: the interplay between life and art worked both ways.

It is just this sense of the seamlessness of personal and creative existence that is underscored in Cage's assertion that, "I think there's a slight difference between Rauschenberg and me ... I have the desire to just erase the difference between art and life, whereas Rauschenberg made that famous statement about working in the gap between the two. Which is a little Roman Catholic from my point of view.... Well he makes a mystery out of being an artist."[46] For Cage, there is no mystery in being an artist: art cannot be segregated from the rest of existence—a "noble," hence liberatory art and a "noble," hence liberatory life are one. [...]

Silent Music

Interviewer: In your Eastern itinerary, first there was India, then the Far East.

Cage: Yes, you could conclude an evolution of that kind from my works. It sometimes seemed to me that I manage to "say" something in them. When I discovered India, what I was saying started to change. And when I discovered China and Japan, I changed the very fact of saying anything: I said nothing anymore. Silence: since everything already communicates, why wish to communicate?[48]

My goal for the remainder of this essay will be to recuperate silence as a means of what I will characterize as a historically specific queer resistance during the Cold War. Silence was much more than conventionally unmusical; it would prove to be a route towards actively challenging the assumptions and prejudices that gave rise to homophobic oppression in the first place.[49] For Cage, silence was an ideal form of resistance, one attuned to the requirements of the Cold War consensus—at least within its originary social historical context.[50] There is both surrender and resistance in these silences, not in a relation of either/or but as both/and. And it is within this complicated nexus of what can be viewed as at once compliance and defiance that the undeniable consistency and congruence to Cage's silence about his sexuality and all those other manifestations of artistic or creative silence—such as *4'33"*—needs to be understood. That Cage's self-silencing was very much in keeping with the requirements of the infamously homophobic McCarthy era, should not obscure the fact that it was also internally and ideologically consistent with Cage's larger aesthetic politics.

The task at hand, then, is to restore the weight and force of the Cold War social context on John Cage while also granting that his ideological convictions were not simply or purely a product of his oppression as a gay man. After all, many similarly oppressed queer artists did not then go on to make silence the touchstone of their aesthetic.[51] Against a web of connections, both personal and political, Cage's many types of silence can be seen as reflecting his queerness—not least through their common repression of expressivity and identity—while no less fully articulating his deeply held aesthetic and political convictions.

Reframing Cage's consistent self-silencing as something other than a timorous refusal to come out of the closet (perhaps even recovering it as a species of politics, however strange, if not self-defeating, it might appear from our contemporary vantage point) may help explain why Cage was so persistently closeted well after the point that life in the closet held any instrumental benefits. When scholars and activists were rooting for John Cage to come out, were we thus asking him to turn his back on his own ideological convictions regarding silence and the work it could do, thereby ignoring the distinction between our political claims on him and his own lifelong principles?[52] Yet it's equally true that Cage was hardly silent about many other aspects of his personal life, detailing his love of mushrooms, various anecdotes about his friendships, even intimate particulars of his daily routine. Why then this silence about his sexuality?

I certainly believe that the easy answer—that Cage's closeted gay identity compelled his infamous anti-expressionism and self-silencing—is at least partially true. Indeed, in correlating his embrace of Zen to his personal "disturbances," he says as much himself. And there is, after all, a lovely economy to the notion that a closeted gay man made anti-expressionism the hallmark of his carrier, culminating in a work of absolute authorial silence. But this notion may also be putting the cart before the horse.

Could it also be the case that Cage's anti-expressionist convictions compelled his closetedness, that his belief in the utility of silence caused him to stifle or at least mute the public acknowledgement of his sexuality? Perhaps, a mix of both factors, his fear of exposure and his belief in the efficacy of silence coexisted without a relation of priority, such that his closetedness and his anti-expressive ideology reinforced one another. I think we can best make sense of Cage's closetedness by analyzing it as both an individual tendency and an ideological conviction, as a social historical phenomenon common among gay men in this era and as a coherent political philosophy. It is precisely this double layered interpretative frame that I next want to explore.

Silent Politics

In what way can silence be understood politically, as a remedy for oppression? I propose that the particular utility of silence as a means of resistance for Cage and his circle was its evasion of a politics of opposition. Not only could closeted homosexuals ill afford to call attention to themselves with an articulated and entrenched oppositional stance, but, according to Cage, actively opposing power would only "Make Matters Worse"—as he claimed in the eponymous series of diary entries from which I've borrowed for the title of this article.[53] Indeed, Cage argues in these entries that any attempt to improve the world will actually only result in worsening the situation you sought to better. But Cage was hardly one to believe that that the world was just fine as it was. His objection wasn't so much with the desire to improve the world (a desire I dare say that animated much of his prodigious output in so many media), as to the best strategies to select in order to bring this desired improvement into practice.

Repeatedly, Cage most powerfully objects to modes of redress which make active opposition to entrenched authority their hallmark. What silence offered was the prospect of resisting the status quo without opposing it. Cage's divorce and subsequent involvement with Cunningham coincided with a very dangerous time for queers in America, a time of long prison sentences, McCarthyite witch-hunts and Cold War hate mongering.[54] Cage knew these dangers well: long before this dangerous time his friend and teacher Henry Cowell had been imprisoned at San Quentin on a trumped up "morals" charge.[55] The fact that silence-as-resistance allowed its author to escape both complicity in dominant culture and detection as a homosexual during this dangerous period was not the least of its charms.

[…] Note that silence achieved these destructuring effects without uttering a sound. Cage's many silences did succeed as a form of resistance. The fact that his work was not discussed at the time as specifically oppositional is in this sense evidence of its discursive success in the consensus-based culture of the fifties. Silence made a statement through the absence of statement. It constituted an appeal to the listener for a new relationship to authority and authoritative forms in music and—this is very much the point—surely in other arenas, too.

Silence, in short, is not another kind of music, but a challenge to the construction of music itself. Neither musical nor unmusical, Cage's silence was quite precisely "other," escaping the binaries that circumscribed the status quo as the sole arena for contestation. As result, it managed to be an anti-authoritative mode that was nonetheless not oppositional. And as an anti-authoritative mode, it revealed the power of the individual to construct meanings unauthorized by dominant culture—and all the while under its very nose. Silence was, in short, seditious.[59]

Cage's silences can thus inaugurate potent "misreadings," seductions towards such profoundly unauthorized interpretations that, for example, a silence can be read instead as a silencing. However, since dominant interests lie above all with preserving authoritative discursive control (as a means of social control), such silences are permitted to flourish precisely because they are not presented as a direct challenge or opposition to authority. Whatever "misreadings" are produced remain the responsibility of the listener, while Cage, ever the Cold War warrior, remains under cover.[60]

[…] Of course, there is a powerful alternative tradition to this Cageian paean to silence-as-resistance, perhaps best represented by Foucault and his careful analysis of relations of power. And surely, the weight of contemporary resistant practice, my own included, falls heavily in line with this Foucauldian tradition. But, as they say, times have changed. Silence-as-resistance was keyed to a context of constraint I have thankfully never experienced. And even Foucault wrote in an oft-quoted passage:

> Silence itself—the things one declines to say, or is forbidden to name, the discretion that is required between different speakers—is less the absolute limit of discourse, the other side from which it is separated by a strict boundary, than an element that functions alongside the things said, with them and in relation to them within over-all strategies. There is no binary division to be made between what one says and what one does not say; we must try to determine the different ways of not saying things, how those who can and those who cannot speak of them are distributed, which type of discourse is authorized, or which form of discretion is required in either case. There is not one but many silences, and they are an integral part of the strategies that underlie and permeate discourses."[66]

Cage would certainly have agreed in principle, and his breakthrough recognition of the coexistence of sound and silence in his *Concerto for Prepared Piano* makes much the same point. But Cage would also surely have differed over Foucault's insistence on determining the import and meanings of that which was left unsaid. For Cage, the unsaid could never have a meaning; it would differ for every (non)speaker.

In fact, Cage was quite specific that simple opposition to dominant culture would never produce any real social change. As he said in an interview:

> It is unimaginable that one particular attitude alone would be able to unleash what you envision under the name revolution. I believe instead that the revolution is in the process of unrolling right before our eyes on all levels—and that we aren't aware of it … Protest movements could quite easily, and despite themselves, lead in the opposite direction, to a reinforcement of law and order. There is in acceptance and non-violence an underestimated revolutionary force. But instead, protest is all too often absorbed into the flow of power, because it limits itself to reaching for the same old mechanisms of power, which is the worst way to challenge authority! We'll never get away from it that way![67]

In short, there is an "underestimated revolutionary force" in modes of resistance that are not oppositional, and equally, the prospect of being coopted ("absorbed into the flow of power") through an opposition that is "itself to reaching for the same old mechanisms of power."

That Cage understood his particular form of acceptance—silence—as an expressly political force is evident in the connections he draws between his composing and the larger social situation at the time in this 1976 book.

1 Dante Alighieri, trans. Allen Mandelbaum. *The Divine Comedy, Inferno*, (Berkeley: University of California Press, 1987), Canto XV: 137. Interestingly, when Cage's friend Robert Rauschenberg illustrated this passage in his *Dante Drawings* he uncharacteristically opted out of the prescribed silence—identifying himself as among the sodomites sentenced to wander over burning sands by outlining his own foot in red at the top of the page.

2 I would like to thank Moira Roth, without whom this essay could not have been written and Kevin Schaub for his love and patience while it was being finished.

3 Interview with Remy Charlip. 4/24/96. The most significant historical account of Cage's gay life, based on two remarkably candid interviews with Cage, is to be found in Thomas Hines, "Then Not Yet "Cage": The Los Angeles Years, 1912–1938" in *John Cage: Composed in America*, ed. Marjorie Perloff and Charles Junkerman (Chicago: The University of Chicago Press, 1994), 65–99. In contrast, as late as 1988, an Architectural Digest spread on Cage and Cunningham photographed them together in the apartment they shared, but referred to them only as "lifelong friends." Caroline Jones does a remarkable analysis of Cage's silence as a means of opposition to the Abstract Expressionist ego in Caroline A. Jones, "Finishing School: John Cage and the Abstract Expressionist Ego," *Critical Inquiry* (Summer 1993), 643–647.

4 Hines "Then Not Yet 'Cage'", 99. Professor Hines was kind enough to let me hear parts of the actual tape recording of the interview, as well as give me the entire unpublished transcript. Despite Richard Kostelanetz's rather scurrilous charges as to its genuineness, I can testify to the authenticity of the tape and transcription.

[…]

28 John Cage, M: *Writings, 67–72*, (Middletown, CT.: Wesleyan University Press, 1973), p. 106.

29 John Cage interviewed by Paul Cummings, p. 36.

30 Philip Brett has argued that music itself constitutes a kind of closet, wherein musicians are free to engage in the most public displays of emotion in exchange for not articulating those emotions verbally. See Philip Brett, "Musicality, Essentialism and the Closet," in *Queering the Pitch* (New York: Routledge, 1994), pp. 9–26.

31 Caroline Jones explicitly correlates Cage's silence to a refusal of the rapacious Abstract Expressionist ego. See Caroline A. Jones, "Finishing School: John Cage and the Abstract Expressionist Ego", pp. 643–47.

32 R. Wood Massi, "Morton Feldman, John Cage and Who", unpublished interview with Morton Feldman (March 3, 1987), p. 9.

33 Cage in Richard Kostelanetz, *Conversing with Cage*. (New York: Limelight Editions. 1988), p. 177.

34 Cage's friend, the composer Morton Feldman recalled in an interview, "Cunningham and Cage did not associate with homosexuals. They associated with homosexuals like Obey, landed-gentry types. John Ashbery, the young poets, Frank (O'Hara), they cruised around. If I went to a party at Frank's, I could have straight friends, or tough Jewish intellectuals like me, Norman Bluhm, Michael Goldberg. He would have all these … And then the party will be, for example, Genet … Atmosphere." R. Wood Massi, "Morton Feldman, John Cage and Who." p. 9.

35 Massi, p. 4.

36 John Cage, *Silence: Lectures and Writings by John Cage* (Middletown, CT.: Wesleyan University Press, 1973), 109.

[…]

48 Cage, *For the Birds*, p. 103.

49 For a related account of resistance among visual artists of the Cage circle, see my "Passive Resistance: On the Critical and Commercial Success of Queer Artists in Cold War American Art", in *L'image* #3, Paris (December 1996), pp. 19–142.

50 Cage's oft-stated defense of what had once been "noise" as simply another (unaccustomed and disempowered) form of music met with much more sympathy than did his defense of silence. The elevation of "noise" only seeks to expand the category of music; the elevation of silence on the other hand could be thought of—and apparently was—as the negation of it. When *4'33"* was first performed, Cage informs us a near riot erupted, a much more forceful protest than met any of his other compositions up until that time. Nonetheless, silence was simply the other face of noise, as noise was the other face of music: and Cage set out quite deliberately to deconstruct these false polarities. His *4'33"* of course sprang from this intuition, and the incidental noises produced by the audience during its performance only served to drive home the point. In his 1949 "Lecture on Nothing," Cage said (his unpredictable silences and idiosyncratic punctuation underscoring his theme), "Noises, too/,/had been discriminated against/; /and being American, … I fought/for noises." See Cage, "Lecture on Nothing" in *Silence: Lectures and Writings by John Cage*, p. 117.

51 Importantly, the circle around Cage, however, did—most notably in the work of Robert Rauschenberg, Jasper Johns and Cy Twombly.

52 A number of scholars asked Cage directly if he was gay. R. Wood Massi, who conducted a number of interviews towards the completion of a doctoral dissertation in musicology at the University of California, San Diego, relates that he asked Cage informally in 1985 at Crown Point Press whether he was gay. Massi reports Cage said, "Yes, but I don't like to be political about it." (Interview with R. Wood Massi October 25, 1998) Massi then interviewed Cage formally at a Cage Conference on February 26th, 1988, and Cage, who was then accompanied by friends, proved evasive. Thomas Hines, in a remarkable five hour interview over two days in May, 1992, was able to record Cage talking explicitly about his gay life.

53 The full title of the multi-part Cage article is "John Cage Diary: How to Improve the World (You Will Only Make Matters Worse)." The first three parts are published in his *A Year from Monday*. Wesleyan University Press: Middletown, Ct. 1967; the next two in his M. Wesleyan University Press: Middletown, Ct. 1973.

54 See John D'Emilio, "The Homosexual Menace: The Politics of Sexuality in Cold War America," in *Passion and Power: Sexuality in History*, pp. 226–240.

55 See Michael Hicks, "The Imprisonment of Henry Cowell", *Journal of American Musicological Society* 44(1991): pp. 92–119.

[…]

59 It is beyond the scope of this essay to follow up on the suggestion that it was left to a man himself marked as unnatural or "other" within the binary authoritative discourse of heterosexuality to develop the potential for resistance inherent in a non-binary third term like silence. This notion comes in for fuller treatment in my forthcoming book, *Opposition, Inc.*

60 I take up the question of the peculiar fit between these "closeted" modes of queer resistance and the Cold War cultural climate in my "Passive Resistance: On the Critical and Commercial Success of Queer Artists in Cold War American Art", *L'image* #3.

66 Michel Foucault, *The History of Sexuality. Volume 1: An Introduction*, trans. Robert Hurley (New York: Pantheon, 1978), p. 27.

67 Cage, *For the Birds*, p. 236.

Branden W. Joseph, "John Cage and the Architecture of Silence" published originally in *October* 81, (Summer 1997) in: *John Cage* [= *October Files* 12], ed. Julia Robinson (Cambridge, Massachusetts: The MIT Press, 2011), pp. 75–79, p. 82, pp. 81–104.

John Cage and the Architecture of Silence

Since the summer of 1954, Cage had lived at the Gatehill Cooperative Community in Stony Point, New York, an experiment in communal living organized to function, in part, as a successor to that aspect of Black Mountain College.[13] Located in Gatehill's upper square, Cage's apartment occupied the western quarter of a duplex that he shared with Paul Williams and the rest of the architect's family. Like the other buildings surrounding the upper square, the Williams-Cage House evinces a high modernist formal sensibility closely akin to that of Marcel Breuer's contemporary domestic architecture. Supported by a weighty central core and barely perceptible wooden columns, the rectangular mass of the house rests, on one side, against the upper slope of a densely forested hillside, while the opposite end of the structure stretches out at some distance above the ground.

The main structure's sense of lightness, which is accentuated by its exceedingly thin lines and windows that run from floor to ceiling, makes the building appear almost to perch atop the site. Contrasting with the building's sylvan environment, the frame is clad in panels of prefabricated, industrial materials, ranging in texture from corrugated aluminum to fiberglass and asbestos.

Separated from the remainder of the building by a free stone wall that John Cage and Vera Williams built by hand, Cage's living quarters, with the exception of a small bath and kitchenette, consisted originally of a single room, the western and southern walls of which were made up almost entirely of vertically sectioned glass windows. While the southern view looks out onto the other buildings at Gatehill, the western wall faces directly onto the steeply climbing hillside. This wall is the most striking aspect of the building, for Williams designed it to slide open, coming to rest in a large wooden frame that stands next to the building as an extension of the facade. It was to this feature that Cage referred when he wrote in "Rhythm Etc.": "Not only the windows, this year, even though they're small, will open: one whole wall slides away when I have the strength or assistance to push it. And what do I enter?" Cage asked, once more taking a swipe at Le Corbusier. "Not proportion. The clutter of the unkempt forest."[14]

While such a specific reference to the Williams-Cage House is unique to Cage's polemic against Le Corbusier, it nonetheless forms part of a larger discursive figuration of glass and glass architecture that surfaces repeatedly throughout Cage's statements and writings. Far from being simply a convenient metaphor, what I would like to argue is that this architectural trope is of particular importance for understanding the specificity of the neo-avant-garde artistic project that Cage pursued throughout the 1950s.

The earliest reference to glass architecture that can be found in Cage's writings occurs in the "Juilliard Lecture" of 1952. There Cage stated with regard to contemporary music, "It acts in such a way that one can 'hear through' a piece of music just as one can see through some modern buildings or see though a wire sculpture by Richard Lippold or the glass of Marcel Duchamp."[15] It is not insignificant that this first reference appeared in 1952, for that year marks the composition of Cage's most famous work, *4'33"*: the manifesto presentation of his definition of silence as the presence of ambient and unintentional noise rather than the complete absence of sound. Indeed, the passage quoted from the "Juilliard Lecture" might well refer to *4'33"*, for, as originally composed, the work consisted solely of an empty time structure of three silent movements through which any sounds emanating from the environment could flow.

Over the years, Cage would more explicitly relate his understanding of silence to the material properties of glass. In a lecture entitled "Experimental Music," given in Chicago in 1957, Cage stated:

> For in this new music nothing takes place but sounds: those that are notated and those that are not. Those that are not notated appear in the written music as silences, opening the doors of the music to the sounds that happen to be in the environment. This openness exists in the fields of modern sculpture and architecture. The glass houses of Mies van der Rohe reflect their environment, presenting to the eye images of clouds, trees, or grass, according to the situation. And while looking at the constructions in wire of the sculptor Richard Lippold, it is inevitable that one will see other things, and people too, if they happen to be there at the same time, through the network of wires. There is no such thing as an empty space or an empty time. There is always something to see, something to hear. In fact, try as we may to make silence, we cannot.[16]

In the way that it subtly interrelates the conceptions of vision and hearing, space and time, and music, sculpture, and architecture, this passage proves much richer and more complex than that in the "Juilliard Lecture." Moreover, in this passage Cage makes a distinction between two modes of openness operating among the constellation of individuals grouped around the notion of transparency. Whereas one looks, as before, through the wire mesh of Lippold's sculptures, in Mies van der Rohes architecture the observation of the environment is to be understood as a result of the reflections cast across the glass surfaces of the building. In this reformulation of transparency in terms of reflection, Cage returned to what was undoubtedly one of the primary sources of his interpretation — the discussion of architectural space presented by László Moholy-Nagy in the book *The New Vision*, the importance of which Cage stressed on more than one occasion.[17]

[...] Cage's reading would have been supported by Moholy-Nagy's text, which described the end limit of spatial relations as the complete dissolution of architecture into its environment. At the end of *The New Vision* Moholy-Nagy speculated that

> a white house with great glass Windows surrounded by trees becomes almost transparent when the sun shines.The white walls act as projection screens on which shadows multiply the trees, and the glass plates become mirrors in which the trees are repeated. A perfect transparency is the result; the house becomes part of nature.[20]

In "Rhythm Etc.," Cage would echo Moholy-Nagy's understanding of a glass building's ability to dematerialize. In apparent reference to Mies's Farnsworth House in Piano, Illinois, Cage stated, "If, as is the case when I look at that building near Chicago, I have the impression it's not there even though I see it taking up space, then module or no module, it's O.K."[21]

[...] In another article [...], Cage made it clear that this notion of space was the same as that he attributed to modern architecture.[37] This fact is significant, for it indicates that behind Cage's aim of collapsing art into life was not a renewed faith in the transgressive facticity of the unassisted readymade but instead an investigation into the modalities of transparency that brought Duchamp closer to Mies van der Rohe. In other words, the Dadaist forebear of the Cagean project was not the *Bottle Rack* but *The Bride Stripped Bare by Her Bachelors, Even* (The Large Glass).

Because of its transparency, Duchamp's *Large Glass* served for Cage as the model of an artwork with no determinate focal point or center of interest. "Looking at the *Large Glass*" Cage explained,

> the thing that I like so much is that I can focus my attention wherever I wish. It helps me to blur the distinction between art and life and produces a kind of silence in the work itself. There is nothing in it that requires me to look in one place or another or, in fact, requires me to look at all. I can look through it to the world beyond.[38]

Beginning with the concept of silence exemplified by *4'33"*, Cage would seek ways of attaining a similar modality of unfocused perception in music.

13 Harris, *The Arts at Black Mountain College*, 156; Calvin Tomkins, *The Bride and the Bachelors* (New York: Penguin, 1968), pp. 121–22.

14 John Cage, "Rhythm Etc.," in Module , Proportion, Symmetry, Rhythem, d. Gyorgy Kepes (New York: George Brazilles, 1966). p. 126.

15 John Cage, "Juilliard Lecture," in Cage, *A Year from Monday*, p. 102.

16 John Cage, "Experimental Music," in Cage, *Silence,* pp. 7–8.
17 Cage stated that Moholy-Nagy's book was extremely influential to his thinking from the 1930s on and that reading it was what attracted him to teach at Moholy-Nagy's Chicago Institute of Design in 1941. See John Cage *Talking to Hans G Helms on Music and Politics* (Munich: S-Press Tapes, 1975). Cage also mentions *The New Vision in Musicage: Cage Muses on Words, Art, Music,* ed. Joan Retallack (Hanover, N.H.: Wesleyan University Press/University Press of New England, 1996), p. 87. It is of interest to note that Cage had spent the summer of 1938 teaching at Mills College in the company of both Kepes and Moholy-Nagy (Tomkins, *The Bride and the Bachelors*, p. 89).
18 In order to include the work of his friend, the sculptor Richard Lippold, Cage had to fudge Moholy-Nagy's definition of space somewhat, for Moholy-Nagy strictly differentiated architectural and sculptural space. In his evaluation of Lippold's constructivist sculptures, Cage would seem to have been following Moholy-Nagys consideration of the Eiffel Tower, which remained sculpture, although it occupied the "borderline between architecture and sculpture" (Moholy-Nagy, *The New Vision* [New York: George Wittenborn, 1947], p. 61).
19 Ibid., p. 62. It should be noted that Moholy-Nagy directly mentions Mies van der Rohe, among others, in the sentence in which this figure is referenced.
20 Ibid., pp. 63–64.
21 Cage, "Rhythm Etc.," p. 128.
[...]
37 "Implicit here, it seems to me, are principles familiär from modern painting and architecture: collage and space. What makes this action like Dada are the underlying philosophical views and the collage like actions. But what makes this action unlike Dada is the space in it" (Cage, "History of Experimental Music in the United States," p. 69–70).
38 Quoted in Moira and William Roth, "John Cage on Marcel Duchamp," *Art in America* 61 (November–December 1973), p. 78.

Legacy / Recordings

William Fetterman, *John Cage's Theatre Pieces: Notations and Performances* (Amsterdam: Harwood Academic Publishers, 1996), pp. 82–83.

Recordings of John Cage's *4′33″*

There are also [...] other mechanically recorded versions of note. The first is a phonograph recording by Gianni-Emilio Simonetti, who performs the three movements according to the urnings in the linguistic score, and follows Tudor's practice of closing and opening the keyboard cover. Since there is no visual cue to denote the beginnings and endings of movements, this is done by closely miked sounds of the keyboard lid in movement (Cage ca. 1980). The second recording is by the Amadinda Percussion Group (Hungary), which consists of a recording of ambient outdoor bird-song in one movement (Cage 1989a). The third audio recording is by the pianist Wayne Marshall, who performs the three movements in the recomposed durations of 1′46″, 1′25″, and 1′22″. When listening to Marshall's CD at high volume, one can hear some sparse ambient sounds reminiscent of a janitor collecting trash in an outer hallway, muffled traffic noise, and soft creakings (Cage 1991c).

The most recent audio recording of *4′33″* is by Frank Zappa, which appears on the double-CD *A Chance Operation: The John Cage Tribute* (1993). This memorial anthology includes performances of Cage's own works as well as original compositions, by such musicians as the Kronos String Quartet, Laurie Anderson, David Tudor, Robert Ashley, Meredith Monk, Yoko Ono, and James Tenney. The producer separated single-movement selections into different yet continuous bands, with the idea that the listener can then make his/her own random choices. This idea obscures Zappa's performance of *4′33″*, as it is separated into five bands. Whether this performance is in five movements, three movements, or one continuous movement is impossible to say, but the five bands have durations of 35″, 1′05″, 2′21″, 1′02″, and 50″, with a total duration of 5′53″. Zappa's recording includes many extraneous sounds, such as distant clinks; muffled, jumbling percussive noises (like those made with a small metal trash can); finger tapping; breathing; and in the fourth band, a short electronic humming vibrato (Cage 1993). True, Cage stated that the total duration of *4′33″* could be any other duration, but the frequency of various sounds makes me wonder whether these are truly "unintended and ambient" or purposefully produced noises. The conclusion of this CD is a one-minute recording (again, unnecessarily broken up into several different, continuous bands) of street sounds found outside of Cage's New York apartment, which perhaps more than Frank Zappa's overly ornate performance, reflects Cage's actual intention of ambient, unintended sounds as the content in this seminal composition.

Kyle Gann, *No Such Thing as Silence. John Cage's 4′33″* (Yale University Press 2010), pp. 188–190, pp. 215–217, pp. 194–205, pp. 209–213.

John Cage's *4′33″*: The Legacy

Cage didn't believe in recordings and wouldn't listen to them, and he doubtless preferred his *4′33″* live and in situ. Nevertheless, as of this writing the John Cage Trust documents about two dozen commercial recordings of *4′33″* [...]. To record the piece forces one to choose an aspect from which to consider it. One can issue a recording of total digital silence and allow the listener to enjoy the sonic phenomena of his or her own home; this most treats the work as a philosophical idea More common, one can perform the piece in front of a microphone, permitting just enough ambient or accidental sound to document that one actually made the gesture; this approach acknowledges the piece's theatrical nature, the mutual awareness between performer and listener. Or one can record four and a half minutes in an intentionally nonsilent environment, allowing the listener to vicariously experience a space other than the one he or she is actually in; this emphasizes the sensuousness of Cage's appreciation of environmental sound. All three strategies have their exemplars.

Many of the recordings are on minor or ephemeral labels. In Gianni-Emilio Simonetti's 1974 recording on Cramps, the beginnings and ends of movements are marked by closings and openings of what sounds like an instrument case, though in the album art the performer is pictured at a piano. In Julie Steinberg's recording on the Music & Arts disc *Non-Stop Flight*, audience applause is heard at the beginning and end, with the silence punctuated by restless shuflings of feet, a few coughs, and a distant clock striking. Frank Zappa's recording on the 1993 two-disc memorial set *A Chance Operation — The John Cage Tribute* (Koch International) gives no hint of human presence save for a thump at the end, as though Zappa has risen from a seated position to signal the end to the recording engineer. Listening to it one summer day, I heard the quiet burbling of the water pump in my fish tank, a steady, sibilant pulsation from the ceiling fan overhead, the hum of my refrigerator, and occasional, irregularly spaced but identical bird chirps from outside. It was quite lovely, surely more sustained and repetitive than Tudor's performance at Maverick — a minimalist version. The movement separations were inaudible.

One disc on the almost unobtainably obscure Korm Plastics label of Amsterdam is titled *45′18″* and contains nine versions of *4′33″* by various performers — or rather, some versions plus some homages to the piece. Performances by Keith Rowe (guitarist for the improvising group AMM) and Pauline Oliveros's Deep Listening Band are as silent as humanly possible, though a human presence is discernible. Sonic Youth guitarist Thurston Moore took *4′33″* as liberating whatever sounds he and other musicians wanted to make, in a "crude setting of instantaneous and improvised music."[1] Jio Shimizu records the vinyl noise of a "silent" record, while the Swiss electronic duo Voice Crack provides faint and distant machine noises. Perhaps most creatively, the electronic duo Alignment (Radboud Mens and Mark Poysden) comes up with electronic metaphors for silence: in three movements they produce steady rasps, echoing clicks, and harsh vibrations that are actually artifacts of various digital recording processes amplified to the max. Never, perhaps, has the audibility of silence been more deafeningly demonstrated.

The use of recording tape to capture sounds for musical use preceded *4′33″* by only a couple of years; in the history of music that employs ambient sound, the influence of *4′33″* cannot be disentangled from that of the vast potential offered by recording technology. Ambient sound and everyday noises were destined to become part of late twentieth-century music even if Cage had never lived, though he had some pull on the direction of aesthetic exploration. Many composers took inspiration from Cage's activities in general, not distinguishing *4′33″* from the larger flow of his ideas. It might be possible to divide the legacy of *4′33″* into three broad areas:

1. the chain of musical events that began with *4′33″*, much of it conditioned by "creative misreadings" of Cage and flowing in directions he would never have envisioned, culminating in minimalism;
2. the more esoteric body of music that deals with environmental sound, some of it with *4′33″* as a direct philosophical impetus, but also a result of advances in technology; and
3. the homages, many of them from pop musicians, which attest to the status of *4′33″* as an iconic work that transcended the avant-garde milieu in which it originated.

The popularization of *4′33″* dissolved the traditionally self-evident boundaries of a piece of music or work of art: the "frame" could now be shifted to any part of life itself, and all phenomena, even the most mundane or rarefied, would be considered materials of art. Liz Kotz has theorized that one of the main significances of *4′33″* was that, in the third, "Tacet" version of the score published by C.F. Peters, it defined a musical composition without using notes or musical notations, only words.[7] This is even more true of the piece Cage wrote in 1962 titled *4′33″(No. 2)*, with the alternate title 0′00″, which simply instructs the performer to perform a disciplined action, with the caveats that the action cannot be the performance of a "musical" composition and that no two performances can involve the same action.[8] Cage dedicated this piece to his student Toshi Ichiyanagi and his wife, Yoko Ono. Ono was a young Japanese woman who had survived wartime deprivations in her native country to move to Scarsdale and attend Sarah Lawrence College. Soon she would become active in the Fluxus conceptual art community; a few years later she would meet and marry John Lennon. Around 1960, the composition of musical pieces defined by words alone started to become rather common in New York and San Francisco avant-garde circles, particularly within the later-so-named Fluxus group; such an instruction was rather jocularly called "the short form." For instance, La Monte Young wrote pieces in which the audience was advised that the performance would last for such-and-such a duration, and that they could do anything they wanted during that duration; in which butterflies were released into the performance area; and, more surrealistically, in which a piano was offered a bale of hay and a bucket of water to eat and drink.[9]

Thus from *4′33″* evolved outward the idea of framing any stretch of time, any experience, even any concept as a work for aesthetic contemplation. Yoko Ono published similar pieces in her 1964 book of concept art *Grapefruit*, directing the reader to play any one note accompanied by the sound of the woods from 5 to 8 am in summer, to listen to the sound of the earth turning, or to ride a bicycle in a concert hall without making any noise.[10]

In 1969 Ono and Lennon released a record of experimental music, *Unfinished Music No. 2: Life with the Lions*, including a track called "Two Minutes Silence," which was exactly that. Clearly the couple were aware of *4′33″* as a predecessor, though Ono had just suffered a miscarriage (of the baby whose heartbeat was captured in the track "Baby's Heartbeat," another Fluxus-style gesture), and the silence can be read as mourning as well. Not so "Toilet Piece/Unknown" on the 1971 Ono album *Fly*, which is a thirty-second recording of a toilet flushing—something that might possibly be heard during an indoor performance *4′33″*.

Asked if there might be anything that is not music, Young replied, "There are probably very still things that do not make any sound. 'Music' might also be defined as anything one listens to."[11] Cage was aware of Young's musical activities and took them seriously. According to an interview with Young in EAR magazine, Cage had told Young that their approaches were "opposite sides of the coin … I'm interested in control and precision and the Yogic approach to concentration, but Cage has … the Zen approach … to clear the mind."[12]

Certainly composers' responses to *4′33″* widened the range of sounds considered musical, as every sound they heard during performances was reimagined as a potential musical phenomenon. The wind and rain at the Maverick Concert Hall were marked by the randomness we associate with nature; but within urban buildings where performances might also take place, many environmental sounds are more repetitive. Listening to or merely thinking about *4′33″* led composers to listen to phenomena that would have formerly been considered nonmusical, including:

- steady, unchanging sounds (such as Young's B and F-sharp "to be held for a long time")
- repetitive processes (fans, motors, and other machinery)
- minute variations appearing in sounds initially heard as static

All of these began to be experimented with by the composers of the 1960s who started out as conceptualist artists and whose work would evolve into a style known as minimalism. *4′33″* has sometimes been referred to as the first, or ultimate, minimalist work.

For instance, a young Steve Reich (b. 1936), whose day job for a while was driving a cab, would surreptitiously record conversations with his riders to get material for sound pieces. In 1965 and 1966 Reich made two pieces, *It's Gonna Rain and Come Out*, based on a tape of a spoken phrase going slowly out of phase with itself. What came to fascinate him was the idea of listening to a gradual process, and he wrote of this as an inheritance from Cage, even as he distanced what he was doing from Cage:

> John Cage has used processes and has certainly accepted their results, but the processes he used were compositional ones that could not be heard when the piece was performed. The process of using the *I Ching* or imperfections in a sheet of paper [which Cage experimented with in the '50s] to determine musical parameters can't be heard when listening to music composed that way. The compositional processes and the sounding music have no audible connection … What I'm interested in is a compositional process and a sounding music that are one and the same thing.[13]

At the beginning of *Silence*, Cage had stated as a motto: "Composing's one thing, performing's another, listening's a third. What can they have to do with one another?"[14] Reich, Philip

Glass, and other minimalists rejected this separation, opting for works in which the composed process was the listening focus. But they did pick up from Cage that a piece could be the result of an impersonal process, that it could result from an action in ways that might not be forseeable. This was as true of *4'33"* as of any of Cage's other works: the chance procedure that determined the movement lengths was an impersonal process, and the composer couldn't anticipate what would actually be heard. Such characteristics typified the early, experimental phase of minimalism as well. Perhaps the most direct influence on subsequent experimental music was that *4'33"* (as well as Cage's other works from *Music of Changes* on) encouraged composers to forget about conventional expressivity and submit themselves to objective processes, such as the two pianists playing the same short motif slowly going out of phase with itself in Reich's *Piano Phase* (1967). In time, the process-oriented minimalism of Reich, Young, Terry Riley, and Glass would balloon into an international movement, take on more intuitive and symphonic characteristics, and become arguably—in the works of John Adams, Arvo Part, Henryk Görecki, Meredith Monk, and dozens of other composers—the most publicly recognized classical music style of the late twentieth century. For all that Cage did not himself find the idiom congenial, *4'33"* occupies a special place in its historical origins.[15]

Within the field of environmental sounds, *4'33"* was a landmark within an ongoing revolution brought about by the availability of recording techniques. Audio-quality electronic tape had appeared in 1947, and French composer Pierre Schaeffer produced the first piece of musique concrete (music consisting of acoustic sounds recorded on tape and manipulated) in 1948: *Etude aux chemins de fer*, recorded from the sounds of trains. In America, Vladimir Ussachevsky and Otto Luening quickly caught up. Other pieces made from recordings of environmental sound would have eventually appeared even without *4'33"*, but the piece did inspire a certain approach, most noticeable in the musique concrete classic *Presque rien no. 1* (1970) by French composer Luc Ferrari, who explicitly credits Cage with having exploded his ideas about music.[16] The work—a recorded landscape of a seaside with voices, boat motors, and so on—could seem like a realization of *4'33"*, though in actuality there is some manipulation in the layering of sounds.

From musique concrète evolved a body of electronic composition known loosely as *acousmatic* music, especially associated with the composing scene in Montreal and including composers such as Francis Dhomont (b. 1926), Denis Smalley (b. 1946), Simon Emmerson (b. 1950), and (depending on how loosely the term is defined) many, many others. The term *acousmatic*, coined by Schaeffer in 1966, is taken from Pythagoras's practice of having students listen to him from behind a screen without being able to see him and refers to using sound separated from its source.[17] According to Jonty Harrison, acousmatic music "admits any sound as potential compositional material, it frequently refers to acoustic phenomena and situations from everyday life and, most fundamentally of all, it relies on perceptual realities rather than conceptual speculation to unlock the potential for musical discourse and musical structure from the inherent properties of the sound objects themselves—and the arbiter of this process is the ear. Because of this, it is unnecessary to have a visual stimulus connected to what is heard—in fact, it is positively detrimental to be encumbered by the visual sense for, without it, the listener's imagination is liberated from the constraints of the physical presence of the sound-producing body."[18] Harrison goes on to say that Pierre Schaeffer "was critical of his own early works, such as the *Etude aux chemins de fer* (1948), precisely because the sound material was too recognisable, too reminiscent of the physical objects which produced them, and he felt that this "referential quality interfered with a truly 'musical' appreciation of the material." One might say, then, that the acousmatic composers, rather than sharing Luigi Russolo's delight in composing for the identifiable noises of everyday machines, took the more abstract approach of *4'33"* in appreciating sound for its own phenomenological qualities.

Opposed to acousmatics are the soundscape composers who value sounds as evocative of a particular time and place, the leading exponent of this being Canada's bestknown experimentalist, R. Murray Schafer (b. 1933). (The idea of environmental sound as art seems to particularly appeal to the Canadian sensibility.) The so-called father of acoustic ecology, Schafer has made the soundscape, the totality of an environment's sound, the central idea of his career. He founded the World Soundscape Project (later the World Forum for Acoustic Ecology), whose affiliates monitor the state of the world's sound environments. Schafer wrote some of his music for specific environments and times of day, starting with his *Music for Wilderness Lake* for twelve trombones of 1979, to be performed on the shore of a specific isolated lake at sunrise or sunset. One of the effects of his massive outdoor operatic cycle Patria (1966–) is a soprano singing from across a lake, a kilometer away from the audience, with other performers seated in canoes. "The big revolutions of musical history," Shafer has said, "are changes of context more than changes of style." Unlike Cage, however, Schafer does not practice a Zen acceptance of whatever he hears; on the contrary, he fights for urban noise reduction statutes and warns, "The world soundscape has reached an apex of vulgarity in our time, and many experts have predicted universal deafness as the ultimate consequence unless the problem can be brought quickly under control." As David Toop has charged, Shafer's aesthetic "seems shot through with a personal aversion to urbanism."[19] Other composers along this line include Barry Truax (b. 1947) and Hildegard Westercamp (b. 1946).

More recent composers like Jonty Harrison (b. 1952) and Paul Rudy (b. 1962) have bridged the gap between the acousmaticians and soundscapers by using the varying recognizability of recorded sounds as a structural component of their works. While it may be tempting to see all of this concern for listening to or recording ambient environments as having been triggered by *4'33"*, it is probably more accurate to say that the desire to incorporate industrial and environmental sounds that first surfaced in the writings and experiments of the Italian Futurists was fed and augmented by the development of recording technology and musique concrete—and that *4'33"* served as a rallying cry, a manifesto, a locus classicus that justified and inspired further experimentation in this direction.

Perhaps more revealing as a legacy, if less profound, are the references to *4'33"* that have spread throughout pop music culture. It seems to have become hip for pop bands to include silent tracks on their albums in homage to Cage. As examples one can name the band Covenant (a 4:33 track on their 2000 disc *United States of Mind*), Ciccone Youth (a one-minute silent track on *The Whitey Album* of 1990), and the Magnetic Fields (a Version of *4'33"* on their 1995 album *The Wayward Bus/Distant Plastic Trees*; the Magnetic Fields have also sometimes played *4'33"* live at concerts.)[20] There is additionally a rock band from Birmingham, England, called 4Minutes33.

[...] A little more than half of the obituaries mentioned *4'33"*. With remarkable frequency, *4'33"* is tagged in the literature as

"John Cage's most misunderstood piece." And yet look at how the work was described by music critics across the United States and in England:

> A work that embodies his musical philosophy most effectively is also probably his most famous and should have a special kind of immortality. It is called *4'30"* [*sic*], and it consists of 4½ minutes of silence. It can be "played" on any instrument or none at all, so long as there is someone to listen to the silence and realize that it is full of sound.
> —Joseph McLellan, *Washington Post*, August 13, 1992

> Typical of the kinds of compositions that set the musical world on its ear are [*sic*] "4 Minutes, 33 Seconds," a 1952 piece that consisted of musicians sitting silently on stage, with the only noises coming from the audience and sounds seeping into the auditorium from outside.
> —Audrey Farolino, *New York Post*, August 13, 1992

> His most famous composition—*4'33"* (1952)—required no instruments whatsoever. The performer was instructed to sit silently on stage for the duration of the piece—appropriately, four minutes and 33 seconds—while the audience listened to whatever sounds took place around it.
> —Tim Page, *New York Newsday*, August 13, 1992

> Mr. Cage came to believe that it should not be an artist's goal to shape the world around him to his own tastes and desires, but, rather, to surrender to the disorder he regarded as the natural state of life.
> Perhaps the most famous expression of this attitude is his *4'33"* (4 minutes, 33 seconds), which may be performed by any instrument or combination of instruments, though no instrument is actually played. At the 1952 premiere, pianist David Tudor sat silently at the keyboard, stopwatch in hand, then retired to the wings at the appointed moment, leaving the mystified audience to their own conclusions.
> —John von Rhein, *Chicago Tribune*, August 13, 1992

> Not only did Cage grant anarchic freedoms to the composer and necessarily also to the performer, he even extended them to listeners, who, in the notorious silent piece *4'33"* (1952), are invited to discover music wherever they may within the ambience of the "performance"—in coughs, grunts, rustles, natural sounds, which acquire new meanings when the context of an "art-work" is added to them.
> —Paul Driver, *The Independent* (London), August 14, 1992

> Like so much of Cage's artwork ... *4'33"* had a philosophical agenda. It was to call attention in a formal context to the richness of ambient sound: to tune an audience's ears to ever present sonic wonders, and hence to enrich lives through meditative awareness. Instant Zen, if you will. And for all those who dismissed the piece without ever hearing it, there were others who found their lives altered.
> —John Rockwell, "Cage Merely an Inventor? Not a Chance," *New York Times*, August 23, 1992

4'33" is often misunderstood—by people who've never heard it, who know nothing about Cage and have no interest in modern music. But imagine any other important avant-garde work from the mid-twentieth century—Olivier Messiaen's *Turangalila*, Boulez's *Le Marteau sans maitre*, Stockhausen's *Gruppen*, Wolpe's *Enactments*, Babbitt's *Philomel*, Glass's *Einstein on the Beach*—and imagine how many of these critics would have described it sympathetically and with understanding. *4'33"* is commonly derided as a joke, a provocation, yet by the time Cage died most critics fully understood that the listener was supposed to appreciate the sounds of the environment in which the piece was performed—and if even the critics got it, the interested public was probably even better informed. It seems to me that *4'33"* is one of the best-understood pieces in avant-garde twentieth-century music. Cage got his point across. Who—aside from Thoreau, perhaps—realized there was so much to listen to?

1 Thurston Moore, quoted in liner notes to *45'18"*, Korm Plastics KP 3005.
[...]
7 Kotz, *Words to Be Looked At*, p. 26.
8 John Cage, *4'33" (No. 2) (0'00")* (New York: C.F. Peters, 1962).
9 Young, *Anthology* (unpaged).
10 Ono, *Grapefruit* (unpaged).
11 Strickland, *Minimalism: Origins*, p. 138.
12 Strickland, *Minimalism: Origins*, p. 162; Ljerka Vidic, "La Monte Young and Marian Zazeela," *EAR*, May 1987, p. 25.
13 Reich, "Music as a Gradual Process," p. 35.
14 Cage, "Experimental Music: Doctrine," in *Silence*, p. 15.
15 Gann, "The Last Barbarian," in *Music Downtown*, p. 130.
16 Ferrari, interview with Dan Warburton.
17 Schaeffer, *Traite des objets musicaux*.
18 Harrison, "Dilemmas, Dichotomies and Definitions."
19 Mcintire, "A Sense of Community," p. 7; *The New Grove Dictionary of Music and Musicians*, Second Edition, s.v. "Schafer, R(aymond) Murray"; Schafer, *Soundscape*, p. 3; Toop, *Haunted Weather*, p. 62, quoted in Mcintire, "Sense of Community."
20 Gross, "Rock/avant convergences."

Exhibition

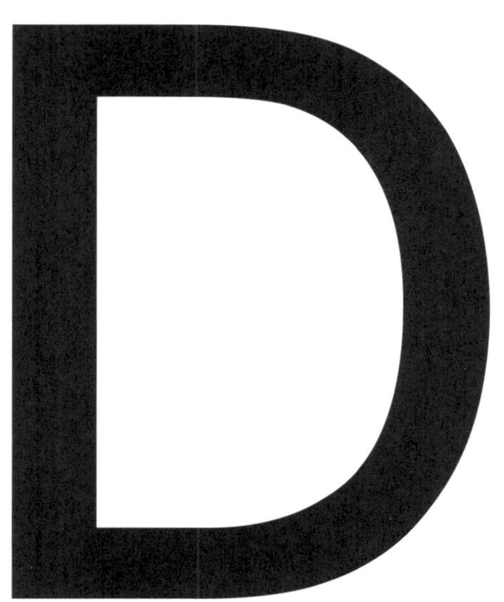

1

All scores and documents by John Cage are presented as facsimile in the exhibition

Works by John Cage

John Cage

Imaginary Landscape No. 4 (March No. 2)

For 12 radios, 24 players, and conductor
4:00 min., 1951

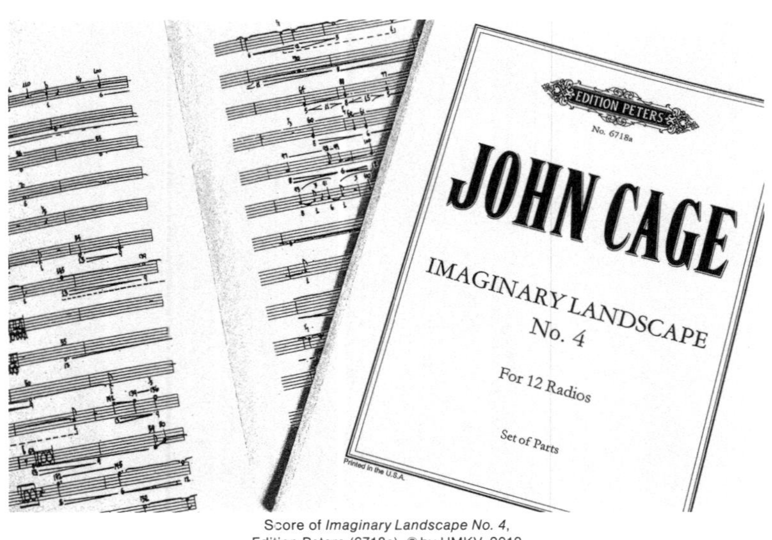

Score of *Imaginary Landscape No. 4*, Edition Peters (6718a), © by HMKV, 2012

Cage's series of five compositions gathered under the title *Imaginary Landscape* uses vinyl discs, audio tape, and radio sets to produce sounds. In *Imaginary Landscape No. 4* two of the performers operate one radio set each, selecting channels and changing the loudness and tone. The score is one of Cage's first to be based on the I Ching and to represent time as a linear measurement—a characteristic later reappearing in the "proportional notation" of *4′33″* (1953). There are far-reaching parallels to *4′33″* (besides their near-identical length): the sounds are determined by extraneous, non-musical factors (radio channels or ambient sounds), which explains why every performance sounds different and is directly related to its time and place. Both pieces—the first with, the second without additional technology—make listeners aware of sounds that usually go unnoticed. The 1951 premiere of *Imaginary Landscape No. 4* was mostly quiet, as it was performed late at night, when most radio stations were already off the air. The piece was performed for the opening of *Sounds Like Silence* and is shown in the exhibition as a video documentation. [DD]

John Cage *4′33″*
Scores and Documents

Woodstock Artists Association

Program for August 29, 1952
Maverick Concert Hall

4′33″ was first performed by pianist David Tudor at Maverick Concert Hall, Woodstock, New York, on August 29, 1952. The last item on the program reads: "4 pieces … john cage. *4′33″,* 30″, 2′23″, 1′40″." The fact that three movements were announced as "pieces" and that *4′33″* appears to be the first of four pieces may be a printing error of relatively low relevance. On the other hand, Tudor himself selected the program and arranged the order. Possibly there has been some confusion about the fourth piece because, besides *4′33″* with its three movements, Tudor also performed Cage's *Water Music* in the same concert. The title of this work is supposed to be changed to the name of the city where one performs the composition, followed by the date of performance.

The durations from the Woodstock program (30″, 2′23″, 1′40″) correspond to Cage's second notational version of *4′33″*, the graphic score dedicated to Irwin Kremen, and probably also to the lost original score. [JT]

→ pp. 86 f

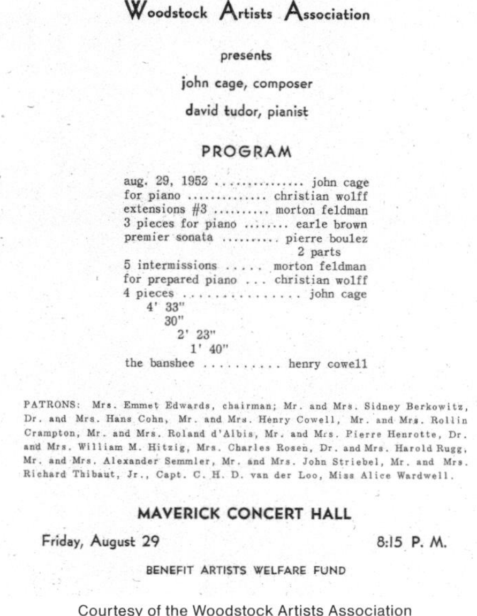

Woodstock Artists Association

presents

john cage, composer

david tudor, pianist

PROGRAM

aug. 29, 1952 .... john cage
for piano .... christian wolff
extensions #3 .... morton feldman
3 pieces for piano .... earle brown
premier sonata .... pierre boulez
2 parts
5 intermissions ..... morton feldman
for prepared piano ... christian wolff
4 pieces .... john cage
4' 33"
30"
2' 23"
1' 40"
the banshee .... henry cowell

PATRONS: Mrs. Emmet Edwards, chairman; Mr. and Mrs. Sidney Berkowitz, Dr. and Mrs. Hans Cohn, Mr. and Mrs. Henry Cowell, Mr. and Mrs. Rollin Crampton, Mr. and Mrs. Roland d'Albis, Mr. and Mrs. Pierre Henrotte, Dr. and Mrs. William M. Hitzig, Mrs. Charles Rosen, Dr. and Mrs. Harold Rugg, Mr. and Mrs. Alexander Semmler, Mr. and Mrs. John Striebel, Mr. and Mrs. Richard Thibaut, Jr., Capt. C. H. D. van der Loo, Miss Alice Wardwell.

MAVERICK CONCERT HALL

Friday, August 29 8:15 P. M.

BENEFIT ARTISTS WELFARE FUND

Courtesy of the Woodstock Artists Association and Museum Archives and Library

John Cage *4′33″*
Scores and Documents

David Tudor

First reconstruction of John Cage's now lost original score of *4′33″* used at its premiere and timing notes for the first reconstructed score of *4′33″*

1982

The original score of *4′33″* is considered lost. Tudor made two reconstructions of the original score from memory, the first one on the occasion of his performance at the Symphony Space *Wall to Wall John Cage* concert on March 13, 1982. This score is chronometrically notated in time-space proportion, meaning that unlike traditional musical scores, the horizontal axis equals the linear passage of time. This reconstruction encompasses fourteen pages with just two single hand-drawn staves per page and no clefs. There are bars every fifteen seconds. As the corresponding timing notes [→ pp. 104 f] for this reconstruction indicate, Tudor took two different sets of durations for *4′33″* into account. The set used in this score (0′33″, 2′40″, 1′20″) might have been chosen according to the durations Cage had attributed to the premiere in his note for the typewritten linguistic version from 1960. [JT]

→ pp. 88 ff

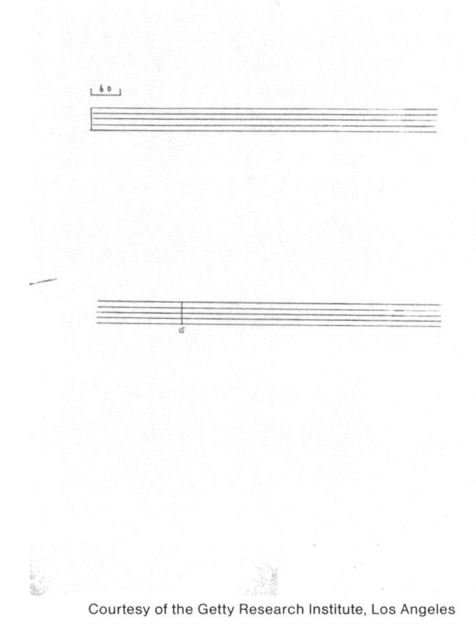

Courtesy of the Getty Research Institute, Los Angeles

John Cage *4′33″*
Scores and Documents

David Tudor

Second reconstruction of John Cage's now lost original score of *4′33″* used at its premiere

1989

David Tudor's second reconstruction of the lost original score was made in 1990 on the occasion of a performance for the video documentation about John Cage *I Have Nothing to Say and I Am Saying it* by Allan Miller and Vivian Perlis for PBS, New York. This version is considered the most accurate reconstruction of the original score. It is written on music paper with staves. He indicated the three movements (0′33″, 2′40″, 1′20″) using red Roman numerals and added page numbers for the eight pages. G (treble) and F (bass) clefs indicate the instrumentation. The score is chronometrically notated in space-time proportion, meaning that unlike in traditional musical scores the horizontal axis equals the linear passage of time: 1 sec. (tempo = 60) equals 2.5 cm. In $\frac{4}{4}$ time signature (four seconds) one measure is equivalent to 10 cm. But the different spacing on pages two, three, and four, and the arrow (turning instruction) on page one were very likely not included in the original but must have been added as a performance aid. [JT]

→ pp. 106 ff

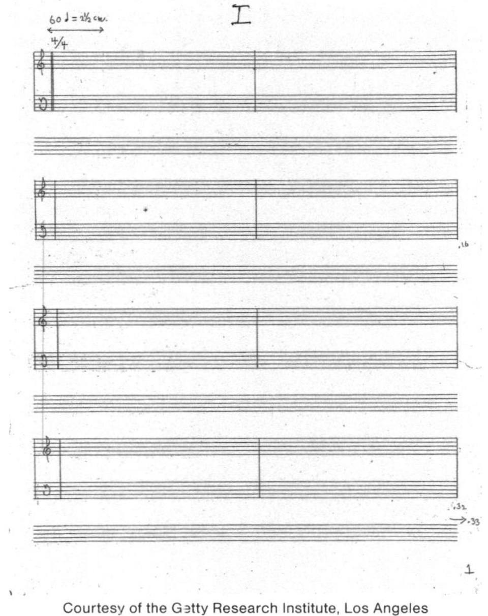

Courtesy of the Getty Research Institute, Los Angeles

John Cage *4′33″*
Scores and Documents

John Cage

4′33″
For Any Inst[r]ument or Combination of Instruments
Graphic score ("proportional notation") dedicated to Irwin Kremen

1953

Cage dedicated this score to visual artist and psychologist Irwin Kremen and gave it to him as a gift for his twenty-eighth birthday on June 5, 1953. It is the oldest notational document of *4′33″* handwritten by Cage. This version contains only vertical lines on blank pages indicating the beginnings and endings of the three movements. The pages are not numbered. Pitch, as indicated by the diastematic system of the original version, is not represented in this notation. Accordingly, the subtitle reads "for any instrument or combinations of instruments." The score closely resembles Robert Rauschenberg's *White Paintings*, its black lines being reminiscent of the gaps between the canvases.

It was first published in reduced size in *Source* magazine in July 1967 causing a distortion of the time-space proportionality of the original manuscript. C.F. Peters published a correct edition in 1993. [JT]

→ pp. 116 ff

John Cage *4′33″*
Scores and Documents

Irwin Kremen

Letter to Larry Austin regarding the publishing of John Cage's graphic score of *4′33″*

1967

This letter written by Irwin Kremen illustrates the page progression of the graphic score of *4′33″*.

→ pp. 168 ff

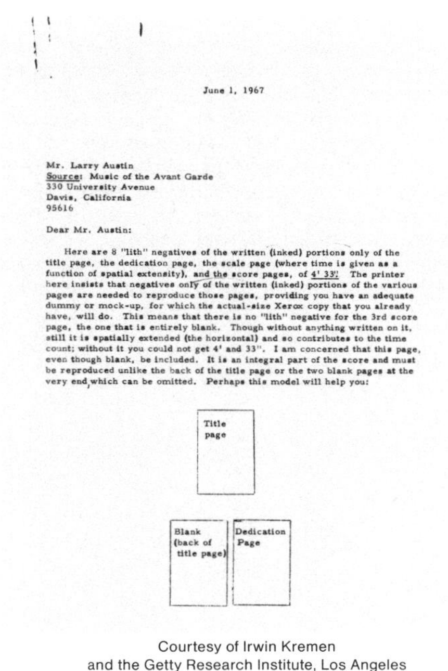

June 1, 1967

Mr. Larry Austin
Source: Music of the Avant Garde
330 University Avenue
Davis, California
95616

Dear Mr. Austin:

Here are 8 "lith" negatives of the written (inked) portions only of the title page, the dedication page, the scale page (where time is given as a function of spatial extensity), and the score pages, of 4' 33". The printer here insists that negatives only of the written (inked) portions of the various pages are needed to reproduce those pages, providing you have an adequate dummy or mock-up, for which the actual-size Xerox copy that you already have, will do. This means that there is no "lith" negative for the 3rd score page, the one that is entirely blank. Though without anything written on it, still it is spatially extended (the horizontal) and so contributes to the time count; without it you could not get 4' and 33". I am concerned that this page, even though blank, be included. It is an integral part of the score and must be reproduced unlike the back of the title page or the two blank pages at the very end, which can be omitted. Perhaps this model will help you:

Courtesy of Irwin Kremen
and the Getty Research Institute, Los Angeles

John Cage *4′33″*
Scores and Documents

John Cage

4′33″
Typewritten linguistic version (Tacet)

ca. 1960

The typewritten linguistic version of *4′33″* was written several years after the graphic score and thus represents the third notational version of Cage's silent composition. But although it was the third version to be composed, it was published first in 1960. Cage had further erased the determining constituents of the former versions. The most important change is the loosening of a rigid time-grid. While the diastematic and the graphic notation allowed non-intentional sounds to appear within determined durations, the linguistic versions allow indeterminate durations. Consequently the typewritten version doesn't come with a title, but with a note, which informs the reader that "[t]he title of this work is the total length in minutes and seconds of its performance" and it may "last any length of time." The set of durations attributed to the historical premiere of the piece contradicts the durations of the graphic score as well as those mentioned in the concert program of the premiere. It is assumed that Cage did not recall the durations of the premiere correctly. [JT]

→ pp. 130 f

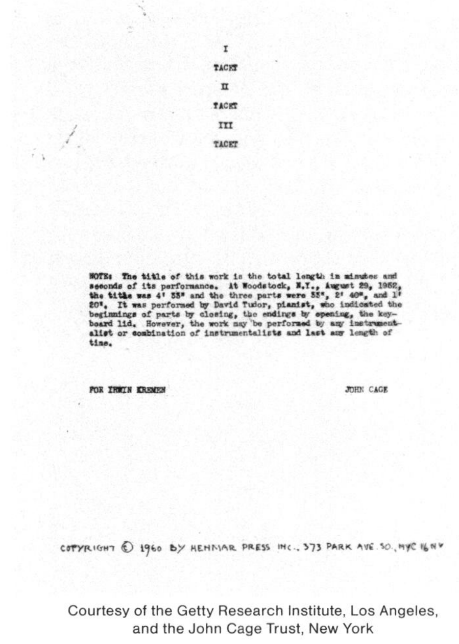

I
TACET
II
TACET
III
TACET

NOTE: The title of this work is the total length in minutes and seconds of its performance. At Woodstock, N.Y., August 29, 1952, the title was 4' 33" and the three parts were 33", 2' 40", and 1' 20". It was performed by David Tudor, pianist, who indicated the beginnings of parts by closing, the endings by opening, the keyboard lid. However, the work may be performed by any instrumentalist or combination of instrumentalists and last any length of time.

FOR IRWIN KREMEN JOHN CAGE

COPYRIGHT © 1960 BY HENMAR PRESS INC., 373 PARK AVE. SO., NYC 16 NY

Courtesy of the Getty Research Institute, Los Angeles,
and the John Cage Trust, New York

John Cage *4′33″*
Scores and Documents

John Cage

4′33″
For Any Instrument or Combination of Instruments

1986

This calligraphic version of the linguistic Tacet notation was made in 1986 when Cage was approached by Peters to provide an autograph of this score. As a reworking of the former typewritten linguistic version it became the fourth and last version of *4′33″*. This handwritten score encompasses three pages instead of one and Cage also changed several details of the notation. In addition to the durations attributed to the premiere already in the typewritten version, Cage mentions the differing durations in the graphic version from 1953. In this way the contradiction of the durations is documented in the score and must be regarded as part of the work from then on. Cage also corrected his statement concerning the overall duration. The length of the whole composition may no longer vary, only the durations of the movements. Thus, he reconstituted the title of *4′33″*, which basically had been discarded in the first linguistic version. [JT]

→ pp. 136 ff

I

TACET

II

TACET

III

TACET

John Cage *4′33″*
Scores and Documents

John Cage

For Wulf Herzogenrath with friendship silently

Handwritten realization score of *4′33″*, red ink on paper
in Wulf Herzogenrath's artists guestbook
Cologne 1986

This performance score of *4′33″* was made by John Cage on August 31, 1986. It was written on the occasion of his performance of the piece in the exhibition *Die 60er Jahre–Kölns Weg zur Kunstmetropole: Vom Happening zum Kunstmarkt*. Cage glued this notation paper into the artists guestbook of Wulf Herzogenrath, the curator of this exhibition. It can be regarded as an autographic realization score of the linguistic Tacet version. Herzogenrath recalls Cage sitting in his office throwing dice to determine the durations for the performance. He came up with a new set of durations: I. 54″, (10″ pause) II. 2′09″ (10″ pause) III. 1′30″. The durations used in the performance are notated in seconds in the left column of the score. Additionally, in the right column, which apparently represents a conversion from seconds to minutes and seconds, the score shows yet another set: 54″, 2′49″, 1′, adding up to 4′43″. [JT]

For the video of this score → pp. 140 f / → pp. 180 f

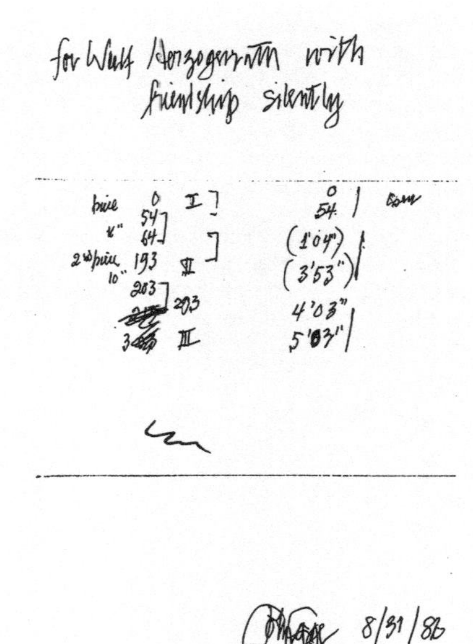

Courtesy of Wulf Herzogenrath

Versions, Derivatives and Sequels of *4′33″* from 1962 to 1992

John Cage

0′00″ (4′33″ No. 2)

Printed version of ink on paper manuscript
one page, 8½ × 11 in. (US Letter)
as published by C.F. Peters in 1962 (EP 6796)

According to the score, the first performance of *0′00″* was the writing of its manuscript, which happened during a concert in Tokyo on October 24, 1962. This causality dilemma of a performance constituting its own notation is reminiscent of the changing title of *4′33″*. Cage's precise and yet highly indeterminate use of language characterizes all silent pieces based on linguistic notation.

Avoiding the self-organization of the musical material—no feedback—Cage attempts a silence full of noises by allowing things to appear with the aid of technology: "In a situation with maximum amplification (no feedback), perform a disciplined action."

0′00″ reappears as *Solo for Voice 8 (0′0″)* in John Cage's *Song Books*, which was published in 1970 by C.F. Peters. In this version, not only has the title been modified, but Cage has also left out the subtitle, dedication, dating, and parts of the instructions. *Solos for Voice 24, 28, 62*, and *63* are variants of *Solo for Voice 8 (0′0″)* denoting with algorhithmic precision that the performer should "engage in some other activity" than before.

0′0″ was the basis for two new compositions, both included in *Song Books* as *Solo for Voice 23. 0′0″ No. 2* and *Solo for Voice 26. 0′00″ No. 2B*. William Fetterman interpreted *0′0″ No. 2* as the written score of *Reunion*, made after the fact, performed by John Cage, Marcel Duchamp, Teeny Duchamp, Gordon Mumma, David Tudor, David Behrman, and Lowell Cross at the Ryerson Theatre in Toronto on February 5, 1968. [JT]

→ pp. 142 f

0′00″
SOLO TO BE PERFORMED IN ANY WAY BY ANYONE

FOR YOKO ONO AND TOSHI ICHIYANAGI
TOKYO, OCT. 24, 1962
John Cage

IN A SITUATION PROVIDED WITH MAXIMUM AMPLIFICATION (NO FEEDBACK), PERFORM A DISCIPLINED ACTION.

WITH ANY INTERRUPTIONS.
FULFILLING IN WHOLE OR PART AN OBLIGATION TO OTHERS.
NO TWO PERFORMANCES TO BE OF THE SAME ACTION, NOR MAY THAT ACTION BE THE PERFORMANCE OF A "MUSICAL" COMPOSITION.
NO ATTENTION TO BE GIVEN THE SITUATION (ELECTRONIC, MUSICAL, THEATRICAL).
10-25-62

THE FIRST PERFORMANCE WAS THE WRITING OF THIS MANUSCRIPT (FIRST MARGINATION ONLY).

THIS IS <u>4′33″ (No. 2)</u> AND ALSO PT. 3 OF A WORK OF WHICH <u>ATLAS ECLIPTICALIS</u> IS PT. 1.

Versions, Derivatives and Sequels of *4′33″* from 1962 to 1992

John Cage (et al.)

Reunion

Collaborative performance
Ryerson Theater
Toronto, March 5, 1968

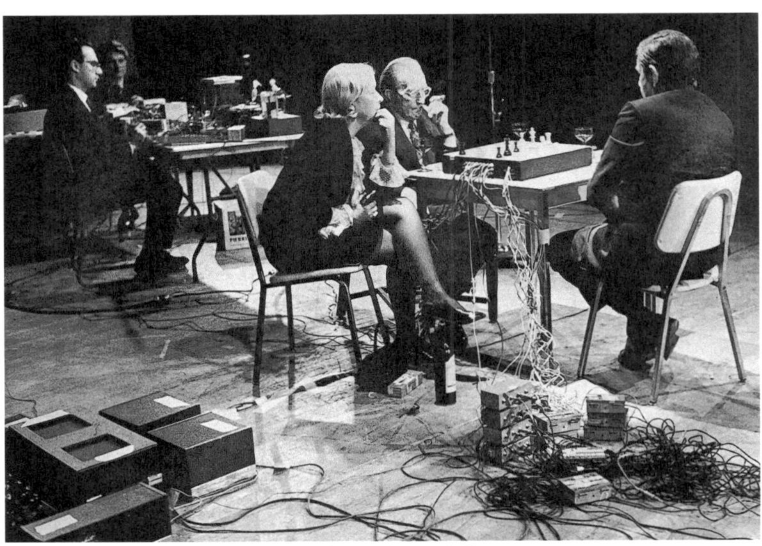

© by Shigeko Kubota, 1968

With John Cage, Marcel Duchamp, and Teeny Duchamp, as well as live electronic music by David Behrman, Gordon Mumma, David Tudor, and Lowell Cross

Opening performance of the Sightsoundsystems Festival in Toronto. Based on a concept developed by Cage, a chess board, on which he played against Marcel and Teeny Duchamp from 8.30 pm to 1 am, was turned into a mixing table for live electronic sounds produced by Behrman, Mumma, Tudor, and Cross. The position of the figures on the board determined which sounds could be heard and how they were distributed in the auditorium. The electronically prepared chessboard and the oscilloscope videos on TV screens were the work of Lowell Cross. The title alludes to the work's social aspect as a gathering of musicians who have previously performed together. Commentators often overlook the fact that Cage not only provided the concept of this performance but also contributed his own sounds. This was a twice updated version of *4′33″* with the title *0′00″ No. 2*. For this purpose, the chessboard was not only fitted with photocells controlling the live sounds through the positioning of the figures, but also with contact microphones which transmitted the sounds of the moving chess figures, which were then amplified and broadcast in the space. [DD]

Versions, Derivatives and Sequels of *4′33″* from 1962 to 1992

Shigeko Kubota

Marcel Duchamp and John Cage

Book
Edition of 500 numbered copies, blue linen cover in blue cardboard slipcase, 1970
Courtesy of Dieter Daniels

This artist's book contains Shigeko Kubota's photographic documentation of the *Reunion* performance in 1968. The black-and-white photographs alternate with Cage's text "36 Acrostics re and not re Duchamp." The slipcase also contains a blue 33 1/4 rpm flexi disc with excerpts from the soundtrack of *Reunion*. [DD]

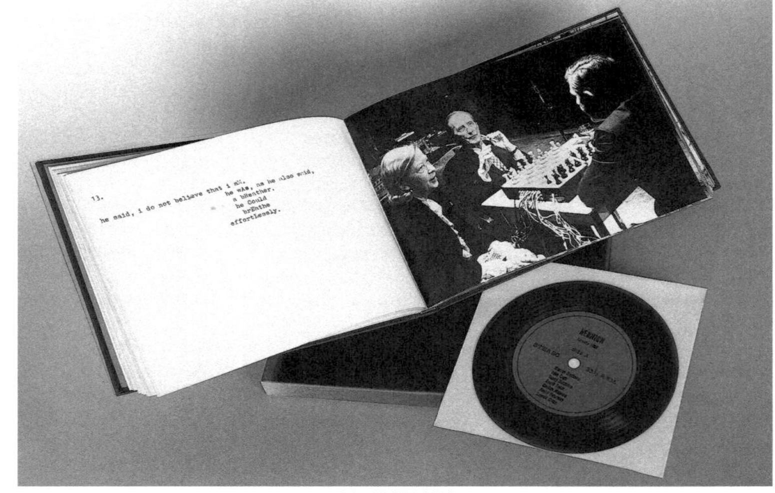

Versions, Derivatives and Sequels of *4′33″* from 1962 to 1992

John Cage

Silent pieces from *Song Books (Solos for Voice 3–92)*

Published by C.F. Peters in 1970
in two volumes (EP 6806a, EP 6806b)

The silent pieces from *Song Books* contain linguistic instructions. *0′00″* reappears as *Solo for Voice 8 (0′0″)* with certain modifications. *Solos for Voice 24, 28, 62*, and *63* are variants of *Solo for Voice 8 (0′0″)*.

0′00″ was the basis for two new compositions, both included in the *Song Books* as *Solo for Voice 23. 0′00″ No. 2* and *Solo for Voice 26. 0′00″ No. 2B. 0′00″ No. 2* can be regarded as the written score of *Reunion*. [JT]

→ pp. 144 ff

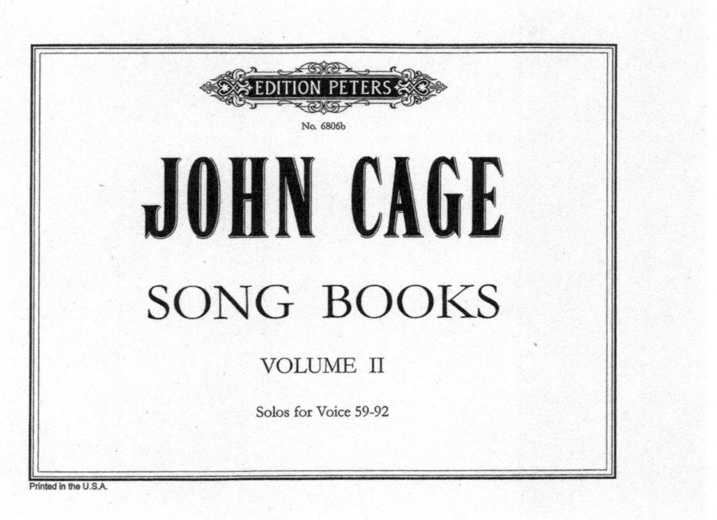

Versions, Derivatives and Sequels of *4′33″* from 1962 to 1992

John Cage

WGBH-TV

4 pages, 8½ × 11 in. (US Letter)
Published by C.F. Peters in 1971

The relationship between *0′00″* and *WGBH-TV* can be seen as derivative. Writing correspondence is regarded as a disciplined action. In this case, the result constitutes a new notation. The score of *WGBH-TV for a Composer and Technicians*–a "composition for TV," as Cage calls it–consists of three items: a handwritten letter from Eva Smerchek from the Caledonia Woman's Club asking for an artistic donation for an auction for the benefit of retarded children, a reply message from John Cage and a sheet with notes for a 30′ telecast written on the back of the original envelope from Smerchek. "This envelope together with your letter and this one of mine will constitute the m[anu]s[cript], to be published by the Henmar Press of C.F. Peters", wrote Cage in his reply. This score has been dedicated to Nam June Paik and published by C.F. Peters in 1971.

The notes indicate how the TV composition is to be recorded: "Camera to focus without movement on work table [–] no face (just ms; hands, etc.) … , microphones … high amplification … (not contact) to pick up sound of work)." [JT]

→ pp. 152 ff

Caledonia Woman's Club
Member of General Federation of Women's Clubs

Dear Mr Cage,
The Caledonia Woman's Club is going to present a Celebrity Auction Sale for the benefit of the Racine County Opportunity Center for Retarded Children.
We are asking prominent people in many fields to help us. Would you as a noted composer donate an item for our auction? Should you decide to help please enclose a card with your name and address.
Please accept our thanks now for your cooperation with our efforts on behalf of Retarded Children.
Sincerely,
Mrs. Eva Smerchek
7634 Hwy 41
Franksville, Wis 53126

Versions, Derivatives and Sequels of *4′33″* from 1962 to 1992

John Cage

One³ = 4′33″ (0′00″) + 𝄞

Manuscript on two sheets
1989

One³ has only been performed by John Cage himself, first on November 14, 1989 in Kyoto Japan and again at Symphony Space in New York, on December 4, 1990. A manuscript draft exists, which must have been made in Acrosanti, where John Cage had participated at the second *Minds for History* conference from October 15 to 19, 1989. Furthermore, a faxleaf including the score is addressed to Yutaka Fujishima from Mimi Johnson of *Artservices*, and is dated October 19, 1989. *One³* represents the last reworking of *4′33″*. Cage asks for an arrangement of the sound system so that "the whole hall is just at the edge of feedback … not actually feeding back, but feeling like it might." David Mayne, whose name, address and phone number appear on the draft manuscript, was involved in filming the conference and also recorded an interview with Cage on the conference. John Cage explained that being on the edge of feedback "is what I think our environmental situation is now.… the world is in a bad situation, and largely through the way we misuse technology." [JT]

→ pp. 156 ff

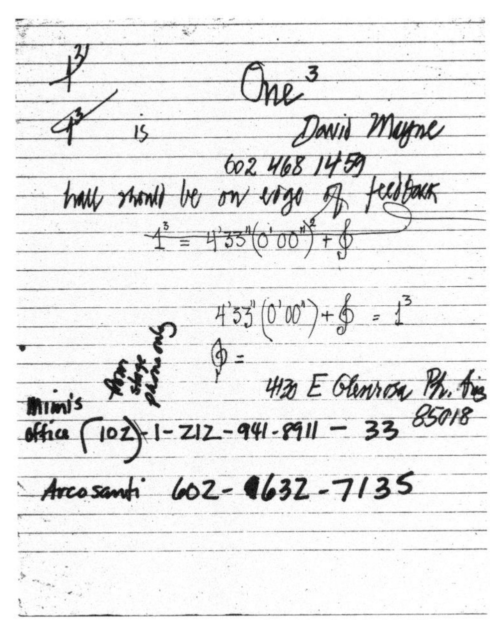

Courtesy of the Music Division of the New York Public Library of the Performing Arts – Astor, Lenox and Tilden Foundations and the John Cage Trust, New York

Versions, Derivatives and Sequels of *4′33″* from 1962 to 1992

John Cage

One^{11}

Excerpts from computer generated score, 1990
Courtesy of Henning Lohner

The score for Cage's first and only film *One^{11}* was computer generated and contains about 250 pages (of which only six exemplary pages are reproduced in the exhibition). The movements of the lights, the camera movements, the angle of view of the lenses, the fades, and the editing of the film were directed based on the I Ching. They are represented in the score as numeric listings and also as computer generated drawings in a grid mapped to the space of the TV studio.

The producer and director of the film was Henning Lohner. The executive producer was Peter Lohner. The light environment was designed and programmed by John Cage and Andrew Culver, who also wrote the software which carried out the I Ching operations for the score. The film *One^{11}* is synchronized with a soundtrack containing Cage's *Composition 103* (for 103 musicians). [DD]

→ pp. 160 ff

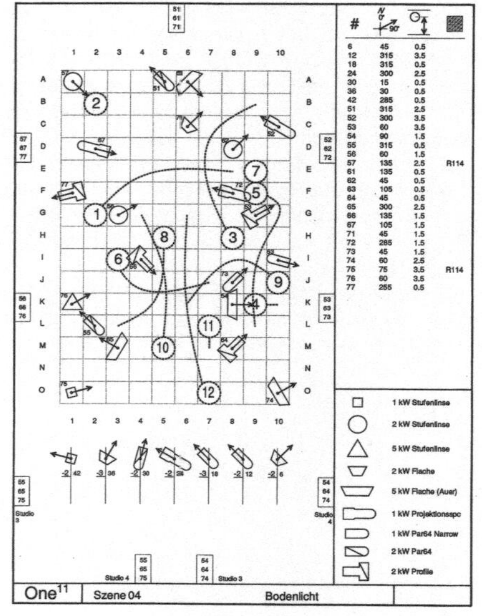

Versions, Derivatives and Sequels of *4′33″* from 1962 to 1992

John Cage & Henning Lohner

One^{11} and 103

Film, original on 35 mm, BluRay / HD video
93:00 min., 1992
Courtesy of Henning Lohner

Created in collaboration with the media artist Henning Lohner, *One^{11}* is the only film ever produced by Cage. It was completed in 1992, the year the composer died. The 90′-long black-and-white film uses as its sole stylistic means a series of spotlights, travelling shots, and the minimal musical composition *103* (for 103 musicians). The conceptual focus of the film is on emptiness. Cage is interested in what can happen in a strictly defined space when chance directs all artistic actions and the artist's personality disappears from the process. For Cage, there is no such thing as an empty space, a premise he visualizes with the help of light and the camera. *One^{11}* thus effectively becomes a visual analogy of the silence in *4′33″*. *One^{11}*, the film, and *103*, the music piece, are played back simultaneously, but there is no connection between the two in terms of content. Both are comprised of seventeen segments, or movements, each of which is based on an average of 1,200 chance operations determined by a computer. The same computer chance-controlled the lighting and the movements of the automated camera crane during the film recording. [FSL]

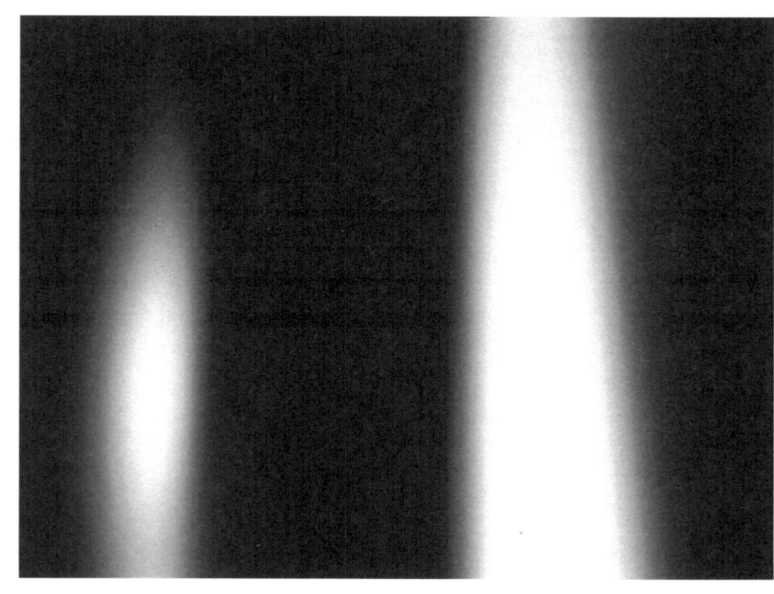

Auctorial Performances of *4′33″* on Video

John Cage

Two versions of *4′33″*, 1972

As part of Nam June Paik, *A Tribute to John Cage*
Video, color, sound, 62:45 min., 1973
Courtesy of Electronic Arts, Intermix, NYC
→ pp. 176 ff

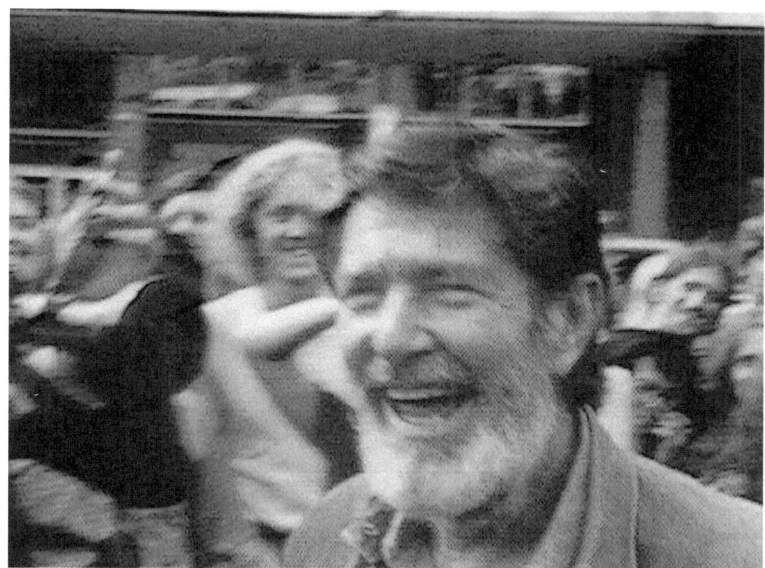

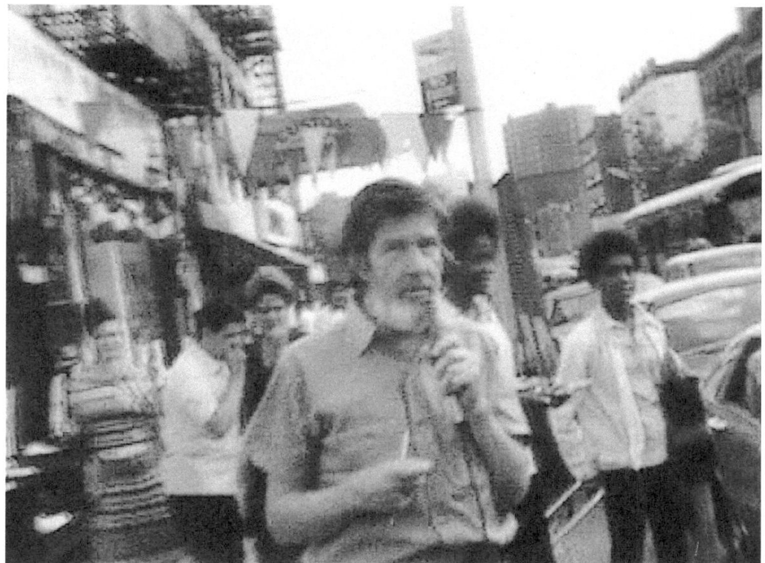

Auctorial Performances of *4′33″* on Video

John Cage

4′33″

Video recording by Klaus vom Bruch of the *4′33″* performance by John Cage
at Kölnischer Kunstverein in front of Sigmar Polke's painting *Schimpftuch*, Cologne
6:12 min., 1986
Courtesy of Klaus vom Bruch

At the opening of the exhibition *Die 60er Jahre–Kölns Weg zur Kunstmetropole: Vom Happening zum Kunstmarkt*, Cage performed a new version of *4′33″*. As an instrument Cage chose an empty glass, which he put upside down on a table. When the performance began, Cage pressed the stopwatch and turned the glass around. After the first and second movements, Cage put the glass upside down again for ten seconds each time to indicate the "pauses" between the movements. The empty glass is a well-known metaphor for silence and emptiness used in Cage's *Lecture on Nothing*, first printed in August 1952: "I have nothing to say and I am saying it and that is poetry as I need it. This space of time is organized. We need not fear these silences,—we may love them. This is a composed talk for I am making it just as I compose a piece of music. It is like a glass of milk. We need the glass and we need the milk. Or again it is like an empty glass into which at any moment anything may be poured." The German media artist Klaus vom Bruch recorded this performance on videotape and added a "countdown" from 4′33″ to 0′00″. [JT]

→ pp. 180 ff
→ pp. 140 f for the notation of this performance

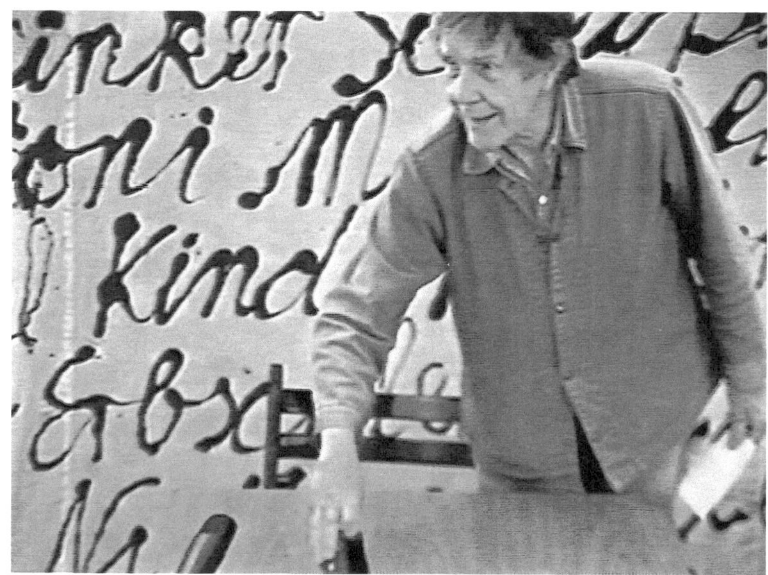

Auctorial Performances of *4′33″* on Video

John Cage

4′33″

Reenactment by David Tudor of the premiere of *4′33″*
for a video documentation by Allan Miller and Vivian Perlis in 1990 (56:00 min.), video, 5:24 min. (excerpt), 1990
Courtesy of Allan Miller and Vivian Perlis for PBS American Masters

For a video documentation about John Cage entitled *I Have Nothing to Say, And I Am Saying It* by Allan Miller and Vivian Perlis for PBS, New York, David Tudor reenacted the premiere of *4′33″* from 1952. Tudor placed his hand-written score on a piano and sat motionless as he used a stopwatch to measure the time of each movement. Just as in the premiere Tudor indicated the beginnings of the movements by closing the keyboard lid, and the endings by opening it. There are also reports that he used a different pedal for each movement. The video performance reflects its medial disposition by inviting the viewers to turn down the volume of their television sets in order to perceive the environmental sounds around them. The score, which had been reconstructed by David Tudor for this performance, is notated in a way that the first page should be turned one second before the end of the first movement. Even if Tudor repeatedly pointed out the importance of actually reading the score, he had, for obvious practical reasons, already turned the page before the beginning of the performance. [JT]

→ pp. 106 f for the notation of this performance

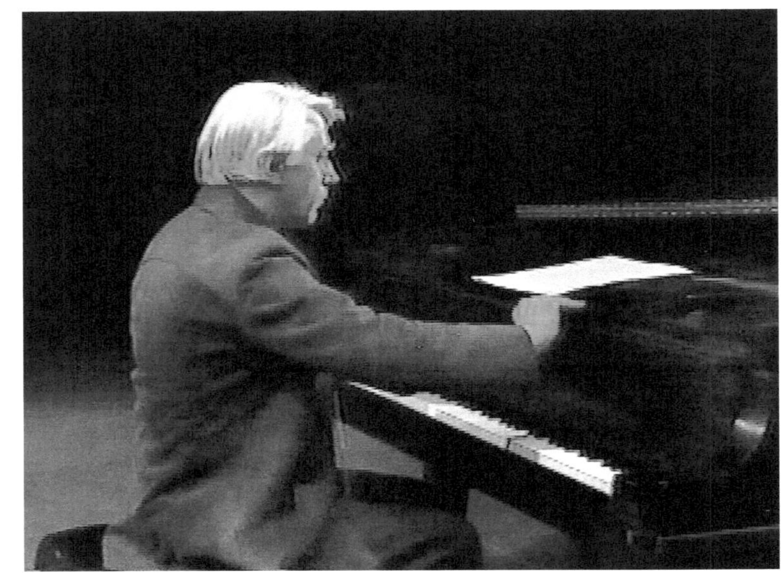

Auctorial Performances of *4′33″* on Video

John Cage & Henning Lohner

4′33″

Video documentation of the performance of *4′33″* at the former German-German border checkpoint Invalidenstraße, Berlin, August 1, 1990
4:33 min., no sound, 1990
Courtesy of private collection Berlin and Los Angeles

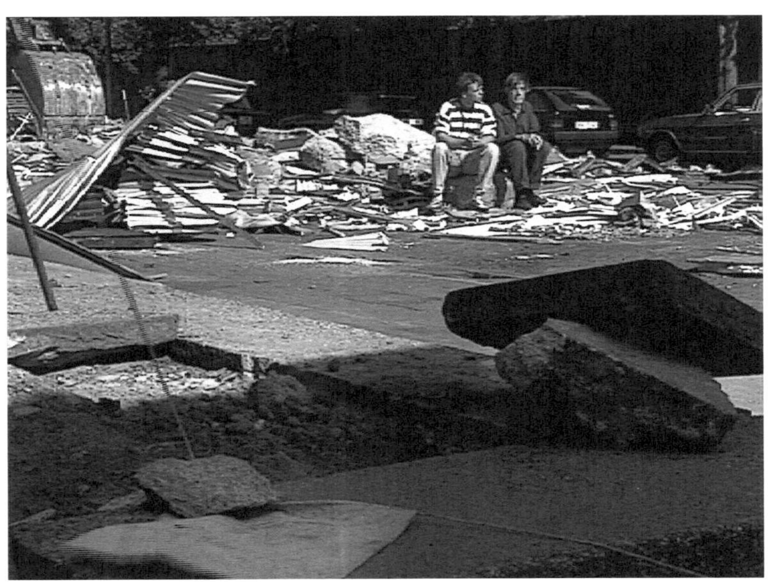

This performance of *4′33″* from 1990 represents an interesting filmic adaptation of the composer's famous piece. Recorded shortly after the fall of the Wall near a former checkpoint on Invalidenstrasse, the film consists of a still sequence shot. In the lower third of the image one recognizes the rubble of the checkpoint, which has been torn down. In the middle of the frame one sees Cage and Lohner sitting silently in front of a crane, which was evidently used to take down the checkpoint. The demolition site is framed by a busy road branching out to the left behind the crane, with a slow but steady and seemingly endless succession of cars winding past. Occasionally the shadow of a passer-by falls on the rubble waiting to be cleared. Instead of staging a classic concert situation and sharpening the audience's senses for ambient sounds, Lohner's filmic adaptation focuses on the two men's silence, whose lack of pathos underlines the historic eventfulness and turns it into a lasting, quiet moment of introspection. All the while the hustle and bustle of everyday life goes on in the background, creating a dynamic momentum that unfurls around a gravitational point in the center of the frame. The video thus becomes a silent, unclichéd, and uncommented metaphor for a historic moment of bliss. [FSL]

→ pp. 182 f

Auctorial Performances of *4′33″* on Video

Merce Cunningham

Enter

Choreography: Merce Cunningham, Music: David Tudor, Décor: Marsha Skinner
Festival d'automne à Paris, Opera de Paris Garnier, November 17, 1992, 60:00 min.
(video recording from the November 19th performance)
Courtesy of The Merce Cunningham Trust and The Jerome Robbins Dance Division,
The New York Public Library for the Performing Arts, Dorothy and Lewis B. Cullman Center

The dance that Cunningham was working on at the time of Cage's death was a commission from the Paris Festival d'automne, and was to be presented in a series of five performances at the Opéra de Paris Garnier, starting on November 17. *Enter* was a long piece, of one hour's duration, and was given each night with a different work from the repertory. Cunningham himself had two solo entrances during the dance; as he told an interviewer, "I stand still in one part, and in the other I try to move." The three static positions that he took at different points on the stage in the first entrance were held for lengths of time that corresponded to the three "movements" of Cage's *4′33″*. There were those who saw *Enter* as a dance about death, but the final leaping section certainly left the audience with a sense of continuing. Cunningham himself admitted, "I miss talking with (Cage), not necessarily about dance, but about so many things, because he always had a fresh way of seeing things." Yet he maintained that the work had not been affected by Cage's death. [DV]

Source: David Vaughan, *Merce Cunningham: Fifty Years / Chronicle and Commentary* (New York: Aperture, 1997), pp. 265–66

Merce Cunningham Dance Company - Dancers: Alan Good, Carol Teitelbaum, Chris Komar, David Kulick, Emma Diamond, Frédéric Gafner (Foofwa d'Imobilité), Helen Barrow, Jean Freebury, Jenifer Weaver, Kimberly Bartosik, Larissa McGoldrick, Merce Cunningham, Michael Cole, Patricia Lent, Randall Sanderson, Robert Swinston.

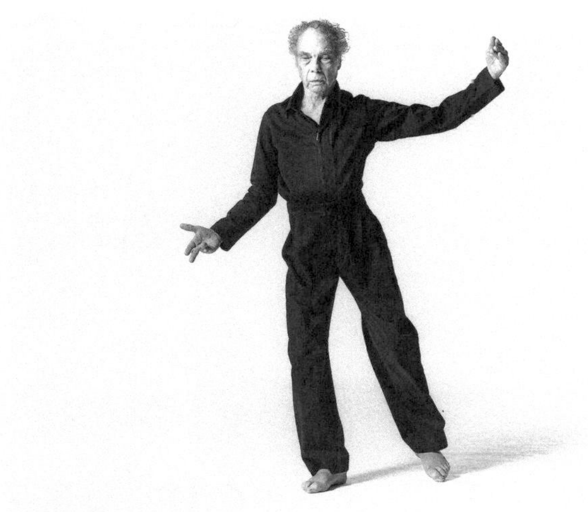

© by Lois Greenfield, 1993

Other Performances of *4′33″* on Video

John Cage

4′33″

BBC Symphony Orchestra, Barbican Hall, London
Video, 9:23 min., 2004

The presenter introduces the performance: "Cage wrote *4′33″* as a piece in three movements where the performer does absolutely nothing, and he wants the audience to absorb the sounds around them, everyone experiencing the piece in a different way therefore, because we all hear things in a different way. Tonight the piece is being presented in full orchestral version conducted by Lawrence Foster. He is going to give a downbeat to each of the three movements. He'll turn pages when he needs to and of course the orchestra will remain silent, we hope, throughout the piece. I don't know if Cage would have been very pleased that this piece is being televised, because, of course, you at home are going to experience this piece in a very different way [applause] to those here in the hall. Well, I promise you, this is the piece that everyone here tonight has come to experience. It really is ... nothing off ... John Cage's *4′33″*." At the end of the performance, the presenter exclaims: "Well, that's one of the most extraordinary performances I have ever experienced here in the Barbican Hall, *4′33″* by John Cage. And, by the way, those of you with stopwatches, and there are many of you out there I know, 4′33″ is the performance time; there was of course time between the movements as well ..." [Transcribed by IA]

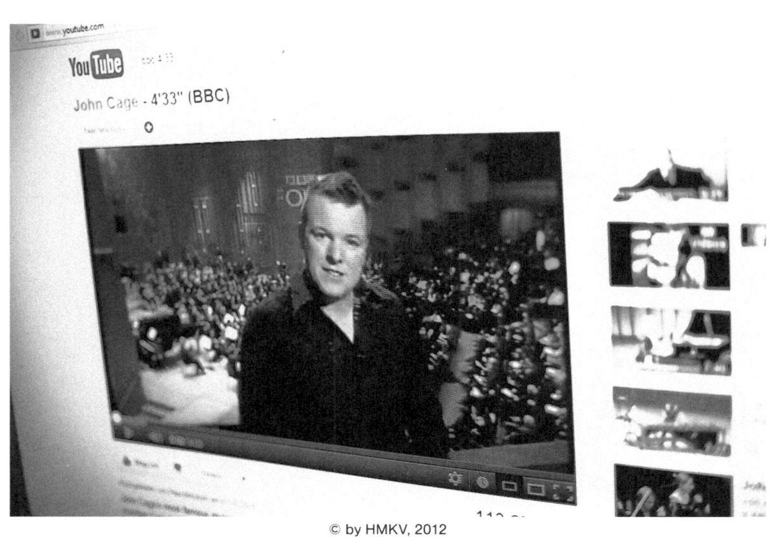

© by HMKV, 2012

Other Performances of *4′33″* on Video

Harald Schmidt & Helge Schneider

4′33″

Performance of *4′33″* in the Harald Schmidt Show, DasErste
December 9, 2010, 7:40 min., 2010
By kind permission of Kogel & Schmidt GmbH, Grünwald /
meine SUPERMAUS GmbH, Mülheim

On December 9, 2010, the German TV presenter Harald Schmidt performed *4′33″* in his *Harald Schmidt Show* together with the well-known musician Helge Schneider, his co-host Katrin Bauerfeind, and the bandleader Helmut Zerlett. The performance received mixed reviews from the public and the media. While some praised it as an ironic comment on the dumbing-down of TV, others were incensed at Schmidt's "refusal to work" and perceived elitism. In contrast to the initial version of the work, *4′33″* was here interpreted as a piano piece for four hands, "accompanied" by a violin and the resident band. The audience in the studio reacted hesitantly, most seeing the performance as one of the presenter's trademark self-referential jokes infused with postmodern irony. They eventually became part of the performance, laughing and applauding during the first two movements, before falling silent in the third movement. [FSL]

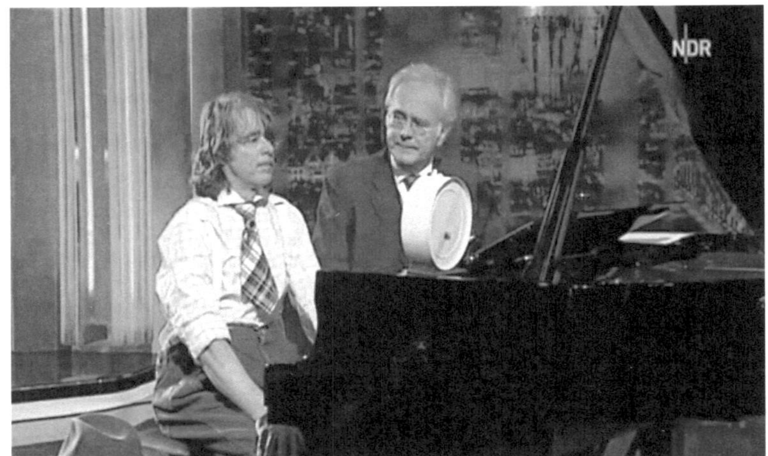

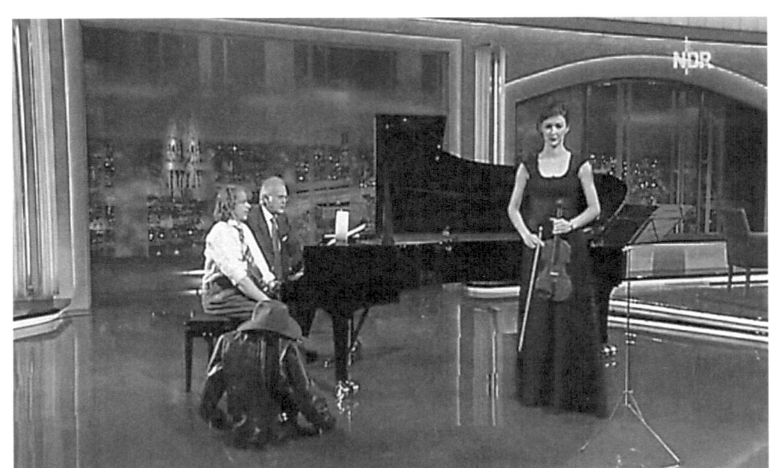

2

Contemporaries of *4′33″*

(ordered alphabetically)

Heinrich Böll

Doktor Murkes gesammelte Schweigen [Murke's Collected Silences]

Frankfurter Hefte, original edition (Vol. 10, Issue 12, December 1955)
Courtesy of Neue Gesellschaft / Frankfurter Hefte, Berlin

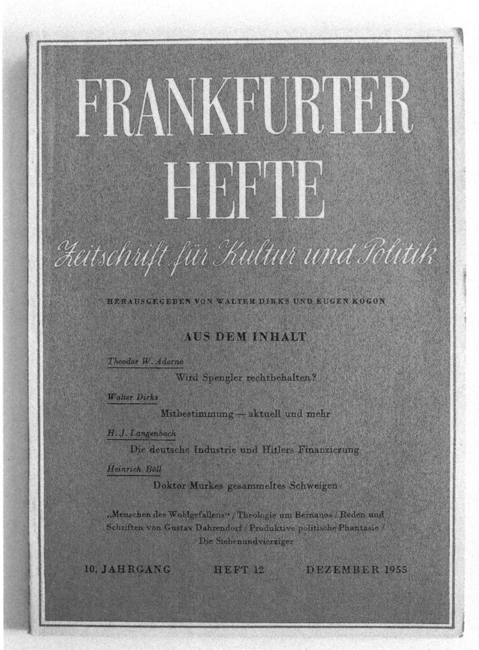

© by HMKV, 2012

Doktor Murkes gesammelte Schweigen [Murke's Collected Silences]

Radio play by Hermann Naber, 50:45 min., 1986,
from: Heinrich Böll, *Kölner Ausgabe,* vol. 9, 1954–55, ed. J.H. Reid
© 2006 by Verlag Kiepenheuer & Witsch GmbH & Co. KG, Cologne
By kind permission of SWR

Heinrich Böll's short story *Murke's Collected Silences* was first published in the *Frankfurter Hefte*, a cultural and political magazine founded in 1946. Murke, who works as an editor at a radio station, is advised by its general director to edit a speech by an acclaimed intellectual with a Nazi past, who wants the word "God" replaced by "the higher Being Whom we revere." Murke has the habit of collecting bits of leftover tape containing nothing but silences, to which he listens at night as a form of relaxation from the loquaciousness of the medium. In the mid-fifties, radio indeed changed from a live to a recorded medium, which allowed for silences to be cut out. As the main protagonist explains: "When I have to cut tapes, in the places where the speakers sometimes pause for a moment–or sigh, or take a breath, or there is absolute silence–I don't throw that away … I splice it together and play back the tape when I'm at home in the evening. There's not much yet, I only have three minutes so far–but then people aren't silent very often."* [IA]

*Quoted from: Heinrich Böll, *The Stories of Heinrich Böll*, trans. Leila Vennewitz (Evanston, Northwestern University Press, 1986), p. 510.

Guy Debord

Hurlements en faveur de Sade [Howling for Sade]

German reconstruction of the film (1952), by Alina Viola Taş and Roberto Ohrt, video, 70:35 min., 2001
Courtesy of Alina Viola Taş

Guy Debord, one of the founding members and leading thinkers of the Situationist International (SI), directed numerous experimental films exploring the possibilities and limitations of the medium. Among the stylistic means he included in his considerations were the reactions of the audience and the black box of the cinema theatre. One of his best-known films is *Howling for Sade*, which caused a scandal when it premiered at the Ciné-club Avant-Garde 52 in the Musée de l'Homme in Paris on June 30, 1952. It shows nothing but a blank screen. The soundtrack consists of voices reading excerpts from legal documents, modernist literature, and newspaper headlines, including ones proclaiming the end of film. The soundtrack and the white image are merely interrupted by several minutes of silence and a pitch-black frame. Loud protest from the audience caused the screening of this "anti-film" to be stopped after ten minutes. It is eighty minutes long in total, of which sixty (and notably the last twenty-four minutes) consist of complete darkness and silence. [FSL]

Yves Klein

Symphonie Monoton–Silence

Composition 1949–61, presented with the following documents:
Score by Yves Klein, 1961 (facsimile)
Staged photo of Yves Klein as conductor in empty concert hall, n.d. [→ fig. 12, p. 37]
Courtesy of Yves Klein Archives

According to Klein, he first had the idea for his *Monotone Symphony* around 1949. It is not clear to what extent it was then worked out as a composition—probably at that stage it could be compared to Cage's idea for a "Silent Prayer" in 1948. Klein gave different durations for the length of the symphony on different occasions, sometimes five to seven, sometimes forty minutes. In 1957, an electronic version of Klein's symphony was realized by Pierre Henry for an exhibition of Klein's monochrome paintings. In 1960 there followed a live performance, accompanying the execution of *Anthropométries* at the Galerie Clert. The final concept from 1961 was titled *Symphonie Monoton–Silence* and comprised two parts, one "symphony" that was simply a D-major chord, and, following that, a silence of the same length, during which the musicians remained motionless in their seats. Klein wrote: "My old Monotone Symphony of 1949... was destined to create an 'after-silence' after all sounds had ended in each of us who were present at that manifestation. Silence ... This is really my symphony and not the sounds during its performance. This silence is so marvelous because it grants 'happenstance' and even sometimes the possibility of true happiness, if only for only a moment, for a moment whose duration is immeasurable. To conquer silence, to skin it and cover oneself with its hide to never be chilled again spiritually." (Yves Klein, *Le vrai devient réalité*, ZERO 3, Düsseldorf, 1960) And elsewhere: "This symphony of forty minutes duration (although that is of no importance, as one will see) consisted of one unique continuous 'sound,' drawn out and deprived of its beginning and of its end, creating a feeling of vertigo and of aspiration outside of time. Thus, even in its presence, this symphony does not exist. It exists outside of the phenomenology of time because it is neither born nor will it die. However, in the world of our possibilities of conscious perception, it is silence—audible presence." (Yves Klein, *Le Dépassement de la problématique de l'art*, La Louvière, Editions de Montbéliard, 1959). [DD]

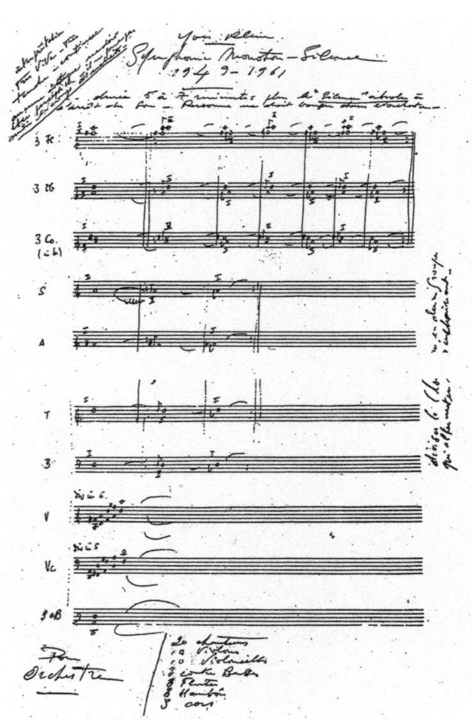

Charles Wilp / Yves Klein

Musik der Leere
[Music Of Emptiness]

LP, n. d. [1959], Sight & Sound Production / Resco
Courtesy of Ursula Block / gelbe MUSIK, Broken Music Archiv, Berlin

This is a vinyl disc published by Wilp under Klein's name without his consent.

List of tracks:

Prince of Space.
Music of Emptiness by Yves Klein

Dance of Emptiness
When The Dutch Arrived, The Indians Were Already There (Tribute To Coney Island)
White Noise
Concert of Vacuum (Tribute)
Frozen Bang (Midnight Train Stop)

Sight & Sound Production

‹Prince of Space›

Musik der Leere
von
Yves Klein.

Charles Wilp
dirigiert das
„Outer Space
Philharmonic Orchestra"

Solist:
Cosmos Berthold Finkelstein
(Helikon)

LP cover

Sight & Sound Production

Tanz der Leere

‹Als die Holländer kamen
waren die Indianer schon da›

‹Weißes Rauschen›

‹Concert of Vacuum›

‹Gefrorener Knall›

Charles Wilp
dirigiert das
„Outer Space
Philharmonic Orchestra"

Original-Soundtrack aus dem
gleichnamigen Film von
Charles Wilp

LP back cover

Robert Rauschenberg

White Paintings

4 paintings
Acrylic on canvas, each 35 1/2 × 35 1/2 in.
2011

Self-Portrait With Four White Paintings

1 painting
Acrylic on canvas, 35 1/2 × 35 1/2 in.
2010

Courtesy of the Museum of American Art Belin

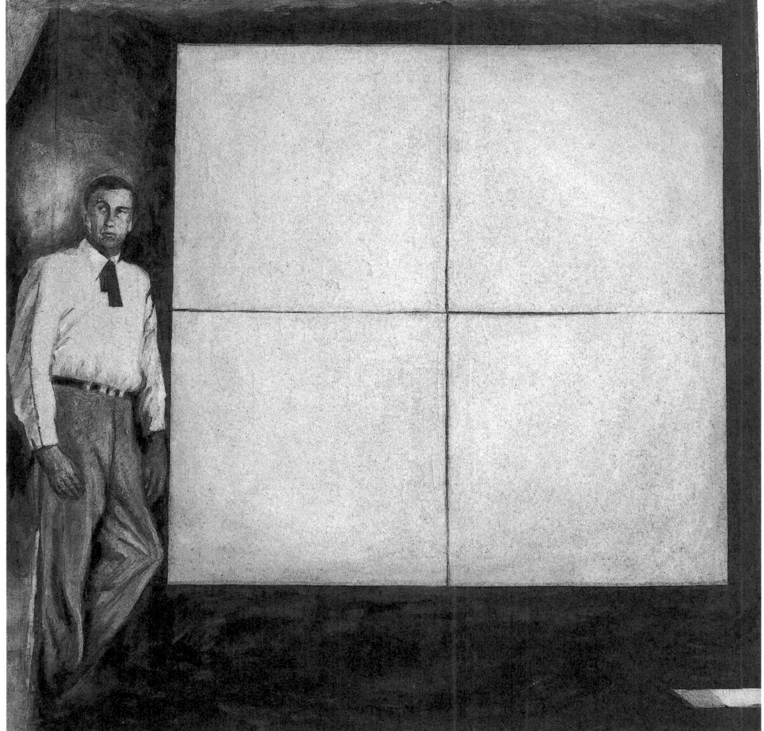

In summer 1951, the American painter Robert Rauschenberg created his first *White Paintings* at Black Mountain College in North Carolina. These monochrome works caused a scandal in the New York art scene, which was then entirely devoted to Abstract Expressionism. Rauschenberg's *White Paintings*, which Cage described as "landing strips for dust motes, light and shadow" (or, alternatively, as "airports for light and shadow"), encouraged the composer to write his "silent piece" *4′33″* the following year. Like Rauschenberg's paintings, *4′33″* is not so much concerned with nothingness or emptiness as with the inevitable presence of something. The four paintings shown here are on loan from the Museum of American Art (MoAA) in Berlin, an educational institution founded in 2004 to collect, preserve, and exhibit reminiscences of modern American art as it was shown in Europe in the fifties and early sixties. [IA]

3

Silence Today

(ordered alphabetically)

Dave Allen

Silent Recording, Hansa Studios Berlin

Audio work, 26:00 min., 2001
Courtesy of Elastic, Malmö
As part of MO's Sound Art Program at Lautsprecher, Dortmunder U, 4th floor, August 1–31, 2012

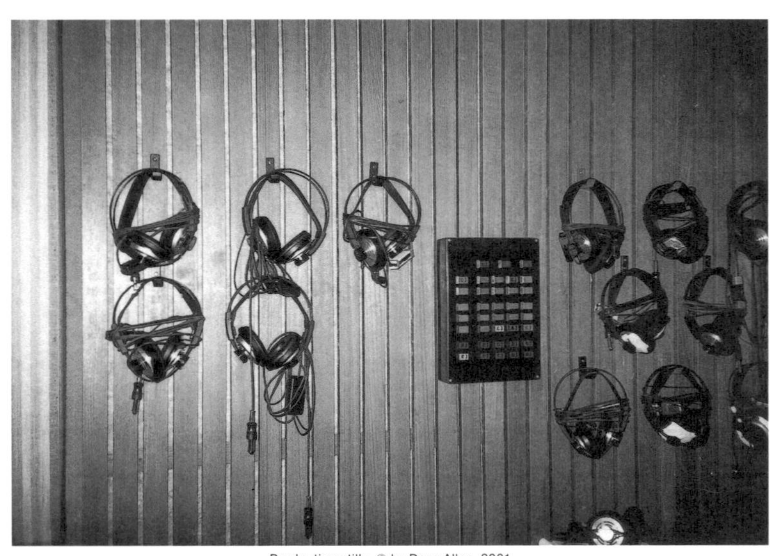

Production stills, © by Dave Allen, 2001

Dave Allen's work is concerned with places which have played an important role in the history of music, from famous concert halls for classical music to recording and radio studios linked to pop culture and its countless anecdotes. While it is often the architecture of these places that creates the conditions for the quality of their musical output, this aspect often disappears behind the personalities who have worked in them. In *Silent Recording, Hansa Studios Berlin* Allen lets listeners experience the physical space as a realm of possibilities by recording the empty and silent recording studio as though it were an instrument. By doing so, he also plays with the myth surrounding the venue as the studio where David Bowie recorded his famous albums *Heroes* (1976) and *Low* (1977). Allen's own recordings are broadcast in the exhibition over a high-end public address system. The "sleeping," abandoned studio thus becomes a space of art where the artistic focus, unlike with Cage's *4'33"*, does not reside in "background noise." In Allen's work each sound essentially remains a possibility for the listener that never materializes. [FSL]

Manon de Boer

Two Times 4′33″

Video installation
35 mm film transferred to video, color, dolby surround sound, 12:33 min., 2008
Courtesy of Manon de Boer and Jan Mot, Brussels

De Boer invited the Brussels-based pianist Jean-Luc Fafchamps to play John Cage's eponymous composition *4′33″* twice in front of a live audience in a studio space in Brussels. Once, with one single still take, the camera films his execution of the "silent" musical composition, complete with the three punctuations indicated on Cage's simple line score at 1′40″, 2′23″, and 30″, which the otherwise still and absorbed Fafchamps interprets by striking a timer. Filmed on 35 mm film, which ensures palpable visual detail, this first part is married to its synchronously recorded ambient sound, which is played in Dolby surround when the work is projected. For the second performance, and the second part of her film, De Boer cut all sound, only interjecting into the filmed performance of *4′33″* with the timer's click at 1′40″ and 2′23″, and 30″. The camera travels in a long pan, which begins where the first section does on Fafchamps, but then moves steadily along every member of his audience and finally travels outside the studio door to show a parochial landscape at the edge of the city center cut through by telephone wires and animated by wind-blown bushes. None of this is heard. Viewed in a cinema setting, the second performance and the second part of the projected film rely on the ambient silence of the live audience. [JM]

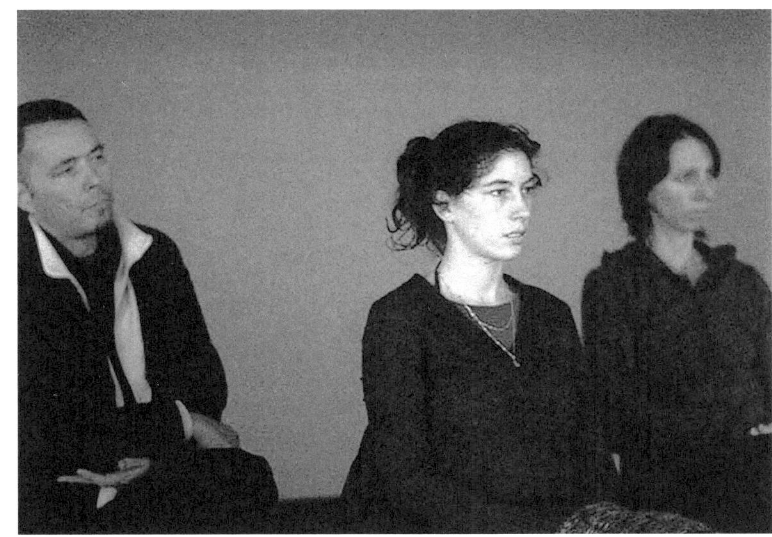

Jens Brand

Stille – Landschaft
[silence/silent–landscape]

Video installation, soundproof and non-resonant room (semi-anechoic chamber), 3:24 min., 2002
Courtesy of Jens Brand

The piece consists of two parts: a video and its presentation in a screening room. The video shows a 360-degree hand camera pan lasting 1:42 min. across the Makgadikgadi Salt Pans in Botswana. The camera movement provides a glimpse of the desert and the external microphone which the artist had installed there. The video shows a place where there are no sounds and where consequently nothing can be heard. The video's images and soundtrack document the silence. The closing credits following the sequence comprising the usual thanks and names last exactly as long as the video itself, but they are not accompanied by a soundtrack.

The video is projected in an especially constructed soundproof, non-reverberating anechoic chamber. The room may be accessed by only one person at a time. The chamber contains a screen, two loudspeakers, a chair, and a footswitch with which the film can be started. The room's very particular acoustic situation enables the viewer to perceive the difference between the recorded silence and the actual absence of sound within the space. The disproportionately long end titles allow the viewer to experience the difference between extreme silence and no sound. [JB]

Realized with generous support of the following institutions and organizations: North Rhine-Westphalian Ministry for Urban Construction and Homes, Culture and Sport, the North Rhine-Westphalian Kunststiftung, the North Rhine-Westphalian Film Office, the Gesellschaft zur Förderung der Westfälischen Kulturarbeit, the Hartware MedienKunstVerein Dortmund, Maerz-Musik, as well as the companies Metzeler, Schaum and soundblocker.

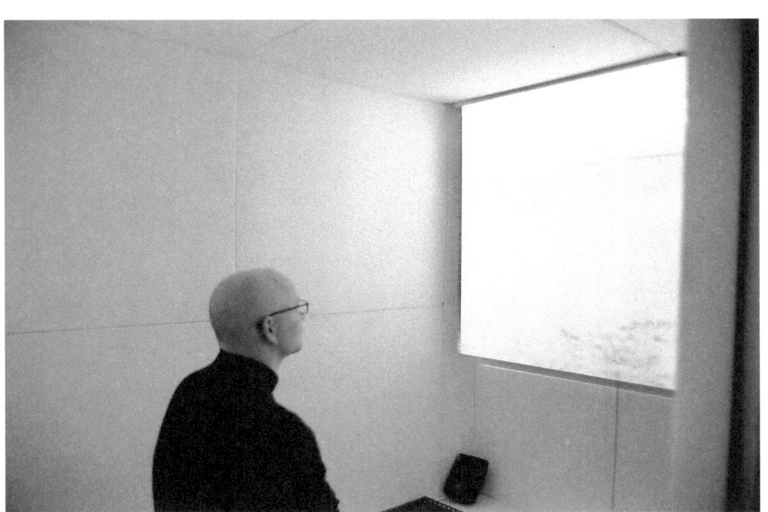

Installation at the Hartware MedienKunstVerein, Dortmund, 2002
© by Sascha Dressler, 2002

Cage Against the Machine

Cage Against the Machine

Action, documentation, promotional material, video, 7:31 min., 2010
Courtesy of Dave Hilliard

Participating musicians: Adam F., Aeroplane, Alexander Wolfe, Alice Russell, Anne Pigalle, Barry Ashworth, Billy Bragg, Bishi, Bon Ningen, Chas Smash, Crystal Fighters, Dane le Sac, Does It Offend You Yeah?, Dub Pistols, Enter Shikari, Fenech Soler, Fyfe Dangerfield, Gallows, Guillemonts, Heaven 17, Imogen Heap, Infadels, Japanese Popsters, Jarra York, John Foxx, John McLure, Kilford The Music Painter, Kooks, Loose Cannons, Man Like Me, Riz MC, Monarchy, Mr. Hudson, Napolean IIIrd, Olly Wride, Orbital, Ou Est Le Swimming Pool, Penguin Prison, Scroobius Pip, South Central, Suggs, Teeth!!!, Tom Alison, Tom Milsom, Unkle, Venus in Furs, Whitey

Concept: Dave Hilliard

Producers: Paul Epworth, Clive Langer, Charlie Rapino

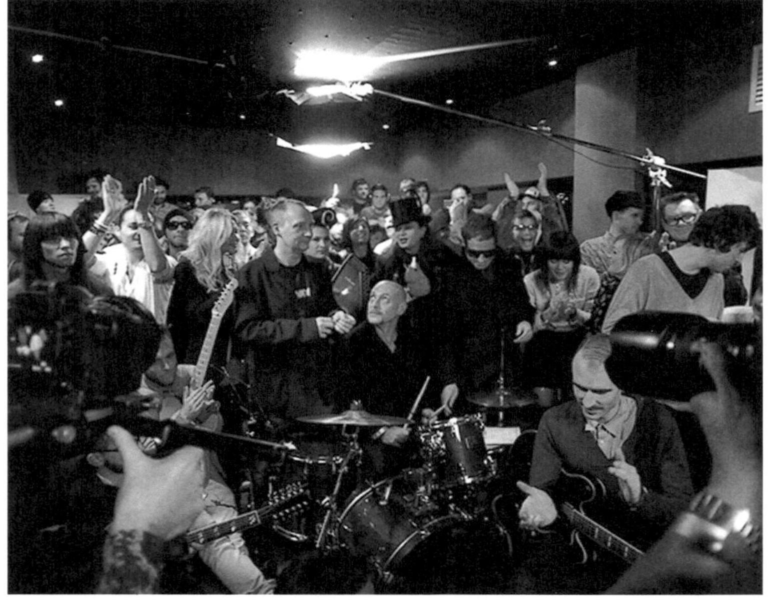

© by Carina Jirsch, 2010

In 2009/10 various artists regrouped under the name Cage Against the Machine to break the stranglehold of *X Factor* candidates on the Christmas charts by subversion. Using activist tactics, they exploited the same social networks (Facebook, Twitter, etc.) as the big media outlets to promote their mock artists and create a media hype. In 2009 the aim of their (successful) campaign against the music industry was to propel the rock song *Killing in the Name* by Rage Against the Machine to number one in the British charts, while in 2010 they tried to reiterate their feat with a specially recorded version of Cage's *4′33″* involving over forty pop musicians from the UK and generated a wider campaign aimed at encouraging people to buy silent recordings. Their single was released on the Wall of Sound label on December 13, 2010 and reached number 21. [FSL]

Martin Conrads

Dr. M's gesammeltes Schweigen (Augsburg Mix) [Dr. M's collected silence (Augsburg Mix)]

Audio work, 3:00 min., 2010
Courtesy of Martin Conrads

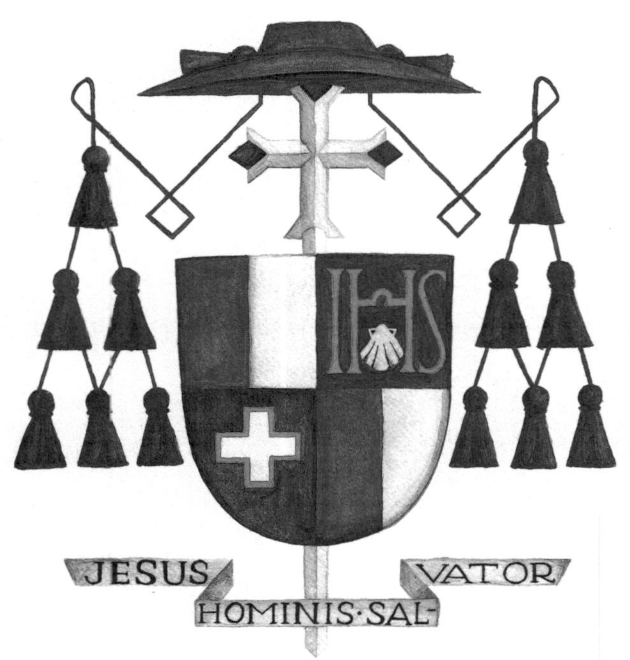

Hand-painted replica of the coat of arms of Bishop Walter Mixa, Bishop of Augsburg 2005–2010
© by Malte Zander, HMKV, 2012

The three-minute audio piece *Dr. M's gesammeltes Schweigen (Augsburg Mix)* (2010) makes use of a radio sermon by the then Augsburg-based Roman Catholic Bishop Dr. Walter Mixa on the topic of "Charity" broadcast on Bayern 1 in 2006. In May 2010, Mixa had to resign as Bishop of Augsburg due to allegations of fraud and violence towards children who had been in his care. In July 2010, the Holy See announced that Mixa "will retire for a time of silence," a time that came to an end when Pope Benedict XVI appointed Mixa a member of the Pontifical Council for the Pastoral Care of Health Care Workers in March 2012. *Dr. M's gesammeltes Schweigen (Augsburg Mix)* was broadcast on Bayern 2 on January 7, 2011 and on September 16, 2011. [MC]

Martin Creed

Work No. 990: A Curtain opening and closing

Fabric, motor,
dimensions variable, 2009
Courtesy of Martin Creed and
Hauser & Wirth

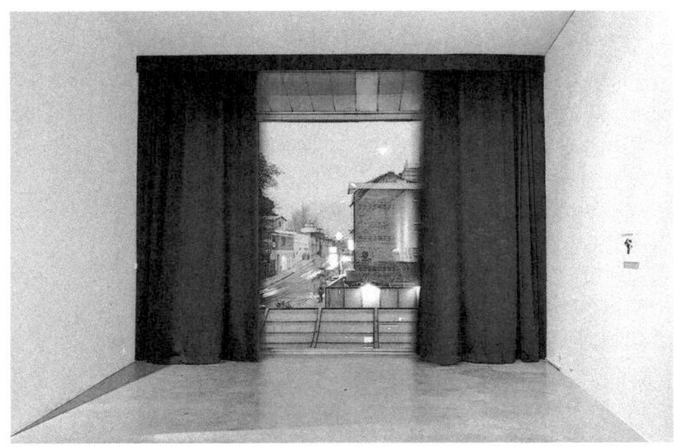

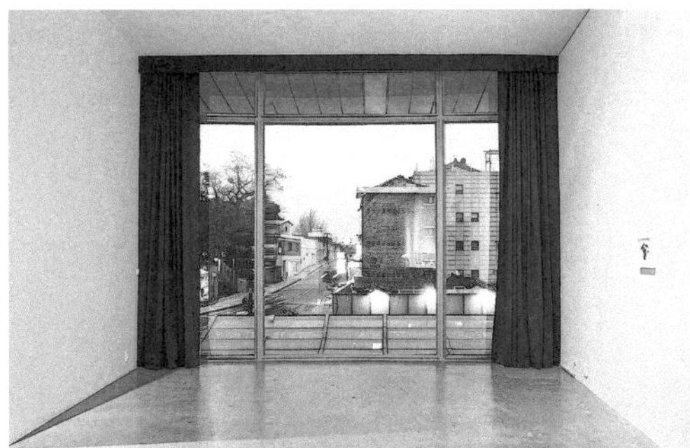

Installation at Artsonje Center, Seoul, Republic of Korea, 2009
© by Myoung-Rae Park, 2009

Martin Creed's *Work No. 990: A Curtain opening and closing* translates and expands on the ideas which led Cage to compose *4'33"*. But Creed does not aim to raise visitors' awareness or change their experience of everyday sounds: instead of sharpening their sense of hearing, he directs their attention to the randomly changing configurations of Dortmund's urban landscape, which—beyond the white cube of the Dortmunder U—is in constant flux. A slowly opening and closing black curtain integrated into the museum architecture is all that he needs to implement one of the many possible visual transpositions of Cage's *4'33"*. The classic notion of the work of art is here dematerialized, as Creed's concept can no longer be assigned to a given traditional medium, which would confer the status of a work of art upon his object. It is therefore the surroundings of the Dortmunder U—the construction sites, roads and train tracks, the passers-by, and the flow of time—which become art. [FSL]

Paul Davis

S.B.D.

Two-channel (stereo) audio work, 4:00 min., 2003
Courtesy of Seventeen Gallery, London & The Sonic Arts Network, UK

"I've always loved to listen to the acapella cuts on 12" singles and check for sounds that you can't pick up in the full mix ... so I thought for the project to make a scratch collage from these sorts of quiet noises—sniffles or throat clears, bleed from the singer's headphones of the instrumental, click tracks, reverb from the vocals that you normally don't hear, etc. I used some little bits from acapella singles by Michael Jackson, Bobby Brown, Ginuwine, and Lil Kim. Because of the low level of the audio, you can also hear other sorts of ephemeral DJ noises like my hands hitting the records. In retrospect I probably should have made it a bit more ridiculous and done a DJ routine with two records of just silence so all you'd hear was vinyl hiss and the 'thump thump thump' of my hands, but I didn't think of it till too late. Hope you like it." [PD]

Source: Nicolas Collins, *A Call for Silence* (2004), CD booklet

Audio only – no illustration

Christopher DeLaurenti

Favorite Intermissions: Music Before and Between Beethoven, Stravinsky, Holst

Audio work, 8:03 min., 2002–2007
Courtesy of the Corette Jepeson Collection
As part of MO's Sound Art Program at Lautsprecher, Dortmunder U, 4th floor, December 1–31, 2012

During intermissions at classical concerts, the musicians often return to the stage. Alone or with others, clarinetists, trumpeters, violinists, and other instruments rehearse difficult passages from the upcoming part of the program. In the course of his research on orchestras around the world, Christopher DeLaurenti secretly recorded these moments. Listeners might wonder why a visual artist should be interested in the cacophony of practicing musicians. DeLaurenti aims to reveal and exhibit unexpected, often overlooked, and hidden musical structures which are closely intertwined with our daily experience of the world. By collecting sounds in a world which, in reference to Cage, he sees as one big symphony, the artist undermines the common understanding of music as a composition comprising notes, melody, and traditional instruments. [FSL]

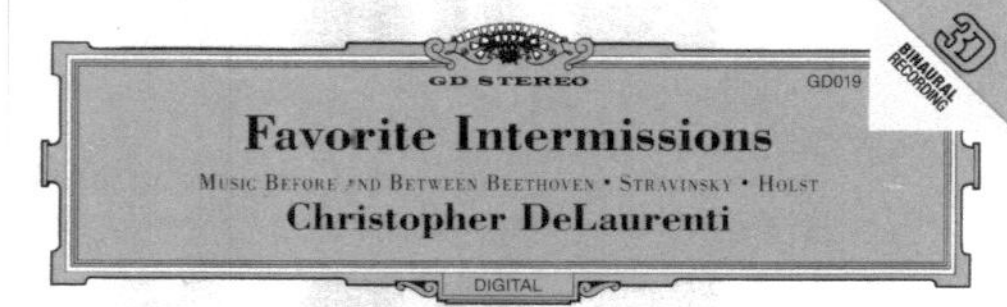

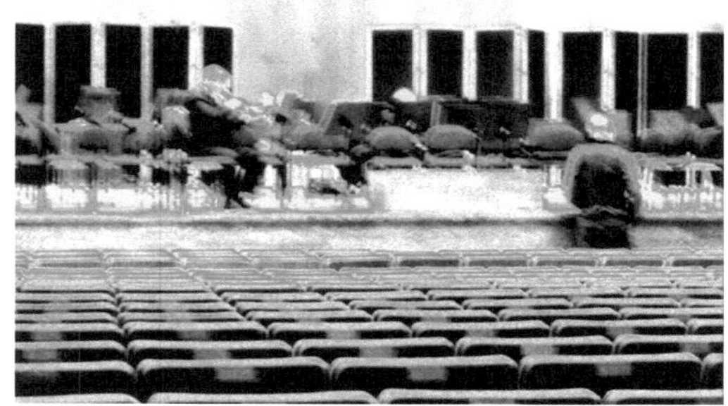

CD cover based on a photo by Ian Vollmer, 2008

Einstürzende Neubauten

Silence Is Sexy

Video documentation of the band's 20th anniversary
Columbiahalle, Berlin, 5:50 min., 2000
Courtesy of Einstürzende Neubauten GbR

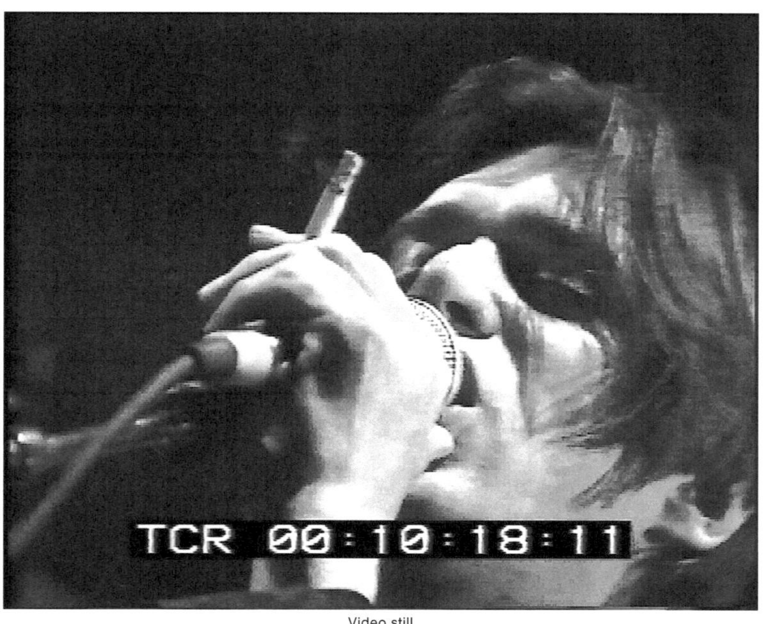

Video still

The Berlin-bred band Einstürzende Neubauten rose to fame in the eighties with a genre of experimental rock that combined elements of noise and industrial music. In 2000, to the surprise of fans and critics alike, they released *Silence Is Sexy*, an album revolving around the notion of silence. Their approach is epitomized by the album's title song, which slowly unfolds from silence. The band are weaving and unraveling minimal musical patterns, opening up a space for sounds which have no place in the mainstream of pop music. Listeners hear people taking a drag from a cigarette, breathing, noises produced in the cavity of the mouth without an actual sound being uttered. This video documents a live performance by the band in Berlin on April 1, 2000. [FSL]

Carl Michael von Hausswolff

4′33″ (81″)

Hand-etched vinyl record, 1996
Courtesy of Carl Michael von Hausswolff

Carl Michael von Hausswolff's work *4′33″ (81″)* is an ironic comment on the critical debates, tributes, and parodies that Cage's paradigmatic piece has inspired. Interpreting *4′33″* as a linear measurement (rather than a measure of time), he transposed this length onto a 7-inch vinyl single. The resulting disc is engraved with an 81-inch-long spiraling groove that encapsulates nothing but silence. From a humorous appropriation of Cage's work, von Hausswolff's unplayable record thus becomes a reflection on the impossibility of recording *4′33″* and, more generally, on the possibility of documenting and archiving music. Cage himself liked the idea that *4′33″* could be interpreted simultaneously as an indication of time and size. The title of von Hausswolff's work alludes to the fact that, in terms of linear measurement, 4′ (minutes or feet) and 33″ (seconds or inches) add up to 81 inches. [FSL]

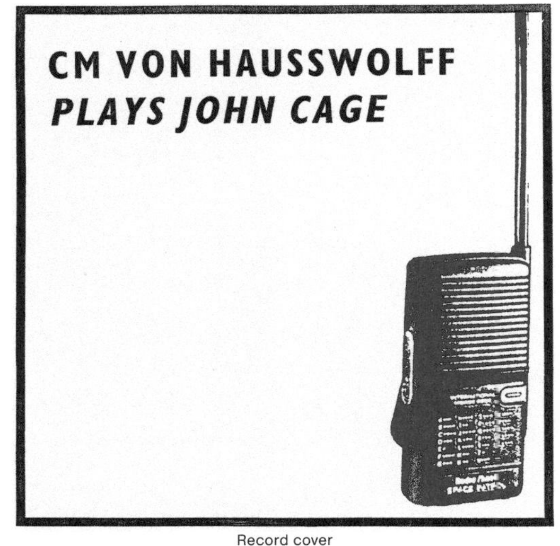

Record cover

Jens Heitjohann

In Begleitung [In the Company of]

4′33″ in twelve versions for one visitor each
Performances in public space, each Sunday 2–6 p.m. (see program schedule)
Courtesy of Jens Heitjohann

The starting point of this project was the question of how I could use Cage's composition *4′33″* to initiate a moment of disruption and confusion in a familiar public environment, which would become a moment of discovery and coming together of strangers. The urban environment of Dortmunder U is marked by a great diversity of contexts ranging from industrial sites and a train station to residential areas developed around churches and monasteries, and the inner city with its busy shopping alleys. Upon entering the building, visitors leave this urban environment behind, but as they walk through the exhibition, it lives on as a memory. Conversely, when leaving the building, it is the exhibition which subsists only in the visitor's mind. The notion of accompaniment at the heart of *In Begleitung* aims to overcome this limitation: the real space of the exhibition, the real space of the city, and their imaginary pendants are intertwined through the practice of walking and enter into a critical dialogue. A performance of *4′33″* provides the framework for an encounter between performers and audience, whose interdependence it puts into focus, and an opportunity for listeners to embark on an encounter with themselves and with the constituents of the situation in which they experience the performance of the piece. I invited twelve inhabitants of Dortmund to create with me a version of *4′33″* in the public space. The choice of venues is determined by their experiences, memories, and everyday life in an environment unknown to me. As companions, they invite members of the audience to follow them and attend a version of *4′33″* performed at a venue they have chosen. [JH]

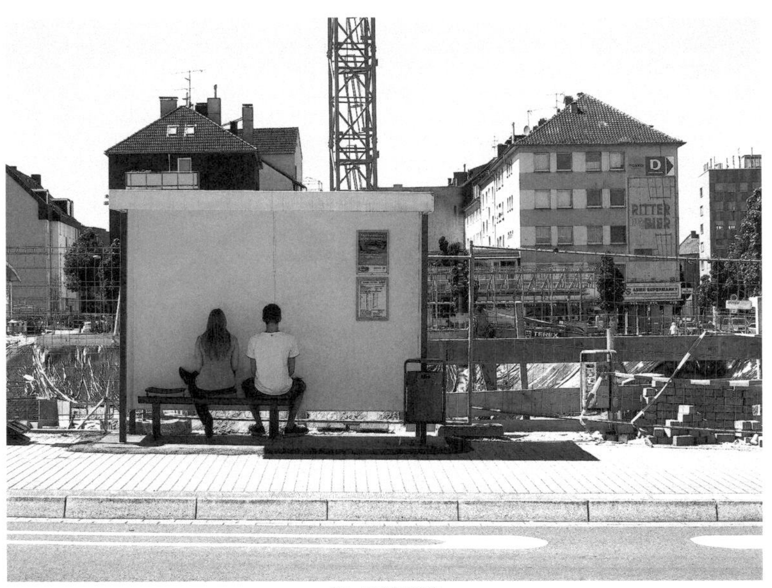
© by HMKV, 2012

Pierre Huyghe

Partition du Silence [Score of Silence]

Set of four prints, music sheets with notations, white frames
16 1/2 × 11 3/4 in. each, 1997
Courtesy of Pierre Huyghe
and Marian Goodman Gallery, New York

With the help of computer software Pierre Huyghe transposed the noises from a CD recording of Cage's *4′33″* into traditional sheet music. These notes may in turn be performed with a conventional musical instrument. From the radical silence of Cage's piece, the artist thus extracts a piece of music that can be played. On the one hand, the sounds occurring during this particular recorded performance are thus precisely facsimilated, while, on the other, Cage's concept is deliberately misinterpreted. The reinterpretation of works from the realms of film, art, music, and literature is characteristic of Huyghe's practice, which revolves around issues of intellectual property. Similarly, the artist's installation *Celebration Park* at Tate Modern in 2006 also referenced *4′33″*: it consisted of a large neon sign proclaiming, "I do not own *4′33″*." [DD]

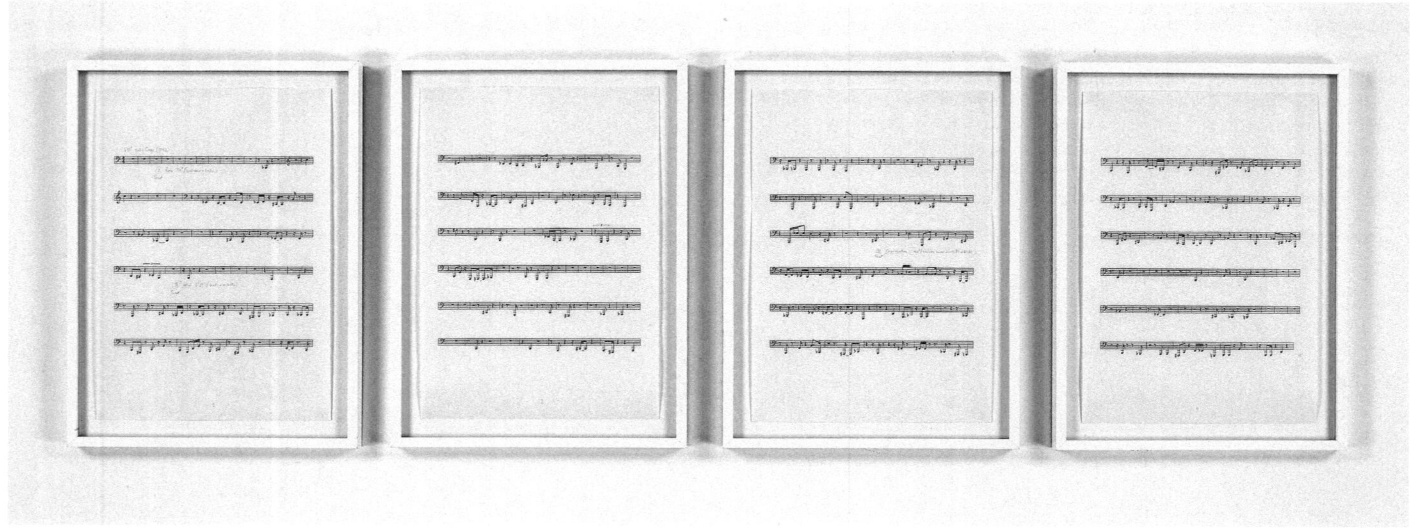

Jonathon Keats

My Cage (Silence for Cellphone)

Conceptual ringtone for mobile phone, digital files
(mp3, Word document, and web links), 4:33 min., 2007
Courtesy of Jonathon Keats
and the Modernism Gallery, San Francisco

Conceptual artist Jonathon Keats has digitally generated a span of silence, four minutes and thirty-three seconds in length, portable enough to be carried on a cellphone. His silent ringtone, freely distributed through special arrangement with Start Mobile, is expected to bring quiet to the lives of millions of cellphone users, as well as those close to them. "When major artists such as 50 Cent ... started making ringtones, I realized that anything was possible in this new medium," says Mr. Keats. "I also knew that another artist, John Cage, had formerly tried, and failed, to create a silent interlude." *My Cage (Silence for Cellphone)* dispenses with performer and piano and auditorium, instead utilizing a continuous stream of silence produced on a computer, and compressed to standard ringtone format. This silence can be heard whenever a call comes through, whether out on the street, at a noisy concert, or in the quiet of home. A remastering of Mr. Cage's classic, *My Cage* is also a remix, according to Mr. Keats. "It introduces serendipity into the equation, delivering performances unpredictably, whenever calls come unexpectedly. You never know." [JK]

Source: press release announcing the project http://rhizome.org/discuss/view/24220/

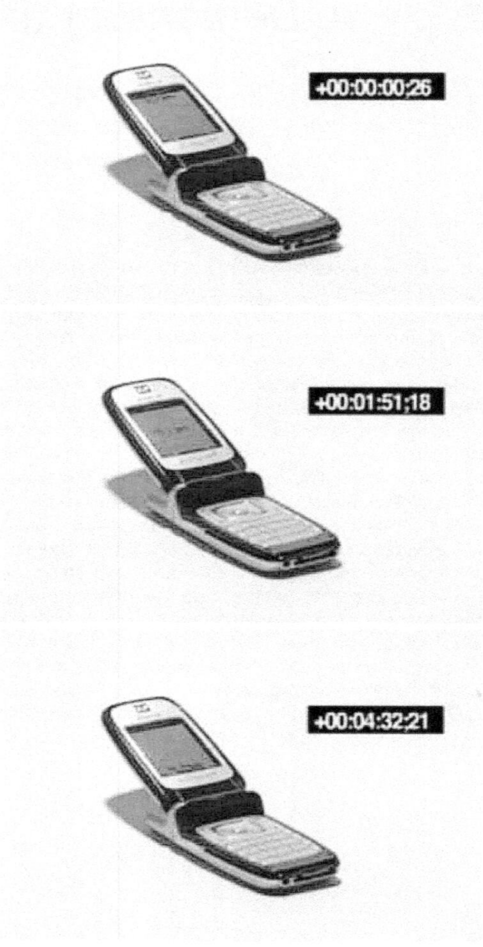

Kollektivnye Deystviya [Collective Actions]

C. A. Jupiter (4.33)

Video documentation of the action, 6–10.33 pm (4 hours 33 minutes), April 13, 1985, Moscow, 12:15 min., 1995
http://conceptualism.letov.ru/KD-ACTIONS-37.htm
Courtesy of Kollektivnye Deystviya

Participants: A. Monastyrski, S. Romashko, S. Letov, S. Hänsgen, G. Kizewalter, I. Yurna, M. K., V. Sorokin
Spectators: V. Sorokin, Yu. Leiderman, I. Bakshtein, M. Konstantinova, I. Nakhova, I. Aleinikov, N. Abalakova, A. Zhigalov, G. Witte

This action took place in a flat in Moscow. Besides the usual furniture, the flat contained six paintings with paralinguistic signs:
1 "Time"– a man looking at a wristwatch
2 "Close your ears"– a man with fingers stuck into his ears
3 "Fifty-fifty"– a one-eyed man
4 "Yes"– a man with bared teeth;
5 "No"– a man with a black hole instead of mouth
6 "No"– a man with his tongue hanging out
The action, which was lit only by torches and a table lamp, consisted of minimalist musical improvisations on various instruments and playing back recordings of these improvisations. Further recordings of trains and a barrel rolling down a street, which Andrey Monastyrski had made near Yauza train station, were also played back. A TV set sitting on a piano was used as a source of light, sound, and images. Occasionally, Monastyrski put on headphones connected to the TV and repeated the Soviet TV evening news. [IA]

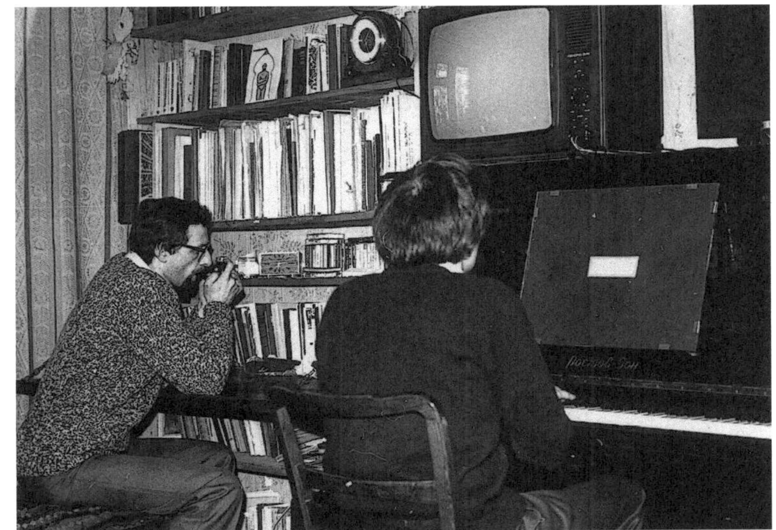
Photo of the action

Christoph Korn

deletion studies

Web-based digital work, 2010
http://www.christophkorn.de/deletion_studie/deletion_studies.html

Christoph Korn's *deletion studies* provides visitors with a visual and audible experience of sounds which are made to disappear by means of a random process of deletion. Sound structures are displayed as audio waves on a computer screen. As more and more parts of these structures are deleted, the screen gradually turns blank, while the sound progressively evolves towards complete silence. The deletion process is computer-generated and based on chance. The sounds to be deleted have been specifically composed and selected for this work. Korn's experimental set-up allows him to analyze how sounds react visually and acoustically to the process of their dissolution. [FSL, CK]

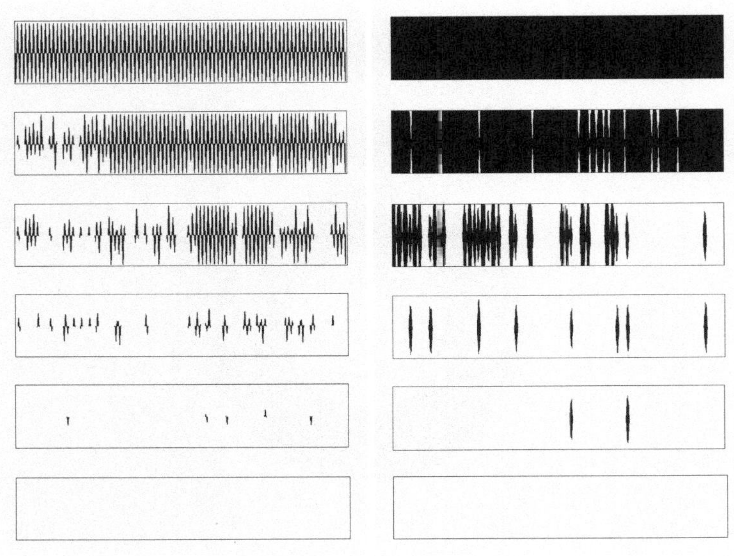
Two examples of a deletion process

Brandon LaBelle

Lecture on Nothing

Audio installation, 54:00 min., 2011
Courtesy of Brandon LaBelle

Brandon LaBelle is an artist, writer, and theorist working with the human voice, sound, and performance. *Lecture on Nothing*, his work in the exhibition *Sounds Like Silence*, takes the shape of a sound installation. Visitors hear the voice of a deaf person (David Kurs) reading out Cage's *Lecture on Nothing* from 1950. In direct reference to the composer's notion of stillness as a means to raise the listener's alertness and awareness of non-musical sounds, LaBelle asks what silence means for people who cannot hear any sounds at all. Simultaneously, his experimental set-up investigates the relationships between performers and their audiences. [FSL]

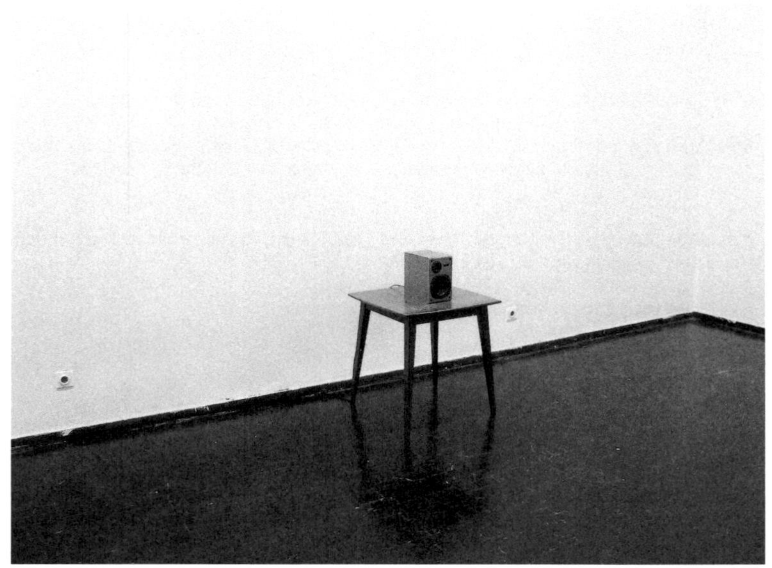

Installation shown at *Dissecting the Ear*, ŠKUC Gallery, Ljubljana, 2009

Christian Marclay

Sound of Silence

Photographys, 12×12 in., 1988
Courtesy of Christian Marclay and Paula Cooper Gallery, NYC

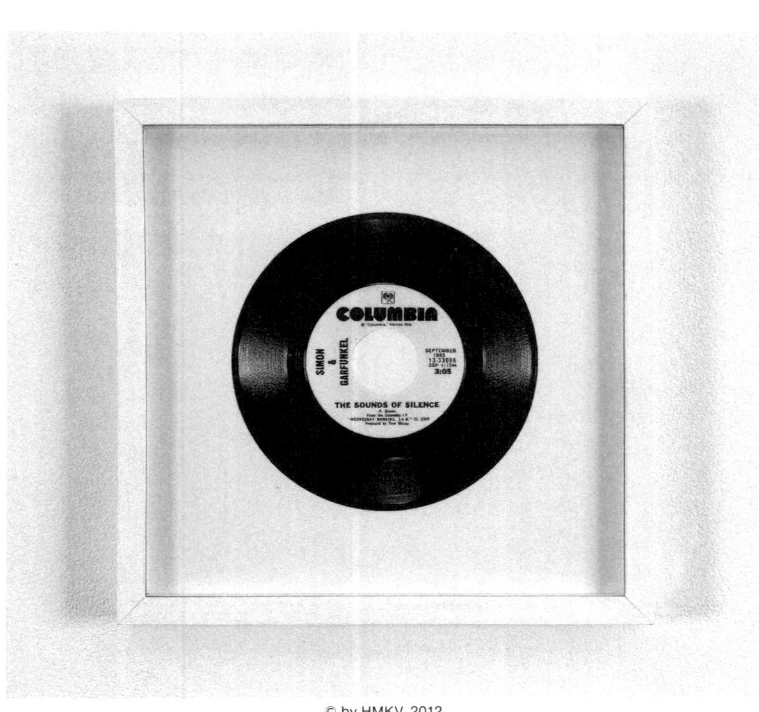

Christian Marclay interrogates the relationship between image and sound in his artistic practice, which ranges from experimental music, photography, collage, and sculpture to video installations. He presents music as an object rendered visible by the technology of the record. The simple photograph *The Sound of Silence* on the cover of Simon and Garfunkel's single of the same name is thus enough to conjure up the idea of this well known duet in the viewer's mind. Marclay refers to the possible existence of an "auditive memory" in humans, while at the same time using photography in its traditional function of representing the immaterial and ephemeral and capturing it in a moment. The title refers not only to the cover shown, but also to the unavoidable "silence" of visual media. [EF]

Source: *See This Sound. Versprechungen von Bild und Ton / See This Sound. Promises in Sound and Vision*, Lentos Kunstmuseum Linz, eds. Cosima Rainer, Stella Rollig, Dieter Daniels, Manuela Ammer (Cologne: Verlag Walther König, 2009), p. 127

Ciprian Mureşan

4′33″

HD Video, 4:33 min., 2008
Courtesy of Ciprian Mureşan and the Andreiana Mihail Gallery, Bucharest

4′33″, 2008, which takes its title and dimensions from John Cage's original 1952 composition, is an alternative view of postindustrialism. Like Cage's original piece, the soundscape of Mureşan's *4′33″* is governed by an eerie stillness, the frozen machines and echo of the departed work force are a somber memorial to a former epoch of productivity. Mureşan's dispute is with a failed utopianism and subsequent social decay that leaves a factory in this languid state—neither communism nor subsequent privatization could prevent this erosion...

It is often the unknown or the unseen that forms the dialogue within Mureşan's art; meanings lie beneath metaphor and insinuation, yet once uncovered there is a frankness that disconcerts the viewer and demands reflection. Mureşan's view is not linear, his inquisition of life is complex and there are no direct answers, instead an unsettling question mark lies over society. [Wilkinson Gallery, press release]

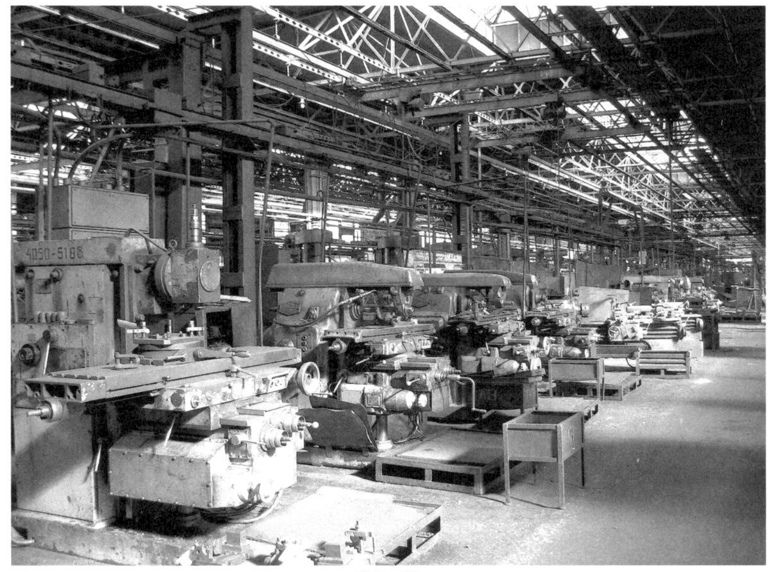

Video still

Bruce Nauman

Mapping the Studio I—All Action Edit (Fat Chance John Cage)

7-channel video installation
unique copy, between 32:00 min. and 84:00 min., 2001
Courtesy of the Friedrich Christian Flick Collection im Hamburger Bahnhof

This installation, consisting of seven large-scale video projections, shows images of the artist's studio in New Mexico, recorded with an infrared camera for one hour every night over several months. The studio was filmed from seven different angles in Nauman's absence. Besides the objects standing or lying about in the studio, the main protagonists are the artist's cat and some mice and moths. Occasionally one hears faint noises or the nightly sounds of the rural surroundings: trees rustling in the wind, a dog barking, heavy rain falling, a train passing by at a distance. The infrared recordings from the camera, which was switched on when the artist left the studio, not only allow him to monitor what happened in his absence, but also visualize what the human eye cannot see in the darkness ... In *Mapping the Studio*, Nauman—like Duchamp with his readymades and Cage with his compositions *4′33″* and *0′00″*—straddles the boundaries of art and non-art. His work investigates the minimal difference between that which has always been present and an art that highlights everyday acoustic or visual events, whether in the artist's studio, the concert hall, or the street. [GK]

Excerpt from: Gabriele Knapstein: "So etwas wie einen leeren Raum oder eine leere Zeit gibt es nicht, es gibt immer etwas zu sehen, etwas zu hören. Bruce Nauman und John Cage," in: *Fast nichts. Minimalistische Werke aus der Friedrich Christian Flick Collection im Hamburger Bahnhof*, eds. Eugen Blume, Gabriele Knapstein, Catherine Nichols, exh. cat. Nationalgalerie im Hamburger Bahnhof, Berlin and Cologne (SMB-DuMont 2005), pp. 48–54.

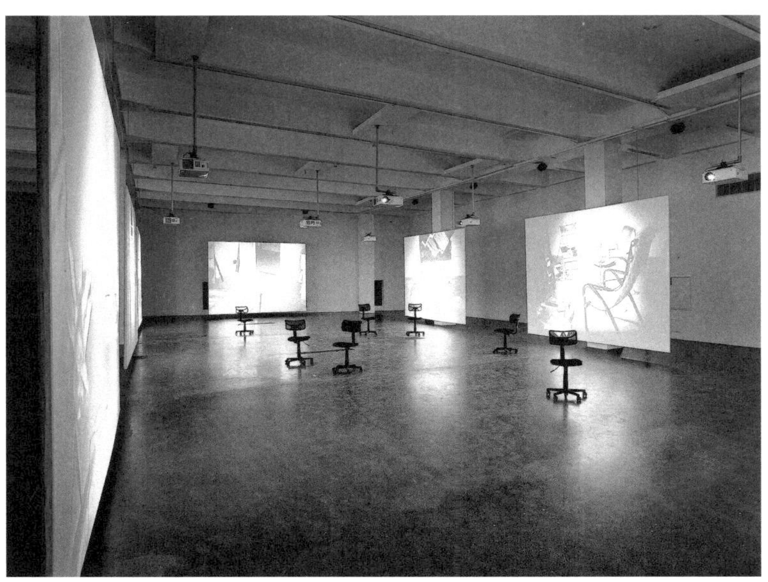

© by Hannes Woidich, HMKV, 2012

Max Neuhaus

Silent Alarm Clock

Prototype, 1979
Courtesy of The Estate of Max Neuhaus

Neuhaus's so-called *Moment* works, such as the *Time Piece Graz* (2003–present) and *Time Piece Beacon* (2005–present) revolve not around presence but rather around absence ... Neuhaus's *Moment* works initially took the form of an unusual consumer product (never put into production): a silent alarm clock he designed in 1979. As Neuhaus described it, the device measured "two by sixteen by one inches with a time display and control buttons on the left side of the larger surface and a round screen covering a small speaker on the far right." Before the time set to awake its listener, the alarm would begin to emit a continuous tone, carefully pitched at the upper limit of the sleeper's range of hearing, a frequency that, Neuhaus explained, "has a very special character. It is there but at the same time almost not there—more of a presence than a sound." Starting at an almost imperceptibly low level, the tone would gradually increase in volume until, at the appointed time, it would suddenly shut off, the abrupt cessation of acoustic stimulus being what would induce wakefulness. Neuhaus's seemingly paradoxical device brings to mind Walter Benjamin's description of "an alarm clock that in each minute rings for sixty seconds." Invoked at the end of his essay on Surrealism, Benjamin's image illustrated the revolutionary face of the new human subject, in whom media technologies thoroughly interpenetrated and enervated the body. Muzak's affective management, which began five years after the publication of Benjamin's essay, is only one, and not the most nefarious, technological attempt to regulate the body on a micropolitical register. Neuhaus's alarm clock, however, reverses the effect of such enervation: the acoustic stimulus is noticed, jolting the sleeper awake, only when it abruptly ceases.

Neuhaus's *Moment* works instigate the same process on a much larger scale, addressing a collective audience within a public realm. Beginning at a nearly inaudible volume, which increases progressively but so slowly as to avoid conscious notice, a tone is suddenly removed, leaving what the artist described as an "aural afterimage ... superimposed on the sounds of the environment—a spontaneous aural memory or reconstruction perhaps, subtle and transparent, engendered by the sound's disappearance." Felt by the body more than perceived by the mind, the sound, which disappears even though one did not realize it was there (much as, one imagines, how Cage's *Silent Prayer* might have impacted a restaurant or shopping mall), is doubly imperceptible. [BJ]

Excerpt from: Branden W. Joseph, "An Implication of an Implication," in: *Max Neuhaus, Times Square, Time Piece Beacon*. Lynne Cooke and Karen Kelley, with Barbara Schröder (New York: Dia Art Foundation, 2009), pp. 59–81.

Nam June Paik

A Tribute to John Cage

Video, 62:45 min., 1973
Courtesy of Electronic Arts Intermix, NYC

Host: Russell Connor
Participants: John Cage, Alvin Lucier, Marianne Amacher, Richard Teitelbaum, Pulsa, Charlotte Moorman, David Behrman, David Tudor
Excerpts from works by Cathy Berberian, Jud Yalkut, Francis Lee, David Rosenboom, Jackie Cassen, Stan VanDerBeek, Alfons Schilling
Producer: New Television Workshop and TV Lab at WNET/Thirteen.

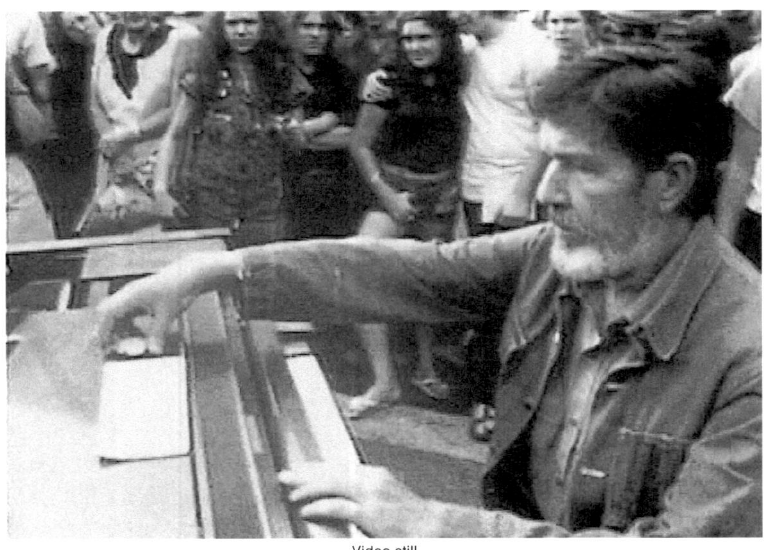

Video still

This experimental TV feature was filmed on the occasion of John Cage's sixtieth birthday in 1972. As one of the main protagonists, the composer is seen performing two versions of *4′33″* himself. The first one is a "classic" interpretation on the piano, but rather than a concert hall, the venue is Harvard Square, a busy crossing in Cambridge, Massachusetts (which the voice-over terms "the Times Square of the American brain"). The second performance is set in Manhattan: "The entire island is, so to speak, a concert hall," as Cage points out in the film. This time it has four instead of the original three movements. With the help of the I Ching, Cage has designated four spots on a map of New York for each of the four movements of *4′33″*. The first is situated in Harlem, the second between 203rd and 204th Street on the Hudson River, the third on Times Square and the fourth on Mitchell Place at Beekman. Each of these places is recorded on video for the duration of the corresponding movement, and it isn't until the four sequences have been assembled and broadcast that the full "silent piece" is achieved. Cage here departs from the "traditional" live performance with a musical instrument by creating a new, medium-specific version of his "silent piece" that is visible and audible only for the TV audience. In doing so, he also redefines the number and length of the movements. The two versions of *4′33″* in this film have been shortened and therefore actually fail to reach four minutes and thirty-three seconds. It also contains a series of entertaining interludes, such as Nam June Paik taking away Cage's microphone on a busy street in Harlem and questioning passers-by on music and ambient noise, with Cage visibly struggling to maintain his composure (this sequence is absent from the 1976 re-edit, which was cut down to twenty-nine minutes). A further reference to *4′33″* are the images of the 1969 Woodstock Festival, since *4′33″* premiered in the same city in 1952. [DD]

→ p. 176 ff

People Like Us (Vicki Bennett)

Cage Silenced

Audio work, 4:33 min., 2004
Courtesy of Vicki Bennett

Vicki Bennett aka People Like Us is a master of appropriation and live-scratching of film and video imagery. For this audio work the artist used an interview with John Cage conducted by the US art critic Richard Kostelanetz in 1978. Among other things, Cage speaks about the techniques he employed in *Writing through Finnegans Wake* (1977) and *Writing for the Second Time through Finnegans Wake* (1977). At the time of the interview Kostelanetz was suffering from severe bronchitis, which explains why he could merely whisper his questions to "Mr Silence," as Bennett points out: "I decided that, since Richard couldn't 'talk,' I would make it so that John Cage didn't say anything either ... So I 'language-removed' John except for guttural sounds, breaths, and so on. As a result Richard Kostelanetz sounds like a lunatic interrogating a bound and gagged John Cage. For 4 minutes and 33 seconds, naturally."* [IA]

*Vicki Bennett in Nicolas Collins, *A Call for Silence* (2004), CD booklet

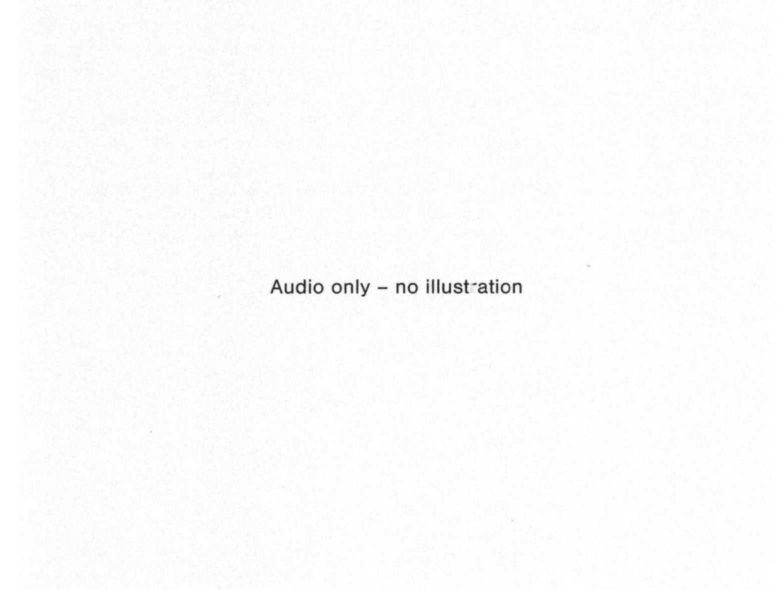

People Like Us (Vicki Bennett)

4′33″: The Movie

Video, 4:33 min., 2011
Courtesy of Vicki Bennett

In this video Vicki Bennett aka People Like Us works with the 1948 Hollywood movie *Key Largo*, directed by John Huston, with Humphrey Bogart, Lauren Bacall, and Edward G. Robinson in the main roles. A disillusioned WWII veteran visits the wife and the father of a soldier from his unit who was killed in combat. The young widow and her father-in-law are running a hotel in Key Largo, Florida, where gangster boss Johnny Rocco has taken a room. As a storm approaches, Rocco and the other guests of the hotel clash. Bennett's video uses only the "speechless" moments during the hurricane (thus heightening the "suspense"), when the cocky gangster played by Robinson reveals himself as a coward. The video quotes Cage: "If something is boring after two minutes, try it for four." [IA]

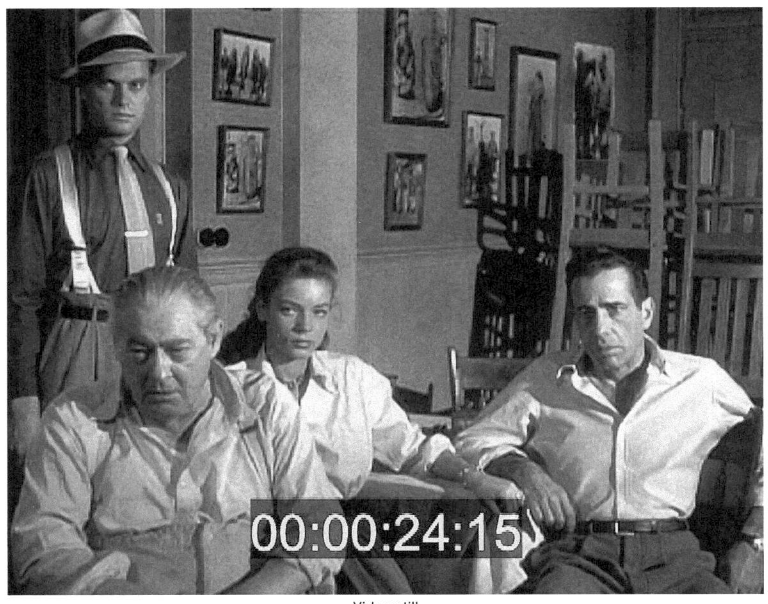

Video still

Hein-Godehart Petschulat

Still

Video, silent news anchor (Ulrich Wickert), 5:23 min., 2004
Courtesy of Hein-Godehart Petschulat

In Hein-Godehart Petschulat's video *Still*, the German anchorman Ulrich Wickert greets viewers from the studio of his late-night news show *Tagesthemen* and then lapses into a long silence. For the purpose of this work, the artist was able to convince the prominent TV presenter to stand still in front of the camera for five minutes. The absence of reports or comments makes for a confusing viewing experience, while opening up a space for individual interpretation. By deliberately foregoing the actual audiovisual broadcasting of news items, Petschulat breaks with viewing conventions and creates a unique TV experiment. The uncanny contrast between the familiar setting of the *Tagesthemen* studio and the speaker's uneasy silence and seeming attempts to make eye contact with viewers heightens their awareness of the flood of images, sounds, and information they must handle every day. [FSL, HGP]

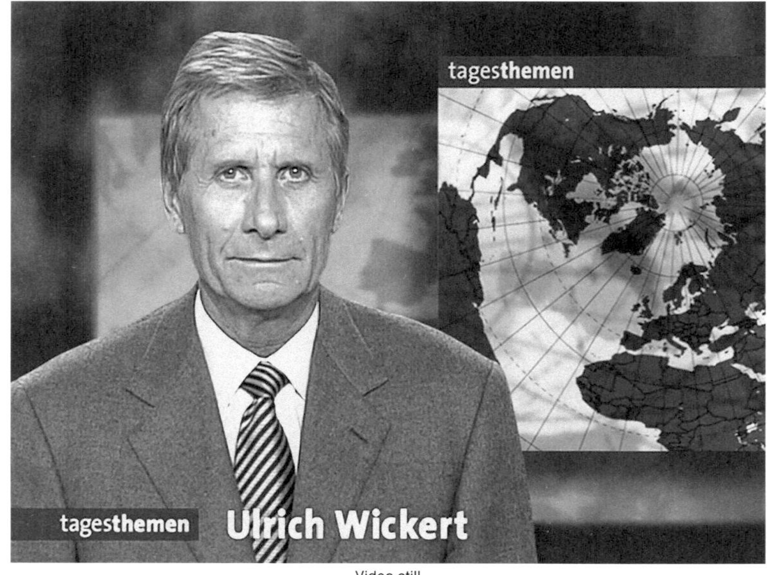

Video still

Matt Rogalsky

Two Minutes Fifty Seconds Silence (for the USA)

Audio work, 2:50 min., 2003
Courtesy of Matt Rogalsky

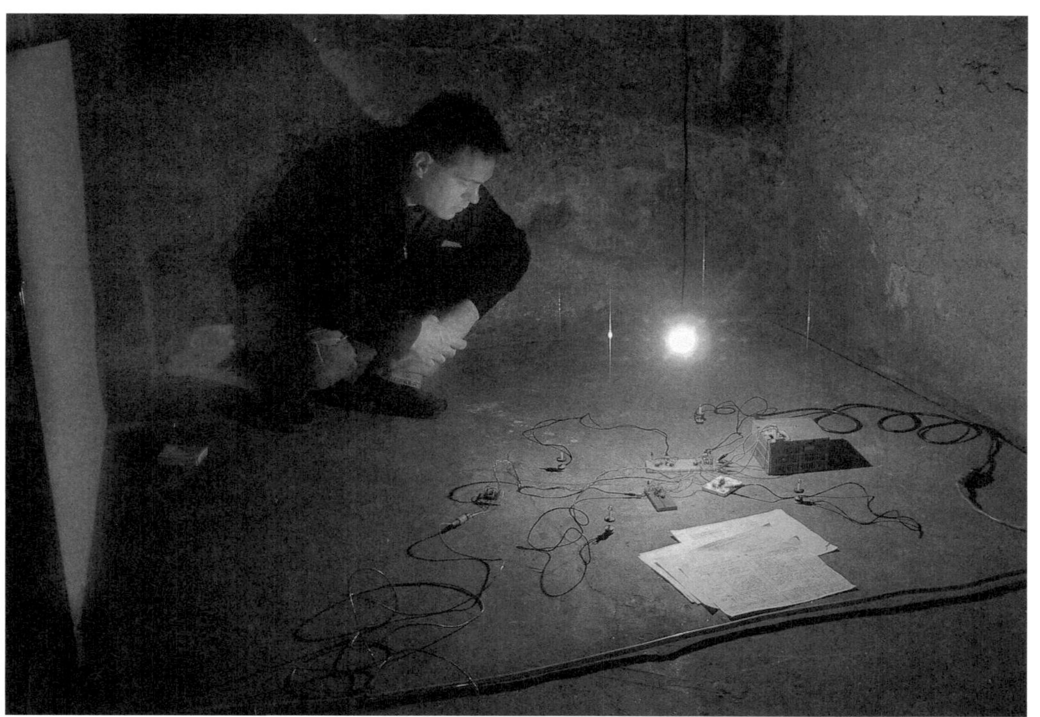

Matt Rogalsky, *When he was in high school in Texas, Eric Ryan Mims used a similar arrangement to detect underground nuclear tests in Nevada*, 2009

A distillation of George W. Bush's address to the world on March 17, 2003, in which he gave Saddam Hussein forty-eight hours to get out of town. Using my own software (written in the SuperCollider programming language), I removed his voice from the 13+ minute speech, leaving only his "silences." The thumping sounds you hear, which a number of people have taken to be a reference to "drums of war," are the reverberations of Bush's voice inside the White House. This piece was first published for free distribution on the web in March 2003 at www.mrogalsky.net and then more widely distributed as part of *Protest Records Vol. 2*, at www.protest-records.com and was subsequently included in the May 2003 illegal art compilation at www.detritus.net. *Maintain Radio Silence*, an article by myself detailing explorations of "silences" distilled in similar ways from radio broadcasts and improvising musicians was published in the journal *Digital Creativity*, Vol. 14 No. 2 (2003). [MR]

Source: Nicolas Collins, *A Call for Silence* (2004), CD booklet

Matthieu Saladin

4′33″ / 0′00″

Audio work, 4:33 min., 2008
maximum amplification of the first release (Cramps, 1974) of *4′33″* by John Cage, performed by Gianni-Emilio Simonetti
Booklet 5 7/8 × 4 1/8 in., Mini CD, Editions Provisoires
Courtesy of Matthieu Saladin

The first published recording of Cage's *4′33″* is by Gianni-Emilio Simonetti and appeared on the Cramps label in 1974. Matthieu Saladin subjects this recording to a similar procedure to that which Cage, in his piece *0′00″ (4′33″ No. 2)* from 1962, proposes applying to everyday sounds: he amplifies the sounds as much as possible. Besides some sporadic, obscure background noises, the soundscape is dominated by the rising, storm-like white noise of the vinyl disc. Saladin thus creates a contemporary digital tribute which transforms *4′33″* itself into *0′00″*. The cover of the artist's mini CD reprises the design of the Edition Peters title page of Cage's scores for *4′33″* and *0′00″*. The minimalist readymade concept was also applied to the pricing, with the disc retailing at □ 4.33. [DD]

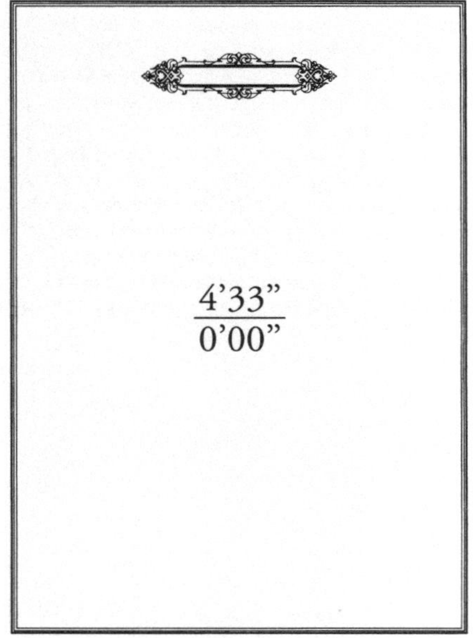

Petri Söderström-Kelley

4 Minutes and 33 Seconds of Uniqueness

Online game, 2009
Courtesy of Kloonigames

In *4 Minutes and 33 Seconds of Uniqueness*, the Finnish computer scientist and game designer Petri Söderström-Kelley asks what the minimum requirements are for creating a computer game from source code. When his game program is executed, it connects itself to a server that checks whether other gamers around the world have executed the game at the same time. If the server recognizes other players, it automatically terminates all running *Uniqueness* programs. Unlike popular multiplayer online games, which are based on the principle of interaction, *4 Minutes and 33 Seconds of Uniqueness* can only be played if the gamer is the sole user on earth running the program. Söderström-Kelley's game was developed as a contribution to a competition launched by the games conference Nordic Game Jam 2009, which ran under the motto, "As long as we have each other, we'll never run out of problems." *4 Minutes and 33 Seconds of Uniqueness* won the 2010 IGF Award for Innovation. [FSL]

Still from online game

Mladen Stilinović

Oduzimanje Nula (Subtracting Zeroes)

Acrylic on panel, 14 pieces
7×5 in., 1993
Courtesy of Mladen Stilinović

Mladen Stilinović (b. 1947) has been working as an artist since the late sixties. From 1975 to 1978 he was a member of Grupa Šestorice Autora (Group of Six Authors), which played a key role in the development of Conceptual Art in Croatia and Yugoslavia. Stilinović often uses the color white and the number zero as symbols of "death." The work shown in this exhibition—literally a zero-sum game—consists of fourteen pages of mathematical operations involving the number zero. In this calculation, more and more zeroes are made to disappear by subtraction until only the division line remains, which in turn vanishes, leaving a blank page. *Subtracting Zeroes* bears a striking resemblance to both Cage's scores of the "silent piece"—specifically *0'00" (4'33" No. 2)*—and the camera and lighting directions for his only film, *One*[11]. Stilinović's "score" should also be read as an ironic or laconic comment on the (violent) political and economic upheaval in (South-)East European countries in the early nineties. [IA]

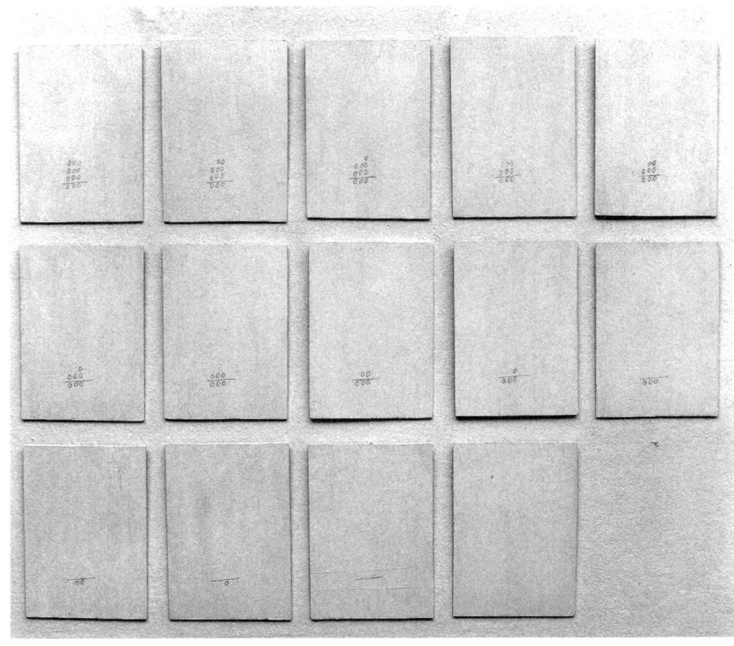

Ultra-red

An Archive of Silence

MP3 album available for free download, Creative Commons Lic.
49:08 min., 2006
Courtesy of Public Record (www.publicrec.org)

"In the worlds of sound art and modern electronic music, Ultra-red pursue a fragile but dynamic exchange between art and political organizing. Founded in 1994 by two AIDS activists, Ultra-red have over the years expanded to include artists, researchers and organisers from different social movements including the struggles of migration, anti-racism, participatory community development, and the politics of HIV/AIDS. Collectively, the group have produced radio broadcasts, performances, recordings, installations, texts and public space actions (ps/o). Exploring acoustic space as enunciative of social relations, Ultra-red take up the acoustic mapping of contested spaces and histories utilising sound-based research (termed Militant Sound Investigations) that directly engage the organizing and analyses of political struggles."
(Ultra-red, mission statement)[1]

1 http://www.ultrared.org/mission.html

"*An Archive of Silence* kicks off with a radical reworking of Mr. Finger's 1986 house track, 'Can You Feel It?' Framed in the context of the AIDS crisis and its impact on gay and African American communities, Ultra-red's reconstruction of the dance classic is bound to generate excitement among MP3 jocks on its 20-year anniversary. For each track on *An Archive of Silence*, Ultra-red began with a different conceptual proposition: sounds from 15-year old AIDS activist videos, site-recordings of places where Rhine was arrested with ACT UP (AIDS Coalition to Unleash Power) in the early 90s, Ultra-red member (and Sony Mao alumni) Eddie Peel practicing the ACT UP manifesto at sites around Los Angeles, a recording of protestors at the 2000 Democratic National Convention chanting 'Silence Equals Death,' and audio collages from Ultra-red's various AIDS-related performances including the SILENT|LISTEN project. The album concludes with a mash-up of a half-dozen recordings of John Cage's famous silent piece, 'Four Minutes and Thirty-Three Seconds.' At the end of *An Archive of Silence*, we hear Cage's voice announce: 'This is the kind of music anybody can make. All you have to do is listen.' For Ultra-red, the same can be said of an AIDS activism for our times."
(Ultra-red, excerpt from press release,[2] September 1, 2006)

2 www.publicrec.org/archive/2-04/2-04-002/2-04-002PR.DOC

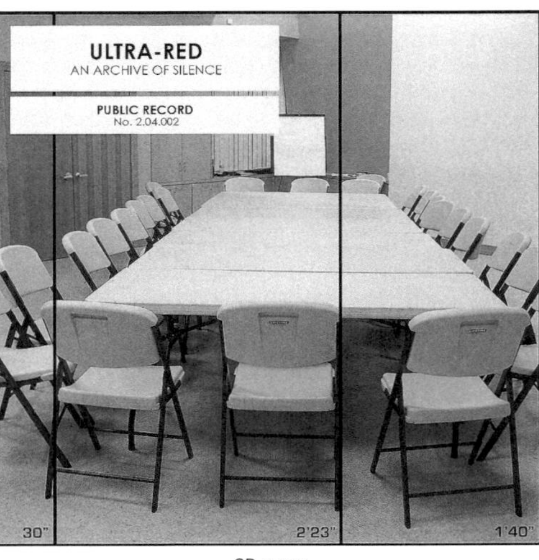

CD cover

Stephen Vitiello

World Trade Center Recordings: Winds After Hurricane Floyd

Audio installation with printed photographs
8:37 min., 1999
Courtesy of Stephen Vitiello and American Contemporary, NYC

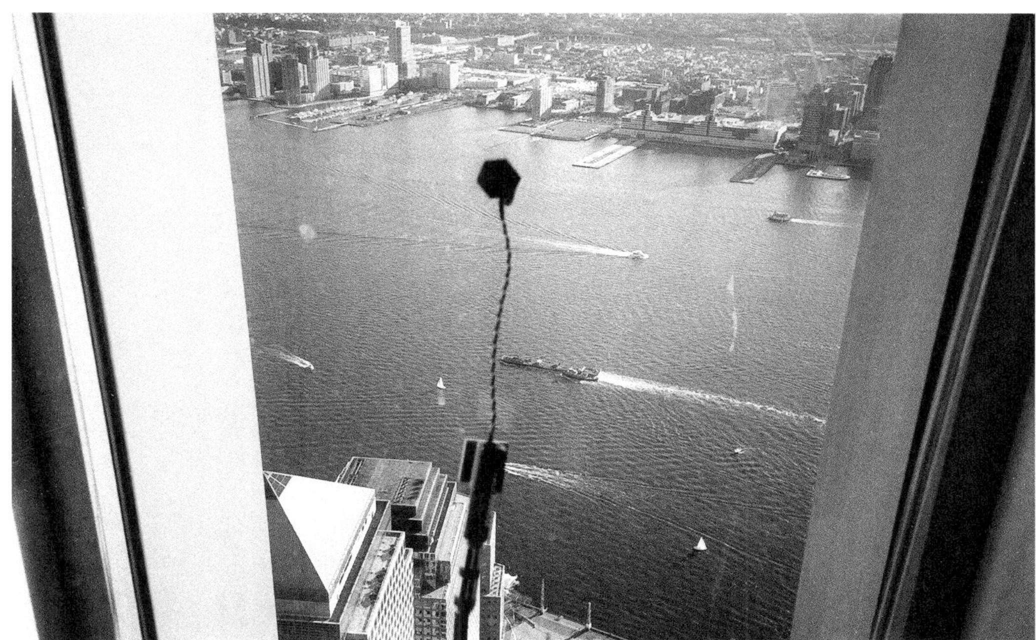

In 1999 the US sound artist Stephen Vitiello completed a six-month residency on the ninety-first floor of One World Trade Center in New York. The first thing that caught his attention was that the windows could not be opened, which explained why all the outside noise was drowned out by the building's air-conditioning system. Vitiello decided to install contact microphones on the safety-glass windows, so as to make audible the vibrations caused by exterior sounds such as planes taking off, church bells, the wind, police sirens, etc. The recording in this exhibition was made in September 1999, when Hurricane Floyd swept over the east coast of the USA with winds of up to 150 miles per hour and wreaked havoc. As though with a stethoscope Vitiello listened to the vibrations of the 110-storey building as it swayed in the hurricane, creaking like a sailing boat and moaning like a wounded animal. [IA]

Gillian Wearing

Sixty Minutes of Silence

Color video projection with sound
60:00 min., 1996
Courtesy of Gillian Wearing and Maureen Paley Gallery, London

"Watching Gillian Wearing's *Sixty Minutes of Silence* (1996) is something of an endurance test. The video shows a group of about thirty police officers seated on stepped benches, as though they're posing for a school photo. As Wearing's title suggests, they have been instructed to sit still and seal their lips for the duration of the shoot. As time wears on, some of them wrinkle their noses or scratch their bums, lost in their own thoughts. You find yourself wondering what's on their minds, and it's not long before you're spinning stories around their fidgety fingers. When sixty minutes have elapsed, one of the officers lets out a scream of anger and relief."[3] *Sixty Minutes of Silence* perpetuates the tradition of *tableaux vivants* introduced at the end of the eighteenth century, which consists of living persons restaging famous paintings or sculptures. Wearing's "living image," however, does not serve to achieve the completion of a movement (as was, historically, the function of tableaux vivants), but is itself an —initially imaginary—moving action, which eventually comes to completion at the end of the sixty minutes. [IA]

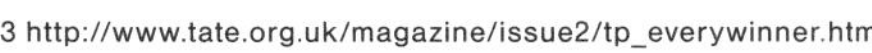

3 http://www.tate.org.uk/magazine/issue2/tp_everywinner.htm

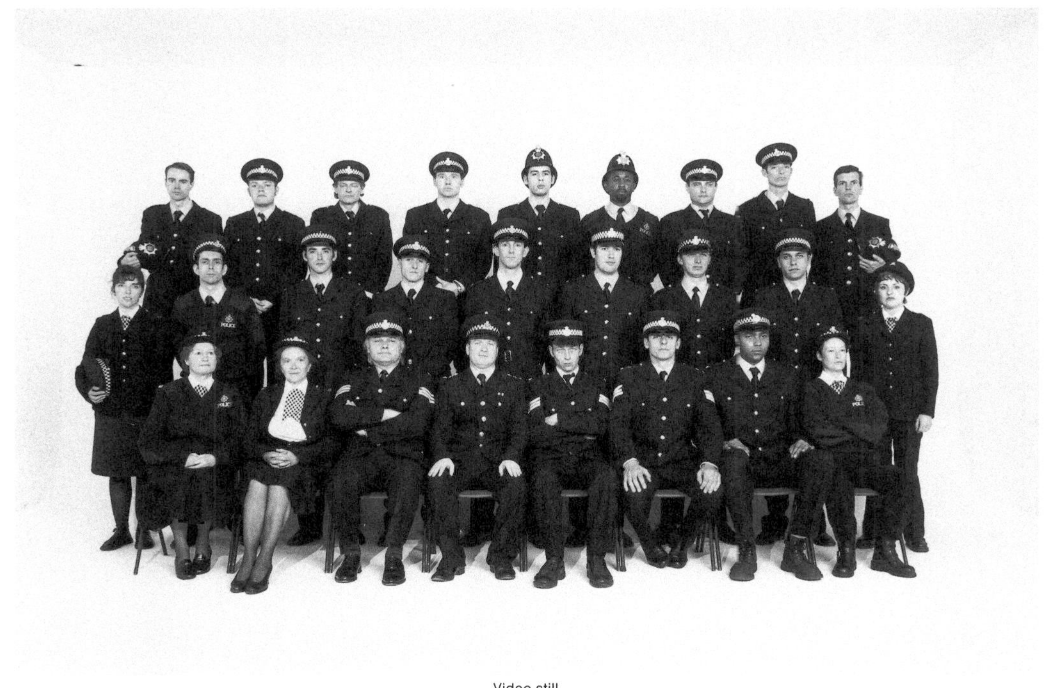

Video still

Dick Whyte

John Cage – 4′33″ (May ’68 Comeback Special)

Video, 5:05 min., 2010
Courtesy of Dick Whyte

The starting point of this video work by Dick Whyte is the unfaltering popularity of Cage's seminal piece. *John Cage – 4′33″ (May ’68 Comeback Special)* assembles recordings of sixty-eight different interpretations of *4′33″* found on YouTube. The videos, by amateur and professional musicians, have been edited into one fast, uncommented sequence. Their part-earnest, part-ironic silence is set off against banal images of everyday life (a sports arena, a busy crossing, an empty train wagon), which implicitly refer to the ambient noises to which Cage wanted to draw our attention when he said that everything was music. The soundtrack of these various recordings of *4′33″*, it appears, is never really silent, but full of background noises: traffic, music, an audience laughing, etc. The countless possibilities of appropriating it in various contexts evidence the timelessness and universality of *4′33″* as an attempt to stem the tide of images and sounds unleashed by the Internet – a gesture of resistance which is not confined to the theoretical realms of art and the avant-garde. [FSL]

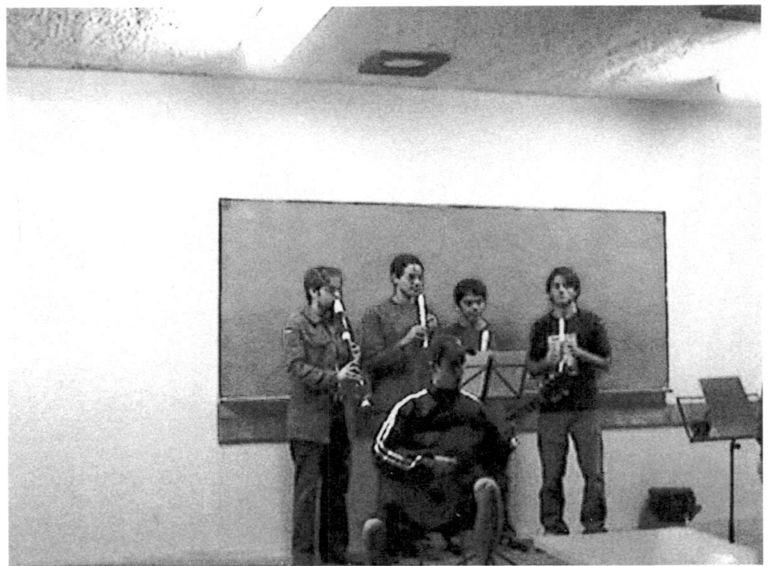

Video still

Appendix

Biographical Notes /
Contributors *Sounds Like Silence*

Colophon

Allen, Dave

*1963 Glasgow, Scotland
media artist
lives and works in Stockholm, Sweden

Arns, Inke

*1968 Bonn, Germany
artistic director of Hartware MedienKunstVerein (HMKV)
and freelance curator and author
lives and works in Dortmund and Berlin, Germany

Böll, Heinrich

*1917 Cologne, Germany,
†1985 Kreuznau-Langenbroich, Germany
writer and Nobel Prize laureate for Literature

Bormann, Hans Friedrich

Professor at the Institute for Theatre and Media
at the University Erlangen, Germany
lives and works in Erlangen, Germany

Brand, Jens

*1968 Dortmund, Germany
media artist
lives and works in Berlin, Germany

Cage Against the Machine

founded in 2009 in London, UK
artist collective

Cage, John

*1912 Los Angeles, USA, †1992 New York City, USA
composer, music theorist, writer, and artist

Conrads, Martin

*1969 Cologne, Germany
author and media artist
lives and works in Berlin, Germany

Creed, Martin

*1968 Wakefield, UK
conceptual artist
lives and works in London, UK

Cunningham, Merce

*1919 Centralia, USA, †2009 New York City, USA
dancer and choreographer

Daniels, Dieter

*1957 Bonn, Germany
Professor of Art History and Media Theory at the Leipzig
Academy of Visual Arts (HGB), author and exhibition curator
lives and works in Leipzig and Berlin, Germany

Davis, Paul

*1977 St Louis, USA
media artist
lives and works in London, UK

de Boer, Manon

*1966 Kodaicanal, India,
media artist
lives and works in Brussels, Belgium,
and Amsterdam, Netherlands

Debord, Guy

*1931 Paris, France, †1994 Bellevue-la-Montagne, France
artist and theoretician,
founder of the Situationist International

DeLaurenti, Christopher

*1967 Seattle, USA
media artist
lives and works in Seattle, USA

Einstürzende Neubauten

founded in 1981 in Berlin, Germany
cult band

Fetterman, William

author of *John Cage's Theatre Pieces: Notations and Performances*
Harwood Academic Publishers, 1996

Gann, Kyle

*1955 in Dallas, USA
composer, new-music critic and musicologist,
lives and works in New York City, USA

Heitjohann, Jens

*1977 Münster (Westphalia), Germany
conceptual artist
lives and works in Leipzig, Germany

Huyghe, Pierre

*1962 Paris, France
media artist
lives and works in Paris, France, and New York City, USA

Joseph, Branden W.

Frank Gallipoli Professor
of Modern and Contemporary Art at Columbia University
lives and works in New York City, USA

Kahn, Douglas

Professor of Media and Innovation at the University of New South Wales, Australia

Katz, Jonathan David

activist, art historian, educator and writer
lives and works in New York, USA

Keats, Jonathon

*1971 New York City, USA
conceptual artist
lives and works in San Francisco, USA,
and Northern Italy

Klein, Yves

*1928 Nice, France, †1962 Paris, France
painter, sculptor, and performance artist

Kollektivnye Deystviya [Collective Actions]

founded in 1976 in Moscow, former USSR
artist collective

Korn, Christoph

*1965 Frankfurt am Main, Germany
media artist
lives and works in Düsseldorf, Germany

Kotz, Liz

critic and art historian
lives and works in Los Angeles, USA

Kubota, Shigeko

*1937 Niigata, Japan
conceptual artist
lives and works in New York City, USA

LaBelle, Brandon

*1969 Memphis, USA
media artist
lives and works in Berlin, Germany

Lohner, Henning

*1961 Bremen, Germany
composer, film maker, media artist,
lives and works in Los Angeles, USA,
and Berlin, Germany

Marclay, Christian

*1955 San Rafael, USA
artist and composer
lives and works in New York City, USA,
and London, UK

Miller, Simon Shaw

Professor at the Birbeck University London
lives and works in London, UK

Mureşan, Ciprian

* 1977
artist
co-editor of VERSION artist run magazine
from 2005 editor of IDEA art+society magazine
lives and works in Cluj, Romania

Nauman, Bruce

*1941 Fort Wayne, USA
conceptual artist
lives and works in Galisteo, USA

Neuhaus, Max

*1939 Beaumont, USA, †2009 Marina di Maratea, Italy
percussionist and sound art pioneer

Paik, Nam June

*1932 Seoul, South Korea, †2006 Miami Beach, USA
media artist and musician

People Like Us (Vicki Bennett)

active since 1991
media artist
lives and works in London, UK

Petschulat, Hein-Godehart

*1981 Schwerin, Germany
media artist
lives and works in Leipzig, Germany

Pritchett, James

musician and musicologist
lives and works in New Jersey, USA

Purho, Petri

*1983 Kouvola, Finland
game designer
lives and works in Helsinki, Finland

Rauschenberg, Robert

*1925 Port Arthur, USA, †2008 Captiva Island, USA
painter and pioneer of Pop Art

Robinson, Julia

Assistant Professor in the Department of Art History
at New York University
lives and works in New York City, USA

Rogalsky, Matt

*1966 Nigeria
media artist
lives and works in Cambridge, UK

Saladin, Matthieu

*1978
researcher and media artist
lives and works in Paris, France

Schmidt, Dörte

*1964
musicologist and author
lives and works in Berlin, Germany

Schmidt, Harald

*1957 Neu-Ulm, Germany
entertainer
lives and works in Cologne, Germany

Schneider, Helge

*1955 Mülheim an der Ruhr, Germany
musician and entertainer,
lives and works between Essen and Mülheim, Germany

Schröder, Julia H.

musicologist and author
lives and works in Berlin, Germany

Stilinović, Mladen

*1947 in Belgrade, Serbia
conceptual artist
lives and works in Zagreb, Croatia

Thoben, Jan

music theorist and art historian
lives and works in Berlin, Germany

Toop, David

*1949 Enfield, UK
author and musician
lives and works in London, UK

Tudor, David

*1962 Philadelphia, USA, †1996 Tomkins Cove, USA
pianist and composer

Ultra-red

founded in 1994 in Los Angeles, USA
sound art collective

Vitiello, Stephen

*1964 New York City, USA
media artist
lives and works in New York, USA

vom Bruch, Klaus

*1952 Cologne, Germany
media artist
lives and works in Munich, Germany

von Hausswolff, Carl Michael

*1956 Linköping, Sweden
media artist, lives and works in Stockholm, Sweden

Wearing, Gillian

*1963 Birmingham, UK
conceptual artist
lives and works in London, UK

Whyte, Dick

has been making visual art since 1997, media artist
lives and works in Wellington, New Zealand

Wilson, Eva

*1982 London, UK, assistant curator of Thyssen-Bornemisza Art Contemporary (TBA21), Vienna, and doctoral research fellow at the Humanities Centre for Advanced Studies "History of the Image and Aesthetics of Evidence", Freie Universität Berlin
lives and works in Berlin, Germany, and Vienna, Austria

Colophon

Exhibition

Sounds Like Silence
John Cage / *4'33"* / Silence Today
1912 – 1952 – 2012

August 25, 2012 – January 6, 2013

Hartware MedienKunstVerein (HMKV)
at the Dortmunder U
Leonie-Reygers-Terrasse
44137 Dortmund, Germany

Concept
Dieter Daniels

Curated by
Inke Arns
Dieter Daniels

Exhibition Architecture
Ruth M. Lorenz (maaskant, Berlin)

Design Information Display
Max Schneider
Frauke Schmidt

Artistic Director HMKV
Inke Arns

Managing Director HMKV
Frauke Hoffschulte

Assistant Curator HMKV
Fabian Saavedra-Lara

Exhibition Production and
Organisation HMKV
Kathleen Ansorg
Andrea Eichardt

Education HMKV
Mirjam Laker

Manager on Duty HMKV
Stephanie Brysch
Lena Schmidt

Accountant HMKV
Simone Czech

Voluntary Social Year
In Culture HMKV
David Groher
Malte Zander

Technical Director HMKV
Stephan Karass

Construction Team HMKV
Matthias Bartikowski
Sanja Biere
Yoko Dupuis
Jens Eberhardt
Sabine Gorski
Kai Kickelbick
Boris Kreinberg
Zeljko Petonjic
Arne Sablinski

Technical Director Dortmunder U
and Advisor
Uwe Gorski

Technical Team Dortmunder U
Timo Kruck
Robin Lockhart
Uli Lueg
Oliver Okunik
Detlev Olschewski

Video Team HMKV
David Figura
Annika Hellmuth

Photography
Hannes Woidich

Graphic Design
labor b designbüro

Artists
Dave Allen (UK)
Heinrich Böll (DE)
Manon de Boer (IN/NL/BE)
Jens Brand (DE)
Klaus vom Bruch (DE)
John Cage (US)
Cage Against the Machine (UK)
Martin Conrads (DE)
Martin Creed (UK)
Merce Cunningham (US)
Paul Davis (US)
Guy Debord (FR)
Christopher DeLaurenti (US)
Einstürzende Neubauten (DE)
Carl Michael von Hausswolff (SE)
Jens Heitjohann (DE)
Pierre Huyghe (FR)
Jonathon Keats (US)
Yves Klein (FR)
Kollektivnye Deystviya
[Collective Actions] (RU)
Christoph Korn (DE)
Shigeko Kubota (JP/US)
Brandon LaBelle (US)
Henning Lohner (DE/US)
Christian Marclay (US)
Ciprian Mureşan (RO)
Bruce Nauman (US)
Max Neuhaus (US)
Nam June Paik (KR/DE/US)
People Like Us
(Vicki Bennett) (UK)
Hein-Godehart Petschulat (DE)
Robert Rauschenberg (US)
Matt Rogalsky (US)
Matthieu Saladin (FR)
Harald Schmidt (DE) &
Helge Schneider (DE)
Petri Söderström-Kelley (FI)
Mladen Stilinović (HR)
Ultra-red (US)
Stephen Vitiello (US)
Gillian Wearing (UK)
Dick Whyte (NZ)

Acknowledgements
The curators / editors wish to thank the following persons and institutions for their generous support:

Ursula Block / gelbe MUSIK Broken Music Archiv, Berlin
The John Cage Trust, New York
Nicolas Collins
Paula Cooper Gallery, New York
The Merce Cunningham Trust and The Jerome Robbins Dance Division, New York
Dorothy and Lewis B. Cullman Center
Edition C.F. Peters, Frankfurt am Main / New York
Marcus Gammel, Deutschlandradio Kultur, Berlin
Getty Research Institute, Los Angeles
Marian Goodman Gallery, New York
Hauser & Wirth, London
Wulf Herzogenrath, Berlin
Yves Klein Archives, Paris
Gabriele Knapstein, Hamburger Bahnhof, Berlin

Sigrid Korbmacher, Bonito TV-Produktionsgesellschaft mbH, Cologne
Irwin Kremen, Durham, North Carolina
Laura Kuhn, The John Cage Trust, New York
Henning Lohner, Berlin / Los Angeles
Andreiana Mihail Gallery, Bucharest
Jan Mot, Brussels
Museum of American Art, Berlin
Sandra Naumann, Berlin
Neue Gesellschaft / Frankfurter Hefte, Berlin
The New York Public Library for the Performing Arts, New York
Music Division of the New York Public Library of the Performing Arts – Astor, Lenox and Tilden Foundations, New York
Till Oellerking, meine SUPERMAUS GmbH, Mülheim
Roberto Ohrt, Hamburg
Maureen Paley Gallery, London
Patrick Peternader, Friedrich Christian Flick Collection im Hamburger Bahnhof
Anna Szczuka, Einstürzende Neubauten GbR
Alina Viola Taş, Istanbul
Jan Thoben, Berlin
Klaus vom Bruch, Munich
Carolina di Vonzo, The Estate of Max Neuhaus
Lynn Wichern, The Merce Cunningham Trust, New York
Regina Wyrwoll, Cologne
Lori Zippay, Electronic Arts Intermix, New York

Radio Broadcast

The exhibition did start in the wee hours of the morning on 24, August 2012 with the radio broadcast *Sounds Like Silence* by Inke Arns and Dieter Daniels on Deutschlandradio Kultur UKW 96,5 (00.05 – 01.00), http://www.dradio.de/dkultur/sendungen/klangkunst/1803282/

CD

The CD *Sounds Like Silence* is published by Gruenrekorder. It contains the radio broadcast by Inke Arns and Dieter Daniels. *Sounds Like Silence*, Gruen 116 (2012), www.gruenrekorder.de

The exhibition is generously supported by

KUNSTSTIFTUNG ➲ NRW

Main funders of HMKV

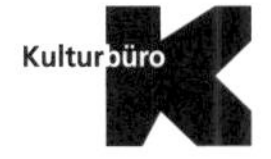

Stadt Dortmund
Kulturbetriebe

Ministerium für Familie, Kinder, Jugend, Kultur und Sport des Landes Nordrhein-Westfalen

Funded by

DSW21

Sparkasse Dortmund

Generously supported by

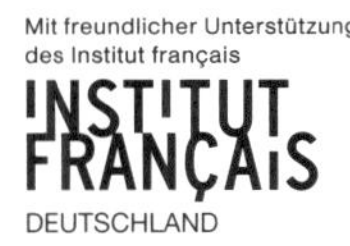

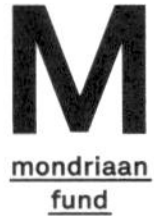

Media partners

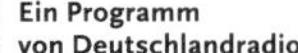

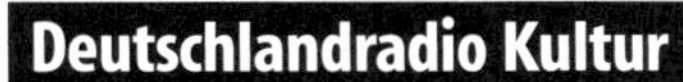

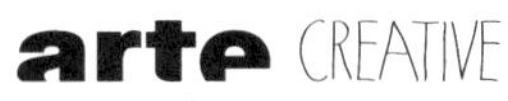

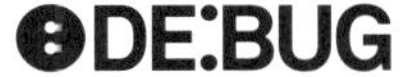

Publication

This book is published on the occasion of the exhibition:

Sounds Like Silence
John Cage / *4′33″* / Silence Today
1912 – 1952 – 2012

August 25, 2012 – January 6, 2013

Hartware MedienKunstVerein (HMKV) at the Dortmunder U

Editors
Dieter Daniels
Inke Arns

Co-Editor for Silence: A Reader
Eva Wilson

Editorial Coordination
Dieter Daniels
Inke Arns
Jan Wenzel

Translations
Lutz Eitel
Patrick (Boris) Kremer

Essays
Inke Arns
Dieter Daniels
Brandon LaBelle
Dörte Schmidt
Julia H. Schröder
Jan Thoben
David Toop

Reader Contributions
Hans-Friedrich Bormann
John Cage
William Fetterman
Kyle Gann
Branden W. Joseph
Douglas Kahn
Jonathan David Katz
Irwin Kremen
Liz Kotz
Simon Shaw Miller
James Pritchett
Julia Robinson

Work Descriptions
Inke Arns (IA)
Jens Brand (JB)
Martin Conrads (MC)
Dieter Daniels (DD)
Paul Davis (PD)
Elisabeth Fritz (EF)
Jens Heitjohann (JH)
Branden W. Joseph (BWJ)
Jonathon Keats (JK)
Gabriele Knapstein (GK)
Christoph Korn (CK)
Jan Mot (JM)
Hein-Godehart Petschulat (HGP)
Matt Rogalsky (MR)
Fabian Saavedra-Lara (FSL)
Jan Thoben (JT)
Ultra-red (UR)
David Vaughan (DV)
Wilkinson Gallery (WG)

Copy-Editing
Simon Cowper

Design
Jakob Kirch
Pascal Storz

Typesetting
Jakob Kirch
Katharina Köhler
Pascal Storz

Image Editing
Carsten Humme

Print / Production
medialis Offsetdruck GmbH, Berlin

Printed in the EU.

Published by
Spector Books
Harkortstraße 10
04107 Leipzig
mail@spectorbooks.com
www.spectorbooks.com

HMKV
Hartware MedienKunstVerein
Hartware MedienKunstVerein (HMKV)
Hoher Wall 15 (office)
44137 Dortmund, Germany
T +49-231-496642-0
F +49-231-496642-29
info@hmkv.de
www.hmkv.de
www.facebook.com/hartwaremedienkunstverein

Second edition, 2018
ISBN: 978-3-940064-41-7

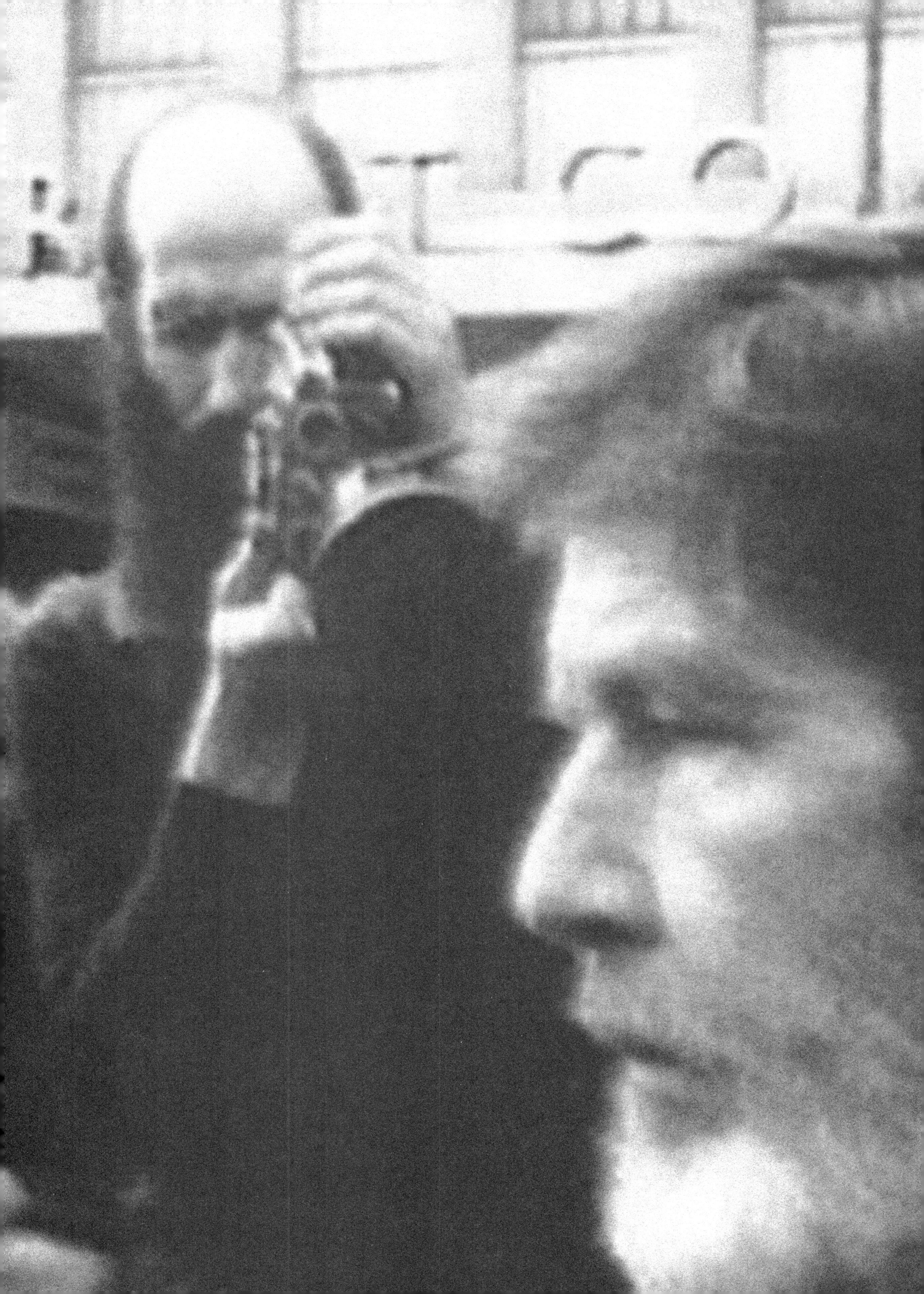

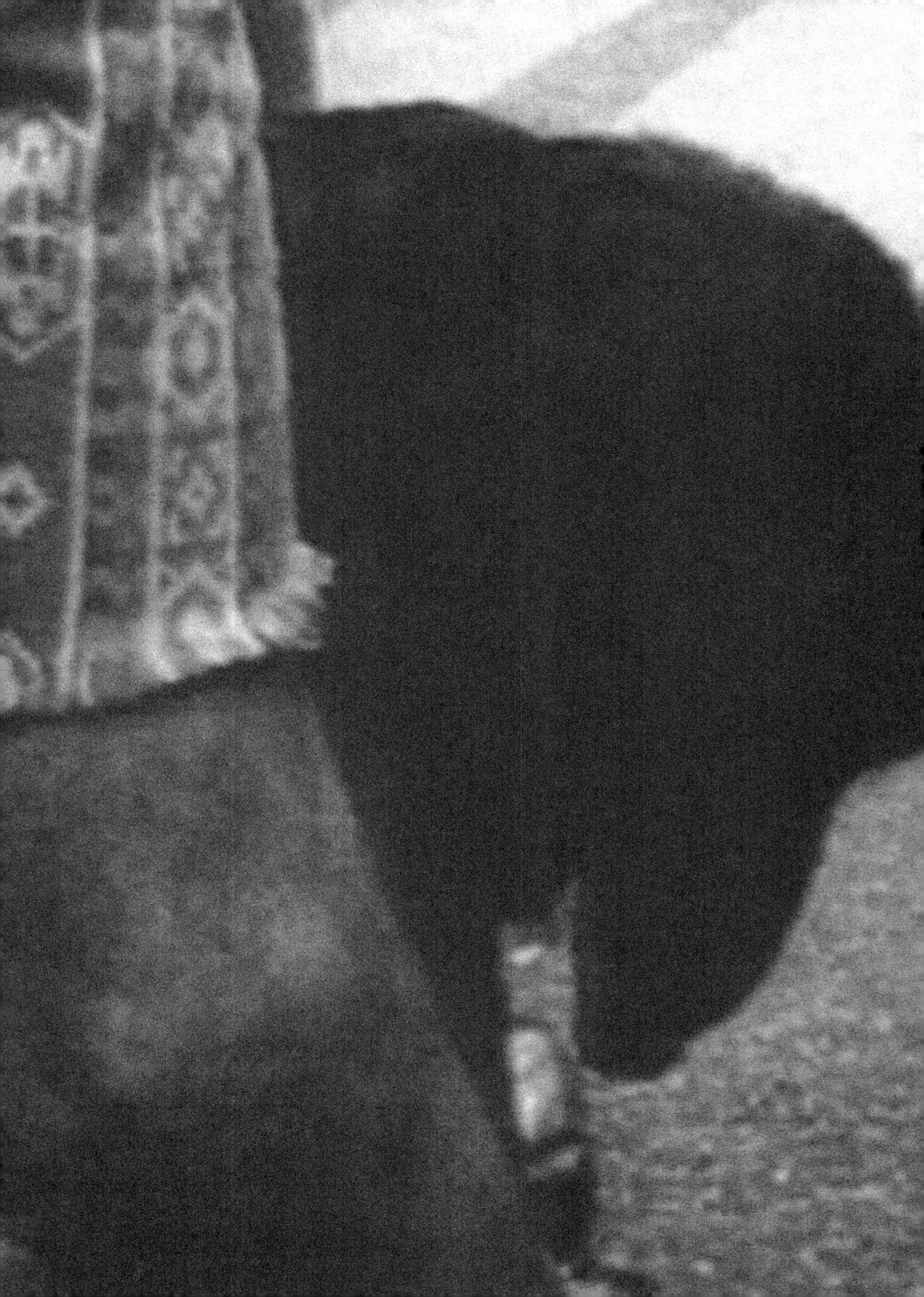

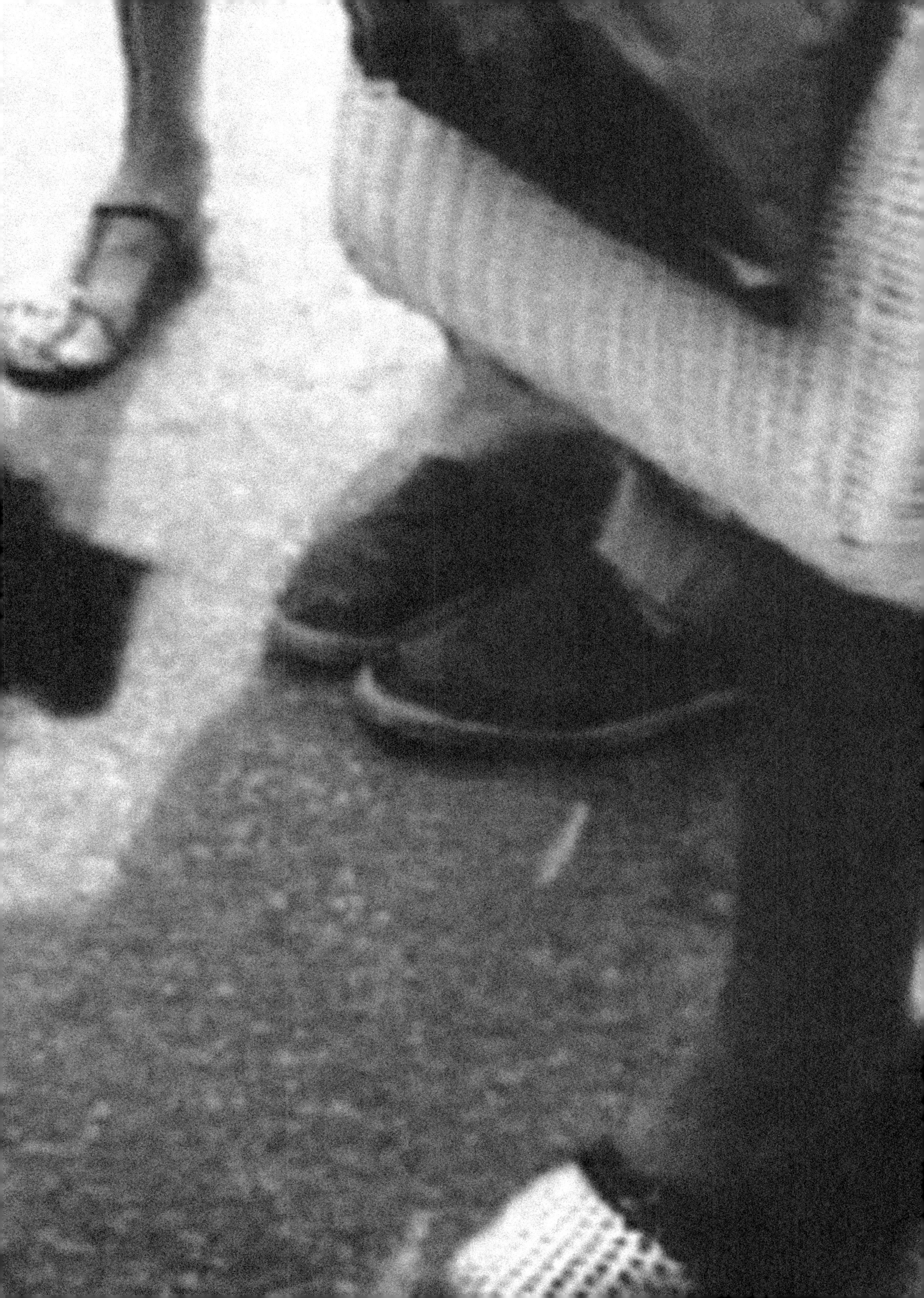

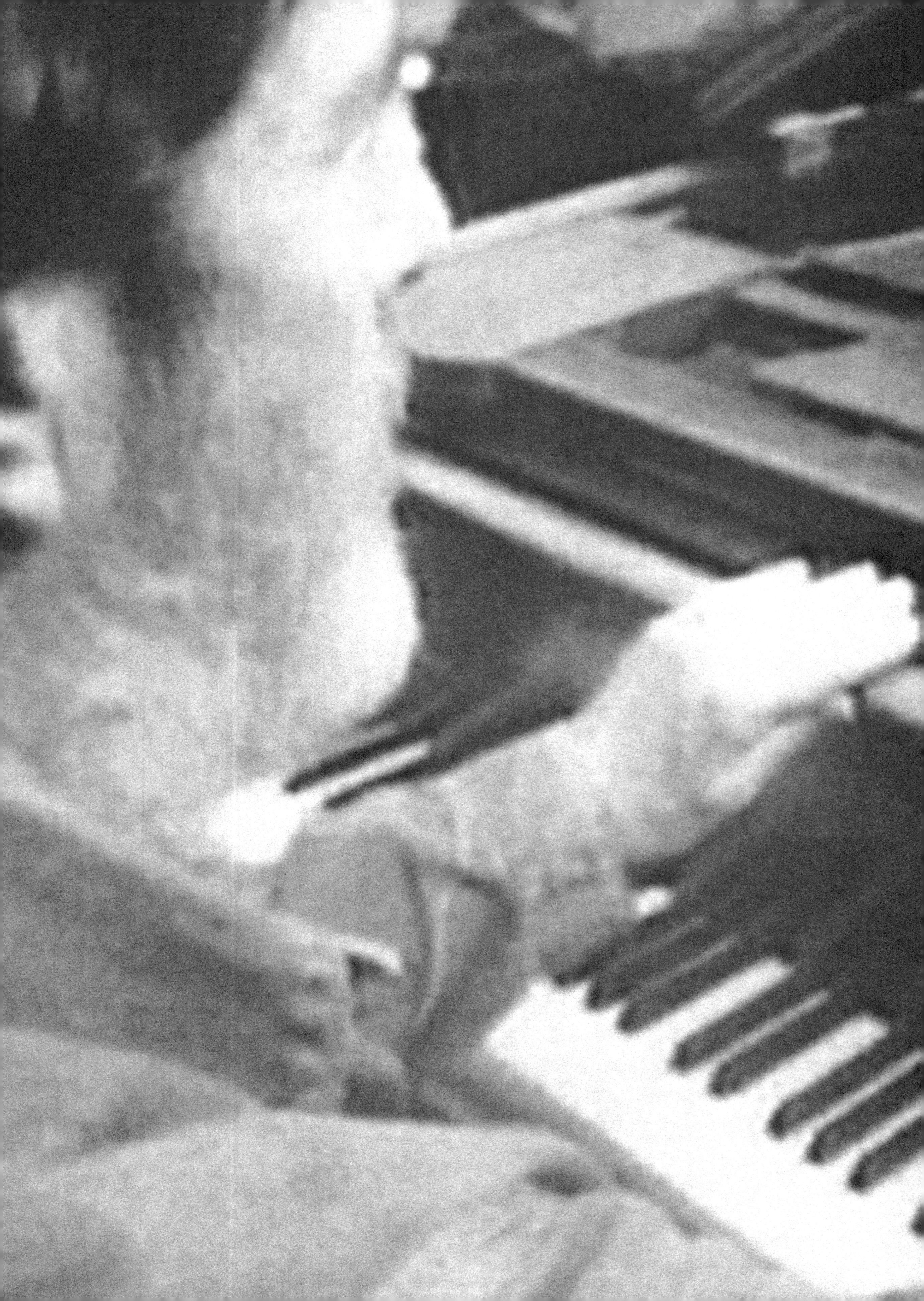

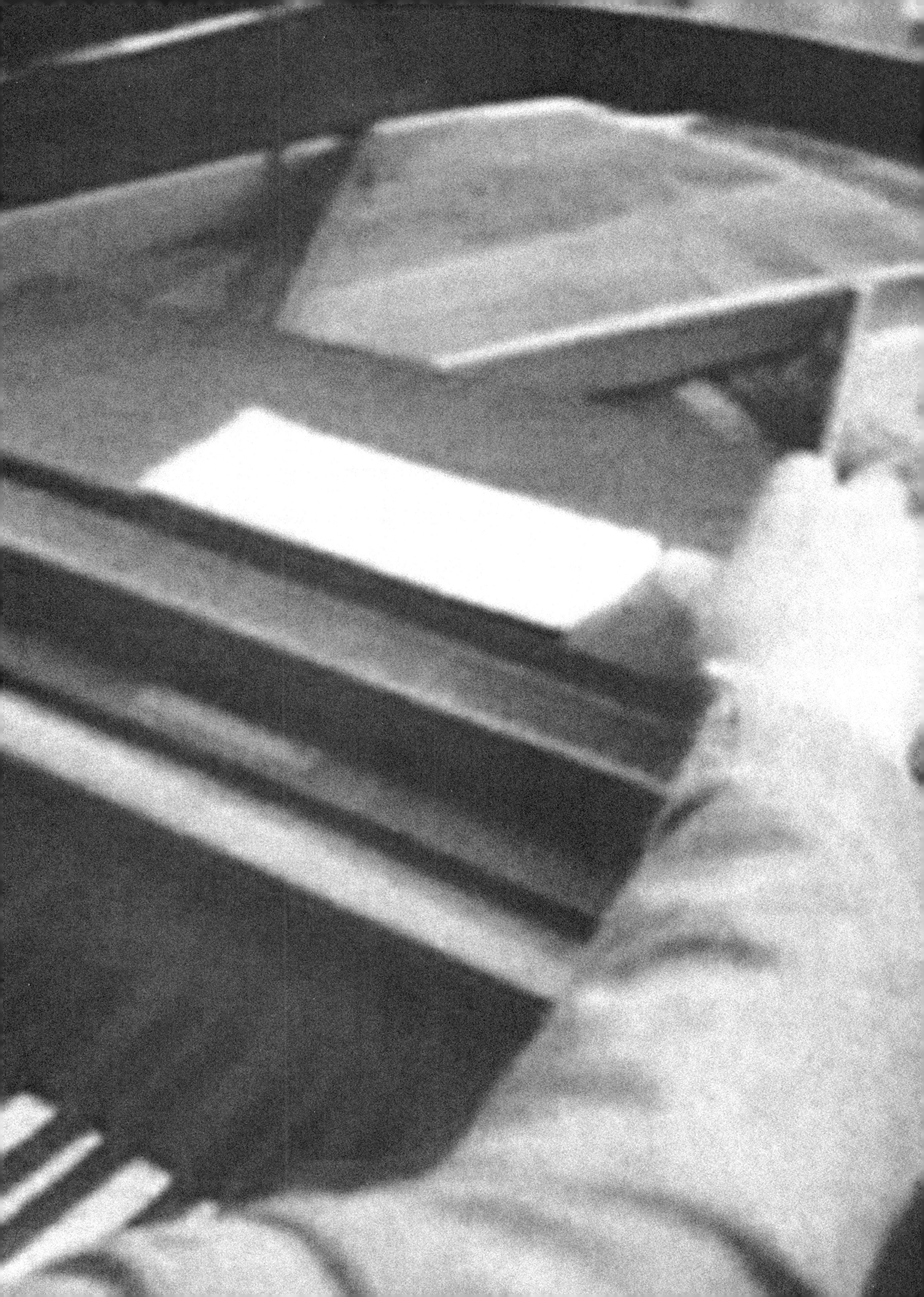

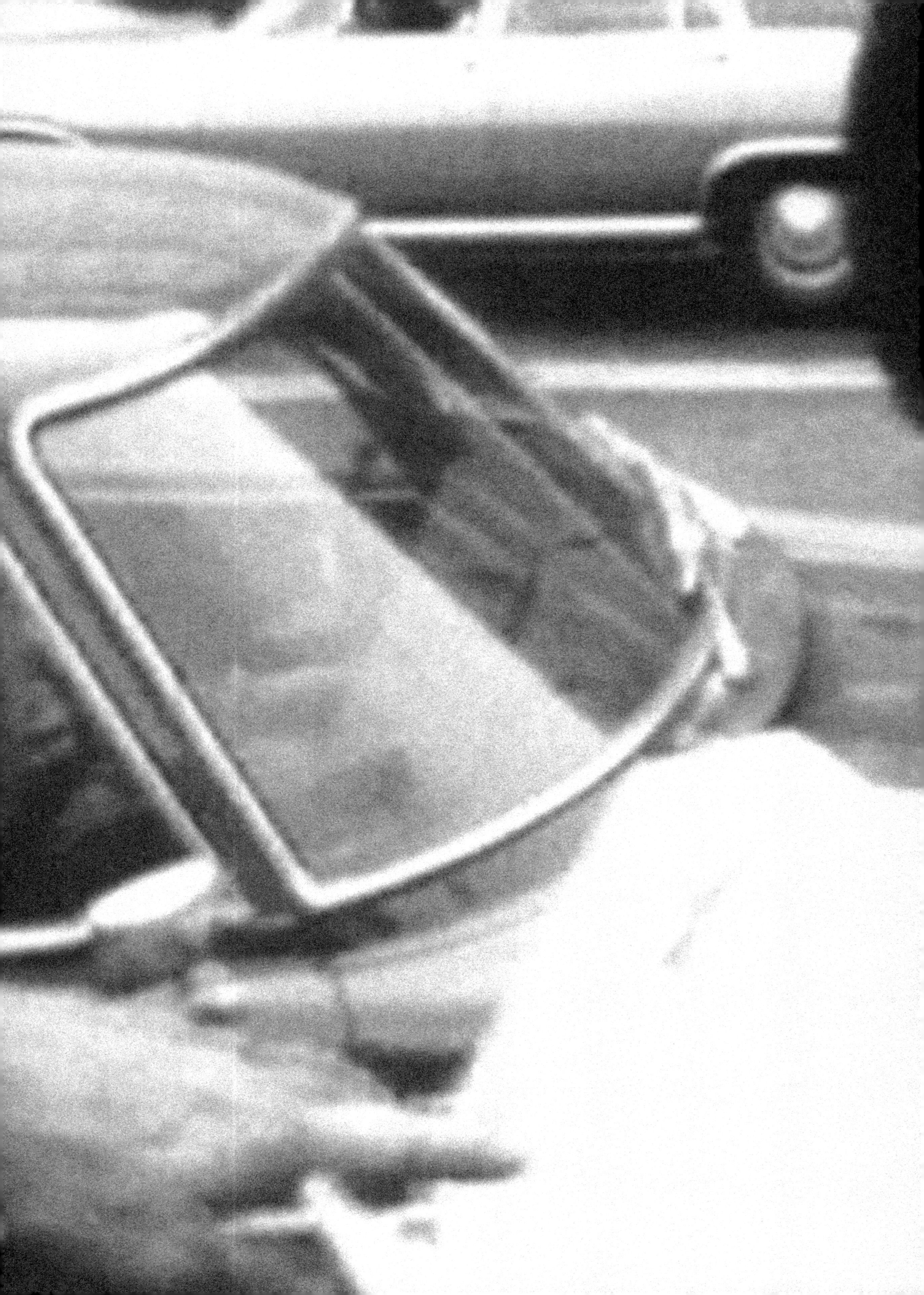

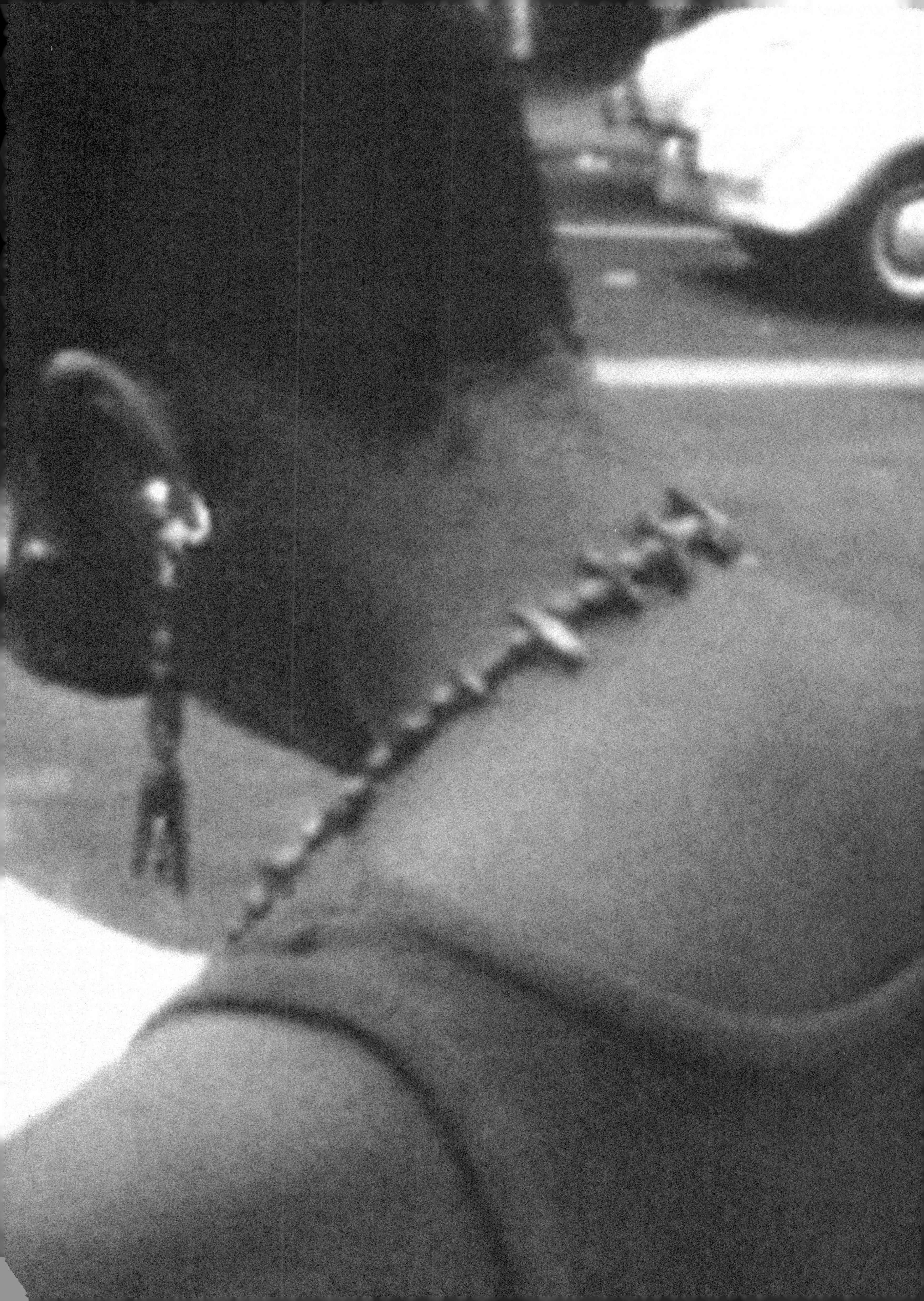

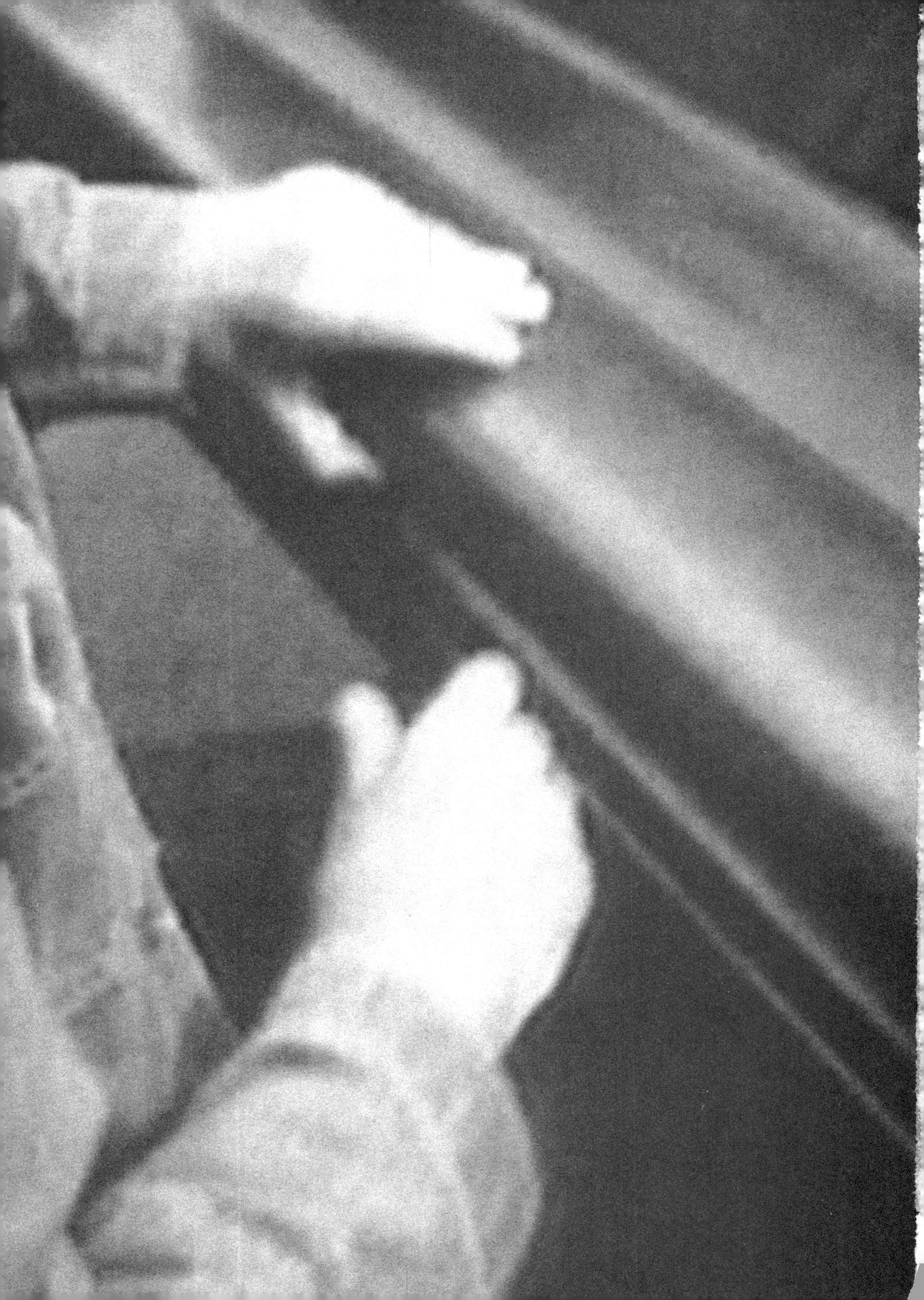